实用英汉-汉英缩略语手册

余富林 主编

东南大学出版社
SOUTHEAST UNIVERSITY PRESS
·南京·

图书在版编目(CIP)数据

实用英汉-汉英缩略语手册 /余富林主编. — 南京：东南大学出版社，2022.7
　　ISBN 978-7-5641-9933-3

　　Ⅰ.①实…　Ⅱ.①余…　Ⅲ.①英语－缩略语－手册　②缩略语－手册－英、汉　Ⅳ.①H313.6-62

　　中国版本图书馆 CIP 数据核字(2021)第 259405 号

责任编辑：周　菊　　责任校对：徐　潇
封面设计：毕　真　　责任印制：周荣虎

实用英汉-汉英缩略语手册
Shiyong Yinghan-Hanying Suolüeyu Shouce

主　　编	余富林
出版发行	东南大学出版社
社　　址	南京市四牌楼 2 号(邮编：210096　电话：025-83793330)
经　　销	全国各地新华书店
印　　刷	江苏凤凰数码印务有限公司
开　　本	880mm×1230mm　1/32
印　　张	22.875
字　　数	1000 千字
版　　次	2022 年 7 月第 1 版
印　　次	2022 年 7 月第 1 次印刷
书　　号	ISBN 978-7-5641-9933-3
定　　价	118.00 元

本社图书若有印装质量问题，请直接与营销部联系，电话：025-83791830。

编 委 会

主　编　余富林

副主编　冯　燕　麻乃文　刘彩霞
　　　　　青　丽　于　捷　雷　刚

编　者　艾泉伶　郭壮丽　孔祥章
　　　　　侯　勇　陈琼芳　龚年华
　　　　　王　芳　王月芳　黄卫君
　　　　　陈海翔　陈莉莉　熊丽红
　　　　　文露云　孔桂珍　余立群
　　　　　钟晓岚　文红梅　黄湘萍

前　言

经过几年的工作，《实用英汉-汉英缩略语手册》已经完稿。

本手册有以下特点：

1. 新。内容新。本手册收录了近年来刚出现的 B&R（一带一路），USMCA（美墨加协议）、FFVD（最终、完全可验证的无核化）、GO（氧化石墨烯），Brexit（英国脱欧）、EPA（日欧经济伙伴关系协定）等缩略语。

2. 全面。它不仅包含中国媒体中常出现的英语缩略语，还包括一般缩略语词典里难以查到读者又特别需要的外贸、标准、体检、汽车、化工、体育、游戏、教育、军事、外交、旅游、高科技、国际关系、地理、安全、金融、收藏等方面的英语缩略语，如 AFS（国际文化交流组织）、ACH（高级战斗头盔）、FRPC（全球人脸识别挑战赛）、FVEY（五眼联盟）、ARWU（世界大学学术排名）、IMO（国际数学奥林匹克竞赛）、GAFA（美国互联网四巨头）、WCO（世界海关组织）、INF（《中导条约》）等，甚至包括口语缩略语，如 gimme（=give me），hafta（=have to）。

3. 外来缩略语多。外来缩略语能弥补英语中的不足，使英语缩略语更加充实。据初步统计，本手册有源于法语、德语、俄语、世界语、拉丁语、韩语、日语、汉语、西班牙语、葡萄牙语、意大利语、保加利亚语、荷兰语、瑞典语、丹麦语、挪威语、芬兰语、印尼语、印地语、土耳其语、蒙古语、阿拉伯语、马来语、希伯来语、阿尔巴尼亚语、匈牙利语、塞-克语、捷克语、乌尔都语、越南语等三十多种语言的缩略语。

4. 实用。基于以上优点，本手册十分实用，是帮助解决我们英语学习甚至日常生活及工作上的缩略语难题的一本难得的工具书。加上有汉英部分，实用性又大大增加。

由于作者能力有限加上涉及领域较多，书中错误难免，望读者、专家指正！

编　者

2020 年 12 月

说　明

1. 本手册以收录实用英语缩略语为主，也收录了三十多种外来的缩略语。凡外来缩略语一般均以方括号注明，如 BNP(Banque Nationale de Paris)巴黎国民银行[法文]，当然还有德文、西班牙文、葡萄牙文、日文、俄文、意大利文等。在此就不一一举例了。

西文用西文字母，但有些文字的字母有一些记号，如西班牙文的 ñ；还有些文字的单词和英文有较大区别，如意大利文中的 e 就可以作为一个单词；而俄文、日文等由于其形状较为特别，我们就将它们拉丁化的字母呈现在本书内，以便于印刷和识别。

2. 正文中缩略语词条结构如下：缩略语＋全称＋中文释义。少数中文释义之后有解释，我们将其置于方括号内，如：A airbus 空中客车[欧洲制造的一种客机名称]。

3. 属于可以替换的内容也用方括号标明，如：HIFU　high-intensity focused ultrasound 海扶刀[高强度聚焦超声肿瘤治疗系统]，中文意思"海扶刀"就是"高强度聚焦超声肿瘤治疗系统"。

4. 圆括号一般表示可有可无，如：GHb　glycosylated hemoglobin 糖(基)化血红蛋白，这里的"基"字可有，也可无。

5. 正文中的缩略语常可大写，也可小写。如果是起专有名词作用的，当然必须大写，如：BIS　British Interplanetry Society 英国星际航行学会。但是作非专有名词的，既可大写，也可小写，如：TD　table data cell 表中数据单元，TD 也可写成 td。

凡　例

1. 本手册排列先英汉、后汉英(部分)。

2. 英汉部分的排列：先是标点、符号、数字开头的缩略语，如"@"" 't was""€""2D""2G"，之后跟英文字母开头的缩略语，最后跟"希腊字母开头"的缩略语。

3. 汉英部分的排列：先排标点、数字、字母开头的英语缩略语，如把"(US)美国教育传播与技术协会 AECT""'海豹'队队员　SEALs'""《当代作家》 CA""10月 Oct""AA 制　AA""CG 动画　CG""β-球蛋白　β-GI"等排在前面，然后接汉语拼音排序。

4. 每个英语缩略语词条一般包括：英语缩略语、缩略语全称、汉语释义，有时加补充说明；而汉英部分中，则把汉语释义提前(含补充说明)如：

  W　　watt 瓦(特)[法定功率计量单位]

  瓦(特)[法定功率计量单位] W　　watt

  UT　　ultra thin 超薄

  超薄 UT　　ultra thin

5. 英汉部分词条按英语字母顺序排列。缩略语相同、全称相同、意思相同而字面表述不同时，合为一个词条；缩略语相同、全称不同、含义不同时，分立为不同词条，如：

  XD　　ex-dividend 无股息/无红利

  YSL　　Yarrow Shipbuilders Ltd 英国亚罗造船有限公司

  YSL　　Young Socialist League 青年社会主义者联盟

6. 方括号用来表示解释性内容或可替换内容；圆括号用来表示可有可无或容易理解的场合；还有一些标点符号不言自明。如：

  TOEIC　　Test of English for International Communication 托业考试[国际交流英语考试]

CGCC　Chinese General Chamber of Commerce 中华总商会[属香港特别行政区]

HT　hyper-threading 超线程(技术)

ATC　Agreement on Textile and Clothing《纺织品与服装协定》

7. 英语缩略语的大小写，常可以互换。如：

u/m　unit of measure 测量单位，这里的 u/m 可以用 U/M，但是作为专有名词用的英语缩略语，一般必须大写。如：

ZAN　Zanzibar 桑给巴尔市[非洲坦桑尼亚城市]

8. 本手册以收录英语缩略语为主，为方便起见，还选用了一些"代字"。如：

VX　Persistent toxic nerve 持续性神经毒气[代字]

ACM　automated checkout machine 自动收款机

9. 本手册以收录英语缩略语为主，为实用，还选用了其他文字的缩略语(含汉语)，如：

PLD　Parti Liberal Démocrate 自由民主党[法文]

WLF　Wulinfeng 武林风[汉语拼音缩略语]

目 录

英汉部分 ·· 1
  标点、符号、数字开头排序 ··· 1
  A ·· 4
  B ·· 36
  C ·· 52
  D ·· 100
  E ·· 114
  F ·· 133
  G ·· 146
  H ·· 158
  I ··· 168
  J ·· 194
  K ·· 197
  L ·· 202
  M ·· 212
  N ·· 229
  O ·· 242
  P ·· 249
  Q ·· 269
  R ·· 272
  S ·· 282
  T ·· 305
  U ·· 319
  V ·· 329

W	334
X	342
Y	343
Z	345
希腊字母开头	347

汉英部分 348
   标点、数字、字母开头排序 348
   A 360
   B 367
   C 381
   D 393
   E 416
   F 418
   G 430
   H 467
   J 481
   K 505
   L 514
   M 527
   N 551
   O 560
   P 565
   Q 568
   R 580
   S 589
   T 614
   W 625
   X 636
   Y 655
   Z 682

参考文献 719
后记 720

英汉部分

标点、符号、数字开头排序

@	at 现成为电子邮件地址中的分隔符
't was	it was 它过去是
't wil	it will 它将是
'til	until 直到
'un	one 一个人或事物
€	Euro 欧元[符号]
©	copyright 版权[符号]
17-KS	17-ketosteroid 17-酮类固醇
17-KS	17-ketosteroid test 17-酮类固醇测定
17-OHCS	17-hydroxycorticosteroids 17-羟皮质类固醇
2019-nCoV	2019-novel coronavirus 二〇一九新型冠状病毒
2D	two dimensions 二维
2G	generation 2 第二代[移动通信系统:含短信]
2H	happy and healthy 文娱与健康
2WD	two wheel drive 二轮驱动
3A	FA,OA,HA 以微电子技术为中心的社会自动化革命[工厂自动化、办公自动化、家庭自动化]
3B	beauty,beast,baby 美女、动物、幼儿[是广告大师奥格威从创意入手提出的广告表现三原则]
3B	beauty,beast,baby 指面孔多变的年轻女子,她们一会儿是美女,一会儿是野兽,一会儿是婴儿
3C	candid,constructive,cooperative 坦率的、建设性的、合作的

1

3C	China, Compulsory, Certification 中国强制性产品认证制度
3C	comforting, curiosity, challenge 舒适、好奇和挑战
3C	communication, computer, control 3C 革命[指实现通信网络化、电脑化、自动控制化的过程]
3Cs(+1C)	courage, capital, capacity (+communication) 勇气、资本、能力(+沟通)[一种商业成功经验]
3D	discontinuous innovation, defensible technology, disruptive business model 不连续的创新思维、防御性技术、颠覆性商业模式
3D	three dimensions 三维
3Dmax	3-Dimensional Studio Max 三维建模软件
3Dmax/3DMax	3D Studio Max 基于 PC 系统的三维动画渲染和制作软件
3G	generation 3 第三代[移动通信系统:含短信、互联网接入]
3H	Healthy, Happy, Harmonious 颐养康复中心(颐康、颐乐、颐和)
3M	Minnesota Mining & Manufacturing Co. 明尼苏达矿业及制造公司
3R	recycle, reuse, refill 环保 3R 原则[再回收、再利用、再填充]
3R	reduce, reuse, recycle 减少、再利用、再循环[环保者的格言]
3T	technology, talent, tolerance 技术、人才、宽容
3Vs	villain, vindicator, victim 危机性新闻故事中的三个主要报道对象:坏人、辩护人、受害者
4C	carat, color, cut, clarity 重量、颜色、切割、透明度[国际上衡量钻石的 4 个标准]
4C	customer, cost, convenience, communication 一种营销理论[顾客、消费、便利、交流]
4D	four dimensions 四维[由空间的长、宽、高和时间坐标组成]
4DP	four dimensional printing 4D 打印
4F	fat, female, forty, family 肥胖,40 岁,有家族史的女性更易得胆结石
4G	generation 4 第四代[移动通信系统:含短信、互联网接入、视频]
4P	people, process, partner, performance 以人为本的公司领导模式[由四部分组成:人、流程、合作伙伴、绩效]
4S	sale, sparepart, service, survey 以四位一体为核心的汽车特许经营模式[包括整车销售(Sale)、零配件供应(Sparepart)、售后服务(Service)和信息反馈(Survey)]

4WD	four wheel drive 四轮驱动
5A	CA,OA,SA,BA,FA 5A(通信、办公、保安、楼宇、消防)智能化写字楼
5-FU	5-fluorouracil 5-氟尿嘧啶
5G	generation 5 第五代[移动通信系统：含短信、互联网接入、超高清视频、智能家居]
5'NT	5'-nucleotidase 5'-核苷酸酶
5R	record，reduce，recite，reflect，review 5R 笔记法[记录、简化、背诵、思考、复习]
5S	strength,sense, swallow, speak,seeing 中风判断五要素[力量,感觉,吞咽,说话,看东西]
5S	Seiri，Seiton，Seisou，Seiketsu，Shitsuke 日本的5S管理法[整理、整顿、清扫、清洁、素养][日文]
5W2H	what，how，why，when，where，who，how much 5W2H 谈判法则[目标、策略、原因、时间、地点、关键人、进展程度，然后达目标]
6A	acceptance，appreciation，affection，availability，accountability，authority 6A 原则[积极正面的教育子女的原则：接纳、赞赏、关爱、有效性、责任、权威]
6S	substantiation，selection，safety，sourcing，standardization，structure 6S 质量措施[实证、选题、安全、来源、标准化、结构]

A

A	Acura 讴歌汽车[日本]
A	abuse 腐败/滥用
A	academic 学术
A	adult 成人
A	airbus 空中客车[欧洲制造的一种客机名称]
A	ampere 安(培)[电流的基本单位]
A	Angström 或 angstrom 埃[光波波长单位]
a	annum 年[拉丁文]
A	atto 阿(托)
A	Singapore-Cambridge General Certificate of Education Advanced Level 新加坡剑桥 A 水准考试
A	academy 学院
A	acceptable 及格[合格]
A	acre 公亩(1公亩＝100平方米或 0.15 市亩)
A	America 美国;美洲
A	artery 动脉
A	article from anthology 专著或论文中析出的文献[参考文献标示字母]
A & P	Agricultural and Pastoral 农牧业的
ACh	acetylcholine 乙酰胆碱
A&HCI	Arts & Humanities Citation Index 艺术与人文科学引文索引
Ar	argon 氩[第18号化学元素]
A/B	Aktiebolag 有限公司[瑞典文]
a/c	air conditioning 空气调节系统
A/C	air conditioning 空调(器)
A/C	account current 往来账户/活期存款账户
a/c NO	account number 账户编号

4

A

A/C	air cleaner 空滤器
A/D, D/A	analog-to-digital 模拟—数字转换
A/DC	analog-to-digital converter 模拟数字转换器
A/ELR	automatic/emergency locking retractor 自动/紧急锁止收卷器[安全带]
A/F	air-fuel ratio 空燃比
A/G	albumin/globulin ratio 白蛋白/球蛋白比值
A/R	Account Receivable 应收账款
A/S	Aktieselkab 联合股份公司[丹麦文]
AA	Algebraic Average 代数平均（AA 制：以前常等于 go Dutch）
AA	Aluminum Association 美国铝业协会
aa	ana 每个[希腊文]
AA	absolute average 绝对平均
AA	ack-ack 高射炮
AA	Alcoholics Anonymous 嗜酒者互诚协会
AA	amino acid 氨基酸
AA	antiaircraft 防空的
AA	each each 聚餐后的 AA 制
AA	acting appointment AA 制
AA	all apart AA 制（中国香港地区用法）
AAA	abdominal aortic aneurysm 腹部主动脉瘤
AAA	anti-adrenal cortex antibody 抗肾上腺皮质抗体
AAA	American Accounting Association 美国会计协会
AAA	American Automobile Association 美国汽车协会
AAA	any advice appreciated 欢迎提出建议
AAA	Asian-African-Latin American 亚洲、非洲、拉丁美洲（的）
AAAA	American Association of Advertising Agencies 美国广告代理协会
AAAI	Association for the Advance of Artificial Intelligence 国际先进人工智能大会
AAAI	American Association for Artificial Intelligence 美国人工智能协会
AAAL	American Academy of Arts and Letters 美国艺术和文学学院
AAAS	American Academy of Arts and Sciences 美国艺术和科学研究院
AAAS	American Association for the Advancement of Science 美国科学促进会

5

A

AABD	African American Biographical Database 非洲美国传记数据库
AAC	advanced audio coding 高级音频编码技术/使用此技术编码的音频格式
AAC	Association of American Colleges 美国大学联合会
AAC	automat and automatic control 自动装置与自动控制
AACM	African-Asian Common Market 亚非共同市场
AACHS	Afro-American Cultural and Historical Society 美国黑人文化及历史学会
AACL	Association of American Correspondents in London 伦敦美国记者协会
AACS	Advanced Access Content System 高级访问内容系统
AACSB	American Assembly of Collegiate Schools of Business 美国工商管理学院联合会
AACSB	American Association of Collegiate Schools of Business 美国商学院协会
AACTE	American Association of Colleges for Teacher Education 美国教师教育学院联合会
AAD	advanced air defense 先进防空导弹
AAD	American Academy of Dentists 美国牙科医师学会
AAD	American Academy of Dermatology 美国皮肤病学会
AAG	Association of American Geographers 美国地理学家协会
AAG	action adventure game 动作冒险游戏
AAHE	American Association for Higher Education 美国高等教育协会
AAHL	Australian Animal Health Laboratory 澳大利亚动物健康实验室
AAHPER	American Association for Health, Physical Education and Recreation 美国卫生、体育及娱乐协会
AAI	atrial inhibited pacing 心房抑制型（起搏）
AAIB	Air Accidents Investigation Branch 英国航空事故调查局
AAL	air auxiliary life 环境辅助生活
AALS	American Association of Language Specialists 美国语言学家协会
AAM	air-to-air missile 空对空导弹
AAMFT	American Association of Marriage and Family Therapists 美国婚姻与家庭治疗师协会
AAMFT	American Association of Marriage and Family Therapy 美国婚姻与家庭治疗协会

A

AAMI	Association for the Advancement of Medical Instrumentation 美国医疗器械促进协会
AAMOF	as a matter of fact 事实上[网络用语]
AAN	amino acid nitrogen 氨基酸氮
AAP	Academy of American Poets 美国诗人协会
AAP	Association of American Publishers 美国出版商协会
AAP	annual acquisition plan 年度采购计划
AAPP	The Association of Asian Parliaments for Peace 亚洲议会和平协会
AAPS	American Association for the Promotion of Science 美国科学促进协会
AAR	against all risks (保险)全险
AAR	air to air refuelling 空中加油
AAR	average annual rainfall 年平均降雨量
AARP	American Association of Retired Persons 美国退休人员协会
AAS	American Academy of Sciences 美国科学院
AAS	Association for Asian Studies 亚洲问题研究学会[美国]
AAS	Australian Academy of Science 澳大利亚科学院
AASB	American Association of Small Business 美国小企业协会
AASE	Australian Associated Stock Exchanges 澳大利亚联合证券交易所
AASHTO	American Association of State Highway and Transportation Officials 美国公路和运输官员协会
AASLD	American Association for the Study of Liver Disease 美国肝脏病研究协会
AASND	American Association for Study of Neoplast Diseases 美国肿瘤病研究协会
AASW	American Association of Scientific Workers 美国科学工作者协会
AATA	Anglo-American Tourist Association 英美旅游协会
AATCLC	American Association of Teachers of Chinese Language and Culture 美国中国语言、文化教师协会
AAU	Association of American Universities 美国大学联合会
AAUN	American Association for the United Nations 美国联合国协会
AAUP	American Association of University Professors 美国大学教授协会
AAV	Amphibious Assault Vehicle 两栖突击车
AAV	adeno-associated virus 腺相关病毒

7

A

AB	actual bicarbonate 实际碳酸氢盐
AB	Agriculture Biologique 法国有机种植认证标志［法文］
AB	Airbus，Boeing 空客、波音（中国轮流购买以求外交平衡）
AB	Artium Baccalaureus 文学士［拉丁文］
AB	Aktiebolag 有限公司［瑞典文］
AB	Anbang Property & Casualty Insurance Co., Ltd. 安邦财产保险股份有限公司
ABA	American Bar Association 美国律师协会
ABB	Asea Brown Boveri Ltd. 阿西布朗勃法瑞公司［瑞典文］
ABBA	Agnetha，Benny，Björn，Anni-Frid 阿巴合唱团［由四位音乐家姓氏首字母组成］
abbr(ev)	abbreviation 缩略语
ABC	activity-based costing 作业成本法
ABC	airway，breathing，circulation 一清二吹三压［口对口呼吸和心脏按压抢救心肌梗死的方法：气道通畅、改善通气、恢复循环］
ABC	American Broadcasting Corporation 美国广播公司
ABC	Australian-born Chinese 澳大利亚出生的华人
ABC	Australian Broadcasting Corporation 澳大利亚广播公司
ABC	automatic coding system 自动编码系统
ABC	ABC Analysis ABC 分类控制法
ABC	Adapt-Borrow-Create 模仿—借用—创新［翻译主张］
ABC	Agricultural Banks of China 中国农业银行
ABC	Airbus，Boeing and COMAC 空客、波音和中国商飞
ABC	American-born Chinese 美国出生的中国人
ABCC	Association of British Chambers of Commerce 英国商会联合会
ABCD	ADM，Bunge，Cargill，Dreyfus 世界粮食四巨头［全世界粮食产量的80％都掌握在世界粮食市场的四大巨头手中，它们是：ADM（美国阿彻丹尼斯米德兰公司）、Bunge（荷兰邦吉集团）、Cargill（美国嘉吉公司）、Dreyfus（Louis Dreyfus）（法国路易达孚公司）］
ABCQ	Associação Brasileira de Contrôle de Qualidade 巴西质量管理协会［葡萄牙文］

A

ABD	all but dissertation 仅差学校论文即可毕业
ABE	actual base excess 实际碱过剩
ABEND	abnormal end 不正常终止（电脑）
ABH	actual bodily harm 实际身体伤害（罪）
ABI	Associated Business Information 联合商业情报
ABI	American-British Intelligence 美英情报（局）
ABNT	Associação Brasileire de Normas Técnicas 巴西产品质量认证标志/巴西技术标准协会［葡萄牙文］
Abp	archbishop 大主教
ABRF	The Association of Biomolecular Resource Facilities 生物分子资源实验室协会
ABS	anti-lock brake system 汽车防抱死制动系统
ABS	asset-backed securities 资产（通常是房地产）抵押债券
ABS	acrylonitrile-butadiene-styrene copolymer 丙烯腈-丁二烯-苯乙烯共聚物［塑料］
ABS	acrylonitrile-butadiene-styrene 丙烯腈
ABS	American Bureau of Shipping 美国船舶局
ABS	anti-skid braking system 防滑移制动系统
ABSW	Association of British Science Writers 英国科学作家协会
ABT	American Ballet Theatre 美国芭蕾舞剧院
ABTA	Association of British Travel Agents 英国旅行社协会
ABU	Asian Broadcasting Union 亚洲广播联盟
ABU Robocon	Asian Broadcasting Union Robot Contest 亚广联地区机器人大赛
ABVP	Akhil Bharatiya Vidyarthi Parishad 全印学生委员会［印地文］
Ac	actinium 锕［第89号化学元素］
ac	ante cibos 饭前【医】［拉丁文］
AC	air conditioning 空气调节系统
AC	Alternating Current 交流电
AC	appellation contrôlée 合格佳酿酒［法国葡萄酒质量管理标记］［法文］
AC	assessment center 评价中心

9

A

AC	airworthiness certification 适航证	
AC	ante Christum 公元前［拉丁文］	
AC/DC/EC	alternating current/direct current/earth current 交流/直流/接地电流	
AC-3	Dolby Surround Audio Coding-3 杜比数码环绕声［美国杜比公司开发的家庭影院多声道数字音频系统］	
ACA	anti-cardiac phospholipids antibody 抗心磷脂抗体	
ACA	anticentromere antibody 抗着丝点抗体	
ACA	Asian Creation Academy 韩国亚洲创意学院	
ACA	The Associate Chartered Accountant 英国皇家特许会计师	
ACAS	Advisory, Conciliation and Arbitration Service 英国咨询、调解与仲裁局	
ACAS	The Asia Contemporary Art Show 亚洲当代艺术展	
ACC	Accident Compensation Corporation 意外事故伤害赔偿局	
ACC	Air Control Center 航空控制中心	
ACC	American College of Cardiology 美国心脏病学会	
ACCA	Associated Chambers of Commerce of Australia 澳大利亚商务联合会	
ACCA	The Association of Chartered Certified Accountants 英国特许公认会计师公会	
ACCEL	American College of Cardiology Extended Learning 美国心脏病学会扩展学习	
ACCESS	American College of Cardiology Extended Study Services 美国心脏病学会推广研究服务部	
ACCESS	automated catalog of computer equipment and software system 计算机设备和软件系统的自动目录	
ACCS	American College of Chest Surgeons 美国胸科医师学会	
ACD	Acute Coronary Disease 急性冠心病	
ACD	*American College Dictionary*《美国大学词典》	
ACD	Asian Clearing Dollar 亚洲决算货币	
ACD	Asian Co-operative Dialogue 亚洲合作对话	
ACD	automatic call distribution 自动呼叫分配［是一种用于处理许多来话呼叫的特殊电话系统］	
ACD	administrative contracting officer 合同管理官	

A

ACE	above customer expectation 高出用户期望
ACE	Allied Command Europe 欧洲盟军司令部
ACE	American Commodity Exchange 美国商品交易所
ACE	American Council on Education 美国教育委员会
ACE	angiotensin converting enzyme 血管紧张素转化酶
ACE	Automated Commercial Environment 自动商业环境
ACEEE	American Council for an Energy Efficient Economy 美国节能经济委员会
ACEI	angiotension converting enzyme inhibitor 血管紧张素转化酶抑制剂
ACFA	American Cat Fanciers Association 美国养猫爱好者协会
ACFTU	All-China Federation of Trade Unions 中华全国总工会
ACG	American College of Gastroenterology 美国胃肠病学学会
ACG	animation, comic, game 动画漫画游戏[通常指电玩游戏或美少女游戏]的总称
ACGA	Asian Corporate Government Association 亚洲公司治理协会
ACH	automated clearing house 自动清算所
ACH	advanced combat helmet 高级战斗头盔
ACHOO Syndrome	Autosomal Dominant Compelling Helio-Ophthalmic Outburst Syndrome 强迫性常染色体显性遗传性日光眼激发综合征
ACHR	American Council of Human Rights 美国人权委员会
ACI	Alloy Casting Institute 美国合金铸造学会
ACI	Advanced Commercial Information 高级商业信息
ACI	Alliance Coopérative Internationale 国际合作联盟[法文]
ACI	American Certificate Institute 美国认证协会
ACI	Automatic Car Identification System 车辆自动识别系统
ACID	atomicity, consistency, isolation and durability 不可再分割性、一致性、隔离性与耐用性
ACIP	Advisory Committee on Immunization Practices (美国)免疫实施咨询委员会
ack	acknowledgment code 确认,应答[是通信中的一个控制码,常在计算机间通联使用]

A

ACL	air cleaner	空气滤清器
ACL	access control list	访问控制表
ACLA	anti-cardiolipin antibody	抗心脂抗体
ACLALS	Association for Commonwealth Literature and Language Studies	英联邦文学和语言研究会
ACLS	American Council of Learned Societies	美国学术团体委员会
ACLU	American Civil Liberties Union	美国公民自由联盟
ACM	adaptable code modulation	自适应编码调制
ACM	Association for Computing Machinery	美国电脑协会
ACM	automated checkout machine	自动收款机
ACMET	Advisory Council on Middle East Trade	中东贸易咨询委员会
ACM-ICP	ACM International Collegiate Programming Contest	美国计算机协会国际大学生程序设计竞赛
ACORD	Advisory Council on Research and Development	研究与发展咨询委员会
ACP	acid phosphatase	酸性磷酸酶
ACP	African, Caribbean & Pacific Countries	非洲、加勒比海和太平洋国家
ACPC	agricultural comprehensive production capability	农业综合生产能力
ACPRA	American College Public Relations Association	美国大学公共关系协会
ACR	albumin-to-creatinine ratio	蛋白/肌酐比率
ACS	Asia Credit Summit	亚信峰会
ACS	American Cancer Society	美国癌症协会
ACS	American Chemical Society	美国化学学会
ACSC	Association for Canada Studies in China	中国加拿大研究会
ACSF	All-China Sports Federation	中华全国体育总会
ACSI	American Consumer Satisfaction Index	美国消费者满意度指数
ACSM	American College of Sports Medicine	美国运动医学会
ACT	activated clotting time	活化凝血时间
ACT	air charge temperature	进气温度
ACT	American College Testing	美国大学入学考试
ACT	aspartate carbamyl transferase	天门冬氨酸转氨甲酰酶
ACT	automated confirmation transactions	自我确认交易
ACT	automatic code translation	自动译码机
ACT	action game	动作类游戏

A

ACTA	Anti-Counterfeiting Trade Agreement《反仿冒贸易协定》
ACTFL	American Council on the Teaching of Foreign Languages 美国外语教学委员会
ACTH	adrenocorticotrophin hormone 促肾上腺皮质激素
ACTR	actuator 传动装置
ACU	American Conservative Union 美国保守主义联盟/美国自然保护联盟
ACU	Asian Currency Unit 亚洲货币单位
ACU	Association of Commonwealth Universities 英联邦大学协会
ACUS	Atlantic Council of the United States 美国大西洋委员会
ACWI	All Country World Index 全球基准指数
AD	Anno Domini 公元[拉丁文]
AD	assembly district 选区
AD	Atopic dermatitis 特应性皮炎，又称遗传过敏性皮炎；自身致敏性皮炎
AD	attack damage 物理伤害
AD	automatic depositor 自动存款机
AD	Accession Document 军事系统报告
AD	active duty 现役[军]
AD	advanced development 先期开发
Ad	advertisement 广告
AD	Alzheimer's Disease 阿尔茨海默氏病
AD	anti-dumping 反倾销
AD	area divide 区域隔离
AD AC	Allegemeiner Dentscher Automobil Club 德国汽车俱乐部[德文]
ad. us. ext	ad usum externum 外用[拉丁文]
ADA	adenosine deaminase 腺苷脱氨酶
ADA	American Dental Association 美国牙科协会
ADA	American Diabetes Association 美国糖尿病学会
ADA	American Dietetic Association 美国营养协会
ADA	US DOD programming language 美国国防部的标准编程语言[代字]
ADAA	Agility Dog Association of Australia 澳大利亚敏捷的狗协会
ADAA	American Dodgeball Association of America 美国躲避球协会[该虚拟组织源于电影躲避球]

A

ADAA	Anxiety Disorders Association of America	美国焦虑症协会
ADAM	androgen deficiency in aging males	老年男子的荷尔蒙缺乏
ADB	Asian Development Bank	亚洲开发银行
ADB	Android Debug Bridge	安卓调试桥
ADC	aide-de-camp	副官［法文］
ADC	analog-digital converter	模数转换器
ADCC	antibody-dependent cell-mediated cytotoxicity	抗体依赖细胞介导的细胞毒作用
Add/addy	address	地址
ADD	attention deficit disorder	注意缺陷多动症
ADE	aerial development establishment	航空发展机构
ADEA	Age Discrimination in Employment Act	《美国就业年龄歧视法案》
ADES	automatic digital encoding system	自动数字编码系统
ADF	Air Defence Force	防空部队
ADH	antidiuretic hormone	抗利尿激素
ADHD	attention deficit/hyperactivity disorder	注意缺陷多动症
ADIS	advanced driver information system	先进驾驶信息系统
ADIUT	Assemblée de directeurs des Instituts Universitaires de Technologie	法国大学科技学院院长联盟［法文］
ADIZ	Air Defense Identification Zone	防空识别区［军］
ADJ	adjuster	调节器/校准器
ADL	Alexander Dannis	亚历山大·丹尼斯公司［英国最大巴士公司之一］
ADL	advance decline line	腾落指标［股市的一种大势分析指标］
Adm	Admiralty	海军部［英国］
Adm	admiral	海军上将
ADM	Archer Daniels Midland Food	阿彻丹尼尔斯米德兰食品
ADM	American Drug Manufactures	美国药品生产商联合会
Admin	administrator	管理员
ADN	any day now	随时［网络用语］
ADP	adenosine diphosphate	腺苷二磷酸
ADP	automatic data processing	自动数据处理
ADPCM	adaptive differential pulse code modulation	自适应差分脉冲编码调制

A

ADR	adverse drug reaction 药品不良反应	
ADR	alternative dispute resolution 非诉讼纠纷解决机制	
ADR	American Depositary Receipts 美国证券存托凭证	
ADS	aerial delivery system 航空运送系统	
ADS	alternative development strategies 变通的发展战略	
ADS	amusement destination state 旅游目的地国家	
ADS	automated data system 自动数据系统	
ADS	anti-dizzy system 防眩目系统	
ADS	accelerator-driven sub-critical system 加速器驱动次临界洁净核能系统	
ADS	Aufmer ksamkeitsdefizit-Syndrom 儿童多动综合征[德文]	
ADSL	analog to digital simulation 模拟数字语言	
ADSL	asymmetric digital subscriber line 不对称电子用户线路	
ADT	airborne data terminal 机载数据终端	
ADT	Atlantic Daylight Time 大西洋夏令时间	
AE	after effect 余波/后效/后果	
AE	account executive 财务经理	
AE	Air Explorer 空气探测器	
AE	American Express 美国运通信用卡	
AE	assistant engineer 助理工程师	
AE	in any event 任何情况下[网络用语]	
AEA	Auto Equipment Association 国际汽车音响超级职业巡回赛	
AE	copper 铜币[代字]	
AEA	Automotive Electric Association 汽车电器协会	
AEC	Atomic Energy Commission 美国原子能委员会	
AECT	Association for Educational Communications and Technology (U. S.) 美国教育传播与技术协会	
AED	automated engineering design 自动工程设计	
AED	automated external defibrillator 自动体外除颤器	
AEDP	automated external defibrillator pacemaker 自动体外除颤仪起搏器	
AEG	Allgemeine Elektrizitats Geselächaft 通用电器公司[德文]	
AEHF	advanced extremely high frequency 先进极高频	

A	AELE	Association Européenne de Libre-Échange ［英文：European Free Trade Association］欧洲自由贸易联盟［法文］
	AEO	authorized economic operator 经认证的经营者
	AERA	American Educational Research Association 美国教育研究协会
	AEROFLOT	Aero Flotilla 苏联民用航空公司［＝Soviet Airlines］
	AES	Advanced Encryption Standard 高级编码标准
	AES	Artificial Earth Satellite 人造地球卫星
	AES	acrylonitrile-ethylene-styrene 丙烯腈-乙烯-苯乙烯共聚物（塑料）
	AESA	active electronically scanned array radar 电子扫描雷达
	AESA	active electronically scanned array (radar) 有源相控阵雷达
	AESC	American Engineering Standards Committee 美国工程标准委员会
	AETD	adaptive engine technique development 自动适应性发动机技术发展
	AEX	Amsterdam Exchange 荷兰阿姆斯特丹证券交易所
	AF	admiral of the fleet 海军元帅
	AF	air force 空军
	AF	Air France 法国航空公司
	AF	audio frequency 音频
	AF	automatic following 自动跟踪
	AFAIAA	as far as I am aware 据我所知［网络用语］
	AFAIC	as far as I'm concerned 就我来说［网络用语］
	AFAICS	as far as I can see 照我看来［网络用语］
	AFAICT	as far as I can tell 照我说［网络用语］
	AFAIK	as far as I know 据我所知［网络用语］
	AFAIR	as far as I recall 就我所能回忆的［网络用语］
	AFB	air force base 空军基地
	AFBE	Asian Forum on Business Education 亚洲管理教育论坛
	AFC	African Football Confederation 非洲足球联合会
	AFC	Air Force Cross 空军十字勋章
	AFC	American Football Conference 美国足球联合会
	AFC	Association Football Club 足球俱乐部
	AFC	Automatic Fare Collection 自动售检票
	AFC	Asian Football Confederation 亚洲足球联合会

A

AFG	Afghanistan 阿富汗[亚洲国家]
AFI	American Film Institute 美国电影学会
AFII	American Federation of International Institutes 美国国际学会联合会
AFK	away from keyboard 不在机旁
AFL	American Football League 美国足球联盟
AFL	Australian Football League 澳大利亚足球联盟
AFL	American Federation of Labor 美国劳工联合会
AFL-CIO	American Federation of Labor - Congress of Industrial Organizations 美国劳联-产联
AFM	atomic force microscope 原子力显微镜
AFM	air flow meter 空气流量计
AFNOR	Association Française de Normalisation 法国标准化协会[法文]
AFP	Agence France-Presse 法新社[法国通讯社][法文]
AFP	associate financial planner 金融理财师
AFP	alpha-fetoprotein 甲胎蛋白
AFR	Advance Filing Rules 预申报制
Afr	African 非洲人
Afr	Africa 非洲
AFR	air-fuel ratio 空燃比
AFRASEC	Afro-Asian Organization for Economic Cooperation 亚非经济合作组织
AFS	active frame stability 主动式底盘稳定性装置
AFS	The American Field Service 国际青年交流组织
AFT	American Federation of Teachers 美国教师联合会
AFTA	ASEAN Free Trade Area 东盟自由贸易区
AFTA	Atlantic Free Trade Area 大西洋自由贸易区
AG	Aktien Gesellschaft 股份公司[德文]
Ag	argentum 银[第 47 号化学元素][拉丁文]
AG	Aktien gesellschaft 股份有限公司[用于德国、瑞士、奥地利等国][德文]
AG	attorney general 首席检察官
AG	about good 较好级(钱币)
AG	silver 银币[代字]
AGBM	antiglomerular basement membrane antibody 抗肾小球基底膜抗体

A

AGC	Asahi Glass Company 旭硝子玻璃集团公司［日本］
AGI	Alliance Graphique International 国际平面设计联盟
AGI	American Geographical Institute 美国地理学会
AGI	Artificial General Intelligence 人工通用智能
AGM	annual general meeting 年会/年度股东大会
AGP	accelerated graphics port 加速图形接口
AGP	Asia Grand Prix 亚洲大奖赛
AGPS	assisted global positioning system 辅助全球卫星定位系统
AGS	American Gem Society 美国宝石学会/美国宝石学会签发的钻石证书
AGT	Art Gallery of Toronto 加拿大多伦多艺术馆
AGTS	Above Ground Transport System 地面运输系统
AGTS	Automated Guideway Transit System 自动导轨运输系统
AGV	automatic guided vehicle 自动引导车
AH	adult humor 成人幽默
aH	attohenry 阿（托亨利）［电感单位］
AH	anno Hegirae 伊斯兰教纪元［拉丁文］
AH	anti-submarine helicopter 反潜直升机
AHA	American Heart Association 美国心脏协会/国际急救证书
AHA	American Historical Association 美国历史协会
AHA	anti-histone antibody 抗组蛋白抗体
AHCPW	Ad Hoc Commission on Prisoners of War （联合国）战俘问题特设委员会
AHE	Association for Higher Education 高等教育协会
A-HKFTA	Australia-Hong Kong Free Trade Agreement《澳港自由贸易协定》
AHL	American Hockey League 美国曲棍球联盟
AHRC	Australian Humanities Research Council 澳大利亚人文学科研究委员会
AHS	automated highway system 自动公路系统
AI	Aptitude Index 学业指数
AI	artificial intelligence 人工智能
AIA	American Institute of Architects 美国建筑师学会
AIA	American International Assurance Co., Ltd. 美国友邦保险有限公司
AIA	Associate of the Institute of Actuaries 保险统计师学会联合会
AIA	Association of International Accountants 国际会计师公会

AIB	Association of International Broadcasting 国际广播协会
AIB	Associate of the Institute of Bankers 英国银行家学会准会员
AIBA	Association Internationale de Boxe Amateur [英文:International Amateur Boxing Association] 国际业余拳击联合会[法语]
AIBO	Artificial Intelligence Robot 人工智能机器人
AIC	Administration of Industry and Commerce 工商局
AIC	Australian Industry Capacity 澳大利亚工业能力
AICA	anti-insulin cell antibody 抗胰岛细胞抗体
AICA	Association Internationale des Critique d'Art 国际艺术评论家协会[法文]
AICPA	American Institute of Certified Public Accountants 美国注册会计师协会
AICR	American Institute for Cancer Research 美国癌症研究院
AID	Artificial Insemination by Donor 供精人工授精
AID	Association Internationale de Développment [英文:International Development Association] 国际开发协会[法文]
AIDMA	attention, interest, desire, memory, action 消费行为学领域的理论模型之一 [引起注意,产生兴趣,唤起欲望,留下记忆,购买行动]
AIDS	Acquired Immune Deficiency Syndrome 艾滋病[获得性免疫缺陷综合征]
AIEE	Association des Instituts d'Études Européennes [英文:Association of Institutes for European Studies]欧洲问题研究联合会[法文]
AIESEC	Association Internationale des Étudiants en Sciences Économiques et Commerciales [英文:International Association of Students of Economic and Commercial Sciences] 国际经济学与商学学生协会[法文]
AIF	Asian Investment Fund 亚洲投资基金
AIFFP	Australian Infrastructure Financing Facility for the Pacific 澳大利亚太平洋基础设施融资基金
AIFS	American Intercultural Affair Society 美国对外文化交流协会
AIG	American International Group(Incorporated) 美国国际集团
AIH	artificial insemination by husband 夫精授精
AIHW	Australian Institute of Health and Welfare 澳大利亚卫生与福利研究院
AIHW	Australian Institute of Health and Welfare 澳大利亚医疗及福利学会
AIIB	Asian Infrastructure Investment Bank 亚洲基础设施投资银行

A

AIIC	Association Internationale des Interprétes de Conférence［英文：International Association of Conference Interpreters］国际会议口译人员/译员协会［法文］	
AIIDE	Artificial Intelligence and Interactive Digital Entertainment 人工智能与交互式数字娱乐大会	
AILA	American Immigrate Lawyer Association 美国移民律师协会	
AILC	Association Internationale de Littérature Comparée［英文：International Comparative Literature Association］国际比较文学协会［法文］	
AIM	aerial intercept missile 空中拦截导弹	
AIM	American Institute of Management 美国管理学会	
AIM	American Institute of Musicology 美国音乐学学会	
AIM	advanced idea mechanics 先进意念力学	
AIME	American Invitational Mathematics Examination 美国数学邀请赛	
AIME	average indexed monthly earnings 平均指数月收入	
AIMR	Association of Investment and Management Research（美国）投资管理和研究协会	
AIMS	American Institute for Myofascial Studies，LLC 美国肌筋膜研究有限公司	
AIMS	Australia Institute of Medical Scientists 澳大利亚医药科学家协会	
AINA	Arctic Institute of North America 加拿大北美北极研究所	
AIP	air injection pump 空气喷射泵	
AIP	American Institute of Physics 美国物理学会	
AIP	Association of Industry of Portugal 葡萄牙工业协会	
AIPAC	American‐Israeli Public Affairs Committee 美国-以色列公共事务委员会	
AIP	air-independent propeller 不依赖空气动力装置	
AIR	as I recall 据我回忆［网络用语］	
AirCell	cell phones on aircraft 机上宽带服务计划	
AIS	air intake system 进气系统	
AIS	Automatic Identification System 自动识别系统	
AISC	American Institute of Steel Construction 美国钢结构学会	
AISI	as I see it 依我看［网络用语］	
AISI	Amerian Iron and Steel Institute 美国钢铁学会	
AIT	advanced intelligent tape 先进智能磁带	
AIT	American Institute in Taiwan 美国在台协会

A

AITA	American International Training Association 美国国际训练协会
AITC	Artificial Intelligence Technology Center 人工智能研究院
AITI	Australian Institute of Translation & Interpretation 澳大利亚翻译学院
AJA	Americans of Japanese Ancestry 日裔美国人
AJAX	asynchronous Java Script and XML 一种创建交互式网页应用的网页开发技术
AJCC	American Joint Committee on Cancer 美国癌症联合会
AJG	American Journal of Gastroenterology 美国胃肠病学杂志
AKA	also known as 也叫作/又名
AKC	American Kennel Club 美国犬舍俱乐部
AKT	all kinds of things 各种各样的东西
al	academic leader 学术导师
Al	aluminium 铝[第13号化学元素]
AL	Arab League 阿拉伯联盟
AL	assessment level 评估等级
ALA	American Library Association 美国图书馆协会
ALAA	Applied Linguistics Association of Australia 澳大利亚应用语言学协会
Alb	albumin 白蛋白[正常值35～50 g/L]
ALB	Albania 阿尔巴尼亚[欧洲国家]
ALCOA	Aluminum Company of America 美国铝业公司
ALD	aldosterone 醛固酮
ALDH	aldehyde dehydrogenase 乙醛脱氢酶
ALF	Animal Liberation Front 动物解放阵线
ALFA Romeo	Anonoma Lombarda Fabbrica Automobili Romeo 阿尔法·罗密欧汽车[意大利文]
ALG	Algeria 阿尔及利亚[非洲国家]
ALGOL	algorithmic language 算法语言
ALIR	Army for the Liberation of Rwanda 卢旺达解放军
ALIS	advanced life information system 先进生命信息系统

A	ALK	anaplastic lymphomatous kinase 间变性淋巴瘤激酶
	ALL	acute lymphocytic leukemia 急性淋巴细胞白血病
	ALP	alkaline phosphatase 碱性磷酸酶
	ALPAC	Automatic Language Processing Advisory Committee 美国语言自动处理咨询委员会
	ALPS	advanced linear programming system 高级线性程序设计系统
	ALS	amyotrophic lateral sclerosis 肌萎缩侧索硬化
	ALS	approach-light system 进场照明系统
	Alt	alternate key 备用键
	ALT	alternator 交流发电机
	ALT	altitude 海拔高度
	ALT	alanine aminotransferase 谷丙转氨酶
	ALTAC	algebraic translator and compiler 代数翻译程序与编译程序
	ALTNTR	alternator 交流发电机
	AM	acrylamide monomer 丙烯酰胺
	Am	americium 镅[第95号化学元素]
	AM	amplitude modulation 调幅
	AM	ante meridien 上午[拉丁语]
	AM	agile manufacturing 敏捷制造
	Am	amylase 淀粉酶
	AM	anti-mine 反雷(的)
	AM	auxiliary memory 辅助存储器
	AMA	anti-mitochondrial antibody 抗线粒体抗体
	AMA	anti-myocardial antibody 抗心肌抗体
	AMANDA	Antarctic Muon and Neutrino Detector Array 南极 μ 介子和中微子探测器阵列望远镜
	AMAP	American Association Against Acronym Abuse 美国反对首字母缩略语协会
	AMAP	as much [many] as possible 尽可能多[网络用语]
	AMAS	autonomous mobile application system 自主移动应用系统
	AMBA	Association of Master of Business Administration 工商管理硕士协会
	AMBW	all my best wishes 致以我所有的祝福[网络用语]

A

AMC	American Mathematics Competitions	美国数学竞赛
AMC	American Movie Corporation	美国电影公司
AMC	asset management company	资产管理公司
AMD	Advanced Micro Devices	超微半导体公司
AMD	acute macular degeneration	急性黄斑变性
AMD	age-related macular degeneration	老年黄斑变性
AMD	automatic master device	自动驾驶系统
AMEX	American Express	美国运通卡
AMEX	American Stock Exchange	美国证券交易所
AMG	Autrecht Melcher Grossaspach	德国 AMG 汽车制造公司［德文］
AMHKY	Association of Mainland and Hong Kong Youth	内地香港青年联合会
AMI	acute myocardial ischemia	急性心肌缺血
AMI	advanced measurement instrument	先进量测仪
AMJ	Assemblée Mondiale de la Jeunesse［英文：World Assembly of Youth］世界青年大会［法文］	
AML	acute myelogenous leukemia	急性髓细胞性白血病
AMMTC	ASEAN Ministerial Meeting on Transnational Crime	东盟打击跨国犯罪部长级会议
AMNH	American Museum of Nature History	美国自然博物馆
AMOLED	active matrix organic light emitting diode	有源矩阵有机发光二极管
amp	ampère	安倍［电流单位］
AMP	analysis of mobility platform	机动平台分析
AMPS	advanced mobile phone service	高级移动电话服务
AMPV	armored multi-purpose vehicle	装甲多用途车辆
AMR	audio/modem riser	声音/调制调解插卡
AMR	antimicrobial resistance	抗微生物药耐药性
AMS	alpha magnetic spectrometer	太空磁谱仪
AMS	American Manifest System	美国仓单系统
AMS	automated manifest system	自动仓单系统
AMS	Auxiliary Medical Service	香港医疗辅助队
AMS	American Mathematical Society	美国数学学会
AMS	American Meteorological Society	美国气象协会

23

A	AMT	advanced metering infrastructure 先进计量基础设施
	AMT	air-mail transfer 航空信汇
	AMT	automated mechanical transmission 机械式自动变速器
	AMTRAM	automatic mathematic translation 自动数学翻译
	AMU	Aix-Marseille Uniersité 艾克斯-马赛大学[法文]
	AMXD	advanced mission extender device 先进任务增程器
	AMY	amylase 淀粉酶
	AN	ammonium nitrate 硝酸铵(炸药)
	ANA	All Nippon Airways 全日本航空公司
	ANA	American Numismatic Association 美国钱币协会
	ANA	antiunclear antibody 抗核抗体
	ANAB	American National Association of Broadcasters 美国国家广播公司协会
	ANAE	α-naphthyl-acetate esterase α-乙酸萘酯酯酶
	ANCA	antineutrophil cytoplasmic antibody 抗中性粒细胞胞浆抗体
	ANC	African National Congress (南非)非洲人国民大会
	ANCC	Article Numbering Center of China 中国物品编码中心
	ANCOM	Andeans Common Market 安第斯共同市场
	AND	Andorra 安道尔[欧洲国家]
	ANERA	Asia, North America Eastbound Rate Agreement 亚洲、北美向东费率协定
	ANG	Angola 安哥拉[非洲国家]
	ANI	automatic number identification 自动号码识别
	ANI	Asian News of International 亚洲新闻国际通讯社
	ANICERTA	Australia New Zealand Closer Economic Relations Trade Agreement 澳新紧密经济关系协定
	ANP	atrial natriuretic polypeptide 心房利钠尿多肽
	ANPR	automatic number plate recognition 自动数字牌识别
	ANS	Anti-Navires-Supersonioue 超音速反舰导弹[法文]
	ANSI	American National Standards Institute 美国国家标准学会
	ANSIC	American National Standard Institute COBOL 美国国家标准研究所制定的C语言标准定义

A

ANT	Antigua and Barbuda 安提瓜和巴布达[北美洲国家]	
ANTBOT	ant robot 蚂蚁机器人	
anti-LP	legionella antibody test 军团菌抗体试验	
ANU	Australian National University 澳洲国立大学	
ANWR	Arctic Natural Wildlife Refuge 国家北极野生生物保护区	
ANZSCO	Australian New Zealand Standard Classification of Occupations 澳大利亚和新西兰标准职业分类	
ANZUS	Australian, New Zealand and United States Treaty 澳大利亚、新西兰、美国安全条约	
AO	Admissions Office 大学入学事务局	
AO	Aktsionernoi Obshestvo 股份公司[俄文]	
AOAC	Association of Official Analytical Chemists 美国官方分析化学家协会	
AOB	any other business 其他事项	
AOC	appellation d'origine contrôlée 法国葡萄酒质量检验特产名酒[法文]	
AOC	Automatic Output Control 自动输出控制	
AOC	Airlines Operation Center 航空公司运行控制中心	
AOL	America On-Line 美国在线服务公司	
AOM	Award of Merit 裁判自行决定奖励给出色犬只[但又没评上 BOB 或 BOS 的]	
AOPA	Aircraft Owners and Pilots Association 航空器拥有者及飞行员协会	
AOSP	automatic operating and scheduling program 自动操作和调度程序	
AOTF	acousto-optical tunable filter 声光可调谐滤光器	
AP	acid phosphatase 酸性磷酸酶	
AP	advanced placement 跳级(生)	
AP	advice and pay 通知付款	
AP	Approved Product 安全标志[合乎标准之意]	
AP	approved product 定型产品	
AP	Associated Press 美联社	
AP	Atypical Pneumonia 非典型病原体肺炎	
AP	navy transport ship 海军运输船[代字]	
AP	Advanced Placement 美国大学预修课程	
AP	ability power 法术伤害	

A	AP	advanced program 先修课程
	APA	American Psychological Association 美国心理学会
	Apabi	author, publisher, area, buyer, Internet 方正公司的中文网络出版整体解决方案[作者、出版社、网络书店渠道、读者、因特网]
	APAC	Asia & Pacific 亚洲太平洋(地区)
	APB	all points bulletin 紧急通知
	APC	Aspirin-phenacetin-caffein 复方阿司匹林[由阿司匹林、非那西汀和咖啡因制成的一种解热镇痛药]
	APC	automatic process control 自动过程控制
	APC	armored personnel carrier 装甲运兵车
	APC	All People's Congress 全国人民大会党[塞拉利昂]
	APCA	Asian and Pacific Cardiac Association 亚太心脏医学研讨会议
	APCSC	Asia Pacific Customer Service Commission 亚太顾客服务协会
	APE	average premium equivalence 平均保费等值
	APEC	Asia-Pacific Economic Cooperation 亚太经合组织
	APECC	Asian-Pacific Economic Consultative Committee 亚太经济协调委员会
	APFA	Asia Pacific Association of Andrology 亚太地区男科学联合会
	APG	Anhui Publishing Group 安徽出版集团
	APHC	Asia Pacific Halal Council 亚太清真理事会
	APHC	Asia Pacific Heart Commission 亚太心脏大会
	API	Air Pollution Index 空气污染指数
	API	application program interface 应用程序接口
	API	American Petroleum Institute 美国石油协会
	APIX	Asia Pacific Internet Exchange 亚太互联网交换中心
	APL	acute promyelocytic leukemia 急性早幼粒细胞白血病
	APM	automated payment machine 自动缴费机
	APM	automated people mover systems 旅客自动捷运系统
	APMA	American Pedopathy Medicine Association 美国足病医学协会
	APMA	Asia-Pacific Musician Association 亚太音乐创作者联盟
	APN	Asian and Pacific Network 亚洲太平洋网络
	APO A-1	apolipoprotein A-1 载脂蛋白 A1
	APO-B	apolipoprotein B 载脂蛋白 B

A

APP	accelerated parellel processing 加速并行处理技术	
APP	application 应用(程序)	
APP	application productivity package 应用生产性软件包	
APP	application 应用(软件)	
APP	Alliance Populaire Progressiste 人民进步联盟[法文]	
APP	Armor Piercing Proof 穿甲试验	
APP	Asian Prewedding Photo 亚裔婚前摄影	
APR	annual percentage rate 年度百分比利率	
Apr	April 4月	
APS	advanced photo system 先进摄影系统	
APS	Akademiche Prüfstelle 德国政府派驻北京的官方办事机构[德文]	
APS	Anparts Selskab 有限责任公司[丹麦－挪威文]	
APSOS	Atmospheric Profiling Synthetic Observation System 大气"激光笔"	
APSOS	Atmospheric Profiling Synthetic Observation System 多波段多大气成分主被动综合探测系统	
APT	Advance Placement Test (美国)跳级考试	
APT	Arbitrage Pricing Theory 套利定价理论	
APT	Advanced Persistent Threat 高级持续性威胁	
APT	automatic picture transmission 自动图像传输	
APTC	American Policy Trade Council 美国汽车贸易政策委员会	
APTS	advanced public transport(traffic) system 先进公共交通系统	
APX	Asia Pacific Exchange 亚太证券交易所	
AQ	Adversity Quotient 逆境情商	
AQ	anquan 安全[汉语拼音"安全"的首字母]	
AQI	Air Quality Index 空气质量指数	
AQS	Air Quality System 空气质量控制系统	
AQSIQ	The General Administration of Quality Supervision, Inspection and Quarantine of the People's Republic of China 中华人民共和国国家质量监督检验检疫总局	
AR	Acknowledgement of Receipt 回执	
AR	Advice of Receipt 取款通知	
AR	Annual Report 年度报告	

A	AR	augmented reality 扩展实景/增强现实技术
	ARA	Automatic Retailers of America 美国自动零售公司
	ARA	Arabic 阿拉伯的
	ARATS	Association for Relations Across Taiwan Straits 海峡两岸关系协会/海协会
	ARBA	American Reference Books Annual《美国工具书年报》
	ARC	American Red Cross 美国红十字会
	ARC	Aeronautical Research Council 英国航空研究委员会
	ARDS	Acute Respiratory Distress Syndrome 急性呼吸窘迫综合征
	ARF	ASEAN Regional Forum 东盟地区论坛
	ARG	Argentina 阿根廷[拉丁美洲国家]
	ARG	arginase 精氨酸酶
	ARK	Noah's Ark 挪亚方舟
	ARK DS	Noah's Ark Operating System 方舟操作系统[鸿蒙操作系统]
	ARM	Advanced RISC Machine 英国 ARM 公司
	ARM	Armenia 亚美尼亚[欧洲国家]
	ARM	Advanced RISC Machines 英国 ARM 公司/英国 ARM 技术/英国 ARM 微处理器/英国微处理器企业/进阶精简报令集机器
	ARM	Acorn RISC Machine 三十二位精简指令集
	ARM	Anti-Radiation Missile 反辐射导弹
	ARMD	aged-related macular degeneration 年龄相关黄斑变性
	ARPA	Advanced Research Project Agency （美国国防部）高级研究计划署
	ARPG	action role playing game 动作角色扮演游戏
	ARPU	average revenue per user 单个用户平均收入
	ARQ	automatic repeat-request 自动重传请求
	arr	arranged by 由……改编
	arr	arrival 到达
	arr	arrive 到达
	ARS	Applied Research System 应用研究系统
	ART	Assisted Reproductive Technologies 辅助生殖技术
	ARTE	Association Relative à la Télévision Européenne 德法公共电视台[法文]
	ARTI	acute respiratory tract infection 急性呼吸道感染

A

ARTI	American Rescue Team International	美国国际救援队
ARV	armored recovery vehicle	装甲修理车
ARWU	Academic Ranking of World Universities	世界大学学术排名
AS	Advanced Subsidiary	高级补充程度考试
As	arsenic	砷[第33号化学元素]
AS	American Samoa	美属萨摩亚[太平洋群岛]
AS	Academy of Science	科学院
AS	access server	访问服务器
AS	Aksjeselskap	有限责任公司[挪威文]
AS	application server	应用服务器
AS	Australian Standard	澳大利亚国家标准
AS	acrylonitrile-styrene resin	丙烯腈-苯乙烯树脂
AS	after sales support	售后服务
AS	ankylosing spondylitis	强直性脊椎炎
AS	armored mobile master-slave system	主从追随式机甲系统
AS/RS	automatic storage and retrieval system	自动化仓储系统
AS/RS	automatic storage and retrieval system	自动化立体仓库
ASA	Advertising Standards Authority	英国广告标准局
ASA	anti-skeletal muscle antibody	抗骨骼肌抗体
ASA	Associate of Society of Actuary	准精算师
ASA	acrylonitrile - styrene - acrylates copolymer	丙烯腈-苯乙烯-丙烯酸酯共聚物[塑料]
ASA	Ambedkar Students Association	印度安贝德卡学生联合会
ASA	American Standard Association	美国标准协会[现为ANSI]
AsAb	antisperm antibody	抗精子抗体
ASAP	as soon as possible	越快越好[网络用语]
ASAS	Automatic Speech Analysis System	自动发音分析系统
ASAT	Anti-Satellite Weapon	反卫星武器
ASBO	antisocial behaviour order	反社会行为令
ASBU	Arab States Broadcasting Union	阿拉伯国家广播组织联盟
ASC	American Security Council	美国安全委员会
ASC	Automatic Switch Center	自动交换中心

A

ASCAP	American Society of Composers, Authors and Publishers 美国作曲家、作家与出版商协会
ASCE	American Society of Civil Engineers 美国土木工程师协会
ASCI	Accelerated Strategic Computing Initiative 美国加速战略计算计划
ASCII	American Standard Code for Information Interchange 美国信息交换标准代码
ASCM	anti-ship cruise missile 反舰巡航导弹
ASCO	American Society of Clinical Oncology 美国临床肿瘤学会
ASD	atrial septal defect 房间隔缺损
ASD	automatic synchronized discriminator 自动同步鉴别器
ASDB	Asian Development Bank 亚洲开发银行
ASE	Association Suisse des Electriciens 瑞士电工协会[法文]
ASEAN	Association of Southeast Asian Nations 东南亚国家联盟
ASEM	Asia-Europe Meeting 亚欧会议
ASES	Asia-Pacific Student Enterpriser Spirit 亚太地区学生企业家精神峰会
ASFV	African swine fever virus 非洲猪瘟病毒
ASIC	application specific integrated circuit 专业集成电路
Asics	anima sana in corpore sano 亚瑟士[日本跑鞋名品牌,源于拉丁语格言,意为健全的精神寓于强健的体魄][拉丁文]
ASIFA	Association Internationale du Film d'Animation 国际动漫电影协会[法文]
ASII	American Science Information Institute 美国科学信息协会
ASIIN	German Accreditation Agency for Study Programs in Engineering, Informatics, Natural Sciences and Mathematics 德国工程、信息科学、自然科学和数学专业认证机构
ASIMO	Advanced Step Innovative Mobility 一种机器人
ASIN	Amazon Standard Identification Number 亚马逊标准标识号[亚马逊随机生成的字母数字组合]
ASIO	Australian Safety Information Organization 澳大利亚安全情报组织
ASKAP	Australian Square Kilometer Array Pathfinder 平方公里阵列望远镜探测器
ASL	argininosuccinate lyase 精氨酸琥珀酸裂解酶
ASM	air-to-surface missile 空对地导弹

ASM	anti-ship missile 反舰导弹
ASM	artificial stock market 人工股票市场
ASMA	anti-smooth muscle antibody 抗平滑肌(自身)抗体
ASML	Advanced Semiconductor Material Lithography 阿斯麦尔
ASML	Advanced Semiconductor Material Lithography 艾司摩尔[中国台湾地区]
ASML	advanced semiconductor material lithography 先进半导体物质光刻机
ASMP	air-sol moyenne portée 中程空对地导弹[法文]
ASMR	autonomous sensory meridian response 自发性知觉经络反应
ASNT	American Society for Nondestructive Testing 美国无损检测学会
ASO	arteriosclerosis obliterans 闭塞性动脉硬化
ASO	antistreptolysin O 抗链球菌溶血素 O
ASP	active server pages 动态服务器网页
ASP	application service provider 应用服务提供商
ASP	Academic Search Premier 学术期刊集成全文数据库
ASPAC	Asian and Pacific Council 亚洲与太平洋地区理事会
ASPCA	American Society for the Prevention of Cruelty to Animals 美国防虐待动物协会
ASPI	Australian Strategic Policy Institute 澳大利亚战略政策研究所
ASQ	American Society for Quality 美国质量协会
ASQC	American Society of Quality Control 美国质量控制学会
ASR	automatic sound recognition 自动语音识别
ASR	anti-schlitten regelung 防滑驱动控制系统[德文]
ASR	anti-slip regulation (control) 防止滑转调节[控制]系统
ASR	automatic speed regulation 自动速度调节
ASRS	air-surveillance radar system 航空监控雷达系统
ASRS	airborne satellite receiving station 机载卫星接收站
ASRS	automatic seat reservation system 自动化订座系统
ASRS	automatic storage/retrieval system 信息自动储存与检索系统
ASRS	aviation safety reporting system 航空安全报告系统
ASRS	Asian Society for Research in Sleeping 亚洲睡眠研究会

A

ASRS	automated support requirements system 自动仓储物流系统	
assc	assistant 助理	
ASSEM	assemble 汇编/装配/组合（编辑）	
Assoc	association 协会	
Asst	assistant 助理的	
ASST	assisten 助理/助手[印尼文]	
ASSY	assembly 总成	
AST	Atlantic Standard Time 大西洋标准时间	
AST	aspartate aminotransferase 天冬氨酸转氨酶	
ASTD	American Society for Training and Development 美国培训与发展协会	
ASTECH	European Sustainable Project for Heating and Cooling Applications 欧洲加热和冷却应用技术的可持续项目	
ASTIA	Document(＝Armed Service Technical Information Agency) Document (美国)军事技术情报局文献	
ASTM	American Society of Testing Materials 美国材料实验学会	
ASU	Airport Security Unit 香港机场特警队	
ASU	Airport Security Unit 机场保安组	
ASU	Airport Security Unit 机场特警队	
ASW	antisubmarine warfare 反潜战	
AT	antithrombin 抗凝血酶	
AT	Aarne Thompson 国际通用的民间故事类型分类法[由芬兰学者阿尔奈和美国学者汤普森提出并修订]	
AT	advanced technology 先进技术	
At	astatine 砹[第85号化学元素]	
AT	automatic transmission 自动液力变速器	
AT	aerial tanker 空中加油机	
AT&T	American Telephone & Telegraph Company 美国电话电报公司	
ATA	actual time of arrival 实际到达时间	
ATA	American Translations Association 美国翻译协会	
ATA	anti-thyroid antibody 抗甲状腺抗体	
ATAC	airborne tactical advantage company 空中战术优势公司	
ATAC	advanced tank and artillery chariot 先进坦克火炮技术展示车	

ATB	all terrain bicycle 全地形自行车
ATB	all the best 祝一切顺利[网络用语]
ATC	Agreement on Textile and Clothing《纺织品与服装协定》
ATC	air traffic control 空中管制
ATCC	American Type Culture Collection 美国典型培养物保存中心
ATE	automatic test equipment 自动测试装置
ATE	Bureau of Alcohol，Tobacco & Firearms 烟酒火器管理局
ATF	automatic transmission fluid 自动变速箱用油
ATFM	air traffic flow management 空中交通流量管理
ATGA	antithyroglobulin antibody 抗甲状腺球蛋白抗体
ATIC	Air Technology Information Center 空中技术情报中心
ATIS	advanced traffic information service 先进的交通信息服务系统
ATLAS	A Toroidal LHC Apparatus 超环面仪器
atm	standard atmospheric pressure 标准大气压[非法定压力、压强、应力计量单位]
ATM	asynchronous transfer mode 异步传移模式
ATM	at the moment 目前[网络用语]
ATM	Automated Teller Machine 自动柜员机/自动提款机
ATMP	Advanced Thermal Grinding Machanical Pulping Process 改良的热磨机械浆方法
ATMS	advanced traffic management system 先进交通管理系统
ATN	augmented transition network 扩充转移网络
ATN	Australian Technology Network 澳大利亚科技大学联盟
ATP	adenosine triphosphate 腺苷三磷酸
ATP	automatic train protection 列车自动保护系统
ATP	Association of Tennis Professional 职业网球协会/国际职业网球联合会
ATR	Advanced Telecommunications Research Institute International 日本国际电气通信基础技术研究所
ATRAC	Adaptive Transform Acoustic Coding 自适应声学转换编码技术
ATS	air control team cooperation system 制空权团队合作系统
ATS	American Technical Service 美国技术学会
ATS	American Television Service 美国电视学会

A

ATS	American Travel Service 美国旅行社	
ATS	Applications Technology Satellite 应用技术卫星	
ATS	Austrian Schilling 奥地利先令[货币名称]	
ATS	automatic train stopping 列车自动停车(装置)	
ATS	automatic transfer switching equipment 自动转换开关电器	
ATS	automatic transfer system 自动转账制度	
ATS	Automobili Turismo e Sport 意大利一家跑车制造商[意大利文]	
ATSB	Australian Traffic and Security Bureau 澳大利亚交通安全局	
ATSC	Advanced Television System Committee 先进电视制式委员会	
ATT	Arms Trade Treaty《武器贸易条约》	
ATT	aspirin tolerance test 阿司匹林耐量试验	
ATV	all terrain vehicle 沙滩车	
ATV	All Terrain Vehicle 全地形车	
ATV	Associated Television (英国)联合电视公司	
ATV	Automatic Transport Vehicle 自动货运飞船	
ATV	Automatic Ticket Vendor 自动售票机	
ATV	advanced tactics vessel 先进战术艇[一种核潜艇]	
ATV	Asia Television Limited 亚洲电视	
ATW	Anti-terror(ism) war 反恐战争	
Au	astronomical unit 天文单位[即地球到太阳的距离(=1.496×10^8 千米)]	
Au	aurum 金[第 79 号化学元素][拉丁文][英文为 gold]	
Au	Australia antigen 澳抗(即乙型肝炎表面抗原)	
AU	about uncirculated 近未流通级(钱币)	
AU	Amsterdam University 荷兰阿姆斯特丹大学	
AU	gold 金币[代字]	
AUCC	Association of Universities and Colleges of Canada 加拿大大专院校联盟;加拿大高等院校协会	
AUD	Australian dollar 澳大利亚元(货币名称)	
Aug	August 8 月	
AUO	African Unity Organization 非洲统一组织	
AURKA	Aurora＋Kinase＋A 极光激酶 A	
AURKB	Aurora Kinase B 极光激酶 B	

A

AURKC	Aurora Kinase C 极光激酶 C
AUS	Australia 澳大利亚[大洋洲国家]
AUT	Austria 奥地利[欧洲国家]
AUTO CAD	automatic computer aided design 自动计算机辅助设计
AUTODIN	automatic digital network 自动数字网络
AV	audio-visual 音频—视频
AVA	Approved Viticultural Area 经认可的葡萄产区[美国葡萄酒质量管理]
AVA	adult video actor 男优
AVA	adult video actress 女优
AVAR	Association of Anti-virns Asia 亚洲反病毒研究者协会
AVCS	Advanced Vehicle Control System 先进汽车控制系统
Ave	avenue 大街
AVG	adventure game 冒险类游戏
AVG	American Volunteer Group 美国志愿援华航空队
AVI	audio video interleaved 是 windows 的一种多媒体文件格式
AVIC	Aviation Industry Corporation of China 中国航空工业集团公司
AVL	approved vendor list 认可的供应商名单
AVLB	armored vehicle launched bridge 架桥装甲车
AVM	around view monitor 全景式监控影像系统
AVP	antiviral protein 抗病毒蛋白(质)
AVS	Audio Video Coding Standard 数字音视频编解码标准
AVSI	Association des Volontaires pour le Service International 国际志愿者协会[法文]
AVT	ad valorem tax 从价税
AVU	The African Virtual University 非洲虚拟大学
AVVID	architecture for voice, video and integrated data 语音、视频及集成数据架构
AW	actual weight 实际重量,实际权数
AW	atomic weapon 原子武器
AW	atomic weight 原子量
AWACS	airborne warning and control system 空中预警及控制系统
AWAK	automated wearable artificial kidney 可穿戴式人工肾脏
AWCIGO	and where can I get one 我在哪儿可得一个?[网络用语]

AWDC	Antwerp World Diamond Center 安特卫普世界钻石中心	
AWHFY	are we having fun yet? 我们(已经)过得很愉快吗?[网络用语]	
AWS S3	Amazon Simple Storage Service 为开发人员和 IT 团队提供安全、耐久且扩展性高的对象存储	
AY	always yours 永远是你的[网络用语]	
AYIE	Asian Youth Invent Expo 亚洲青少年发明展	
A-Z Test	Ascheim-Zondek Test 阿—宗二氏试验[妊娠检查]	
az	azure 天蓝色	
AZE	Azerbaijan 阿塞拜疆[欧洲国家]	
AZT	zidovudine 叠氮胸苷/齐多夫定[一种抗艾滋病药物]	

B	B type ultrasonic diagnose [examination] B 型超声诊断(仪)	
b	barn 靶恩[非法定面积单位,1 靶恩＝10^{-28}平方米]	
B	boron 硼[第 5 号化学元素]	
B	Thailand Baht 泰国铢[货币]	
B	black 黑色	
B to B	business to business 商家对商家[电子商务的一种形式]	
B to B to C	business to business to customer 商家到商家到客户[电子商务的一种形式]	
B to G	business to government 商家对政府[电子商务的一种形式]	
B	Balenciaga 巴黎世家服饰	
B	Bentley 英国宾利汽车	
B	blue 蓝色	
B	Brabus 美国巴博斯汽车	
B&B	Bed & Breakfast 含早餐旅馆	
B&H	Bosnia and Herzegovina 波斯尼亚和黑塞哥维那[欧洲国家,又称波黑]	

B&Q	Richard Block and David Quayle 百安居(用公司两创始人的姓的首字母)
B&R	The Belt and Road 一带一路
B. T. O.	big time operator 游手好闲、浪费时间、无所事事的人
B/L	bill of lading 提单
B/O	brought over 结转
B/R	bill receivable 应收票据
B/S	bore/stroke 缸径/行程
B/S	bore-to-stroke 缸径行程比
B/S	browser/server 浏览器/服务器模式
B/W/H	bust/waist/hips 胸围/腰围/臀围[简称三围]
B2B	business to business 商家对商家[电子商务的一种形式]
B2C	business to customer 商家对客户[电子商务的一种形式]
B2G	Business to Government 商家对政府[电子商务的一种形式]
B4N	bye for now 再见[网络用语]
BA	Bachelor of Arts 文学学士
Ba	barium 钡[第 56 号化学元素]
BAA	Basketball Association of America 美国篮球协会
BAA	broad-agency announcement 广泛机构公告
BAC	Blood Alcohol Concentration 血液酒精浓度
BAC	by any chance 也许/万一[网络用语]
BACA	Bikers Against Child Abuse 反霸凌机车帮
BACP	British Association for Counselling and Psychotherapy 英国咨询和心理治疗协会
BACR	British Association for Cancer Research 英国肿瘤研究协会
BAF	Bo'ao Asian Forum 博鳌亚洲论坛
BAF	bunker adjustment factor 燃油附加费/油价调整指数附加费
BAFTA	The British Academy of Film and Television Arts 英国电影和电视艺术学院
BAH	Bahamas 巴哈马[北美洲国家]
Baha	bone anchored hearing aid 骨锚式助听器
BAI	Bertelsmann Asia Investments 贝塔斯曼亚洲投资基金
BAII	La Banque asiatique d'investissement pour les infrastructures 亚洲基础设施投资银行[法文]

BAK	back at keyboard 回到电脑旁[网络用语]
BAM	broadcasting AM 午前广播
BAME	Black，Asian，and minority ethnic 非裔、亚裔及其他少数族裔
BAMF	Bundesamt für Migration und Flüchtlinge 联邦移民与难民(事务)局[德文]
BAMS	Broad Area Maritime Surveillance 广域海上无人监视
BAN	Bangladesh 孟加拉国[亚洲国家]
BAN	Basel Action Network 巴塞尔行动网络
BAP	blood bone alkaline phosphatase 骨源性碱性磷酸[酯]酶
BAR	Barbados 巴巴多斯[北美洲国家]
Bart	baronet 准男爵
BAS	brake assistant system 刹车辅助系统
BAS	Berlin Air Show 柏林航空展
BASA	Bilateral Air Safety Agreement 双边航空安全协定
BASF	Badische Anilin & Soda-Fabrik AG 巴斯夫公司[德文]
BASIC	beginners all-purpose system instruction code 初学者通用指令码
BASO	basophil 嗜碱性粒细胞
BAT	British-American Tobacco 英美烟草公司
BAT	Baidu, Alibaba, Tencent 超一流规模的互联网公司[百度、阿里巴巴、腾讯]
BAT	battery 蓄电池
BATJ	Baidu, Alibaba, Tencent, Jingdong 百度、阿里巴巴、腾讯、京东为代表的巨头企业
BAW	bulk acoustic wave 体声波
BAW	Beijing Automobile Works 北京汽车制造有限公司
BB	baby 婴儿
BB	be back 要回来[网络用语]
BB	blemish balm 遮瑕膏
BB	bye-bye 再见[网络用语]
BB	Bed & Breakfast 含早餐旅馆
BB	buffer base 缓冲碱
BB	Blue Book 蓝皮书
BB	Buy Box 黄金购物车[购买按钮]
BBA	Belgium Banker Association 比利时银行家学会

B

BBA	building block approach 模块方式
BBA	Benz，BMW，Audi 德国豪车三巨头[奔驰、宝马、奥迪]
BBAV	Banco Bilbao Vizcaya Argentaria 西班牙毕尔巴鄂比斯开银行[西班牙文]
BBB	blood buffer base 血液缓冲碱
BBC	British Broadcast Corporation 英国广播公司
BBCC	Beauty and the Best Cosmeceutical Company Ltd. 瑞士苏黎世药妆开发公司
BBCCB	Balasore Bhadra Central Cooperative Bank 巴拉索巴德拉中央合作银行
BBE	background block error 背景误差
BBFN	bye bye for now 再见[网络用语]
BBIAB	be back in a bit 一会儿就回来[网络用语]
BBIAM	be back in a minute [moment] 一会儿就回来[网络用语]
BBIAS	be back in a second 一会儿就回来[网络用语]
BBIT	building block integrated test 跨团队子系统间的集成测试
BBL	be back later 稍后便回来[网络用语]
BBN	Broad Band Networks（北京）宽带网公司
BBN	bye bye now 再见[网络用语]
BBO	barium borate 硼酸钡
BBO	beta-barium borate 偏硼酸钡
BBO	β Bab204 [Beta-Barium Borate] 低温相偏硼酸钡
BBP	butyl benzyl phthalate 邻苯二甲酸丁苄酯
BBQ	barbecue 烤肉野餐
BBR	burnt beyond repair 烧得无法修理[网络用语]
BBS	be back soon 很快回来[网络用语]
BBS	bulletin board system 电子公告栏系统
BBT	basal body temperature 基础体温
BBT	bombardment 轰炸/炮击
BBT	bright beer tank 清酒罐
BBW	big beautiful woman 非常美的女人[网络用语]
BC	Bachelor of Commerce 商学士
BC	bar code 条码（技术）
BC	before Christ 公元前

BC	Binary Code 二进制代码
BC	Beijing Culture 北京文化
BC	bicycle club 自行车俱乐部
BC	blue chips 蓝筹股
BC	buyer's credit 买方信贷
BCA	budget control act 预算控制法案
bcc	blind carbon copy (to) 密件抄送
BCC	black carbon copy 秘密副本,秘密抄送
BCCI	Bank of Credit and Commerce International 国际商业信贷银行
BCCI	Bankcard Consumption Confidence Index 银行卡消费信心指数
BCE	before the Common Era 公元前
BCG	bacillus calmette-guerin 卡介苗
BCG	Boston Consulting Group 波士顿咨询集团/波士顿咨询公司
BCH	Banco Central Hipotecario 哥伦比亚中央抵押银行［西班牙文］
BCH	Bose, Chaudhuri & Hocquenghem type of code 博斯-乔赫里-霍克文黑姆码
BCI	Business Competitiveness Index 企业竞争力指数
BCI	brain computer interface 脑机接口
BCIM	Bangladesh, China, India, Myanmar 孟中印缅经济走廊
BCM	Bank of Communications 交通银行
BCN	Blockchain Consensus Network 区块链共识网络
BCS	Bank of Changsha 长沙银行
BCS	Board Certified in Securities 德国有机认证标志
BCS	Bureau of Ceylon Standard 斯里兰卡标准局
BCT	Business Chinese Test 商务汉语考试
BCU	Banco Central del Uruguay 乌拉圭中央银行［西班牙文］
BD	Blu-ray Disc 蓝光光盘
BD	Baidu 百度［汉语拼音缩略语］
BDA	Beijing Economic-technological Development Area 北京经济技术开发区
BDA	Blu-ray Disc Association 蓝光光盘协会
BDA	British Dental Association 英国牙科协会
BDA	British Diabetes Association 英国糖尿病协会

B

BDA	British Dietetics Association 英国营养协会	
BDA	Business Data Analysis 业务数据分析	
BDA	Bund Deutscher Architekten 德国建筑联合会[德文]	
BDA	Bundesvereinigung der Deutschen Abeitgeberverbände 德国雇主协会联邦联合会[德文]	
BDA	Dr Bohai Zhang，Duncan Alark Associates 博达克咨询有限公司	
BDB	Bharat Diamond Bourse 印度孟买巴拉特钻交所	
BDCA	border defence cooperation agreement 边境防务合作协议	
BDCI	Brand Design of China International 中国国际品牌设计（年展）	
BDD	behavior-driven development 行为驱动开发	
BDI	Burundi 布隆迪[非洲国家]	
BDN	Broadband Digital Network 宽带数字网	
BDNF	brain-derived neurotrophic factor 脑源性神经营养因子	
BDP	beclomethasone dipropionate 二丙酸倍氯米松	
BDS	Beidou System 北斗导航系统	
BDS	Bălgarski dár Žaven Standart 保加利亚标准局[保加利亚文]	
BDS	Beidou Navigation Satellite System 中国北斗卫星导航系统	
BDTC	Big Data Technology Conference 大数据技术大会	
BE	Bachelor of Engineering 工学士	
BE	Bank of England 英格兰银行	
BE	base excess 碱过量	
Be	beryllium 铍[第4号化学元素]	
BE	Bill of Exchange 汇票	
BE	Blue Efficiency 蓝色高效能	
BE	British Empire 英帝国	
BE	bad ending 悲剧结尾	
BEA	Le Bureau d'Enquêtes et d'Analyses 法国民航安全调查分析局[法文]	
BEC	Business English Certificate 商务英语证书	
BECA	Berlin Expo Center Airport 柏林机场会展中心	
BEI	butanol-extractable iodine 丁醇提取碘	
BEL	Belgium 比利时[欧洲国家]	
BEN	Benin 贝宁[非洲国家]	

BeOS	BE Operating System	由美国 Be 公司研制的一种个人计算机操作系统
BEPC	Beijing Electron Positron Collider	北京正负电子对撞机
BETT	Business English Translation Test	商务英语翻译考试
BF	Belgian Franc	比利时法郎［比利时 2002 年前的货币］
BF	baby's father	孩子他爸
BF	be forever	永远
BF	bentonite flocculation test	皂土絮状试验
BF	best friend	最好的朋友
BF	boy friend	男友
BFA	Bachelor of Fine Arts	美术学士
BFA	Bo'ao Forum for Asia	博鳌亚洲论坛
BFF	best friend forever	永远最好的朋友
BFF	Binary Flip-Flop	二进制触发器
BFG	big friendly grin	友好的露齿大笑［网络用语］
BFG	BF Goodrich	美国百路驰轮胎公司
BFG	Buffett Financial Group	巴氏财团
BFGF	basic fibroblast growth factor	碱性成纤维细胞生长因子
BFM	business frequency modulation	商业频道
BFN	bye for now	再见
BFP	biologic false positive	生物假阳性
BfR	Bundesinstitut für Risikobewertung	德国联邦风险评估研究所［德文］
BFSU	Beijing Foreign Studies University	北京外国语大学
BFT	Biofeedback Therapy	生物反馈疗法
BFT	Business Foreign Language Test	全国出国培训备选人员外语考试
BfV	Bundesamt für Verfassungsschutz	德国联邦宪法保卫局［德文］
BG	business group	业务集团
BG	bank guarantee	银行担保
BG	Bis Gleich	一会儿回来［德文］
BG	blood group	血型
BG	bluish green	青绿色
BG	boy and girl	男女恋/异性恋
BGA	British Geriatrics Association	英国老年协会

BgC3	Bill Gates Company Three 盖茨的公司
BGI	Beijing Genomics Institute 华大基因（北京基因组研究中心）
BGM	background music 背景音乐
BH	Boeing helicopter 波音直升机
Bh	bohrium 铍［第 107 号化学元素］
BHAG	big，hairy，audacious goal 宏伟目标
Bhd	Berhad 股份有限公司［马来文］
BHPI	big data house price index 大数据房价指数
BHT	Butylated Hydroxy Toluene 丁基羟基甲苯
BHU	Bhutan 不丹［亚洲国家］
BI	bismuth 铋［第 83 号化学元素］
BI	behaviour identity 行为识别
BI	Birds International 鸟类国际
BI	business intelligence 商务智能/商业智能
BIC	best in class 班上最好的［网络用语］
BIC	Biometrics Institute Congress 生物识别学会年会
BICBW	but I could be wrong 但我可能错了［网络用语］
BICC	British Institute Centre of China 全英高校中国研究中心
bid	bis in die 每日两次［拉丁文］
BID	British Intelligence Department 英国情报部
BID	Business Improvement District 经济开发区
BIE	Bureau of International Exhibition 国际展览局
BIF	basis in fact 以事实为依据［网络用语］
BIG	Best In Group 犬组冠军
BIL	bilirubin 胆红素
BIL	brother in law 姐夫；妹夫；妻舅［网络用语］
BIL	urine bilirubin 尿胆红素
BIL	bilirubin test 胆红素实验
Bil	serum bilirubin 血清胆红素
BIM	building information modeling 建筑信息模型
BIMBA	Beijing University International Master of Business Administration 北京大学国际 MBA 项目

BIN	bank identification number 银行标识号	
BION	believe it or not 信不信由你[网络用语]	
BIOS	Basic Input Output System 基本输入输出系统	
biotech	biology technology 生物技术	
Bio-X	Biology-X 生物学与其他学科相结合形成的交叉学科	
BIR	Bureau of Intelligence and Research 情报研究局	
BIR	Bureau of International Recycling 国际回收局	
BIS	Best In Show 全场犬类总冠军	
BIS	Bank for International Settlements 国际清算银行	
BIS	Bureau of Indian Standards 印度标准局	
BIS	Board of Industry and Security 工业与安全局	
BIS	British Information Service 英国情报处	
BIS	British Interplanetary Society 英国星际航行学会	
BIS	Bureau of Industry and Security 工业和安全局	
BIS	Business Information System 商业情报系统	
BISDN	Broadband Integrated Services Digital Network 宽带综合业务数字网络	
BISFA	Bureau International pour la Standardisation des Fibres Artificielles 国际化学纤维标准局[法文]	
BISS	Best In Specialty Show 某一犬种单独展的冠军	
BIT	Beijing Institute of Technology 北京理工大学	
BIT	bilateral investment treatment 双边投资协定	
BIV	Bovine Immunodeficiency Virus 牛免疫缺损病毒	
BIV	built-in variable (plumbing) 内置的变量(管道)	
biz	business 生意	
BJP	Bence-Jones Protein 本周蛋白	
BJJ	Bruce Lee, Jackie Chan, Jet Lee 中国三位武打艺人(李小龙,成龙,李连杰)	
BJP	Bharatiya Janata Party (India) 印度人民党	
BJPIS	Best Junior Puppy In Show 全场特幼犬冠军	
BJT	bipolar junction transistor 双载子晶体管	
BJT	bipolar junction triode 双极型三极管	
BK	because 因为;由于[根据英文单词读音缩略][网络用语]	
Bk	berkelium 锫[第 97 号化学元素]	

B

BKI	Biro Klasifikasi Indonesia 印度尼西亚船级社[印尼文]
BKM	business knowledge management 商业知识管理
BL	Boys Love 男性间的恋爱[或称蔷薇;耽美;少年爱。不完全等同于男同性恋]
BL	belly laugh 哈哈大笑;纵情大笑[网络用语]
BLD	urine occult blood 尿潜血
Bldg E	building engineer 建筑工程师
BLIS	Bilingual Laws Information System 香港双语法例资料系统
BLOG	web Log 博客
BLOGGER	Web Logger 写博客的人
BLR	Belarus 白俄罗斯[欧洲国家]
BLT	bacon, lettuce and tomato 熏猪肉、生菜、番茄三明治
BLU	blue 蓝色
Blvd	boulevard 大道
BM	Body Maintenance 塑身
BMBPF	bovine milk basic protein fraction 牛奶碱性蛋白成分
BMC	British Medical Council 英国医学委员会
BMC	Bio Med Centre 生物医学中心
BMC4I	battle management/command control, communications, compute's and intelligence 战斗管理/指挥、控制、通信、计算机和情报[军队自动化指挥系统]
BMD	ballistic missile defense 弹道导弹防御系统
BMD	bone mineral density 骨矿物质密度
BMDW	Bone Marrow Devices of World 国际骨髓库
BMI	Body Mass Index 体重指数[以体重 kg/身高 m^2 表示]
BMJ	British Medical Journal《英国医学杂志》
BMOC	big man on campus 校园里的大人物[网络用语]
BMP	Bitmap 位图
BMP	Boyevaya Mashina Pekhoty 步兵战车(俄文)
BMPT	Boievaia mashina poddierzhki tankov 坦克火力支援战车[俄文]
BMR	basal metabolic rate 基础代谢率
BMS	Brand Management System 品牌管理系统

BMTIPG	brilliant minds think in parallel gutters 英雄所见略同[网络用语]
BMus	Bachelor of Music 音乐学士
BMW	Bayerische Motoren Werke 宝马汽车[原意为德国巴伐利亚汽车公司][德文]
BMW	bus, metro, walk 在大城市，人们出门上班，不少人是先乘公交车到最近的地铁站，出了地铁，再走一段路才到单位，这些人被称为 BMW 一族
BMX	bicycle motocross 小轮车/越野自行车
bn	billion 十亿
BN(O)	British National (Overseas) Passport 英国国民（海外）护照
BNB	British National Bibliography 英国国家书目
BNC	British National Corpus (Collection) 英语国家语料库
BND	Bundesnachrichtendienst 德国联邦情报局[德文]
BNDDIS	band display 波段显示
BNEC	British National Export Council 英国国家出口委员会
BNF	big name fan 名人迷[网络用语]
BNI	business network intelligence 商务网络智能
BNI	Butterfly Network Inc 蝴蝶网络公司
BNP	British National Party 英国国家党
BNP	brain natriuretic Peptide 脑钠肽
BNP	Banque Nationale de Paris 巴黎国民银行[法文]
BNU	Beijing Normal University 北京师范大学
BO	body odour 体臭
BO	Burn Out 发怒族[因工作过分紧张而精神抑郁和脾气暴躁的人]
BOA	British Olympics Association 英国奥委会
BOB	Best of Breed 单一犬种冠军[同 BOV]
BOB	best of the best 精英中的精英[网络用语]
BOB	Bank of Beijing 北京银行
BOBO	Bourgeois Bohemia 波波族[布尔乔亚和波希米亚缩写组合]
BOBS	Betswana Bureau of Standards 博茨瓦纳标准局
BOC	but of course 当然[网络用语]
BOC	Bank of China 中国银行

BOCI	Bank of China International 中银国际
BOCOM	Bank of Communications 交通银行
BOD	bandwidth on demand 按需分配宽带
BOD	biochemical oxygen demand 生化需氧量
BOD5	five-day biochemical oxygen demand 5日生化需氧量
BOE	Bank of England 英格兰银行
BOF	birds of a feather 一丘之貉[网络用语]
BOGOF	buy one, get one free 买一送一
BOL	Best of luck 好运气[网络用语]
BOL	Bolivia 玻利维亚[南美洲国家]
BOLL	Bolinger Bands 布林线指标[其波动的上下限随股价浮动]
BOM	bill of material 物料清单
BOPY	bivalent oral poliovirus vaccine 二价口服脊髓灰质炎疫苗
BOS	basic operation system 基本操作系统
BOS	Best Opposite Sex 单一犬种最佳相对性别[同BOB不同性别的最佳犬只]
BOSS	Business & Operation Support System 业务运营支持系统
BOT	back on topic 回来谈这个话题[网络用语]
BOT	balance of trade 金融贸易收支差额
BOT	Botswana 博茨瓦纳[非洲国家]
BOT	build, operate, transfer 建设、运营、转让[是一种新兴的投资融资方式]
BOTC	British Overseas Territories Citizen 英国海外领土公民
BOTE	back of the envelope 信封背面[网络用语]
BOV	Best of Variety 单一犬种冠军[同BOB]
BOY	beginning of year 年初
BP	beeper 无线寻呼机
BP	blood pressure 血压
BP	British Petroleum 英国石油公司
BP	bust point 乳点
BP	blood press 血压
BP	Border Patrol 边境巡逻队
BPA	Business Publications Audit 国际权威发行量认证机构

BPA	bisphenol A 双酚 A
BPC	blood platelet count 血小板计数
BPCE	Banque fédérale des banques populaires＋Caisse nationale des caisses d'épargne 法国 BPCE 银行集团［法文］
BPH	benign prostatic hyperplasia 良性前列腺增生
BPI	Bribe Payers Index 行贿指数
BPI	Buying Power Index 购买力指数
BPI	Banco Português de Investimento 葡萄牙投资银行［葡萄牙文］
BPI	Bard Prison Initiative 巴德学院监狱项目
BPIS	Best Puppy In Show 全场幼犬冠军
BPJPH	Badan Penyelenggara Jaminan Produk Halal 政府清真产品认证机构［印尼文］
BPO	bipolar offset 双极性偏移
BPO	British Post Office 英国邮政总局
BPO	business process outsourcing 商业流程外包
BPR	business process reengineering 业务流程重组
bps	bits per second 比特/秒［数据传输速率单位］
Bps	bytes per second 字节/秒［传输速率单位］
BPSK	binary phase shift keying 二进制相移键控
Bq	becquerel 贝可［放射性活度单位］
Bq	Becquerel 贝可（勒尔）［法定放射性活度计量单位］
BQ	behavior quotient 行为商（数）
BQ	body quotient 体商
Br	British 英国的
Br	bromine 溴［第 35 号化学元素］
BR	best regards 祝好
BR	born rich 出生富有
BR	brown 棕色
BRA	brassiere 胸罩
BRA	Brazil 巴西［南美洲国家］
BRAIN	brain research through advancing innovative neurotechnologies 通过推动创新型神经技术的大脑研究

B

BRAS	broadband remote access service 宽带远程接入服务
BRASS	Business Reference and Services Section 商业参考与服务小组
BRB	be right back 马上回来［网络用语］
BRC	British Retail Consortium 英国零售商协会（认证）
BRCA	breast cancer susceptibility gene 乳腺癌易感基因
Brexit	Britain exiting from the EU 英国脱欧
BRG	bearing 轴承
BRI	The Belt and Road Initiative 一路一带倡议
BRICS	the countries of Brazil，Russia，India，China and South Africa 金砖五国（指巴西、俄罗斯、印度、中国和南非）
BRICS	bank，reform，inclusiveness，confidence，sense of gain 银行、改革、包容、信心和获得感
BRICS	The Belt and Road，respect，innovation，cooperation，seeking common ground while shelving differences 一带一路，尊重，创新，合作，求同存异
BRKT	bracket 支架
BRM	Biological Response Modifier 生物反应调节剂
BRN	Bahrain 巴林［亚洲国家］
BRN	brown 棕色
brPK	brownish pink 棕红色
BRS	Bulgaria Register of Shipping 保加利亚船舶登记局
BRT	Bus Rapid Transit 快速公交系统
BRU	Brunei 文莱［亚洲国家］
BRV	Blue Run Ventures 蓝驰创投
BS	body suit 紧身衣裤
BS	blood sugar 血糖
BS	brain storming 脑力激荡
BSA	body surface area 体表面积
BSA	Business Software Association 商务软件联盟
BSA	Bachelor of Science in Agriculture 农业科学学士
BSA	Boy Scouts of America 美国童子军
BSA	British Society of Aesthetics 英国美学学会
BSATs	biological select agents and toxins 生物选择剂和毒素

BSC	balanced scorecard 平衡记分卡	
BSC	British Secretary of Cambridge 剑桥 BSC 秘书证书考试	
B-school	business school 商学院	
BSCI	Business Social Compliance Initiative 商业社会标准认证	
BSD	Berkeley Software Design 伯克利软件设计[国际一种广泛使用的免费操作系统]	
BSE	Bovine Spongiform Encephalopathy（即 mad cow disease）牛海绵状脑病[即疯牛病]	
BSEC	Black Sea Economic Cooperation 黑海经济合作组织	
BSF	border security force 边防保安队[印度]	
BSG	big smiling grin 露齿大笑[网络用语]	
BSG	broad sweeping generalization 广泛的概括[网络用语]	
BSHS	British Society for the History of Science 英国科学史学会	
BSI	British Standards Institution 英国标准学会	
BSI	British Standards Institution 英国认证标志	
BSkyB	British Sky Broadcasting 英国天空广播公司	
BSM	modern shipbuilding model 现代造船模式	
BSO	Birmingham Symphony Orchestra 英国伯明翰交响乐团	
BSO	Boston Symphony Orchestra 美国波士顿交响乐团	
BSO	Bournemouth Symphony Orchestra 英国伯恩茅斯交响乐团	
BSOD	blue screen of death 死亡的蓝屏[网络用语]	
BSP	Blog service provider 博客服务提供商	
BSP	Business Service Platform 商业服务平台	
BSP	Business Source Premier 商业资源电子文献全文数据库	
BSR	Blood Sedimentation Rate 血沉降率	
BSS	British Standard Specification 英国标准规范	
BSS	Broadcast Satellite Service 广播卫星业务	
BSS	Business Support System 商务支持系统	
BST	Business Software Technology 商业软件技术	
BSV	boshivideo 液晶拼接屏	
BT	bass tuba 低音大号、低音大喇叭[音响]	
BT	Bit Torrent 比特流[pnp 下载，又称变态下载]	

BT	botulinus toxin 肉毒杆菌毒素
BT	British Telecommunications 英国电信公司
BT	building-transfer 建设—移交模式
BT	Black Temple 黑暗神殿
BT	bleeding time 出血时间
Bt	Btcry 1 Ah 农杆菌介导转基因
BTA	Best Time Available 广告黄金收视时间
BTA	border tax adjustment 边界税收调整
BTA	British Tourist Authority 英国旅游局
BTA	but then again 但另一方面[网络用语]
BTA	British Textile Agreement《英国纺织品协定》
BTB	business to business 商家对商家[电子商务的一种形式]
BTC	BitCoin 比特币
BTC	business to customer 商家对消费者[电子商务的一种形式]
BTCC	British Touring Car Cup 英国房车赛
BTD	breaking talent and ability of drug 突破性药物资格
BTE	bachelor of textile engineering 纺织工程学士
BTG	Bitcoin Gold 比特币黄金
BTG	British Tecnology Group 英国科技集团
BTG	Bitcoin Gold 显卡挖矿
BTS	Bangkok rail transit system 曼谷轨道交通系统
BTV	Beijing Television 北京电视台
BTW	by the way 顺便问一下[网络用语]
BU	Boston University 美国波士顿大学
Bud	Budweiser 百威啤酒
BUL	Bulgaria 保加利亚[欧洲国家]
BULATS	Business Language Testing Service 博思考试
BUN	blood urea nitrogen 血(液)尿素氮
BUR	Burkina Faso 布基纳法索[非洲国家]
BURN-Proof	buffer underrun proof 防刻死技术
BUSH	bushing 衬套

BUX	bucks（美元）的类似音，意为美元［网络用语］
BV	Besloten Vennootschap 私人有限公司［荷兰文］
BV	Bottega Veneta 葆蝶家［意大利奢侈品牌］
BV	Bureau Veritas 法国船级社［法文］
BVI	British Virgin Islands 英属维尔京群岛
BVRAAM	Beyond Visual Range Air-Air Missile 超视距空对空导弹
BW	business warehouse 商业（信息）仓库
BWAPI	Brood War Application Programming Interface 开发《星球争霸》竞赛时广泛使用的应用编程界面
BWB	blended wing body 翼身融合体
BWC	biological Weapons Convention《禁止生物武器公约》
BWC	body weight change 体重变化
BWC	Business Weekly Corporation 商业周刊公司
BWL	bursting with laughter 笑破肚皮［网络用语］
BYD	Biyadi 比亚迪（车）［汉语拼音缩略语］
BYD	Build Your Dreams 比亚迪［英文：构筑你的梦想］
BYKTA	but you knew that already 不过你已知道那件事了［网络用语］
BYOB	Bring Your Own Bag 自备购物袋［环保人士常用］
BYOB	Bring your Own Booze 自带酒
BYR	Belarusian Rouble 白俄罗斯卢布［白俄罗斯货币］

C	Carbon 碳［第 6 号化学元素］
C	computer 电脑
C	consumer 消费者；最终用户
C	coulomb 库（仑）［电荷量单位名称］
C	cycle 周［非法定频率计量单位］

C

℃	centigrade 摄氏度[法定摄氏温度计量单位]
C	classified 分类的
C&LC	capitals and lower case 大写字母和小写字母
C	center 中心
C	collected papers 论文集[参考文献标示字母]
C	complement 补体
C	coupe 双门小汽车
C#	C SHARP 面向对象编程语言
C&A	Chage & Aska 日本二人组合乐队
C&A	Clemens and August Brenninkmeyer 西雅衣家(荷兰人布伦尼克迈耶兄弟品牌服装)
C. A.	Consumers' Association 消费者协会
C. E. T.	Common External Tariff 统一对外税率
C. V. S.	Computer Vision Syndrome 电脑视频终端综合征
C. W.	curb weight 整备质量
C/A	capital account 资本账户
C/A	current account 经常项目
C/O	carried over 转入
C/O	cash order 现金订货
C/OL	conference proceeding on line 网上会议录[电子文献标示略语]
C/S	case 情形/病例
C/S	client/server 客户机/服务器模式
C++	C plus plus C++语言
C2B	Consumer to Business 客户对商家[电子商务的一种形式]
C2C	Customer to Customer 客户对客户[电子商务的一种形式]
C2C	consumer to consumer 消费者对消费者[电子商务的一种形式]
C2C	Copy to China 拷贝至中国
C2F	consumer to factory 消费者对工厂[电子商务的一种形式]
C2M	Consumer to Manufacture 用户直连工厂
C3I	system of command, control, communication and intelligence 指挥、控制、通信和情报系统[军队自动化指挥系统]
C4	military explosive 军用炸药[代字]

C4	plastic bomb 塑料炸弹[代字]
C40	40 Cities Climate Leadership Group 40 城市气候领袖群
C4D	cinema 4D 4D 电影
C4ISR	command, control, communication, computer, intelligence, surveillance, reconnaissance 军队自动化指挥系统(指挥、控制、通信、计算机、情报、监视、侦察)
C5+1	5 countries (Kazakhstan, Uzbekistan, Turkmenistan, Kyrgyzstan, Tajikistan)＋USA 五个国家(哈萨克斯坦、乌兹别克斯坦、土库曼斯坦、吉尔吉斯斯坦、塔吉克斯坦)与美国的对话机制
Ca	calcium 钙[第 20 号化学元素]
CA	carbohydrate antigen 糖抗原
CA	chartered accountant 特许会计师
CA	*Chemical Abstracts*《化学文摘》
CA	chronological age 生理年龄
CA	Civil Aviation 民航
CA	Condyloma Acuminatum 尖锐湿疣
CA	current account 往来账户
CA	current assets 流动资产
CA	Chang'an 长安汽车[中国:汉语缩略语]
CA	chartered accountant 特许会计师/公认会计师
CA	*Contemporary Author*《当代作家》
CA	catecholamine 儿茶酚胺
CA	cellulose acetate 乙酸纤维素
CA	Certificate Authority 证书授权中心
CA19-9	carbohydrate antigen 19-9 糖抗原 19-9
CAA	The Citizenship Amendment Act《公民身份修正法案》
CAA	Certificate Authority Authorization 证书颁发机构授权
CAAC	Civil Aviation Administration of China 中国民用航空局[其前身为 General Administration of Civil Aviation of China(中国民用航空总局)]
CAAS	China Automotive Systems, Inc. 中国汽车系统股份公司
CAB	Conformity Assessment Body 符合性评定机构
CAB	The Citizenship Amendment Bill《公民身份修正议案》

C

cabal	cabbala 秘密的事情［希伯来文］
CAC	center of account control 账户管理中心
CAC	Codex Alimentarius Commission 国际食品法典委员会/国际营养标准委员会
CAC	Certificate d' Aptitute au Championnat 国家选美冠军大赛［法文］
CAC	Certificate d'Aptitude au Championnat 国家选美冠军纸质证书［法文］
CAC	Chery Automobile Corporation Limited 奇瑞汽车有限公司［中国］
CAC	compagnie des agents de change 证券经纪人公司［法文］
CACA	Central After-Care Association 病后护理和治疗中心协会
CACE	Committee of American Culture and Education 美国文化教育委员会
CACFO	China Association of Chief Financial Officers 中国总会计师协会［原名 CIGA］
CACIB	Certificado de Aptitud al Campeonato Intenacional de Belleza 国际选美冠军［西班牙文］
CACIB	Certificate d' Aptitude au Championnat International de Beauté 国际选美冠军资质证明［法文］
CACIB	Credit Agricole Corporate and Investment Bank 东方汇理银行
CACM	Central American Common Market 中美洲共同市场
Cad	Cadillac 美国卡迪拉克汽车
CAD	Canadian dollar 加拿大元［货币符号］
CAD	cash against documents 凭单据付款
CAD	Central Culture District 中央文化区
CAD	computer aided detection 计算机辅助探测
CAD	contract award date 合同签订日期
CAD	coronary artery disease 冠心病
CAD	computer aided design 计算机辅助设计
CADBM	China Association of Decorative Building Materials 中国建筑装饰装修材料协会
CADPE	comprehensive alcohol-drug prevention education 酒精-麻醉剂综合预防教育
CADR	clean air delivery rate 洁净空气量
CADRE	Committee of American Diabetes Research and Education 美国糖尿病研究与教育促进会

CAE	computer aided education 计算机辅助教育
CAE	computer aided engineering 计算机辅助工程
CAE	computer aided experiment 计算机辅助实验
CAE	computer-assisted electro-cardiography 计算机辅助心电图描记
CAEA	Chinese-American Entrepreneurs Association 美国华人创业者协会
CAF	calcium activated factor 钙激活因子
CAF	Central African Republic 中非共和国[非洲国家]
CAF	cost assurance and freight 到岸价格[成本加保险费运费]
CAF	Charities Aid Foundation 英国慈善援助基金会
CAF	Confederation of African Football 非洲足球联合会
CAF	currency adjustment factor 币值调整附加费/汇率调整附加费/货币（贬值）附加费
CAF	currency and bunker adjustment factor 货币和燃油附加费
CAF	current adjustment factor 货币附加费
caff	caffeine 咖啡因
CAFR	comprehensive annual financial report 综合年度财政报告
CAG	card game 卡片类游戏
CAG	chief accountant group 首席会计师团体
CAGR	compound annual growth rate 复合年均增长率
CAHE	China Association of Higher Education 中国高等教育学会
CAI	computer-aided instruction 计算机辅助教学
CAIU	Child Abuse Investigation Unit 香港虐儿罪案调查组
CAL	computer aided learning 计算机辅助学习
CAL	conversational algebraic language 对话式代数语言
Cal/EPA	Environmental Protection Agency, California 加州环境保护署
CALC	China Association of Life Concerning 中国关怀生命协会
CALO	Cognitive Assistant that Learns and Organizes 基于人工智能来实现智能助手的项目
CALP	cognitive academic language proficiency 认知学术语言能力
Cal-Red	calcium-red 钙红色
CAM	Cambodia 柬埔寨[亚洲国家]
CAM	computer aided management 计算机辅助管理

C

CAM	computer aided manufacture 计算机辅助制造
CAM	computer aided measurement 计算机辅助测量
CAMA	China Architecture Media Award 中国建筑传媒奖
CAMC	Committee on the American Mathematics Competitions 美国数学竞赛委员会
CAMEL	capital adequacy, asset quality, management, earnings, liquidity 骆驼评级法(包括：资本充足率、资产管理、经营管理水平、盈利水平、流动性)
CAMEL+	CAMEL+sensitivity to market risk 骆驼评级法的发展版(增加了"市场风险敏感度")
CAMIC	*Central American Model Investment Code*《中美洲投资法典范本》
cAMP	cyclic adenosine monophosphate 环磷酸腺苷
CAMT	College of Arts, Media and Technology 艺术、传媒与技术学院
Can	Canadian Dollar 加拿大元[货币符号]
CAN	Canada 加拿大[北美洲国家]
CAN	Chinese Article Number 中国货物编码
CAN	computer area net 电脑控制区[局]域网
CAN-DO	Cleaning up, Arranging, Neatness, Discipline, Ongoing Improvement 日本的5s管理法的英文表达法
CANR	Contemporary Author New Revision Series 当代作家最新修订版丛书
CANVAS	Center of Action of Non-Violence and Strategy 非暴力行为和战略中心
CAO	chief accuracy officer 首席精算官
CAO	chief administrative officer 首席行政官
CAO	chief art officer 首席艺术官
CaO_2	oxygen content in arterial blood 动脉血氧含量
CAP	common agriculture policy 共同农业政策
CAPEX	capital expenditure 资本支出
CAPI	China Association for the Promotion of Investment 中国投资发展促进会
CAPM	capital asset pricing model 资本资产定价模型
CAPP	China Art Platform of Performance 中国行为艺术平台
CAPS	China Area Position System 中国区域定位系统
Car	carotene 胡萝卜素

CARB	California Air Resources Board 加利福尼亚空中资源委员会
carbo	carbohydrate 碳水化合物
Care	Cooperative for American Remittances to Europe 美国援助欧洲合作组织（现改名为 Cooperative of Assistance and Relief Everywhere 四方援助救济社）
CARICOM	Caribbean Community and Common Market 加勒比共同体和共同市场
CARR	carrier 载体
CARS	credibility, accuracy, reasonableness, support 因特网研究资源评价的著名指标体系[包括：可信性、准确性、合理性、支持度]
CAR-T	chimeric antigen receptor t-cell immunotherapy 嵌合抗原受体 T 细胞免疫疗法
CARTA	Central American Free Trade Agreement 中美洲自由贸易协定
CAS	Canadian Anesthetists' Society 加拿大麻醉师学会
CAS	Chemical Abstract Service 化学文摘社
CAS	China Association for Standardization 中国标准化协会
CAS	Chinese Academy of Sciences 中国科学院
CAS	Close Air Support 近距离空中支援
CAS	Communication Automation System 通信自动化系统
CAS	Control Automation System 控制自动化系统
CAS	College of ASEAN Studies 东盟学院
CAS	Court of Arbitration for Sports 体育仲裁法庭
CASBAA	Cable and Satellite Broadcasting Association of Asia 亚洲有线与卫星电视广播协会
CASC	China Aerospace Science and Technology Corporation 中国航天科技集团公司
CASCF	China-Arab States Cooperation Forum 中阿（拉伯）合作论坛
CASE	computer-aided software engineering 计算机辅助软件工程
CASE	computer-aided systems engineering 计算机辅助系统工程
CASHK	Civil Aid Service of Hong Kong 香港民众安全服务队
CASS	Chinese Academic of Social Sciences 中国社会科学院
CAST	computer-assisted scanning techniques 计算机辅助扫描技术
CAST	China Association for Science and Technology 中国科学技术协会

CASU	Cooperative Association of Suez Canal Users	苏伊士运河使用者合作协会
CAT	Cambridge Academy of Translation UK	英国剑桥翻译协会
CAT	category	分类
CAT	College Ability Test	美国大学能力测验
CAT	computer aided translation	计算机辅助翻译；电脑翻译
CAT	computer assisted testing	计算机辅助测试
CAT	computer assisted trading	计算机辅助贸易
cat	catalogue	目录/一览表
CAT	cold agglutination test	冷凝集试验
CAT	computer adaptive test	计算机自适应测试
CATA	Civil Aviation and Transport Association	民航与运输协会
CATARC	China Automotive Technology and Research Center	中国汽车技术研究中心
CATC	computer-aided traffic control	计算机辅助交通管制
CATF	China-Air Task Force	美国驻华空军特遣队
CATI	computer-aided telephone investigation	计算机辅助电话调查（系统）
CATIA	computer-graphics aided three-dimensional interactive application	计算机图形辅助三维交互应用
CATIC	China National Aero-Technology Import & Export Corporation	中航科技进出口有限责任公司
CATO	Cantonese Teenager Organization	广州青年组织
CATO	Caribbean Area Treaty Organization	加勒比地区公约组织
CATOBAR	catapult-assisted takeoff/barrier operations	弹射起飞/拦阻索助降系统
CATTC	computer-aided translation and transmission competition	计算机辅助翻译与传播大赛
CATTI	China Accreditation Test for Translators and Interpreter	全国翻译专业资格（水平）考试
CATV	community antenna television	共同天线电视；有线电视
CAV	common aerospace vehicle	通用航空航天飞行器
CAV	constant angular velocity	恒定角速度
CAVE	Caller Verification	呼叫者声纹识别
CB	C++ Builder	是 Borland 公司开发的集成开发环境
CB	call back	回电［网络用语］

C

CB	Celestial Being 仙人/拥有高达战士的私设武装组织[天人]	
CB	Certification Bodies Scheme 认证机构体系	
CB	certification body 认证机构	
CB	cnBeta COM 网友媒体与言论平台	
CB	College Board 美国大学理事会	
CB	Commercial Bank 商业银行	
CB	crushing blow 决定性打击	
CBA	Chinese Basketball Association 中国篮球协会	
CBA	Chinese Buddhist Association 中国佛教协会	
CBA	cytometric bead assay 流式微球技术	
CBBA	Chinese Bodybuilding Association 中国健美协会	
CBC	China Boxing Champion 中国拳击锦标赛	
CBC	Canadian Broadcasting Corporation 加拿大广播公司	
CBC	Central Bible College 中部圣经学院	
CBD	China Biographical Database 中国传记数据库	
CBD	cash before delivery 交货前付款	
CBD	central business district 中央商务区	
CBDB	China Biographical Database Project 中国历代人物传记资料库	
CBE	Certificate of Business English 商务英语证书[澳大利亚政府和其他英联邦国家认可]	
CBE	Commander of the Order of the British Empire 英帝国勋章奖的司令勋位/大英帝国勋章/司令勋章	
CBI	Central Bureau of Investigation 中央调查局	
CBI	China Business Index 中国企业品牌竞争力指数	
CBI	content-based instruction 内容依托式教学法	
CBIRC	The China Banking and Insurance Regulatory Commission 中国银行管理委员会	
CBIUS	Chinese Buyer Investment in the United States 中资企业赴美投资	
CBM	category business management 商业管理人员范畴	
CBM	chemical-biological munitions 化学生物武器	
CBM	Chinese Biological Medicine 中国生物医学文献数据库	
CBM	cubic metre 立方米	

C

CBMA	computer-based music analysis 基于计算机的音乐分析
CBO	Chinese Basketball Open 中国业余篮球公开赛
CBO	Congressional Budget Office 国会预算办公室
CBO	Chief Brand Officer 首席品牌官
CBO	Chief Business Officer 首席商务官
CBO	China Basketball Organization 中国篮球组织
CBO	Chinese Basketball Open 中国篮球公开赛
CBOT	Chicago Board of Trade 芝加哥贸易委员会
CBP	Customs and Border Protection 海关及边境保护局
CBS	cash before shipment 付款后装船
CBS	Centraal Bureau van Statistiek 荷兰中央统计局［荷兰文］
CBS	Columbia Broadcast System 美国哥伦比亚广播公司
CBSCT	cord blood stem cell transplantation 脐血造血干细胞移植
CBSA	Canadian Border Service Administration 加拿大边境服务局
CBSF	China Bus System of the Future 新能源与智能公交系统
CBT	Chicago Board Trade 美国芝加哥交易所
CBT	Cognitive Behavioral Therapy 认知行为疗法
CBU	California Baptist University 美国加州浸会大学
CBX	computerized branch exchange 程控交换
CC	Challenge Certificate 挑战赛
CC	carbon copy 副本
CC	colour compensation filter 彩色补偿滤光镜
CC	contra credit 对开信用证
CC	Cultural Creative 文化创造族［指反对物欲享受、追求心理健康，希望以自身价值创造新文化方式的人］
CC Index	China Cotton Index 中国棉花价格指数
CC	cabrio-coupe 敞篷车和硬顶轿车的混合体
CC	carbon copy 抄送
CC	central club 中央俱乐部
CC	combustion chamber 燃烧室
CC	commercial company 商业公司
CC	common code 通用准则

C

CC	corruption control（index）腐败控制指数
CC	credit card 信用卡
CCA	Cement and Concrete Association 水泥和混凝土协会［英］
CCA	China Consumer's Association 中国消费者协会
CCA	Circuit Court of Appeals 美国巡回上诉法院
CCA	Committee for Conventional Armaments 联合国常规军备委员会
CCA	combining cholalic acid 结合胆酸
CCAD	China Commerce Art Designer 中国商业美术设计师
CCAS	Committee of Concerned Asian Scholars 美国关心亚洲学者委员会
CCAV	CCTV＋Aoyun "奥运"流行语［反映了部分观众对 CCTV 和"奥运"的不满］
CCB	China Construction Bank Financial Leasing 建行融资租赁
CCB	China Construction Bank 中国建设银行
CCB	Commercial Crime Bureau 香港商业罪案调查科
CCC	Cloud Call Center 云呼叫中心
CCC	Customs Co-operation Council 关税合作理事会
CCC	China Compulsory Certification 中国强制性产品认证标志
CCCEC	China Coal Complete sets of Equipment Co., Ltd. 中国煤炭设备成套有限公司
CCCEU	China Chamber of Commerce in European Union 欧盟中国商会
CC-CMM	customer center-capability maturity model 客户中心能力成熟度模型
CCCPC	Central Committee of the Communist Party of China 中国共产党中央委员会
CCD	charge coupled device 电荷耦合器件
CCD	Conference of Committee on Disarmament 裁军委员会会议（通称日内瓦裁军委员会）
CCD	Central Cultural District 中央文化区
CCDA	Cisco Certified Design Associate 思科认证网络设计师
CCDI	China Culture Big Data & Basic Data Industry 中国文化大数据产业项目
CCDP	Cisco Certified Design Professional 思科认证资深设计工程师
CCEC	Canada China Education Council 加拿大中国教育委员会
CCEC	China Commodity Exchange center 中国商品交易中心

C

CCEC	China National Complete Engineering Corporation 中国成套工程有限公司
CCER	China Center of Economic Research 中国经济研究中心
CCET	Carnegie Commission on Educational Television 卡内基教育电视委员会
CCF	China Computer Federation 中国计算机协会
CCG	Center for China and Globalization 中国与全球化智库
CCG	China Coast Guard 中国海警部队
CCG	Center for China and Globalization 中国与全球化智库
CCG	Cross Communication Group 综合服务广告集团
CCI	Commodity Channel Index 顺势指标
CCI	Continuous Commodity Index 大宗商品信心指数
CCIB	China Commercial Inspection Bureau 中国商检标志
CCIB	China Commercial Inspection Bureau 中国进出口商品检验局
CCIC	China National Import and Export Commodities Inspection Corporation 中国进出口商品检验总公司
CCIC	China Certification & Inspection (Group) Co., Ltd. 中国检验认证(集团)有限公司
CCIC	China Commodity Inspection Corporation 中国商品检验公司
CCIC	China Crime Information Center 中国犯罪信息中心
CCIC	cultural and creative industrial clustering 文化创意产业集聚
CCID	China Center for Information Industry Development 中国电子信息产业发展研究院
CCIE	Cisco Certified Internetwork Expert 思科认证网络专家
CCIEE	China Center for International Economic Exchanges 中国国际经济交流中心
CCII	Chinese Character Code for Information Interchange 信息交换用汉字编码集,一种汉字编码
CCIM	Certified Commercial Investment Member 注册商业投资师
CCIP	customer common investment plan 客户共同投资计划
CCIR	Consultative Committee on International Radio 国际无线电咨询委员会
CCISSR	Center of China Insurance and Society Security Research 中国保险与社会保障研究中心
CCITT	Consultative Committee on International Telegraph and Telephone 国际电报电话咨询委员会

63

CCL	Commerce Control List 商业管制清单	
CCMC	Chinese Career Manager Certification 职业经理人资格证书	
CCMC	Coordination Commerce Management 协调商务管理	
CCMD	Carnegie Committee for Music and Drama 卡内基音乐和戏剧委员会	
CCMT	China CNC Machine Tool Fair 中国数控机床展览会	
CCNA	Cisco Certified Network Associate 思科认证网络工程师	
CCNP	Cisco Certified Network Professional 思科认证资深网络工程师	
CCO	Chief Culture Officer 首席文化官	
CCOCF	China Culture Overseas Communication Forum 中华文化海外传播论坛	
CCO	Chief Communications Officer 首席宣传官	
CCOIC	The China Chamber of International Commerce 中国国际商会	
CCOS	China Climate Observation System 中国气候观测系统	
CCP	Chinese Communist Party 中国共产党	
CCPIT	China Council for the Promotion of International Trade 中国国际贸易促进委员会	
CCPL	Creative Commons Public License 知识共享组织公共许可	
CCPS	Party School of the Central Committee of CPC 中共中央党校	
Ccr	endogenous creatinine clearance rate 内生肌酐清除率	
CCR	central control room 中央控制室	
CCRA	certified credit risk analyst 注册信贷风险分析师	
CCRE	Canadian Council for Research in Education 加拿大教育研究委员会	
CCR-Expanded	Current Chemical Reaction Expanded 化学反应式数据库	
CCS	Combined Chiefs of Staff 美国国防部参谋长联席会议	
CCS	Cabinet Committee on Security 内阁安全委员会	
CCS	Center for Chinese Studies 汉语研究中心	
CCS	China Classification Society 中国船级社	
CCSC	China Classification Society Certification 中国船级社质量认证公司	
CCSD	Chinese Continental Scientific Drilling 中国大陆科学钻探工程	
CCSI	Chinese Customer Satisfaction Index 中国用户满意度指数	
CCSST	Canada-China Society for Science and Technology 加拿大—中国科学技术协会	

CCSTV	China Countryside TV 中国山寨电视
CCSVC	credit card service 信用卡客服
CCT	Common Customs Tariff 共同海关税则
CCT	content creation tool 多媒体制作工具
CCT	Cambridge Committee of Translation 剑桥翻译委员会
CCT	combat control team 作战引导队
CCTA	Chinese Communications Transportation Association 中国交通运输协会
CCTV	China Central Television 中国中央电视台
CCTV	Closed Circuit Television 闭路电视
CCU	Cardiac Care Unit 心脏监护病房
CCU	Coronary Care Unit 冠心病监护病房
CCW	close combat weapon 近战武器（游戏）
cd	candela 坎（德拉）[发光强度国际单位制基本单位]
Cd	cadmium 镉[第48号化学元素]
CD	Certificate Deposit 大额可转让定期存单
CD	Certificate of Delivery 交货单存款证明
CD	compact disc 光碟/激光唱盘
CD	conference on disarmament 裁军谈判会议
CD	Christain Dior 迪奥女装
CD	Committee Draft 委员会草案
CD	compact disc 光盘[电子文献标示字母]
CD	Crohn's disease 克罗恩病
CD4/CD8	Thelper cells/T killer cells 细胞亚群 CD4/CD8
CDAC	Conference on Dialogue of Asian Civilizations 亚洲文明对话
CDB	China Development Bank 国家开发银行/国开行
CDC	Centers for Disease Control and prevention 疾病（预防）控制中心
CDC	Continuous Damping Control 持续减震控制（系统）
CDC	committee for developing countries 发展中国家委员会
CDC	Customer Research & User Experience Design Center 用户研究与体验设计中心

CDE	Centro de Espoloro kaj Dokument［英文：Research and Documentation Center］研究和文献中心［世界语］
CDER	Center of Drug Evaluation and Research 药物评价与研发中心
CDF	corn dietary fiber 玉米膳食纤维
CDF	China Duty Free 中国免税
CD-I	compact disc interactive 激光唱片交互式光盘
CDIO	Conceive Design Implement Operate 工程教育模式
CDLI	China Designer of Light Industry 中国轻工业设计师
CDM	cash deposit machine 现金自动存款机
CDM	Clean Development Mechanism 清洁发展机制
CDM	collaborative decision making 协同决策
CDMA	code division multiple access 码分多路访问/码分多址
CDMB	China Digital Multimedia Broadcasting 中国数字多媒体广播
CDM-EB	Executive Board of Clean Development Mechanism 清洁发展机制执行理事会
CDMO	Contract Development Manufacture Organization 定制研发生产
CDN	content delivery network 内容传递网络
CDN	content delivery network 内容分发网络
CDNA	complementary DNA 互补 DNA
CDNS	Cadence Design System, Inc. 纳斯达克股票代码
CDO	Chief Diplomatism Officer 首席外交官
CDO	collateralized debt obligation 担保债务凭证
CDP	capability development plan 能力发展计划
CDPC	Chinese Disease Prevention and Control 中国疾病预防控制
CDPD	cellular digital packet data 蜂窝数字分组数据
CDPF	China Disabled Persons' Federation 中国残疾人联合会
CDPS	central data processing system 中央数据处理系统
CD-R	compact disc recordable 可录光盘
CDR	capital-to-debt ratio 资本与债务比率
CDR	change design request 更改设计请求
CDR	Chinese Depository Receipt 中国存托凭证

CDR	conceptual design report 概念设计报告	
CDRC	Commodity Development Research Centre 中国大宗商品发展研究中心	
CDRL	contractor data requirements list 承包商技术数据需求	
CDS	central dynamic store 中央动态存储器	
CDS	credit default swap 信用违约互换	
CDSF	Chinese Dance Sport Federation 中国体育舞蹈联合会	
CDU	Christlich-Demokratische Union 基督教民主联盟［德文］	
CDV	Committee Draft for Vote 委员会投票草案	
CD-R	compact disc-recordable 可写光盘	
CD-ROM	compact disc read-only memory 只读光盘	
CD-RW	compact disc-rewritable 可擦写光盘	
Ce	Cerium 铈［第58号化学元素］	
CE	Collier's Encyclopedia《科利尔百科全书》	
CE	compact embedding 嵌入式视窗操作系统	
CE	Conformity of Europe 欧盟质量认证标志	
CE	Consumer Electronics 消费类电子产品	
CE	Council of Europe 欧洲委员会/欧洲理事会	
CE	creative editing 创造性编辑［网络用语］	
CE	Customer Engineer 用户工程师	
CE	cellulose plastics, general 通用纤维素塑料	
CE	Communauté Européenne 欧共体有机产品质量认证标志［法文］	
CE	Communauté Européenne 欧盟/欧洲共同体［法文］	
CEA	Canadian Education Association 加拿大教育协会	
CEA	carcinoembryonic antigen 癌胚抗原	
CEA	Centre Européen de la Culture［英文：European Cultural Center］欧洲文化中心［法文］	
CEA	College English Association 大学英语协会	
CEA	Consuming Electronics Association（美国）消费电子协会	
CEA	cost effectiveness analysis 成本效益分析	
CEA	Council for Educational Advance 英国发展教育委员会	
CEAC	Computer Education and Certification 国家信息化计算机教育认证	
CEB	China Everbright Bank 中国光大银行	

CEB	Comité Electrotechnique Belge 比利时电工技术委员会［法文］
CEBE	Certified Exam of Business Engineers 电子商务工程师认证考试
CeBIT	Centrum der Büro- und Informationstechnik 汉诺威国际信息及通信技术博览会［德文］
CEBR	Centre for Economics and Business Research Ltd. 经济与商业研究中心
CEC	China Electronic Company 中国电子信息产业集团公司
CECA	Comprehensive Economic Co-operation Agreement 两岸综合性经济合作协议
CECC	Central Epidemic Command Center 中央流行疫情指挥中心
CECC	Congressional Executive Commission on China 美国国会及行政当局中国委员会
CECC	CENEL EC Electronic Components Committee 欧洲电工标准化委员会电子器件委员会
CECC	CENEL EC Electronic Components Committee 欧洲电子元器件质量认证标志
CECF	Chinese Export Commodities Fair 中国出口商品交易会
CECP	China Energy-saving Center of Products 中国节能产品认证中心
CED	Customs and Excise Department 香港海关
CED	Committee for Economic Development 美国经济发展委员会
CEDA	Committee for Economic Development of Australia 澳大利亚经济发展委员会
CEDO	Centre for Educational Development Overseas 英国海外教育发展中心
CEE	Commission Économique pour l'Europe ［英文：Economic Commission for Europe］欧洲经济委员会［法文］
CEE	Communauté Économique Européenne ［英文：European Economic Community］欧洲经济共同体［法文］
CEEC	Central East Europe Countries 中东欧国家
CEEP	Centre Européen d'Études de Population ［英文：European Center for Population Studies］欧洲人口问题研究中心［法文］
CEG	China E-Sports Game 中国电子竞技运动会
CEG	China Europe-sports Game 中欧对抗赛
CEH	Certificated Ethical Hacker 道德黑客认证

C

CEI	Certified Environmental Institute 注册环境研究院
CEI	China Economic Information 中国经济信息(网)
CEIBS	China Europe International Business School 中欧国际工商管理学院
CEIC	China Economic Intelligence Committee 中国经济情报委员会
CEIF	Council of European Industrial Federation 欧洲工业联合会委员会
CELA	Center of Evaluation of Language and Academics 语言与学术评估中心
CELAC	Comisión Económica de Latinoamérica y el Caribe 拉丁美洲和加勒比经济委员会[西班牙文]
CELS	Certificates in English Language Skills 剑桥英语技能考试
CEMA	Council for Economic Mutual Assistance 经济互助委员会
CEMPMC	China E-Marketing Professional Managers Certification 中国网络营销职业经理人认证(管理办公室)
CEN	Comité Européen de Normalisation 欧洲标准化委员会[法文]
CENEL	Comité Européen de Coordination des Normes Electriques 欧洲电气标准协调委员会[现已改为:CENELEC][法文]
CENELEC	Comité Européen de Normalisation Electrotechnique 欧洲电工标准化委员会[法文]
CEO	Chief Executive Officer 首席执行官
CEP	China Economic Panel 中国市场调查
CEP	China Economy Probe 中国经济调查
CEPA	Closer Economic Partnership Arrangement 内地与港澳地区关于建立更紧密经贸关系安排
CEPI	Coalition for Epidemic Peparedness Innovations 流行病应对创新联盟[挪威]
CEPS	Centre for European Policy Studies 欧洲政治研究中心
CERN	Conseil Européen pour la Recherche Nucleaire 欧洲核子研究委员会[法文]
CERNET	China Educational and Scientific Research Network 中国教育科研网
CERNET	China Education and Research Network 中国教育和科研计算机网
CES	China Economic Summit 中国经济高峰会
CES	China Electronics Show 中国电子消费展
CES	consumer electronics show 消费电子产品展览会
CES	International Consumer Electronics Show 国际电子消费展

CESI	Chinese Electronics Standardization Institute 中国电子技术标准化研究所
CESL	China-Europe School of Law 中欧法学院
CESM	Community Earth System Model 地球系统模式
CET	College English Test 大学英语考试
CET	Centre Européen de Traduction [英文: European Translation Center] 欧洲翻译中心[法文]
CETA	Comprehensive Economical Trade Agreement 加拿大与欧盟全面经济与贸易协定
CETA	Centre d'Études pour la Traduction Automatique [英文: Center for the Study of Automatic Translation] 自动化翻译研究中心[法文]
CETC	China Electronic Technology Corporation 中国电子科技集团公司
CETEX	Committee on Contamination of Extra-Terrestrial Exploration 宇宙探测污染委员会
CETI	Certificate of English Translation and Interpreting 英语翻译资格证书
CETTIC	China Employment Training Technical Instruction Center 职业岗位培训合格证书
CETV	China Entertainment Television 华娱电视台
CETV	China Education Television 中国教育电视台
CEUCA	Customs and Economic Union of Central Africa 中非关税和经济同盟
Cf	californium 锎[第 98 号化学元素]
CF	compact flash, 压缩内存[又叫 CF 卡, 一种在掌上电脑和数码相机上使用的大容量存储设备]
C&F	Cost and Freight 成本加运费价格
CF Micro	continue focus micro 全程微距
CF	call forwarding 来电转接
CF	Center Frequency 中心频率
CF	Central African Republic 中非共和国[非洲国家]
CF	commercial film 广告影片
CF	compact flash 紧凑式闪存
CF	cresol-formaldehyde (resin) 甲酚-甲醛树脂
CF	Cross Fire《穿越火线》[韩国游戏名]
CF	customer feedback 订单评价

CFA	chartered [certified] financial analyst 特许金融分析师
CFA	Changfeng Automobile 长丰汽车制造股份有限公司[中国]
CFAT	cash flow after taxes 税后现金流量
CFC	chloro fluorohydrocarbon 氯氟烃
CFCA	China Finance Certification Authority 中国金融认证中心
CFCSR	Chinese Federation for Corporate Social Responsibility 中国企业社会责任同盟
CFD	computational fluid dynamics 计算流体动力学
CFD	Congress for Democracy 民主大会
Cfd	frequency dependent compliance 频率依赖顺应性
CFDA	Council of Fashion Designers of America 美国时尚设计委员会
CFDA	Country Food and Drug Administration 国家食品与药品管理局
CFF	Cambodian Freedom Fighters 柬埔寨自由斗士组织
CFFEX	China Financial Futures Exchange 中国金融期货交易所
CFIA	Canada Food Inspection Agency 加拿大食品检验局
CFIUS	Committee on Foreign Investment in the United States 美国外国投资委员会
CFLAC	China Federation of Literary and Art Circles 中国文学艺术界联合会
CFLC	College of Foreign Languages and Cultures 外语与文化学院
CFLP	China Federation of Logistics & Purchasing 中国物流与采购联合会
CFM	Certified of Financial Management 财务管理认证
CFM	communications fraud management 通信欺诈管理
CFN	countrywide finance net 全国金融综合信息服务网
CFN	Chinese Frame Net 汉语框架网[参 FN]
CFO	Calling For Orders 停泊待命[船即到港口后,听候指令]
CFO	Chief Financial Officer 首席财务官,财务总经理
CFP	Certified Financial Planner 注册金融策划师
CFP	Ciguatera Fish Poisoning 鱼肉毒素
CFP	China Foto Press 国务院新闻办公室图片库/中国图片代理机构
C-FPWV	carotid-femoral pulse wave velocities 颈动脉-股动脉搏动波速度
CFR	Code of Federal Regulations 联邦条例法规
CFR	Council on Foreign Relations 美国对外关系委员会/外交关系协会

CFRM	Certified Financial Risk Manager 注册金融风险管理师
CFS	Chronic Fatigue Syndrome 慢性疲劳综合征
CFS	The Center for Food Safety 食品安全中心
CFS	Committee of Foods Safety 粮食安全委员会
CFS	container freight station 集装箱货运站
CFSAN	Center for Food Safety and Applied Nutrition 食品安全和应用营养中心
CFT	cross-functional team 跨职能团队
CFTC	Commodity Futures Trade Committee 商品期货交易委员会/期货交易管理委员会
CFTC	Commodity Futures Trading Commission 商品期货交易委员会
CFU	colony-forming unit 菌落形成单位
CFX	cefoxitin 头孢西丁
CG	computer graphics 电脑绘画
CG	computer game 电脑动漫
CG	Computer Graphics CG 动画
CG	capital goods 资本财货
CG	Convenzione di Ginevra (22 Agosto 1864)《日内瓦公约》(1864.8.22)[意大利文]
CG	cholyglycine 甘胆酸
CGA	color graphics adapter 彩色图形适配器
CGA	Canadian Gas Association 加拿大煤气协会/加拿大燃料产品质量认证标志
CGA	certified general accountant 注册会计师
CGCC	Chinese General Chamber of Commerce 中华总商会[属香港特别行政区]
CGH	comparative genome hybridization 比较基因组杂交
CGI	common gateway interface 通用网关接口
CGI	computer generated imagery 电脑成像技术
CGIL	Confederazione Generale Italiana de Lavoro [英文：Italian General Confederation of Labor] 意大利总工会[意大利文]
CGMW	Commission for the Geological Map of the World 世界地质地图委员会
CGO	Chief Game Officer 首席游戏官

C

CGO	Chief Government Officer 首席沟通官	
CGO	Congo 刚果(布)[非洲国家]	
CGPI	China Global Philanthropy Institute 深圳国际公益学院	
CGPI	corporate goods price index 企业商品交易价格指数	
CGSB	Canadian General Standards Board 加拿大建材产品质量认证标志/加拿大中央标准理事会	
CGT	capital gains tax 资本所得税	
CGT	compensated gross ton 修正总吨	
CGT	Confédération Générale du Travail 法国工会总同盟[法文]	
CGT	compensated gross tonnage 修正总吨	
CGTN	China Global Television Network 央视中国国际电视台/中国环球电视网	
CH	Champion ACK赛制比赛中完成15个胜利积分的犬只,又称登陆冠军V	
CH	Changhe 昌河汽车[中国景德镇:汉语缩略语]	
CH	channel 频道/声道	
CH	clearing house 清算所	
ch	central heating 集中供热	
Ch	cholesterol 胆固醇	
CH50	50% complement hemolytic activity 百分之五十补体溶血活性	
CHA	Chad 乍得[非洲国家]	
CHA	Community Health Association 社区健康协会	
CHAU	choiced about uncirculated 精选近未流通级(钱币)	
CHD	congenital heart disease 先天性心脏病	
Che Min	Chemistry and Mineralogy Analysis 化学与矿物学分析仪	
CHE	cholinesterase 胆碱酯酶	
CHF	Confederatio Helvetico fran(s) 瑞士法郎[法文]	
CHI	Chile 智利[南美洲国家]	
CHI	closed-head injure 闭合性颅脑损伤	
CHI	China Railway High-speed 中国铁路高速列车	
CHIC	China International Clothing & Accessories Fair 中国国际服装博览会	
CHIME	Canadian Hydrogen Intensity Mapping Experiment 加拿大射氢强度映射团队	

Chimerica	China + America 中美国
China GBN	China Golden Bridge Net 中国金桥网
China MARC	China Machine Readable Cataloging Format 中国机读目录格式
China TELECOM	China Telecom Group Corporation 中国电信集团公司
CHINA TELECOM	China Telecommunications Corporation 中国电信集团公司
CHINANET	China Network 中国公用计算机互联网
CHINA-VALS	CHINA-value and life style 中国（消费者）生活形态模型
Chindia	China + India 中印[中国＋印度]
Chinglish	Chinese English 中式英文
CHIPS	Clearing House Interbank Payment System 银行间票据交换支付系统
CHIS	Chinese Hospital Information System 中国医院信息系统
CHIS	Covent human intelligence sources 秘密情报信源
CHMBR	chamber 气门室
CHMS	choiced mint state 精选未流通级（钱币）
CHN	China 中国
CHO	Chief Homepage Officer 首席网页制作官
CHO	Chief Human Resource Officer 人力资源总监
CHO	Chinese Hamster Ovary 中国仓鼠卵巢
CHO	cholesterol 胆固醇
CHP	chemical polishing 化学抛光
CHR	Commission on Human Rights 联合国人权委员会
CHRD	Chinese Human Rights Defenders 中国人权捍卫者网络
CHSSCI	China Humanities Social Sciences Citation Index 中国人文社会科学论文索引
CHTF	China HI-TECH Fair 中国高新技术交易会
CHVF	choiced very fine 精选优美级（钱币）
CHXF	choice extremely fine 精选极美级（钱币）
CI	certificate of insurance 保险凭证
CI	Composite Index （统计）景气综合指数
CI	Corporate Identity 公司形象/企业识别
Ci	Curie 居里（非法定放射性活度计量单位）

C

CI	color index 颜色指数
CIA	Central Intelligence Agency 美国中央情报局
CIA	Certified Internal Auditor 国际注册内部审计师
CIA	Commerce and Industries Association 工商协会
CIA	Computer Industry Association 计算机行业协会
CIA	Construction Industries Association 建筑工业协会
CIAA	Chinese Industry Association for Antimicrobial Materials & Products 中国抗菌材料及制品行业协会
CIADLC	Comité International pour la Diffusion des Arts et des Letters par le Cinéma [英文：International Committee for the Diffusion of Arts and Literature through Cinema] 国际电影传播文艺作品委员会[法文]
CIAM	Chartered Insurance Agency Manager 美国特许营业部经理
CIAM	Confédération Internationale des Association de Musiciens 国际音乐创作者委员会[法文]
CIB	China Investment Bank 中国投资银行
CIB	Industrial Bank Co.,Ltd. 兴业银行
CIB	Criminal Intelligence Bureau 刑事情报科
CIBNE	Certified International Business Negotiation Expert 注册国际商务谈判专家认证
CIC	Commerce Identification Code 运营商标识码
CIC	customer interaction center 客户互动中心（系统平台）
CIC	carcinogen identifying commission 致癌物质鉴定委员会
CIC	circulating immune complexes 循环免疫复合体
CICA	Certificate in Company Administration 公司管理认证
CICA	cervical internal carotid artery 颈内动脉
CICA	Conference on Interaction and Confidence-Building Measures in Asia 亚洲相互协作与信任措施会议
CICIR	China Institute for Contemporary International Relations 中国现代国际关系研究院
CICP	Committee to Investigate Copyright Problems 美国版权问题调查委员会
CICR	Comité Internacional de la Cruz Roja 国际红十字会[西班牙文]

CICR	Comité International de la Croix-Rouge 国际红十字会[法文]
CICT	Conseil International du Cinéma et de la Télévision [英文：International Film and Television Council] 国际电影和电视委员会[法文]
CICT	Colombo International Container Terminal 科伦坡国际集装箱码头
CICV	Comitê Internacional da Cruz Vermelha 国际红十字会[葡萄牙文]
CID	central information district 中央信息区
CID	Compensative Import Duty 补偿性进口税
CID	Commission for International Development 国际开发委员会
CID	Committee for Industrial Development 工业发展委员会
CID	Criminal Investigation Division 刑事侦查局
CID	Criminal Investigation Department 刑事侦缉处
CIDA	Canadian International Development Agency 加拿大国际开发署
CIDA	Comité Intergouvernmental du Droit d'Auter [英文：Intergovernmental Copyright Committee] 政府间版权委员会[法文]
CIE	Commission internationale de l'eclairage 国际照明委员会[法文]
CIE	Committee of International Ex(am)（英国剑桥大学）国际考试委员会
CIE	Chinese Institute of Electronics 中国电子学会
CIEC	China International Energy Center 中国国际能源控股有限公司
CIEC	Conference on International Economic Cooperation 国际经济合作会议
CIECS	Certification of International E-Commerce Specialist 国际电子商务师职业资格认证
CIEE	Council on International Educational Exchanges（美国）国际教育交流理事会
CIEG	Committee for International Economic Growth 国际经济增长委员会
CIEP	counter immunoelectrophoresis 对流免疫电泳
CIF	Certificate in International Finance 国际金融证书
CIF	cost, insurance and freight 成本加保险费、运费价格/到岸价格
CIFA	counterintelligence field activity 反情报活动局/反情报战地行动
CIFAR	Canadian Institute for Advanced Research 加拿大高级研究院
CIFC	China Internet finance Conference 中国互联网金融联盟
CIFCO	China International Futures Investment Co., Ltd. 中国中期投资股份有限公司

C

CIFIT	China International Fair for Investment and Trade 中国国际投资贸易洽谈会
CIFTIS	China International Fair for Trade in Services 中国国际服务贸易交易会
CIG	China Insurance Group 中国保险集团
CIG	China Internet Group 中国互联网集团
CIG	Capital Investment Group 资金投资集团
CIGA	Chinese Institute of General Accountants 中国总会计师协会（现已更名为 CACFO）
CIGS	Cu、In、Ga、Se 薄膜太阳能电池[由铜、铟、镓、硒组成]
CIH	Confucius Institute Headquarters (Hanban) 孔子学院总部[国家汉办]
CIHAF	China International Real Estate & Architectural Technology Fair 中国国际房地产与建筑科技展览会（简称"中国住交会"）
CII	Chartered Insurance Institute 英国皇家特许保险学会
CIIE	China International Import Expo 中国国际进口博览会
CIIF	China International Industrial Fair 中国国际工业博览会
CILIP	the Chartered Institute of Library and Information Professionals 英国图书馆与信息专家注册协会
CIM	computer integrated manufacture 计算机集成制造
CIM	Convention Concerning International Carriage of Goods by Rail《国际铁路货物运输公约》
CIMS	computer-integrated manufacturing system 计算机集成制造系统
CINS	child in need of supervision 需监管的孩子
CIO	Chief Information Officer 首席信息主管/首席信息官
CIO	color in the office 商用彩色
CIOCS	communications input/output control system 通信输入/输出控制系统
CIP	cataloguing in publication 在版编目
CIPC	Certified International Psychological Consultant 注册国际心理咨询师
CIPD	Chartered Institute of Personnel and Development 英国特许人事和发展协会
CIPE	Center for International Private Enterprise 国际私企中心
CIPS	Cross-border Interbank Payment System 人民币跨境支付（业务）系统
CIPS	Canadian Information Processing Society 加拿大信息处理学会

CIPUC	Criminal Investigation Police University of China	中国刑事警察学院
CIQ	China Entry-Exit Inspection and Quarantine Bureau	中国出入境检验检疫局
CIS	Cartographic Information Services	地图信息服务中心
CIS	Chinese Industrial Standards	中国工业标准
CIS	Clinic Information System	临床管理信息化
CIS	Commonwealth of Independent States	独立国家联合体
CIS	corporate identify system	企业形象设计
CIS	corporation identity system	企业识别系统
CISA	commissioner of information system audit	信息系统审计师
CISAC	Confédération Internationale des Sociétés d'Auteurs et Compositeurs	国际作家和作曲家协会联合会[法文]
CISAR	China International Search and Rescue	中国国际救援队
CISM	Conseil International du Sport Militaire	国际军事体育运动委员会/国际军事体育理事会[法文]
CISRT	China International Search and Rescue Team	中国国际救援队
CISS	Comité International des Sports Silencieux	国际聋哑人体育运动委员会[法文]
CIT	Cambridge Information Technology	英国剑桥信息技术
CIT	California Institute of Technology	加州理工学院[美国]
CITES	campus information technologies and educational services	校园信息技术和教育服务
CITES	Convention on International Trade in Endangered Species	濒危野生动植物种国际贸易公约
CITIC	China International Trust and Investment Corporation	中国国际信托投资公司
CITIC	China CITIC Bank	中信银行
CITL	The Community Independent Transaction Log	欧盟独立交易登记系统
CITO	chief information technology officer	首席信息技术官
CITS	China International Travel Service	中国国际旅行社
CityU	City University of Hong Kong	香港城市大学
CIUTI	Conférence Internationale Permanente d'Instituts Universitaires de Traducteurs et Interprètes	国际大学翻译学院联合会[法文]

C

CIV	Côte d'lvoire [英文：Ivory Coast] 科特迪瓦[非洲国家]
CIVETS	Colombia, Indonesia, Vietnam, Egypt, Turkey, South Africa 灵猫六国,其国名分别为：哥伦比亚、印尼、越南、埃及、土耳其和南非
CIW	Certified Internet Webmaster 认证互联网络大师
CJFD	China Journals Full-text Database 中文期刊全文数据库
CJNG	Cartel de Jalisco Nueva Genracion 新生代哈里斯科州卡特尔[西班牙文]
CJOL	China Job Online 中国人才热线
CJR	*Columbia Journalism Review*《哥伦比亚新闻评论》
CK	conductive keratoplastry 传导性角膜成形术
CK	creatine kinase 肌酸激酶
CK	Calvin Klein 卡尔文·卡莱时装
CK-BB	creatine kinase BB isoenzyme 脑型肌酸激酶同工酶
CKD	completely knocked down 现场装配
CK-MB	MB isoenzyme of creatine kinase 心肌型肌酸激酶同工酶
CK-MM	MM isoenzyme of creatine kinase 肌型肌酸激酶同工酶
CKO	chief knowledge officer 首席知识官
CKP	crank shaft position 曲轴位置
CKU	China Kennel Union 中爱联合纯种犬文化发展中心
Cl	chlorine 氯[第17号化学元素]
CL	contract logistics 合同物流
CLA	conjugated linoleic acid 共轭亚油酸
CLAM	China Low Activation Martensitic 中国低活化马氏体钢
CLAM	China Low Activation Martensitic 中国抗中子辐照钢
CLD	Central Living District 中央生活区
CLEO	Conference on Lasers and Electro-Optics 激光及光电会议
CLEP	China Lunar Exploration Program 中国探月
CLI	Customer Loyalty Index 客户忠诚指数
CLIC	China Language Intelligence Conference 中国语言智能大会
CLIP	compiler language for information processing 信息处理编译程序语言
CLM	Chinese language module 中国语言模型
CLO	chief learning officer 首席学习官
CLO	chief law officer 首席律师

CLV	constant linear velocity 恒定线速度
CM	credit memo 贷记通知单
Cm	curium 锔[第96号化学元素]
CM	chylomicron 乳糜微粒
CMA	cash management account 现金管理账户
CMA	Certified Management Accountant 美国注册管理会计师(认证)/管理会计认证
CMA	China Medical Association 中华医学会
CMA	China Metrology Accreditation 中国计量认证
CMA	China Meteorological Administration 中国气象局
CMAC	China Maritime Arbitration Commission 中国海事仲裁委员会
CMA-CGM	Companie Maritime d'Affertment—Companie General Maritime 法国达飞海运集团[法文]
CMANO	Command Modern Air/Naval Operations 指挥:现代海空行动
CMB	cosmic microwave background 宇宙微波背景辐射
CMBC	China Minsheng Bank Co. Ltd 中国民生银行
CMC	China National Machinery Import and Export Corporation 中国机械进出口(集团)有限公司
CMC	carboxymethyl cellulose 羧甲基纤维素
CMC	Central Military Commission 中央军事委员会
CMC	Communication and Multimedia Commission 通信和多媒体委员会
CMC	Crisis Management Center 危机管理中心
CMCC	China Mobile Communications Group Co., Ltd. 中国移动通信集团有限公司
CMCC	Committee of Missile Contingent Capacity 导弹应对能力委员会
CMCGC	China Mobile Communications Group Co. Ltd. 中国移动通信集团有限公司
CMCPI	Coalición Méxicana por la Corte Penal Internacional 墨西哥联盟的国际刑事法院[西班牙文]
CMDPDH	Comisión Méxicana de Defensay Promoción de los Derechos Humanos 墨西哥人权捍卫和促进委员会[西班牙文]
CME	Chicago Mercantile Exchange 芝加哥商业交易所

C

CMEA	Council for Mutual Economic Assistance 经济互助委员会
CMF	color, material & finishing 有关产品颜色、材质与工艺基础的认知
CMF	continuous micro filtre 连续微滤
CMF	computer network military force 网络作战部队
CMF	continuous membrane filtration 连续膜过滤技术
CMFA	China Mixed Fighting Alliance 中国综合格斗联盟
CMG	China Media Group 中央广播电视总台
CMM	Capability Maturity Models 企业生产能力成熟度模型
CMM	Commission for Maritime Meteorology 联合国海洋气象学委员会
CMM	coordinate measuring machine 三坐标测量机
CMMB	China Mobile Multimedia Broadcasting 中国移动多媒体广播
CMMQ	Chinese Career Manager Certification 中国营销经理人职业资格认证
CMMS	Chinese Market and Media Study 中国市场与媒体研究
CMN	China Mobile Net 中国移动互联网
CMO	Central Meteorological Observatory（中国)中央气象台
CMO	chief market officer 首席市场官
CMO	Chinese music opera 中国音乐剧
CMO	Contract Manufacturing Organization 合同生产组织
CMO	collateralized mortgage obligation 担保抵押证券
CMOS	complementary metal-oxide semi-conductor 互补金属氧化物半导体
CMP	camshaft position 凸轮轴位置
CMP	chemical mechanical polishing 化学机械抛光
CMP	chiral mobile phase 手性流动相法
CMR	Cameroon 喀麦隆［非洲国家］
CMS	cash management service 现金管理服务
CMS	conversational monitor system 会话式监督系统
CMS	cruise missile submarine 巡航导弹潜艇
CMT	chartered market technocrat 特许市场技术师
CMT	Chicago Merchandise Trade 芝加哥商品交易所
CMTL	Computer Memory Tester Lab 美国计算机内存模块与主机板测试认证标志
CMTL	Computer Memory Test Lab 美国专业计算机内存测试实验室

CMV	cytomegalovirus 巨细胞病毒
CMWA	China Medical We-Media Association 中国医疗自媒体联盟
C-myc	Cancer-myc 癌基因
CMYK	cyan, magenta, yellow, black 用于印刷的四分色：青、洋红、黄、黑
CN	cellulose nitrate 硝酸纤维素
CN	China 中国国家代码
Cn	copernicium 鿔[第112号化学元素]
CNACPQ	China National Accreditation Council for Products Quality 中国产品质量认证委员会
CNAL	Canadian National Accelerator Laboratory 加拿大国家加速器实验室
CNAL	China National Accreditation Board for Laboratories 中国实验室国家认可委员会
CNAPS	China National Automatic Payment System 中国现代化支付系统
CNAS	Center of New America Safety 美国新安全中心
CNAS	China National Accreditation Service for Conformity Assessment 中国合格评定国家认可委员会
CNAS	Civil Navigation Aids System 民用导航辅助系统
CNC	Centre National de la Cinematographie 法国国家电影中心[法文]
CNC	China NetCom 中国网络通信有限公司
CNC	computer numerical control 计算机数字控制
CNC	communication network control 通信网络控制
CNC	computer number control 计算机数字控制机床
CNC	computerized numerical control machine 数控机床
CNCA	Certification and Accreditation Administration of the P.R.C. 中国国家认证认可监督管理委员会
C-ncap	China-New Car Assessment Programme 五星安全认证/中国新车评价规程
CNCC	China National Computer Congress 中国计算机大会
CNCERT/CC	China National Internet Emergency Center 国家计算机网络应急技术处理协调中心
CNCOFIEC	China National Cereals, Oils and Foodstuffs Import and Export Corporation 中国粮油食品进出口总公司

C

CNCSI	China National Customer Satisfaction Index 中国国家顾客满意度指数
CNE	computer net engineer 网络工程师
CNF	cellulose nano fibre 纤维素纳米纤维
CNG	*China National Geography*《中国国家地理》
CNG	compressed natural gas 压缩天然气
CNGI	China Next Generation Internet 中国下一代互联网工程
CNGO	Committee on Non Governmental Organization 联合国非政府组织委员会
CNGV	compressed natural gas vehicle 压缩天然气汽车
CNH	Chinese Yuan in Hongkong 离岸人民币
CNI	Coalition for Networked Information 网络信息联盟
CNIEC	China National Import and Export Corporation 中国进出口总公司
CNKI	China National Knowledge Infrastructure 中国知识基础设施（工程）/中国知网
CNMA	China Non-prescription Medicine Association 中国非处方药物协会
CNN	Cable News Networks 美国有线（电视）新闻网
CNN	Convolution Neural Network 卷积神经网络
CNNIC	China Internet Network Information Center 中国互联网信息中心
CNO	chief negotiating officer 首席谈判官
CNOOC	China National Offshore Oil Corporation 中国海洋石油总公司/中海油
CNPC	China National Petroleum Corporation 中国石油天然气集团公司/中石油
CnPunk	China Punk 中式朋克，一种摇滚乐
CNR	communication and network riser 通信与网络升级卡
CNR	carrier to noise ratio 载噪比
CNR	China National Radio 中央人民广播电台
CNR	China Northern Locomotive & Rolling Stock Industry (Group) Corporation 中国北车；中国北方机车车辆工业集团公司
CNR	China Northern Railway 中国北方机车厂
CNRC	Conseil national de recherches Canada 加拿大国家研究委员会[法文]
CNRS	Centre National de la Recherche Scientifique [英文: National Center for Scientific Research]（法国）国家科学研究中心[法文]

CNRS	Centre National de la Recherche Scientifique	国家科学研究中心[法文]
CNRS	China National Reader Survey	中国全国读者调查
CNRS	Chinese National Registration System	中国公民信息登记系统
CNS	Canadian News Service	加拿大新闻社
CNS	Chinese Nutrition Society	中国营养学会
CNS	central nervous system	中枢神经系统
CNTA	The China National Tourism Administration	中国国家旅游局
CNTV	China Network Television	中国网络电视台
CNVD	China National Vulnerability database	中国国家信息安全漏洞共享平台
CNWM	China National Wildlife Management	中国野生动物经营利用管理专用标识
CNY	Chinese Yuan	人民币（符号）
CNYK	China Youth K	全国青少年卡丁车运动委员会（K 为 carting car 的变异缩略语）
CO	Center Output	中置输出（音响）
Co	cobalt	钴[第 27 号化学元素]
CO	carbon monoxide	一氧化碳
CO	Central Office	中央办公室
CO	College of Optometry	视光学院
CO	Concert Orchestra	音乐会管弦乐团
CO_2 CP	carbon dioxide combining power	二氧化碳结合力
COA	China Oil Association	中国油脂学会
COA	Chinese Orthopaedic Association	中华医学会骨科学分会
COA	International Congress of Chinese Orthopaedic Association	中华骨科学术会议国际学术大会
COB	chip on board	板上芯片
COB	close of business	停止营业
COBOL	common business-oriented language	通用商业语言
COC	carrier's owned container	承运人箱
COC	Certificate of Conformity	伊拉克 COC 符合性认证标志
COC	Codes of Conduct in the South China Sea	《南海行为准则》
COCOM	Coordinating Committee on Export Control	巴黎统筹委员会
COD	chemical oxygen demand	化学需氧量

C

COD	collect on delivery 货到付款
COD	*The Concise Oxford Dictionary*《简明牛津词典》
COD	Congo(D. R) 刚果(金)[非洲国家]
CODAG	combined diesel and gas turbine (propulsion) 柴油机和燃气轮机组合动力系统
CODAP	control data assembly program 控制数据汇编程序
CODATA	Committee on Data for Science and Technology 国际科学技术数据委员会
code promo	un code promotionnel 折扣码[法文]
COK	the Cook Islands 库克群岛[大洋洲新西兰属岛屿]
COL	Colombia 哥伦比亚[南美洲国家]
COL	colour 尿液颜色
COM	Comoros 科摩罗[非洲国家]
COM	computer output microfilm 计算机输出缩微胶片
COMAC	The Commercial Aircraft Corporation of China, Ltd. 中国商用飞机有限责任公司
COMCASA	Communication Compatible and Security Agreement《通信兼容与安全协议》
COMDEX	Computer Dealer Exhibition 计算机分销商展览会
COMET	Committee for Middle East Trade 中东贸易委员会[英国]
COMEX	Commodities Exchange 商品交易所[美国]
COMIT	Compiler of Massachusetts Institute of Technology 麻省理工学院的编译程序
CompTIA	Computer Technology Industry Association 计算机技术工业协会
COMSEA	Common Market of Southeast Africa 东南非共同市场
COMTRAN	commercial translator 商用翻译程序
ConA	concanavalin A 伴刀豆凝集素 A
CONCACAF	Confederation of North, Central American and Caribbean Football 中北美及加勒比足球协会
CONCACAF	Confederación Norte-Centroamericana y del Caribe de Fútbol 中北美及加勒比足球联合会[西班牙文]
con-call	conference call 电话会议

CONIE	Comisión Nacional de Investigacion del Espacio 国家空间研究委员会[西班牙文]
CONMEBOL	Confederación Sudamericana de Fútbol 南美洲足球协会/南美足联[西班牙文]
CONSOL	consolidation 集装箱拼箱
CONT	control 控制
CONTRAN	control translator 控制翻译程序
COO	country of origin 产品来源国
COO	chief operation office 首席经营官
Co-op	Co-operative Education 带薪实习课程
COPAC	the CURL Online Public Access Catalogue 英国大学及研究图书馆联盟在线联合目录
COPANT	Comisión Pan-americana de Normas Técnicas 泛美技术标准委员会[西班牙文]
COPD	chronic obstructive pulmonary disease 慢性阻塞性肺部疾病
COPUOS	Committee on the Peaceful Uses of Outer Space 和平利用外层空间委员会
CoQ10	Coenzyme Q10 辅酶 Q10
CORAL	computer on-line real-time applications language 计算机联机实时应用语言
Cos	Cosplay 动漫角色扮演
COS	cosine 余弦
COSCO	China Overseas Shipping Corporation 中国远洋运输总公司
cose c	cosecant 余割
COSIP	Consejo Superior de la Iniciativa Privada 私营事业最高委员会[西班牙文]
cosmeceutical	cosmetic pharmaceutical product 药用化妆品
COSO	Committee of Sponsoring Organizations 发起组织委员会
COSPAR	Committee for Space Research 空间研究委员会
Cosplay	costume play 动漫角色扮演
Cot	cotangent 余切
COTIF	Convention de relative aux Transports Internationaux Ferroviaires 《国际铁路货物运输公约》[法文]

C

COTIP	Committee of Translation and International Promotion of Traditional Chinese Culture 中医药研究促进会传统文化翻译与国际传播专业委员会
COUR	Committee of University Resource 大学资源委员会
COVID-19	coronavirus disease 2019 新冠肺炎
Cox	cyclooxygenase 环氧合酶
CP	carotid pulse 颈动脉
CP	cerebral palsy 大脑性麻痹
CP	chemically pure 化学纯
CP	chronic pyelonephritis 慢性肾盂肾炎
CP	commercial paper 商业票据
CP	Communist Party 共产党
CP	corpulmonale 肺心病
CP	creatine phosphate 磷酸肌酸
CP	cyclophosphamide and prednisone 环磷酰胺和泼尼松［化疗方案］
CP	customs police 海关警察
CP	ceruloplasmin 血浆铜蓝蛋白
CP	computer program 计算机程序［电子文献标示字母］
CP	coterie partner 同人配对
CP	couple 夫妻配对［一般是漫画同人拿来自配的］
CP	coupling 配对
CP	C-peptide 连接肽［体检用语］
CP	The Commercial Press 商务印书馆
CP/DK	computer program on disk 磁带软件［电子文献标示略语］
CPA	certified public accountant 注册（公共）会计师
CPA	chartered patent agent 特许专利代理人
CPA	Chinese phonetic alphabet 汉语拼音字母
CPA	Commonwealth Parliamentary Association 英联邦议会联合会
CPAC	Conservative Political Action Conference 保守政治行动会议
CPACRFC	Chinese People's Association for Cultural Relations with Foreign Countries 中国人民对外文化协会
CPAH	para-aminohippurate clearance 对氨基马尿酸清除率

CPAM	China International Exchange and Promotion Association for Medical and Health Care 中国医疗保健国际交流促进会
CPAM	Caisse Primaire d'Assurance Maladie 基层疾病保险金管理处［法文］
CPAM	Committee of Purchasers of Aircraft Material 飞机材料购买者委员会
CPAPD	Chinese People's Association for Peace And Disarmament 中国人民争取和平与裁军协会
CPB	Central Planning Bureau 中央计划署
CPB	China Patent Bureau 中国专利局
CPB	Clea de Peau Beaute 肌肤之钥化妆品［日本品牌］［法文］
CPB	Consumer Protection Bureau 消费者保护局
CPB	Corporation for Public Broadcasting 公共广播公司
CPBM	Chinese Pharmacy Benefit Management 中版药品福利管理
CPBS	Central People's Broadcasting Station 中央人民广播电台
CPC	the Communist Party of China 中国共产党
CPC	composite pass card 复合通行卡
CPCI-S	Conference Proceedings Citation Index-Science 科学会议录引文索引
CPCI-SSH	Conference Proceedings Citation Index-Social Science & Humanities 社会与人文科学会议录引文索引
CPD	center park district 中央公园区
CPD	computer produced drawing 计算机绘图
CPDC	Committee on the Present Danger: China 应对中国当前危险委员会
CPE	customer premises equipment 用户终端设备
CPE	Cambridge English: Proficiency 专业英语证书
CPE	chlorinated polyethylene 氯化聚乙烯
CPEC	China-Pakistan Economic Corridor 中巴经济走廊
CPEC	Children Parenting Education Centre 儿童家长教育中心
CPEC	California Post-secondary Education Commission 加利福尼亚中学后教育委员会
CPEC	China-Pakistan Economy Corridor 中巴经济走廊
CPES	Comprehensive Program for Ebola Survivors 埃博拉幸存者综合计划
CPG	Central People's Government （中国）中央人民政府
CPI	clear and pure index 清廉指数

C

CPI	Conference Papers Index	美国会议论文索引
CPI	commodity price index	商品价格指数
CPI	consumer price index	消费者价格指数
CPI	cost performance index	价格表现指数
CPIC	China Pacific Insurance Corporation	中国太平洋保险公司
CPIFA	Chinese People's Institute of Foreign Affairs	中国人民外交学会
CP-ISRA	Cerebral Palsy International Sport and Recreation Association	国际脑瘫人体育和休闲运动协会
CPK	creatine phosphokinase	肌酸磷酸激酶
CPL	Cyberathelete Professional League	电子职业联赛
CPM	Certified Property Manager	国际注册资产管理师
CPM	Concentrated Purchasing Management	集中采购管理
CPMA	Chinese Preventive Medical Association	中华预防医学会
CPMI	China Property Management Institute	中国物业管理协会
CPMIEC	China Precision Machinery Import-Export Corporation	中国精密机械进出口公司
CPN	*China Philately News*	《中国集邮报》
CPO	chief procurement officer	首席采购官
CPO	chief privacy officer	首席隐私官
CPO	chief programme officer	首席程序官
CPP	Certified Purchasing Professional	专业采购人员认证
CPPCC	Chinese People's Political Consultative Conference	中国人民政治协商会议
CPPM	Certified Purchasing Professional Manager	专业采购经理认证
CPPU	Child Protection Policy Unit	香港保护儿童政策组
CPR	cardio-pulmonary resuscitation	心肺复苏术
CPS	come-pay-stay	先交费[一种网络游戏模式]
CPSC	Consumer Product Safety Commission	美国消费品安全委员会
CPSIA	Consumer Product Safety Improvement Act	《消费品安全改进法案》
CPSR	Cosmetic Product Safety Report	化妆品安全报告
CPT	computer network police team	网络执法分队
CPT	Curricular Practical Training	美国政府允许学习期间使用的实习许可

CPTPP	Comprehensive Progressive Trans-Pacific Partnership 全面与进步跨太平洋伙伴关系协定	
CPU	Central Processing Unit 中央处理器	
CPUOS	Committee of the Peaceful Uses of Outer Space 联合国和平利用外层空间委员会	
CPV	canister purge valve 碳罐净化阀	
CPV	Cape Verde 佛得角[非洲国家]	
CPV	certified public valuer 资产评估师	
CPV	concentrating photovoltaics 聚光光伏	
CPVC	chlorinated polyvinyl chloride 氯化聚氯乙烯	
CPVG	certified public valuer of gem 珠宝资产评估师	
CQ	collaboration quotient 合拍商数	
CQ	courage quotient 胆(略)商(数)	
CQ	creation quotient 创造力商数	
CQC	China Quality Certification Centre for Import and Export 中国进出口质量认证中心	
CQI	Customer Quality Index 客户质量指数	
CQO	chief quality officer 首席质量官	
Cr	creatinine 肌酐/肌酐(血)[生化检查项目之一]	
CR	critical 危急的	
CR	change request 变革请求	
Cr	chromium 铬[第24号化学元素]	
CR	College of the Rockies 落基山学院	
CR	complete remission 完全缓解	
CR	compression ratio 压缩比	
CR	consumer reports 消费者报告	
CR	conditioned reflex 条件反射	
CR	connect request 连接请求[网络用语]	
cr	calorie restricted 热量限制类药物/限制热卡	
CR4	Four-firm Concentration Rate 四企业集中度	
CR929	China Russia 929 中俄联合开发的CR929宽体客机	
CRAM	card random access memory 卡片随机存取存储器	

C

CRB	Commodity Research Bureau 商品调查局
CRB	Criminal Record Bureau 香港刑事记录科
CRBA	China National Registration Board for Auditors 中国认证人员国家注册委员会
CRBC	China Railway and Bridge Company 中国路桥工程公司
CRBI	Commodity Research Bureau Index 商品调查指数
CRC	cyclic redundancy check 循环冗余码校验
CRC	Costa Rica 哥斯达黎加[北美洲国家]
CRCC	China Railway Construction Corporation Limited 中国铁建股份有限公司
CRE	creatinine 肌酸
CRF	case report form 病例报告表
CRF	corticotropin-regulating factor 促肾上腺皮质激素调节因子
CRFTG	China Radio Film and Television Group 中国广播影视集团
CRH	corticotropin releasing hormone 促肾上腺皮质激素释放激素
CRH	China Railways High-speed 中国高速铁路
CRI	China Radio International 中国国际广播电台
CRIC	Commercial Radio International Committee 国际商业无线电委员会
CRISP	computer retrieval of information on scientific projects 科学计划信息计算机检索
CRISPR	clustered regularly interspaced short palindromic repeats 基因剪刀/基因编辑技术
CRM	Customer Relationship Management 客户关系管理
CRM	call recording monitor 呼叫记录监视器
CRM	Canadian Royal Mounties 加拿大皇家骑警
CRM	Centre of Research of Machine 机械研究中心
CRM	computer resources management 计算机资源管理
CRM	cost reduction management 降低成本的管理
CRM	courtesy reply mail 礼貌回复邮件
CRNET	China Railway Network 中国铁路网
CRO	chief research officer 首席分析官
CRO	chief roadshow officer 首席路演官[网络用语]
CRO	Contract Research Organization 合同研究组织

C

CRO	Croatia 克罗地亚[欧洲国家]
CRO	chief risk officer 首席风险控制投资师
CROPI	Children's Rights Organization Plan International 儿童权利组织国际计划
CRP	C-reactive protein C反应蛋白
CRP	Center of Refinery in Paragua 帕拉瓜河的炼油中心
CRP	chiral reagent derivatization 手性试剂衍生化法
CRPA	C-reactive protein antiserum C-反应蛋白抗血清
CRPF	Central Reserve Police Force (India) 印度中央后备警察部队
CRPS	complicated region pain syndrome 复杂区域疼痛综合征
CRRC	China Railway Rolling Stock Corporation 中国中车股份有限公司
CRRT	continuous renal replacement therapy 连续性肾脏替代治疗
CRS	China Railway Schedule 中国铁路时刻
CRS	computer reservation system （航空）计算机订座系统
CRS	Congressional Research Service 美国国会调查部
CRS	credits 贷款（复数）
CRS	Comité des Recherches Spatiales 空间研究委员会[法文]
CRS	Croatian Register of Shipping 克罗地亚船舶登记局
CRS	cash recycling system 自动（循环）存取款机
CRS	central reservation system 中央预订系统
CRS	child restraint system 儿童专用安全装置
CRS	China Rescue & Salvage 中国救捞
CRS	Common Reporting Standard 共同申报准则
CRS	common reporting standard 共同税务汇报系统
CRS	common reporting standard 统一报告标准
CRS	computer reservation system 计算机预订系统
CRSA	Chinese Radio Sports Association 中国无线电运动协会
CRSA	Concrete Reinforcement Steel Association 钢筋混凝土协会
CRT	cathode ray tube 阴极射线管
CRT	clot retraction test 血块收缩试验
Crufts Qualifier & CAC	Crufts Qualifier & Certificate d' Aptitude au championnat 英国卡夫犬类资格赛

C

CR-V	city recreation vehicle 城市休闲车	
CRvanguard	China Resource Vanguard Co., Ltd. 华润万家（超市）	
CS	capital stock 股本	
CS	cash settlement 现金结汇	
CS	counter strike 反击	
CS	cryptographic system 密码系统	
CS	current strength 当前实力	
Cs	caesium 铯[第 55 号化学元素]	
CS	cop shop（＝police station）警察局[网络用语]	
CS	*Counter-Strike*《反恐精英》[电子游戏名]	
CS	Central Secretariat 中央秘书处	
CS	city of sustainability 可持续城市	
CSA	Canadian Standards Association 加拿大标准协会	
CSA	China Software Association 中国软件联盟	
CSA	Chinese Space Agency 中国航天局	
CSA	Chinese Stomatological Association 中华口腔医学会	
CSA	Cambridge Scientific Abstracts 美国剑桥科学文摘社	
CSA	Community Supported Agriculture 社区支持农业	
CSA	Canadian Standards Association 北美电子、电器产品质量认证标志	
CSAIL	Computer Science and Artificial Intelligence Laboratory 计算机科学与人工智能实验室	
CSBA	Center for Strategic and Budgetary Assessments 战略与预算评估中心	
CSBA	Center for Strategic and Budgetary Analysis 战略和预算分析中心	
CSC	China Scholarship Council 国家留学基金管理委员会	
CSC	container service charge 集装箱服务费	
CSC	cosecant 余割	
CSC	comprehensive self-check 综合自校验	
CSC	configuration switching control 配置转换控制	
CSCL	computer-supported collaborative learning 计算机辅助和支持的协作学习	
CSCW	computer supported cooperative work 计算机支持的协同工作	
CSD	Correctional Services Department 香港惩教署	

C

CSDC	China Software Development Centre	中国软件开发中心
CSDL	Chinese National Science Digital Library	中科院国家科学数字图书馆
CSDN	China Social Development Network	中国社会发展互联网
CSDN	Circuit Switching Data Network	电路交换数据网络
CSDR	Center for Strategic and Defense Research	战略与防务研究中心
CSE	Certificate of Secondary Education	中等教育证书［英国］
CSE	China's Standards of English	中国英语能力等级量表
CSF	carrier strike force	航母打击部队
CSF	central switching facility	中央交换设施
CSF	close supporting fire	近距支援火力
CSF	coastal surveillance force	海岸监视部队
CSF	combat support force	战斗支援部队
CSF	cerebrospinal fluid	脑脊液
CSF	colony stimulating factor	集落刺激因子
CSF	combined support fund	联合支持基金
CSF	Cross Strait Ferry	海峡轮渡
CSF	Fujian Cross Strait Ferry Corporation	福建海峡高速客轮航运有限公司
CSG	coronavirus study group	冠状病毒研究小组
CSG	carrier strike group	航母打击群
CSI	Computer Simulated Instruction	计算机模拟教学
CSI	crime scene investigation	犯罪现场调查
CSI	Customer Satisfaction Index	顾客满意指数
CSIAT	Certificate of Shanghai Interpretation Accreditation Test (Intermediate Level) 上海市英语中级口译资格证书	
CSIC	Canadian Society of Immigration Consultants	加拿大移民顾问协会
CSIC	China Shipbuilding Industry Corporation	中船重工
CSIRO	Commonwealth Scientific and Industrial Research Organization 澳大利亚联邦科学与工业研究组织	
CSIS	Center for Strategic and International Studies	（美国）战略及国际问题研究中心
CSM	Certified Scrum Master	优普丰敏捷教练认证
CSM	*Christian Science Monitor*	《基督教科学箴言报》（美国）

C

CSM	Committee on Safety of Medicines 药物安全委员会	
CSM	contemporary shipbuilding model 当代造船模式	
CSM	CVSC-SOFRES Research MEDIA 中国广视索福瑞媒介研究	
ČSN	Československých Státních Norem 捷克电气产品质量认证标志/前捷克斯洛伐克标准化与计量局[捷克文]	
CSNet	China Satellite Network 中国卫星网络	
CSO	Contract Sales Organization 合同销售组织	
CSO	Chief System Officer 首席系统官	
CSO	Chief Security Officer 安全总监,首席安全官	
CSO	Chicago Symphony Orchestra 美国芝加哥交响乐团	
CSO	Commonwealth Scientific Office 英联邦科学署	
CSOC	China Sun Oil Company 中国太阳石油公司	
CSOC	China Shipbuilding and Offshore International Corporation 中国船贸	
CSOC	Critical Systems Operations Center 关键系统操作中心	
CSP	commercial service provider 商业服务供应商	
CSP	computer simulation program 计算机模拟程序	
CSP	chiral stationary phase 手性固定相法	
CSP	Concentrating Solar Power 聚光太阳能发电	
CSPI	Center for Science in the Public Interest 公共利益科学中心/美国公众兴趣科学中心	
CSR	corporate social responsibility 企业社会责任	
CSR	claim settlement rate 理赔率	
CSRC	China Securities Regulatory Commission 中国证券监督管理委员会	
CSS	cascading style sheet 串联样式表	
CSS	Central Security Service 中央安全署	
CSSC	China State Shipbuilding Corporation Limited 中国船舶集团有限公司	
CSSCI	*Chinese Social Science Citation Information*《中文社会科学引文索引》	
CSSRC	Canadian Social Sciences Research Council 加拿大社会科学研究委员会	
CST	Central Standard Time 中部标准时间	
CST	computer simulation technique 计算机模拟技术	
CSTC	China Shipbuilding Trade Co., LTD. 中国船舶工业贸易公司	
CSTC	China Standard Technical Services Co., Ltd 中国标准技术开发公司	

CSTNET	China Science and Technology Network 中国科技网
CSTPCD	Chinese Science and Technology Papers and Citation Databases 中国科技论文与引文数据库
CSU	Christlich-Soziale Union 基督教社会联盟[德文]
CSU	Central South University 中南大学
CSU	Civil Service Union 英国公职人员联合会
CSUSA	Copyright Society of the United States of America 美国版权协会
CT	Computer Telephone 电脑电话
CT	Computerized Tomography CT 扫描
CT	computerized tomography 计算机(辅助)段层摄影术
CT	counter terrorist 反恐警察[网络用语]
CT	calcitonin 降钙素
Ct	carat 克拉[钻石计量单位]
CT	clotting time 凝血时间
CT	codman triangle 骨膜三角
CTA	China Testing Alliance 中国质量检验联盟
CTA	CT angio(arterio)graphy CT 血管造影
CTA	CT angio(arterio)graphy 计算机断层血管造影术
CTAD	United Nations Conference on Trade and Development 联合国贸易与发展会议
CTAIS	China Taxation Administration Information System 中国税收征管信息系统
CTB	Commonwealth Telecommunications Board 英联邦电信委员会
CTB	Citybus 城巴[香港]
CT B/L	Combined Transport Bill of Lading 联合运输提单
CTBT	Comprehensive Nuclear Test Ban Treaty《全面禁止核试验条约》
CTBTO	Preparatory Commission for the Comprehensive Nuclear-Test-Ban Treaty Organization 全面禁止核试验条约组织筹备委员会
CTBTO	Comprehensive Nuclear-Test-Ban Treaty Organization 全面禁止核试验条约组织
CTBU	Chongqing Technology and Business University 重庆工商大学
CTBUH	The Council on Tall Building and Urban Habitat 国际高层建筑与城市住宅协会

C

CTC	common toxicity criteria 一般毒性标准
CTC	Consumer to Consumer 消费者对消费者[电子商务的一种形式]
CTC	United Nations Security Council Counter-Terrorism Committee 联合国安全理事会反恐怖主义委员会
CTCA	China Telecom Certification Authority 中国电信认证中心
CTCC	China Touring Car Championship 中国房车锦标赛
CTCF	The China Toilet Culture Forum 中国厕所文化论坛
CTE	chronic toxic encephathy 慢性中毒性脑病
CTF	Children Trust Fund 儿童信托基金
ctg	cotangent 余切
CTG	Casino Table Game 赌场表的游戏
CTI	computer telephone integration 电脑电话集成；电脑语音合成技术
CTI	Chinese Testing International 汉考国际
CTL	cytotoxit T lymphocyte 细胞毒性 T 淋巴细胞
CTM	Cognitive Teaching Method 认知教学法
CTMP	Chemi-thermal mechanical pulp 化学热磨机械浆
CTnI	cardiac troponin I 心肌肌钙蛋白
CTO	chief technology officer 首席技术官
CTO	combined transport operator 联运经营人
CTP	Computer to Paper 电脑直接印刷
CTPF	China Translation Profession Forum 中国翻译职业交流大会
CTR	click through ratio 点击（通过）率
CTR	container 集装箱
CTRU	Counter Terrorism Response Unit 香港反恐特勤队
CTS	China Travel Service 中国旅行社
CTS	communication technology satellite 通信技术卫星
CTS	computerized typesetting system 电脑排版系统
CTS	China Travel Service 中国旅行总社
CTSI	China Transport Production Index 中国运输生产指数
CTT	capital transfer tax 资本转移税
CTT	completion of TU transmission 传输单元传输完毕
CTV	Canadian Television 加拿大电视新闻台

CU	calculated unit 计量单位
CU	Cambridge University 剑桥大学
CU	Consumers Union (美国)消费者联盟
CU	see you 再见[网络用语]
CU	CVS for you 你的便利店
CU	The Customs Union 海关联盟
CU	Columbia University 美国哥伦比亚大学
CU	Cornell university 美国康奈尔大学
Cu	cuprum 血清铜[拉丁文]/铜[第29号化学元素][拉丁文]
CUB	Cuba 古巴[北美洲国家]
CUBA	China University Basketball Association 中国大学生篮球协会
CUC	Communication University of China 中国传媒大学
CUHK	The Chinese University of Hong Kong 香港中文大学
CULV	consumer, ultra, low, voltage 消费超低压处理器笔记本
CUMC	Columbia University Medical Center 哥伦比亚大学医学中心
CUN	Charter of the United Nations《联合国宪章》
CUP	common underlying proficiency model 公有潜在能力模型
CUPL	China University of Political Science and Law 中国政法大学[旧称,现称 ZUC]
CUR	Committee of University Resource 大学资源委员会
CUR	urea clearance rate 尿素清除率
CURL	Consortium of University and Research Libraries 英国大学及研究图书馆联盟
CUSPEA	China US Physics Examination and Application 中美联合培养物理类研究生计划
CUTIN	cutting 插入编辑
CUW	Clean Up World "使世界清洁起来"组织
CV	Commanditaine Vennootschap 合伙有限公司[荷兰文]
CV	closed volume 闭合容积
CV	curriculum vitae 简历[拉丁文]
CV	voice character 配音演员
CVCC	compound vortex controlled combustion 复合控制涡流燃烧式发动机

C

CVD	cardio vascular disease 心血管疾病
CVD	compact video disc 激光视频光盘
CVD	chemical vapor deposition 化学气相沉积
CVD	countervailing duties 抵消性关税/反倾销税
CVJ	constant velocity joint 万向节
CV-LX	aircraft carrier，conventionally powered 常规动力航母[代字]
CVO	Chief Value Officer 首席价值官[网络用语]
CVOM	commercial vehicle operation/fleet management 营运车辆调度管理系统
CVR	cockpit voice recorder 驾驶舱语音记录器
CVS	convenience store 便利店
CVSC	Central Viewer Survey & Consulting Company 央视调查咨询公司
CVT	continuously variable transmission 无级变速传动/无级自动变速器
CVTC	continuous variable timing control 连续可变气门正时控制
CVTCU	CVT control unit 无极自动变速器控制单元
CW	Clan War 团队战
CW	clockwise 顺时针方向
CWGC	China Worldbest Group Co., Ltd. 中国华源集团有限公司
CWI	China Welfare Institute 中国福利会
CWM	certified wealth manager 特许财富管理师
CWO	chief web officer 首席网络官
CWQC	company-wide quality control 全公司质量控制
CWSA	China Well-Off Society Association 中国小康建设研究会
CWTV	China Web TV 中国网络电视
CWUR	Center for World University Rankings 世界大学排名中心
CWYL	chat with you later 过后跟你聊[网络用语]
CY	container yard 集装箱堆场
CYA	Canadian Youth Association 加拿大青年协会
CYA	China Youth Ambassador 中国青年大使
CYFRA21-1	cytokeratin fragment 19 细胞角蛋白片段 19
CYL	Communist Youth League 共产主义青年团
CYL	cylinder 气缸

CYP	Cyprus 塞浦路斯[欧洲国家]
CYS	Cyprus Organization for Standards and Control of Quality 塞浦路斯标准与质量管理局/塞浦路斯产品质量认证标志
CYTS	China Youth Travel Service 中国青年旅行社
CZ	Czech 捷克[欧洲国家]
CZBANK	China Zheshang Bank Co., Ltd. 浙商银行
CZE	Czech Republic 捷克共和国[欧洲国家]

d	deci 十进分数单位的词头名称"分",表示的因数为 10−1
D	Daihatsu 大发汽车[日本]
D	Defense 国防
D	diopter 屈光度[−5·5D 就是 550 度的近视]
D	trial data 试验数据
D	Danmarks Elektriske Materielkontrol 丹麦电气认证标志/丹麦电气设备检验委员会[丹麦文]
D	dark 浊色
D	diesel 柴油机
D	dissertation 学位论文[参考文献标示字母]
D	dreadful 差[不好]
D	drive 前进挡
D&C	dilatation and curettage 宫颈扩张及刮宫术
D&D	Decontamination and Decommissioning 去污及服役[停用]
D&D	Dungeons and Dragons 地下探宝游戏
D(em)	Democrat 美国民主党员
D.M.E.	design, measure, evaluate 设计、测量、评价[是把流行病学、医学统计学原理和方法应用于临床研究的设计、数据的测定,效果的评价]
D/N	debit note 借项清单

D

D/O	delivery order 提货单
D20	Dairy 20 奶业 20 强
D5	DVD5 单面单层光碟
D9	DVD9 单面双层光碟
da	deca 十进倍数单位的词头名称"十"的符号,表示的因数为 101
D/A	document against acceptance 承兑交单
DA	day after acceptance 承兑后若干天后付款
DA	debit advice 借款通知单
DA	deposit account 存款账户
DA	desk accessory 桌面附件
DA	development aid 发展援助
DA	discharge afloat 船上卸货
DA	dopamine 多巴胺
DA	duck's arse 鸭尾巴式发型
DA	*Dictionary of Americanisms*《美语词典》
DAA	data access arrangement 数据入口装置
DAAD	Democratic Alliance Against Dictatorship (泰国)反独裁民主联盟
DAB	Digital Audio Broadcasting 数字音频广播
DAB	*Deutsches Apothekerbuch* [英文:*German Pharmacopoeia*]《德国药典》[德文]
DAB	*Dictionary of American Biography*《美国人名词典》
DAC	digital to analog converter 数字模拟转换器
DAC	Diamond Administration of China 中国钻石管理局
DACA	Deferred Action for Childhood Arrivals 童年抵美国者暂缓遣返
DAE	*Dictionary of American English*《美国英语词典》
DAF	decay accelerating factor 衰变因子
DAF	delivered at frontier 边境交货
DaF	Deutsch als Fremdsprache 德语托福考试[德文]
DAH	Disordered Action of the Heart 心律不齐
DAI	*Dissertation Abstracts International*《国际学位论文文摘》
Daks	Dad and Slacks 德克斯长裤
DALY	Disability Adjusting Life Years 伤残调整生命年

Danskin	dance+skin 紧身舞衣
DAPP	decentralized application 去中心化应用
DAR	Deutscher Akkreditierungs Rat 德国认证机构,是世界六家权威的国家认证机构之一[德文]
DARPA	Defence Advanced Research Projects Agency 美国国防部高级研究计划署
DART	data automatic rescheduling technique 自动数据再调度技术
DAS	*Dictionary of American Slang*《美国俚语词典》
DAS	Delphi automotive systems 德尔福汽车系统
DAS	digital avionics system 数码航电系统
DAS	direct at sea 海洋废物处理
DAS	disposal attached storage 直接方式存储
DASH	Dietary Approaches to Stop Hypertension 得舒饮食[防高血压健康饮食]
DAT	digital audio tape 数字音频磁带
DATANET	data network 数据网
DATS	District Anti-Triad Squa 香港警区反三合会行动组
DAX	Deutscher Aktienindex 德国重要的股票指数[德文]
DB	Daimler Benz AG 戴姆勒·奔驰股份公司[德文]
Db	dubnium 𨧀[第 105 号化学元素]
DB	deadbeat 不负责任的
DB	data bank 数据库[电子文献标示字母]
DB/MT	data bank/magnetic tape 磁带数据库[电子文献标示略语]
DB/OL	data bank on line 联机网上的数据库[电子文献标示略语]
dB;db	decibel 分贝[表示功率比和声音强度的单位]
DBA	Doctor of Business Administration 工商管理博士
DBD	deadbeat dad 不负责任的爸爸
DBE	Dame Commander of the Order of the British Empire 大英帝国统治的女士指挥官/爵士级别的司令勋章(女)
DBF	digital beam former 数字波束形成
DB Hi Tek	Dongbu High Technology Co., Ltd. 东部高科株式会社
D-Bil	direct bilirubin 直接胆红素

D

DBK	dibike 迪比科移动电源[汉语拼音缩略语]
DBM	Development Bank of Mongolia 蒙古开发银行
DBMS	Data Base Management System 数据管理系统
DBP	dibutyl phthalate 邻苯二甲酸二丁酯[增塑剂]
DBS	Development Bank of Singapore 星展银行
DBS	direct broadcasting by satellite 卫星直播
DBTC	Dalian Beida Technology (Group) Co., Ltd. 大连北大科技(集团)股份有限公司
DBTC	debitcoin 借方币
DC	digital camera 数字相机
DC	direct current 直流电
DC	dendritic cell 树突状细胞
DC	Detective Comics 美国 DC 漫画公司
DC	differential count 白细胞分类计数
DC	District Council 区议会[英国]
DC	doctor of chiropractic 按摩医师
DC/EP	digital currency electronic payment 数字化货币
DCC	digital compact cassette 数码盒式磁带
DCC	dynamic circulation corpus 动态流通语料库
DCC	document control center 文控中心
DCCI	Data Center of China Internet 中国互联网数据中心
DCCT	diabetes control and complications trial 糖尿病及其并发症控制试验
DCD	data carrier detection 数据载波检测
DCD	data collecting device 数据收集设备
DCD	decoder 译码器
DCE	domestic credit expansion 国内信用膨胀
DCEP	Digital Currency Electronic Payment 数字货币
DCF	discounted cash flow 现金流量贴现
DCGAN	Deep Convolutional Generative Adversarial Networks 深度卷积世代对抗网络
DCI	digital cinema initiators 数字电影倡导联盟(规范)
DCI	Director of Central Intelligence 中央情报主任

DCIS	ductal carcinoma in situ 导管原位癌
DCIS	Defence Criminal Investigation Service 美国国防部刑事调查局
DCM	dilated cardiomyopathy 扩张型心肌病
DCN	design change notice 设计变更通知
DCP	data collection platform 数据收集平台
DCP	digital content provider 数字资源内容提供者
DCR	design change request 设计变更需求
DCS	dispose control system 分散控制系统
DCT	double clutch transmission 双离合器变速器
DD	deadline date 截止日期
D/D	demand draft 即期汇票
D-D	D-dimer D-二聚体
DDC	destination delivery charge 目的地交货费
DDD	direct distance dialing 长途直接拨号
DDD	domestic direct dial 国内电话直拨
DDD	double chambers-double chambers-double 房室全能型（心脏起搏器）
DDE	dynamic data exchange 动态数据交换
DDG	guided missile destroyer 导弹驱逐舰[代字]
DDH	destroyer, anti-submarine helicopter 反潜直升机驱逐舰[代字]
DDHD	digital dynamic high device 数字动态高清芯片
DDN	digital data network 数字数据网
DDP	Desistance and Disengagement Programme 断念与脱离项目
DDP	delivered duty paid 完税后交货价
DDR	Dance Dance Revolution 跳舞机
DDR	Double Data Rate 双倍速数据（传输速）率
DDR	direct drive 直接驱动
DDS	Deep Diving System 深潜系统
DDT	dichloro-diphenyl-trichloroethane 滴滴涕[一种杀虫剂]
DDT	depth, distance and time 深度、距离和时间
DEA	disposable e-mail address 一次性的电子邮箱地址
DEA	draft environmental assessment 环境评估草案
DEA	Drug Enforcement Administration 毒品管制局/毒品强制执行管理局

D

DEA	Drug Enforcement Agency 禁毒署
Dec	December 12月
DEHM	di (2-ethylhexyl) maleate 顺丁烯二酸二(2-乙基己)酯
DEHP	di (2-ethylhexyl) phthalate 邻苯二甲酸二(2-乙基己基)酯
DEHP	diethyl hydrogen phosphide 二乙基磷化氢
DEM	Deutsche Mark 德国马克[货币][德文]
DEMO	demonstration 演示,示范
Demo	demonstration 演示板
DEN	Denmark 丹麦[欧洲国家]
DEPC	diethyl pyrocarbonate 焦碳酸二乙酯
DES	Data Encryption Standard 数据加密标准
Desertopia	desert utopia 荒漠乐园
DEVGRU	Naval Special Warfare Development Group 海军特种作战研究组
DF	Delivery Forward (有本金交割)远期外汇合约
DF	dongfeng 东风[汉语拼音缩略语]
DFAT	Department of Foreign Affairs and Trade 外交贸易部
DFAT	Direct Fluorescent Antibody Technique 直接荧光抗体技术
DFC	direct flight control 直接飞行控制
DFG	Diagnosis Related Group 按疾病诊断相关分担付费
DFID	Department for International Development 英国国际发展部
DFKI	Deutsche Forschungszentrum für Künstliche Intelligenz GmbH 德国人工智能研究中心[德文]
DFS	disease-free survival 无病生存期
DFS	duty-free shops 免税商店
DFS	Department of Field Support 联合国外勤资助部
DG	dark green 深绿色
DGA	Délégation Générale à l'Armement 武器装备总署[法文]
DGAC	Direction Générale de l'Aviation Civile 民航总局[法文]
DGAD	anti-dumping and allied duties 反倾销和联合税收理事会
DGCCRF	Direction bénérale de la concurrence de la consommation et de la répression des fraudes 竞争、消费和打击舞弊总局[法文]
DGF	dry geothermal formation 干热岩体

DHA	dehydroascorbic acid 脱氢抗坏血酸	
DHA	dehydroacetic acid 脱氢乙酸	
DHC	Diamond High Council 比利时钻石高阶议会	
DHE	design human engineering 人体设计工程学	
DHEA	dehydroepiandrosterone 脱氢表雄酮	
DHL	Adrian Dalsey, Larry Hillblom, Robert Lynn 美国敦豪速递公司	
DHR	dry hot rock 干热岩	
DHS	Department of Homeland Security 国土安全部	
DHT	dihydrotestosterone 双氢睾酮	
DHV	Deutscher Hundesportverband 德国犬运动协会[德文]	
DHWG	Digital Home Working Group 数字家庭工作组	
DI	DNA index DNA 指数	
DIA	Defense Intelligence Agency 美国国防情报局	
DIA	Documentation Internationale des Accidents 国际事故文献(法文)	
DID	Department of International Development 国际发展部	
DIDP	di-iso-decyl phthalate 邻苯二甲酸二异癸酯[增塑剂]	
DIF	direct investment fund 直接投资基金	
DIFF	differential 差速器	
DIGICCY	digital currency 数字货币	
DII	Derwent Innovations Index 英国德温特世界专利索引	
DIM	design information manual 设计资料手册	
DIMM	digital image memory module 数字图像存储模板	
DIN	Deutsche Industrie Normen 德国工业标准 [英文: German Industry Standards][德文]	
DIN	Deutsche Institut für Normung 德国标准化学会/德国产品质量认证标志[德文]	
DIN-DVGW	Deutsche Institut für Normung—Deutsche Verein von Gas und Wasserfachmännern 德国煤气与自来水产品质量认证标志[德文]	
DINK	Double Income and No Kids 丁克族[有双薪收入而没有孩子的夫妇]	
DIS	Defense Intelligence Service 国防情报局	
DIS	digital indoor system 室内数字系统	

DIS	Draft International Standard 国际标准草案
diss	dissertation 学位论文
DIU	defense innovating unit 国防创新单元
DIY	Do It Yourself 自己动手做
DJ	Disc Jockey 流行音乐节目主持人
DJ	Daniel Jones 丹尼尔·琼斯[英国语音学家]
DJ	Department of Justice 司法部
DJ	Doctor Juris 法学博士[拉丁文]
DJ	Don Juan 唐璜[转义:淫荡者]
DJI	Djibouti 吉布提[非洲国家]
DJI	Dajiang Innovations 大疆创新
DJI	Dow-Jones Index 道琼斯指数
DJIA	Dow Jones Industrial Average (Stock Index) 道琼斯工业平均(股票价格指数)
DJUA	Dow Jones Utility Average 道琼斯公用事业平均指数
DK	don't know 不知道[网络用语]
DK	dark 深色
DK	disk 磁盘[电子文献标示字母]
DK	Dorling Kindersley 英国DK(多林金德斯利)出版公司
DKK	Danish Krone 丹麦克朗[丹麦货币单位][丹麦文]
DKNY	Donna Karan New York 唐可娜儿时装
DKr	Danish Krone 丹麦克朗[丹麦货币单位][丹麦文]
DLCO	diffusing capacity of the lungs for carbon monoxide 肺一氧化碳弥散量
DLH	Deutsche Luft Hansa 德国航空公司[德文]
DLL	dynamic link library 动态链接库
DLNA	Digital Life Network Association 数字生活网协会
DLO_2	diffusing capacity of the lungs for oxygen 肺氧弥散量
DLP	digital light processor 数码光处理
DLT	distributed ledger technology 分布式分类账技术
DM	Design Manual 设计手册
DM	Deutsche Mark 德国马克[德国货币单位][德文]
DM	diabetes mellitus 糖尿病

DM	Department of Management	联合国管理事务部
DM	direct mail advertising	直接邮件广告
DM	direct marketing	免费直投广告
DM	driver motor	驱动马达
DM	drowsiness monitor	驾驶防瞌睡监视器
DMA	Direct Memory Access	直接存取存储器
DMA	Dominica	多米尼加[北美洲国家]
DMAX	demand maximum	需求最大值
DMAX	density maximum	最大密度
DMB	digital multimedia broadcasting	数字多媒体广播
DMCA	Digital Millenium Copyright Act	美国数字千年版权法案
DMD	digital micromirror device	数字微镜器件
DME	distance measuring equipment	测距仪
DME	Dubai Merchandise Exchange	迪拜商品期货交易所
DMEM	Dulbecco modified Eagle medium	由 Dulbecco 改良的 Eagle 培养基
DMG	digital media group	数码媒体集团
DMI	desktop management interface	桌面管理接口
DMI	directional movement index	趋向指数
DMK	Dravida Munnetra Kazhagam	德拉维达进步联盟党[印地文]
Dmm	decimillimetre(s)	丝米[非法定长度计量单位 1 丝米＝0.1 毫米＝0.00001 米]
DMMA	dimercaptomandelic acid	二巯基扁桃酸
DMR	data management routines	数据管理程序
DMS	database management system	数据库管理系统
DMS	digital microwave system	数字微波系统
dmsh	diminish	减少
DN	domain name	域名
DNA	deoxyribonucleic acid	脱氧核糖核酸
DNA	digital network application	数字化设备在网络接连中的应用
DNA	digital network architecture	数字网络结构[一种用于网络体系结构的协议]
DNA	Digbrain Network Authentication	挖大脑网络认证服务

DNC	direct numerical control 直接数字控制
DNI	Director of National Intelligence 国家情报主任
DNMT	DNA methyltransferases DNA 甲基转移酶
DNS	distributed network server 分布式网络系统服务器
DNS	Domain Name System 域名系统
DNS	data network service 数据网络业务
DNS	Doppler Navigation System 多普勒导航系统
DNS	digital network system 数字网络系统
DNS	Domain Name Server 域名服务器
2,4-DNT	2,4-Dinitrotoluene 二硝基甲苯(炸药)
DNV	Det Norske Veritas 挪威船级社[挪威文]
DO	Department of the Interior 内务部
DO	Directorate of Operations 美国中央情报局作战处
DOAJ	Directory of Open Access Journals 开放获取期刊目录
DOC	Department of Commerce (美国)商务部
DOC	Declaration on the Conduct of parties in the South China Sea《南海各方行为宣言》
DOCA	deoxycorticosterone acetate 醋酸脱氧皮质酮
DOCA	dynamic object computing architecture 分布式对象计算架构
DOD	Department of Defense 国防部
DODIIS	DOD (Department of Defense) Intelligence Information System 国防部情报信息系统
DOE	Department of Energy (美国)能源部
DOE	design of experiments 实验设计
DOE	designated operational entity 指定经营实体
DOHC	double overhead camshaft(engine) 双顶置双凸轮轴(发动机)
DOJ	Department of Justice 美国司法部
DOKA	Doppelkabine 德国多卡模板公司[德文]
DOKA	Doppelkabine 双机仓[德文]
DOKR	Deutsches Olympiadekomitee für Reiterei 德国马术奥委会[德文]
DOM	Dominican Republic 多米加共和国[北美洲国家]
DOMS	delayed onset muscle soreness 延迟性肌肉酸痛

DOM-SAT	domestic satellite 国内通信卫星
Dop	Doppler 多普勒(效应)
DOP	developing-out paper (摄影)显相纸
DOP	diabetes osteoporosis 糖尿病并发骨质疏松症
DOR	date of rank 服役日期
DOS	disk operating system 磁盘操作系统
DOS	Department of State 国务院
DOS	desktop operation system 桌面操作系统
DOS	digital operating system 数字操作系统
DOT	Department of Transportation 交通部
DOT	Directly-Observed Treatment Strategy 直接观察治疗策略
DOTA	defense of the ancients 守护古物[树,遗址]
DOTC	Defense Office of Trade Control 国防贸易管制局
DP	diastolic pressure 舒张压
dp	degradable plastics 可分解塑料
DPA	Deutsche Presse Agentur 德意志新闻社[德文]
DPA	doctor of public administration 公共管理博士
DPA	Department of Political Affairs 联合国政治事务部
DPA	Diamond Production Association 钻石生产商协会
DPD	diver propulsion device 蛙人推进装置
DPDB	digital planting demonstration base 数字化种植示范基地
Dpi	data processing installation 数据处理设备
DPI	discretionary/disposable personal income 个人可支配收入
DPI	dots per inch 每英寸的点数
DPKO	Department of Peacekeeping Operations 联合国维持和平行动部
DPM	data processing machine 数据处理机
DPM	Detroit People Mover 底特律自动轨道交通系统
DPM	Deutsche Produktion Meisterschaft 德国量产房车赛[德文]
DPMA	data processing management association 数据处理管理协会
DPMO	Defense POW (Prisoner of War)/MP (Missing Personnel) Office 国防部战俘与失踪人员办公室
DPO	documentary payment order 跟单付款委托书

D

DPOS	delegated proof of stake 委托权益证明
DPP	data processing platform 数据处理平台
DPS	data path software 数据路径软件
DPV	diver propulsion vehicle 蛙人推进器
DQ	disqualify 取消资格
DQ	Dairy Queen 冰雪王后（连锁快餐店）
DQ	daring quotient 胆商
dq	direct question 直接提问
Dr	debtor 借方，收方
Dr	discount rate 贴现率
Dr	doctor 博士/医生
Dr	drawer 出票人
DR	deposit receipt 存款收条
DR	depositary receipts 存托凭证
DR	dividend right 股票除息除权
DR	delivery room 产房；分娩室
Dr	Drake Captain 德雷克船长［箱包商标］
DR	dark red 深红色
DR	Darry Ring　DR戒指
DR	digital radiography 数字放射线照相术
DRAM	dynamic random access memory 动态随机存取存储器
DRC	Digital Reality Creation 数码精密显像/数字逼真重建
DRC	data record control 数据记录控制
DRC	development and research center 发展研究中心
DRG	diagnosis related group 诊断相关组
DRL	Department of Right and Labour 人权劳动局
DRM	digital rights management 数字版权管理
DRM	digital rights management 内容数字版权加密保护技术
DRS	dual ram system 两阶段进气系统
DRV	Deutsche Reiterliche Vereinigung 德国马术协会［德文］
DS	dancer （酒吧）领舞
DS	Dansk Standardiseringsrad 丹麦标准协会/丹麦非电气产品质量认证

标志[丹麦文]
Ds	darmstadtium 鐽[第 110 号化学元素]
DS&DS	dual sim & dual standby 双卡双待
DSA	Defense Space Agency 国防航天局
DSA	Driving Standards Agency 驾驶标准局
DSA	digital subtraction angiography 数字减影血管造影术
DSB	dispute settlement body 争端解决机构
DSBS	Digital Satellite Broadcasting System 数字卫星广播系统
DSC	Defense Supply Center 国防部采购中心
DSC	digital system camera 数码相机
DSC	drive stability control 驾驶稳定性控制/动态稳定性控制
DSC	differential scanning calorimetry 差示扫描量热法
DSC	Doctor of Science 理学博士
DSCS	defense-satellite communication system(s) 国防卫星通信系统
dsDNA	double stranded DNA 双链脱氧核糖核酸
DSE	Diploma of Secondary Education 香港中学文凭考试
DSG	direct shift gearbox 直接换挡变速器
DSH	Deutsche Sprachpruefung für den Hochschulzugang auslaendischer Studienbewerber 外国申请留学德国人员高校入学德语考试[德文]
DSHK	Disciplined Services of Hong Kong 香港纪律部队
DSL	digital simulation language 数字模拟语言
DSL	digital subscriber line 数字用户线路
DSN	deep space network 深空天线网络
DSP	Defense Support Program 美国国防支援计划
DSP	Defense Satellite Program 国防卫星计划
DSP	digital signal process 数字信号处理芯片
DSP	digital signal processing 数字信号处理(技术)
DSP	digital signal processor 数字信号处理器
DSP	DSP Media 韩国 DSP 娱乐公司
DSS	decision support system 决策支持系统
DSS	Diplomatic Security Service 外交保安局
DST	department of science and technology 科学技术部门

D

DSU	dispute settlement usage	争端解决规则和程序
DSVD	Digital Simultaneous Voice and Data	数字化同步话音和数据
DT	data terminal	数据终端
DT	Department of the Treasury	财政部
DTC	depositary transfer check	存款转账支票
DTC	Datang Coin	大唐币
DTCs	disseminated tumor cells	播散肿瘤细胞
DTE	data terminal equipment	数据终端设备
DTH	delayed type hypersensitivity	迟发型超敏反应
DTH	direct to home	直接到户
DTI	Doctor of Translation and Interpreting	翻译博士学位
DTL	diode-transistor logic	二极管-晶体管逻辑
DTM	Deutsche Tourenwagen Meisterschaft	德国房车(大师)赛［德文］
DTMF	dual tone multi-frequency	双音多频
DTR	data terminal ready	数字终端就绪
DTR	defense terrestrial reactor	国防地面核反应堆
DTR	digital trunked radio	数字集群无线电
DTR	disk transfer rate	磁带传输率
DTS	digital theater system	数字影院立体声系统
DTS	Detective Training School	香港警校
DTS	drain the swamp	排光沼泽里的水/彻底改变美国的政治生态［引申义］
DTV	digital television	数字电视
DU	Duke University	杜克大学
DUFL	Dalian University of Foreign Languages	大连外国语大学
DUKW	amphibious truck	水陆两用汽车［代字］
dunno	don't［doesn't］know	不知道［口语］
DUREX	durability, reliability, excellence	杜蕾斯(安全套)
DV	digital video	数字视频；数字摄像机
DVB	digital video bandwidth	数字视频带宽
DVB	digital video broadcasting	数字视频广播
DVB-H	Digital Video Broadcasting-Handheld	手持地面无线/数字视频广播——手持
DVB-H	Digital Video Broadcasting-Terrestrial	地面无线/数字视频广播——地面
DVBS	Digital Video Broadcasting System	数字视频广播系统

DVB-SH	Digital Video Broadcasting-Satellite Services to Handhelds 移动电视发送卫星
DVD	digital video disc 数字视频光盘
DVD	digital versatile disc 数字多功能光盘
DVD	digital virtual disc 数字虚拟磁盘
DVD	digital virus disease 数字病毒病
DVD-R	DVD Recordable 刻录光盘
DVD-RDL	DVD-Recordable data left 不能重复刻录光盘
DVD-ROM	DVD-Read Only Memory 只读数字激光视盘机/高密度只读光盘
DVD-RW	DVD-Rewritable 可重写光碟
DVGW	Deutsche Verein von Gas und Wasserfachmännern 德国煤气与供水技术协会[德文]
DVR	digital video recorder 数字录像机
dvr	diver 潜水员
DVT	deep vein thrombosis 深静脉血栓形成
DW	Deutschen Werft AG 德国船厂[德文]
DWI	driving while intoxicated 醉酒开车
Dy	dysprosium 镝[第 66 号化学元素]
DYFI	Democratic Youth Federation of India 印度民主青年联合会

e	electronic 电子
E	exa 艾(可萨)[一个十进倍数的词头名称,其表示因数为 1018]
E	Externalized language 外表化语言
E	electronic sportsmen 电子竞技人
E	economic 经济型的
E	edge 比较主流的无线网络传输方式
E	electronic 电子的

E	erythrocyte 红细胞
E	exceed expectation 超乎期待/较好
e. g.	exempli gratia 例如[拉丁文]
E. T.	extra-terrestrial 外星人
E1	estrone 雌酮
E2	estradiol 雌二醇
E3	Electronic Entertainment Expo 电子娱乐博览会
E3	Echelon 3 第 3 梯队
E3	estriol 雌三醇
EA	electronic arts 电子艺术
EA	Electronic Arts 美国艺电公司[美国游戏巨头]
EA	English Association 英语协会
EA	Esperanto Association 世界语协会
EA-6B	Grumman electronic-intelligence-gathering aircraft（Intruder）格鲁曼电子情报收集飞机[又名：入侵者收集飞机]
EAA	Engineers and Architects Association 美国工程师和建筑师协会
EAA	European Athletic Association 欧洲田径协会
EAC	Education Advisory Committee 教育咨询委员会
EAC	Ehrlich ascitic carcinoma 艾氏腹水癌
EACL	emergency action checklist 紧急行动的清单
EACL	European Association of Chinese Linguistics 欧洲的中国语言学会
EACL	European Chapter of the Association for Computational Linguistics 欧洲计算语言学协会
EACM	East African Common Market 东非共同市场
EACR	European Association for Cancer Research 欧洲肿瘤研究协会
EACRFC	EAC rosette forming cell EAC 玫瑰花结形成细胞
EADS	European Aero Defence System 欧洲宇航防务公司
EAEA	European Atomic Energy Agency 欧洲原子能机构
EAEU	Eurasian Economical Union 欧亚经济体联盟
EAI	enterprise application integration 企业应用集成
EAM	emergency action message 紧急发射指令
EAM	enterprise asset management 企业资产管理

EAN	European Article Number 国际物品编码协会(借用"欧洲物品编码协会"的 EAN)	
EAN	European Article Number 欧洲物品编码协会	
EAP	employee assistance program 员工辅助计划	
EAP	English for Academic Purpose 学术用英语	
EAP	environmental analysis and planning 环境分析与规划	
EAP	Environmental Agency of Protection 环境保护署	
EAP	Employee Assistance Program 员工帮助计划	
EAP	Experiment Aeroplane Program 实验飞机项目	
EAR	Export Administration Regulation《出口管理条例》	
EARN	European Academic and Research Network 欧洲学术和研究网络	
EAS	electronic automatic switch 电子自动开关	
EAS	electronic article system 电子防盗系统	
EAS	enterprise application system 企业应用系统	
EAS	East Asia Summit 东亚峰会	
EASA	European Aviation Safety Agency 欧洲航空安全局	
EATR	enhancing automatic tactics robot 强动力自动战术机器人	
EB	electron beam 电子束	
EB	electronic business 电子商务	
EB	*Encyclopaedia Britannica*《大英百科全书》(亦称《大不列颠百科全书》)	
EB	Exabyte 艾字节[1 EB＝10 亿 GB(千兆字节)]	
EB	excess burden 超额负担	
EB	electronic bulletin board 电子公告[电子文献标示字母]	
EB	endorsable bond 可背书债券	
EB	epidermolysis bullosa 大疱性表皮松解症	
EB	Ettore Bugatti 布加迪汽车标志[源于艾托里·布加迪]	
EB	extendible bond 可延期债券	
EB/OL	electronic bulletin board online 网上电子公告[电子文献标示略语]	
EBA	elementary business administration 初级工商管理	
EBA	English Bowling Association 英格兰保龄球协会	
EBA	emergency brake assistant 紧急制动辅助系统	
EBAF	emergency bunker adjustment factor 紧急燃油附加费	

E

e-bank	electronic bank 电子银行	
E-BANK	electronic bank 网上银行	
Ebay	electronic bay 电子港湾/易趣	
EBD	electronic brakeforce distribution 电子制动力分配系统	
EBD	electronic braking distribute 电子制动分配系统	
EBIC	European Banks of International Company 欧洲国际银行	
EBIT	earnings before interest and taxes 付息抽税前收益	
EBITDA	earning before interest, taxes, depreciation and amortization 未计利息、税收、折旧、摊销前时收入	
Ebl	erythroblast 有核红细胞	
EBMA	The European Baking Machinery Association 欧洲烘烤机械协会	
E-BOM	engineering bill of material 工程物料清单	
E-book	electronic-book 电子书籍	
EBPP	electronic bill process and payment 电子账单处理与支付系统	
EBSCO	Elton B. Stephens Company 埃尔顿·B.斯蒂芬斯公司	
EBSF	European Bus System of the Future 欧洲未来交通系统	
EBU	English Bridge Union 英格兰桥牌联合会	
EBU	European Badminton Union 欧洲羽毛球联合会	
EBU	European Boxing Union 欧洲拳击联合会	
EBU	European Broadcasting Union 欧洲广播联盟	
EBV	Epstein-Barr virus EB病毒	
EBV	electron bombarded vehicle 电子轰击式推进装置	
EBV	electronic brake varioplex 电子制动可变多路传输器	
EBV	Elektronische Bremskraft vertung Gerät 电子制动分配装置[德文]	
EBYC	European Bureau for Youth and Childhood 欧洲青少年儿童局	
EC	electronic combat 电子战	
EC	electronic commerce 电子商务	
EC	emergency contraception 紧急避孕	
EC	English Corner 英语角	
EC	European Community 欧洲共同体	
EC	Enzyme Commission of IUB 国际生物化学协会酶学委员会	
ECA	Economic Commission for Africa 联合国非洲经济委员会	

ECA	Electronic Components Association 美国电子元器件协会	
ECA	Economic Commission for Africa 非洲经济委员会	
ECA	export credit agency 出口信贷机构	
ECAC	European Civil Aviation Community 欧洲民航联盟	
ECAFE	Economic Commission for Asia and the Far East 亚洲及远东经济委员会	
E-cash	electronic cash 电子现金	
ECB	European Central Bank 欧洲中央银行	
E-CBD	electronic central business district 电子化商务中心区	
ECC	error correction code 纠错码	
ECC	European Coordinating Committee 欧洲协调委员会	
ECCO	ECCO'let 爱步鞋［丹麦产］	
ECCO	European Cancer Conference 欧洲肿瘤年会	
EC-Council	Electronic Commercial Council 电子商务顾问国际委员会	
ECDS	Electron Commercial Draft System 中国电子商业汇票系统	
ECE	Economic Commission for Europe 欧洲经济委员会	
ECE	Export Council for Europe 对欧洲出口委员会［英国］	
ECF	elemental chlorine free 无元素氯	
ECFA	Economic Co-operation Frame Agreement 海峡两岸经济合作框架协议	
ECFTUC	European Confederation of Free Trade Unions in the Community 欧洲共同体自由工会联合会	
ECG	electrocardiogram 心电图	
ECHA	European Chemicals Agency 欧洲化学品管理局	
ECHR	European Court of Human Rights 欧洲人权法院	
ECIS	European Community Information Service 欧洲共同体新闻处	
ECL	emitter coupled logic 发射极耦合逻辑	
ECLA	Economic Commission for Latin America 拉丁美洲经济委员会	
ECLAC	Economic Commission for Latin America and Caribbean 拉丁美洲和加勒比地区经济委员会	
E-Class	electronic class 电子教室	
ECM	electronic counter measures 电子对抗措施	
ECM	European Common Market 欧洲共同市场	
ECM	extracelluar matrix 细胞外基质	

E

ECMA	European Computer Manufactures Association 欧洲计算机制造商协会
ECME	Economic Commission for the Middle East 中东经济委员会
ECMO	extracorporeal membrane oxygenator 体外膜肺/体外膜氧合器
ECN	engineer change notice 工程变更通知
ECNR	emigration check not required 不须移民出境检查
ECO	ecology, conservation, optimization 节能模式（由英语生态、节能、优化三个单词的首字母构成）
ECOCERT SA	Ecological Certificate SA 法国国际生态认证中心
Econ J	*Economic Journal*《经济季刊》[英国]
Econ R	*Economic Review*《经济评论》半月刊[英国]
ECOSOC	Economic and Social Council 联合国经济及社会理事会
ECPS	European Centre for Population Studies 欧洲人口研究中心
ECR	efficient consumer response 有效消费者反应
ECR	emigration check required 移民出境检查
ECR	engineer change request 工程变更需求
ECRIS	European Crime Record Information System 欧洲犯罪记录信息系统
ECRL	East Coast Rail Link 东海岸铁路
ECRN	European Center of Research Nuclear 欧洲核子研究中心
ECS	elastic compute service 云服务器
ECS	electronic chart system 电子海图系统
ECS	electronic commerce system 电子商务系统
ECS	electronic control system 智能控制系统
ECS	electronic countermeasure system 电子对抗系统
ECS	environmental control system 环境控制系统
ECSC	enterprise capital settlement center 企业资金结算中心
ECT	electrochemotherapy 电化学疗法
ECT	electroconvulsive therapy 电休克疗法
ECT	emission computerized tomography 发射型计算机断层成像
ECT	enteric coated tablet 肠溶片剂
ECTC	European Counter-Terrorism Centre 欧洲反恐中心
ECU	electronically controlled unit 电子控制装置
ECU	European currency unit 欧洲货币单位

ECU	Ecuador 厄瓜多尔[南美洲国家]	
ECU	eletronic control unit 电子控制装置	
ECU	engine control unit 电子控制单元/发动机控制装置	
ECVN	Electronic Commerce, Vietnam 越南电子商务网	
ECVT	electro-continuously variable transmission 电子控制无级变速器	
ECWA	Economic Commission for Western Asia 联合国西亚经济委员会	
ED	effective dose 有效剂量	
ED	erection dysfunction 男子勃起功能障碍	
ED	estate duty 财产税	
ED	export declaration 出口申报单	
ED	extra duty 累进税	
Ed	education 教育	
Ed	edition 版本	
EDA	European Defence Administration 欧洲防务局	
EDA	electronic design automation 电子设计自动化	
EDC	European Defense Community 欧洲防务共同体	
EDC	eau de cologne 古龙水(香精含量 4%~8%)[法文]	
EDD	*English Dialect Dictionary*《英语方言词典》	
EDDE	electric defragment dispelling equipment 电力碎片消除器	
EDF	emergency decontamination facility 紧急净化设备	
EDF	European Development Fund 欧洲开发基金会	
EDGE	enhanced data rate for GSM Evolution 增强型速率 GSM 演进技术	
EDI	electronic data interchange 电子数据交换	
EDL	electronic differential locking 电子差速锁定	
EDM	enterprise decision management 企业决策管理	
EDMF	European Drug Management Federation 欧洲药品管理联合会	
EDM	email direct marketing 电子邮件营销	
EDM	engine development model 工程开发模型	
EDO	enhanced data-out ram 数据增强输出内存	
EDP	electronic data processing 电子数据处理	
EDP	eau de parfum 浓香水(香精含量 15%)[法文]	
EDQM	European Drug Quality Management 欧洲药品质量管理局	

EDS	electronic data systems 电子数据系统
EDS	electronic differential system 电子差速锁
EDS	egg drop syndrome 减蛋综合征
EDS	Education,demand,self-study 大学英语教学中强调人文教学:思想品德、文化修养和精神品格
EDSAC	electronic delay storage automatic computer 延迟存储自动电子计算机
EDT	eau de toilette 淡香水(香精含量 8%～15%)[法文]
EduHK	The Education University of Hong Kong 香港教育大学
EDVAC	electronic discrete variable automatic computer 离散变量自动电子计算机
EE	electronic engineering 电子工程(学)
EE	electrical engineer 电子工程师
EE	Everything Everywhere 英国 EE 电信公司
EEA	European Economic Area 欧洲经济区
EEC	European Economic Community 欧洲经济共同体
EEC	East Economic Corridor 东部经济走廊
EEF	East Economic Forum 东方经济论坛
EEG	electroencephalogram 脑电图
EEOC	Equal Employment Opportunity Commission 均等就业机会委员会
EER	energy efficiency ratio 能量效率比
EES	engine evaluation system 引擎评价系统
EEV	energy efficiency vehicle 低油耗汽车
EEV	energy efficiency vehicle 环境友好汽车
EEV	energy efficiency vehicle 省油车
EEV	enhanced environmentally friendly vehicles and engines 强化的环境友好车辆和发动机
EEZ	Exclusive Economic Zone 专属经济区
EF	eau fraiche 清淡香水(香精含量 1%～3%)[法文]
EFCC	Economic & Financial Crimes Commission 金融犯罪委员会
EFF	electronic front fund 电子前沿基金
EFL	English as a Foreign Language 作为外语的英语
EFM	electronic fuel-management system 电子燃油控制系统
EFMD	European Foundation for Management Development 欧洲管理发展基金会

EFP	electronic field production 电子现场节目制作
EFP	electronic field program production 电子现场节目制作
EFQM	European Foundation for Quality Management 欧洲质量管理基金
EFSA	European Food Safety Authority 欧盟食品安全局
EFSM	European Financial Stable Mechanism 欧洲金融稳定机制
EFSP	European Financial Steady Fund 欧洲金融稳定基金
EFT	electronic funds transfer 电子资金转账
EFT	erythrocyte osmotic fragility test 红细胞渗透脆性试验
EFTA	European Free Trade Association 欧洲自由贸易联盟
EFU	Europaische Frauenunion［英文：European Union of Women］欧洲妇女联合会［德文］
EFU	European Football Union 欧洲足球联盟
EG&S	ecological goods and service 生态产品和服务（功能）
EGA	enhanced graphics adapter 增强型图形适配器
EGA	European Golf Association 欧洲高尔夫球协会
EGCG	epigallocatechin gallate 表没食子儿茶素没食子酸酯
EGF	epidermal growth factor 表皮生长因子
EGFR	epidermal growth factor receptor 表皮生长因子受体
EGG	electrogastrogram 电气描记图
EGG	electrogastrogram 胃电图
EGO	educational growth opportunities 教育发展机会
EGP	English for General Purposes 通用英语
EGR	exhaust gas recirculation 废气再循环
EGS	enhanced geothermal system 增强性地热系统
EGT	ethanol gelation test 乙醇凝胶试验
EGY	Egypt 埃及［非洲国家］
EHA	European Hydrogen Association 欧洲氢协会
EHF	Ebola hemorrhagic fever 埃博拉出血热
EHF	extra high frequency 极高频
EHP	effective horse power 有效功率
EHS	environment, health, safety 健康,安全与环境一体化管理
EHS	Environment, Health, Safety 环境管理体系［环境、健康、安全］

E

EHT	Event Horizon Telescope	事件视界望远镜
EI	electrical inspectorate	电气检验
EI	Economic Internationalism	经济国际主义
EI	endorsement irregular	背书不符
EI	education index	教育指数
EI	Engineer Index	《工程索引》
EIA	Environmental Investigation Association	环境调查局
EIA	enzyme immunoassay	酶免疫测定
EIA	Electronic Industry Association	美国电子工业协会
EIA	Agua Sierra de Cazorla S. A. Explotaciones Internacionales Acuiferas	西班牙国际饮用水开发股份有限公司[西班牙文]
EIA	Electronic Industries Association	电子工业协会
EIA	Energy Information Administration	美国能源信息署
EIA	Engineering Industries Association	发动机工业协会
EIA	environmental impact assessment	环境影响评估
EIB	European Investment Bank	欧洲投资银行
EIB	Export-Import Bank	进出口银行
EICU	emergency intensive care unit	重症监护病房
eID	electronic identity	(公民网络)电子身份标识
EIP	enterprise information portal	企业信息门户
EIS	European Information Service	欧洲信息服务中心
EIS	Electronic Information System	电子信息系统
EISA	extended industry standard architecture	扩展工业标准结构
E-journal	electronic journal	电子刊物
EL INT	electronic intelligence	电子情报
EL	electronics	电子设备/电子学
EL	exchange line	调换线路/用户回线
EL	extra line	附加线路/特殊线路
ELA	Evaluation of Language and Academics	语言与学术评估中心
ELCC	European Lung Cancer Conference	欧洲肺癌会议
ELEC	European League for Economic Cooperation	欧洲经济合作联盟
ELETO	The Hellenic Society for Terminology	希腊术语协会

ELF	extra low frequency 极低频
ELI	Examen Linguistique Individuel 法语水平考试[法文]
ELISA	enzyme-linked immuno sorbent assay 酶联免疫吸附试验
ELL	English language learning 英语学习
ELN	Ejército de Liberación Nacional 哥伦比亚民族解放军[西班牙文]
ELOT	The Hellenic Organization for Standardization 希腊标准化组织
ELP	electronic learning product 电子教学产品
ELSI	extremely Large Scale integrated circuit 超大规模集成电路
ELT	*English League Teaching*《英语教学》[英国]
ELT	euglobulin lysis test 优球蛋白溶解试验
em	emerald 祖母绿[宝石]
EM	effective microbe 有效微生物群
EM	electron microscope 电子显微镜
EM	electronic music 电子音乐
EM	emission 排放
em	embark 上船
EMA	Europe Music Awards 欧洲音乐奖
EMA	European Medicine Association 欧洲药物管理局
EMA	European Monetary Agreement 欧洲货币协定组织
EMAC	electromagnetic arresting cable 电磁阻拦索
E-mail	electronic mail 电子邮件
EMALS	electro-magnetic aircraft launch system 机载电磁发射系统
EMBA	Executive Master of Business Administration 高级管理人员工商管理硕士学位
EMBASE	Excerpta Medical Database 医学文摘数据库
EMC	Electrical Manufacturers Council 电器制造商理事会[美]
EMC	Electromagnetic Certificate 电磁兼容认证[现已被 CCC 认证代替]
EMC	Electronic Magnetic Compatible 电磁兼容性
EMC	Export Management Company 出口管理公司
EMC	enterprise management center 企业管理中心
EMC	Richard Egan and Roger Marino Co. 易安信公司/EMC 公司
Em-Drive	electromagnetism drive 电磁推进系统

E

EMEA	Europe，Middle-East and Africa 欧洲、中东和非洲
EMH	Efficient Market Hypothesis 有效市场假说
EMMA	Executive Master of Medicine Administration（高层管理人员）药业管理硕士课程班
EMP	Electromagnetic pulse 电磁脉冲
EMR	electromagnetic radiation 电磁辐射
EMR	Electronic Medical Record 电子医疗记录/电子病历
EMR	Energy and Miner Region 加拿大防爆、电气等认证标志
EMR	energy and miner region 能源矿产局
Ems	emergency switch 应急开关
EMS	engine management system 发动机控制系统
EMS	environmental management system 环境管理体系
EMS	European Monetary System 欧洲货币体系
EMS	experiment management system 实验管理系统
EMS	express mail service 全球邮政特快专递
EMS	electronical manufacturing services 电子制造服务业
EMS	enhanced message service 增强型短信服务
EMT	epithelial-mesenchymal transition 上皮细胞间质转换
EMUI	Emotion User Interface 华为手机操作系统［英文:情感使用者界面］
EMVCo	Europay, Mastercard Visa Cooperation 欧陆卡/万事达卡/维萨卡联合组织
EN	Economic Nationalism 经济国家主义
EN	El Niño 厄尔尼诺现象［西班牙文］
EN	enteral nutrition 肠内营养
EN	European Standards 欧洲标准
EN	European 欧洲的
ENA	Ecole Nationale d'Administration 法国国立行政学校［法文］
ENA	extractable nuclear antigens 血清可提取的核抗原抗体
ENACT	Environmental Action for Survival 环境问题行动委员会［美国］
ENASA	Empresa Nacional de Autocamiones SA 恩普雷萨国家汽车公司［西班牙文］
Ency Brit	*Encyclopaedia Britannica*《不列颠百科全书》
ENG	electronic news gathering 电子新闻收集

ENG	engine 发动机
Engnese	English Chinese 英文式中文
ENIAC	electronic numerical integrator and calculator 电子数字积分计算机 [1946 年美国制造的第一台通用计算机的名称]
ENIAC	Electronic Numerical Integrator And Computer 埃尼阿克[电子数字积分计算机:第一台通用计算机]
ENIT	Ente Nazionale Italiano per il Turismo [英文: Italian State Tourist Office] 意大利国家旅游局[意大利文]
ENKS	Kurdish National Council 库尔德全国委员会
ENS	Ecole normale superieure de Paris 巴黎高师[法文]
ENT	ear, nose and throat 耳鼻喉(科)
ENV	envelopes 轨道线
EO	eosinophil 嗜酸性粒细胞
EOB	End of Business 营业停止[网络用语]
EOD	explosive ordnance demolition 拆弹部队
EOD	end of the day 下班前
EOD	Explosive Ordanance Disposal 香港爆炸品处理科
EOFT	erythrocyte osmotic fragility test 红细胞渗透脆性试验
EOH	end of overhaul 大修结束
EO-IR	electro-optical-infrared 电子—光学—红外
EOQ	European Organization for Quality 欧洲质量组织
EOS	electro-optical system 光电系统
EOS	Egyptian Organization for Standardization 埃及标准化组织/埃及质量认证标志
EOS	eosinophil 嗜酸性粒细胞
EOSC	eosinophil count 嗜酸粒细胞直接计数
EOSG	Executive Office of the Secretary General 联合国秘书长办公室
EOT	End of Transmission 通话结束
EOTA	European Organisation for Technical Approvals 欧洲技术认可组织
EOTP	European Organization for Trade Promotion 欧洲贸易促进组织
EP	European Parliament 欧洲议会
EP	extended playing record 细碟(时长 15～20 分)

E

EP	electronic patrol (aircraft) (飞机)电子巡逻
EP	epoxy resin 环氧树脂
EPA	Economic Partnership Agreement 经济伙伴关系协定
EPA	Economic Planning Agency 经济规划机构
EPA	eicosa-pentaenoic acid 二十碳五烯酸
EPA	Environmental Protection Agency 美国环境保护署/美国汽油、柴油发动机认证标志
E-Paper	electronic paper 电子文档
EPC	engineering-procurement-contruction 工程-采购-施工总承包模式
EPC	European Patent Convention 欧洲专利条约
EPC	Economic Policy Committee 经济政策委员会
EPC	Esso Petroleum Company 埃索石油公司
EPCO	excogitation, purchaser, construction, operation 设计、采购、施工、运营一体化
EPCO+PM	excogitation, purchaser, construction, operation and prospecting management 设计、勘察管理、采购、施工和运营一体化
EPD	electronic panel display 平板显示器
EPDM	ethylene propylene diene monomer 三元乙丙橡胶
EPEC	enteropathogenic Escherichia coli 肠致病性大肠埃希菌
EPG	electronic program guide 电子电视节目指南
EPI	Expanded Programme on Immunization 免疫扩展计划
EPI	epidemic 流行病
EPIS	Entrepreneur Personal Identity System 企业家形象识别系统
EPLD	erasable programmable logic device 可擦可编程逻辑器件
EPLF	Europe Lump Floor 欧洲木地板
EPM	Energy Efficiency & Productive Maintenance 能效与生产维护管理
EPM	ethylene-propylene copolymer 乙烯-丙烯共聚物[塑料]
EPO	erythropoietin 促红细胞生成素
EPO	European Patent Office 欧洲专利局
EPP	enhanced parallel port 增强性并行端口
EPR	Einstein-Podolsky-Rosen paradox EPR 悖论(爱因斯坦、波多尔斯基和罗森为论证量子力学的不完备性而提出的一个悖论)

EPR	engineering power reactor 工程动力反应堆
EPS	electric power steering 电动助力转向系统
EPS	earnings per share 每股收益
EPS	electrical power steering 电气动力转向
EPS	electronic publishing system 电子出版系统
EPS	emergency power supply 应急电源
EPS	electronic power steering 电子控制动力转向系统
EPS	emergency power supply 备用电源
EPS	Ethernet for Plant Automation 开放性实时以太网标准
EPS	expandable polystyrene 发泡性聚苯乙烯[塑料]
EPS	financial planning system 财政规划系统
EPSR	Electrical Products Safety Regulation 电器产品安全规范
EPSS	electronic performance support system 电子绩效支持系统
EPT	English Proficiency Test（中国）出国进修人员英语水平考试
EPWS	Expatriate Professional Women's Society 外籍职业女性协会
EPZ	export processing zone 出口加工区
EQ	Emotion Quotient 情商
EQ	equalization 均衡（音响）
EQA	European Quality Award 欧洲质量奖
EQP	European Quality Premium 欧洲质量奖金
EQULS	European Quality Improvement System 欧洲质量改进系统
Er	erbium 铒[第 68 号化学元素]
ER	Early Reflection 早期反射[指只经过一次反射的回声][音响]
ER	export rebate 出口退税
ER	extended range 延长航程
ER	estrogen receptor 雌激素受体
ERA	Economic Research Association 美国经济研究会
ERA	Equal Rights Amendment 平等权利修宪案
ERA	Energy Research Abstracts《能源研究文摘》
ERA	Emergency Relief Administration 紧急情况缓解委员会
ERCP	endoscopic retrograde cholangiopancreatography 内镜逆行胰胆管造影
ERDA	Energy Research and Development Administration 能源研究和发展署报告[美国四大科技报告之一]

E

ERET	erythrocyte rosette formation test	E 玫瑰花结形成试验
ERIC	Education Resource Information Center	美国教育资源信息中心
ERM	employee relations management	员工关系管理
ERM	exchange rate margin	汇率范围
ERM	exchange rate mechanism	汇率机制
EROFS	Extendable Read-Only File System	超级文件系统
ERP	electronic road pricing	电子道路收费
ERP	error recovery program	差错恢复程序
ERP	enterprise resource planning	企业资源计划
ERS	economic research service	经济研究局
ERV	expiratory reserve volume	补呼吸量
Es	einsteinium	锿[第 99 号化学元素]
ES	electronic sports	电子竞技
ESA	European Space Agency	欧洲航天局
ESA	The Entertainment Software Association	游戏软件协会
ESAC	electronic spark advance control	电子点火提前控制
ESC	European Society of Cardiology	欧洲心脏病学年会
ESC	Eurovision Song Contest	欧洲歌唱大赛
ESC	electronic stability control	电子稳定控制系统
ESCAP	Economic and Social Commission for Asia and the Pacific	(联合国)亚洲及太平洋经济社会委员会
ESDI	enhanced small device interface	增强型小设备接口
ESDP	European Safety and Defence Policy	欧洲安全与防务政策
ESEA	E-Sports Entertainment Association	电子竞技娱乐协会/电子文体协会
e-shipping	electric shipping	电子货运
E-shop	electronic shop	电子商店
ESI	Environmental Sustainable Index	环境可持续指数
ESI	Educational Services, Inc.	教育服务有限公司
ESI	Essential Science Indicators	基本科学指标/基本科学指标数据库
eSIM	embedded subscriber identification module	嵌入式 SIM 卡
ESIT	École Supérieure d'Interprètes & de Traducteurs	巴黎高翻学院[法文]
ESL	English as a Second Language	作为第二语言的英语

ESM	European Steady Mechanism 欧洲稳定机制
ESM	educational simulation model 教育模拟模型
ESM	European Sports Media 欧洲体育媒体联盟
ESMO	European Society for Medical Oncology 欧洲肿瘤内科学会
ESO	executive stock options 股票期权
ESO	European South Observation 欧洲南方天文台
ESOL	English for Speakers of Other Languages 操其他语言者的英语课程
ESOP	Employee Stock Ownership Plan 员工持股计划
ESP	electronic stability program 电子稳定程序
ESP	English for Special Purpose 专门用途英语
ESP	Espanola Peseta 西班牙比塞塔[西班牙货币符号][西班牙语]
ESP	European Studies Project 欧洲研究项目
ESP	Spain（西班牙文为：España）西班牙[欧洲国家]
ESP	electronic stability program 电子稳定系统
Esp	Esperanto 世界语
ESPN	Entertainment and Sports Programming Network 美国娱乐与体育节目电视网
ESPO	The Eastern Siberia—Pacific Ocean Oil Pipeline 东西伯利亚—太平洋运输管道
ESP	endoscopic sphinctero papillectomy 内镜下括约肌乳头切开术
ESR	erythrocyte sedimentation rate 血沉
ESS	emergency survival system 紧急救生系统
ESS	*Encyclopedia of the Social Sciences*《社会科学百科全书》
ESSA	Earth Station，South Africa 南非地面站
ESSA	employment service systems administrator 就业服务系统管理员
ESSA	English School Swimming Association 英语学校游泳协会
ESSO	Standard Oil of New Jersey 埃索石油（根据首字"S""O"的发音形成的缩略语）
EST	English for Science and Technology 科技英语
EST	Estonia 爱沙尼亚[欧洲国家]
EST	express sequence tag 表达序列标签
ESU	English Speaking Union 伦敦英语口语联盟
ESWC	Electronic Sports World Cup 电子竞技世界杯
ESWL	extracorporeal shockwave lithotripsy 体外冲击波碎石术

E

et al	et alii 以及别的[拉丁文]
ETA	European Technical Approvals 欧洲技术认可[认证]
ETA	estimated time of arrival 预计到达时间
e-talking	electric talking 电子论坛
etc	et cetera 等等[拉丁文]
ETC	electronic toll collection 电子收费系统
ETCP	electronic toll collection park 智慧停车
ETD	Electronic Theses and Dissertations 电子学位论文项目
ETD	estimated time of departure 预计离开时间
ETF	Exchange Traded Fund 交易型开放式指数基金/交易所交易基金
ETH	Ethiopia 埃塞俄比亚[非洲国家]
ETH	Eidgenössische Technische Hochschule 瑞士联邦理工学院[德注]
ETL	English Language Teaching 英语语言教学
ETL	Electrical Testing Laboratory 电气测试实验室/美国职业安全与健康认证标志
ETOPS	extended operations 延程运行
ETP	elective termination pregnancy 选择性终止妊娠
ETS	Educational Testing Service 美国教育考试服务中心
ETS	emergency trip system 汽轮机跳闸保护系统
ETS	Emission Trading Scheme 欧盟碳排放交易体系
ETSI	European Telecommunications Standards Institute 欧洲通信标准协会
ETTBL	English Translation Test of Business Language 商务英语翻译证书考试
ETX	end of text character 文本结束符
EU	European Union 欧盟
Eu	europium 铕[第63号化学元素]
EU Pro Su	Europe Production Sun 欧洲太阳能制造业联合会
EU	Emergency Unit 香港冲锋队
EUCCC	European Union Chamber of Commerce in China 中国欧盟商会
EUI	unit injector 泵喷嘴
eUICC	embedded universal integrated circuit card 智能计量嵌入式通用集成电路卡
EUIPO	European Union Intellectual Property Office 欧盟知识产权局

EUR	Euro 欧元［货币符号］
Eurasia	Europe and Asia 欧亚大陆
EUREKA	European Research Coordination Agency 欧洲调查协调署
Euro NCAP	European New Car Assessment Program 欧洲新车评估体系
EUROPAMA	The European Packaging Machinery Association 欧洲包装机械协会
EUV	extreme ultraviolet 极端紫外
EUVL	extreme ultraviolet lithography 极紫外光刻
eV	electronic volt 电子伏(特)［能量单位名称］
EV	electric vehicle 电动汽车
EV71	enterovirus type 71 七一型肠道病毒
EVA	economic value added 经济增加值
EVA	extravehicular activity (宇航)出舱活动
EVA	ethylene-vinyl acetate copolymer 乙烯-乙酸乙烯酯共聚物［塑料］
EVAP	evaporate 蒸发
EVD	enhanced versatile disc 新一代高密度数字激光视盘
EVR	electronic video recorder 电子录像机
EVS	electric vehicles security 电动汽车安全
EVS-GTR	Electric Vehicles Security-Global Technology Regulation 电动汽车安全全球技术法规
EVSL	early voluntary sectoral liberalization 部门提前自愿自由化
EW	electronic warfare 电子战
EWA	East and West Association 东西方协会
EWG	Executive Working Group (北约)执行工作组
EWG	environmental work group 环境工作组织
eWTP	e-Commerce Wireless Transfer Protocol 电商无线传输协议
eWTP	electronic World Trade Platform 世界贸易电子平台
EXE	executable file 执行文件的扩展名
EXH	exhaust 排气
exot	exotic 外来词
EXP. Date	expiration date 失效期
expo	exposition 博览会

EZ	Euro Zone 欧元区	
E-zine	electronic magazine 电子杂志	

f; F	Facebook 脸书	
F	Fahrenheit 华氏(温度)[德文]	
F	farad 法(拉)[法定电容计量单位]	
F	femto 飞(母托)[十进分数单位的词头名称,其表示因数为 10~15]	
F	Florin 荷兰盾[荷兰货币]	
F	fluorine 氟[第 9 号化学元素]	
F	Fudi 福迪汽车[中国佛山:汉语缩略语]	
F	floor 建筑物的楼层	
F	fine 精美级(钱币)	
F/O	first officer 大副	
F1	formula Ⅰ 一级方程式锦标赛	
F-15SE	Fighter-15 Silent Eagle 美国波音公司的"沉默鹰"战斗机	
F5WC	Football 5 World Cup 五人制世界杯足球	
FA	face amount 票面金额,面值	
FA	factory automation 工厂自动化	
FA	focus aid 辅助聚焦	
FA	Electronics Fair 消费电子展	
FA	fair 一般级(钱币)	
Fa	fatty acid 脂肪酸	
FA	Football Association 足球协会	
FAA	Federal Aviation Administration 联邦航空管理局	
FACA	Fellow of the Association of Certified Accountants 联邦注册会计师协会成员	
FACC	French American Capital Corporation 法美资本公司	
Facekini	face bikini 脸基尼	

FACT	fully automatic compiling technique 全自动编译技术	
FACT	foundation for accountability and civic trust 问责与公民信任基金	
FACT	Functional Assessment of Cancer Therapy Scales 癌症治疗等级的功能评估	
FADE	FAA/airline data exchange 美国联邦航空管理局航空数据交换协议	
FAFC	Fashion Athletes Fitness Club 时尚健儿健身俱乐部	
FAFSA	Free Application for Federal Student Aid 联邦政府助学金免费申请	
FAI	Fédération Aéronautique Interationale 国际航空联合会[法文]	
FAIMER	Foundation for Advancement of International Medical Education and Research 联合国国际医学教育研究促进基金会	
FAIR	Facebook Artificial Intelligence Research 脸书人工智能研究	
FAIR	Fundamentals of Artificial Intelligence Research 人工智能研究的基础	
FAK	freight all kinds 同一税率	
FALab	Future Architecture Lab 未来建筑实验室	
FAM	foreign air mail 国外航空邮件	
Family	forgiveness, appreciation, model, intimacy, listening, you 幸福家庭的秘诀[宽恕,欣赏,榜样,亲密,聆听,爱你自己]	
FANID	fan identification 球迷身份证	
FAO	Food and Agricultural Organization of the United Nations 联合国粮农组织	
FAO	Foreign Affairs Office 外事处	
FAQs	frequent asked questions 常见问题及回答	
FAR	failure analysis report 故障分析报告	
FARC	Fuerzas Armadas Revolucionarias de Colombia 哥伦比亚革命武装力量[西班牙文]	
FAS	Federation of American Scientists 美国科学家联合会	
FAS	fetus alcohol syndrome 胎儿酒精综合征	
FAS	fire alarm system 火灾报警系统	
FASB	Financial Accounting Standards Boards 美国财务会计准则委员会	
FASEB	Federation of American Societies of Experimental Biology 美国实验生物学协会联盟	
FAST	face, arm, speech, time 国际上识别中风的 FAST 法[观察微笑时面部	

	有无歪斜,双手平举,观察是否无力垂落,有无说话口齿不清,有上述情况第一时间求助]
FAST	Five-hundred-meter Aperture Spherical radio Telescope 500米口径球面射电望远镜/中国天眼
FAST	Fleet Antiterrorism Security Team 舰队反恐安全组
FAT	file allocation table 文件分配表
FATCA	Foreign Account Tax Compliance Act 外国账户税收遵从法
FATF	Financial Action Task Force on Money Laundering 反洗钱金融特别行动组[西方七国首脑会议设置机构]
FATF	Financial Action Task Force 金融行动特别工作组
FAX	facsimile 传真(系统)/用传真机传送
FB	fullback 后卫
FB	facebook 脸书
FB	feedback 反馈
Fb	fibrinogen 纤维蛋白原
FB	first blood 一血
FBA	Fashion Business Association 时尚商务总会
FBA	Fulfillment By Amazon 亚马逊物流
FBG	fiber bragg gratings 光纤布拉格光栅
FBG	fasting blood glucose 空腹血糖
FBI	Federal Bureau of Investigation 美国联邦调查局
FBL	fly bar less system 无副翼系统/无平衡标系统
FBL	fly bar less(head) 传统的无副翼旋翼头式
FBO	foreign building office 外宾楼(办公室)
FBP	Federal Bureau of Prison 联邦监狱管理局
FBS	fasting blood sugar 空腹血糖[参见 FBG]
FC	fighting championship 格斗锦标赛
FC	fiscal coordination 财政协调
FC	flight control 飞行控制
FC	football club 足球俱乐部
FC	franchise chain 特许连锁
FC	fighter China 中国枭龙战斗机

FC	front company 影子公司	
FC(E)V	fuel cell electric vehicle 燃料电池提供动力来源的电动汽车	
FCA	Failure Criticality Analysis 故障致命性分析	
FCA	Financial Conduct Authority 英国金融行为监管局	
FCAE	Fellow of Canadian Academy of Engineering 加拿大工程院院士	
FCAS	future combat aviation system 未来作战航空系统	
FCC	Federal Communications Commission 联邦通信委员会	
FCC	Federal Communications Commission (美国)联邦通信委员会	
FCC	Federal Communications Commission 美国无线电频率装置认证标志	
FCC	Foreign Correspondents Club 外国记者协会	
FCCA	Fellowship of Chartered Certified Accountants 特许公认会计师成员	
FCCC	Foreign Correspondents Club of China 驻华外国记者协会	
FCCC	Framework Convention on Climatic Change 气候变化框架公约	
FCD	final committee draft 最终委员会草案	
FCDR	failure cause data reporting 故障原因数据报告	
FCDR	fuel-cutoff-in-drive 驾驶时燃料切断	
FChFP	Fellow Chartered Financial Practitioner 国际注册特许财务策划师	
FCHV	fuel cells hybrid vehicle 燃料电池混合动力汽车	
FCI	Federación Cynológica Internacional 国际犬业协会[西班牙文]	
FCI	Federazione Colombotila Italiana 意大利信鸽饲养者协会[意大利文]	
FCI	Fédération Cynologique Internationale 世界犬业联盟[法文]	
FCI-ES	FCI-Europasieger FCI 欧洲冠军[德文]	
FCIC	Fellow of the Chemical Institute of Canada 加拿大化学协会会员	
FCL	full container load 整箱	
FCM	flow cytometry 流式细胞术	
FCM	food contact material 食品接触材料	
FCore	function core 功能核心	
FCS	facsimile communications system 传真通信系统	
FCS	fire control system 火控系统	
FCS	FAA Cloud Service 美国联邦航空管理局云服务	
FCS	functional checkout set 功能检验装置	
FCUK	French Connection United Kingdom 英国年轻人的时装品牌	

F

FCV	fuel cell vehicles 燃料电池汽车
FD	floppy disk 软磁盘
FD	freeze-drying 冻干（技术）
FD	functional dyspepsia 功能性消化不良
FD&C	Food, Drug and Cosmetic Act《联邦食品、药品及化妆品法案》
FDA	Food and Drug Administration（美国）食品与药品管理局
FDCA	Food, Drug and Cosmetic Act《联邦食品、药品及化妆品法案》
FDCPA	Fair Debt Collection Practices Act《公平债务催收作业法》
FDD	floppy disk drive 软盘驱动器
FDD	frequency-division duplex 频分双工方式
FDFRC	Fudan University Development Financial Research Center 复旦发展研究院金融研究中心
FDI	foreign direct investment 外国直接投资
FDIC	Federal Deposit Insurance Corporation 联邦储蓄保险公司
FDIS	Final Draft International Standard 国际标准最终草案
FDMA	frequency division multiple access 频分多路
FDMA	frequency division multiple address 频分多址
FDP	fibrinogen degradation product 纤维蛋白原降解产物
FDR	flight data recorder 飞行数据记录器
FDS	Fusion Design Study 聚变相关设计研究
FDS	Fusion Digital Simulation 深度集成数字仿真
FDT	Florists' Transworld Delivery 花卉商全球速递
Fe	ferrum［英文：iron］铁［第 26 号化学元素］［拉丁文］
FE	Fiscal Efficiency 财政效率
FEA	failure effect analysis 故障影响分析
FEA	finite element analysis 有限元分析
Feb	February 2 月
FEC	Foreign Exchange Certificate 外汇兑换券
FEC	Federal Election Commission 联邦选举委员会
FEC	forward err correction 纠错编码
FECT	Financial English Certificate Test 金融英语证书考试
Fed	Federal Reserve System 美国联邦储备委员会

FED	field emission display 场发射显示	
FedEx	Federal Express Corp. 联邦快递公司	
FEDS	Foreign Economic Development Service 对外经济开发局[美国]	
FEER	*Far East Economic Review*《远东经济评论》	
FEFC	Far East Freight Conference 远东货运工会	
FEG	Force Escort Group 港警队护送组	
FEI	Fédération Equestre Internationale 国际马术联合会[法文]	
Fembot	female type robot 女性机器人	
FEN	ferroprotein 血清铁蛋白	
FEN	Fédération Equestre Nationale 德国马术协会[法文]	
FEP	Federal Entrepreneur Immigration Program 企业家移民计划	
FET	future and emerging technology 未来和新兴技术	
FEU	forty foot equivalent unit 40 标箱	
FEU	Forty-foot Equivalent Units 四十英尺当量单位	
FEV	forced evolutionary virus 强迫进化病毒	
FEV1	forced expiratory volume in one second 一秒钟用力呼气量	
FF	fortune forum 财富论坛	
FF	French Franc 法国法郎[法国 2002 年前的货币]	
FF	Faraday' Future 法拉第未来[一家全球化互联网智能出行生态企业]	
FF	filtration fraction 滤过分数	
FF	financial freedom 金融自由度指数	
FF	Ford Foundation 福特基金会	
FFA	free fatty acid 游离脂肪酸	
FFDCA	Federal Food, Drug and Cosmetic Act《联邦食品、药品及化妆品法案》	
FFG	Guided Missile Frigate 导弹护卫舰	
FFT	Fast Fourier Transform 快速傅立叶变换	
FFT	Finite Fourier Transform 有限傅立叶变换	
FFVD	final, fully-verified denuclearization 最终完全可验证的无核化	
fg	fibrinogen 纤维蛋白原	
FG	full grade 全面评级	
FGA	Fellowship of Gemological Association 英国宝石协会会员	
FGF	fibroblast growth factor 成纤维细胞生长因子	

F

FGFA	fifth generation fighter aircraft 俄印第五代战斗机
FHD	full high definition 全高清
FHKI	Federation of Hong Kong Industry 香港工业总会
FHLMC	Federal Home Loan Mortgage Corporation 联邦住房贷款抵押公司[简称"房地美"]
FI	fiscal integration 财政一体化
FI	fake intelligence 假情报
FI	Finland 芬兰[欧洲国家]/芬兰电气认证标志
FI	format identifier 格式标识符
fi	free in 买方不负担装货费用
FIA	Fédération Internationale de l'Automobile 国际汽车联合会[法文]
FIAP	Fédération Internationale de l'Art photographique 国际摄影艺术联合会[法文]
Fiat	Fabbrica Italiana Automobile Torino 菲亚特汽车[原义:意大利都灵汽车厂][意大利文]
FIBA	Fédération Internationale de Basketball Amateur 业余篮球国际联盟[法文]
FIBT	Fédération Internationale de Bobsleigh et de Tobogganing [英文:International Bobsleighing and Tobogganing Federation] 国际雪橇滑雪联合会[法文]
FIC	Fédération Internationale de Canoe 国际皮划艇联合会[法文]
FICO	financial control 财务管理
FIDH	Fédération Internationale des Droits de I'Homme 国际人权联盟[法文]
FIE	foreign invested enterprise 外资企业
FIE	Fédération Internationale d'Escrime 国际击剑联合会[法文]
FIFA	Fédération Internationale de Football Associations [英文:International Association Football Federation] 国际足球联合会[法文]
FIFO	first-in first-out 先进先出(法)
FIFRA	Federal Insecticide, Fungicide and Rodenticide Act《联邦杀虫剂、杀真菌剂和灭鼠剂法案》
FIFS	financial innovation and financial stability 金融创新与金融稳定
FIG	Fédération Interationale de Gymnastique [英文:International Gymnastic Federation] 国际体操联合会[法文]

FIGO	Fédération Internationale de Gynecologie et d'Obstetrique 国际妇产科联盟[法文]
FIH	Fédération Internationale de Hockey[英文：International Hockey Federation]国际曲棍球联合会[法文]
FIJ	Fiji 斐济[大洋洲国家]
FIL	father-in-law 岳父/公公[网络用语]
FILA	Fédération Internationale de Lutte Amateur[英文：International Amateur Wrestling Federation]国际业余摔跤联合会[法文]
Fin Tech	*Finance Technology*《金融科技》
FINA	Fédération Internationale de Natation Association 国际泳联[法文]
FIO	for information only 仅供参考
fio	free in and out 买方不负担装卸货费用
fios	free in, out and stow 买方不负担装卸和理仓费
FIPSE	Fund for the Improvement of Postsecondary Education 高等教育改善基金
FIQ	Financial Intelligence Quotient 财商
FIR	far infrared 远红外线
FIR	far infrared radiation 远红外辐射
FIRRMA	The Foreign Investment Risk Review Modernization Act 外资投资风险审查现代化法案
FIS	Fédération Internationale de Ski[英文：International Ski Federation]国际滑雪联合会[法文]
FISH	fluorescence in situ hybridization 荧光原位杂交
FISU	Federation of International Students of University 国际大学生体育联合会
FIT	Fédération Internationale des Traducteurs[英文：International Federation of Translators]国际翻译工作者联合会[法文]
FITA	Fédération Internationale de Tirà l'Arc[英文：International Federation for Archery]国际射箭联合会[法文]
FITC	fluorescein isothiocyanate 异硫氰酸荧光素
FIU	Florida International University 美国佛罗里达国际大学
FIVB	Fédération Internationale de Volley-Ball[英文：International Volleyball Federation]国际排球联合会[法文]

F

Fl	Formula One(Grand Prix)1 世界一级方程汽车锦标赛
Fl	Flerovium 铁[第 114 号化学元素]
FLAC	free lossless audio codec 无损音频压缩编码
FLG	flange 凸缘
FLT	fork lift truck 叉车
FLTR	filter 滤清器
fm	femtometer 飞米[法定长度计量单位,1 飞米＝10^{-15} 米]
Fm	fermium 镄[第 100 号化学元素]
FM	flight modification 航班变更
FM	fibrin monomer 纤维蛋白单体
FM	frequency modulation 调频
FMCG	Fast-moving Consumer Goods 快速消费品
FMEA	failure mode and effect analysis 失效模式与影响分析/故障模式与影响分析
FMGE	Foreign Medical Graduate Exam 外国医学毕业生考试
FMIS	form interface management system 格式接口管理系统
fMRI	Functional Magnetic Resonance Imaging 功能核磁共振成像
FMS	Federal Maritime Commission 美国联邦海事委员会
FMTV	family of medium tactical vehicles 中型战术车辆族
FMV	full-motion video 全动态影像
FMVP	Final Most Valuable Player 总决赛最有价值运动员
FN	fiscal neutrality 财政中性
FN	Fabrique Nationale des Armes de Guerre 国营军火工厂[比利时][法文]
FN	file number 文件号
FN	foreign national 外国侨民
FN	Frame Net 框架网[计算机词典编纂项目]
FNC	Fox News Channel 福克斯新闻频道
FO	first officer 大副
fo	free out 买方不负担卸货费用
FOA	free on airport 机场交货价
FOB	free on board 离岸价格/船上交货价格
FOBS	fractional orbital bombardment system 部分轨道轰炸系统

FOCAC	Forum on China-Africa Cooperation 中非合作论坛
FOF	Fund of Fund 母基金
FOF	fund of fund 基金中的基金
FOMC	Federal Open Market Committee 联邦公开市场委员会
FOMO	fear of missing out 怕错过
FON	fiber optic network 光纤网络
FOR	free on rail 车上交货价格/铁路交货价格
Forex	foreign exchange 外汇
FORMAC	formula manipulation compiler 公式处理编译程序
FORTRAN	formula translation 公式转换语言
FOS	factor of safety 安全系数
FOSM	first-order second-moment 一次二阶矩法
FP	Flocky Pet 宠物博览会
FP	foreign policy 外交政策
FPC	flexible plate of circuit 柔性电路板
FPDA	Five-Power Defense Arrangements 五国联防协议[包括澳大利亚、新西兰、新加坡、马来西亚和英国]
FPE	Swedish Federation of Professional Employees 瑞典专业雇员协会
FPGA	field programmable gate array 现场可编程门阵列
FPO	Fight against Prostitution 与卖淫斗争委员会
FPS	first-person shooter game 第一人射击类游戏
FPS	frames per second 每秒帧数（电视图像的）
FPSA	free prostate-specific antigen 游离前列腺特异性抗原
FPSO	floating production, storage and offloading unit 海上浮式生产储卸油装置
FPT	Faliya peach taste 法利雅调配威士忌
FPUA	female pick-up artist 撩汉达人
FQ	Financial Quotient 财商
Fr	francium 钫[第87号化学元素]
FR	Frankfurter Rundschau《法兰克福评论报》（德文）
FR	front 前部
FRA	France 法国[欧洲国家]

F

frag	fragment 碎片
framedia	frame media 窗框媒介
FRAND	fair，reasonable，and non-discriminatory terms 公平、合理和不带歧视性的条款
FRB	Federal Reserve Bank 美国联邦储备银行
FRB	fast radio burst 快速电波爆发
FRC	Fault Reporting Center 故障报告中心
FRC	Federal Radio Commission 联邦无线电委员会
FRC	Foreign Relations Committee 外交关系委员会
FRC	functional residual capacity (of lungs) 肺功能残气量
FRCC	financial risk control center 财务风险控制中心
FRE	Freddie Mac 美国费雷德马克公司（即房地美）[又称 FHLMC]
FRESH	fun，rich，education，safety，health 未来十年的产业趋势：娱乐、财富管理、教育、安全、健康
FRF	French Franc 法国法郎[货币]
FRI	Friday 星期五
FR-M	Financial Risk Manager 金融风险管理师证书/金融风险管理师
FRP	fiberglass-reinforced plastics 玻璃钢/玻璃纤维增强塑料
FRPC	Face Recognition Prize Challenge 全球人脸识别挑战赛
FRQ	frequent 频繁的
FRS	Federal Reserve System 美联储
FRS	flexible response strategy 灵活反应战略
FRSC	Fellow of the Royal Society of Canada 加拿大皇家协会会员
FRTIB	Federal Retired Thrift Investment Board 联邦退休储蓄投资委员会
Fru	fructose 果糖
FRWF	fresh wharf 淡水码头
FS	foundation suite 基础套件
FSA	Fellow of the Society of Actuary 北美精算师
FSA	Free Syrian Army 叙利亚自由军
FSA	Financial Service Authority 英国金融服务管理局
FSA	Food Standards Agency 英国食品标准局
FSA	frozen section analysis 冰冻切片检查

FSB	Federal Safety Bureau 俄罗斯联邦安全局
FSB	front side bus 前端总线
FSC	Force Search Cadre 香港重点及搜查队
FSC	forest stewardship council 森林管理委员会
FSH	follicle-stimulating hormone 促卵泡（成熟）激素
FSI	Foreign Service Institute 美国外交学院
FSI	foreign service institute 驻外事务处机构
FSM	The Federated States of Micronesia 密克罗尼西亚联邦政府[太平洋一地区]
FSO	Fabryka Samochodów Osobowych 乘用汽车厂[波兰文]
FSR	feasibility study report 可行性研究报告
FSR	fast supply (restaurant) ready 快速配额餐包
FSRIO	Food Safety Research Information Office 食品安全研究信息办公室
Ft	foot 英尺[非法定长度计量单位 1 英尺＝12 英寸＝0.3048 米]
FT	faint 昏倒[网络用语]
FT	*Financial Times*《金融时报》
FT	forces terrestres 陆军[法文]
FT$_3$	free triiodothyronine 游离三碘甲腺原氨酸
FT$_4$	free thyroxine 游离甲状腺素
FT$_4$I	free thyroxine index 游离甲状腺指数
FTA	Free Trade Agreement 自由贸易协定
FTA	Free Trade Area 自由贸易区
FTA	Free Trade Association 欧洲自由贸易协会
FTA	Freight Transport Association 货运协会
FTAA	Free Trade Area of Americas 美洲自由贸易区
FTA-ABS	fluorescent treponemal antibody absorption (test) 荧光密螺旋体抗体吸收实验
FTAC	Foreign Trade Arbitration Commission 外贸仲裁委员会[中国]
FTC	Fair Trade Commission 公平贸易委员会[英国]
FTC	Federal Trade Committee 美国联邦贸易委员会
FTC	Flight Test Center 飞行试验中心
FTD	Foreign Technology Department 外国技术处

F

FTFY	Fixed that for you 当你不小心弄错时帮你改正[网络英语]
FTG	fight technology game 格斗类游戏
FTKs	Freight Ton Kilometers 货运吨千米
FTP	file transfer protocol 文件传输协议
FTP	funds transfer pricing 资金转移定价
FTRIB	the Federal Thrift Retirement Investment Board 联邦退休节俭储蓄投资委员会
FTS	fructosamine 果糖胺
FTSE	failed to sustain engraftment 支撑移植物植入失败
FTSE	Financial Times Stock Exchange 富时指数公司
FTSE100	Financial Times Stock Exchange 100 Index 富时100指数[英国最权威最有代表性的股价指数]
FTTB	fiber to the building 光纤到大楼
FTTH	fiber to the home 光纤到家庭
FTTO	fiber to the office 光纤到办公室
FTTZ	fiber to the zone 光纤到小区
FTZ	Free Trade Zone 自由贸易区
FU	fiscal union 财政同盟
FU	Fudan University 复旦大学
FUD	fear，uncertainty，doubt 一种心理恐怖战术[由"恐惧""不确定""怀疑"的英文首字母构成]
FUE	follicle unit extration 无痕植发
FUNAI	Fundação Nacional dos Indios 全国印第安人基金[葡萄牙文]
FV	Network Virtualization 网络虚拟化
FV	face value 票面金额
FVC	Forced Vital Capacity 用力肺活量
FVEY	Five Eyes Alliance 五眼联盟（由美、英、加、澳、新组成）
FVIFA	final value if annuity 年金的终值系数
FVP	first vice president 第一副总裁
FW	Flylions whisky 菲朗氏调配威士忌
FW	forward 转发
FWC	flight warning computer (airbus) 计算机[空客的飞行警告]

FWD	front wheel drive 前轮驱动
FWIW	for what it's worth 不论真伪
FX	foreign exchange 外汇
FX	flight cancellation 航班取消
FYI	for your information 供参考
FYP	Forum for Young Professionals 年轻专业人士论坛
FYR	for your reference 供参考
FZ	Free Zone (港口的)自由区

G

g	gram 克[法定质量计量单位]
G	GB gigabyte 吉字节
G	General audiences all ages admitted 美国电影协会制定的电影分级制中的大众级,无裸体、性爱场面,吸毒与暴力场面也很少
G	Giga 吉[咖][十进倍数单位的词头名称,其表示的因数为 109]
G	Global System for Mobile Communications 全球移动通信系统
G	general 资料汇编[参考文献标示字母]
G	Ginetta 英国吉列塔汽车
G	good 良好级(钱币)
G	granular cell 颗粒细胞
G	green 绿色
g/cm²	gram/square centimeter 克/平方厘米
G1	Best In Group 犬组冠军
G-2	military intelligence section of Army Corps 陆军参谋部二部[代字]
G2B	Government to Business 政府对企业[电子商务]
G5	Group of Five (Universities) 英国五大名校:牛津大学(University of Oxford),剑桥大学(University of Cambridge),帝国理工(Imperial

G

	College London),伦敦政治经济学院(London School of Economics and Political Science)和伦敦大学学院(London's Global University)
G6PD	glucose 6-phosphate dehydrogenase 葡萄糖-6-磷酸脱氢酶
G7	Group of Seven 七国集团[1975年由美国、日本、法国、英国、德国、意大利和加拿大七国组成]
G8	Group of Eight 八国集团[即在G7的基础上加上俄罗斯]
Ga	gallium 镓[第31号化学元素]
GA	glycated albumin 糖化白蛋白
GAAP	generally accepted accounting principles 公认的会计准则
GAB	Gabon 加蓬[非洲国家]
GAB	Government Approval Board 政府批准委员会
GACC	General Administration of Customs,P. R. China 中国海关总署
GAE	General American English 通用美国英语
GAFA	Google,Apple,Facebook,Amazon 美国互联网四巨头:谷歌、苹果、脸书、亚马逊
GAIA	The Global Alliance for Incinerator Alternatives 全球垃圾焚烧替代联盟
GAIA	The Global Anti-Incinerator Alliance 全球反垃圾焚烧联盟
GAITC	Global Artificial Intelligence Technology Conference 全球人工智能技术大全
gal	gallon 加仑[非法定液量单位],1加仑＝4.546升
GaL	galactose 半乳糖
GAM	Gambia 冈比亚[非洲国家]
GaN	gallium nitride 氮化镓
GANS	generative adversarial networks 生成式对抗网络
GAO	General Accounting Office 美国总审计局
GAO	general accounting officer 总会计师
GAO	General Auditing Office 审计总署
GAP	Good Agricultural Practice 良好农业规范
GAP	Group for the Advancement of Psychiatry 精神病学促进小组
GAPDH	gluceraldehyed-3-phosphate dehydrogenase 甘油醛-3-磷酸脱氢酶
GAPI	gateway application programming interface 网关应用软件编程接口

gar	garage 飞机库/汽车库/汽车修理厂
gas	gasoline 汽油
GATT	General Agreement on Tariffs and Trade 关税及贸易总协定（现已被WTO所取代）
GaWC	Globalization and World Cities Research Network 全球化及世界城市研究网络
GaWC	Globalization and World Cities 世界城市评级机构
GAZ	Gorkovsky Avtomobilny Zavod 嘎斯汽车［俄国］
Gazprom	Gazovaia promeishliennosti 俄气/煤气工业［俄文］
GB	GigaByte 吉字节［千兆字节,计算机内存储单位］［1 GB＝1 024 MB,1 MB＝1 024 KB］
GB	Great Britain 大不列颠
GB	Guobiao 中国（国家）标准［汉语拼音缩略语］
GB	green blue 蓝绿色
GB/T	Guo Biao/Tui 推荐性国家标准［汉语拼音缩略语］
GBA	Golden Bridge Award 金桥奖
GBE	Dame or Knight of the Grand Gross of the British Empire 大英帝国大十字勋位夫人或骑士
GBI	Ground-Based Interceptor 陆基拦截器
GBII	Gaogong Lithium Battery Industry Institute 高工锂电产业研究所
GBK	Guojia Biaozhun Kuozhanma 国家标准扩展码［汉语拼音缩略语］
GBNet	Golden Bridge Net 中国金桥网
GBP	Great Britain Pound 英镑［英国货币］
GBR	Great Britain 英国［欧洲国家］
GBS	Guinea-Bissau 几内亚比绍［非洲国家］
GBU	Global Boxing Unit 全球拳击队
GBU	general-purpose bomb unit 多用途炸弹装置
GBU-39SDB	guided bomb unit-39 small diameter bomb 小直径制导炸弹
GC	Golf Club 高尔夫球俱乐部
GCC	Gulf Cooperation Council 海湾阿拉伯国家合作委员会/海湾合作委员会/科威特认证标志/沙特认证标志

GCE	General Certificate of Education 普通教育证书
GCHQ	Government Communications Headquarters 英国政府通信总部
GCI	general capital increase 普遍增资
GCI	Global Competitiveness Index 全球竞争力指数
GCI	Growth Competitiveness Index 成长竞争力指数
GCID	Global Catalog Identifier 全球目录识别
GCL	Government Confessional Loan 政府优惠贷款
GCP	Good Clinical Practice 药品临床试验管理规范
GCS	Global Classification System 全球分类系统
GCSE	General Certificate of Secondary Education 中学教育普通证书
GCT	Graduate Candidate Test 在职人员硕士研究生入学资格考试
GCT	Grand Central Terminal 美国纽约中央火车站
GCU	ground control unit 地面控制设备
GCV	ground combat vehicle 地面战车
Gd	gadolinium 钆[第 64 号化学元素]
GD	good design 优秀设计
GD	gaming disorder 游戏成瘾
GD	guanase 鸟嘌呤酶
GDB	Guangdong Development Bank 广东发展银行
GDF	Gaz de France 法国天然气公司[法文]
GDH	glutamate dehydrogenase 谷氨酸脱氢酶
GDI	gasoline direct injection 燃油直接喷射
GDP	Gross Domestic Product 国内生产总值
GDS	ground display system 地面显示系统
GDS	Global Distribution Service 全球配送服务
GDS	Global Distribution System 全球分销系统
GDT	ground data terminal 地面数据终端
GDUF	Guangdong University of Finance 广东金融学院
GDUFE	Guangdong University of Finance and Economics 广东财经大学
GE	General Electric Company 通用电气公司
Ge	germanium 锗[第 32 号化学元素]
GE	graphic equalizer 图示均衡器(音响)

GEC	Genius Education Centre	香港专才教育中心
GECAS	General Electric Capital Aviation Services	美国通用资本航空服务
GECOM	general compiler	通用编译程序
GED	General Equivalency Diploma	高中毕业文凭
GEF	Global Environment Facility	全球环境基金
GEIS	General Electric Information Services	通用电子信息服务
GEM	Growth and Emerging Market	新兴市场
GEM	Growth Enterprise Market	创业板
Gem MS	Gem Mint State	珍宝级（钱币）
gem	gemstone	宝石
GEM	Global Entrepreneurship Monitor	全球创业观察
GEMS	Global Environmental Monitoring System	全球环境监测系统
Gen	general	将军
gen	general	普通
GEO	Georgia	格鲁吉亚［欧洲国家］
GEO	Group on Earth Observations	地球观测组织
GEQ	Equatorial Guinea	赤道几内亚［非洲国家］
GER	Germany	德国［欧洲国家］
GESB	The General Scientific Board	科学总委员会
GET	Global Ecommerce Training	全球跨境电商人才培训联盟
GF	girl friend	女朋友
GF	gravity force	重力
GFCI	Global Finance Center Index	全球金融中心指数
GFG	Global Financial Group	环球金融集团
GFI	Global Financial (Integrity) Institute	全球金融诚信组织
GFI	gas-flow indicator	煤气表
GfK	Gesellschaft für Konsum-，Markt-und Absatzforschung	捷孚凯［德文］
GfK	Gesellschaft für Konsum-，Markt-und Absatzforschung	消费、市场及销售研究协会［德文］
GFMS	Gold Fields Mineral Services	黄金矿业服务公司
GFP	global fighting power	全球战力
GFP	green fluorescent protein	绿色荧光蛋白

GFPTRI	Guangzhou Fiber Products Testing and Research Institute 广州纤维产品检测研究院	
GFR	glomerular filtration rate 肾小球过滤率	
GFS	graphical file system 图形文件系统	
GFSI	Global Food Safety Initiative 全球食品安全倡议（认证）	
GG	gamma globulin 丙种球蛋白	
GG	Guccio Gucci 古驰时装	
GGE	generalized glandular enlargement 全身性淋巴结肿大	
GGI	government-guaranteed investment 政府担保的投资	
GGT	gamma-glutamyl transpeptidase γ-谷氨酰转肽酶	
GGV	Granite Global Ventures 纪源资本	
GH	growth hormone 生长激素	
GHA	Ghana 加纳[非洲国家]	
GHB	gamma hydroxybutyrate γ-羟基丁酸盐	
GHb	glycosylated hemoglobin 糖（基）化血红蛋白	
GHbA1	glycosylated hemoglobin A1 糖基化血红蛋白 A1	
GHRE	growth hormone-releasing factor 生长激素释放因子	
GHRIH	growth hormone-releasing-inhibiting hormone 生长激素释放抑制激素	
Gi	gilbert 吉（伯）[磁通势单位]	
GI	general input 总输入量	
GI	glycogen index 糖原指数	
GI	government issue 政府出版物	
GIA	Gem Institute of America 美国宝石学院	
GIA	Gemological Institute of America 美国宝石研究所/世界最权威的宝石鉴定书	
GIF	graphics interchange format 图形交换格式	
GIF	Gen Ⅳ International Forum 创Ⅳ国际论坛	
GIF	Global Integration Framework 全球一体化框架	
GIH	Global Infrastructure Hub 全球基础设施中心	
GII	Global Information Infrastructure 全球信息基础设施	
GIL	gas-insulated transmission line 气体绝缘输电线路	
GILT	globalization, internationalization, localization, translation 全球化、国	

际化、本地化和翻译

gimme	give me 给我［口语］
GINA	Global Initiative for Asthma 全球哮喘防治创议
GIPC	Government Information ProCessing 政府信息处理
GIS	Geographical Information System 地理信息系统［又称资源与环境信息系统］
GIS	gas insulator switchgear 气体绝缘全封闭组合电器
GIS	geo-information software 地理信息软件
GIS	Gruppo d'Intervento Speciale 意大利空军特别行动勤务组［意大利文］
GIS	Special Interventions Group 特别行动勤务组
GITS	Government Information Technology Service 美国政府信息技术服务小组
GIUK	Greenland-Iceland-UK 格陵兰—冰岛—英国
GIV	Global Industry Vision 全球产业展望
GJB	Guo Jun Biao 军用国家标准（汉语拼音缩写）
GJM	Gorkha Janmukti Morcha 廓尔喀人民族独立运动组织［印地文］
GK	Grace Kelly 格蕾丝·凯利［美国女演员摩纳哥王妃］
GKC	Guangdong Kennel Club 广东犬类俱乐部
gkw	God knows what 天知道
GL	Germanischer Lloyd 德国劳氏船级社［德文］
GL	girl's love 女同性恋
GL	Guy Laroche 姬龙雪服装
GLAC	GNSS and LBS Association of China 中国卫星导航定位协会
GLAM	graying, leisured, affluent and married 中年富翁［指头发苍白、有闲的、富有的已婚者］
GLD	gold 金色
GLDH	glutamic dehydrogenase 谷氨酸脱氢酶
Glitterati	glitter literati 明星；高层
GloWbE	The Corpus of Global Web-Based English 英语翻译语料库
GLP	genuine leather product 真皮标志产品
GLP	Good Laboratory Practice 标准实验室规范
GLSV	Great Lakes Symposium on VLSIC 大湖研讨会的超大规模集成电路

G

GLU	glucose 葡萄糖
GLU	glucosuria 血糖
GLU	glucose 空腹血糖/尿糖
Glu	glucose 葡萄糖
GM	General Motors Corporation 美国通用汽车公司
GM	genetically modified 转基因（遗传改造）
GM	game manager 游戏管理员
GM	general manager 总经理
GMAC	Graduate Management Admission Council 管理专业研究生入学考试委员会
Gmail	Google mail 谷歌邮件
GMAT	Graduate Management Admission Test 管理专业研究生入学考试
GMBA	Global Master of Business Administration 国际工商管理硕士
GmbH	Gesellschaft mit beschränkter Haftung 股份有限公司［德文］
GM(C)	General Motors Corporation 美国通用汽车公司
GMD	Global Missile Defence (system) 全球导弹防御系统
GMDSS	global maritime distress and safety system 全球海上遇险与安全系统
GMF	genetically modified food 转基因食品
GML	geography markup language 地理标示语言
GMO	genetically modified organism 转基因有机体
GMP	Good Manufacturing Practice 优良制造标准
GMPCS	Global Mobile Personal Communication by Satellite 全球卫星移动个人通信
GMQ	Good Merchantable Quality 上等销售品质
GMS	Great Mekong Subregion Economic Co-operation 大湄公河次区域经济合作
GMS	Google Mobile Service(Certified) 谷歌移动服务（认证）
GMT	Greenwich Mean (astronomical) Time 格林尼治（天文）标准时间
GMV	gross merchandise value 交易总额
GN	Good night 晚安
GNA	Government of National Accord 利比亚民族团结政府
GNE	Gross National Expenditure 国民总支出

153

GNEP	Global Neuclear Energy Partnership 全球核能伙伴计划
GNH	Gross National Happiness 国民幸福总值
GNI	Gross National Income 国民总收入
GNMT	Google Neural Machine Translation 谷歌神经机器翻译系统
GNP	Gross National Product 国民生产总值
GNSS	Global Navigation Satellite System 全球导航卫星系统
GNW	gross national wealth 国民财富总额
GNW	Gross National Welfare 国民总福利
GO	graphene oxide 氧化石墨烯
GO	graphite oxide 氧化石墨
GOD	game on demand 点播游戏
GOED	Government Office of Economic Development 政府经济发展办公室
gok	God only knows 天知道
Gomx-3	Gomspace-3 丹麦 Gomspace 公司与欧洲航天局合作的 3 号微型卫星
GONGO	Government Organized NGO 政府组织的非政府组织
gonna	going to 将要去[口语]
GOP	Grand Old Party 老大党[指美国共和党]
GOST	Gosudarstvennyj Obscesojuznyi standart 苏联国家标准[俄语]
GOT/AST	glutamic-oxaloacetic transaminase/aspartate aminotransferase 谷草转氨酶/天冬氨酸转氨酶
gotta	got to 去[口语]
GOW	Grand Old Woman 维多利亚女王[别称]
GP	Gallup Poll 美国盖洛普民意测验
GP	general partner 一般合伙人
GP	general practitioner 全科医生
GP	grace period 宽限期
GP	grand-prix 国际汽车大奖(最高奖)
Gp Capt	Group Captain 英国空军上校
GPA	grade point average 学分加权平均分[又称 WAM]/成绩平均值
GPG	goals per game 场均进球数[足球]
GPI	genuine progress indicator 真实发展指数
GPIC	Gulf Petrochemical Industries Co. 海湾石化工业公司

GPL	GNU Public License 开放公共源码许可协议
GPMI	Global Purchasing Manager Index 全球采购经理指数
GPP	general plant projects 一般工厂项目
GPP	generic packetized protocol 普通包装协议
GPP	gyro pitch position 陀螺俯仰位
GPP	generation partner program 第……代合作伙伴计划
GPP	Generation Partnership Plan X 代伙伴计划
GPP	glycosylated plasma protein 糖化血浆蛋白
GPPi	Global Public Policy Institute 全球公共政策研究所
GPPS	general purpose polystyrene 通用聚苯乙烯[塑料]
GPRS	general packet radio service 通用无线分组业务
GPS	Global Positioning System 全球定位系统
GPSS	general purpose systems simulator 通用系统模拟程序
GPT	general preferential tariff 普通优惠关税
GPT/ALT	glutamic pyruvic transaminase/alanine aminotransferase 谷丙转氨酶/丙氨酸转氨酶
GPU	graphic processing unit 图像处理器
GPU	general processing unit 通用处理器
GPW	general purpose Willys 威力斯万能车
GQT	Guangzhou Quality Supervision and Testing Institute 广州质量监督检测研究院
GR	gear ratio 传动比
GRAIL	gravity recovering and interior library 重力恢复和内部实验室
GRE	Graduate Record Examination 美国研究生入学考试
GRE	Greece 希腊[欧洲国家]
GRN	Grenada 格林纳达[北美洲国家]
GROM	grommet 金属孔眼
GRP	glass reinforced plastic 玻璃钢/玻璃增强塑料
GRP	gross rating point 总收视点/总收视率百分点
GRP	ground relay panel 接地继电器盘
GS	Germany Safety 德国安全(认证标志)
GS	Geprufte Sicherheit 安全性已认证[德国安全认证标示][德文]

GS1	Global Standard 1	国际物品编码协会（1973年由美国统一代码委员会建立的组织）
GSA	Global Semiconductor Association	全球半导体联盟
GSB	Ghana Standards Board	加纳标准局/加纳认证标志
GSCS	Global Satellite Communication System	全球卫星通信系统
GSE	Government-Sponsored Enterprise	政府支持的企业
GSH	glutathione	谷胱甘肽
GSHKL	Grand Seasons Hotel Kuala Lumpur	吉隆坡盛季酒店
GSK	Glaxo Smith Kline	英国葛兰素史克公司
GSK	glycogen sythase kinase	糖原合成酶激酶
GSKT	gasket	垫圈
GSL	Global Star League	世界明星对抗赛
GSLV	geosynchronous satellite launch vehicle	地球同步卫星运载火箭
GSM	Global System for Mobile Communication	全球移动通信系统
GSM-R	Global System for Mobile Communication of Railway	全球铁路数字移动通信系统
GSOH	good sense of humour	丰富的幽默感
GSOMIA	Japanese and South Korean Military Intelligence Protection Agreement	《日韩军事情报保护协定》
GSP	Good Supplying Practice	《药品经营质量管理规范》
GSP	Generalized System of Preference	普惠制
GSP	glycated serum protein assay	糖化血清蛋白测定
GSRN	Global Service Relation Number	全球服务关系代码
GSS	General Social Survey	综合社会调查
GST	glutathione-S-transferase	谷胱甘肽-硫转移酶
GST	goods and services tax	商品与服务税
GSV	Global Silicon Valley	全球硅谷
GSVC	Global Social Venture Competition	全球社会风险竞赛
Gt	great	大
GT	grand tourer	大型旅游车
GT	gross tonnage	总吨
GTA	Gurkland Territory Administration	印度廓尔喀兰领地管理局

G

GTC	gas turbine compressor 燃气轮机压缩机
GTC	grand touring car 高性能旅游乘用车
GTC	great telescope of celestial 大型天文望远镜
GTC	ground traffic centre 地面交通中心
GTC	general time counter 通用时间计数器
GTC	general traffic centre 综合交通换乘中心
GTC	global trade centre 全球商品交易中心
GTC	global translator community 全球翻译社区
GTCC	German Touring Car Cup 德国房车锦标赛
GTCs	Government Training Centres 政府培训中心
GTF	general trust fund 普通信托基金
GTF	glucose tolerance factor 葡萄糖耐受量因子
GTF	geared turbofan 齿轮传动涡扇发动机
GTL	Gem Testing Laboratory of Great Britain 英国宝石测试实验室
GTL	Gemological Trade Laboratory 宝石贸易实验室
GTOC X	The 10th edition of the Global Trajectory Optimisation Competition 第十届国际空间轨道设计大赛
GTT	Global Title Translation 全局码
GTT	glucose tolerance test 糖耐量试验
GTT	The General Theory of Terminology 普通术语学
GUA	Guatemala 危地马拉[中美洲国家]
GUUAM	Georgia, Ukraine, Uzbekistan, Azerbaijan, Moldova 古阿姆[由格鲁吉亚、乌克兰、乌兹别克斯坦、阿塞拜疆、摩尔多瓦五国成立的非正式的地区联盟]
GUFS	Guangdong University of Foreign Studies 广东外语外贸大学
GUI	graphical user interface 图形用户界面
GUI	Guinea 几内亚[非洲国家]
GUM	Guam 关岛[太平洋美国所属岛屿]
GUY	Guyana 圭亚那[南美洲国家]
GVA	gross value added 附加总值/加值
GW	Gale Warning 烈风警报
GW	gross weight 毛重/总重量

GWH	Great Western Highway 大西部公路[澳大利亚新南威尔士]
GWICC	Great Wall International Cardiovascular Disease Conference 长城国际心血管病会议
GXV-T	ground X vehicle technology 地面 X 战车技术
GY	green yellow 绿黄色

H	Hafei 哈飞汽车[中国哈尔滨:汉语缩略语]
h	hecto 百[十进倍数的词头名称,其表示的因数为 102]
h	hour 小时
H	Hardness 金属硬度[代号]
H	Henry 亨(利)[法定电感计量单位]
H	hydrogenium 氢[第 1 号化学元素]
H	Honda 日本本田汽车
H	hyperloop 超级高铁
H	Hyundai 韩国现代汽车
H&M	Hennes & Mauritz AB 海恩斯与莫里斯服装、化妆品[瑞典]
H&M	hull and machinery 船体与机械设备
H. S. Code	The Harmonized System Code 协调制编码
ha	hectare 公顷[非法定面积计量单位,1 公顷=10 000 平方米]
HA	hemagglutination 血细胞凝集,血凝反应
HA	home automation 家庭自动化
HA	hazel 褐色
HAA	hepatitis associated antigen 肝炎相关抗原
HAA	hepatitis associated antibody 肝炎相关抗体
HAAb	hepatitis A antibody 甲型肝炎抗体
HAAg	hepatitis A antigen 甲型肝炎抗原
HACCP	Hazard Analysis and Critical Control Point 危害分析和关键控制点

H

Hackathon	hacker marathon 黑客马拉松
hafta	have to 必须[口语]
HAG	Kaffee Handels Aktien Gesellschaft 黑格(脱咖啡因咖啡)[德文：原意为咖啡贸易公司]
HAL	Hindustan Aeronautics Limited 印度斯坦航空公司
Hale-D	high altitude, long-endurance-debris 高空长航时的"碎片"
HAND	have a nice day 过得开心；玩得高兴[网络用语]
HAP	hospital acquired pneumonia 医院获得性肺炎
HARQ	hybrid automatic repeat request 混合自动重传请求
Harv	Harvard University 哈佛大学
HASBRO	Hassenfeld Brothers 孩子宝(玩具)
HAT	heterophil agglutination test 嗜异性凝集试验
HAV	hepatitis A virus 甲型肝炎病毒
HAV-IgM	hepatitis A virus immunoglobulin M 甲肝抗体
Hb COT	carboxyhemoglobin test 碳氧血红蛋白试验
HB	Brinell Hardness 布氏硬度
Hb	hemoglobin 血红蛋白
HbA2	minor fraction of adult hemoglobin 血红蛋白 A2
HbA1C	glycosylated hemoglobin 糖化血红蛋白[另见 GHb]
HBcAb	hepatitis B core antibody 乙型肝炎核心抗体
HBcAg	hepatitis B core antigen 乙型肝炎核心抗原
HBeAb	hepatitis B e antibody 乙型肝炎 e 抗体
HbeAg	hepatitis B e antigen 乙型肝炎 e 抗原
HbF	alkali-resistant hemoglobin determination 抗碱血红蛋白测定
HBO	Home Box Office 总部位于纽约的有线网络媒体公司
HBO	hyperbaric oxygen 高压氧
HBP	health benefit program 保健福利
HBP	human brain protein 人脑蛋白
HBsAb	hepatitis B surface antibody 乙型肝炎表面抗体
HBsAg	hepatitis B surface antigen 乙型肝炎表面抗原
HBV	hepatitis B virus 乙(型)肝(炎)病毒
HC	human clone 人体克隆

HC	hydrocarbon 碳氢化合物
HC	Halal certification 清真认证
HC	human code 人体密码
HC	hydrocarbon 碳氢化合物
HCC	hepatic cell carcinoma 肝细胞癌
HCC	hepatocellular carcinoma 肝癌
HCC	hepatoma carcinoma cell 肝癌细胞
HCF	highest common factor 最大公因子
HCG	human chorionic gonadotrophin 人绒毛膜促性腺素
HCG	hypersecretory chronic gastritis 高分泌性慢性胃炎
HCHS	Hinsdale Center High School 美国欣斯代尔中心高中
HCI	human-computer interaction 人机交互
HCM	hypertrophic cardiomyopathy 肥厚型心肌病
HCO₃⁻	supercarbonate 碳酸氢盐
HCSW	hypersonic convention strike weapon 高超音速常规打击武器
HCT	haematocrit 血细胞比容
HCTS	Hong Kong China Travel Service 香港中国旅行社
HCVAb	hepatitis C virus antibody 丙肝抗体
HD	hard disk (计算机) 硬盘
HD	high definition 高清晰度
HD	high density 高密度
HDAC	histone deacetylase 组蛋白脱乙酰酶
HDC	Home Digital Center 家庭数据中心
HDC	Halal Industry Development Corporation 清真产业发展局
HDCD	high definition compact disk 高清晰度光碟
HDD	hard disk drive 硬盘驱动器
HDD	high density data 高密度数据
HDD	high-precision drive 高精度驱动器
HDD	holographic disk drive 全息磁盘驱动器
HDF	high density ferroalloy 高密度航空合金
HDI	Human Development Index 人类发展指数
HDL	Hardware Description Language 硬件描述语言

HDL	high density lipoprotein 高密度脂蛋白
HDL-C(h)	high density lipoprotein cholesterol 高密度脂蛋白胆固醇
HDMI	high-definition multimedia interface 高清晰度多媒体接口
HDPE	high density polyethylene 高密度聚乙烯[塑料]
HDR	high definition radio 高清广播
HDR	high definition recorder 高清摄像机
HDR	high-dynamic rang 高动态范围(图像)
HDR	hot direct rolling 直接热轧制
HDSL	high-speed digital subscriber line 高速数字用户线路
HDSPA	high-speed downlink packet access 高速下行的分组接入
HDTV	high-definition TV 高清晰度电视
HDVAb	hepatitis delta virus antibody 丁型肝炎抗体
HDVD	high-density digital video disk 压缩版 DVD
HDVS	high definition video system 高清晰度视频系统
HDW	Howaldtswerke-Deutsche Werft GmbH 德国霍瓦特造船厂[德文]
HE	Her/His Excellency 阁下
HE	Higher Education 高等教育
HE	happy ending 大团圆结局/喜剧结尾
He	helium 氦[第 2 号化学元素]
HEAC	Higher Education Advisory Center (英国)高等教育咨询中心
HEC	Ecole des Hautes Etudes Commerciales 巴黎高等商学院[法文]
HEEC	Higher Education Expo of China 中国高等教育博览会
HeLa	Henrietta Lacks strain of cancer cells 海拉癌细胞株
HEMC	Higher Education Mega Center 广州大学城
HEO	High Earth Orbit 高地球轨道
HEPA	high efficiency particulate air filter 高效空气过滤器
HER	exercise heart rate 运动心率
HER2	human epidermal growth factor receptor-2 人表皮生长因子受体-2
HERA	Heavy Engineering Research Association 重工业研究协会
HET	heavy equipment transporter 重型设备运输车
HET	home entertainment center 家庭娱乐中心
HEV	hybrid electric vehicle 混合动力[内燃机、电动机]汽车

HEVAb	hepatitis E virus antibody 戊肝抗体
Hf	hafnium 铪[第 72 号化学元素]
HF	high frequency 高频
HF	Hall of Fame 名人堂
HF	The Heritage Foundation 美国传统基金会
HFAARP	High Frequency Active Auroral Research Program 高频主动极光研究项目
HFC	hybrid fiber coax 混合光纤同轴电缆
HFC	Halal Foundation Center 清真食品研究中心(总部在香港)
HFCI	Halal Food Council International 国际清真食品理事会
HFE	Human Factors Engineering 人的因素工程学
HFEA	Human Fertilisation and Embryology Authority 人类受精与胚胎学管理局
HFESS	High Frequency Electromagnetic Simulation System 高频电磁仿真系统
HFGWOTHR	high frequency ground wave over the horizon radar 高频地波超视距雷达
HFI	Hangzhou Finance Investment Company 杭州金融投资公司
HFMD	hand, foot, mouth disease 手足口病
HFOTHR	high frequency over-the-horizon radar 高频超视距雷达
HFSWOTHR	high frequency sky wave over the horizon radar 高频天波超视距雷达
Hg	hydrargyrum 汞[第 80 号化学元素][拉丁文]
HGB	hemoglobin 血红蛋白
HGB	glycosylated hemoglobin 糖化血红蛋白
HGF	hepatocyte growth factor 肝细胞生长因子
HGH	human growth hormone 人体生长激素
HGP	Human Genome Project 人类基因组计划
HGVAb	hepatitis G virus antibody 庚肝抗体
HH	hypogonadotropic hypogOnadism 低促性腺素性功能减退症
HHA	hao hao ai 一种蜂浆纸[源于汉语拼音"好好爱"]
HHAG	Helvetia Holding AG 瑞士持股银行
HHP	household pet 宠物

HHS	Department of Health and Human Services 卫生及公共服务部
HHS	Health and Human Services 保健与人事服务(部)
HIAA	Health Insurance Association of America 美国医疗保险协会
HID	High intensity discharge 高强度放电
HIF-1	hypoxia inducible factor-1 缺氧诱导因子-1
HI-FI	high-fidelity 高保真(度)
HIFU	high-intensity focused ultrasound 海扶刀[高强度聚焦超声肿瘤治疗系统]
HIIT	high-intensity interval training 高强度间隙训练法
HIPC	the heavily indebted poor countries 重债国
HIPS	high impact polystyrene 高抗冲聚苯乙烯[塑料]
HIRA	handheld infrared alarm 袖珍红外报警器
HIRC	health insurance review committee 健康保险审查委员会
HIS	hard-working, intelligence, silence 勤劳、聪明、宁静
HIS	hospital information system 医院信息系统
HIT	Harbin Institute of Technology 哈尔滨工业大学
HIT	Heavy Industry, Taxilia 巴基斯坦塔克西拉重工业
Hi-Tech	high technology 高科技
HIV	human immunodeficiency virus 人类免疫缺陷病毒;艾滋病病毒
HKADC	Hong Kong Arts Development Council 香港艺术发展局
HKAS	Hong Kong Attestation Service 香港认证服务中心
HKBU	Hong Kong Baptist University 香港浸会大学
HKCEE	Hong Kong Certificate of Education Examination 香港中学会考
HKCMAC	Hong Kong Chinese Medicine Authentication Centre 香港中药检定中心
HKCTU	Hong Kong Confederation of Trade Unions 香港工会联盟
HKD	Hong Kong Dollar 港元[货币]
HKEX	Hong Kong Exchange 香港交易所
HKFRMA	Hong Kong Financial Risk Manager Association 香港金融风险管理师协会
HKFSD	Hong Kong Fire Service Department 香港消防处
HKFTU	Hong Kong Federation of Trade Unions 香港工会联合会
HKG	Hong Kong (中国)香港

HKGFS	Hong Kong Government Flying Service 香港特区政府飞行服务队
HKIF	Hong Kong Investment Fund SP 香港投资基金
HKMA	Hong Kong Monetary Authority 香港金融管理局
HKPCA	Hong Kong Professional Coaching Association 香港专业辅导协会
HKPF	Hong Kong Police Force 香港警务处
HKSAR	Hong Kong Special Administration Region 香港特别行政区
HKU	The University of Hong Kong 香港大学
HKUST	The Hong Kong University of Science and Technology 香港科技大学
HLA	Human Leucocyte Antigen 人类白细胞抗原
HLA-A	human leukocyte antigen A 人类白细胞 A 抗原
HLB	hard lock ball bearing 轴承专用螺丝
HLN	Hard Lock nut 哈德洛克螺母
HLS	Hard Lock screw 哈德洛克螺丝
HM	Heimlich's Maneuvers 美国海姆立克急救法
HM	hull and machinery 船体与机械设备
HMG-CoA	hydroxyl-methyl-glutaryl coenzyme A 羟基甲戊二酸单酰辅酶 A
HML	Hypertext Markup Language 超文本标识语言
HMMWV	high mobility multipurpose wheeled vehicle 高机动多用途轮式车辆
HMO	Health Maintenance Organization 卫生维护组织
HMO	heart minute output 心脏每分钟搏出量
HMS	Huawei Mobile Services 华为移动服务
HMS	Her Majesty's Ship Queen Elizabeth 伊丽莎白女王号
HMS	Her[His] Majesty's Ship 英国皇家海军舰艇
HMX	homocyclonite 奥克托今[炸药]
HNA	Hainan Airlines 海南航空
HNC	hierarchical network of concepts 概念层次网络
HNC	Higher National Certificate（英国职业技术教育）国家高级合格证书
HNCM	hypertrophic nonobstructive cardiomyopathy 肥厚型非梗阻性心肌病
HND	Higher National Diploma（英国）国家高等教育文凭
HNWI	high-net-worth individual 高净值人士
Ho	Holmium 钬［第 67 号化学元素］
HO	head office 总公司；总部

HOA	hands off-automatic 自动装置;不用手动
HOL	Home On Line 家庭在线
HOL	House of Lords 上议院[英国]
HON	Honduras 洪都拉斯[北美洲国家]
HONET	home optical network 家庭光纤网络
HOPE	Hormuz Peace Effort 霍尔木兹和平动议
HOPEN	hope+open 我国自主版权的嵌入式操作系统[希望+开放]
HoReCa	hotel, restaurant, cafe/catering 餐馆
HOS	sperm hypoosmotic swelling experiment 精子低渗肿胀试验
HP	helicobacter pylori 幽门螺杆菌
HP	hewlett packard (美国)惠普公司
HP	high performance 高性能
HP	high potency 高效能
HP	hit point 生命力
HP3	heat flow and physical properties probe 热流和物理性质探测仪
HPA	Health Protection Agency 英国卫生防护局
HPC	hand personal computer 手提个人电脑
HPC	high performance computer 高性能计算机
HPC	high performance computing 高性能计算
HPCIA	highest priority critically important antimicrobial 最高优先级的重要抗菌药物
HPL	high-level programming language 高级编程语言
HPM	high power microware 高功率微波
HPS	hazardous polluting substance 危险污染物质
HPS	hydraulic power steering 普通液压助力动力转向系统
HPV	human papilloma virus 人乳头瘤病毒
HQ	Health Quotient 健康商数[指一个人的健康智慧及对健康的态度]
HQMC	Headquarters Marine Corps 海军陆战队总部
hr	hour 小时
HR	Human Resource 人力资源
HR	House of Representatives 美国众议院
HR	Hellenic Register 希腊船级社

HR	Hoog Rendement 荷兰煤气认证标志[荷兰文]
HR	household refuse 生活垃圾
HR	human right 人权
HRA	Health Risk Appraisal 健康风险评估
HRA	health risk assessment 健康风险评价
HRA	human resource accounting 人力资源会计
HRA	human resource allocation 人力资源配置
HRA	Human Rights Association 人权协会
HRA	hydrogeological risk assessment 水文地质风险评估
HRA	hypersonic research airplane 高超音速研究飞机
HRD	human resource development 人力资源开发
HRD	Hoge Raad voor Diamant 钻石 HRD 证书[荷兰文]
HRD	human resource director 人力资源总监
HREF	hypertext reference 超文本参考
HRG	Harbin Industry University Robot Group 哈尔滨工业大学机器人集团
HRM	human resource management 人力资源管理
HRP	horseradish peroxidase 辣根过氧化物酶
HRS	Hawaii Revised Statutes 夏威夷修订的律例
HRT	hormone replacement therapy 激素替代疗法
HRW	Human Rights Watch 人权观察/人权监察站
Hs	hassium 镙[第 108 号化学元素]
HS	harmonized system 海关编码[简称,详称见另一个 HS]
HS	high seas 公海
HS	hospital ship 医院船
HS	House System 住宅体制
HS	International Convention for the Harmonized Commodity Description and Coding System 海关编码[即《商品名称及编码协调制度的国际公约》]
HSA	human serum albumin 人血清白蛋白
HSB	hue, saturation, brightness 一种色彩模型[色调+饱和度+亮度]
HSBC	Hong Kong and Shanghai Banking Corporation 香港汇丰银行
HSC	hematopoietic stem cell 造血干细胞
HSD	Homeland Security Department 国土安全部

H

HSE	Health, Safety, Environment 健康、安全、环境一体化管理体系
HSI	Hang Seng Index 恒生指数
HSI	Homeland Safety Investigation Bureau 国土安全调查部门
HSK	Hanyu Shuiping Kaoshi 汉语水平考试[汉语拼音缩略语]
HSP	highly sensitive person 高度敏感的人[网络用语]
HSP	High-Speed Printer 高速打印机
HSPs	heat shock proteins 热休克蛋白
HSR	heat shock response 热休克反应
HSR	high-speed railway 高速铁路
HSRCC	High Speed Railway Contractor Consortium 中印尼高铁合同承包商联合体
HST	Hostage Supply Team 人质救援组
HSV	high speed vessel 高速船
HT	high technology 高科技
HT	hyper-threading 超线程（技术）
HT	Huobi Token 火币全球通用积分
Ht	haematocrit 红细胞比容
5-HT	5-hydroxy tryptamine (serotonin) 5-羟色胺
HTC	High Technology Computer Corporation 宏达国际电子股份有限公司[台湾]
HTC	high-throughout computing 高吞吐量计算
HTC	Hollerith Type Computer 霍尔瑞斯型计算机
HTLV	human T-cell lymphotropic virus 人类嗜T[淋巴]细胞病毒
HTLV-1	human T-cell lymphotropic virus type-1 人类嗜T[淋巴]细胞病毒-1
HTML	hyper text markup language 超文本标记语言
HTOL	horizontal takeoff and landing 水平起飞和着陆
HTPC	home theater personal computer 家庭影院电脑
HTRDP	high Technology Research and Development Program 高科技研究和发展项目
HTS	Hayyat Tahriral—Sham 沙姆解放组织[土耳其文]
HTT	Hyperloop Transportation Technologies 超环线运输技术；被动磁悬浮技术

HTTP	hyper text transfer protocol 超文本传输协议
HTTPS	hyper-text transfer protocol server 超文本传输协议服务器
Hubo	Humanoid Robot 仿人机器人［韩国产］
HUD	holographic up display 全息平视显示器
HUFS	Hankuk University of Foreign Studies 韩国外国语大学
HUGO	Human Union of Gene Organization 人类基因组组织
HUN	Hungary 匈牙利［欧洲国家］
HUS	hemolytic uremic syndrome 溶血性尿毒症综合征
HUST	Huazhong University of Science and Technology 华中科技大学
HUVEC	human umbilical vein endothelial cell 人脐静脉内皮细胞
HVA	homovanillic 高香草酸
HVAC	heating, ventilation and air conditioning 空气调节系统［是包含温度、湿度、空气清净度及空气循环的控制系统］
HVC	hardware video conference 视频会议硬件
HVD	high-definition video decoder 高清数字电影播放机
HW	Huawei 华为企业［中国著名民企］
HWP	health & wealth planner 健康财富规划师
HXMT	Hard X-ray Modulation Telescope 硬X射线调制望远镜
HYP	Harvard, Yale and Princeton Universities 哈佛大学、耶鲁大学和普林斯顿大学［美国］
Hypermedia	hypertext multimedia 超媒体
Hz	hertz 赫兹［法定频率计量单位］

i	Internet 互联网
I	iodine 碘［第53化学号元素］
I&N	immigration and naturalization 移民并加入国籍
I DO	International Dangerous Organization 国际危险品组织

I

i. e.	id est 换言之[拉丁文]
I/O	input/output 输入/输出
IA	information appliance 信息化家电
IA	international agent 国际代理
IAA	International Association of Actuaries 国际精算师协会
IAAC	individual all-around competition 个人全能比赛
IAAF	individual all-around finals 个人全能决赛
IAAF	International Amateur Athletic Federation 国际业余田径联合会
IaaS	infrastructure as a service 基础设施即服务
IAATO	International Association of Antarctic Tour Operators 国际南极旅游组织协会
IAB	Industry Advisory Board 工业咨询委员会[英国]
IAB	Institut für Arbeitsmarkt-und Berufsforschung 劳动力市场和职业研究所[德文]
IAC	Indian Airlines Corporation 印度航空公司
IAC	International Air Convention 国际航空协定
IAC	International Aquatic-speed Competition 世界水上极速运动大赛
IACAC	Inter-American Commercial Arbitration Commission 泛美商业仲裁委员会
IACF	International Automobile Club Federation 国际汽车俱乐部协会
IACM	The Institute for the Advancement of Chinese Medicine Ltd. 中医药研究所
IACS	International Association of Classification Societies 国际船级社协会
IAD	Internet addictive disease 网络成瘾症
IAEA	Institute of Asian Economic Affairs 日本亚洲经济研究所
IAEA	International Atomic Energy Agency 国际原子能机构
IAEGHCRF	IA Ecoflex Global Health Care Renaissance Fund 全球医疗复兴基金
IAF	International Astronautical Federation 国际宇航联合会
IAF	International Automobile Federation 国际汽车联合会
IAG	International Aviation Group 国际航空集团
IAHA	immune adherence hemagglutination assay 免疫吸附血凝测定
IAI	Israel Aircraft Industries, Ltd. 以色列航空航天工业公司

IAIC	International Artificial Intelligence Center 国际人工智能中心
IAMCR	International Association for Mass Communication Research 国际大众传媒研究协会
IANSA	Instituto Azucarero Nacional, S. A. 全国糖业股份公司［智利，西班牙文］
IAP	internet access provider 互联网接入提供商
IAP	In-App Purchase 应用程序内购买
IAPMO	International Association of Plumbing and Mechanical Officials 国际管道机械理事会/国际管道机械产品质量认证标志
IAPR	The International Association for Pattern Recognition 国际模式识别会议
IARC	International Agency for Research on Cancer 国际癌症研究机构
IARFC	International Association of Registered Financial Consultants 国际认证财务顾问师协会
IARU	International Alliance of Research Universities 国际研究型大学联盟
IAS	intelligent assessing system 智能测评系统
IAS	intelligent authoring system 智能创作系统
IAS	International Accounting Standards 国际会计准则
IAS	Internet addiction syndrome 互联网成瘾综合征
IATA	International Air Transport Association 国际航空运输协会
IATE	Interactive Terminology for Europe 欧盟内部的术语库
IATF	International Automotive Task Force 国际汽车工业特别工作组
IAU	International Astronomical Union 国际天文学联合会
IB	International Baccalaureate 国际文凭
IB	Identification Bureau 香港鉴证科
IB	initial program 预料课程
IB	Istanbul Banka 土耳其伊斯坦布尔银行［土耳其文］
IBA	International Baseball Association 国际棒球联合会
IBA	International Bar Association 国际律师协会
IBA	Internet Business Forum 因特网商业论坛
IBAN	International Bank Account Number 国际银行账户号码
IBBY	International Board on Books for Young People 国际青少年读物委员会；国际儿童读物联盟

IBC	International Bar Council 国际律师协会
IBC	International Biographical Centre 国际传记中心
IBC	International Business Center 环球商务中心
IBC	International Broadcast Center 国际广播中心
IBD	inflammatory bowel disease 炎症性肠病
IBF	International Badminton Federation 国际羽毛球联合会
IBF	International Boxing Federation 国际拳击联合会
IBGE	Instituto Brasileiro de Geografia e Estatistica 巴西地理统计局［葡萄牙文］
I-Bil	indirect bilirubin 间接胆红素
IBK	Industrial Bank of Korea 韩国中小企业银行
IBM	International Business Machines Corporation 国际商用机器公司
IBN	Institut Belge de Normalisation 比利时标准化学会［法文］
IBO	International Baccalaureate Organization 国际文凭组织
IBO	International Biology Olympaid 国际生物学奥林匹克竞赛
IBO	International Boxing Organization 国际拳击组织
IBOR	inter bank offered rate 银行同业拆借利率
IBP	Iowa Beef Packers 美国艾奥瓦牛肉罐头
IBRD	International Bank for Reconstruction and Development 国际复兴开发银行
IBRO-Kemali	International Brain Research Organization-Kemali 国际脑研究组织-凯默理
IBS	irritable bowel syndrome 肠易激综合征
IBSA	International Blind Sports Association 国际盲人体育联盟
IBS－D	irritable bowel syndrome with diarrhea 腹泻型肠易激综合征
IBU	International Biathlon Union 国际冬季两项全能联盟
IBU	International Boxing Union 国际拳击联盟
IBU	International Broadcasting Union 国际广播联合会/国际广播联盟
IBY	International Book Year 国际图书年
IBZ	Interkulturelles Bildungszentrum e. V. an der Universitaet Duisburg-Essen 德国 IBZ 德语培训学校［德文］
IC	integrated circuit card 集成电路卡/智能卡

IC	intelligence chip 智能芯片
IC	inspiratory capacity 深吸气量
IC	integrated circuit 集成电路
ICA	Interbank Card Association 银行卡协会
ICA	International Ceramic Association 国际陶器协会
ICA	International Colour Gem Association 国际彩色宝石协会
ICAA	Investment Counsel Association of America 美国投资顾问协会
ICAC	International Cotton Advisory Committee 国际棉花咨询委员会
ICAC	Independent Committee Against Corruption 香港廉政公署
ICAD	International Commercial Art Designer 国际商业美术设计师职业资格认证
ICADA	International Commercial Art Designer Association 国际商业美术设计师协会
ICAN	International Campaign to Abolish Nuclear Weapons 国际废除核武器运动
ICANN	The Internet Corporation for Assigned Names and Numbers 互联网名称与数字地址分配机构
ICAO	International Civil Aviation Organization 国际民航组织
ICAP	International Carbon Action Partnership 国际碳行动伙伴组织
ICBC	Industrial and Commercial Bank of China 中国工商银行
ICC	International Chamber of Commerce 国际商会
ICC	International Committee for the Coordination of Sports for the Disabled 国际残疾人体育协调委员会
ICC	International Computation Center 国际计算中心
ICC	International Criminal Court 国际刑事法院
ICC	intrahepatic cholangiocarcinoma 肝内胆管癌
ICCA	International Conference and Convention Association 国际大会与会议协会
ICCA	International Conference on Control and Automation 国际控制和自动化会议
ICCC	International Conference on Computer and Communication 国际计算机通信会议
CCITT	Comité Consultatif International pour Télégraphie et Téléphonie 国际电报电话咨询委员会 [法文]

ICD	Immune Complex Disease 免疫综合征
ICD	intrauterine contraceptive device 宫内避孕器
ICD	International Classification of Diseases 国际疾病分类(法)
ICD	International Cooperation for Development 国际发展合作(组织)
ICD	isocitrate dehydrogenase 异柠檬酸脱氢酶
ICD-O	International Classification of Diseases for Oncology 国际疾病分类学—肿瘤学
ICDP	International Continental Scientific Driving Plan 国际大陆科学钻探计划
ICE	Internet Communication Engine 互联网通信引擎
ICE	Immigration and Customs Enforcement 移民与海关执法(局)
ICE	Intercontinental Exchange 洲际交易所
ICE	The International Corpus of English 国际英语语料库
ICF	Independent Cat federation 独立猫类联盟
ICFF	International Contemporary Furniture Fair 国际现代家具展
ICG	impedance cardiogram 阻抗心电图
ICG	indocyanine green 靛氰绿滞留实验
ICG	International Crisis Group 国际危机组织
ICHPER	International Council for Health, Physical Education and Recreation 国际卫生、体育与文娱理事会
ICHR	International Council for Human Rights 国际人权委员会
ICI	Imperial Chemical Industries 帝国化学公司[英国]
ICIA	International Communication Information Association (美国)国际通信信息协会
ICIF	International Cultural Industries Fair 国际文化产业博览交易会
ICIJ	International Consortium of Investigative Journalist 国际调查记者协会
ICIT	Institute for Critical Infrastructure Technology 美国关键基础设施技术研究所
ICITF	International Cultural Industry Trade Fair 国际文化产业博览交易会
ICJ	International Court of Justice 联合国国际法院
ICL	Imperial College London 帝国理工大学[英国]
ICL	Institut de Chimie de Lyon 里昂化学工业公司[法文]

ICLA	International Comparative Literature Association 国际比较文学协会
ICLE	International Corpus of Learner English 国际英语学习者语料库
ICM	the International Congress of Mathematicians 国际数学家大会
ICM	l'Institut de la Communication et des Médias 传媒学院［法文］
ICMA	Institute of Cost and Management Accountants 成本和管理会计师学会
ICMA	International City Management Association 国际城市管理协会
ICO	International Coal Organization 国际煤炭组织
ICO	Illinois College of Optometry 伊利诺伊视光学院
ICO	information, coordination and organization 信息、协调及组织
ICO	in-house computing option 内部计算选项
ICO	initial coin offerings 初始货币供应
ICO	initial coin offering 名义筹资/首次代币发售
ICO	integration and coordination office 集成和协同办公
ICO	International Coffee Organization 国际咖啡组织
ICO	International Council of Ophthalmology 国际眼科理事会
ICOI	The International Congress of Oral Implantologists 国际口腔种植医师学会
ICONIEC	Instituto Colombiano de Normas Técnicas 哥伦比亚产品质量认证标志［西班牙文］
ICONIEC	Instituto Colombiano de Normas Técnicas 哥伦比亚技术标准协会［西班牙文］
ICP	International Center of Photography （纽约）国际摄影中心
ICP	international comparison program 国际比较项目
ICP	Internet Content Provider 网络内容服务商
ICPA	International Profession Certification Association 国际认证协会
ICPC	Independent Corrupt Practice Commission 独立腐败行为委员会
ICPC	Interstate Compact on the Placement of Children 《关于儿童安置的州际契约》
ICPC	International Collegiate Programming Contest 国际大学生程序设计竞赛
ICPO	International Criminal Police Organization 国际刑（事）警（察）组织
ICQ	I seek you 一种国际流行的网络即时通信软件
ICRC	International Committee of the Red Cross 国际红十字委员会

ICS	International Channel Shanghai 上海外语频道
ICSA	International Computer Security Association 国际计算机安全协会
ICSO	International Commonwealth Support Organization 国际公益扶持组织
ICSS	improved contact support set 改进型联络支援装置
ICSS	Internet Connection Secure Server 因特网连接安全网服务系统
ICSS	The International Centre for Sport Security 国际运动安全中心
ICSU	International Council of Scientific Unions (联合国教科文组织)国际科学协会理事会
ICT	International Coffee Tasting 国际咖啡品鉴大赛
ICT	in circuit tester 在线测试仪
ICT	in-circuit test 电路内测试
ICT	information and communication technology 信息与通信技术
ICT	Institute of Computer Technology 计算机技术研究所
ICTR	International Centre for Theatre Research 国际戏剧研究中心
ICTSB	Information and Communiction Technologies for Standardization Board 信息和通信技术标准委员会
ICTV	International Commercial Television 乌克兰国际商业电视台
ICU	intensive care unit 重症监护室
ICU	Indonesian Council of Ulama 印度尼西亚乌拉玛委员会
ICYMI	In case you missed it 我再说一次,以防万一[网络用语]
ID	identification 识别
ID	identity card 身份证
ID	international data 国际数据
ID	iron deficiency 缺铁症
ID	Immigration Department 香港入境事务处
IDA	iron deficiency anemia 缺铁性贫血
IDA	International Development Association 国际开发协会
IDC	International Design Contest 国际设计大赛
IDC	International Data Corporation 国际数据公司
IDC	International Documentation Center 国际文献资料中心
IDC	Internet Data Center 互联网数据中心
IDCP	International Dolphin Conservation Program 国际海豚保育计划

IDCP	Islamic Dawah Council of the Philippines 菲律宾伊斯兰宣教理事会
IDD	international direct dial 国际直拨(电话)
IDD	iodine deficiency disorders 碘缺乏症
IDDC	Implanting Complex Cases Diagnosis Design Center 牙齿种植复杂病例诊断设计中心
IDE	integrated development environment 集成开发环境
IDE	integrated drive electronics 集成驱动器电子设备/综合驱动器电子设备
IDEA	International Design Excellence Awards 国际最佳工业设计奖
IDEF	International Defence Engineer Fair 国际防务工业展
IDF	indigenous defense fighter 本土制造防御战机
IDF	International Dairy Federation 国际乳制品业联合会
IDF	International Diabetes Federation 国际糖尿病联盟
IDFC	International Development Finance Co. 国际开发金融公司
IDFL	International Down & Feather Laboratory 国际羽绒羽毛检测实验室
IDG	International Data Group 国际数据集团
IDI	Inherent Defects Insurance 住宅质量保证保险［又称"潜在缺陷保险"］
IDIEM	Instituto de Investigaciones'y Ensayos de Materiales 材料强度试验研究价［智利,西班牙文］
IDL	International Date Line 国际日期变更线
IDMA	International Diamond Manufactures Association 国际钻石制造商协会
IDNS	Internet domain name system 互联网域名系统
IDP	Internet directory provider 互联网目录提供商
IDP	International Development Program 国际开发署
IDPSF	International Disabled Persons' Sports Federation 国际残疾人体育联合会
IDS	information detection system 信息检测系统
IDS	intrusion detecting system 入侵检测系统
IDSA	Interactive Digital Software Association 互动数字软件协会
IDSF	International Dance Sport Association 世界体育舞蹈协会
IDSIA	Instituto Dalle Molle di Studi sul l'Intelligenza Artificiale 人工智能研究所［法文］
IDTC	Indian Diamond Trade Center 印度钻石交易中心
IE	industrial engineering 工业管理

IE	information extraction 信息摘录
IE	Imperial Energy 帝国能源公司
IE	industrial engineer 从事工业工程的人
IE	infectious endocarditis 感染性心内膜炎
IEA	International Energy Agency 国际能源署
IEBS	International Electronic Business Affairs 国际电子商务师
IEC	International Electrotechnical Commission 国际电工委员会
IEC	intraepithelial carcinoma 上皮内癌
IECQ	International Electrotechnical Commission of Quality 电子认证标志
IECQ	International Electrotechnical Commission of Quality 国际电气技术质量委员会
IED	improvised explosive device 简易爆炸装置
IEEE	Institute of Electrical and Electronics Engineers 电气和电子工程师协会
IEEPA	International Emergency Economic Powers Act 国际紧急经济权利法案
IELTS	International English Language Testing System 雅思考试
IEM	Intel Extreme Masters 英特尔极限大师杯赛
IEP	Internet equipment provider 网络设备提供商
IEP	Ireland pound 爱尔兰镑［爱尔兰货币］
IEP	immunoelectrophoresis 免疫电泳
IF	ice fog 冰雾
IF	Industries Forum Design 汉诺威工业设计论坛奖
IF	international freeman 国际自由人
IFA	indirect fluorescent antibody test 间接荧光抗体试验
IFA	International Fair Annual 国际展览年会
IFAD	International Fund for Agricultural Development 国际农业发展基金会
IFANCA	Islamic Food and Nutrition Council of America 美国伊斯兰食品营养委员会
IFAT	indirect fluorescent antibody test 间接荧光抗体实验
IFAW	International Fund for Animal Welfare 国际爱护动物基金会
IFBAS	integrated farming and biological areas 综合农业和生物多样性区域
IFBB	International Federation of Bodybuilders 国际健美联合会
IFC	International Finance Corporation 国际金融公司
IFES	International Federation for Exhibition Services 国际展览服务协会

IFFHS	International Federation of Football History and Statistics 国际足球历史和统计联合会
IFHR	International Federation for Human Rights 人权国际联合会
IFJ	International Federation of Journalists 国际新闻工作者联合会
IFL	Informed For Life 非商业性质的新汽车安全试验组织
IFLA	International Federation of Landscape Architects 国际景观设计师协会
IFLA	International Federation of Library Associations 国际图书馆协会联合会
IFMA	International Federation of Muay Thai Amateur 泰拳业余爱好者国标联合会
IFMA	International Financial Management Association 国际财务管理协会
IFO	Institut für Wirtschaftsforschung 经济研究学会[德文]
IFoA	Institute and Faculty of Actuaries 英国精算师协会
IFOAM	International Federation of Organic Agriculture Movement 国际有机农业运动联合会
IFOP	Institut Français de I'Opinion Publique 法国民意调查所[法文]
IFP	Institut Français du Petrole 法国石油研究院[法文]
IFPI	International Federation of the Phonographic Industry 国际唱片业协会
IFPRI	International Food Policy Research Institute 国际粮食政策研究所
IFRCRCS	International Federation of Red Cross and Red Crescent Societies 红十字会与红新月会国际联合会
IFRS	International Financial Reporting Standards 国际财务报告准则
IFS	International Food Standard 国际食品标准（认证）
IFS	integrated financial services 集成财经服务
IFS	integrated financial statement 综合财务报表
IFS	International Finance Square 国际金融中心
IFS	International Foundation for Science 国际科学基金会
IFS	International Fund of Science 国际科学基金
IFSA	International Federation of Strength Athletes 国际大力士联盟
IFSC	International Federation of Surgical College 国际外科学会联合会
IFSCC	International Federation of Societies of Cosmetic Chemists 国际化妆品化学家学会联盟

IFSIDP	International Federation of Sports for Intellectual Disabled Person 国际智力残疾人体育联盟
IFT	International Federation of Translators 国际翻译家联合会
IG	Inspector General 监察长（公署）
IG	invictus game 坚忍不拔的博弈
IG	Invictus Gaming iG 电子竞技俱乐部
Ig(A,D,E,G,M)	immunoglobulin(A,D,E,G,M) 免疫球蛋白(A,D,E,G,M)
IGBT	insulated gate bipolar transistor 绝缘栅双极型晶体管
IGC	intellectually gifted children 神童
IGEO	International Geography Olympiad 国际地理奥林匹克竞赛
IGF	insulin-like growth factors 胰岛素样生长因子
IGF	International Golf Federation 国际高尔夫球联盟
IGI	International Gem Institute 国际宝石学院
IGI	International Gemological Institute 国际宝石学院
IGI	International Gemological Institute 世界最权威的宝石鉴定书
IGMP	Internet Group Management Protocol 互联网组管理协议
IGN	ignition 点火
IGSO	Inclined GeoSynchronous Orbit 倾斜地球同步轨道
IGSS	Inclined GeoSynchronous Satellite 倾斜地球同步卫星
IGTT	intravenous glucose tolerance test 静脉葡萄糖耐量实验
IGU	International Geography Union 国际地理联合会
IH	infectious hepatitis 传染性肝炎
IH	Ionosphere Heater 电离层加热器
IHA	indirect hemagglutination antibody 间接血细胞凝集抗体
IHC	immunohistochemistry 免疫组织化学
IHC	International Help for Children 国际儿童援助组织
IHF	International Handball Federation 国际手球联合会
IHIA	International Halal Integrity Alliance 国际清真诚信联盟
IHIT	integrated homicide investigation team 凶案调查组
IHO	International Humanitarian Organization 国际人权组织
IHO	International Hydrographic Organization 国际水文学组织
iHQ	Sidus HQ 韩国较大的娱乐公司

IHS	information handling services 信息处理集团
II	icterus index 黄疸指数
II	income index 收入指数
IIAC	The International Institute of Coffee Tasters 国际咖啡品鉴者协会
IIC	International Institute of Communications 国际通信学会
IIC	International Integrated Circuit 国际集成电路研讨会
IIEP	International Institute of Educational Planning 国际教育计划研究中心
IIF	Institute of International Finance 国际金融协会
IIFRC	International I-Ching Fengshui Research Center 国际易学风水研究中心
IIHF	International Ice Hockey Federation 国际冰球联合会
III	International Institute of Interpreters 国际译员协会[联合国]
IIIC	immediate imagery interpretation center 紧急图像判读中心
IIM	Indian Institutes of Management 印度管理学院
IIOC	Independent International Organization for Certification 国际独立认证组织
IIRS	Institute for Industrial Research and Standards 爱尔兰产品质量认证标志
IIRS	Institute for Industrial Research and Standards 爱尔兰工业研究和标准学会
IISS	International Institute for Strategic Studies 国际战略研究所
IIT	Indian Institute of Technology 印度理工学院
IJERPH	*International Journal of Environmental Research and Public Health* 《国际环境研究与公共卫生》(杂志)
IJF	International Judo Federation 国际柔道联合会
IKEA	Ingvar Kamprad Elmtaryd Agunnaryd 宜家家居(公司创始人姓名和位置的首字母组合)[瑞典文]
IKMC	International Kids Model Contest 国际少儿模特大赛
IKO	Innovation, Knowhow and Originality 日本 IKO 轴承(I 表示革新、K 表示技术、O 表示创意)
IL	import license 进口许可证
il	illegal immigrant 非法移民
IL	insulator 绝缘体
IL-2	interleukin-2 白细胞介素-2

I

ILA	Innovation and Leadership in Aerospace 航空和航天的革新和领军者
ILC	International Labour Conference 国际劳工大会[联合国]
ILC	International Law Commission 国际法委员会
ILCUN	International Law Commission of United Nations 联合国国际法委员会
ILF	International Leadership Foundation 国际领袖基金会
ILLIAC	Illinois Automatic Computer 伊利诺伊自动计算机
ILO	International Labour Organization 国际劳工组织
ILO	International Labor Office 国际劳工局
ils	illegal immigrants 非法移民
ILS	instrument landing system 仪表着陆系统
ILSI	International Life Sciences Institute 国际生命科学研究所
ILSP	The Institute for Language and Speech Processing 话语加工研究所
IM	instant messaging 即时通信
IM	ideal money 虚拟货币
IMA	Indian Medical Association 印度医学协会
IMAP	Internet Mail Access Protocol 互联网邮件访问协议
IMAX	Image Maximum 巨幕(影像系统)
IMBA	International Master of Business Administration 国际工商管理硕士
IMBO	in my biased opinion 依我带偏见的看法[网络用语]
IMC	integrated marketing communications 整合行销传播
IMCO	Inter-Government Maritime Consultative Organization 政府间海事协商组织[现改为:"国际海事组织"IMO]
IMD	International Institute for Management and Development 瑞士国际管理发展学院
IMD	institute of management and development 管理发展研究所
IMDB	The Internet Movie Database 互联网电影数据库
IMDG Code	International Maritime Dangerous Goods Code 国际海运危险品法规
IMEI	International Mobile Equipment Identifier 国际移动设备标识符
IMF	International Monetary Fund 国际货币基金组织
IMG	International Management Group 国际管理集团
IMHO	in my humble opinion 在我看来[网络用语]

181

IMI	International Management Institute 国际管理学院
IML	Integrated Memory Logic Limited 集成逻辑存储公司
IMLS	Institute of Medical Laboratory Sciences 医学实验室科学协会
I'mma	I'm going to 我将;我要[口语]
immig	immigration 外来移民/移居
IMO	in my opinion 在我看来[网络用语]
IMO	initial miner offerings 虚拟数字资产
IMO	International Maritime Organization 国际海事组织
IMO	International Mathematical Olympiad 国际数学奥林匹克竞赛;奥数
IMPACT	inventory management program and control technique 库存管理程序与控制技术
IMPM	international master in practicing management 国际实践管理硕士
IMQ	Instituto Italiano del Marchio di Qualita 意大利产品质量认证标志[意大利文]
IMQ	Instituto Italiano del Marchio di Qualita 意大利质量标志学会[意大利文]
IMR	infant mortality rate 婴儿死亡率
IMRT	intensity modulated conformal radiation therapy 强度调制适性放疗
IMS	information management system 信息管理系统
IMS	irritable male syndrome 男性易怒综合征
IMS	International Magic Society 国际魔术协会
IMS	International Magicians Society 国际魔术师协会
IMS	International Mythological Society 国际神话学协会
IMS	Information Management System 信息管理系统
IMSI	International Mobile Subscriber Identity 国际移动用户标识
IMSI	International Mobile Subscriber Identification Number 国际移动用户识别码
IMT	International Mobile Telecommunication 国际移动通信
IMT	International Military Tribunal 国际军事法庭
IMT	intelligence multi-functional terminal 智能多功能终端
IMTV	interactive multimedia television 交互式多媒体电视
IMU	International Mathematics Union 国际数学联盟
IMU	International Muslim Union 国际穆斯林联盟

I

IN	in fashion 时髦
In	indium 铟[第 49 号化学元素]
in	inch 英寸
InSight	Interior Exploration using Seismic Investigations, Geodesy and Heat Transport 洞察号[即:利用地震、大地测量和热流的火星内部结构探测器]
IN	internal node 内部节点
INA	Indonesia 印度尼西亚[亚洲国家]
inc	including; included 包括
Inc	incorporated 股份有限公司
INC	Indian National Congress 印度国家议会
ince	insurance 保险(费)
incl	including; included 包括
ind	independent 独立的
IND	India 印度[亚洲国家]
Ind	index 索引
Ind	index 指数
Ind	indicator 指示剂/指示器
INDPRK	In Democratic People's Republic of Korea 走进朝鲜
INE	Shanghai International Energy Exchange 上海国际能源中心
INF	Intermediate-Range Nuclear Forces Treaty《中导条约》
infl	inflammable 易燃的
INFOL	information-oriented language 面向信息的语言
ING	International Netherlands Group 荷兰国际集团
INJ	injector 喷油器
iNKT	internal Natural Kill T-cell 体内不变的自然杀伤 T 细胞
INMETRO	Instituto Nacional de Metrologia, Normalização e Qualidade Industrial 巴西国家计量、标准化和工业质量协会[葡萄牙文]
INN	Instituto Nacional de Normalizacion 智利国家标准局[西班牙文]
INR	international normalized ratio 国际标准化比值
INS	inertial navigation system 惯性导航系统
INS	iodine number and saponification number factor 碘值与皂化值因数
INS	Immigration and Naturalization Service 移民局

INS	Immigration and Naturalization Service, USA 美国移民归化局
INS	instagram 照片墙（一款社交应用）
INS	insulin 胰岛素
INSEE	Institut national de la statistique et des études économiques 全国统计与经济研究所[法文]
INSEP	Institut National du Sport et de l'Education Physique 法国国立体育运动学院[法文]
INSS	Institute for National Strategic Studies 国家战略研究所
INST	instruction 说明书
INSTC	International North-South Transportation Corridor 国际南北运输走廊
INSTEX	Instrument for Supporting Trade Exchanges 贸易往来支持工具
INSUL	insulator 隔热垫/减震垫
INT	intake 进气
int	interior 内部
INT	international 国际的
INTA	International Trademark Association 国际商标协会
Intel	Integrated Electronics（美国）英特尔芯片制造公司
Intel	intelligence 英特尔（微型电子计算机）
INTELSAT	International Telecommunications Satellite Organization 国际通信卫星组织
Internic	Internet Network Information Center 互联网网络信息中心
Interpol	International Criminal Police Organization 国际刑警组织
Intl CH	International Champion 国际永久冠军
InTT	insulin tolerance test 胰岛素耐量实验
inv	invention 发明
inv	investment 投资
IOA	Irish Organic Association 爱尔兰有机商品委员会
IOA	Irish Organic Association 爱尔兰有机认证标志
IOC	International Olympic Committee 国际奥林匹克运动委员会
IOC	Indian Oil Company 印度石油公司
IOD	Indian Ocean Dipole 印度洋偶极子

IODP	Integrated Ocean Drilling Program 综合大洋钻探计划
IODP	International Ocean Development Program 国际大洋发现计划
IOI	International Olympiad in Informatics 国际信息学奥林匹克竞赛
IOL	International Olympiad in Linguistics 国际语言学奥林匹克竞赛；奥语
IOM	Institute of Medicine （美国）医学研究所
IOM	International Organization for Migration 国际移民组织
IOPP	International Oil Pollution Protection 国际防止油污证书
IOS	input-output switch 输入输出开关
IOS	International Organization for Standardization 国际标准化组织
IOS	Internet operation system 因特网操作系统
iOS	iPhone Operation System 美国思科公司网络设备操作系统注册商标
IoT	Internet of Things 物联网
IOTF	International Obesity Task Force 国际肥胖专案小组
IOU	I owe you 借条/我欠你的
IP	inhalable particle 可吸入颗粒物
IP	insurance policy 保险单
IP	Internet Phone 互联网电话
IP	Internet Protocal 互联网协议
IP	inertia processional 当量惯量
IP	information processing 信息处理（程序）
IP	Institute of Petroleum 美国石油产品标志
IP	Institute of Petroleum 石油协会
IP	Institute of Physics 物理学会
IP	intellectual property 知识产权
IP	Interface Protocol 因特网协议
IPA	*International Pharmaceutical Abstracts*《国际药学文摘》
IPA	International Phonetic Alphabet 国际音标
IPA	International Publishers Association 国际出版商协会
IPAC	Institute for Policy Analysis of Conflict 冲突政策分析研究所
IPAM	intellectual property asset management 知识资产管理系统
IPATA	Independent Pet and Animal Transportation Association 宠物与动物运送机构

IPB	Institut Pertanian Bogor 茂物农学院[印尼文]
IPB	International Public Bads 国际公害品
IPC	International Paralympic Committee 国际残疾人奥林匹克委员会
IPC	International Patent Classification 国际专利分类法
IPCC	Intergovernmental Panel on Climate Change 联合国政府间气候变化专门委员会
IPCC	Independent Police Complaints Council 投诉警方独立监察委员会
IPD	integrated product development 集成产品开发
IPEN	International PoPs Elimination Network 国际清除持久性有机污染物网络
IPF	idiopathic pulmonary fibrosis 特发性肺纤维化
IPGP	International Physics Group of Paris 巴黎全球物理研究所
ipi	interior point intermodal 内部联运
IPL	Internet Public Library 虚拟公共图书馆
IPL	information processing language 信息处理语言
IPM	Instituto Politécnico de Macau 澳门理工学院[葡萄牙文]
IPMP	International Project Management Profession 国际项目管理专业资质认证
IPMT	integrated portfolio management team 集成组合管理团队
IPN	isopropyl nitrate 硝酸异丙酯
IPO	Initial Public Offering 首次公开发行股票
IPO	International Projects Office 国际规划局
iPod generation	Insecure, Pressured, Overtaxed and Debt-ridden generation 一代"朝不保夕、压力巨大、负担沉重、债台高筑"的人
IPP	information processing platform 信息处理平台
IPP	Internet platform provider 网络平台提供商
IPPC	International Plant Protection Convention 国际植物保护公约
IPR	intellectual property right 知识产权
IPRO	International Patent Research Office 国际专利研究处
IPS	inches per second 每秒英寸
iPS	induced pluripotent stem cells 诱导多功能干细胞
IPS	Industry Policy Studies 产业政策研究院

I

IPS	information processing system 信息处理系统	
IPS	impact-resistant polystyrene 抗冲击聚苯乙烯［塑料］	
IPS	Institute of Policy Studies 政策研究院	
IPS	Interim Payment System 期中支付系统	
IPSC	International Payment Service Company 国际支付服务公司	
IPSO	International Plan of Seas and Oceans 国际海洋计划	
IPT	integrated project team 集成产品开发团队	
IPT	International People's Tribunal 国际人民法庭	
IPTV	intelligent personal television 智能个人电视	
IPTV	Internet Protocol TV 百视通/大电视/网络电视	
IPV	inactivated polio vaccine 灭活的脊髓灰质炎疫苗	
IPV	Internet Protocol Version 互联网协议版本	
IQ	import quota 进口配额	
IQ	intelligence quotient 智商	
IQM	Industrial Quality Management 工业品质管理学	
IQSCS	International Quality Safety Control System 国际质量安全管理体系	
Ir	iridium 铱［第 77 号化学元素］	
IR	information retrieval 信息检索	
IR	Iran 伊朗［亚洲国家］	
IR	industrial robot 工业机器人	
IR	integrated resort 综合度假区	
IR	investor relations 投资者关系	
IRA	Individual Retirement Account（美国）个人退休账户	
IRA	intravenous renal arteriography 经静脉肾动脉造影术	
IRANOR	Instituto Español de Normalizacion 西班牙标准化协会［西班牙文］	
IRC	International Red Cross 国际红十字会	
IRC	Internet Relay Chat 互联网在线聊天	
IRC	International Rescue Committee 国际救援委员会	
IRCA	International Railway Congress Association 国际铁路协会	
IRCC	Immigration, Refugees and Citizenship, Canada 加拿大联邦移民、难民及公民部	
IRGC	Islamic Revolutionary Guard Corps 伊朗伊斯兰革命卫队	

IRI	International Republic Institute 国际共和研究所
IRI	insulin radioimmunoassay 胰岛素放射免疫测定
IRI	Ionosphere Research Instrument 高离层研究仪器
IRL	Ireland 爱尔兰［欧洲国家］
IRL	in real life 现实生活中［网络用语］
IRNA	Islamic Republic News Agency 伊斯兰共和国通讯社
IRO	International Refugee Organization 国际难民组织
IRQ	Iraq 伊拉克［亚洲国家］
IRR	Interest Rate Risk 利率风险
IRR	Internal Rate of Return 内部收益率/内含报酬率
irr	irregular 不规则的
IRS	information retrieval system 信息检索系统
IRS	intelligent room system 房间智能化系统
IRS	Indian Register of Shipping 印度船级社
IRS	Internal Revenue Service 国税局
IRSCI	Internal Revenue Service Criminal Investigation 国税局刑事调查处
IRTS	International Radio and Television Society 国际广播与电视协会
IRV	inspiratory reserve volume 补吸气量
IS	Interlinking System 相互间连接系统
Is	Island(s); Isle 岛
Is N	Isaac Newton 艾萨克·牛顿［英国物理学家］
ISA	International Seabed Authority 国际海底管理机构
ISA	individual savings account 个人储蓄账户
ISA	industry standard architecture 工业标准结构/工业标准体系结构
ISA	instruction set architecture 指令集架构
ISA	International Standards Association 国际标准协会
ISA	Industry Subversive Alliance 产业颠覆联盟
ISAB	International Safety Advice Bureau（美国）国际安全顾问委员会
ISACA	Information System Auditing and Control Association（国际）信息系统审计与控制协会
ISAF	International Security Assistant Force 国际安全援助部队
ISAPS	International Society of Aesthetic Plastic Surgery 国际美容整形外科学会

I

ISASL	International Standard Atmosphere Sea Level 海平面国际标准大气压	
ISBN	International Standard Book Number 国际标准书号	
ISC	China Internet Security Conference 中国互联网安全大会	
ISC	Indian subcontinent 印度次大陆	
ISC	insider stock compensation 内线股票补偿	
ISC	integrated supply chain 集合供应链	
ISC	International Supercomputing Conference 国际超级计算大会/世界超算大会	
ISC	International Supercomputing 国际高性能计算机	
ISC	Internet Security Committee 互联网安全大会	
ISC	Internet Society of China 中国互联网协会	
ISCCC	Information Security Certification Center of China 中国信息安全认证中心	
ISCO	International Standard Classfication Occupations 国际技术移民职业列表	
ISDA	International Swaps and Derivatives Association 国际交易与衍生品协会	
ISDB-T	Integrated Services Digital Broadcasting-Terrestrial Transmissions 综合业务数字广播-地面传输	
ISDN	integrated service digital network 综合业务数据网	
ISDS	Investor-State Dispute Settlement 投资人与国家的纷争解决条款	
ISDS	International Series Data System 国际丛书资料系统	
ISE	internal secret file 内部保密文件	
ISF	Importer Security Filing 进口安全申报	
ISF	International Softball Federation 国际垒球联合会	
ISFA	International Scientific Film Association 国际科学电影协会	
ISG	Information Service Group 信息服务组	
ISH	Information Super Highway 信息高速公路	
ISI	Institute for Scientific Information 科学情报研究所	
ISI	Inter-Symbol Interference 码间干扰	
ISI	Institute for Scientific Information 美国科学情报研究所	
ISI	Indian Standards Institution 印度标准学会	
ISI	Indian Standards Institution 印度产品质量认证标志	
ISIC	International Student Identity Card 国际学生证	

ISIN	International Securities Identification Number 国际证券识别编码
ISIT	Institut Supérieur d'Interprétation et de Traduction 巴黎跨文化管理与公关学院[法文]
ISL	Iceland 冰岛[欧洲国家]
ISM	Institute for Supply Management 供应管理协会
ISMA	International Securities Market Association 国际证券市场协会
ISMS	information security management system 信息安全管理体系
ISMWSF	International Stoke Mandeville Wheelchair Sports Federation 国际斯托克·曼德维尔轮椅运动联合会
ISO	International Standardization Organization 国际标准化组织
ISO	International Organization of Standardization 国际标准化组织
ISOD	International Sports Organization for the Disabled 国际伤残人体育组织
ISODE	ISO development environment 国际标准化组织开发环境
ISP	Internet services provider 互联网服务提供商
ISP	independent study program 独立选修
ISP	integral spiritual psychology 整合灵性心理学
ISPA	International Sleep Products Association 国际床上用品协会
ISPWP	The International Society of Professional Wedding Photographers 国际专业婚礼摄影师协会
ISR	Information Search Ranking 信息搜索排名
ISR	Intelligence, Surveillance, and Reconnaissance 情报、监视和侦察
ISR	Israel 以色列[亚洲国家]
ISRC	International Standard Recording Code 国际标准音像制品编码
ISRI	Institute of Scrap Recycling Industries 美国废品回收工业协会
ISS	International Space Station 国际空间站
ISS of BC	The Immigration Services Society of British Columbia 加拿大大不列颠哥伦比亚省移民服务协会
ISS	International Student Service 国际学生服务处
ISSCC	International Solid-State Circuits Conference 国际固态电路峰会
ISSM	Information System Service Management 信息系统服务管理
ISSN	International Standard Serial Number 国际标准连续出版物编号

I

ISTIC	Institute of Scientific and Technical Information of China 中国科学技术信息研究院
ISTP	Index to Scientific & Technical Proceedings《科技会议录索引》
ISU	International Skating Union 国际滑冰联盟
ISU	The International Salvage Union 国际打捞协会
ISV	independent software vendor 独立软件开发商
IT	Indian Institute of Technology 印度理工学院
IT	information technology 信息技术
IT	idle time 空闲时间
IT	international tender 国际招标
ITA	Information Technology Association 信息技术协会
ITA	International Touring Alliance 国际旅游联盟
ITA	Italy 意大利[欧洲国家]
ItaaS	information technology as a service 信息技术即服务
ITAR	International Traffic in Arms Regulation 国际军火交易条例
ITBP	Indo-Tibetan Border Police 印藏边境警察部队
ITC	International Trade Centre 国际贸易中心
ITC	International Trade Commission (美国)国际贸易委员会
ITC	Inland Transport Committee 内陆运输委员会
ITC	International Trade Commission 国际贸易委员会[英国]
ITER	International Thermonuclear Experimental Reactor 国际热核聚变实验堆(计划)
ITF	International Tennis Federation 国际网球联合会
ITF	International Taekwondo Federation 国际跆拳道联盟
ITF	International Trade Fair 国际贸易博览会
ITF	International Transport Federation 国际运输联盟
ITFCA	International Track and Field Coaches Association 国际田径教练联合会
ITIC	Information Technology Industry Council 信息技术产业委员会
ITIC	International Teacher Identity Card 国际教师证
ITIF	Information Technology & Innovation Foundation 信息技术与创新基金会
ITM	International Trade Commission 国际贸易委员会
ITN	Independent Television News (英国)独立电视新闻公司

ITO	input-transformation-output 输入—转换—输出
ITO	International Telecommunication Office 国际电信局
ITO	Internet technology officer 网络技术官
ITP	Internet technology provider 互联网技术及方案供应商
ITQI	International Taste & Quality Institute 国际风味暨品质评鉴所
ITR	Iranian Transaction Regulations 伊朗交易法规
ITS	information transmission system 信息传输系统
ITS	intelligent transport system 智能交通系统
ITT	inductance type transducer 电感式传感器
ITT	International Telephone and Telegraph Corporation 国际电报电话公司
ITT	iodine tolerance test 碘耐量试验
ITTF	International Table Tennis Federation 国际乒乓球联合会
ITTO	International Tropical Timber Organization 国际热带木材组织
ITU	Intensive Therapy Unit 重症病房
ITU	International Telecommunications Union 国际电信联盟
ITU	International Telecommunications Union 国际电信联盟标志
ITU-R	International Telecom Union-Radio 国际电信联盟无线部
ITU-R	International Telecom Union-Telecome 国际电信联盟通信部
ITV	industrial television 工业（用）电视
ITV	instructional television 教学电视
ITV	Independent Television 英国独立电视台
IU	Indiana University 美国印第安纳大学
IU	international unit 国际单位
IUAC	The International Union Against Cancer 国际抗癌联盟
IUB	International Union of Biochemistry 国际生物化学协会
IUCN	International Union for Conservation of Nature 国际自然保护联盟/世界自然保护联盟
IUCNNR	International Union for Conservation of Nature and Natural Resources 国际自然及自然资源保护协会
IUD	intrauterine device 避孕环
IUPA	International Union of Police Associations 国际警察协会
IUPAC	International Union of Pure and Applied Chemistry 国际理论和应用化

	学联合会
IUPAP	International Union of Pure and Applied Physics 国际理论和应用物理联合会
IUPR	Imagery Understanding and Pattern Recognition 图像理解和模式识别
IUPT	International Union of Public Transport 国际公共交通联会
IURC	International Committee of the Red Cross 国际红十字会
IUT	l'Institut universitaire de technologie 大学工艺研究所[法文]
IUUF	illegal, unreported, uncontrolled fishing 非法、不报告、不管制捕捞
IUVM	International Union of Virtual Media 国际虚拟媒体联盟
IVF	in vitro fertilization 体外受精
IVF	International Volleyball Federation 国际排球联合会
IVHS	intelligent vehicle highway system 智能车路系统
IVOD	interactive video on demand 交互式视频点播
IVQ	International Vocational Qualification 国际职业资格证书
IVR	interactive voice response 交互式语音应答
IWAS	International Wheelchair and Amputation Sports Federation 国际轮椅和截肢运动联合会
IWBF	International Women's Boxing Federation 国际女子拳击联合会
IWC	International Watch Company 万国手表[瑞士]
IWC	International Whaling Commission 国际捕鲸委员会
IWF	International Weightlifting Federation 国际举重联合会
IWS	International Wool Secretariat 国际羊毛秘书处
IWYF	International World Youth Friendship 国际世界青年友谊会
IXDC	International Experience Design Committee 国际体验设计协会
IYF	International Youth Federation 国际青年联盟
IYF	International Youth Fellowship 国际青年奖学金
IZA	International Zinc Association 国际锌协会

J	journal 期刊文章[参考文献标示字母]
J/OL	journal on line 网上期刊[电子文献标示略语]
JA	Jockey Association 美国赛马协会
JA	Junior Achievement 国际青年成就组织
JAC	Jianghuai Automobile Company 江淮汽车[中国合肥]
JACC	Journal of the American College of Cardiology 美国心脏病学会杂志
JAIC	joint artificial intelligence center 联合人工智能中心
JAKIM	Jabatan Kemajuan Islam Malaysia 马来西亚伊斯兰教发展署[马来文]
JAL	Japan Airlines 日本航空公司
JAM	Jamaica 牙买加[北美洲国家]
JAMA	Journal of the American Medical Association 美国医药协会杂志
Jan	January 1 月
JAN	Japanese Article Number 日本货物编码
JAPATIC	Japan Patent Information Center 日本特许情报中心
JARI	Japan Automobile Research Institute 日本汽车研究所
JARI	Jiangsu Automation Research Institute 江苏自动化研究所
JARI-USV	Jiangsu Automation Research Institute 战斗型多用无人艇[源于江苏自动化研究所]
JAS	Japanese Agricultural Standard 日本农林标准
JAS	Japanese Agricultural Standard 日本有机产品、食品质量认证标志
JBC	Japan Broadcasting Corporation 日本广播公司
JBIC	Japanese Bank of International Co-operation 日本国际协力银行
JBL	James Bullough Lansing 美国詹姆斯·布洛·兰辛公司[以工程师名字命名]
JBL	*Journal of Business Law*《法学杂志》[英国]
JBSA	Joint Base San Antonio 圣安东尼奥联合基地

J

JCB	Japan Credit Bureau Card 日财卡/吉士美卡
JCB	Joseph Cyril Bamford 杰西博挖掘装载机
JCCC	Joint Committee on Contemporary China 国会现代中国问题联合委员会[美国]
JCEA	Japan China Economic Association 日中经济协会
JCL	Japanese Confederation of Labor 全日本劳动总同盟
JCN	justice communications network 司法通信网
JCN	justice crisis network 司法危机网
JCR	Journal Citation Report 期刊引用报告
JD	Jingdong 京东[汉语拼音缩略语]
JDAM	joint direct attack munition 联合直接攻击弹药
JDI	Japan Display Inc 日本显示公司
JDI	Juvenile Delinquency Index 未成年人犯罪指数
JEA	Japan Education Association 日本教育协会
JEDEC	Joint Electron Device Engineering Council 电子工程设计发展联合会/电子器件工程联合委员会
JEDI	Joint Enterprise DoDIIS Infrastructure 企业防务联合基础设施
JERC	Japan Economic Research Center 日本经济研究中心
JERI	Japan Economic Research Institute 日本经济研究所
JET	Joint European Torus 欧洲共同体联合聚变中心
JETDS	joint electronics type designation system 联合电子系统型号标志系统
JETRO	Japan Extention Trade Organization 日本贸易振兴机构
JF	Joint Fighter 枭龙[中巴联合生产的战斗机]
JGE	just good enough 够好就行
JGR	*Journal of Geophysical Research*《地球物理研究杂志》[美国]
JGU	Japanese Geomorphological Union 日本地貌联盟
JHU	Johns Hopkins University 约翰·霍普金斯大学
JIB	Japan International Bank 日本国际银行
JICA	Japanese International Co-op Agency 日本国际合作署
JINR	Joint Institute for Nuclear Research 俄罗斯杜布纳联合核研究所
JIPO	Jordan Investment Promotion Office 约旦投资促进局
JIS	Japanese Industrial Standards 日本工业标准

JIS	Japanese Industrial Standards 日本矿产品、工业品质量认证标志
JISC	Joint Information Systems Committee 联合信息系统委员会
JISC	Japanese Industrial Standard Committee 日本工业标准委员会
JIT	just-in-time 准时化
JIT	joint investigation team 联合调查小组
JITC	Joint International Trade Center 联合国际贸易中心
JITF	Japanese International Trade Fair 日本国际商品展览会
JITPA	Japan International Trade Promotion Association 日本国际贸易促进协会
JKC	Japanese Kennel Club 日本犬舍俱乐部/日本狗舍俱乐部
JL	Johnson Line 约翰逊航线
JL	just looking 只是看看（并非真正购物）
JLPT	Japanese Language Proficiency Test 日语能力测试
JLS	Jack the Lad Swing 摇摆不定男生[英国男孩团体]
JLS	Jean-Louis Scherrer 让·路易·雪莱服饰
JLTV	joint light tactical vehicle 联合轻型战术车辆
JN	Japan Navy 日本海军
JNCC	Japan's National Cancer Centre 日本国家癌症中心
JNJ	Johnson and Johnson 强生医药公司
Jnr	junior 年少者
JOC	*Journal of Commerce*《商业日报》[英国;美国]
JOCV	Japan Overseas Cooperation Volunteer 日本海外协力事业团
JOR	Jordan 约旦[亚洲国家]
JP	*Japanese Pharmacopoeia*《日本药典》
JP(E)G	joint photographic experts group 联合图像专家组[一种图像压缩标准]
JPAC	Joint POW［Prisoner of War］/MIA［Missing in action］Accounting Command 美国国防部战俘及战斗失踪人员联合调查司令部
JPEG	joint photographic experts group 联合图像专家组规范
JPL	Jet Propulsion Laboratory 喷气推进实验室
JPM	JP Morgan Chase Bank, New York 摩根大通银行
JPN	Japan 日本[亚洲国家]
JPO	junior professional officer 青年专业人员
JPY	Japanese Yen 日元[货币]

K

Jr	junior 年少者	
JR	Japanese Railway 日本铁路(公司)	
JRC	Japan Red Cross 日本红十字会	
JSA	Joint Security Area 联合警备区	
JSC	Japan Ship Centre 日本航运中心	
JSC	Jiuquan Space Center 酒泉宇航中心	
JSX	Jakarta Stock Index 雅加达证券指数	
JSYK	just so you know 让你知道一下［网络用语］	
JTBC	Joongang Tongyang Broadcasting Company 中央东洋广播公司	
JTC	Joint Technical Committee 联合技术委员会	
JTC	Junior Team Canada 加拿大青少年团体	
JTC	Junior Training Center 青少年训练中心	
JTF	Joint Task Force 联合特遣队	
JU	Jilin University 吉林大学	
Jul	July 7月	
Jun	June 6月	
JUSE	Japanese Union of Scientists and Engineers 日本科学家和工程师联合会	
JV	joint venture 合资经营/合资企业	
JVC	Japan Victor Company 日本胜利公司	
JWG	Joint Working Group 联合工作组	
JYP	Jin Young Park Entertainment 韩国JYP娱乐公司	

K	Karat Gold 克金,黄金与其他金属熔合而成的合金［纯金为24K(即100％含金量)］
K	Kelvin 开(尔文)［法定温度计量单位］
K	ketamine 氯胺酮［一种具有镇痛作用的静脉全麻药物;一种毒品］

K	killer cell	免疫细胞
K of S	King of Spain	西班牙国王
K	kalium	钾[第19号化学元素][拉丁文]
K	kickboxing	踢拳击
K	kilo	千(＝1000)
K	Karakoram	喀喇昆仑山
K	Korean Bureau of Standards	韩国产品质量认证标志
K	kungfu	功夫
K	potassium	钾[第19号化学元素]
K-1	Karate-1	日本国内最有影响的搏击比赛
K-12	kindergarten to 12th grade	中小学及学前教育的
K9	canine	狗
KAAV	Korea armoured amphibious vehicle	韩国两栖装甲车
KAB	korrektiruemaia aviachionnaia bomba	校正(航空)炸弹[俄文]
KADIZ	Korean Air Defense Identification Zone	韩国防空识别区
KAS	Knowledge Assessing System	学科测评系统
KAS	Knowledge Acquisition System	知识获取系统
KASDAQ	Korean Association of Security Dealers Automated Quotations	科斯达克[韩国创业板]
KATI	Korean Association of Translation and Interpretation	韩国口笔译协会
KAZ	Kazakhstan	哈萨克斯坦[亚洲国家]
kb	kilobit	千比特
KB	kilobytes	千字节[计算机存储单位][另参GB]
KBBF	$KBe_2BO_3F_2$	氟代硼铍酸钾/非线性光学晶体
KBE	Knight Commander of the Order of the British Empire	英国骑士官勋章[男]/爵级司令勋位
kbit	kilobit	千比特
kbps	kilobits per second	千位每秒/千比特/秒[数据传输速率]
kBps	kilobytes per second	千字节/秒[数据传输速率]
KBS	Kenya Bureau of Standards	肯尼亚标准局[现称KEBS]
KBS	Korean Broadcasting System	韩国电视台[旧称]
KBS	Korean Bureau of Standards	韩国标准局

K

KBS	Korean Bureau of Standards 韩国产品质量认证标志
KC	Kennel Club 狗舍俱乐部[英国]
KC	King's Counsel（英国）皇家律师
KCA	Key Certification Authority 密钥认证机构
KCC	Kennedy Cultural Center 美国肯尼迪文化中心
KCI	Korea Composite Index 韩国综合指数
KCIC	Kereta Cepat Indonesia China 中国和印尼的合资公司
KCNA	Korean Central News Agency [N. K.] 朝鲜中央通讯社
KDI	Korea Development Institute 韩国开发研究院
KEBS	Kenya Bureau of Standards 肯尼亚标准局
KEBS	Kenya Bureau of Standards 肯尼亚产品质量认证标志[旧称：KBS]
KEBS	Korean Broadcasting System 韩国电视台[现称]
KEKS	knowledge engineering and knowledge science 知识工程与知识科学
KEMA	N. V. tot Keuring van Electrotechnische Materiale 荷兰电工材料协会[荷兰文]
KEMA	N. V. tot Keuring van Electrotechnische Materiale 荷兰电工产品质量认证标志[荷兰文]
KEN	Kenya 肯尼亚[非洲国家]
Kengine	knowledge engine 知识引擎
KET	ketone 尿酮体
KET	β-ketobutyric acid β-丁酮酸
KETI	Korea Electrical Testing Institute 韩国电器试验研究所
KFC	Kentucky Fried Chicken 肯德基[炸鸡快餐]
KFDA	Korean Food and Drug Administration 韩国产品质量认证标志
KFDA	Korean Food and Drug Association 韩国食品药品监督管理局
KFKR	Kim Fook Korean Restaurant 金福饭店
K-Food	Korea-Food 韩国食品
KFOR	Kosovo Peacekeeping Force 驻科索沃国际安全部队
KfW	Kreditanstalt für Wiederaufbau 复兴信贷银行[德文]
KG	Kommanditgesellschaft 无限、有限股份两合公司[德文]
kg/cm²	kilogram/square centimeter 千克/平方厘米
KGL	KPL G-League 王者荣耀职业发展联赛

kgs	kilogram(s) 千克
KGZ	Kyrgyzstan [或 Kirghizstan] 吉尔吉斯斯坦[亚洲国家]
KH-11	Key Hole-11 "锁眼"-11 侦察卫星
KHZ	kilohertz 千赫[法定频率计量单位]
KI	Karolinska Institute 瑞典卡罗琳斯卡学院
KI	potassium iodide 碘化钾
Ki67	proliferating cell-associated unclear antigen 增殖细胞相关抗原
KIA	killed in action 作战阵亡人士
KiB	Kibibyte 千字节
kidult	kid adult 老小孩
KIFV	Korean infantry vehicle 韩国步兵战车
KIM	knowledge and innovation management 知识创新管理
kinda	kind of 有点儿[口语]
KIPO	Korean Intellectual Property Office 韩国知识产权局
Kiron	Chiron 德国非政府组织[德文]
KISS	keep it simple, stupid 最简/单纯
KIST	Korea Institute of Science and Technology 韩国科学技术研究院
KISTI	Korea Institute of Science and Technology Information 韩国科学技术情报研究院
KIV	keep it view 注意事态变化
KJ	kilojoule 千焦耳[功的单位]
KK	Kabushiki Kaisha 股份有限公司[日文]
KKH	Karakorum Highway 喀喇昆仑公路
KKR	Kohlberg Kravis Roberts & Co. L. P. KKR集团
KLBD	Kashrut Division of the London Beth Din 伦敦贝斯丁的犹太教饮食分支机构
KLIC	key letters in context 上下文中的关键字母
KLM	Koninkijke Luchtvaart Maatschappij 皇家荷兰航空公司[荷兰文]
KLSE	Kuala Lumpur Stock Exchange 吉隆坡证券交易所
KM	kilometer 千米 [长度单位]
KM	knowledge management 知识管理
km/h	kilometer/hour 千米/小时

KMC	Knowledge Management Center 中国知识管理中心
KMT	Kuomintang 国民党
Know-bot	knowledge robot 知识机器人
knw	know 知道
KO	knock out（拳击）击倒
KOL	key opinion leader 关键意见领袖（微博上有话语权的人或微博红人大号）/网络名人
KOL	Kings of Leon 狮王
KONICA	Konishiroku＋camera 柯尼卡相机（公司名＋camera）
KOR	Korea(R.O) 韩国［亚洲国家］
Kosher	Kosher Certificate 洁食认证/犹太认证
KOZA	Kooza 藏在盒子里的宝藏
KP	kitchen police 帮厨兵
KP	key point 要点
Kpa	kilopascal 千帕斯卡［压强单位］
kph	kilometres per hour 千米每小时
KPI	Key Performance Indicator 关键绩效指标
KPL	King Professional League 王者荣耀职业联赛
KPO	key punch operator 键控穿孔操作员
K-POP	Korea-Pop 韩国流行音乐
KPT	Korean Proficiency Test 韩国语能力测试
KPTT	kaolin partial thromboplastin time 高岭土部分凝血活酶时间
KPU	Kwantlen Polytechnic University 加拿大昆特兰理工大学
Kr	krypton 氪［第36号化学元素］
KR	Korean Register of Shipping 韩国船级社
KRC	Kawasaki Rail Car 日本川崎重工
KRKPL	Korea King Pro League 王者荣耀韩国职业联赛
KSA	Saudi Arabia 沙特阿拉伯［亚洲国家］
KSA	Korea Standards Association 韩国标准协会
KSE	Korea Stock Exchange 韩国证券交易所
KSEW	Karachi Shipyard & Engineering Works 卡拉奇造船及机械制造厂
KSK	ethyl iodoacetate 催泪瓦斯［乙烷基三碘乙酸］

KSS	Korabelny Snaryad "Strela" 舰载型 Shchuka 导弹[俄文]
KT	kiloton(s) 千吨(相当于千吨 TNT 的爆炸力)
KT	Korea Telecom 韩国通信
KTCT	Kitchen Table Charities Trust 餐桌慈善信任基金
KTF	Kauai Test Facility 考爱岛导弹试验靶场
KTH	Kungliga Tekniska Hogskolan[英文:Royal Institute of Technology] 瑞典皇家理工学院[瑞典文]
KTO	Korean Tourism Organization 韩国旅游发展局
KTTC	K Tatal Tri-state Coverage K 全三态覆盖
KTV	Karaok TV 卡拉 OK 包房
KUW	Kuwait 科威特[亚洲国家]
KVA	Korean Veterans Association 朝鲜退伍军人协会
KVS	kernel video sharing 核心视频共享
kW	kilowatt 千瓦[功率单位]
KW	Korean War 朝鲜战争
kW·h	kilowatt hour 千瓦时
KWIC	key word in context 上下文内关键词
KWSC	Karachi Water and Sewerage Commission 卡拉奇给水与排污委员会
Kybo	keep your bowels open 保持健康
KYC	knowing your consumer 认识你的客户
KZ	Konzentrationslager 集中营[德文]

L	Landwind 陆风汽车[中国南昌]
L	liability 负债
L	Luft 空气[德文]
L	liter 升[容量与体积单位]
L	latitude 纬度

L

L	LEXUS 日本雷克萨斯汽车
L&W	living and well 某人健在
L(O)C	Library of Congress 美国国会图书馆
La	lanthanum 镧［第 57 号化学元素］
LA	lactic acid 血清乳酸
LA	law agent 法律代理人
LA	lightning arrester 避雷针
LAA	lymphadenoma associated antigen 淋巴瘤相关抗原
lab	low-alcohol beer 低度酒精啤酒
Lab	Labour 工党
LAB	laboratory 实验室
LAC	line of actual control 实际控制线
LaC	lactose 乳糖
LacZ	β-galactosidase gene β-半乳糖苷酶基因
LAE	leadership ability evaluation 领导能力评价
LAFTA	Latin American Free Trade Association 拉丁美洲自由贸易联盟
LAK	lymphokine activated killer cell 淋巴因子激活的杀伤细胞
Lamb	Lamborghini 兰博基尼汽车［意大利文］
LAMOST	Large Sky Area Multi-Object Fiber Spectroscopy Telescope 大天区面积多目标光纤光谱天文望远镜
LAN	local area network 局域网络
LAO	Laos 老挝［亚洲国家］
LAP	leukocyte alkaline phosphatase 白细胞碱性磷酸酶
LAP	London Airport 英国伦敦机场
LAPB	line access protocol balanced 链路访问协议平衡
LARC	Livermore Automatic Research Computer 利弗莫尔自动研究计算机
LAS	League of Arab States 阿拉伯国家联盟
LASER	light amplification by the stimulated emission of radiation 激光
LAT	Latvia 拉脱维亚［欧洲国家］
LAT	Language Ability Test 语言能力综合测评
LAT	living apart together 分开同居者
LAV	lavatory 洗手间

LB	life boat 救生船
LB	light blue 浅蓝色
LB	Lebanon 黎巴嫩[亚洲国家]
lBA	International Basketball Association 国际篮球协会
LBA	Libya 利比亚[非洲国家]
LBDA	Language Big Data Alliance 语言大数据联盟
LBO	leveraged buy out 融资收购
LBO	LiB305 [Lithium Triborate crystal] 三硼酸锂晶体
LBR	Liberia 利比里亚[非洲国家]
lbs	librae 磅[拉丁文]
LBS	location based services 定位系统
lbw	leg before wicker 腿碰球[极球运动]
lc	loco citato 引文中[拉丁文]
LC	Letter of Credit 信用证
LC	lower case 小写字体
LC50	median lethal concentration 半数致死浓度
LCA	low cost airline 廉价航空公司
LCA	large corporation account 大公司客户
LCAC	landing craft, air cushion 气垫登陆艇
LCAT	lecithin-cholesterol acyltransferase 卵磷脂-胆固醇酰基转移酶
LCC	low cost carrier 廉价航空
LCC	Life Cycle Cost 全生命周期成本
LCCI	London Chamber of Commerce and Industry 伦敦工商会所
LCCIEB	London Chamber of Commerce and Industry Exam Board 伦敦工商会所考试局
LCD	lowest common denominator 最小公分母
LCD	liquid crystal diode 液晶二极管
LCD	laser compact disc 激光视听盘
LCD	Ley de Competencia Desleal 不正当竞争法[西班牙文]
LCD	liquid crystal display 液晶显示（器）
LCL	less than car load 零担货物装载/拼箱/少于整箱装载
LCM	landing craft medium 中型登陆艇

L

LCM	laser-captured microdissection 激光捕获显微切割
LCM	least common multiple 最小公倍数
LCM	liquid crystal module 液晶模块
LCP	link control protocol 链路控制协议
LCP	liquid crystal polymer 液晶聚合物[塑料]
LCS	littoral combat ship 濒海战斗舰
LCS	located communications system 定位通信系统
LCSD	Leisure and Cultural Services Department 香港康乐及文化事务署
LCT	latest closing time 最迟停止营业时间
LCT	latest completing time 最迟完成时间
LCU	landing craft, utility 通用登陆艇
LCU	large close-up 大型特写镜头
LCU	length of the cervix uteri 子宫颈长度
LCV	light commercial vehicle 轻型商务用车
LCVP	landing craft, vehicle, personnel 车辆及人员登陆艇
LCVR	liquid crystal variable retarder 液晶可变延迟器
LD	Lada 拉达汽车[俄国]
LD	learning disorder 学习障碍
LD	laser disc 激光视盘
LD	liquid display 液晶显示器
Lda	Sociedade Industrial de Lacticinios de Angola, Lda 安哥拉乳业有限公司[葡萄牙文]
LDC	least developed country 最不发达国家
LDC	less developed country 欠发达国家
LDG	landing 登陆/着陆
LDG	lodge 小旅馆
LDH	lactate dehydrogenase 乳酸脱氢酶
LDL	low density lipoprotein 低密度脂蛋白
LDL/HDL	low density lipoprotein/high density lipoprotein 低密高密比
LDL-C(h)	low-density lipoprotein cholesterol 低密度脂蛋白胆固醇
LDMOS	laterally diffused metal oxide semiconductor 横向扩散金属氧化物半导体
LDOCE	*Longman Dictionary of Contemporary English*《朗文当代英语辞典》

LDP	lane departure prevention automotive 车道偏离修正系统
LDPC	low density parity check code 低密度奇偶校验码
LDPE	low density polyethylene 低密度聚乙烯［塑料］
LDR	low-dynamic range 低动态范围（图像）
LDs	learning disabilities 无学习能力
LDTEL	long distance telephone 长途电话
LE	lead engineer 首席工程师
LE	labour exchange 职业介绍所
LE	latent energy 潜能
LE	law efficiency 法律效率
LE	less or equal 小于或等于
LE	lupus erythematosus 红斑狼疮
LEC	lupus erythematosus cell 红斑狼疮细胞
LED	light emitting diode 发光二极管
LEED	Leadership in Energy and Environmental Design 能源与环境设计认证
legit	legitimate 合法
LEGO	leg godt 乐高玩具［丹麦文：意为"好好玩"］
LEH	Lehman Brothers Holdings Inc 雷曼兄弟公司
LEI	life expectancy index 预期寿命指数
LeM	*Le Monde*［英文：*The World*］法国《世界报》［法文］
Lemme	let me 让我［口语］
LEMOA	Logistics Exchange Memorandum of Agreement《后勤交换协议备忘录》
LEMV	long-endurance multiplex vessel 长航时多情报飞行器
LEP	limited English proficiency 英语程度不足
LEP	large electron positron collider 大型正负电子对撞机
LEP	lowest effective power 最低有效功率
LEQ	less than or equal 小于或等于
LERU	League of European Research Universities 欧洲研究型大学联盟
LES	Lesotho 莱索托［非洲国家］
LEU	leukocyte 白细胞
LEU	leucocyte 尿白细胞

L

LEV	low emission vehicle 低排放汽车/低污染汽车
LF	low fat 低脂肪
LFD	low fat diet 低脂肪饮食
LFW	Labled Faces in the Wild 人脸数据库
LG	life is good 乐喜金星［由 Lucky Goldstar 衍生成］
LG	landing gear 飞机起落架
LG	light green 浅绿色
LG	Lucky Goldstars 韩国 LG 集团（直译：喜乐金星）
LGBT	large gear box treatment 大型减速处理器
LGBT	lesbian, gay, bisexual and transgender 同性恋、双性恋及变性者
LGBTQ	lesbian, gay, bisexual, transgender, queer 性少数群体
LGRs	local government reports 地方政府报告
LGT	liquid gas tank 液化气储罐
lh	left hand 左手
LH	luteinizing hormone 促黄体生成激素
LHC	Large Hadron Collider 大型强子对撞机
Li	lithium 锂［第 3 号化学元素］
Li	lengthening or wheelbase lengthening 长款或轴距加长
LI	life insurance 人寿保险
LIB	liberation 解放
LIB	library 程序库/文件库
LIB	library 图书馆
LIBOR	London Inter Bank Offered Rate 伦敦银行间拆放利率
lic	licence 特许（证）
LIE	Liechtenstein 列支敦士登［欧洲国家］
Lieut	lieutenant 陆军中尉，海空军上尉
LIF	leukocyte inhibitory factor 白细胞抑制因子
LIF	leukemia-inhibitory factor 白血病抑制因子
Lifi	Light Fidelity 可见光通信
LIGO	Laser Interferometer Gravitational-Wave Observatory 激光干涉引力波天文台

LII	Librarian's Internet Index 图书馆因特网索引
LIN	linear 线性的
LINC	Language Instruction for Newcomers in Canada 加拿大新移民的语言教学
LINUS	logical inquiry and update system 逻辑询问和更新系统
LINX	London Internet Exchange 伦敦国际互联网交换中心
LIP	life insurance policy 人寿保险单
LIP	lipase 血清脂肪酶
LIQ	liquor 烈性酒
LISA	Library and Information Science Abstracts 图书馆学情报学文摘
LISP	list processing 表处理语言
Lit	lire italiane 意大利里拉[货币]
LITASTOR	light tapping storage 光分支存储器
LITEX	Light Technology Corp 莱泰克灯泡
LITPOLUKRBRIG	Lithuania, Poland, Ukraine Brigade 立陶宛、波兰、乌克兰联合作战旅
ll	line 行[复数]
LL	land line 地面通信线/地面运输线
LLAP	live long and prosper 健康长寿,财源滚滚
LLD	Legum Doctor 法学博士[拉丁文]
LLDPE	linear low density polyethylene 线型低密度聚乙烯[塑料]
LLM	Legum Magister 法律硕士[拉丁文]
LLNL	Laurence Livemore National Laboratory 劳伦斯·利弗莫尔国家实验室
lm	lumen 流(明)[法定光通量计量单位]
LM	liberation movement 解放运动
LM	Lincoln Memorial 美国林肯纪念馆
LM5SLV	Long March 5 Series Launch Vehicle 冰箭
LM5SLV	Long March 5 Series Launch Vehicle 大火箭
LM5SLV	Long March 5 Series Launch Vehicle 长征五号系列运输火箭
LMDPE	linear medium density polyethylene 线型中密度聚乙烯[塑料]
LME	London Metal Exchange 伦敦金属交易所

L

LMG	liquefied methane gas 液化沼气
LMS	learning management system 学习管理系统
LN	Line 韩国 Line 公司的股票代码
LN	the League of Nation 国际联盟
LNA	Libyan National Army 利比亚国民军
LNG	liquefied natural gas 液化天然气
Lo	low 低档
LO	lubricating oil 润滑油
LOA	list of agreement 协议书
LOA	leave of absence 休假
LOC	line of control 实际控制线
LOD	limit of detection 淘汰检出限
LOD	*Little Oxford Dictionary*《牛津小词典》[英国]
LOF	Listed Open-ended Fund 上市型开放式基金
LOH	loss of heterozygosity 杂合性丢失
LOL	laugh-out-loud 非常滑稽的
LOL	*League of Legends*《英雄联盟》
LOL	lots of laugh 大笑
LONG	longitude 经度
LOP	list of parts 零件目录
LOQ	limit of quantity 定量下限
LOT	large orbiting telescope 大型轨道望远镜
LOT	laser optical transmission 激光传输
LP	Limited Partnership 有限合伙公司
LP	Labour Party 英国工党
LP	Liberal Party 英国自由党
LP	limited partner 有限合作人
LP	long-playing 密纹唱片
LP	liquefied petroleum 液化石油
LP(a)	lipoprotein 血清脂蛋白(a)
LPAT	latex particle agglutination test 乳胶颗粒凝集试验
LPD	amphibious transport dock 两栖作战船坞登陆舰[代字]

LPG	liquefied petroleum gas 液化石油气
LPL	League of Legends Pro League 英雄联盟职业联赛
LPN	licensed practical nurse 注册护士
LPO	lipid peroxides 过氧化脂/血清过氧化脂质
LPO	London Philharmonic Orchestra 伦敦爱乐乐团
LPPOM	Lembaga Pengkajian Pagan, Obat-obatan dan Kosmetika 食品、药品和化妆品研究协会[印尼文]
LPR	loan price interest 贷款市场报价利率
LPR	loan prime rate 贷款基础利率/贷款市场报价利率
LPS	lipase 血清脂肪酶
LP-X	lipoprotein-X 脂蛋白 X
Lr	lawrencium 铹[第 103 号化学元素]
LR	living room 起居室
LR	Lloyds Register of Shipping 英国劳氏船级社
LRASM	long-range antiship missile 远程反舰导弹
LRH	luteinizing hormone-releasing hormone 促黄体生成激素释放激素
LRHW	long-range hypersonic 远程高超音速武器
LRO	Lunar Reconnaissance Orbiter 月球勘测轨道器
LRT	light rapid transit 轻轨
LRT	light rail train 轻轨列车
LRUH	low diversity, related diversity, unrelated diversity, high diversity 低度多元化,相关多元化,不相关多元化,高度多元化
LS	long shot 远景
LS	loudspeaker 扩音器
LSCM	laser scanning confocal microscope 激光扫描共聚焦显微镜
LSD	lysergic acid diethylamide 麦角酰二乙胺[一种迷幻药]
LSE	local search engine 本地搜索引擎
LSE	London School of Economics and Political Science 伦敦(政治)经济学院
LSE	London Stock Exchange 伦敦股票交易所
LSI	large scale integration 大规模集成电路
LSP	loans support plan 贷款支持计划
LT	large tug 大型拖船

LT	low temperature 低温
Ltd	limited 有限责任公司
LTE	Long Term Evolution 长期演进技术(2010年12月之后被正式称为4G)
LTE	line terminator equipment 线路终端设备
LTO	linear tape-open 开放线性磁带
LTR	long term reserve 长期储备
LTS	long term store 长期储存
LTT	lymphocyte transformation test 淋巴细胞转化试验
LTU	Lithuania 立陶宛[欧洲国家]
Lu	lutetium 镥[第71号化学元素]
LU	Lingnan University 岭南学院
lub	lubrication 润滑剂
LUI	language user interface 语音用户界面
LUPA	Leadership of Open Source University Promotion 全国开放源代码高校推进联盟
LUR	London Underground Railway 伦敦地下铁道[英国]
Lux	luxury; luxurious 豪华/奢侈
LUX	Luxembourg 卢森堡[欧洲国家]
LUX	luxury cars 豪华汽车
LV	laser vision 激光视盘
LV	Louis Vuitton 路易威登皮具
Lv	Livermorium 鿫[第116号化学元素]
LVCP	Livemore Valley Charter Preparatory 美国利弗莫尔(峡谷)中学
LVG	love game 恋爱养成游戏
LVMH	Louis Vuitton Moët Hennessy 路易·威登集团[法文]
LVN	licensed vocational nurse 持证职业护士
LW	long wave 长波
LWM	low water mark 低水位标志
LWP	leave with pay 带薪休假
LWP	light water processor 轻量级水净化器
Lx	lux 勒(克斯)[法定光照度计量单位]
LYM	lymphocyte 淋巴细胞
Lys	lysosome 溶酶体

M

M	Mach number 马赫数[指某速度相对音速的倍数]
M	man 男人
M	May 5 月
M	mega 兆，十进倍数单位词头名称[其表示的因数为 106]
M	metre 米[长度单位]
M	Machiavellian Politics 美国权力操弄的马基雅维利政治
M	Mazda 日本马自达汽车
M	monocyte 单核白细胞
M	monograph 专著[参考文献标示字母]
M	monsieur 先生[法文]
M	morality and political meritocracy 中国的道德与贤能政治
M	Mosler 美国莫斯勒汽车
M&A	mergers and acquisitions 并购/兼并收购
M&M	Forrest Mars and Bruce Murries 玛氏朱古力豆
M&S	Marks and Spencer 玛莎公司
M. B. E	Member of the Order of the British Empire 大英帝国员佐勋位
m. o.	mail order 邮购
M. S. Ed	Master of Science in Education 教育理学硕士
M/C	master cylinder 主缸
M/CD	monograph/compact disc 光盘图书[电子文献标示略语]
M/T	mail transfer 信汇
M/T	metric ton 公吨
M/V	motor vessel 机动船
M1A1	US main battle tank 美国主战坦克[代字]
M2	Broad Money 广义货币(供应量)
M24	American Military Sniper Rifle 美国 M24 狙击步枪

M

MAA	Mathematical Association of America 美国数学协会
MAA	market allowance application 上市许可申请
MAB	Man and Biosphere 人与生物圈
MAC	multiaccess computer 多存取计算机
MAC	multiple address code 多地址代码
MAC	make-up art cosmetics 彩妆艺术化妆品
MAC	Make-up Art Cosmetics 魅可[彩妆艺术化妆品]
MAcc	master of accountancy 会计学硕士
MACD	moving average convergence and divergence 指数平滑移动平均线
MACOS	Macintosh Operating System 麦金托希操作系统
MACR	missing aircraft report 失事飞机报告
MAD	Madagascar 马达加斯加[非洲国家]
MAD	material analysis data 材料分析资料
MADR	minimum adult daily requirement 成人最低日需求量
MAE	mean absolute error 平均绝对误差
MAGIC	machine for automatic graphics interface to a computer 计算机自动图形接口机
MagR	magnetoreceptor 磁感应蛋白
mAh	milli-Ampere hour 毫安时
MAH	Marketing Authorization Holder 药品上市许可持有人制度
MAHLI	Mars Hand Lens Imager 火星手持透镜成像仪
MAI	Multilateral Agreement of Investment 多边投资协议
MAIC	most advantageously involved country 最受益国家
Maj	major 少校
MAL	methyl alcohol 甲醇
Man Utd	Manchester United Football Club 曼彻斯特联合足球俱乐部
Man	mannose 甘露糖
MAN	Maschinen fabrica Augsburg Nürnberg 曼卡车[原意:奥格斯堡-纽伦堡机械制造公司][德文]
MAN	Maschinenfabrik Augsburg Nürnberg 奥格斯堡-纽伦堡机械工厂[德文]
MANA	manner 常识[日本人多用]
MANDS	maintenance and supply 维修与供应

213

MANIAC	mathematical analyzer, numerical integrator and computer 数学分析器、数值积分器和计算机
MANIF	manifold 歧管
MAO	monoamine oxidase 单胺氧化酶
MAP	manifold air pressure 歧管空气压力
MAP	Military Assistance Program 美国军事援助计划
MAPC	Minnesota Association of Private Colleges 美国明尼苏达私人学院协会
MAPI	Message Application Process Interface 消息应用处理接口
MAPK	mitogen-activated protein kinase 丝裂原激活的蛋白激酶
MAPP	Microsoft Active Protections Program 微软的积极保护项目
MAQ	money allowance for quarters 房租津贴
Mar	March 3月
Mar CO	Mars Cube One 火星立方星一号
MAPK	mitogen-activated protein kinase 丝裂原激活的蛋白激酶
MARC	machine-readable catalog 机读目录,由美国国会图书馆销售
MARCOS	Jem Marsh, Frank Costin 马科斯小汽车
MARS	Mild Acute Respiratory Syndrome 温和急性呼吸综合征
MARS	the Machine-Assisted Reference Section 机器辅助服务部
MAS	Malaysia 马来西亚[亚洲国家]
MASH	medical army surgical hospital 军事外科医院
MAST	marine and aerial safe technology 海空防卫及安全系统科技
Mastcam	mast camera 桅杆相机
Master CNE	master computer net engineer 高级网络工程师
MATLAB	matrix laboratory 矩阵实验室
MATV	master antenna television 共用天线电视
MAW	Malawi 马拉维[非洲国家]
MAX	maximum 最大值
MB	megabyte 兆字节[计算机存储单位][另参 GB]
Mb	myoglobin 血清肌红蛋白
MBA	master of business administration 工商管理硕士
MBBF	Globe Mobile Broadband Forum 全球移动宽带论坛
MBBS/BMBS	Bachelor of Medicine & Bachelor of Surgery 临床医学学士

MBBS/BMBS	Medicinae Baccalaureus/Baccalaureus Chirurgiae 临床医学学士[拉丁文]	
MBC	management by creation 价值创造型经营	
MBC	Munhwa Broadcasting Corporation 韩国文化放送株式会社[韩国大型传媒企业]	
MBD	minimal brain dysfunction 轻微脑机能障碍	
MBE	Member(of the Order)of the British Empire 大英帝国勋章获得者	
MBG	Multinational Banking Group 多国性银行集团	
MBMS	multi broadcast multimedia service 多媒体广播多播技术	
MBO	management buyout 管理层收购	
MBO	management by object 目标管理	
MBO	management by organization 组织管理	
MBP	milk basic protein 牛奶碱性蛋白	
MBP	myelin basic protein 髓鞘碱性蛋白	
Mbps	megabits per second 兆位(比特)每秒	
Mbps	megabytes per second 兆字节每秒	
MBS	Malawi Bureau of Standards 马拉维标准局	
MBS	Malawi Bureau of Standards 马拉维认证标志	
MBS	methacrylate-butadiene styrene 甲基丙烯酸-丁二烯-苯乙烯共聚物[塑料]	
MBT	main battle tank 主战坦克	
MbT	myoglobin test 肌红蛋白试验	
MBTA	Massachusetts Bay Transit Authority 美国马萨诸塞州海湾交通局	
MC	Master of Ceremony 节目主持人	
MC	Master of Commerce 商学硕士	
MC	material control 物料管理/物控/物料控制	
MC	methyl cellulose 甲基纤维素[塑料]	
MC	microphone controller 控制麦克风的人[即说唱者]/舞台上带动气氛的人	
MC	microcircuit 芯片	
MC	moisture content 含水量	
MC	molten core 熔火之心	

Mc	moscovium 镆[第115号化学元素]
MCA	micro channel architecture 微通道结构
MCA	Music Company of America 美国音乐公司
MCA	Military Chaplain's Association 军事牧师协会
MCA	Music Corporation of America 美国音乐社团
MCAI	multimedia computer-assisted instruction 多媒体计算机辅导教学系统
MCAO	multi-congugate adaptive optics 多层共轭自适应光学
MCAS	maneuvering characteristics augmentation system 操纵特性增强系统
MCBIHP	Malaysia-China (Beijing) International Halal Products 马中（北京）国际清真商品贸易中心
MCC	Medical Consulting Committee 印度医学咨询委员会
MCC	mean corpuscular constants 红细胞平均常数
MCC	motor control center 电机控制中心
MCD	mean corpuscular diameter 红细胞平均直径
MCDBA	Microsoft Certified Data-Base Administrator 微软认证数据库管理员
MCDPHR	Mexican Commission for the Defence and Promotion of Human Right 墨西哥人权捍卫和促进委员会
mcg	microgram 微克
MCH	mean corpuscular hemoglobin 平均红细胞血红蛋白（含量）
MCH	metal ceramics heater 金属陶瓷发热体
MCHC	mean corpuscular hemoglobin concentration 平均红细胞血红蛋白浓度
MCI	Microwave Communication Inc. （美国）微波通信公司
McJobs	McDonald's Jobs 低工资、无前途的工作
MCM	Mode Creation Munich 欧洲新奢侈时装品牌[1976年创建于慕尼黑]
MCM	metal commodity manager 金属商品经理
MCO	miscellaneous charge order 多种项目结算凭证
MCP	Microsoft Certified Professional 微软认证专家
MCPS	Microsoft Certified Product Specialist 微软认证产品专家
M-CR	mission capable rate 任务执行率
MCRC	Mission of Central Raid Control 中央防空管理所
MCRRS	Mobile Clean Recovery and Revolving System 移动式清洁回收与循环系统

M

MCRWV	microwave 微波
MCS	microwave communication system 微波通信系统
MCS	mobile checkout station 流动检查站
MCSA	Medical Computer Services Administration 医学计算机服务管理处
MCSC	Music Copyright Society of China 中国音乐著作权协会
MCSD	Microsoft Certified Solution Developer 微软认证方案开发员
MCSE	Microsoft Certified System Engineer 微软认证系统工程师
MCT	Microsoft Certified Teacher 微软认证教师
MCT	mean corpuscular thickness 平均红细胞厚度
MCV	mean corpuscular volume 平均红细胞体积
MCV	mean cell volume 平均红细胞体积
MD	marketing director 市场总监
MD	Medicine Doctor 医学博士
MD	mini disc 微型碟，微型唱片
MD	missile defence 导弹防御（系统）
MD	muscular dystrophy 肌肉萎缩症
Md	mendelevium 钔［第 101 号化学元素］
MDA	Moldova 摩尔多瓦［欧洲国家］
MDAA	Mutual Defense Assistance Agreement《美日共同防御援助协定》
MDC	more developed country 较发达国家
MDF	medium density fibre board 中密度纤维板
MDM	Mobile Device Management 移动设备管理
Mdm	Madam 夫人
MDM	master data management 主数据的管理
MDMA	methylenedioxymethamphetamine 亚甲基二氧甲基苯丙胺
Mdme	Madame 夫人［法文］
MDP	management development plan 管理人才发展计划
MDPE	medium density polyethylene 中密度聚乙烯［塑料］
MDR	multidrug resistance 多药耐药
MDRT	The Million Dollar Round Table 百万圆桌会议［全球寿险精英的最高盛会］
MDS	myelodysplastic syndrome 骨髓增生异常综合征

MDU	Multiple Dwellers Unit 多住户单元
MDV	Maldives 马尔代夫[亚洲国家]
MDV	Music Dance Video 音乐舞蹈影片
ME	method engineering 方法改善
ME	Ministry of Environment 环境部
ME	Management Engineering 管理工程学
ME	Master of Engineering 工程硕士
ME	Myalgic Encephalomyelitis 肌痛性脑脊髓炎
me too	that applies to me, too 我也是
ME	machine engineer 设备工程师
ME	maximum effort 最大努力
ME	mechanical engineer 机械工程师
MEA	Ministry of External Affairs (India) 印度外交部
MED	minimal erythema dose 最小红斑量
Medicaid	Medical Aid 医疗辅助计划
MEE	Magyar Electrotechnikal Egyesulet 匈牙利电工协会[匈牙利文]
MEFV	maximal expiratory flow volume curves 最大呼气流量容积曲线
MEI	main economic indicators 主要经济指标
MEL	master equipment list 主要设备清单
MEMS	micro-electro-mechanical system 微电子机械系统
MENA	Middle East News Agency (埃及)中东通讯社[埃及国家通讯社,设在开罗]
MEO	marine engineering office 海洋工程局
MEQ	morningness eveningness questionnaire 问卷评估法
MER	maximum efficient rate 最大有效率
Mer	mercury 水银
MERS	Middle East Respiratory Syndrome 中东呼吸综合征
MES	manufacturing execution system 制造执行系统
MET	metabolic equivalent 代谢当量
meth	methane 甲烷
METI	Messaging to Extra-Terrestrial Intelligence 外星智能通讯
Metro	Metropolitan Railway 地下铁道

M

Mets	New York Mets 纽约大都会队
MEX	Mexico 墨西哥[北美洲国家]
MF	medium frequency 中频
MF	melamine-formaldehyde resin 蜜胺甲醛树脂[塑料]
MFA	master of fine arts 艺术硕士专业学位
MFAS	multi-function active sensor 多功能主动传感器
MFC	multifunction component 多功能元件
MFC	marginal factor cost 边际要素成本
MFG	manufacturing 制造
MFi	made for iphone[或 ipod 或 ipad] 苹果根据 iPhone 等产品的认证
MFI	multipoint fuel injection 多点燃油喷射
MFLOPS	million floating-point operations per second 每秒百万次浮点运算
MFLR	muffler 消声器
MFN	Most Favored Nations 最惠国
MFS	manned flying system 载人飞行系统
Mg	magnesium 镁[第 12 号化学元素]
mg	milligram(s) 毫克
MG	myasthenia gravis 重症肌无力
MG	magazine advertising 杂志广告
MG	*Manchester Guardian* 《曼彻斯特卫报》[英国]
MG	Morris Garage 英国名爵汽车
M-G	Morris-Garage 莫里斯汽车[英国竞赛用车]
mg/cig	milligrams per cigarette 每支香烟的(焦油)毫克数
mg/m³	milligram per cubic meter of air 每立方米空气[灰尘,烟气或雾霜]毫克数
mg/kg	milligram(me)/kilogram 毫克/千克
mg/l	milligram per liter 毫克/升
MGF	Mechanical Growth Factor 机械生长因素
MGH	Massachusetts General Hospital 美国麻省总医院
MGL	Mongolia 蒙古[亚洲国家]
MGM	Metro-Goldwyn-Mayer (美国)米高梅电影制片公司
MGO	methylglyoxal 食用甲基乙二醛

MGO TM400+	methylglyoxal TM400+ 每公斤的食用甲基乙二醛产品含量至少为 400 毫克,作用为帮助人体提高消化功能
Mgr	Monsignor 阁下[法文]
MGS	Marcasite 曼古银珠宝佩饰
MHA	Member of the House of Assembly 议会议员
MHz	megahertz 兆赫(兹)[法定频率计量单位]
MI	Military Intelligence (英国)军事情报(处)
MI	Mind Identity 理念识别
MI	multiple intelligence 多元智能
MI 5	Military Intelligence 5 军情五处
MI 6	Military Intelligence 6 军情六处
MI	manufacturing index 制造业活动指数
MI	mind identity 理念识别
MI	mitral insufficiency 二尖瓣关闭不全
MI	mutual information 相互信息
MIA	Migration Institute of Australia 澳大利亚移民协会
MIA	missing in action 作战中失踪人员
MIB	Master of International Business 国际工商硕士
Mib	mebibit 兆比特
MiB	mebibyte 兆字节
MIBG	Meta-Iodo Benzy Guanidine 间碘苄胍
MIBS	Macquarie Innovative Business Society 麦考瑞大学商业创新协会
MIC	Ministry of Information and Communication 信息与通信部
MIC	many integrated cores 集成多核架构处理器
MIC	mature industrial countries 成熟的工业国
MIC	Ministry of Information and Communication 韩国信息及通信产品质量认证标志
MIC	Ministry of Information and Communication 信息及通信部门
MIC	Mitsubishi International Co., Ltd. 日本三菱国际公司
MIDI	musical instruction digital interface 音乐教学数字界面
MIDI SYSTEM	Musical Instruction Digital Interface System 乐器数字接口系统

M

MIDL	multiple information divided link 多功能信息分发系统
MIF	Market Intervention Fund 市场干预基金
MiG	Mikoyan i Gurevich 米格[苏联飞机设计师米高扬和格列维奇两人姓的首字母缩略语][俄文]
Mij	Maatschappij 公司[荷兰文]
MIL	malfunction indicator lamp 故障指示器灯
MILS	minimum international labour standards 最低国际劳保标准
MIMO	man in, machine out 人工输入, 机器输出
MIMO	many-input and many-output 多输入多输出
min	minimum 最小的
min	minute(s) 分钟
min	mobile interactive media 移动互动媒体
MIND	Mediterranean Diet 地中海饮食
Minero	mine robot 探矿机器人[海底无人深潜器]
MINS	minor(s) in need of supervision 需监护的未成年人
MIP	minimum import price 最低进口价格
MIPS	million instructions per second 每秒百万条指令
MIS	management information system 管理信息系统
MIT	Massachusetts Institute of Technology (美国)麻省理工学院
MJ	movie jockey 电影栏目主持人
MJ	marijuana 大麻
MJ	Michael Jackson 迈克尔·杰克逊[美国流行音乐巨星]
MKD	Macedonia 马其顿[欧洲国家][现称 NMKD 北马其顿]
ml	millilitre 毫升
MLA	Modern Language Association 美国现代语言协会
MLAP	migrant legal action program 移民法律行动计划
MLB	Major League Baseball 美国职业棒球大联盟
MLB	mini-land bridge 小陆桥/小陆桥运输
MLC	Microsoft (Authorized Window) Learning Center 微软授权视窗应用学习中心
MLF	media language format 媒体语言格式
MLF	medium-term lending facility 中期借贷便利

MLI	Mali 马里[非洲国家]	
MLM	multi-level marketing 传销	
MLT	Malta 马耳他[欧洲国家]	
MLTSSL	Medium and Long-term Strategic Skills List 中长期战略技术清单	
MLV	magnetic levitation vehicle 磁浮列车	
MM	malignant melanoma 恶性黑色素瘤	
MM	material management 物料管理	
MM	Maybach Manufaktur 德国迈巴赫汽车	
MM	mind master 心灵支配者	
MM	*Mingguan Mahasiswa* 印尼《大学生周报》[印尼文]	
MMA	mixed martial arts 综合格斗[是一种规则极为开放的竞技格斗运动]	
MMC	money market certificate 货币市场存单	
MMC	multi media card 多媒体卡	
MMC	multimedia controller 多媒体控制器	
MMC	multimedia memory card 多媒体内存卡	
MMDA	Metro Manila Development Agency 马尼拉城市发展局	
MMEA	Malaysia Maritime Enforcement Agency 马来西亚海事执法机构	
MMEF	mean maximum expiratory flow 平均最大呼气流量	
mmHg	millimeter mercury column 毫米水银柱	
MMI	multimedia interface 多媒体接口	
MMI	modernization management system 现代化管理系统	
MMIC	monolithic microwave integrated circuit 单片微波集成电路	
MMM	Maison Martin Margiela 马丁·马拉吉服饰	
mmol/l	millimol/litre 毫摩尔/升	
MMORPG	massive multiplayer online role playing game 大型多人在线角色扮演游戏	
MMP	matrix metalloproteinase 基质金属蛋白酶	
MMP	mysterious motorist program 神秘顾客访问	
MMS	Multimedia Messaging Service 多媒体短信	
MMTA	Mobile Multimedia Technology Alliance 移动多媒体技术联盟	
MMUK	Men's Make-Up UK 男性化妆品	
Mn	manganese 锰[第25号化学元素]	

M

MN	metanephrine 3-甲氧基肾上腺素
MNB	Mongolian National Broadcast 蒙古国家公共电视台
MNC	multinational corporation 跨国公司
mNGS	metagenomics next generation sequencing 二代高通量测序技术
MNO	Mobile Network Operator 移动运营商
MNO	multimedia network operator 多媒体网络运营商
MNP	mobile number portability 移动号码携带
Mo	molybdenum 钼[第 42 号化学元素]
MO	mobile office 移动办公[任何时间地点,利用 IT 工具都可上班,甚至兼职数份工作]
MOAB	massive ordnance air burst（美国）大型燃料空气炸弹（或称炸弹之母）
MOAB	mother of all bombs 炸弹之母[或称大型燃料空气炸弹]
MOAH	mineral oil aromatic hydrocarbons 芳香烃矿物油
MODS	multiple organ dysfunction syndrome 多脏器功能障碍综合征
MODS	multiple organ dysfunction score 多器官功能障碍评分
MOF	multiple organ failure 多脏器功能衰竭综合征
MOKV	multi-object kill vehicle 多目标杀伤器
Mol	molecule 摩(尔)[法定物质的量计量单位]
mol/l	mol/litre 摩尔/升
MON	Monaco 摩纳哥[欧洲国家]
MON	Monday 星期一
Mon	monocyte 单核白细胞
MONA	Museum of Old and New Art 新闻艺术博物馆[国际赌神 David Walsh 所设]
MONO	monocyte 单核细胞
MOOCs	massive open online courses 慕课[大规模网络公共课]
MOP	Macao Pataca 澳门元[货币]
MOP	Massive Ordnance Penetrator 巨型钻地弹
MoPOP	Museum of Pop Culture 流行文化博物馆
MOR	Morocco 摩洛哥[非洲国家]
Mose	Modulo Sperimentale Elettromeccanico 实验电动机械模块[意大利文]
MOSH	mineral oil saturated hydrocarbons 饱和烃矿物油
MOSS	Mozilla Open Source Support 支持开源和自由软件运动的计划

MOT	management of technology 技术管理	
MoT	Ministry of Transport 英国运输部	
MOT	motilin 胃动素	
MOTO	Motorola 摩托罗拉(电子产品)	
MOU	memorandum of understanding 谅解备忘录	
MOX	mixed-oxide (uranium and plutonium) 混合氧化物[铀和钚]	
MOZ	Mozambique 莫桑比克[非洲国家]	
MP	melt & pour 融化再制制皂法	
MP	megapixel 百万像素	
MP3	MPEG 1 Layer 3 一种音频压缩格式[或称第三代声音文件压缩格式]	
MP4	MPEG 1 Layer 4 一种音视频压缩格式[或称第四代声音文件压缩格式]	
MPA	Master of Public Administration 公共管理硕士	
mpa	mega pascal 兆帕[压强单位,1 帕=1 牛顿/米^2]	
MPA	macro prudential assessment 宏观审慎管理框架/宏观审慎评估	
Mpa	megapascal 百万帕(斯卡)	
MPACC	master of professional accounting 专业会计硕士	
MPC	monetary policy committee 货币政策委员会	
MPC	multimedia personal computer 多媒体个人计算机	
MPC	Manpower and Personnel Council 人力及人事委员会	
MPE	Master of Physical Education 体育硕士	
MPEG	Moving Picture Experts Group 运动图像专家组[一种压缩比较大的活动图像和声音压缩标准]	
MPF	melamine/phenol formaldehyde resin 蜜胺/苯酚甲醛树脂[塑料]	
MPF	mobile protection fire 机动保护火力	
mpg	miles per gallon 每加仑英里数	
MPH	Master of Public Health 公共卫生硕士	
mph	miles per hour 每小时英里数	
MPI	Macao Polytechnic Institute 澳门理工学院	
MPI	Magnetic Particle Inspection 磁振造影	
MPLS	Multiple Protocol Label Switch 多协议标记交换	
MPPC	multimedia pocket personal computer 多媒体口袋式个人电脑	
MPR	materials resource planning 材料资源计划	

M

MPS	master production schedule 主生产计划
MPS	microprocessor system 微处理器系统
MPS	multi-purpose sedan 多功能轿车
MPU	micro-processing unit 微处理器
MPV	mean platelet volume 平均血小板体积
MPV	multi-purpose vehicle 多用途汽车
MPY	Maatschappij 公司[荷兰文]
MQ	mental quotient 心灵商
MQ	memory quotient 存储商数
MQ	merit quotient 指数系数
MQ	morals quotient 道德商数
Mr	mister 先生
MR	mixture reality 混合现实
MRA	Magnetic Resonance Angiography 核磁共振血管造影
Mrabo	Mobile Rabo 移动博客
MRAM	Magnetic Random Access Memory 磁随机读写存储器
MRAP	mine resistant ambush protected 防地雷反伏击车
MRB	material review board 材料评审委员会
MRE	Meal Ready to Eat 快餐
MRI	magnetic resonance imaging 磁共振造影/磁共振成像
MRI	Mauritius 毛里求斯[非洲国家]
MRJ	Mitsubishi Regional Jet 三菱支线喷气式飞机
MRO	Maintenance, Repair and Operations 维护、维修和使用
MRO	Media Relation Officer 媒体新闻联络店
MRP	marginal revenue of product 边际收益产品
MRP	Material Requirement Plan 物料需求计划
MRP	manufacturing resource plan 制造资源计划(系统)
Mrs	mistress 夫人
MRS	marginal rate of substitution 边际替代率
MRSA	methicillin resistant staphylococcus aureus 耐甲氧西林金黄色葡萄球菌
MRSE	meticillin resistant staphylococcus epidermidis 耐甲氧西林表皮葡萄球菌
MRT	mass rapid transit 大众高速交通

MRU	Mauritius 毛里求斯[非洲国家]
MS	Master Degree 硕士学位
MS	Master of Science 理科硕士
MS	Microsoft 微软公司
MS	Mobile Station 移动站
MS	memory stick 记忆棒
MS	mint state 未流通级（货币）
MS	mitral stenosis 二尖瓣狭窄
MS	Morgan Stanley 摩根士丹利
MS	multiple sclerosis 多发性硬化（症）
MSA	Maritime Safety Administration 海事局
MSAR	Macao Special Administrative Region 澳门特别行政区
MSB	medium-small business 中小企业
MSC	mobile switch center 移动交换中心
MSC	Military Staff Commission 安理会军事参谋团
MSCI	Morgan Stanley Capital International 美国明晟指数公司/摩根士丹利资本国际
MSD	mean square displacement 均方位移
MSDN	Microsoft Developer Network 微软开发者网
MSDS	material safety data sheet 材料安全数据一览表
MSEA	Macromolecule Science and Engine Award 大分子科学与工程奖
MSF	Medecins Sans Frontiers [英文：Doctors without Borders] 无国界医生组织[法文]
MSG	message 签收短信通知
MSH	melanocyte-stimulating hormone 促黑激素
MSI	medium scale integration 中规模集成电路
MSI	Micro Star International 微星公司
MSI	mid-season invitational 季中邀请赛
MSL	Mars Scientific Laboratory 火星科学实验室
MSM	men who have sex with men 男同性恋者
MSN	Microsoft Service Network 微软网络服务
MSNBC	Microsoft National Broadcast Corporation 美国微软全国广播公司

MSO	multiple system operator 多系统操作员
MSR	manufacturing specification request 生产规范要求
MSRP	manufacturer's suggested retail price 厂商建议提出的零售价
MSS	Ministry of State Security 国家安全部
MSSM	Master of Society Servant Management 社会行政管理硕士
MSU	Michigan State University 美国密歇根州立大学
MSU	Moscow State University 俄罗斯国立莫斯科大学
mSV	millisievert 毫西弗[辐射量单位,1毫西弗等于1000微西弗 μSV]
MSW	Master of Society Work 社会工作硕士
MSZ	Magyar Szabvány 匈牙利标准化局[匈牙利文]
MSZ	Magyar Szabvány 匈牙利认证标志[匈牙利文]
MSZH	Magyar Szabvány ügyi Hivatal 匈牙利标准局[匈牙利文]
Mt	Meitnerium 鿏[第109号化学元素]
MT	management trainee 管理培训生
MT	motor tanker 运油汽车[船]
MT	motor towboat 小型机动牵引汽艇
MT	magnetic tape 磁带[电子文献标示字母]
MT	mechanical transmission 机械变速器
MTA	Metropolitan Transit Authority 大都会运输署
MTA	Metropolitan Transportation Authority 纽约大都会运输署
MTBF	mean time between failure 平均故障间隔时间
MTC	manual semi-automatic toll collection 人工半自动收费通道
MTF	modulation transmission function (摄影)模量传递函数
MTI	Master of Translation and Interpreting 翻译硕士
MTN	Mauritania 毛里塔尼亚[非洲国家]
MTP	mail transfer protocol 协议交换邮件
MTR	Mass Transit Railway 港铁
MTS	Manager Testing Solution 管理者胜任素质测评(系统)
MTS	multispectral aiming system 多光谱瞄准系统
MTS	message transfer service 信息传送业务
MTS	Mobile Tele Systems 俄罗斯移动通信系统公司
MTSS	minimum telephone service standard 最小电话服务标准

MTT	methyl thiazolyl tetrazolium 甲基噻唑基四唑
MTU	maximum transport unit 最大传输单元
MTU	Motoren und Turbinen Union GmbH 德国安特优公司[德文]
MTU	motorno-transmissionnaia ustanovka 发动机传动装置(公司)[俄文]
MTV	music television 音乐电视
MUD	multiple user dialogue 多人对话
MUD	multiple user dimension 多用户层面
MUG	music game 音乐类游戏
MUI	Majelis Ulama Indonesia 印度尼西亚乌拉玛委员会[印尼文]
MUIS	Majils Ugama Islam Singapura 新加坡伊斯兰宗教理事会[印尼文]
MULS	Minnesota(University)Union List of Serials 美国明尼苏达(大学)期刊联合目录
MUNCOPUOS	Model United Nations Committee on the Peaceful Uses of Outer Space 模拟联合国和平利用外层空间委员会
MUST	military unshock trousers 军用防休克裤
MUTV	Manchester United Television 曼联电视台
MV	million volts 百万伏(特)
MV	Music Video 音乐视频[一种用动态画面配合歌曲演唱的艺术形式]
MV	Master of Valuation 资产评估硕士
MVCF	movie commercial film 电影广告
MVD	microvessel density 微血管密度
MVP	Most Valuable Player 最有价值的运动员
MVV	maximal ventilatory volume 最大通气量
MW	medium wave 中波
MW	megawatts 兆瓦(特)
MWC	Mobile World Congress 移动世界大会
MYA	Myanmar 缅甸[亚洲国家]
MYO	myoglobin 血清肌红蛋白
M-zone	Motive Zone 动感地带

N	Newton 牛(顿)[法定力、重力计量单位]
N	nitrogen 氮[第7号化学元素]
N	normal 正常
N	New York N 股[我国在纽约发行的股票]
N	New York 纽约
N	not resistant to oil 非耐油
N	neutral 空档
N	neutrophil 嗜中性粒细胞
N	newspaper article 报纸文章[参考文献标示字母]
n	Nippon 立邦漆[Nippon 原义:日本]
N	Norges Elektriske Materiell Kontroll 挪威电气材料检验所[挪威文]
N	Norges Elektriske Materiell Kontroll 挪威电气产品质量认证标志[挪威文]
N.W.	net weight 净重
n/a	not applicable 不适用的
N/A	no account 无此账
N/A	not applicable 不适用
N/A	not available 不可用
N/OL	newspaper on line 网上报纸[电子文献标示略语]
Na	natrium (英文名称是 sodium) 钠(第11号化学元素)[拉丁文]
NA	network address 网址
NA	Not Applicable 不适用的
NAA	Newspaper Association of America 美国报业协会
NAACP	National Association for the Advancement of Colored People 全国有色人种促进会
NAATI	National Accreditation Authority for Translators and Interpreters 澳大利亚翻译资格认可局

nab	no-alcohol beer 无酒精啤酒
NAB	National Australian Bank 澳大利亚国民银行
NAC	neoadjuvant chemotherapy 初始化疗
NAD	nicotinamide adenine dinucleotide 烟酰胺腺嘌呤二核苷酸
NAETI	National Accreditation Examinations for Translators and Interpreters 全国外语翻译证书考试
NAFFP	National Association of Frozen Food Packers 全国冷冻食品包装商协会
NAFLD	non-alcoholic fatty liver disease 非酒精性脂肪性肝病
NAFSA	Association of International Educators [原全称为:National Association of Foreign Student Affairs] 国际教育工作者协会
NAFSA	National Association of Foreign Student Advisers 全国外国学生顾问协会
NAFTA	North America Free Trade Agreement 北美自由贸易协定 [现在被USMCA代替]
NAI	National Association of Internet 美国网络联盟
NAM	Namibia 纳米比亚 [非洲国家]
NAM	Non-Aligned Movement 不结盟运动
NAP	network access point 网络接入点
NAP	neutrophil alkaline phosphatase 中性粒细胞碱性磷酸酶
NAR	National Association of Realtors 全国房地产经纪人协会
NARS	National Agricultural Research System 国家农业科研系统
NARS	National Archives and Records Service 国家档案文件局
NARS	National Automated Response System 全国自动回复系统
NAS	National Academy of Sciences (美国)国家科学院
NAS	national airspace system 国家空域系统
NAS	National Adoption Society 全国领养协会
NAS	network affiliated storage 网络附属存储
NAS	Noise Abatement Society 噪声控制协会
NASA	National Aeronautics and Space Administration (美国)国家航空航天局
NASCAR	The National Association for Stock Car Auto Racing 美国全国赛车协会
NASD	National Association of Securities Dealers 全美证券交易商协会
Nasdaq	National Association of Securities Dealers Automated Quotations 纳斯达

N

		克（指数）
NATO	Northern Atlantic Treaty Organization	北大西洋公约组织
Nb	niobium	铌［第41号化学元素］
NB	narcotics bureau	毒品调查科
NB	nota bene	注意［拉丁文］
NBA	National Banking Association	美国全国银行业协会
NBA	National Basketball Association	美国国家篮球协会/美国职业篮球联赛
NBAR	National Bureau of Asian Research	国家亚洲研究局（美国非营利组织）
NBC	National Broadcast Corporation	美国全国广播公司
NBC	new basic car	新基准轿车
NBCP	The National Bureau of Corruption Prevention of China	中国预防腐败局
NBDL	NBA Development League	国家篮球发展联盟
NBER	National Bureau of Economic Research	全国经济研究所
NBG	no bloody good	不好
NBL	Naval Biological Laboratory	美国海洋生物实验室
NBL	National Basketball League	国家篮球联盟
NBR	Norges Byggstandardiseringsrad	挪威建筑标准化委员会［挪威文］
NBS	National Board of Standards	国家标准局
NBT	National Ballet Theatre	英国国家芭蕾舞团
NBT	nitroblue tetrazolium test	氮蓝四唑试验
NC	network computer	网络计算机
NC	Comite Estatal de Normalization	古巴国家标准化委员会［西班牙文］
NC	Niagara College	尼亚加拉学院
NC	Norton Commander	诺顿命令管理器
NCA	National Composition Association	美国国家作品协会
NCA	Nicaragua	尼加拉瓜［北美洲国家］
NCA	National Crime Agency	国家打击犯罪局
NCAA	National Collegiate Athletic Association	美国国家大学体育总会/全国大学体育协会
NCAP	New Car Assessment Program	新车鉴定程序
NCAR	National Center for Atmospheric Research	国家大气研究中心
NCB	National Tech Committee of the Biotechnology	全国生物科技管理专业委

员会

NCBI	National Centre of Biological Information 美国国立生物信息中心	
NCC	National Computing Center 全国计算中心	
NCC	National Cadet Corps 国民志愿服务团	
NCC	National Climate Center 国家气候中心	
NCEP	National Center for Environment Predicting 国家环境预测中心	
NCH	normal charge 正常费用	
NCI	National Cancer Institute 美国全国癌症研究所	
NCI	National Council of Importers 全国进口商协会	
NCI	National Cancer Institute 国立癌症研究所	
NCIP	novel coronavirus-infected pneumonia 新型冠状病毒感染的肺炎	
NCIS	Naval Criminal Investigation Service 海军犯罪调查组	
NCL	Norwegian Cruise Line 诺唯真游轮	
NCLH	Norwegian Cruise Line Holding Company 诺唯真游轮控股公司	
NCNA	New China News Agency 新华通讯社	
NCNE	National Certification of Network Engineer 国家网络技术水平考试	
NCO	non-commissioned officer 军士	
nCoV	novel coronavirus 新型冠状病毒	
NCP	network control protocol 网络控制协议	
NCP	novel coronavirus pneumonia 新冠肺炎	
NCPM	non-critical phase matching 非临界相位匹配	
NCR	no carbon required (paper) 无碳复写纸（不用复写纸可复写）	
NCRE	National Computer Rank Examination 全国计算机等级考试	
NCS	National Clandestine Service 美国国家秘密行动处	
NCSA	National Center for Supercomputing Application 美国国家超级计算机应用中心	
NCSA	National Computer Security Association 国家计算机安全协会	
NCT	National Car Test 国家汽车检测	
NCT	National Curriculum Test 国家课程考试	
NCTFS	National Conference on Terminological Formation and Standardization 中国术语学建设暨术语规范化会议	
NCV	nano cellulose vehicle 环保木制汽车	

N

Nd	neodymium 钕[第 60 号化学元素]	
NDA	New Drug Application 新药申报	
NDA	National Democratic Alliance 印度全国民主联盟	
NDAA	National Defense Authorization Act《国防授权法案》	
NDARC	National Drug and Alcohol Research Centre 国家毒品及酒精研究中心	
NDE	Near Death Experience 濒死体验	
NDI	Non-Government Development Item 非政府开发项目	
NDI	Numerical Designation Index 数字指示索引	
NDI	National Democratic Institute 全国民主协会	
NDLTD	Networked Digital Library of Theses and Dissertations 国际博硕士论文数字图书馆	
NDP	New Democratic Party 新民主党	
NDTV	New Dehli Television 印度新德里电视台	
NE	north-east(ern) 东北方(的)	
Ne	neon 氖[第 10 号化学元素]	
NE	noradrenaline 去甲肾上腺素	
NEA	National Energy Agency 国家能源局	
NEC	Nippon Electric Company 日本电气公司	
NECCS	National English Contest for College Students 全国大学生英语竞赛	
NED	Netherlands 荷兰[欧洲国家]	
NED	National Endowment for Democracy 国家民主(捐赠)基金会	
NED	*New English Dictionary* [=*Oxford English Dictionary*]《牛津大词典》[英国]	
NEDC	New European Driving Cycle 新的欧洲行驶(油耗)循环(综合油耗计算循环)	
NEEA	National Educational Examinations Authority 国家教育部考试中心	
NEET	Not in Employment, Education or Training 尼特族[指一些不升学,不就业,不参加培训无所事事的青年族群]	
neg	negative 否定的	
NEMKO	Norges Elektriske Materiell Kontroll 挪威电气材料检验所[挪威文]	
NEMKO	Norges Elektriske Materiell Kontroll 挪威电气产品质量认证标志[挪威文]	
NEO	Near Earth Object 近地天体	

NEO	naval embarkation officer 海军装载军官
NEO	non-combatant evacuation operation 撤侨/非战斗人员撤离行动
NEP	Nepal 尼泊尔［亚洲国家］
NEPAD	The New Partnership for Africa's Development 非洲发展新伙伴计划
NESC	National English Speaking Competition 国家英语演讲比赛
NEST	network endogenous security testing ground 网络内生安全试验场
NEST	National Employment Savings Trust 国家职业储蓄信托
NEST	nuclear emergency support team 核紧急支援组
NET	navigation warfare evaluation team 导航战鉴定小组
NEUT	neuter granulocyte 中性粒细胞
NF	AFNOR（Association Française de Normalisation）法国标准化协会［法文］
NF	AFNOR（Association Française de Normalisation）法国产品质量认证标志［法文］
NFA	National Futures Association 全国期货协会
NFC	near field communication 近距离无线通信技术/短距离高频天线通信/近场通信
NFC	no frequency conversion 无频率变换
NFC	not from concentrate 非浓缩还原汁
NFDM	non-fat dried milk 脱脂奶粉
NFL	National Football League（美国）全国职业橄榄球大联盟
NFPDP	National Forest Plant and Development Plan 国家森林种植发展规划
NFTC	National Foreign Trade Council 国家对外贸易委员会［美国］
NFV	Network Functions Virtualization 网络功能虚拟化
NFV	no further visits 不得进一步参观［访问］
NF-κB	nuclear factor-κB 核因子-κB
NG	net grade 净评级
NG	nitro-glycerine 硝化甘油［炸药］
NG	no good 无用
NGA	National Geography Agency 国家地理情报局
NGC	Numismatic Guaranty Corporation 美国钱币鉴定、分级、评分的公司
NGF	nerve growth factor 神经生长因子
NGH	National Guild of Hypnotists Inc. 国家催眠师协会

NGI	Next Generation Internet 下一代互联网
NGIT	Norwegian Government Institute of Technology 挪威国家理工学院
NGO	Non-Governmental Organization 非政府组织
NGR	Nigeria 尼日利亚[非洲国家]
NGS	next generation sequencing 下一代测序
NGSC	new generation of subway car 新一代地铁车辆
NGTC	National Gemstone Testing Center 国家珠宝玉石质量监督检验中心
Nh	nihonium 钅尔[第113号化学元素]
NHK	Nippon Hoso Kyokai［英文：Japan Broadcasting Corporation］日本广播公司［日文］
NHL	National Hockey League 全国冰球联盟
NHN	Naver and Hangame Network Corp 韩国互联网集团［由 Naver 和 Hangame 两家公司组成］
NHS	National Health Service 英国国家卫生局
NHTSA	National Highway Traffic Safety Administration 全国公路交通安全管理局
NI	national income 国民收入
Ni	nickel 镍[第28号化学元素]
NI	noise index 噪音指数
NIA	National Immigration Administration 国家移民管理局
NIA	National Institute Aging 国立老年研究所
NIAID	National Institute of Allergy and Infectious Diseases 过敏与传染病研究所
NIAID	National Institute of Allergies and Infectious Diseases 国家敏感症和传染病学会
NIAS	Nevada Institute for Autonomous Systems 内华达州自动系统研究所
NIAS	Nutrition International Advanced Studies 营养学国际研修
NIC	newly-industrializing country 新兴工业化国家
NIC	Network Interface Card 网卡
NICU	Neonatal [Newborn] Intensive Care Unit 新生儿加强监护病房
NID	New International Dictionary (Webster's)《新韦氏国际英语大词典》[美国]

NIDS	Network Intrusion Detection System 网络入侵检测系统
NIE	newly-industrializing economics 新兴工业化经济
NIG	Niger 尼日尔[非洲国家]
NIH	USA National Institutes of Health 美国国立卫生研究院
NII	National Institute of Informatics 国立情报学研究所
NII	Netherlands Industrial Institute 荷兰工业协会
NIIT	National Institute of Information Technology 印度国家信息技术研究院
NIKKATSU	Nippon Katsudo Shashin 日本电影公司[日文]
NIKON	Nippon Kogaku KK 尼康相机[日文,意为日本光学工业株式会社]
NILK	no income lots of kids 无收入多子女(家庭)
NIQ	National Informatization Quotient 国家信息化指数
NIS	National Innovation System 国家创新系统
NIS	National Intelligence Service 国家情报局
NIS	Nigerian Industrial Standards 尼日利亚产品质量认证标志
NIS	Nigerian Industrial Standards 尼日利亚工业标准
NIST	National Institute of Standards and Technology 国家标准和技术协会
NIT	nitrate 硝酸盐
NIT	nitrite 尿亚硝酸盐
Nitto	Nitto Denko Co., Ltd. 日东电工有限公司
NJ	Net Jockey 网络节目主持人
NK	Nippon Kaijikyokai 日本海事协会[日文]
NKr	Norwegian Krone 挪威克朗[货币单位]
NKVD	Narodnei Kamisariat Vnutrennih Diel 苏联内务人民委员会[俄文]
NL	Netherlands 荷兰[欧洲国家]
NLC	National Library of China 中国国家图书馆
NLG	natural language generation 自然语言生成
NLP	natural language processing 自然语言处理
NLU	natural language understanding 自然语言理解
nm	nanometer 纳米[又称毫微米＝10亿分之一米]
NMD	Nimodipine 尼莫地平[药]
NMD	National Missile Defense System 国家导弹防御体系
NMDP	National Marrow Donor Program 美国国家骨髓库

NMET	non-medical education and training 非医学教育和训练
NMET	National Matriculation English Test 全国普通高等学校英语统一招生考试
NMFS	National Marine Fisheries Service 美国国家海洋渔业局
NMKD	North Macedonia 北马其顿[欧洲国家,前称马其顿]
NMN	Nicotinamide Mononucleotide 烟酰胺单核苷酸[延缓衰老的药]
NMR	Nuclear Magnetic Resonance 核磁共振
NN	Nomen Nescio 某某[拉丁文]
NNC	non-nuclear countries 无核(武器)国家
NNCC	China National Narcotics Control Commission 中国国家禁毒委员会
NNN	Nonaligned News Network 不结盟运动新闻网
NNN	Nihon News Network 日本新闻网
NNP	Net National Product 国民生产净值
NNTP	Network News Transfer Protocol 网络新闻传送协议
No	nobelium 锘[第102号化学元素]
No	north(ern) 北方(的)
NO	nitrogen oxide 氮氧化合物
NOA	not otherwise authorized 未另行授权
NOA	notice on availability 到货通知
NOAA	National Oceanic and Atmospheric Administration 美国国家海洋和大气管理局
NOE	not otherwise enumerated 不另行说明
NOFT	notification of foreign travel 国外旅行通知书
NOI	National Olympiad in Informatics 全国青少年信息学奥林匹克竞赛
NOIP	National Olympiad in Informatics in Provinces 全国青少年信息学奥林匹克联赛
NOM	Norma Oficial Mexicana 墨西哥产品质量认证标志[西班牙文]
NOM	Norma Oficial Mexicana 墨西哥官方标准[西班牙文]
NOR	Norway 挪威[欧洲国家]
NOS	network operating system 网络操作系统
NOS	not otherwise specified 不另行说明/未另行规定
NOSS	Navy Ocean Surveillance Satellites 海军海洋监视系统

NOV	November 11月	
NOW	National Organization of Women 美国全国妇女组织	
NOW	National Orchestra of Wales 威尔士国家交响乐团	
Np	neptunium 镎[第93号化学元素]	
NP	new pattern 新模式/新式样/新型	
NP	No Parking 禁止停车	
NP	notary public 公证员	
NPA	Natural Product Association (美国)天然产品协会	
NPC	National People's Congress (中国)全国人民代表大会	
NPC	nasopharyngeal carcinoma 鼻咽癌	
NPC&CPCC	National People's Congress and Chinese People's Political Consultation Conference 全国人民代表大会和中国人民政治协商会议(简称"两会")	
NPD	narcissistic personality disorder 病态自恋个性	
NPD	new product development 新产品开发	
NPE	new product engineer 新产品工程师	
NPI	new product introduction 新产品导入	
NPIC	Nuclear Power Institute of China 中国核电力研究所	
NPL	neoproteolipid 新蛋白脂质	
NPO	non-profitable organization 非营利组织	
NPR	National Population Register 国民人口登记册	
NPR	National Public Radio 美国全国公共广播电台	
NPR	natriuretic peptide receptor 钠尿肽受体	
NPS	net promoter score 净推荐值	
NPS	National Park Service 国家公园管理处	
NPSE	National Public Servant Examination 国家公务员考试	
NPT	Nuclear Non-proliferation Treaty《核不扩散条约》	
NPU	neural-network processing unit 神经网络处理单元	
NPU	Northwestern Polytechnical University 西北工业大学	
nr	near 靠近	
NR	national record 全国纪录	
NRA	National Rifle Association 全国步枪协会	
NRA	Non-Resident Account 境外企业人民币结算账户	

N

NRA-ILA	National Rifle Association-Institute for Legislative Action 美国步枪协会-立法行动研究所
NRC	National Referral Center 全国咨询中心
NRC	National Register of Citizens 国家公民登记册
NRC	National Research Council 国家科学研究委员会
NRC	Nuclear Regulatory Commission 核管理委员会
NRCC	National Republican Campaign Committee 美国共和党竞选委员会
NRCC	National Republican Congressional Committee 美国全国共和党国会委员会
NRCC	National Research Council of Canada 加拿大国家科学研究委员会
NRCC	network routing control center 网络路由选择控制中心
NRDC	Natural Resources Defense Council 自然资源保护协会
NREL	National Renewable Energy Laboratory 国家可再生能源实验室
NRF	The National Retail Foundation 国家零售基金会
NRIC	National Register of Indian Citizen 印度公民国家登记簿
NRJ	National Radio de Jeunes 法国 NRJ 电台(法国最大电台)[法文]
NRO	Non Recurring Charges 一次性费用
NRO	National Reconnaissance Office 国家侦查局
NRSRO	nationally recognized statistical rating organization 全国认定的评级组织
NRTL	National Recognized Testing Lab 国家认可实验室
NRU	Nauru 瑙鲁[太平洋岛国]
NRV	nutrient reference value 营养素参考值
ns	nanosecond 毫微秒[一毫微秒等于十亿分之一秒]
NS	Navier-Stokes 纳维-斯托克斯(方程)
NS	Newspaper Resource 报纸资源数据库
NS	Norsk Standard 挪威标准[挪威文]
NS	Norsk Standard 挪威产品质量认证标志[挪威文]
NSA	National Security Agency 美国国家安全局
NSA	non-standalone 非独立组网
NSAID	non-steroid antiinflammatory drug 非固醇类抗炎药
NSB	National Security Board 国家安全分部
NSC	National Security Committee 国家安全保障协会

NSC	National Security Council 国家安全委员会[美国]
NSCLC	non-small cell lung cancer 非小细胞肺癌
NSCLC-NE	non-small cell lung caner with neuroendocrine properties 神经内分泌型的非小细胞肺癌
NSE	neurone specific enolase 神经元特异性烯醇化酶
NSE	non-specific esterase 中心非特异性酯酶染色
NSF	National Science Foundation 国家科学基金会
NSF	National Sanitation Foundation 美国国家卫生基金会
NSF	Norges Standardiserings-Forbund 挪威标准化协会[挪威文]
NSFC	National Science Fund Committee 国家自然科学基金委员会
NSFL	not safe for life 日常不宜[网络用语]
NSFW	not safe for work 办公室不宜[网络用语]
NSO	The Nigerian Standards Organization 尼日利亚标准组织
NSS	navigation satellite system 卫星导航系统
NSSS	National Safety Space Strategy 美国国家安全太空战略
NSWDG	Naval Special Warfare Development Group 海军特战开发大队
NT	national treatment 国民待遇
NTCE	National Teacher Certificate Examination 中小学教师资格考试
NTI	Nuclear Threat Initiative 核威胁倡议
NTJ	National Theatre of Japan 日本国家剧院
NTN	Toyo Bearing Mfg Co., Ltd. （日本）东洋轴承制造公司
NTN	National Tax Number Certificates 全国税号证书
NTN	National Training Number Certificates 全国实习号证书
NTP	National Toxicology Program 国家毒理学计划
NTRI	Nutrisystem Inc 纳斯达克证券交易所
NTSB	National Transportation Safety Board 全国运输安全委员会
NTSC	National Television Systems Committee 全国电视制式委员会
NTT	Nippon Telegraph and Telephone Corporation 日本电信电话株式会社
NTU	Nanyang Technological University 新加坡南洋理工大学
NTUA	The National Technical University of Athens 雅典国立科技大学
NTV	Niezavisimei Tielievidienie 独立电视台[俄文]

N

NTV	Nippon Television 日本电视台
NU	Nanjing University 南京大学
NU	Nankai University 南开大学
NUC	National Union Catalog 美国全国联合书目
NUCMC	National Union Catalog of Manuscript Collections 美国国会图书馆手稿文献联合目录
NUS	National University of Singapore 新加坡国立大学
NV	Naamloze Vernootschap 有限股份公司［荷兰文］
NVDA	NVIDIA Corporation 英伟达半导体公司
NVOCC	non-vessel operating common carrier 无船经营的公共承运人
NVQ	National Vocational Qualification 国家职业资格（证书制度）
NW	north-west(ern) 西北方(的)
NWA	Northwest Airlines，Inc（美国）西北航空公司
NWFB	New World First Bus 新巴［香港］
NWIP	New Work Item Proposal 新工作项目提案
NWS	nuclear weapon states 有核（武器）国家
NXP	nonlinear exponential increase ratio 非线性而指数级增长
NXP	NXP semiconductors 荷兰恩智浦半导体公司
NY	New York 纽约
NYBOT	New York Board of Trade 纽约商品交易所
NYC	New York City 纽约市
NYCT	New York City Transit 纽约市公共交通局
NYMEX	New York Mercantile Exchange 纽约商品交易所
NYSE	New York Stock Exchange 美国纽约证券交易所
NYT	New York Times《纽约时报》［美国］
Nyy	New York Yankees 纽约洋基队
NZD	New Zealand Dollar 新西兰元［货币］
NZG	National Zoological Gardens of South Africa 南非国家动物园
NZHEA	New Zealand Higher Education Alliance 新西兰高等教育联盟
NZL	New Zealand 新西兰［大洋洲国家］
NZQA	New Zealand Qualifications Authority 新西兰学历认证局

O	oxygen 氧[第8号化学元素]
O	osteoporosis 骨质疏松症
O	orange 橙色
O	outstanding 完美[杰出]
o. n. o.	or near/nearest offer 可还价
O/Y	Osakeyhtiö 有限公司[芬兰文]
O2	On & On 英国O2电信公司
O2-C	oxygen content 氧含量
O2O	online to offline 线上线下/在线离线
O2sat	oxygen saturation 氧饱和度
OA	office automation 办公自动化
OA	osteoarthritis 骨性关节炎
OANA	Organization of Asia-Pacific News Agencies 亚洲-太平洋通讯社组织
OAPEC	Organization of Arab Petroleum Exporting Countries 阿拉伯石油输出国组织
OAS	Organization of American States 美洲国家组织
OASDI	old-age, survivors, and disable insurance [social security] 老年、遗嘱及残障保险[社会安全]
OAU	Organization of African Unity 非洲统一组织
OB	occult blood 隐血/潜血
OB	old boy 校友
OBCs	other backward classes 其他落后阶层
OBD	off-board diagnostics 离车诊断/车载自动诊断系统
OBE	Officer of the Order of the British Empire 荣获英帝国勋章的军官
OBE	Order of the British Empire 英帝国勋章
obit	obituary 讣文
Ö-BJS	Österreichischer Bundesjugendsiger 奥地利联盟青年冠军[德文]

O

OBM	Original Brand Manufacturer 原始品牌制造商
Ö-BS	Österreichischer Bundessinger 奥地利联盟冠军[德文]
OC	oral contraceptive 口服避孕药
OC	Overseas Chinese 华侨
OCA	Olympic Committee of Asia 亚洲奥林匹克理事会
OCAS	Organization of Central American States 中美洲国家组织
OCBs	Oligoclonal Bands 脑脊液寡克隆区带
OCC	ocean camouflage clothing 海洋迷彩服
OCC	oil consuming countries 石油消费国
OCC	Office of the Control of the Currency 货币监理署
OCC	Oxford Corpus Collection 牛津语料库
OCD	obsessive compulsive disorder 强迫症
OCHA	United Nations Office for the Coordination of Humanitarian Affairs 联合国人道主义事务协调厅
OCI	Organization of the Islamic Conference 伊斯兰会议组织
OCLC	Online Computer Library Center 国际联机计算机图书馆中心，在线图书馆中心
OCLC	Ohio College Library Center 俄亥俄大学图书馆中心
OCR	optical character recognition 文字识别/光符识别
Oct	October 10 月
OCT	octane 辛烷
OCT	ornithine carbamoyl transferase 鸟氨酸氨甲酰转移酶
OCT	Overseas Chinese Town 华侨城
OCTB	Organised Crime and Triad Bureau 香港有组织罪案及三合会调查科
OD	overdose 过量
OD	olive drab 草绿色
OD	operations director 运营总监
OD/OS	oculus dexter/oculus sinister 右眼/左眼（测试眼睛时的标志）
ODA	Official Development Assistance 政府开发援助
ODA	Overseas Development Assistance 海外开发援助
ODA	Overseas Development Administration 海外开发署
ODD	orphan drug designation 孤儿药物认定

ODEE	*Oxford Dictionary of English Etymology*《牛津英语语源学词典》[英国]	
ODEP	*Oxford Dictionary of English Proverbs*《牛津英语谚语词典》[英国]	
ODI	overseas direct investment 海外直接投资	
ODM	original design manufacturer 原始设计制造商	
ODNI	Office of the Director of National Intelligence 国家情报主任办公室	
ODP	Offshore Drilling Platform 海上钻井平台	
ODP	Offshore Drilling Project 大洋钻探工程	
ODR	Order Defect Rate 订单缺陷率	
OEA	Observatoire Européen Austral 欧洲南方天文台[法文]	
OECD	Organization for Economic Cooperation and Development 经济合作与发展组织	
OED	*Oxford English Dictionary*《牛津英语词典》[也叫《新英语词典》]	
OEHHA	The Office of Environmental Health Hazard Assessment 美国加州环境健康危害评估办公室	
OEM	original equipment manufacturer 原始设备制造商	
OEM	original equipment manufacture 委托代工	
OER	open educational resource 开放教育资源	
OF	optical fibre 光学纤维	
OFAC	Office of Foreign Assets Control 海外资产管理办公室	
OFC	Oceanian Football Confederation 大洋洲足球联合会	
OFDM	orthogonal frequency division multiplexing 正交频分复用	
OFE	open financial exchange 开放金融交易	
oft	often 时常	
OG	online game 网络游戏	
Og	oganesson 鿫[第 118 号化学元素]	
OG	orange green 橙绿色	
OG	organic glass 有机玻璃	
OGTT	oral glucose tolerance test 口服葡萄糖耐量试验	
OH	other half 伴侣	
OHMS	On His [Her] Majesty's Serve 英国公函免付邮费戳记	
OHP	overhead projector 投影仪	
OHSA	Occupational Health Safety System 职业卫生安全体系	

O

OHSMS	Occupational Heath Safety Management Systems 职业健康安全管理体系
OHT	overhead transparency 投影胶片
OHV	overhead valve 预置气门
OIC	Organisation Internationale du Commerce [英文：International Trade Organization] 国际贸易组织[法文]
OICA	Organisation Internationale des Constructeurs d'Automobiles 国际汽车制造商协会[法文]
OICW	objective individual combat weapon 目标单兵作战武器
OIE	Office of International Epizootics 国际兽疫学办公室
OIF	Organisation Internationale de la Francophonie 法语国家国际组织[法文]
OINK	one income no kids 单收入无子女夫妇
OIOS	Office of Internal Oversight Services 联合国内部监督事务厅
OIRT	Organisation Internationale de Radiodiffusion et de Télévision 国际广播电视组织
OIV(V)	Office International de la Vigne et du Vin [英文：International Vine and Wine Office] 国际葡萄与葡萄酒局[法文]
OJ	orange juice 橙汁
OK	okay 好的
OK	orthokeratology 角膜塑形镜，是通过改变角膜形状来达到矫正近视目的的一种硬性隐形眼镜
OK	Otto Kraste 合格（德国人 Otto Kraste 是优秀质量检测员，他所检测的汽车无质量问题，每部合格车均写上他的姓名缩写 OK）
ÖKO TEST	ÖKOtex Test 国际生态纺织品研究与发展协会制定的安全测试标准
OKR	Objective and Key Results 目标与关键结果法
OL	office lady 白领女性
OL	online 在线/网上
ol ol	olive oil 橄榄油
OL	on-line 联机网络[电子文献标示字母]
OLA	Office of Legal Affairs 联合国法律事务厅
OLAP	online analysis and processing 在线分析处理
OLE	object lining and embedding 目标链接嵌入
OLED	organic light-emitting diode 有机发光二极管

OM	Odyssey of the Mind 头脑奥林匹克
OMA	Oman 阿曼[亚洲国家]
OMA	object management architecture 对象管理体系
OMF	office of management and finance 管理和金融办公室
OMFIF	Official Monetary Finance Institute Forum 国际货币金融机构官方论坛
OMG	Oh, my God 我的天啊!
OMP	osteoblast milk protein 造骨牛奶蛋白
OMS	Organisation Mondiale de la Santé[英文: World Health Organization]世界卫生组织[法文]
OMX	Office Max 欧洲七国证券交易所的运营商和所有者
ÖN	Österreichischer Normunsinstitut 奥地利标准化协会[德文]
ÖN	Österreichischer Normunsinstitut 奥地利认证标志[德文]
ONDCP	Office of National Drag Control Policy 国家毒品控制政策办公室
ONF	open network foundation 开放网络基金会
ONGC	Oil and Natural Gas Company 石油天然气公司
ONS	oral nutritional supplement 口服营养增补剂
ONUESC	Organisation des Nations Unies pour l'Éducation, la Science et la Culture [英文: United Nations Educational, Scientific and Cultural Organization] 联合国教科文组织[法文]
OOB	out of balance 失去平衡
OODA	observation, orientation, decision and action 观察、熟悉[判断]、决策、行动(循环)
OOTD	outfit of the day 已经过时
OOTO	out of the office 不在办公室
OOU	out of use 无用
Op	opus 编号乐曲
OP	operation 运营
OP	out of print 绝版
OPA	Outward Processing Arrangement 外发加工方式
OPA	optical parametric amplifier 光学参量放大器
OPC	oil producting countries 石油生产国
OPCW	Organization for the Prohibition of Chemical Weapons 禁止化学武器组织

O

OPEC	Organization of Petroleum Exporting Countries 石油输出国组织
OPEC plus	Organization of Petroleum Exporting Countries plus 非石油输出国组织成员国
OpenCL	Open Computing Language 开放运算语言
OpenGL	Open Graphics Library 功能强大、调用方便的底层图形库
OpenNI	Open Natural Interaction 开放式的自然交互
OpenCV	Open Source Computer Vision Library 基于发行的跨平台计算机视觉库
OPF	One Planet Foundation 一个地球自然基金会
OPO	optical parametric oscillator 光学参量振荡器
OPT	Optimized Production Technology 最优生产技术
OPT	Optional Practical Training 毕业前后用的实习许可
OPT	Optional Practical Training 可选择的实践训练
OPTEX	operational test and evaluation 操作试验与鉴定
OR	operational room 手术室
OR	official referee 审查人
OREO	cream+chocolate 奥利奥(夹心饼干)
ORF	observation research fund 观察研究基金会
ORF	official representation fund 官方代表基金
ÖRF	Österreichischer Rundfunk 奥地利广播电视公司[德文]
ORR	objective relief rate 客观缓解率
ORR	objective response rate 客观应答率
ORV	off-road vehicle 越野车辆
OS	occupation safeguard 行业质量保证体系
OS	operating system 操作系统
Os	osmium 锇[第76号化学元素]
OS	only son 独生子
OS	operational sheets 操作说明书
OS	overall survival 总生存率
OSA	obstructive sleep apnea 阻塞性睡眠呼吸暂停
OSAT	Occupation Skill Association of Test 中国职业技能鉴定中心
OSB	oriented strand board 定向刨花板/欧松板

OSCE	Organization for Security and Cooperation in Europe	欧洲安全与合作组织
OSCs	overseas Chinese students	中国留学生
OSD	on-screen display	屏幕菜单调节
OSF	off-shore fund	境外基金
OSHMS	Occupational Safety and Health Management System	职业安全健康管理体系
OSI	open system interconnection	开放系统互联
OSI	Office of Special Investigation	美国空军特别调查局
Osm	osmosis	渗透性
OSP	official selling price	官方售价
OSS	Operating Support System	操作支持系统
OSS	Office of Strategic Services	美国战略服务局
OST	Original Sound Track	原声碟
OSTA	Occupational Skill Test Association	（劳动和社会保障部）职业技能鉴定中心
OSTP	Office of Scientific and Technical Policy	科学与技术政策办公室
OT	old tuberculin test	旧结核菌素试验
OT	overtime	加班
OT	Oyu Tolgoi	奥尤陶勒盖铜金矿项目[蒙古文]
OTA	other trading authority	其他交易授权
OTA	online travel agent	在线旅行社/在线旅游代理商
OTA	over the air	空中下载
OTC	Over The Counter	非处方药
OTC	one-stop inclusive tour charter	单点包机旅游（包括一切费用）
OTC	Organization for Trade Cooperation	贸易合作组织
OTC	over-the-counter	场外交易市场
OTCS	over-the-counter securities	场外交易的证券
OTCT	over-the-counter trading	场外交易
OTEC	ocean thermal energy conversion	海洋热能转换
OTO	Office of Trade Ombudsman	日本贸易申诉局
OTS	Office of Thrift Supervision	美国储蓄管理局

P

OTT	operational training test 操作培训测试
OTT	over the top 超过限额
OU	Oxford University 牛津大学[英国]
OUP	Oxford University Press 牛津大学出版社[英国]
outta	out of 在……之外[口语]
OVD	Optical Video Disc 视频光盘
ÖVE	Österreichischer Verband für Elektrotechnik 奥地利电气技术协会[德文]
ÖVE	Österreichischer Verband für Elektrotechnik 奥地利电气认证标志[德文]
Oxbridge	Oxford＋Cambridge 牛津＋剑桥
Oxfam	Oxford Committee for Famine Relief 牛津饥荒救济物质委员会
OY	Osakeyhti 有限公司[芬兰文]
OY	orange yellow 橙黄色
OYH	overhead projector 投影仪
OZ	ounce 盎司[非法定质量计量单位，1 盎司＝28.35 克]
Oz	Australia 澳大利亚

P	page 页
P	parking 停放处；车辆停放、船只停泊的标志
P	phosphorus 磷[第 15 号化学元素]
P	penny 便士
P	photoshop 修图
P	piano 轻柔地[意大利文]
p and h	postage and handling 邮资和手续费
p and p	postage and packing 邮资和包装费
p-book	paper-book 纸质书
P	parking 停车挡
P	park 公园

P	park 停车场
P	patent 专利[参考文献标示字母]
P	pink 粉红色
P	poor 低于平均[不佳]
P	progesterone 黄体酮/孕酮
P	purple 紫色
P&G	Procter & Gamble 宝洁
P&I	protection and indemnity 保赔
P&P	plug and play 即插即用传感器
P&R	park and ride 停车换乘
P(A-a)O2	alveolar-arterial oxygen tension difference 肺泡气和动脉血氧分压差
p. a.	per annum 每年[拉丁文]
P. A.	paper ass 没头脑的人
P. T.	passenger train 客车
P/B	price-book ratio 市净率
P/B	price-to-book ratio 市净[账]率
P/E	price-earnings 国内市盈率,股价利润率
P/E	price earnings ratio 本益比/市盈率
P+R/P&R	park and ride 停车换车
P2P	point to point（网络）点对点
P4	Protect 4 生物安全四级实验室的不规范简称
P-50	oxygen half-saturation pressure of hemoglobin 血红蛋白半饱和分压
PA	Press Association Ltd 英国报纸联合社
Pa	Protactinium 镤[第91号化学元素]
PA	Protection Grade of UVA PA 指数
PA	Protection Grade of UVA 防紫外线 UVA 标准
Pa	Pascal 帕（斯卡）[标准压强单位,1 帕＝1 牛顿/米^2]
PA	personal assistant 私人助理
PA	public address system 广播系统
PA	Physics Abstracts《物理学文摘》[美国]
PA	polyamide nylon 聚酰胺尼龙
PA	prothrombin activity 凝血酶原活性

PA	Psychological Abstracts《心理学文摘》[美国]	
PA	pyruvic acid 血清丙酮酸	
PaaS	platform-as-a-service 服务器平台服务	
PABA	para-aminobenzoic acid 对氨基苯甲酸	
PAC	pilotless aircraft 无人驾驶飞行器	
PAC	parent, adult, children 家长、成人、小孩	
PAC	political action committee 政治行动委员会	
PAC	Pakistan Aeronautical Complex 巴基斯坦航空联合体	
PAC	platelet associated complement 血小板相关补体	
PAC	press arbitration commission 仲裁委员会	
PAC-3	Patriot Advanced Capability-3 爱国者三型先进导弹系统	
PACE	Parliamentary Assembly of the Council of Europe 欧洲委员会议会大会	
PACE	precision analog computing equipment 精密模拟计算设备	
PaCO$_2$	partial pressure of carbon dioxide in artery 动脉血二氧化碳分压	
PACS	Picture Archiving and Communications System 医学影像传送与储存系统	
PACs	Political Action Committees 政治行动委员会[特殊利益集团的代言人]	
PAD	peripheral arterial disease 外周动脉疾病	
PAD	Prithvi Air Defense 印度普里特维防御飞行器	
PADAM	partial androgen deficiency in aging men 中老年男性雄激素部分缺乏综合征	
PADS	Partia Aleanca Demokratike Shqiptare 阿尔巴尼亚民主联盟党[阿尔巴尼亚文]	
PADS	performance analysis display system 性能分析显示系统	
PADS	personnel automatic data system 人事自动数据系统	
PADS	pneumatic air distribution system 气动空气分配系统	
PAdT	platelet adherence test 血小板黏附试验	
PAE	phthalic acid ester 邻苯二甲酸酯	
PAE	polyarylether 聚芳醚[塑料]	
PAEK	polyaryletherketone 聚芳醚酮[塑料]	
PAEs	phthalic acid esters 邻苯二甲酸酯类化合物	
PAF	platelet activating factor 血小板活化因子	
PAgT	platelet agglutination test 血小板聚集试验	

PAH(s)	polycyclic aromatic hydrocarbon(s)	多环芳烃
PAHO	Pan American Health Organization	泛美卫生组织
PAI	polyamide imide	聚酰胺-酰亚胺[塑料]
PAIGA	platelet associated Ig A	血小板相关免疫球蛋白A
PAIGG	platelet associated Ig G	血小板相关免疫球蛋白G
PAIGM	platelet associated Ig M	血小板相关免疫球蛋白M
PAK	Pakistan	巴基斯坦[亚洲国家]
PAK	Polyester alkyd resins	聚酯醇酸树脂
PAL	phase alternating (by) line	彩电帕尔制/相位变化线/逐行倒相制
PAL	program assembly language	程序汇编语言
PAN	Panama	巴拿马[北美洲国家]
PAN	polyacrylonitrile	聚苯烯腈[塑料]
PANA	Pan-African News Agency	泛非新闻社
PANA	Pan-Asian Newspaper Alliance	泛亚新闻社[设在香港]
PAO	peak acid output	胃酸分泌峰值
PAO	polyalphaolefin	聚α-烯烃
PAO2	alveolar oxygen partial pressure	肺泡氧分压
PaO2	arterial oxygen tension	动脉血氧分压
PAP	People's Action Party	人民行动党
PAP	prostate acid phosphatase	前列腺酸性磷酸酶
PAR	Paraguay	巴拉圭[南美洲国家]
PAR	phrased array radar	相控阵雷达
PARP	poly (ADP-ribose) polymerase	多腺苷二磷酸核糖聚合酶
PAS	Pacific Astronomical Society	太平洋天文学会
PAS	periodic acid-schiff stain	高碘酸希夫染色/糖原染色
PAS	publicly available specification	可公共提供的规范
PASMIN	Paralled Adaptive Structured Mesh Applications Infrastructure	并行自适应结构网格应用支撑软件框架
PASU	polyarylsulfone	聚芳砜[塑料]
Pat	Pataca	澳门元[货币]
PAT	profit after tax	税后利润
PAT	polyarylate	聚芳酯[塑料]

P

PATH	Ping'an, Alibaba, Tencent, Huawei 智慧城市代表企业:平安、阿里巴巴、腾讯、华为
PAUR	polyester polyurethane 聚酯型聚氨酯[塑料]
PAV	Poste Avion[英文:air mail]航空邮件[法文]
PAW	parents are watching 爸妈在看我玩电脑[网络用语][暗号]
PAWA	Pan-American Women's Association 泛美妇女协会
PAYE	pay as you earn 支付所得税
Pay-TV	pay television 收费电视
PB	personal best 个人最好成绩
PB	payment balance 支付差额
Pb	plumbum 铅[第82号化学元素][拉丁文]
PB	polybutene-1 聚丁烯-[1][塑料]
PB	purple blue 紫蓝色
PBA	Professional Bowlers Association 职业保龄球手协会
PBC	The petroleum brokerage company 石油经纪公司
PBC	The People's Bank of China 中国人民银行
PBGEA	Philippines Banana Growers and Exporters Association 菲律宾蕉农暨出口商协会
PBI	protein bound iodine 蛋白结合碘
PBM	pharmacy benefit management 药品福利管理
P-BOM	production bill of material 生产物料清单
PBR	price-book ratio 市净率
PBR	price-to-book ratio 市净[账]率
PBS	Public Broadcasting Service (美国)公共广播公司
PBT	polybutylene terephthalate 聚对苯二甲酸丁二醇酯[塑料]
PC	personal computer 个人电脑
PC	politically correct 政治上正确:能符合大多数选民的立场,引申不得罪人的立场,有时有挖苦之意
PC	postal code 邮政编码
PC	police constable 警员
PC card	printed circuit card 印刷电路卡
PC Plod	Police Constable Plod 警员[对警察的一种幽默称呼]

PC	polycarbonate 聚碳酸酯(塑料)
PC	production certification 生产许可证
PC	production control 生产管理/生产控制
PC	project committee 项目委员会
PCA	Partners Cooperation Agreement 伙伴合作协定
PCA	patient-controlled analgesia 病人自控镇痛
PCA	parietal cell antibody 壁细胞抗体
PCA	Permanent Court of Arbitration 海牙常设仲裁法院
PCAS	post-cardiac arrest syndrome 心脏骤停后综合征
PCAT	plasma recovery-calcium time 血浆复钙时间
PCB	polychlorinated biphenyls 多氯联苯
PCB	printed circuit board 印刷电路板
PCBA	printed circuit board assembly 成品线路板/印刷电路板组件
PCC	poison control center 中毒控制中心；毒品控制中心
PC-DOS	Personal Computer Disk Operating System 个人计算机磁盘操作系统
PCE	personal consumption expenditure 个人消费支出
PCEDM	Petro China Exploration Development Model 中国石油勘探开发数据模型
PCG	publishers communication group 美国出版商传播机构
PCG	phonocardiogram 心音图
PCI	Patent Citation Index 专利引文索引
PCI	peripheral component interconnect 外围部件互连
PCI	peripheral controller interface 外围控制器接口
PCI	Pollution Control Index 污染控制指数
PCI	percutaneous coronary intervention 经皮冠状动脉介入治疗
PCISIG	peripheral component interconnect special interest group 外围设备互连专业组
PCL	printer control language 打印机控制语言
PCM	power train control module 动力系统控制模块
PCM	pulse coding modulate 脉冲编码调制
PCMCIA	Personal Computer Memory Card International Association 个人电脑存储卡国际协会

PCN	Personal Communication Network	个人通信 PET(E)网络
PCNA	proliferating cell nuclear antigen	增殖细胞核抗原
PCO	pest control operation	有害生物防治
PCOS	polycystic ovary syndrome	多囊卵巢综合征
PCP	primary care provider	初级护理机构
PCP	primary care physician	初级护理医师
PCP	Partido Comunista del Perú	秘鲁共产党[西班牙文]
PCPS	percutaneous cardiopulmonary support	经皮心肺辅助法
PCR	polymerase chain reaction	聚合酶链反应
PCR	pathologic complete response	病理学完全缓解
PCS	print contrast signal	印刷对比度
PCSO	police community support officer	社区服务警察
PCT	Patent Cooperation Treaty	《专利合作条约》
PCT	platelet constrict volume	血小板比积
PCT	prothrombin consumption time	凝血酶原消耗时间
PCV	positive crankshaft ventilation	曲轴强制通风器
PCX	Pacific Exchange (stocks)	太平洋证券交易所
Pd	palladium	钯[第46号化学元素]
PD	Parkinson disease	帕金森病
PD	Police Department	警察局
PD	progressive disease	进展期疾病
PD	Pulse Doppler (radar)	脉冲多普勒(雷达)
PDA	Personal Digital Assistant	个人数字助理
PDA	Personal Digital Assistant	掌上电脑
PDB	protein data bank	蛋白质数据库
PDC	Professional Development Collection	教育核心期刊全文数据库
PDCA	plan, do, check, act	按计划、执行、检查、行动顺序进行质量管理
PDE-5	phosphodiesterase-5	5型磷酸二酯酶
PDF	portable data file	可移植数据文件
PDF	portable document format	可移植文档格式
PDI	personal disposable income	个人可支配收入
PDI	pre-delivery inspection	交付前检查[售前服务]

PDM	product data management 产品数据管理
PDO	protected designation of origin 受保护的原产地名称
PDP	plasma display panel 等离子体显示板
pdq	pretty damn(ed) quick 火速
PDR	Physicians' Desk Reference《医师手册》[美国]
PDSH	Partia Demokratike Shqiptare 阿尔巴尼亚民主联盟党[阿尔巴尼亚文]
PDT	Pacific Daylight Time 太平洋夏令时间
PDT	parfum de toilette 淡香精(香精含量15%)[法文]
PDT	photodynamic therapy 光动力疗法
PDT	portable data terminal 便携式数据采集终端
PDU	Police Dog Unit 警犬队
PDVSA	Petroleo de Venezuela SA 委内瑞拉石油公司[西班牙文]
PDW	Personal Defense Weapon 单兵自卫武器
PDW	platelet distribution width 血小板体积分布宽度
PE	physical education 体育课
PE	polyethylene 聚乙烯[打包食品的塑料袋的标注]
PE	price earnings ratio 市盈率
PE	price-to-earnings (ratio) 价格收益率
PE	project engineer 项目工程师
PE	physical examination 体检
PE	positive energy 正能量
PE	private equity 私募股本
PE	process engineer 工艺工程师
PE	production engineer 产品工程师
PE	protein electrophoresis 脑脊液蛋白电泳
pec	pectorals 胸肌
PEC	petroleum exporting countries 石油输出国
PECC	Pacific Economic Cooperation Conference 太平洋经济合作理事会
PECC	Provincial Emergency Coordination Centre 省紧急协调中心
PEEK	polyetheretherketone 聚醚醚酮[塑料]
Peerenting	peer+parent 同伴式父母
PEG	percutaneous endoscopic gastrostomy 经皮内镜下胃造瘘术

PEG	Panda Electronic Group 熊猫电子集团有限公司
PEH	Premium Eagles Holding LLC 美国盈鹰控股有限公司
PEI	polyetherimide 聚醚酰亚胺[塑料]
PEI	Prince Edward Island 加拿大爱德华王子岛
PEINP	Prince Edward Island National Park 加拿大爱德华王子岛国家公园
PEK	polyether ketone 聚醚酮[塑料]
PEMEX	Petróleos Mexicanos 墨西哥石油公司[西班牙文]
PEP	post exposure prophylaxis 艾滋阻断药
PER	price earnings ratio 本益比/市盈率
PERT	program evaluation and review technique 计划评估审查技术
PES	polyether sulfone 聚醚砜[塑料]
PESA	passive electronically scanned array (radar) 无源相控阵雷达
PESCO	permanent structural cooperation 永久的结构性合作
PET	Professional English Test 专业英语考试
PET	Public English Test 公共英语考试
PET	positron emission tomography 正电子发射断层扫描装置/正电子发射断层摄影术
PET	petrol 汽油
PET	petrol 石油
PET	polyester 聚酯
PET	polyethylene terephthalate 聚对苯二甲酸乙二(醇)酯[塑料]
PET	Primary English Test 英语入门考试
PETA	People for the Ethical Treatment of Animals Association 善待动物组织
PETA	people for the ethical treatment of animals 善待动物的人
PET-CT	positron emission tomography-computed tomography 肿瘤雷达
PET-CT	positron emission tomography-computed tomography 正电子发射计算机断层显像
PETN	pentaerythrite tetranitrate 太安[炸药]
PETROBRAS	Petróleo Brasileiro 巴西石油公司[葡萄牙文]
Petronas	Petroliam Nasional Bhd 马来西亚石油公司[马来文]
PETS	Public English Test System 全国英语等级考试
PEUR	polyether urethane 聚醚型聚氨酯[塑料]

PEVC	private equity venture capital fund 私募及创投	
PF	phenol-formaldehyde resin 酚醛树脂	
PF3T	platelet factor Ⅲ test 血小板第三因子试验	
PFI	Physical Fitness Index 身体健康指数	
PFI	port fuel injected (system) 进气道燃油喷射系统	
PFLOPS	peta floating-point operations per second 每秒千万亿次浮点运算	
P-FMEA	production failure mode & effect analysis 生产失效模式与效应分析	
PFS	progression life survival 进展生存期	
PG	public goods 公共产品	
PG	plasminogen 纤溶酶原	
PGA	Professional Golfers' Association of America 美国职业高尔夫球协会	
PGA	Project of Global Access 全球通用证书项目	
PGAS	polyglandular autoimmune syndrome 多（内分泌）腺性自身免疫综合征	
PGC	professional generated content 专业原创内容	
PGD	prenatal genetic diagnosis 产前遗传学诊断	
PGI	protected geographical indication 受保护的地理标志	
PGI	Petro-Geotech Incorporated 加拿大石油地质工程技术有限公司	
PGI	Platinum Guild International 国际铂金协会	
PGL	ProGamer League 职业电子竞技职业选手联赛	
PGR	population growth rate 人口增长率	
PGTL	Pakistan Gem Trade Laboratory 巴基斯坦宝石贸易实验室	
pH	potential hydrogen 氢离子浓度指数	
PH	phone 打电话	
PH	phone 电话	
PH	potential hydrogen 尿酸碱度	
PH	public house 酒吧	
PHC	public health care 公共卫生保健	
PHEIC	Public Health Emergency of International Concern 国际关注的突发公共卫生事件	
PHEV	parallel-hybrid electric vehicle 并联混合动力电动汽车	
PHODIR	photonic-based fully digital radar 基于光子的全数字雷达	
PHR	Profession of Human Resource 人力资源专业认证	

P

PHR	permanent hair remove 长久性脱毛
PHS	personal handy phone system 无线电话
PHS	Public Health Service （美国）公共卫生署
PHV	plug in hybrid vehicle 插电式混合动力车
phys ther	physical therapy 物理疗法
PI	principal investigator 主要研究者
PI	pulse interaction 脉中感应
PI	polyimide 聚酰亚胺［塑料］
PI3K	phosphatidylinositol 3-kinase 磷脂酰肌醇 3-激酶
PIA	Personal Information Assistant 个人信息助理
PIBA	Programa de desarrollo Integrado de Buenos Aires 布宜诺斯艾利斯行动计划［西班牙文］
PICC	People's Insurance Company of China 中国人民保险公司
PICU	pediatric intensive care unit 儿童重症监护室
PICU	perinatal intensive care unit 围产期重症监护室
PICU	pulmonary intensive care unit 肺科重症监护室
PIF	Paper Industry Federation 造纸工业联合会
PIF	prolactin release inhibiting factor 催乳素释放抑制因子
PIF	public investment fund 公共投资基金
Pig/HLJ/18	African swine fever virus strain 非洲猪瘟病毒毒株
PIM	Personal Information Management 个人信息管理
PIMCO	Pacific Investment Management Co. 太平洋投资管理公司
PIN	Personal Identification Number 个人身份识别号码
PINC	property income certificate 财产收入证书
PINPOINT	personal identification number＋point 精确定位器
PIRLS	Progress in International Reading Literacy Study 全球学生阅读能力进展研究
PISA	Programme for International Student Assessment 学生能力国际评估计划
Pitts Co Vacc	Pittsburgh Coronavirus Vaccine 匹兹堡冠状病毒疫苗
PJ	pararescue jumper 伞兵援救员
pjs	Peutz-Jeghers Syndrome 波伊茨-耶格综合征

PK	Player Killing 指游戏中玩家相互格斗，引申指对决
PK	pyruvate kinase (assay) 丙酮酸激酶
PKC	Public Key Cryptosystem 公共密钥密码系统
PKD	Peace-Keeping Deed (UN) 联合国维和行动
PKI	public key infrastructure 公开密钥基础设施
PKM	Peshawar to Karachi Motorway 白沙瓦到卡拉奇高速公路
PKM	personal knowledge management 个人知识管理
PKU	Peking University 北京大学
PKU	phenylketonuria 苯丙酮尿症
Pl	place 街道
Pl	plaza 广场
pl	plural 复数
PL	product liability 产品责任
PLA	People's Liberation Army of China (中国)人民解放军
plc	public limited company 公开股份公司
PLC	power line communication 电力线通信
PLC	power line conditioner 电力调节器
PLC	power loading control 动力负载控制
PLC	power-line carrier 电力线载波
PLC	programmable logic controller 可编程逻辑控制器
PLC	public listed company 公开上市公司
P-LCR	platelet large cell ratio 大血小板比值
PLD	Parti Libéral Démocrate 自由民主党[法文]
PLDT	Philippine Long Distance Telephone Company 菲律宾长途电话公司
PLE	Palestine 巴勒斯坦[亚洲国家]
PLG	plasminogen 纤溶酶原
PLGA	plasminogen activity 纤溶酶原活性
PLM	product lifecycle management 产品生产周期管理
PLM	programming language for microcomputer 微型计算机程序设计语言
PLOS	Public Library of Science 公共科学图书馆
PLSS	portable life-support system 便携式生命维持系统
PLT	platelet 血小板(计数)

P

PLU	player labour union 玩家工会	
PLW	Palau 帕劳[大洋洲国家][代字]	
PM	Prime Minister 总理	
PM	Private Message 网络论坛中的站内短消息	
PM	Production Management 生产管理	
Pm	Promethium 钷[第 61 号化学元素]	
PM	fine particulate matter 细颗粒物（如 PM2.5 指大气中直径小于或等于 2.5 微米的颗粒物）	
PM	periodic maintenance 定期维修	
PM	plant management 工厂管理/设备管理	
PM	precious metal 贵金属	
PM	procedures manuel 程序手册	
PM	project management 项目管理	
PMA	Pharmaceutical Manufacturers Association 药品生产商协会	
PMC	Panasonic Mobile Communications 个人移动通信	
PMC	portable media center 便携式媒体中心	
PMC	project management contract 项目管理承包	
PMC	production & material control 生产和物料控制	
PMI	private mortgage insurance 私人抵押保险	
PMI	Project Management Index 工程管理指数	
PMI	Project Management Institute 美国项目管理协会	
PMI	Purchasing Manager Index 采购经理人指数	
PMMA	polymethyl methacrylate 聚甲基丙烯酸甲酯[塑料]	
PMMI	The Packaging Machinery Manufactures Institute 美国包装机械制造协会	
PMO	Postal Money Order 邮政汇票	
PMO	Project Management Office 项目管理办公室	
PMP	portable media player 便携式媒体播放器	
PMP	Project Management Professional 项目管理专业人员认证	
PMRF	Pacific Missile Range Facility 太平洋导弹靶场设施	
PMS	premenstrual syndrome 经前期综合征	
PMS	poly(alpha-methyl styrene) 聚 α-甲基苯乙烯[塑料]	

PMT	premenstrual tension 经前紧张征
PNA	Philippine News Agency 菲律宾通讯社
PNA	The Pakistan National Alliance 巴基斯坦国家联盟
PNAS	*Proceedings of the National Academy of the Sciences of the United States of America* 《美国科学院院报》
PNC	Police Negotiation Circle 香港警察谈判小组
PNDD	Pacte National Pour la Démocratie et le Développement 民主与发展全国同盟［法文］
PNG	Portable Network Graphic Format 网络图形格式
PNG	persona non grata 不受欢迎的人
PNOC	Philippine National Oil Co. 菲律宾国家石油公司
PNR	passenger name record 乘客姓名记录
PNT	position, navigation and timing 定位、导航与授时
PNTR	Permanent Normal Trade Relations 永久性正常贸易关系
Po	polonium 钋［第84号化学元素］
PO	purchase order 订单
PO	the Post Office 邮政部门
PO$_2$	partial pressure of oxygen 氧分压
POC	proof of concept 概念验证
POGO	Project On Government Oversight 政府监督项目组织
POL	Poland 波兰［欧洲国家］
PolyU	The Hong Kong Polytechnic University 香港理工大学
POM	polyoxymethylene 聚甲醛［塑料］
POP	popular 流行的
POP	point of presence 因特网接入点
POP	post office protocol 邮政办公协议
POP	point of promotion 促销焦点（广告）
POPs	persistent organic pollutants 持久性有机污染物
POR	Portugal 葡萄牙［欧洲国家］
POS	point of sale (terminal) 销售点终端机；电子收款机
POSCO	Pohang Iron and Steel Co., Ltd. 韩国浦项制铁公司
POSH	polyolefin oligomeric saturated hydrocarbons 聚烯烃低聚饱和烃

P

POWER	Professional Organized for Women's Equal Rights 职业人员争取妇女平等权利组织[象征该组织有力量]
POX	peroxidase 过氧化物酶
PP	pages 页码
PP	polyphenyl 聚苯
PP	paddle paddle 百度飞桨
PP	polypropylene 聚丙烯[塑料]
PP	product plan 生产计划
PPA	phenyl propanolamine 苯丙醇胺[曾用来做某些感冒药的一种成分]
PPA	polyphthalamide 聚邻苯二（甲）酰胺[塑料]
PPAR	passive phased array radar 无源相控阵雷达
PPE	personal protective equipment 个人防护设备
ppi	pixels per inch 每英寸像素
PPI	Producer's Price Index 生产者物价指数
ppm	part per million 百万分之一
PPMA	The Process and Packaging Machinery Association 英国加工与包装机械厂商贸易协会
PPO	polyphenylene oxide 聚苯醚[塑料]
PPP	Pollute Pays Principle 环保污染付费原则
PPP	Purchasing-Power Parity 购买力平价[相对购买力指标]
PPP	partenarist public-privé 政府和社会资本合作模式[法文]
PPP	Public-Private Partnership 政府与社会资本合作
PPP	personal projects page 个人项目页
PPP	plasma protamine precipitating 血浆鱼精蛋白沉淀
PPP	point to point protocol 点到点协议
PPP	project portfolio prioritization 专案组合优化管理系统
PPP	projects, plans and policy 项目、计划和政策
PPP	public-private-partnership 公私合作模式
PPR	Pinault Printemps Redoute 法国皮诺家族[法文]
PP-R	polypropylene random copolymer 聚丙烯无规共聚物[塑料]
PPRB	Police Public Relation Bureau 香港警察公共关系科
PPS	progressive power steering 渐进式动力转向

PPS	Parliamentary Private Secretary 议会私人秘书
PPS	picture perception system 图像感知系统
PPS	picture pickup system 摄像系统
PPS	pictures per second 每秒钟画面数
PPS	polyethylene sulfide 聚亚苯基硫醚[塑料]
PPS	Pre-Production Shop (development) 发展生产车间
PPSU	polyethylene sulfone 聚苯砜[塑料]
PPT	Power Point 一种演示文稿图形程序
PPT	program processing table 程序处理表
PPV	pay-per-view 每收视一次的付费
PQDD	Pro Quest Digital Dissertation 美国博硕士论文数据库
PQE	product quality engineer 产品质量工程师
PQI	Patent Quotation Index《专利引文索引》
PQS	project quantity surveyor 项目数量检验员
PR	Personal Record 个人履历
Pr	praseodymium 镨[第59号化学元素]
PR	proportional representation 比例代表制
PR	public relation 公共关系
PR	pattern recognition 模式识别
PR	page rank 网页级别
PR	Pakatan Rakyat 人民联盟[马来文]
PR	partial response 部分缓解
PR	poor 差等级(钱币)
PR	product review 针对产品的评价
PR	purchase requisition 请购单
PR	pure risk 纯粹风险
PR	purple red 紫红色
PRA	plasma renin activity 血浆肾素活性
PRAB	Program Risk Assessment Board 项目风险评估委员会
PRAC	Program Risk Assessment Committee 项目风险评估委员会
PRB	Population Reference Bureau 人口问题参考资料局
PRCA	pure red blood cell regeneration barrier anemia 单纯红细胞再生障碍性贫血

P

PRDR	Parti Républicain pour la Démocratie et Ranouveau 争取民主与革新共和党[法文]
Prep	preparation 大学预科的一年级学生
prep	pattern reversal evoked potential 图像倒转诱发电位
PRF	prolactin releasing factor 催乳素释放因子
PRI	Partido Revolucionario Institucional 革命制度党[西班牙文]
PRI	Public Radio International 国际公共广播电台
PRISM	program reliability information system for management 管理程序可靠性信息系统
PRK	Korea (D.P.R.) 朝鲜[亚洲国家]
PRK	photorefractive keratectomy 激光光学角膜切削术
PRL	prolactin 催乳素
PRM	Partner Relationship Management 伙伴关系管理
PRM	professional risk management 专业风险管理
PRMIA	Professional Risk Manager International Association 国际风险管理师协会
Pro	professional 专业人员
PRO	protein 蛋白质
PRO	urine protein 尿蛋白
Pro-E	Pro-engineer 美国参数技术公司旗下的 CAD/CAM/CAE 一体化的三维软件
pro-e	professional engineer 专业工程师
PROM	programmable read-only memory 可编程只读存储器
PRP	public relation personnel 公关人士
PRS	Poland Register of Shipping 波兰船舶登记局
PRT	Personal Rapid Transit 个人捷运系统
PRT	plasma recalcification time 血浆复钙时间
PS	pub show 酒吧秀
PS	photo service 照片服务
PS	Photoshop 由 Adobe 公司开发的一种图像编辑软件
PS	plastic surgery 整形外科
PS	play station 游戏工作站
PS	presensitized plate 预涂感光版,一种预先涂有感光性膜层的印刷版

PS	Philippine Standards 菲律宾标准	
PS	Philippine Standards 菲律宾产品认证标志	
ps	photoshop 照片处理	
PS	polystyrene 聚苯乙烯[塑料]	
PS	postscriptum 附言[拉丁文]/又及[拉丁文]	
ps	postscript 附言	
PS	post 补充说明	
PS	processor storage 处理器存储器	
PS	product or service 高新技术产品或服务	
PS	project system 项目管理	
PSA	prostate-specific antigen 前列腺特异抗原	
PSA	Peugot Société Anoryme 法国标致雪铁龙[法文]	
PSA	Product Standards Agency 菲律宾产品标准局	
PSA	psoriatic arthropathy 牛皮癣性关节炎	
PSAT	Preliminary Scholastic Aptitude Test（美国）学业能力倾向初步测验；大学预考	
PSB	Productivity and Standards Board 新加坡认证标志	
PSB	Productivity and Standards Board 新加坡生产力及标准质量会议	
PSC	putonghua shuiping ceshi 普通话水平测试[汉语拼音缩略语]	
PSCUS	Pursuing Tracing Survey of Chinese University Students 中国大学生追踪调查	
PSE	psychological stress evaluator 心理压力测评器	
PSE	Public Service Employment 公共服务职业	
PSE	Public Service Employment 日本产品质量认证标志	
PSHEE	personal, social, health and economic education 个人、社会、健康和经济教育	
psi	pound per square inch 磅/平方英寸	
PSI	per square inch 每平方英寸	
PSI	Personalized System of Instruction 个性化教学法	
PSI	pollutant standard index 污染标准指数	
PSI	Pakistan Standards Institution 巴基斯坦标准学会	
PSI	Pakistan Standards Institution 巴基斯坦产品认证标志	

PSK	phase shift keying 高阶调制
PSL	pledged supplementary lending 抵押补充贷款
PSP	play station portable 掌上游戏机
PST	Pacific Standard Time 太平洋标准时间
PST	provincial sales tax 省销售税
PSTN	Public Switched Telephone Network 公用交换电话网
PSU	polyphenylene sulfone 聚亚苯基砜[塑料]
PSV	public service vehicle 公共(交通)车辆
PT	part-time 兼职
PT	physical training 体格锻炼
PT	Particular Transfer 特别转让
PT	Perséroan Torbetas 有限公司[印尼文]
Pt	platinum 铂[第76号化学元素]
PT	pneumatic tubes 超级高铁
PT-76	Soviet amphibious tank 苏联的水陆两栖坦克
PTA	parent-teacher association 家长教师联盟会
PTA	part-time assistant or analyst 兼职助理
PTA	preferential trade agreement 特惠贸易协定
PTA	preferential trade area 特惠贸易区
PTA	purified terephthalic acid 精对苯二甲酸
PTC	photographic type composition 照相排字
PTC	World Snooker Player Tour Championship 世界斯诺克球员巡回锦标赛
PTC	Parameter Technology Corporation 参数技术公司
PTCS	percutaneous transhepatic cholangioscopy 经皮经肝胆管镜检查
Pte	private 二等兵
PTFE	polytetrafluoroethylene 聚四氟乙烯[塑料]
PTH	parathyroid hormone 甲状旁腺激素
PTHrP	parathyroid hormone-related protein 甲状旁腺激素相关蛋白
PTI	Press Trust of India 印度报业托拉斯
PTLA	*Publishers Trade List Annual* 《美国出版商目录年报》
PTO	patent and trademark office 专利商标局
PTO	please turn over 见下页

PTOP	partner to partner 伙伴对伙伴的关系
PTQ	put together quickly 高速装配
PTS	Police Training School 香港警校
PTSD	post-traumatic stress disorder 创伤后应激障碍
PTU	Police Tactical Unit 香港警察机动部队
PTV	pay television 付费电视
PTV	projection television 背投电视
PTVIP	platinum very important person 最高级贵宾
PTW	permissible total weight 最大允许总质量
Pty	proprietary 公司［多用于澳大利亚和南非］
Pu	plutonium 钚［第 94 号化学元素］
PU	Peking University 北京大学
PU	polyurethane 聚氨酯［塑料］
PU	Princeton University 普林斯顿大学［美国］
PU	purple 紫色
PU6	University of Paris 6 法国巴黎第六大学
PUA	pick-up artist 搭讪艺术家（用搭讪来骗人的人）
PubArt	Art for Public 艺术属公众
PUFA	polyunsaturated fatty acid 多不饱和脂肪酸
PUGC	professional user generated content 专业用户原创内容
PUK	personal unblocking key 个人解锁码
PUMP	Political Upwardly Mobile Personality 政治行情看涨
PUR	Puerto Rico 波多黎各［北美洲国家］
PUS	Pharmacopoeia of the United States《美国药典》
PUZ	puzzle game 益智类游戏
PV	peak value 峰值
PV	per value 按价值
PVAL	polyvinyl alcohol 聚乙烯醇［塑料］
PVC	polyvinyl chloride 聚氯乙烯［塑料］
PVDC	polyvinyl dichloride 聚偏（二）乙烯［塑料］
PVDF	polyvinylidene fluoride 聚偏（二）氟乙烯［塑料］
PVE	player vs environment 玩家对抗环境

PVH	Philips-Van-Heusen 美国 PVH 服装集团(世界第二大服装集团)
PVIFA	present value if annuity 年金的现值系数
PVM	Process Virtual Machine 流程虚拟机
PVM	products value management 产品价值管理模式
PVoC	Pre-Export Verification of Conformity to Standards 出口前产品与标准的符合性验证
PVOC	Pre-Export Verification of Conformity 货物出口前符合性认证[东非国家常用]
PVP	payment v payment 支付对支付
PVR	personal video recorder 个人视频录像机
PVS	persistent vegetative state 持续性植物人状态
pw	per week 每周
PW	Physics World 物理世界
PWA	person with AIDS 艾滋病患者
PWB	print wiring board 印刷电路板
PX	post exchange 小卖部
PX	p-xylene 对二甲苯
PYD	Partiya Yekîtiya Demokrat 民主联盟党[土耳其文]
PZL	puzzle game 解谜类游戏

Q	cute 聪明、漂亮、可爱、招人喜欢、酷[英语谐音缩略语]
Q	qiyebiaozhun 企业标准[汉语拼音缩略语]
Q	question 问题
Q	quality 质量
Q	queen 皇后/女王
Q&A	question and answer 问与答
q. d.	quasi dictum 仿佛是说[拉丁文]

QA	quality assessment 质量评价
QA	quality assurance 品质保证/质量保证
QAA	Quality Assurance Agency for Higher Education 高等教育质量保证署
QAM	quadrature amplitude modulation 正交振幅调制
QAO	Quality Assurance Office 质量保证局
QAT	Qatar 卡塔尔[亚洲国家]
QC	Queen's Counsel 王室法律顾问
QC	quality control 品质管理/质量控制
QCC	Quality Control Circle 质量管理圈/品质管理圈
QCD	quality control division 质量检查处
QCDS	Quality Control Directive Special 质量控制特别指令
QCDS	Quality Cost Delivery Service 品质成本交期服务
qd	quaque die 每天[拉丁文]
QDII	Qualified Domestic Institutional Investors 合格境内机构投资者
QDOS	Quick and Dirty Operating System 快速粗制操作系统
QDR	Quadrennial Defense Review 国防战略评估
QE	quality engineer 品质工程师
QE	quantitative easing 量化宽松（货币政策）
QE	quantum electronics 量子电子学
QED	quod erat demonstrandum 证明完毕[拉丁文]
QFF	quick frozen foods 快冻食品
QFII	Qualified Foreign Institutional Investors 合格境外机构投资者
QFT	quoted for truth 赞同（别人的话）（引用别人话时"以此为证"）[网络用语]
qh	quaque hora 每小时[拉丁文]
qid	quarter in die 每日四次[拉丁文]
QIHC	Qianhai Investment Holding Company 前海投资控股公司
QL	quality level 质量水平
QM	quality management 质量管理
QM	quality manual 品质手册
QMS	Quality Management System 质量管理体系
QNB	quinuclidinyl benzilate 毕兹

Q

QNB	3-quinuclidinyl benzilate 二苯羟乙酸-3-奎宁环酯
qns	quantum ono sufficiat 量不足[拉丁文]
QOL	quality of life 生命质量/生活质量/生存质量
QPSK	quadrature phase shift keying 正交相移键控
QQ	Oh, I seek you→OICQ→QQ 即时聊天工具
QQC	quality and quantity certificate 质量和数量证书
QQE	quantitative and qualitative monetary easing 质化和量化的货币宽松政策
QR	quality review 质量检查
QR	quick reaction 快速反应
QR Code	Quick Response Code 二维码
QR	quick response 二维码
QR	quick response 快速响应(码)
QRF	quick reaction force 快速反应部队
QS	quality safety 质量安全
QS	quality service 质量服务
qs	quantum sufficiat 足量[拉丁文]
qt	quart 夸脱[液量单位]
QTL	quantitative trait loci 数量性状遗传位点
qtz	quartz 石英
QU	Qingdao University 青岛大学
QueSST	quiet supersonic technology 安静超音速技术
qv	quod vide 参见该条[拉丁文]
QVM	Qualified Vehicle Modifier 有资质的车辆改装商
QZ	quartz 水晶
QZSS	Quasi Zenith Satellite System 准天顶卫星系统

R	Rely 威麟汽车[中国]	
R	Riich 瑞麒汽车[中国:汉语缩略语]	
R	Regina 女王[拉丁文]	
R	restricted 限制级的	
R	retinene 视黄醛	
R	Rex 国王[拉丁文]	
R	river 河流	
R	royal 王室的	
R	rare 稀有	
R	Échelle Réaumur Lieaomier 列氏温标[法文]	
R	red 红色	
R	registered trade mark 注册商标	
R	report 报告[参考文献标示字母]	
R	Republican 共和党(党员)	
R	respiration 呼吸	
R	reverse 倒挡	
R	roentgen 伦琴(照射计量单位)	
R&B	Rhythm & Blues 节奏布鲁斯[黑人流行音乐]	
R&D	research and development 研究与开发	
R&D	Research and Development Department 研发部	
R&R	rescue and resuscitation 救生	
R&R	Rolls Royce 劳斯莱斯汽车[英国]	
r. h.	right hand 右手	
R/T	revenue ton 运费吨	
Ra	radium 镭[第88号化学元素]	
RA	Registration Authority 注册机构	

R

RA	research assistant 美国研究助理[高等教育机构为研究生设置的支薪职位]
RA	resident assistant 住院医生助手
RA	residence advisor 宿舍舍监
RA	rheumatic arthritis 风湿性关节炎
RA	rheumatoid arthritis 类风湿性关节炎
RAA	risk-based approach to assessment 基于风险控制的院校评审
RABF	Robust Adaptive Beam Forming 鲁棒自适应波束
RAC	race game 竞速类游戏
RAC	Royal Automobile Club 英国皇家汽车俱乐部
RAC	Rubber Association of Canada 加拿大橡胶协会
RAF	Royal Air Force 英国皇家空军
RAII	resource acquisition is initialization 资源获取就是初始化
RAIU	radioactive iodine uptake 放射性碘摄取率
RAL	Russian Airlines 俄罗斯航空公司
RAM	Random Access Memory 随机存取存储器
RAM	radar absorbing material 雷达吸波材料
RAPM	risk-adjusted performance measure 风险调整后的绩效指标
RAS	Remote Access Service 远程访问服务
RAS	rail adapter system 导轨适配系统
RASD	Reference and Adult Services Division 参考与成人服务分会
RATU	Regional Anti Triad Unit 香港总区反三合会行动组
RB	regular budget 经常预算
Rb	rubidium 铷[第37号化学元素]
RB	Red Bull 红牛[饮料]
RBC	ragdoll breed club 猫犬俱乐部
RBC	rechargeable battery cell 可充电电池
RBC	red blood cell 红细胞
RBC	regional broadband consortia 区域宽带联盟
RBC	regional building committee 区域建设委员会
RBC	regional business center 区域商业中心
RBC	requirements based collection 基于需求搜集
RBC	Rhythm and Blues Cafe 音乐和蓝调咖啡馆[美国辛辛那提]

RBC	risk based capital 基于风险资本
RBC	Royal Bank of Canada 加拿大皇家银行
RBC	rural broadband coalition 农村宽带联盟
RBC	Russia Business Council 俄罗斯商务委员会
RBC	Ryukyu Broadcasting Corporation 琉球广播公司
RBCT4	red blood cell total thyronine concentration 红细胞甲状腺浓度测定
RBD	Recreational Business District 旅游商业街
RBF	renal blood flow 肾血流量
rBGH	Recombinant Bovine Growth Hormone 重组牛生长激素
RBIS	Reserve Best In Show 全场犬类后备总冠军[即亚军]
RBN	Regional Business News 区域商业文献全文数据库
RBR	Review of Business Research 回顾商业研究
RBS	Royal Bank of Scotland 苏格兰皇家银行
rBST	Recombinant Bovine Somatotropin 重组牛生长激素
RC	radio control 无线电控制
RC	Roman Catholic 天主教
RC	Red Cross 红十字会
RC	reticular cell 网状细胞（计数）
RCA	Radio Corporation of America 美国无线电公司
RCAC	RCA Communications Inc. 美国无线电通信公司
RCEP	Regional Comprehensive Economic Partnership 区域全面经济伙伴关系
RCI	resident cost inspection 居民消费调查
RCIC	Red Cross International Committee 红十字国际委员会
RCLS	Ramapo Catskill Library System RC 图书馆体系
RCMP	Royal Canadian Mounted Police 加拿大皇家骑警
RCO	reduce the cost 降低造价
RCTC	Research Center for Toilet Culture 厕所文化研究中心
RCU	Regional Crime Unit 香港重案组
Rd	road 路[用于书面地址]
RD	radio 广播电台
RD	*Reader's Digest* 《读者文摘》[美国]
RDA	recommended daily allowance 每日推荐摄入量标准

R

RDI	research, development and innovation 研发和创新
RDIF	Russia Direct Investment Fund 俄罗斯直接投资基金
RDK	rapid displaying kitchen 快速展开式野战厨房
RDS	Radio Data System 无线数据系统
RDS	Relational Database Service 阿里云关系数据库
RDU	Rassemblement pour la Démocratie et UNI 民主团结联盟[法文]
RDW	red cell distribution (width) 细胞分布宽度
RDX	Hexogen 黑索金[炸药]
RE	religious education 宗教教育
Re	rhenium 铼[第75号化学元素]
RE	real estate 房地产
Re	reply 回复
RE	Robot Erectus 新加坡研发的仿人机器人
RE	Royal Exchange 伦敦交易所
REACH	Registration, Evaluation, Authorization and Restriction of Chemicals 化学品注册、评估、许可和限制
REAP	Rural Education Action Program 农村教育行动项目
Rec(p)t	receipt 收据
recd	received 收到
recd	recorded 记录
RECEIVED B/L	received for shipment bill of landing 待装运提单
RECIST	Response Evaluation Criteria in Solid Tumor 实体肿瘤疗效评估标准
REF	Research Excellence Framework 科研卓越框架
Ref	reference 参照
refr	refrigerate 冷藏
REITs	real estate investment trusts 房地产信托基金
REITs	real estate investment trusts 不动产投资信托公司
REM	rapid eye movement 快速眼动
REMP	Research Group for European Migration Problems 欧洲移民问题研究组织
rep	representative 代表

Res	Resveratrol 白藜芦醇
Ret	reticular cell 网状细胞（计数）
Reuters	Reuters News Agency 路透社[英国通讯社]
Revd	reverend 尊敬的
RF	radio frequency 射频技术
RF	reserve fund 准备基金
RF	right fullback（足球）右后卫
Rf	rutherfordium 𬬻[第104号化学元素]
RF	rheumatoid factor 类风湿因子
RFAB	rapid facilities of assembly and blend 快速组装和混合设施
RFC	Registered Financial Consultants 认证测验报名表
RFD	Rassemblement des Forces Démocratiques 民主力量联盟[法文]
RFI	Radio France Internationale 法国国际广播电台[法文]
RFI	request for information 信息邀请书
RFID	radio frequency identification devices 无线射频识别/射频识别技术
Rg	roentgenium 𬬭[第111号化学元素]
RGB	red, green, blue 工业界的一种颜色标准[三基色:红、绿、蓝]
RGN	registered general nurse 注册普通护士
RGU	Rating Group Ukraine 乌克兰独立民意调查机构
RH	relative humidity 相对湿度
RH	right 右边
RH	Regal House 瑞阁堡葡萄酒
Rh	Rh type Rh血型（检查）
RH	rhesus blood group Rh血型/猕猴血型
Rh	rhodium 铑[第45号化学元素]
RIA	radioimmunoassay 放射免疫分析
RIA	Russian Information Agency 俄罗斯新闻社
RIGS	radioimmunoguided surgery 放射免疫导向手术
RIKEN	RIkagaku Kenkyusho [英文: Institute of Physical and Chemical Research] 日本理化学研究所[日文]
RINA	Registo Italiano Navade 意大利船级社[意大利文]
RINOs	Republicans in Name Only 名义上的共和党

R

RIP	Requiescat In Pace 愿灵安息[拉丁文]	
RIS	rail interface system 导轨接口系统	
RISC	reduced instruction set computer 简化指令集计算（机）	
RISE	rotation and interior structure experiment 旋转和内部结构实验	
RISUG	Reversible Inhibition of Sperm Under Guidance 印度男性避孕药[英文意为在引导下对精子进行可逆抑制]	
RIU	Regional Intelligence Unit 香港总区情报组	
RKE	remote keyless entry 遥控门禁系统	
RKV	re-design kill vehicle 重新设计的杀伤器	
RLEST	real estate 房地产	
RLND	regional lymph node dissection 区域淋巴结清扫	
RM	Record Management 记录管理	
RMA	Revolution in Military Affairs 军事革命	
RMB	renminbi 人民币[汉语拼音缩略语]	
RMPU	Regional Missing Person Unit 香港失踪人口调查组	
RMS	re-multiple sclerosis 复发性多发性硬化症	
Rn	radon 氡[第 86 号化学元素]	
RNA	ribonucleic acid 核糖核酸	
RNAi	ribonucleic acid interference 核糖核酸干扰	
RNG	Royal Never Giveup RNG 电子竞技俱乐部	
RNP	ribonucleoprotein 核糖核蛋白	
RNRD	Rassemblement National pour la Reforme et le Developpement 全国改革与发展联盟[法文]	
RO	reproduction number 病毒再生繁殖数	
ROA	return on assets 资产回报率/资产收益（率）	
Robocon	robot contest 机器人大赛	
ROC	return on capital 资本收益率	
ROCA	Returned Overseas Chinese Association 归国华侨联合会	
ROCN	Randonneurs of China 中国不间断骑行协会	
ROE	Rate of Exchange 汇率	
ROE	return on equity 股本收益	
ROE	return on equity 股东权益报酬率/净资产收益率	

ROG	receipt of goods	货已收到凭证
ROI	return on investment	投资回报
ROI	rate of interest	利(息)率
ROI	return of investment	投资利润
ROI	return on investment	投资回报率
ROM	Read Only Memory	只读存储器
ROR	rate of return	报酬率
ROS	return on sales	销售收益率
ROSC	restoration of spontaneous circulation	自发循环恢复
Rostec	Rostekhnologii	俄罗斯国家技术集团[俄文]
Rostec	Rossiiskaia Tehnika	俄技集团[俄文]
ROTC	Reserve Officers' Training Corps	预备役军官训练团
ROUS	hemosiderin	尿含铁血黄素实验
ROYGBIV	red, orange, yellow, green, blue, indigo, violet	赤橙黄绿青蓝紫(色)
RP	real property	不动产
RP	reference price	参考价格
RP	retail price	零售价
RP	return premium	退还保险费
RP	received pronunciation	标准发音
RP	reddish purple	红色
RP	reinforced plastics	增强塑料
RPF	renal plasma flow	肾血浆流量
RPG	Rocket-Propelled Grenade	火箭助推榴弹发射器
RPG	report program generator	报表程序的生成程序
RPG	role-playing game	角色扮演游戏
RPHA	reversed passive hemagglutination	反向被动凝血反应
RPI	retail price index	零售物价指数
Rpm	revolutions per minute	每分钟转数
RPMI-1640	Rosewell Pack Memorial Institute-1640	罗斯威尔派克纪念研究所开发的培养基
RPN	risk priority number	风险优先数
RPO	recruitment process outsourcing	招聘流程外包

RPQ	request for price quotation 请求报价单
RPR	rapid plasma reagent 快速血浆反应素（实验）
RPR	Rassemblement pour la République 保卫共和联盟［法文］
RPS	Radiation Protection Standards 辐射防护标准
RQ	respiratory quotient 呼吸指数
RQ	Royal Photographic Society（英国）皇家摄影学会
RQB	Recognized Qualifying Bodies 英国审计师资格
RQFII	RMB Qualified Foreign Institutional Investors 人民币合格境外投资者
RR	rear 后部
RR	rate of return on capital 资本利润率
RR	Rolls-Royce 英国劳斯莱斯汽车
RRC	radio resource controller 无线电资源控制器
RRC	rotate right through carry 带进位循环右移
RRSP	registered retirement saving plan 注册退休储蓄计划
RS	remote sensing 遥感技术
RS	Reed-Solomon 里德-所罗门码
RS	Republic Services 共和废品处理公司
RS	Russian Maritime Register of Shipping 俄罗斯船舶登记局
RSA	Republic of South Africa 南非［非洲国家］
RSA	radar signature analysis 雷达信号特征分析
RSA	Ron Rivest, Adi Shamir, Leonard Adleman 算法加密系统［以发明者的姓氏首字母命名］
RSA	Royal Society of Arts 英国皇家艺术学会
RSB	Recognized Supervisory Body 承认监管机构
RSD	relative standard deviation 相对平均偏差
RSDS	Regional Special Duty Squad 香港特别职务队
RSE	relationships and sex education 两性关系和性教育
RSG	realtime strategy game 即时战略类游戏
RSI	repetitive strength injure 重复性外力伤害
RSI	rationalization, standardization, interoperability 合理化、标准化及相互适应性
RSI	relative strength index 相对强弱指标

RSIS	Singapore Rajaratnam School of International Studies 新加坡拉惹勒南国际研究院
RSIU	Remote Sensing Imagery Understanding 遥感图像理解
RSL	Rieter-Scragg Ltd 英国立达公司
RSPCA	Royal Society for the Prevention of Cruelty to Animals 英国防止虐待动物协会
RSS	Really Simple Syndication 简易信息聚合，也称聚合内容
RSS	Rashtriya Swayamasevak Sangh 国民志愿服务团［印地文］
RSS	received signal strength 接收信号强度
rss	root-sum square 和的平方根
RSSS	Regional Surveillance & Support Squad 香港总区跟踪及支援组
RSVP	Répondez s'il vous plait 请回复［法文］
RT	retweet 转推［用于所转发的消息前］
RT	részesedési társaság 控股公司［匈牙利文］
Rt Hon	Right Honourable 阁下
Rt Rev(d)	Right Reverend 尊敬的［尊称主教］
RT	Russia Today 今日俄罗斯
RT	Russian Television 俄罗斯电视台
rT3	reverse triiodothyronine 反式三碘甲腺原氨酸
RTA	road traffic accident 道路交通事故
RTF	rich text format 普适文本格式
RTGS	Real Time Gross Settlement 实时全额支付系统
RTI	Round Table International 国际圆桌会议
RTI	radiotehnicheskii institut 无线电技术研究所［俄文］
RTL	Radio Télévision Luxembourgecise 卢森堡广播电视台［法文］
RTL	Radio-Tolbiac (Zulpich) en Lutte 法国 RTL 电台［法文］
RTL	Radio-Télévision Luxembourg 卢森堡广播电视台［德文］
RTL	real time logistics 实时物流
RTL	Radio and Television of Luxembourg 卢森堡广播电视台
RTM	registered trade mark 注册商标
RTP	reinforced thermoplastics 增强热塑性塑料
RT-PCR	reverse transcription-polymerase chain reaction 逆转录聚合酶链反应

R

RTS	ready-to-send 准备发送
RTS	ready-to-serve 发送请求
RTS	realtime strategy 即时战略游戏
RTS	residence time, temperature and speed 驻留时间、温度和速度
RTT	radio transfers technology 无线电传输技术
RTT	realtime tactics 即时战术游戏
RTTV	Russia Today Television 今日俄罗斯电视台
RTV	restaurant television 有高级视听设备的餐厅
Ru	ruthenium 钌[第44号化学元素]
ru	Russia 俄罗斯
RUB	rubber 橡胶
RUB	Russian Ruble 俄罗斯卢布
RUC	Renmin University of China 中国人民大学
RUS	Russia 俄罗斯[欧洲国家]
RUSA	Reference and User Services Association 参考与用户服务协会
RV	rated voltage 额定电压
RV	recreation vehicle 休闲车
RV	receipt voucher 收据
RV	residual volume 残气容积
RVH	right ventricular hypertrophy 右心室肥大
Rw	Rongwei 荣威汽车[中国:汉语缩略语]
RW	raw white 本白色
RWA	Rwanda 卢旺达[非洲国家]
RWA	rural wireless operator association 农村无线运营商协会
RWCS	reasonable worst case scenario 可接受底线
RWE	Rheinisch-Westfaetisches Elektriritaets-werk AG 德国RWE股份公司
RX	rising 瑞星软件
RXR	retinoid X receptor 类视黄醇X受体
RY	red yellow 红黄色

S		Austrian Schilling 奥地利先令［奥地利货币］
S		second 秒［时间单位］
S		small 小号
S		sulfur 硫［第 16 号化学元素］
S		Saint 圣人
S		saloon 厢式小汽车
S		sedan 轿车
S		Shuanghuan 双环汽车［中国石家庄；汉语缩略语］
S		siemens 西门子［电导单位］
S		south(ern) 南方的
S&P		Standard and Poor's 标准普尔［美国的信用评级机构］
S		SEMKO［见 SEMKO 条］
S		session 访问量
S		SEV［见 SEV 条］
S		specification 标准［参考文献标示字母］
S		Standards Association of New Zealand 新西兰标准协会
S		Standards Association of New Zealand 新西兰产品质量认证标志
S		Suzuki 日本铃木汽车
S&L		savings and loan association 房屋互助协会
S&L		savings and loan 储蓄和贷款
S&P 500		Standard & Poor's 500 标准普尔 500 种股票指数
S&P		Standard & Poor's 标准普尔（股票价格）指数
S. A.		Società Anonima 有限公司［意大利文］
S/AN		styrene-acrylonitrile plastics 苯乙烯-丙烯腈塑料
S/MS		styrene-α-methyl styrene plastics 苯乙烯-α-甲基苯乙烯塑料
S/N		shipping note 装运单

S/O	shipping order 装货单
S/S	steam ship 蒸汽船
SA	savings account 储蓄账户
SA	social accountability 社会责任
SA	South Africa 南非
SA	Science Abstracts《科学文摘》
SA	Sociedad Anónima 股份公司[西班牙文]
SA	Sociedade Anónima 股份公司[葡萄牙文]
SA	Société Anonyme 有限公司[法文]
SA	Special Ale 特色淡啤
SA	standalone 独立组网
SA8000	Social Accountability 8000 社会责任标准体系[一种质量认证]
SAA	Saudi Arabian Airlines 沙特阿拉伯航空公司
SAA	South African Airways 南非航空公司
SAA	South Atlantic Anomaly 南大西洋异常区
SAA	Standards Association of Australia 澳大利亚标准协会
SAA	Standards Association of Australia 澳大利亚产品质量认证标志
SAA	Syria Arabia Army 叙利亚阿拉伯陆军
SAAB	Svenska Aeroplan Aktiebolaget 瑞典萨博汽车公司[瑞典文]
SAALT	South Asian Americans Leading Together 美国南亚人联盟
SAARC	South Asia Association of Regional Co-operation—Bangladesh, Bhutan, Maldives, Nepal, India, Pakistan, Sri Lanka 南亚地区性合作联盟：[由孟加拉国、不丹、马尔代夫、尼泊尔、印度、巴基斯坦、斯里兰卡等国组成]
SaaS	Software as a Service 中国软件运营服务
SABIC	Saudi Basic Industries Corporation 沙特基础工业公司
SABS	South African Bureau of Standards 南非标准局
SABS	South African Bureau of Standards 南非产品质量认证标志
SAC	Smith Aviation Club 史密斯航空俱乐部
SAC	security access controller 安全接入控制器
SAC	Standardization Administration of the P. R. C. 国家标准化管理委员会
SAC	Syria Arabian Coalition 叙利亚阿拉伯人联盟

SACD	super audio compact disc 超级音频光盘
SACO	Sino-America Co. Organization 中美合作组织
SAD	seasonal affective disorder 季节性情感障碍
SAD	special action department 特别活动科
SAE	stamped addressed envelope 回邮信封
SAE	Society of Automobile Engineers 美国汽车工程师学会
SAF	Syria Armed Forces 叙利亚武装力量
SAFE	Silvoarable Agroforestry For Europe 欧洲林农业
SAFE	Solar Energy Association For Europe 欧洲太阳能联盟
SAFER	Société d'Aménagement Foncier et d'Etablissement Rural 土地整治及乡村建设公司[法文]
SAG-AFTRA	the Screen Actors Guild and the American Federation of Television and Radio Artists 美国演员工会和广播电视艺人联合会
SAI	Social Accountability International 社会责任国际组织
SAIC	Shanghai Administration of Industry and Commerce 上海市工商管理局
SAIC	Shanghai Automotive Industry Corp. Group 上海汽车集团股份有限公司
SAIT	Samsung Aggregative Institute of Technology 三星综合技术院
SAL	semi-active laser 半主动激光器
SAM	security account management 安全账户管理
SAM	Sample Analysis at Mars 火星样本分析仪
SAM	signal acquisition/activation module 信号采集控制模块
SAN	styrene-acrylonitrile copolymer 苯乙烯-丙烯腈共聚物[塑料]
SANA	Syrian Arab News Agency 阿拉伯叙利亚通讯社
SANZ	Standards Association of New Zealand 新西兰标准协会
SANZ	Standards Association of New Zealand 新西兰产品质量认证标志
SAP	safety assessment plan 安全评估计划
SAP	symbolic assembly program 符号汇编程序
SAP	system assembly program 系统汇编程序
SAP	system assurance program 系统担保程序
SAP	Systemalyse und Programmentwicklung 五人公司[1972年创][德文]

SAP	systems applications and products in data processing 系统应用技术和产品的数据处理
SAP	Systems, Applications and Product in Data Processing ERP 企业管理解决方案的软件名称
SAR	synthetic aperture radar 合成孔径雷达
SAR	safety analysis report 安全分析报告
SAR	search and rescue 搜索救援服务/搜索救援队
SAR	Special Administrative Region 特别行政区
SAR	stop and reverse 抛物线指标/抛物转向[止损]指标
SAR80	Singapore Assault Rifle 80 80式新加坡突击步枪
SARI	Severe Acute Respiratory Infection 严重急性呼吸道感染[新型冠状病毒]
SARL	Sociedade Anónima de Responsabilidadem Limitada 有限责任公司[葡萄牙文]
SARS	severe acute respiratory syndrome 严重急性呼吸综合征
SARS AIDS(HIV)	Severe Acute Respiratory Syndromes, Acquired Immune Deficiency Syndrome, Human Immunodeficiency Virus 超乎寻常厉害的事物[以非典、艾滋病、人类免疫缺陷病毒引申]
SARS-CoV-2	SARS-coronavirus-2 严重急性呼吸综合征冠状病毒2型
SAS	Special Air Service Regiment 英国空军特种部队
SAS	Statistical Analysis System 统计分析系统(语言)
SAS	special air service regiment 特种空中勤务团
SASE	self-addressed stamped envelope 回邮信封
SASMO	Syrian Arab Organization for Standardization and Metrology 叙利亚阿拉伯标准化与计量组织
SASO	Saudi Arabian Standards Organization 沙特阿拉伯标准局
SASS	South African Standard Specifications 南非标准规范
SASS	South African Standard Specifications 南非产品认证标志
Sat	Saturday 星期六
SAT	Scholastic Assessment Test 学术能力评估测试
SAT	Standard Assessment Test 标准课业测评考试(现称NCT)
SAT	subcutaneous adipose tissue 皮下脂肪组织

SATCOM	satellite communications 卫星通信	
SatO2	oxygen saturation 氧饱和度	
SAUC	South Asia Union Catalogue 南亚洲联合目录	
SAW	surface acoustic wave 面声波(滤波器)	
SB	shangyebiaozhun 商业标准[汉语拼音缩略语]	
SB	Silence Breaker 沉默击破者	
SB	Security Branch 安保部	
SB	savings bank 储蓄银行	
SB	sky blue 天蓝色	
SB	special branch 政治部	
Sb	stibium 锑[第51号化学元素][拉丁文]	
SB	styrene-butadiene copolymer 苯乙烯-丁二烯共聚物[塑料]	
SB	super boy 超级男孩	
SB	super boy 喷气机驾驶员	
SBA	Street Basketball Association 街头篮球联盟	
SBAS	satellite-based augmentation system 星基增强服务	
SBC	Swiss Broadcast Corporation 瑞士广播公司	
SBC	standard bicarbonate radical 标准碳酸氢根	
SBCVC	Softbank China Venture Capital 软银中国资本	
SBE	standard base excess 标准碱过剩	
SBGC	Softbank Group Corp 软银集团	
SBI	State Bank of India 印度国家银行	
SBIGs	subject based information gateways 基于学科的信息门户	
SBME	simulation based medical education 模拟医学教育	
SBS	Satellite Broadcasting Service 卫星广播服务	
SBS	sick building syndrome 大楼综合征	
SBS	Seoul Broadcasting System 首尔电视台	
SBS	styrene-butadiene-styrene block copolymer 苯乙烯-丁二烯-苯乙烯嵌段共聚物[塑料]	
SBSS	space-based space surveillance 天基航天监视(系统)	
SBU	Small Boat Unit 香港小艇队	
SC	Solidarno 团结工会[波兰文]	

Sc	scandium 钪[第21号化学元素]
SC	solidarity center 团结中心
SC	sour crude 含硫原油
Sc	school certificate 中学毕业证书[英国]
SC	securities commission 证券委员会
SC	subcommittee 分委员会
SC	super charger (super charged) 增压器(超增压的)
SC	Supercomputing Conference 超级计算大会
SCALP	système de croisière conventionnel autonome à longue portée 自主远射程巡航导弹[法文]
SCAQMD	South Coast Air Quality Management District 南海岸空气质量管理区
SCC	squamous cell carcinoma 鳞状细胞癌
SCC	supervisor control console 管理员控制台
SCC	Satellite Control Center 卫星控制中心
SCC	Standards Council of Canada 加拿大标准协会
SCD	sudden cardiac death 心源性猝死
SCDA	Student Career Development Association 大学生职业发展协会
SCE HKBU	School of Continuing Education Hong Kong Baptist University 香港浸会大学持续教育学院
SCF	stem cell factor 干细胞因子
SCHIP	State Children Health Insurance Program 州儿童医疗保险
Schufa	Schutzgemeinschaft für allgemeine Kroditssicherung 一般信贷安全保护协会[德文]
SCI	Science Citation Index 科学引文索引
SCID	severe combined immunodeficiency 严重综合性免疫缺陷
SCIE	Science Citation Index Expanded《科学引文索引》网络版
sci-fi	science fiction 科幻小说
SCIP	Shanghai Chemistry Industry Park 上海化学工业园区
SCM	security consultative meeting 安全协商会议
SCM	Shanghai Conservatory of Music 上海音乐学院
SCM	single chip micyoco 单片机
SCM	software configuration management 软件配置管理

SCM	supply chain management 供应链管理
SCM	supply chain manager 供应链管理经理
SCO	Shanghai Cooperation Organization 上海合作组织
ScotLond	Scotland and London 苏格兰和伦敦[支持英国不脱欧的]
SCQF	Scottish Credit and Qualifications Framework 苏格兰学分和学历体系
SCQI	supporter continuous quality improvement 供应商质量持续改善
SCr	serum creatinine 血清肌酸酐
SCS	special collection service 特别搜集服务
SCS	sales configuration system 销售配置系统
SCS	Standard Chinese System 标准汉字系统
SCT	staphylococcal clumping test 葡萄球菌凝集试验
SCUFN	South-Central University for Nationalities 中南民族大学
SCUFN	Sub-Committee On Undersea Feature Names 国际海底地名管理机构
SCUK	Shell Chemicals UK Limited 壳牌化学品公司英国分公司
SD	secure digital card 安全数字记忆卡
SD	standard definition 标准清晰度
SD	sales and distribution 销售与分销
SD	sleeping disturbance 睡眠障碍
SD	special delivery 快递
SD	stable disease 病情稳定
SD	Swedish Democrat 瑞典民主党
SDA	Storage Data Association 存储数据协会
SDA	Security Digital Card Association 安全数字卡协会[又称SD存储卡协会]
SDA	shaft drive axis 手柄驱动轴
SDA	State Drug Agency 国家药监局
SDB	Shenzhen Development Bank 深圳发展银行
SDB	State Development Bank 中国国家开发银行
SDC	Secure Digital Card 安全数字卡
SDF	Syria Democratic Forces 叙利亚民主军
SDH	sorbitol dehydrogenase 山梨醇脱氢酶
SDHC card	secure digital high capacity card 大容量内存卡
SDI	Selective Dissemination of Information 信息选择传播

S

SDI	Serial Digital Interface	数字串行接口
SDI	Strategic Defense Initiative	战略防御计划
SDIC	State Development & Investment Corp Group	中国国家开发投资公司
SDK	software development kit	软件开发工具包
SDLP	Social Democratic and Labour Party	社会民主工党[北爱尔兰]
SDMI	standardization data management information	标准化数据管理情报
SDN BHD	Sendirian Berhad	有限公司[马来文]
SDN	software definition network	软件定义网络
SDN	specially designated national	特别指定国民
SDO	Standard Development Organization	标准制定组织
SDPA	Shenzhen Dogs Protection Association	深圳犬类保护协会
SDR	Special Drawing Rights	特别提款权
SDRAM	Synchronous Dynamic Random Access Memory	同步动态存储器
SDS	safety data sheet	安全数据表
SDS	sudden death syndrome	猝死综合征
SDSC	San Diego Supercomputer Center	圣迭戈超级计算中心
SDSC	Strategic and Defense Studies Centre	战略与防务研究中心
SDS-PAGE	sodium dodecylsulfate-polyacrylamide gel electrophoresis	十二烷基硫酸钠-聚丙烯酰胺凝胶电泳
SDTV	standard definition television	标准清晰度电视
SDU	Special Duties Unit	特别任务连/飞虎队
SE	south-east(ern)	东南方(的)
SE	scramjet engine	超声速燃烧冲压式发动机
Se	selenium	硒[第34号化学元素]
SE	stock exchange	股票交易所
SE	storage element	存储器单元
SEAC	standard electronic automatic computer	标准电子自动计算机
SEAD	Salzburg Experiment Academy of Dance	奥地利萨尔茨堡实验舞蹈学院
SEALs	United States Navy Sea, Air and Land Teams	美国海军三栖特种部队
sec	second	片刻/秒
sec	secant	正割
SEC	Securities and Exchange Commission	美国证券和交易委员会

SEC	Social Ecommerce Chain 社交电商链
SEC	Sunshine English Club 阳光英语俱乐部
Sec(y)	secretary 秘书
SECAM	sequence couleur a memorie 顺序彩色与存储电视制式[法文]
SECAM	Sequence de Couleurs avec Memoire 法国色康制[彩色电视系统][法文]
SECAM	sequential colour and memory 顺序彩色与存储电视制式
SECAM	sequential couleur a memoire 顺序传送彩色与存储[法文]
SED	surface conduction electron emitter display 表面传导电子发射显示
SEE	Society of Entrepreneurs & Ecology 阿拉善 SEE 生态协会
SEER	surveillance, epidemiology, and end results 癌症的检测、流行病学及其最后结果
SEF	Straits Exchange Foundation 海峡交流基金会
SEIRS	susceptibles, exposed, infectives, recovered 生物学数学模型[易感者、感染而未发病者、染病者、恢复者]
SEK	Swedish krona 瑞典克朗[货币]
SEM	School of Economics and Management 经管学院
SEM	search engine marketing 搜索引擎营销
SEMKO	Svenska Electriska Materiel-kontroll-Anstalten 瑞典电气产品质量认证标志[瑞典文]
SEMKO	Svenska Electriska Materiel-kontroll-Anstalten 瑞典电气设备检验所[瑞典文]
Sen	senator 参议员
SEN	Senegal 塞内加尔[非洲国家]
SEN	sensor 传感器
SENSE	Space Environment Nanometer Satellite of Experiment 空间环境纳米实验卫星
SEO	search engine optimization 搜索引擎优化
Sep	September 9 月
SEP	standard essential patent 标准必要专利
SEQ	safety, efficiency, quality 安全、高效、高质量
SESKO	Suomen Sahkötecknillinen Standardisoimiskomitea 芬兰电工标准委员会[芬兰文]

S

SET	secure electronic transaction 安全电子交易协议
SET	Secure Electronic Transfer 电子商务交易安全协议
SET	Spoken English Test 英语口语测试
SETI	Stock Exchange of Thailand Index 泰国证交所指数
SETI	Search for Extraterrestrial Intelligence 寻找外太空星球智慧生命计划
SEU	single event upsets 单一混乱事件
SEV	Schweizerischen Elektrotechnischen Verein 瑞士产品质量认证标志[德文]
SEV	Schweizerischen Elektrotechnischen Verein 瑞士电工协会(=ASE)[德文]
SEVIS	student and exchange visitor information system 学生与人员互访信息系统
SEZ	Special Economic Zone 经济特区
SF	Schweizer Fernschen 瑞士国家电视台[德文]
SF	science fiction 科幻小说[或电影等]
SF	Swiss Franc 瑞士法郎[瑞士2002年前的货币]
SF	Scuderia Ferrari 法拉利车队[意大利文]
SF	Special Forces 陆军特种部队
SF	Special Forces 绿色贝雷帽
SFC	San Francisco Chronicle《旧金山记事报》[美国]
SFC	specific fuel consumption 耗油率
SFDA	State Food and Drug Administration 国家食品药品监督管理局
SFHA	Scottish Federation of Housing Association 苏格兰住房协会联盟
SFL	School of Foreign Languages 外语学院
SFOR	Stabilization Force 联合保护稳定部队[欧洲波黑军队]
SFR	saliva flow rate 唾液流率
SFR	Société Française de Radiotéléphonie 法国最大的电信运营商之一[法文]
SFS	Suomen Standardisoimisliittory 芬兰标准协会[芬兰文]
SFS	Suomen Standardisoimisliittory 芬兰非电气产品质量认证标志[芬兰文]
SFTA	Semiconduct Facilities Technology Academy 半导体设施技术学院
SFX	special effects 特技效果
SG	Softbank Group 软银集团
SG	smart grids 智能电网
Sg	seaborgium 𨭎[第106号化学元素]
SG	sea green 海绿色

SG	Société Générale 法国兴业银行［法文］
SG	specific gravity 尿比重
SGA	Special General Assembly 联合国特别大会
SGLT-2	sodium-dependent glucose transporters 2 纳-葡萄糖协同转运蛋白 2
SGML	Standard Generalized Markup Language 标准通用置标语言
SGO	guanase 鸟嘌呤酶
SGS	safe-guard system 安全防护系统
SGS	Société Générale de Surveillance S. A. 法国认证标志［法文］
SGS	Société Général de Surveillance 通用鉴定公司［法文］
SGS	Société Générale de Surveillance Holding S. A. 瑞士通用公证行［法文］
Sgt	sergeant 中士
SH	security harbor 安全港
SHD	smart handheld devices 智能手持设备
SHDSL	single-pair high bit rate DSL (digital subscriber line) 单对线高速数字用户线
SHF	super high frequency 超高频
SHF	shaft 轴
SHLH	sitting here laughing hysterically 坐在这里歇斯底里地笑［网络用语］
SHR	Star Horn Royal Club 星之号角皇族战
SHRIMP	Short-Range Independent Microrobotic Platforms 独立微机器人平台计划
SI	Système International 国际单位制［法文］
Si	silicon 硅［第 14 号化学元素］
SI	safety index 安全指标（行业）
SI	saturation index 饱和指数
Si	silicone plastics 有机硅塑料
SIA	Semi-conductor Industry Association 半导体行业协会
SIAM	Society for Industrial and Applied Mathematics (美国)工业和应用数学协会
SIC	silicon carbide 碳化硅
SIC	standard industrial classification 标准企业分类法
SICT	Shantou International Container Terminal Co., Ltd. 汕头国际集装箱码头有限公司

SID	security identifiers 安全标识符
SID	source identification 来源识别码
SID	Society for Investigative Dermatology 皮肤病研究会
SIDS	sudden infant death syndrome 婴儿急性死亡综合征
SIgA	salivary immunoglobulin A 唾液免疫球蛋白 A
SIgG	salivary immunoglobulin G 唾液免疫球蛋白 G
SII	Standards Institution of Israel 以色列标准学会
SII	Standards Institution of Israel 以色列产品质量认证标志
SIIA	Software & Information Industry Association 软件和信息业协会
SIL	silica 硅质
SIL	special import license 特别进口许可证
SIM	subscriber identification module 用户识别模块
SIM	simulation game 模拟经商[养成]游戏
SIMeID	Subscriber Identification Module electronic identity 公安部公民网络电子身份标识
SIMS	stellar inertial measurement system 星体惯性测量系统
SIMULA	simulation language 模拟语言
sin	sine 正弦
SIN	Singapore 新加坡[亚洲国家]
SIN	social insurance number 社会保险号
SINGAIR	Singapore Airlines Ltd 新加坡航空公司
Singlish	Singapore English 新加坡英语
Sinopec	China Petroleum & Chemical Corporation 中国石化(公司)
SIP	standard inspection procedure 标准检验程序
SIPC	Shell International Petroleum Company 英国国际壳牌石油公司
SIPRI	Stockholm International Peace Research Institute 斯德哥尔摩国际和平研究所
SIPROS	simultaneous processing operating system 并行处理操作系统
SIRIM	Standards & Industrial Research Institute of Malaysia 马来西亚标准与工业研究学会
SIRIM	Standards & Industrial Research Institute of Malaysia 马来西亚产品质量认证标志

SIS	system information service 系统信息服务
SIS	Secret Intelligence Service 英国秘密情报局[又称军情六处 MI6]
SIS	space and information system 空间和信息系统
SIS	Sri Lanka Industry Standards 斯里兰卡产品质量认证标志
SIS	Sri Lanka Industry Standards 斯里兰卡工业标准
SIS	Sveriges Industriens Standardiserings kommission 瑞典非电气产品质量认证标志[瑞典文]
SIS	Sveriges Industriens Standardiserings kommission 瑞典工业标准化委员会[瑞典文]
SISIR	Singapore Institute of Standards and Industrial Research 新加坡标准与工业研究院
SISIR	Singapore Institute of Standards and Industrial Research 新加坡产品质量认证标志
SISU	Shanghai International Studies University 上海外国语大学
SISU	Sichuan International Studies University 四川外国语大学
SIUF	China(Shenzhen) International Brand Underwear Fair 中国(深圳)国际品牌内衣展
SJU	Shanghai Jiaotong University 上海交通大学
SK	secure key 加密密钥
SK	satellite killer 反卫星武器
SKA	Square Kilometre Array 平方公里射电阵
SKU	stockkeeping unit 库存量单位
SL	source language 源语言[被译语言]
SL	sport & luxurious 运动娱乐和豪华型汽车
SL	super lightweight 超轻型
SL&C	shipper's load and count 发货人装箱计数
SLA	second language acquisition 第二语言习得
SLA	Service-Level Agreement 服务水平协议
SLAP	serum leucine aminopeptidase 血清亮氨酸氨基肽酶
SLE	Sierra Leone 塞拉利昂[非洲国家]
SLE	super low frequency 超低频
SLE	systemic lupus erythematosus 系统性红斑狼疮

SLF	Standing Lending Facility 常备借贷便利
SLG	simulation game 模拟经商[养成]游戏
SLG	strategy game 策略游戏
SLIP	serial line IP 串行 IP
SLN	single lock nut 单一螺母
SLNB	sentinel lymph node biopsy 前哨淋巴结活检
SLO	Slovenia 斯洛文尼亚[欧洲国家]
SLO	short-term liquidity operations 短期流动性调节工具
Slo(v)	Slovenia 斯洛文尼亚[欧洲国家]
Slo(v)	Slovakia 斯洛伐克[欧洲国家]
SLPP	The Sierra Leone People's Party 塞拉利昂人民党
SLT	student loan institution 学生贷款资金
SLUFAE	surface-launched unit, fuel air explosive 地面发射单元,燃料空气炸药
SLV	satellite launching vehicle 卫星运载火箭
SM	sadism and masochism 施虐与受虐狂
Sm	samarium 钐[第 62 号化学元素]
SM	stock market 股票市场
SM	storage mark 存储标志
SM	somatomedin 生长介素
SM	Star Museum 明星博物馆[韩国一家娱乐公司名称]
SMA	Shanghai Maple Automobile 上海华普汽车
SMA	simple moving average 简单移动平均线
SMA	Society of Management Accountants 管理会计师协会
SMA	smooth muscle antibody 抗平滑肌抗体
SMA	Spectrum Manager of Australia 澳大利亚频谱管理局
SMA	spinal muscular atrophy 脊髓性萎缩
SMA	Submillimeter Array (Radio Telescope) 次毫米阵列(射电望远镜)
SMART	special, measurable, achievable, result-oriented, timed 青少年领袖能力培养计划[包括:明确具体的、可衡量评估的、可实现的、结果导向的、有时间限制的几个方面]
SMART	specific, measurable, attainable, relevant, time-based 目标管理的 SMART 原则[明确性、衡量性、可达到、相关性、期限性]

SMb	serum myoglobin 血清肌红蛋白
SMB	The Standardization Management Board 标准化管理局
SMBC	The Sumitomo Mitsui Banking Corporation 日本三井住友银行
SMBH	super massive black holes 超大质量黑洞
SMC	sheet molding compound 片状模塑料
SME	small and medium-sized enterprise 中小型企业
SMEDI	small and medium-sized enterprise development index 中小企业发展指数
SMEE	Shanghai Microelectronics Equipment Co 上海微电子装备公司
SMEX	small explorer 小型探索者计划
SMH	shaking my head 摇头表示失望［网络用语］
SMHS	Shri Maharaja Hari Singh 创伤救治中心［印地文］
SMIC	Semiconductor Manufacturing International Corporation 中芯国际集成电路制造有限公司
SMOS	semiconductor memory operating system 半导体存储操作系统
SMP	standard management processor 标准管理程序
SMPV	small multi-purpose vehicle 小型多功能汽车
SMR	San Marino 圣马力诺［欧洲国家］
SMS	short messaging service 短信息服务
SMS	system management server 系统管理服务器
SMS	styrene-α-methyl styrene copolymer 苯乙烯-α-甲基苯乙烯共聚物［塑料］
SMSA	standard metropolitan statistical area 标准大城市统计区
SMSE	small and medium scale enterprise 中小企业
SMT	surface mounting technology 表面贴装技术
SMTP	simple message transfer protocol 简单邮件传输协议
SMTWTFS	Sunday, Monday, Tuesday, Wednesday, Thursday, Friday, Saturday 星期天、星期一、星期二、星期三、星期四、星期五、星期六
SMV	space motor vehicle 空间机动飞行器
SN	serial number 序号
SN	Science News《科学通讯》［英国季刊］
SN	shipping note 装运单

S

Sn	stannum 锡[第50号化学元素,英文为 tin][拉丁文]
SN	stock number 股票编号
SNA	system network architecture 系统网络架构
SNA	system of national accounts 国民账户制度
SNB	Swiss National Bank 瑞士国家银行
SNC	Syrian National Council 叙利亚全国委员会
SNC	Sociedad en Comandita 两合公司[西班牙文]
SNCF	Société Nationale des Chemins de Fer Français 法国国营铁路公司[法文]
SNG	satellite news gathering 卫星新闻采集
SNOBOL	string-oriented symbolic language 面向字符串的符号
SNP	Scottish National Party 苏格兰民族党
SNP	single nucleotide polymorphism 单核苷酸多态性
Snr	senior 大/老
SNR	signal noise ratio 信噪比
SNS	Social Networking Services 社交网络服务
SNS	social networking site 社交网站
SNS	Syrian National Standard 叙利亚产品质量认证标志
SNS	Syrian National Standard 叙利亚国家标准
SNTO	Swiss National Tourist Office 瑞士国家旅游局
SNU	Seoul National University 韩国首尔国立大学
So	south(ern) 南方的
SO	symphony orchestra 交响乐团
SO	sulphur dioxide 二氧化硫
SOAP	simple object access protocol 简单对象访问协议
SOAP	symbolic optimum assembly programming 符号最优汇编程序
SOAR	special operations aviation regiment 特种作战航空团
soc	statement of condition 借贷对照表
soc	system on chip 片上系统
SOC	society 协会
SoC	system-on-chip 系统单晶片
SOC	Shell Oil Company 美国壳牌石油公司
SOC	Standard Oil Company 美国美孚石油公司

SOCA	Stamp Out Crime Authority 杜绝犯罪行为署
SOCO	Society for Community Organization 香港社区组织协会
SOD	superoxide dismutase 超氧化物歧化酶
SOFA	ROK-US States of Forces Agreement 韩美驻军地位协定
SOFOFA	Sociedad de Fomento Fabril 智利工厂发展协会[西班牙文]
SOHC	single overhead camshaft (engine) 顶置单凸轮轴发动机
SOHO	small office home office 在家办公
SOL	Solomon Islands 所罗门群岛[太平洋岛国]
SOL	Skilled Occupation List 职业清单
SOM	Somalia 索马里[非洲国家]
SOMTC	ASEAN Senior Officials Meeting on Transnational Crime 东盟打击跨国犯罪高官会议
SON	Standard Organization of Nigeria 尼日利亚标准局
SONCAP	Standards Organization of Nigeria Conformity Assessment Program 尼日利亚强制性合格评定程序
SONCAP	Standard Organization of Nigeria Conformity Assessment Programme 尼日利亚标准局认证
SOP	standard operating procedure 标准操作流程
SOP	standard operation procedure 标准作业程序
Soph	sophomore 大学二年级学生/中学二年级学生
SORT	special operations reaction team 特别行动反应组
SOS	Save Our Souls 国际通用的无线电求救信号的通俗写法
SOS	silicon on sapphire 硅蓝宝石技术
SOWT	special operations weather team 特种作战气象队
SOX	semiconductor index 半导体质数
SP	service provider 服务提供商
SP	shrinkage pressure 收缩压
SP	stress protein 应激蛋白
SP	sales promotion 促销
SP	session percentage 访问量百分比
SP	Special Publications 专门出版物
SP	sponsored products 亚马逊的产品广告

SP	structured programming 结构化编程
SP	support publications 辅助出版物
SPA	Società per Azioni 股份公司(意大利文)
SpA	Società per Azioni 股份公司(意大利文)
SPA	Solus Par Aqua 水疗[拉丁文]
SPA	sunburn preventive agent 晒伤防护剂
SPA	serum prealbumin 血清前白蛋白
SPBS	solar power building system 太阳能建筑系统
SPC	Singapore Petroleum Corporation Private Limited 新加坡石油公司
SPC	sodium percarbonate 过氧碳酸钠
SPD	Society of Publication Designers 出版设计协会
SPD	Sozialdemokratische Partei Deutschlands 德国社会民主党[德文]
SPDB	Shanghai Pudong Development Bank 上海浦东发展银行
SPE	serum protein electrophoresis 血清蛋白电泳
SPE	Solar-Energy & Photovoltaic Application Expo 太阳能光伏应用博览会
SPE	specific esterase stain 特异性酯酶染色
Spec	specification 规格
SPECT	single photon emission computed tomography 单光子发射计算机断层成像
SPF	sun-protection factor 防晒因子
SPFA	Sparekassen Faaborg 金融信息传输系统[丹麦文]
SPG	sport game 体育类游戏
SPHR	Senior Profession of Human Resource 高级人力资源专业认证
SPIEF	St. Petersburg International Economic Forum 圣彼得堡国际经济论坛
SPIF	Share Price Index Futures 股票价格指数期货
SPMC	Shanghai Port Machinery Co., Ltd. 原上海港机股份有限公司
SPO	secondary public offering 再次公开发行新股票
SPQR	small profits and quick returns 薄利多销
SPR	strategic petrol reserve 战略石油储备
SPRING	Standards, Productivity and Innovation Board 新加坡生产力及标准委员会
SPRITS	Sichuan Provincial Research Institute of Thai Studies 四川省泰语研究所

SPS	sanitary and phytosanitary 动植物卫生检疫措施
SPS	special purpose securities 特设证券
SPSS	Statistical Package for the Social Science, Statistical Product and Service Solution 社会科学统计软件包,统计产品与服务解决方案
SPT	sport 运动类游戏
SPT	Scout Portal Toolkit 侦察门户工具包
SPT	serum prothrombin time 血清凝血酶原时间
SPV	special-purpose vehicle 特殊用途媒介物;特别目的载体
SQ	sexual quotient 性商
sq	square 平方
Sq	square 广场
SQ	soul quotient 灵商
SQA	Software Quality Assurance 软件质量保证
SQA	Strategic Quality Assurance 策略品质保证
SQC	Scottish Qualification Certificate 苏格兰资格证书
SQE	supplier quality engineer 供应商品质工程师
SQL	Structured Query Language 结构化查询语言
SQuAD	Stanford Question Answering Data set 美国斯坦福大学发起的机器阅读理解顶级赛事
Sr	strontium 锶[第38号化学元素]
Sr	senior 老/大
SR	super rare 超级稀有
SSR	superior super rare 特级超稀有[因为super无比较级]
Sr HS	senior high school 高级中学[美国]
SR	Saturday Review《星期六评论》[美国]
SR	sovereign risk 主权风险
SR	speculative risk 投机性风险
SRB	Serbia 塞尔维亚[欧洲国家]
SRF	Schweizer Radio and Fernsehen 瑞士国家广播电视集团[德文]
SRF	Syria Revolutionary Front 叙利亚革命阵线
SRI	socially responsible investing 社会责任投资
SRI	Sri Lanka 斯里兰卡[亚洲国家]

S

SRL	Sociedad de Responsabilidad Limitada 股份有限公司[西班牙文]	
SRL	Società a responsabilità limitata 有限责任公司[意大利文]	
SRPG	strategy role-playing game 策略角色扮演游戏	
SRS	self-regulating system 自动调节系统	
SRS	speech recognition system 语音识别系统	
SRT	special reaction team 特别反应组	
SRV	sport recreational vehicle 运动型休闲车	
SRV	small recreation vehicle 小型休闲车	
SS	security services 安全服务	
SS	secret service 情报部门	
SS	solid suspension 固态悬浮物	
SS	saints 圣徒	
ss	steamship 轮船	
SS	sjögren syndrome 干燥综合征	
SS	somatostatin 生长激素抑制素	
SS-A	sjögren syndrome-A antigen 干燥综合征 A 抗原	
SSA	Social Security Administration 社会保障总署	
SSA	standard spending assessment 标准开支评估	
SSAG	Sweden Society of Anthropology and Geography 瑞典人类学和地理学会	
SSAT	Secondary School Admission Test 美国中学入学考试	
SS-B	sjögren syndrome-B antigen 干燥综合征 B 抗原	
SSB	swimmer support boat 蛙人支援艇	
SSC	social security card 社会安全卡	
SSCI	Social Science Citation Index 社会科学引文索引	
SSCI	Scientific Systems Co. Inc. 科学系统公司	
SSD	solid state disk 固态硬盘	
SSD	solid state driver 固态驱动器	
SSD	Strategy Security Department 战略安全部	
SSE	Shanghai Securities Exchange 上海证券交易所	
SSH	secure shell 安全外壳协议	
SSI	small scale integration 小规模集成电路	

SSI	Sky Service Incorporation 美国太空服务公司
SSID	storage service identifier 存储服务标识符
SSL	secure sockets layer 安全套接层
SSN	social security number 社会安全卡号码
SSO	standard-setting organization 标准制定组织
SSO	Scottish Symphony Orchestra 苏格兰交响乐团
SSP	sea solar power 海洋太阳能
SSS	Super Special Stage 汽车拉力赛中为观众及方便电视转播而设的路段
SST	satellite-to-satellite tracking 卫星对卫星跟踪
SST	space sun telescope 空间太阳望远镜
SST	super-sonic transport 超音速运输机
SSTA	Solid State Technology Association 固态技术协会
SSVEP	steady-state visually evoked potential 稳态视觉诱发电位
ST	space telescope 太空望远镜
ST	special treatment 股票特别处理
St	saint 圣人
St	state 州
st	stone 英石［英国重量单位＝14 磅或 6.35 千克］
st	street 街
St	street 街
St Ex(ch)	Stock Exchange 证券交易所
ST	safe toy 安全玩具
ST	safe toy 日本玩具质量认证标志
ST	SGS＋Thomson 意法半导体集团
STA	Superior Taste Award 顶级美味大奖
STAQ	Securities Trading Automated Quotation System 全国证券交易自动报价系统
STAR	Scientific and Technical Aerospace Report 宇宙航行科技报告
STAR	Standardized Testing and Reporting Program 标准化测试与报告计划
START	Strategic Arms Reduction Treaties《削减战略武器条约》(美国与苏联签订的)
STB	set top box 电视机的机顶盒

STB	serum total bilirubin 血清总胆红素
STC	Satellite Test Center 美国卫星试验中心
STD	sexually transmitted disease 性传染疾病
STD	subscriber trunk dialling 长途直拨电话
STEM	science, technology, engineering and maths 理工
STEM	science, technology, engine and maths 科学、技术、工程、数学
STEP	standard terminal executive program 标准终端执行
STF	smooth trans focus 影像平滑
STG	shooting game 射击类游戏
STGT	simplified thromboplastin generation test 简易凝血活酶生成试验
STH	somatotropic hormone 生长激素
STI	sexually transmitted infection 性传播感染
STK	SIM Card Tool Kit 用户识别模块卡开发工具包
STL	serum total lipoid 血清总脂
STL	standard template library 标准模板库
STM	scanning tunnel microscope 扫描隧道显微镜
STO	Syria Turkmen Column 叙利亚土库曼纵队
STOL	short take-off and landing （飞机）短距离起落
STOVL	short take-off and vertical landing aircraft 短距离起飞与垂直降落飞机
STP	standard temperature and pressure 标准温度和压力
STR	smile, talk, raise 中风判断三个词［要求：患者笑一下，说一个简单句子，举起双手。如果患者不能做好其中任何一个，请立即送患者入医院］
STT	serial thrombin time 连续凝血酶时间
STV	satellite television 卫星电视
STV	stereoscopic television 立体电视
STV	subscription television 收费电视
SU	Shanghai University 上海大学
SU	Stanford University 斯坦福大学［美国］
SUA	serum uric acid 血清尿酸
SUBLAN/ADNS	Submarine, Atlantic/Automated Data Network System 海军大西

		洋潜艇专用自动化数据网络系统
SUD	Sudan 苏丹[非洲国家]	
SUI	Switzerland 瑞士[欧洲国家]	
SUN	Sunday 星期日	
Sun	Sunday 星期天	
SUN	serum urea nitrogen 血清尿素氮	
SUP	Syriac Union Party 叙利亚联盟党	
sup OS	superior operation system 高级操作系统	
Supreme SAT	Supreme Satellite 斯里兰卡卫星公司	
Supt	superintendent 警司	
SUSTech	South University of Science and Technology 南方科技大学	
SUV	sports utility vehicle 运动型多功能车	
SV	serve 服务	
SV	svensk 瑞典人[丹麦—挪威文]	
SV	El Salvador 萨尔瓦多[南美洲国家]	
SV	Sandi Arabian Airlines 沙特阿拉伯航空公司	
SV	save 拯救	
Sv	sievert 希沃特[辐射剂量单位]	
SVAC	Shanghai Volkswagen Automotive Company 上海大众汽车公司	
SVD	Soviet sniper rifle 苏联狙击步枪	
SVGA	super video graphic array 超级视频图形阵列	
SVOD	Staggered VOD 交错视频点播	
SVW	Shanghai Volkswagen 上海大众	
SW	short wave 短波	
SW	south-west(ern) 西南方(的)	
SW	Security Wing 保安部/保安处	
SW	Sunwell Plateau 太阳井高地	
SWAG	swagger 行事调调很酷	
SWAK	sealed with a kiss 以吻封信	
SWAP	Shared Wireless Access Protocol 共享无线接入协议	
SWAT	special weapons and tactics 特种武器和战术	
Sway	office sway "直观、有效的表达观点的工具"的简化版	

SWE	Sweden 瑞典[欧洲国家]
SWIFT	Society for Worldwide Interbank Financial Telecommunication 环球银行金融电信协会
Swinglish	Swiss English 瑞士英语
SWOT	strengths, weaknesses, opportunities, threats 优势、劣势、机会、威胁[前两者是内部条件的优劣,后两者是外部条件的优劣,通过分析,制定策略]
SWP	Star Wars Program 星球大战计划
SWS	Slow Wave Sleep 慢波睡眠
SWZ	Swaziland 斯威士兰[非洲国家]
SXO	serum xanthine oxidase 血清黄嘌呤氧化酶
SYB	start your business 创办你的企业
synd	syndicate 企业联合组织/辛迪加
SYR	Syria 叙利亚[亚洲国家]
SYSU	Sun Yat-Sen University 中山大学
SZMG	ShenZhen Media Group 深圳广播电影电视集团

T	telephone 电话
T	Tesla 特(斯拉)[法定磁感应强度计量单位]
T	thymus 胸腺
T	Tesla 美国特斯拉汽车
T	Tata 印度塔塔汽车
T	testosterone 睾(丸)酮
T	Toyota 日本丰田汽车
T	trainer 教练机
T	turbo 涡轮增压器
T	turquoise 青绿色

T/L	total loss 全损
t'other	the other 两者中的另一个
T2 S	TARGET 2-Securities 泛欧证券交收综合技术平台
T3	triiodothyronine 三碘甲腺原氨酸
T3U	triiodothyronine uptake test 三碘甲状腺原氨酸摄取试验
T4	thyroxine 四碘甲腺原氨酸
Ta	tantalum 钽[第 73 号化学元素]
TA	teaching assistant（美国）教师助理[高等教育机构为研究生设置的支薪职位]
TA	transmission adapter 传输衔接适配器
ta	thank you 谢谢
TA	Territorial Army 国防义勇军
TA	traffic agent 运输代理人
TA	transfer agent 过户转账代理人
TA	Translators' Association 翻译家协会
TAB	table game 桌面类游戏
Tablet PC	tablet personal computer 平板电脑
TAC	Thai Airways Company 泰国航空公司
TACIS	Technical Assistance to the Commonwealth of Independent States 对独联体技术援助
TACT	textual analysis computing tools 语料分析计算工具
TAFE	technical and further eduction 澳大利亚全国通用的职业与继续教育
TAG	technical advisory group 技术咨询组
TALIS	Teaching and Learning International Survey 国际教学调查
tan	tangent 正切
TAN	Tanzania 坦桑尼亚[非洲国家]
TAO	Office of Tailored Access Operations 获取特定情报办公室[或称：陶小组]
TAP	time of arrived police 警察到达犯罪现场所需的时间
TAR	thrust-augmented rocket 加大推力的火箭
TARGET	Trans-European Automated Real-time Gross Settlement Express Transfer System 泛欧实时全额自动清算系统

TAS	tactical analysis system 战术分析系统	
TASS	Telegrafnoie Agenstvo Sovietskavo Soyuza 塔斯社[苏联通讯社][俄文]	
TAST	TOFEL Academic Spoken Test 托福学术口语考试	
TAT	transactivation and transcription 超激活和转录	
TAT	tetanus antitoxin 破伤风抗毒素	
TAT	total adipose tissue 总脂肪组织	
TATP	triacetone triperoxide 熵炸药	
TB	terabyte 万亿字节	
Tb	terbium 铽[第65号化学元素]	
TB	thermal balance 热平衡	
TB	tuberculosis 肺结核病	
Tb	terabit 太比特	
TB	treasury bond 国库券	
TBA	to be announced 待宣布	
TBA	total bile acid 总胆汁酸	
TBC	to be confirmed 待确认	
TBC	The Boeing Company 美国波音飞机公司	
TBD	to be decided [determined] 待定	
TBG	table game 桌面类游戏	
TBG	tactics boosting glide 战术助推滑翔	
TBG	The Brilliant Green 绿乐园[日本乐队]	
TBG	thyroxine-binding globulin 甲状腺素结合球蛋白	
TBH	to be honest 说实话	
TBM	full face rock tunnel boring machine 全断面硬岩掘进机	
tbp	true boiling point 真沸点	
TBS	talk between ships 舰船间无线电通话	
TBS	Tokyo Broadcasting System 东京广播公司	
tbs	Tanzania Bureau of Standards 坦桑尼亚产品质量认证标志	
TBS	Tanzania Bureau of Standards 坦桑尼亚标准局	
TBT	trade barriers of technics 贸易技术壁垒	
TBT	toluidine blue rectification test 甲苯胺蓝纠正试验	
Tc	technetium 锝[第43号化学元素]	

TC	triglyceride 甘油三(酸)酯
TC	Trusteeship Council 联合国托管理事会
TC	Technology Commission 中国信息安全标准化技术委员会
TC	tactical center 战术中心
TC	technical committee 技术委员会
TC	total cholesterol 总胆固醇
TC	type certification 型号合格证
TCA	TESOL International Association China Assembly 世界英语教师协会中国大会
TCC	torque converter clutch 液力变扭离合器
TCD	transcranial doppler sonography 经颅多普勒超声
TCE	total customer experience 全面客户体验
TCF	telescopic tube 伸缩套管
TCF	Test de Connaissance du Français 法语知识测试[法文]
TCF	totally chlorine-free 全无氯
TCFL	Teaching Chinese as a Foreign Language 对外汉语教学
TCG	The Tunisian Combatant Group 突尼斯战斗团
TCG	trading card game 集换式卡牌游戏
TCH	Tokyo Clearing House 日本东京票据交易所
TCI	Telecommunications Corporation of Iran 伊朗电信公司
TCI	The Children's Investment Fund 英国儿童投资基金
TCL	Today China Lion 中国 TCL 电子有限公司
TCM	Traditional Chinese Medicine 中医
TCM	Turner Classic Movie 特纳经典电影
TCO	Tjanstemannens Central Orgnisation 瑞典显示器产品质量认证标志[瑞典文]
TCO	Tjanstemannens Central Orgnisation 瑞典专业雇员协会[瑞典文]
TCO	total cost of ownership 总体拥有成本
TCO$_2$	total carbon dioxide 二氧化碳总量
TCP	transmission control protocol 传输控制协议
TCP	telecommunication program 远程通信程序
TCP/IP	transmission control protocol/internet protocol 传输控制协议/网际协议

T

TCPP	tris（2-chloropropyl）phosphate 磷酸三(二氯丙基)酯
TCS	transmission control system 变速器控制系统
TCS	track control system 跟踪控制系统
TCS	traction control system 牵引力控制系统/驱动力控制系统
TCSOL	Teaching Chinese to Speakers of Other Languages 对外汉语教学
TCT	thin-prep cytology test 液基薄层细胞学检查
TCU	transmission control unit 变速器控制装置
TD	Test Director 一种测试管理工具
TD	time deposit 定期存款
TD	time draft 远期汇票
TD	trade diversion 贸易转向
TD	Teachta Dála 爱尔兰共和国的众议院议员[爱尔兰文]
TD	technique development 技术发展
TD	technology data 技术资料
TD	Test Director 测试工程师
TD	touchdown 触地
TD	transmission delay 延时
TD	table data cell 表中数据单元
TD	team death match 团队竞技
TD	Test Daily 每日一考
TD	tower defence 塔内防守
TDC	technology data centre 技术资料中心
TDC	Trade Development Council 香港贸易发展局
TDD	test-driven development 测试驱动开发
TDD	time division duplex 时分双工
TDK	Tokyo Denki Kagaku 日本TDK集团[日文]
TDMA	time division multiple access 时分多路
TDMA	time division multiple address 时分多址
TDR	talent directional recommendation 人才定向推荐
TDR	technical data report 技术数据报告
TDR	time domain reflectometry 时域反射
TDR	time relay reflectometry 时间延迟反射

Te	tellurium 碲[第52号化学元素]	
TEA	Trade Expansion Act 扩大贸易法[美国]	
TEC	Toyo Engineering Corp 日本东洋工程公司	
TEC	Translational English Corpus 翻译英语语料库	
TEC	Technical Education Council 工业教育委员会	
TEC	Toyo Electric Co 日本东洋电气公司	
tech	technical college 科技大学	
tech	technology 技术	
TechX	technology X 德知航创:无人机研发团队	
TED	technology, entertainment, design 科技、娱乐、设计	
TED	Technology, Entertainment, Design 技术、娱乐、设计[美国一家私有非营利机构的名称]	
ted	transferred electron device 电子传递设备	
TEE	Tertiary Entrance Examination 澳大利亚大学录取考试	
TEE	Technical Chamber of Greece 希腊技术协会	
TEF	Test d'Evaluation de Francais 法语水平测试[法文]	
TEFL	Teaching English as a Foreign Language 作为外语的英语教学	
TEFLON	polytetrafluoroethylene 特氟龙[聚四氟乙烯]	
TEG	effluent gas treatment system 废气处理系统	
TEG	thermo-electric generator 热电发电机/温差发电机	
tel	telephone number 电话号码	
Tel	telephone 电话(号码)	
telco	telecommunications company 电信公司	
Telstra	Telecom Australia 澳大利亚电信公司	
TEM	transmission electron microscope 透射电子显微镜	
temp	temperature 温度	
temp	temporary employee 临时雇员	
TEOTWAWKI	the end of the world as we know it 可以毁灭现有人类社会机构和规范的灾难性事件	
TEPCO	Tokyo Electric Power Co., Ltd. 日本东京电力公司	
ter	terrorist 恐怖分子	
TERCOM	terrain contour matching 地形匹配(制导)	

TESL	Teaching English as a Second Language 英语作为第二语言的教学
TESOL	Teaching English to Speakers of Other Languages 对外英语教学
TESP	Teaching English for Specific Purposes 专门用途英语教学
TEU	Twenty-Foot Equivalent Units (inter modal shipping container) 国际标准箱单位(集装箱多式联运)
TEU	twenty-foot-equipment unit 货柜/集装箱
Tev-Dem	Tevgera Civaka Demokratîk 争取民主社会运动[库尔德文]
TF	task force 任务组
TF	Task Force 香港特遣队
TF	tax free 免税
TF	Trans Flash 微型 SD 卡(安全数字卡)
TFC	total fixed costs 总固定成本
TFT	thin film transistor 薄膜晶体管
TFT-LCD	thin film transistor liquid crystal display 薄膜晶体管液晶显示屏
TG	triglyceride 甘油三酯
TGE	Tokyo Grain Exchange 日本东京谷物交易所
TGIF	Thank God. It's Friday 谢天谢地,又到星期五了。
TGL	temporary general license 临时一般许可证
TGT	TARGET 塔吉特[参见 TARGET 条]
TGT	thromboplastin generation test 凝血活酶生成实验
TGV	train à grande vitesse 高铁[法文]
Th	thorium 钍[第 90 号化学元素]
THA	Thailand 泰国[亚洲国家]
THA	total hip arthroplasty 全髋关节置换术
THB	Thailand Baht 泰国铢[货币]
THC	tetrahydrocannabinol 四氢大麻酚
the three Rs	reading, writing and arithmetic 初等教育三要素:读、写、算
THERMO	thermostat 恒温
THLDL	Tsing Hua lingdaoli 清华领导力[汉语拼音缩略语]
THLDL	think, link, do, leadership 知行合一成就领导力[知识思考、连接、行动、领导力]
tho'	though 虽然

three D	length, width, depth 三维:长、宽、高
Three UK	three United Kingdom 三英国(电信公司)
thru	through 直到
Thu	Thursday 星期四
thx	thanks 感谢
Ti	titanium 钛[第22号化学元素]
Ti	tumor inducing 肿瘤诱导
TI	topological insulators 拓扑绝缘
TI	Transparency International 国际透明组织
TIA	transient ischemic attack 短暂性脑缺血发作
TIA	trading investment area 贸易投资区
Tib	tebibit 太比特[二进制计算机内存或数据单位]
TiB	tebibyte 太字节[二进制计算机内存或数据单位]
TIBC	total iron-binding capacity 血清总铁结合力
Tibit	tebibit 太比特[二进制计算机内存或数据单位]
TIFF	tagged image file format 标签式图像文件格式
TIG	tetanus immunoglobulin 破伤风免疫球蛋白
til	until 直到
TIL	today I learned 每天学点知识(在分享时加个TIL)[网络用语]
TIL	tumor infiltrating lymphocyte 肿瘤浸润淋巴细胞
TILLING	Targeting Induced Local Lesions IN Genomes 基因组靶向定位诱导损伤技术
TIM	ticket issue machine 自动售票机
TIPS	target instant payments settles 目标即时支付结算
TIPS	Technology and Information Promotion System 联合国技术信息促进系统
TIPS	Terrorism Information and Prevention System 恐怖主义情报预防系统
Tis	tumor in situ 原位肿瘤
TISI	Thai Industrial Standards Institute 泰国产品质量认证标志
TISI	Thai Industrial Standards Institute 泰国工业标准协会
TJ	Teheran Journal《德黑兰日报》[伊朗]
TJK	Tajikistan 塔吉克斯坦[亚洲国家]
TKI	tyrosine kinase inhibitor 酪氨酸激酶抑制剂

TKM	Turkmenistan 土库曼斯坦［亚洲国家］
Tl	thallium 铊［第 81 号化学元素］
TL DR	too long, didn't read 太长了,没看,先留个言［网络用语］
TL	target language 目标语言
TL	total loss 全损
TL	translation 翻译
TLC	tender loving care 亲切的照顾
TLS	Times Literary Supplement《泰晤士报文学副刊》［英国］
TLV	troop landing vessel 部队登陆舰
TM	Tianma 天马汽车［中国保定:汉语缩略语］
Tm	thulium 铥［第 69 号化学元素］
TM	theme music 主题音乐
TM	trade mark 商标
TM	transcendental meditation 超脱沉思/打坐［佛教］
TMB	technical management board 技术管理局
TMC	thick molding compound 厚片模塑料
TMD	theater missile defense (system) 战区导弹防御系统
T-men	tax men 税务人员
TMI	too much information 信息过多
TMK	Trupat Mbrojtese to Kosoves 科索沃阿尔巴尼亚保护部队［阿尔巴尼亚文］
TMO	telegraphic money order 电汇单
TMP	template metaprogramming 模板元编程
TMP	Thermal Mechanical Pulp 热磨机械浆
TMP	transmembrane pressure 跨膜压差
tmr	tomorrow 明天
TMR	trademark registration 商标注册
TMSR	Thorium Molten Salt Reactor Nuclear Power System 钍基熔盐堆核能系统
TMT	technology, media, telecom 科技、媒体、通信［以互联网链接起来的新兴行业］
TMT	telecommunications, media and technology 电信、传媒、技术
TN	technology network 技术网络
TN	treasury note 国库券

TNC	transnational company	跨国公司
TNE	transnational enterprise	跨国企业
TNF	tumor necrosis factor	肿瘤坏死因子
TNF-α	tumor necrosis factor-α	肿瘤坏死因子-α
TNG	Touch'n Go	蚂蚁金服与马来西亚支付服务提供商
TNGA	Toyota New Global Architecture	丰巢概念
TNM	primary tumor, regional nodes, metastasis (tumor staging) 癌症分类法（根据肿瘤、淋巴结和转移情况）	
TNS	Taylor Nelson Sofres	特恩斯市场研究公司
TNS	Transit Navigation System	横越导航系统
TNS	transparent network substrate	透明网络底层
TNT	Thomas National Transport	世界著名快递与物流公司，总部位于荷兰
TNT	Trans-national terrorism	跨国界恐怖主义
TNT	trinitrotoluene	三硝基甲苯[又名：梯恩梯炸药]
TNT	Turner Network Television	特纳电视网
TNW	The New Walford Guide to Reference Resources	新沃尔福特参考资料指南
TOC	test of cure	试验治疗
TOEFL	Test of English as a Foreign Language	托福考试[指美国举办的母语为非英语者的英语水平考试]
TOEIC	Test of English for International Communication	托业考试[国际交流英语考试]
TOG	Togo	多哥[非洲国家]
TOHO	Tiny Office Home Office	袖珍家庭企业
TOL	Tower of London	伦敦塔[英国]
TOP	The Olympic Partner Programme	TOP计划/奥运计划
TOP	time, occasion, place	TOP原则[要求穿戴与不同的时间、场合、地点相适应]
TOPE	Test of Professional English	职业英语考试[美国为母语为非英语国家的企业、政府部门和英语学习者开发的一项考试]
TOPV	trivalent oral poliovirus vaccine	三价口服脊髓灰质炎疫苗
TORQ	torque	转矩
TOS	tape operating system	磁带操作系统

TOS	Tencent operating system 腾讯操作系统
TOT	Transfer-Operate-Transfer 移交—经营—移交[一种国际流行的项目融资方式]
TOT	trust of trusts 组合信托
TOU	The Open University 开放大学
TP	terminal printing 终端打印
TP	total protein 总蛋白
TP	typical pneumonia 典型肺炎
TP	trade protocol 贸易意向书
TPA	tissue peptide antigen 组织多肽抗原
TPA	Trans-Pacific Airlines 美国太平洋航空公司
TPC	Tianfu Park City 天府公园城市
TPE	Taipei 台北[中国台湾地区]
TPE	thermoplastic elastomer 热塑性弹性件
TPF	transaction processing facility 事务处理机制
TPHA	treponema pallidum hemagglutination assay 梅毒螺旋体血凝试验
TPI	treponema pallidum immobilization assay 梅毒螺旋体制动测定
TPM	trusted platform module 安全芯片
TPN	total parenteral nutrition 全肠外营养
TPP	Trans-Pacific Partnership Agreement《跨太平洋伙伴关系协定》
TPS	TOYOTA production system 日本丰田公司生产系统管理模式
TPS	temporary protected status 临时保护身份
TPSA	tissue polypeptide specific antigen 总前列腺特异性抗原
TPSEPA	Trans-Pacific Strategic Economic Partnership Agreement《跨太平洋战略经济伙伴关系协定》[TPP 的前身][由新西兰、新加坡、智利和文莱四国发起]
TPU	tensor processing unit 张量处理器
TPU	thermoplastic polyurethane 热塑性聚氨酯(弹性体)
TQM	Total Quality Management 全面质量管理,以前用 TQC(Total Quality Control)
TQS	Total Quality Service 全面质量服务
TR	trust receipt 信托收据
TR	technical report 技术报告

TRAC	traction control system 驱动力控制系统
TRC	Truth and Reconciliation Commission 真相与调解委员会[南非组织]
TRC	traction control system 驱动力控制系统
TRI	Trinidad and Tobago 特立尼达和多巴哥[北美洲国家]
TRIPS	Agreement on Trade-Related Aspects of Intellectual Property Rights《与贸易有关的知识产权协定》
TRK	tropomyosin receptor kinase 原肌球蛋白受体激酶
TRPG	table role playing game 桌上角色扮演游戏
TS	tank ship 油船
TS	technical specification 技术规范
Ts	tennessine 鿬[第117号化学元素]
TSA	total sialic acid 血清总唾液酸
TSA	Transportation Security Administration 运输安全管理局
TSA	Transportation Security Agency 运输安全局
TSA	Transportation Service Authority 运输服务管理局
TSD	Technical Service Department 香港技术支援组
TSE	Test of Spoken English 英语口语测试
TSE	Taiwan Stock Exchange 中国台湾股票交易所
TSE	Tokyo Stock Exchange 日本东京股票交易所/日本东京证券交易所
TSE	Toronto Stock Exchange 加拿大多伦多证券交易所
TSE	Turk Standardlari Enstitusu 土耳其标准学会[土耳其文]
TSE	Turk Standardlari Enstitusu 土耳其产品质量认证标志[土耳其文]
TSG	tumor suppressor gene 肿瘤抑制基因
TSH	thyroid-stimulating hormone 促甲状腺激素
TSH-RE	thyroid-stimulating hormone-releasing factor 促甲状腺激素释放因子
tsmc	Taiwan Semiconductor Manufacturing Co., Ltd. 台湾积体电路制造股份有限公司
TSP	thrifty savings plan 节俭储蓄计划
TSP	total suspended particle 总空中悬浮物
tsp(s)	teaspoon 一茶匙(的量)
TSS	traffic safety service 交通安全性服务
TSS	trailer stability system 汽车拖车稳定系统

TSU	this side up 勿倒置
TT	telegraphic transfer 电汇
TT	Tik Tok 抖音
TT	Tavan Tolgoi 塔温陶勒盖（巨型煤矿）[蒙古国][蒙古文]
TT	tetanus toxoid 破伤风类毒素
TT	thymol turbidity test 麝香草酚浓度试验
TT	transit trade 过境贸易
TT	triangular trade 三角贸易
TTA	travel time authorized 旅行时间授权
TTB	telegraphic transfer bought 电汇买进
TTBS	Trinidad and Tobago Bureau of Standards 特立尼达和多巴哥标准局
TTBS	Trinidad and Tobago Bureau of Standards 特立尼达和多巴哥产品质量认证标志
TTC	triphenyl tetrazolium chloride 氯化三苯基四氮唑
TTH	thyrotropic hormone 促甲状腺激素
TTIP	Trans-Atlantic Trade and Investment Partnership 跨大西洋贸易与投资伙伴协议
TTO	tactics technology office 战术技术办公室
TTP	time to progression 至进展时间
TTP	time to progress 肿瘤进展时间
TTS	text to speech 文字—语言转换
TTX	table top exercise 桌面演习
TTX	tetrodotoxin 河豚毒素
TTYL	talk to you later 以后再聊
T-U	Teller-Ulam T－U 构型[美国用的氢弹构型，比我国于敏构型落后]
TU	Tianjin University 天津大学
TU	Tongji University 同济大学
TU	transmission unit 传输单元
TU	Tsinghua University 清华大学
TUC	tuck 糕点
TUC	Trades Union Congress 英国职工大会
TUM	Technical University of Munich 德国慕尼黑工业大学

TUN	Tunisia 突尼斯［非洲国家］
TUNEL	TdT mediated nick end labeling TdT 介导的缺口末端标记法
TUR	Turkey 土耳其［亚洲国家］
TURB	turbidity 尿透明度
TÜV SÜD	Technischer Überwachungsverein, süddeutsch 南德国技术监督联合会［德文］
TüV	Technischer Überwachungsverein 德国安全认证标志之一［德文］
TüV	Technischer Überwachungsverein 技术监察协会［德文］
TV	television 电视（机）
TVB	Television Broadcasts Limited 香港电视广播有限公司
TVBS	Television Broadcast Satellite （中国台湾地区）无线卫星电视台
TVC	total variable costs 总可变成本
TVC	thrust vectoring control 推力矢量控制
TVC	thrust vector converter 矢量推力
TVCF	television commercial film 电视广告影片
TVET	Technical and Vocational Education and Training College 职业技术教育与培训学院
TVM	TRON Virtual Machine 波场虚拟机
TVN	television news 电视新闻
TVNZ	Television New Zealand 新西兰电视台
TVOC	total volatile organic compounds 总挥发性有机物
TVP	textured vegetable protein 组织性植物蛋白/素肉
TVR	Trevor 英国特雷弗汽车
TWA	Trans-World Airlines Inc 美国环球航空公司
TWE	test of written English 英文写作测试
TWN	Taiwan 中国台湾地区
tx	thanks 感谢
TXA2	thromboxane A2 血栓素 A2

U

U	uranium 铀[第92号化学元素]
U	USB Flash Disk 移动存储盘
U	you 你，您，你们[网络用语]
U	universal 普通的适合所有观众的影片
U	unit 单位
u/m	unit of measure 测量单位
U/W	underwriters 承销人
U19	Under 19 十九岁以下（国家队）
U20	Under 20 二十岁以下（国家队）
U23	Under 23 二十三岁以下（国家队）
UA	uninterruptible autopilot 不间断自动驾驶系统
UA	uric acid 尿酸
UAA	United Arab Airlines 阿拉伯航空
UAE	United Arab Emirates 阿拉伯联合酋长国[亚洲国家]
UAH	Ukrainian Hryvnia 乌克兰格里夫纳[乌克兰货币单位]
UALB	urinary albumin 尿微量白蛋白
UAM	United American Mechanics 美国机械学、力学联盟
UAM	urban air transport 城市空中交通
UAMY	urine amylase 尿淀粉酶
UAP	unidentified aerial phenomena 无法解释的空中现象
UAP	upper atmosphere phenomena 高层大气现象
UAS	unmanned aerial surveillance 无人空中监视
UAS	unmanned aerospace surveillance 无人宇宙空间监视
UASUTM	Unmanned Aircraft System UTM 无人机系统交通管理平台
UAV	unmanned air vehicle 无人驾驶飞机
UAW	United Automobile Workers 美国汽车工人工会

UAZ	Ulianovskii Avtomobilinei Zavod 乌里扬诺夫汽车制造厂［俄文］	
UB	ultra blue 深蓝	
UB	University of Barcelona 西班牙巴塞罗那大学	
UBC	unclaimed baggage centre 无人认领行李中心	
UBC	University of British Columbia 大不列颠哥伦比亚大学	
UBG	urobilinogen 尿胆素原	
UBI	universal basic income 普遍的基本收入	
U-boot	Unterseeboot 潜艇［德文］	
UBS	Union Bank of Switzerland 瑞士联合银行	
UC	The University of Copenhagen 丹麦哥本哈根大学	
UC	ubiquitous computer 无处不在的电脑	
UC	ulcerative colitis 溃疡性结肠炎	
UC	Unified Communications 统一通信［指把计算机技术与传统通信技术融为一体的新通信模式］	
UC	unit cooler 冷却机组	
UC	University of California 加利福尼亚大学	
UC	University of Chicago 芝加哥大学	
UC	upper case 大写	
UC	user code 用户码	
UC	you see 你知道（的谐音）	
UCA	urine catecholamine 尿儿茶酚胺	
UCAS	uniform cost accounting standards 统一成本的会计标准	
UCAS	Universities and Colleges Admissions Service 大学和学院招生服务中心	
UCAS	University of Chinese Academy of Sciences 中国科学院大学	
UCASS	University of Chinese Academy of Social Sciences 中国社会科学院大学	
UCB	University of California，Berkeley 加州大学伯克利分校［美国］	
UCC	Uniform Code Council 美国统一代码委员会	
UCC	Universal Copyright Convention《世界版权公约》	
UCD	University College Dublin 都柏林大学	
UCF	ultracentrifuge 超速离心机	
UCG	ultrasonocardiography 超声心动图	
UCI	Union Cycliste Internationale［英文：International Cycling Union］国际

U

	自行车联合会[法文]
UCLA	University of California, Los Angeles 加利福尼亚大学洛杉矶分校[美国]
UCLES	University of Cambridge Local Examinations Syndicate 剑桥大学考试委员会
UCS	The Union of Concerned Scientists 忧思科学家联盟
UCS	Unified Computing System 统一计算机系统
UCSB	University of California, Santa Barbara 加利福尼亚大学圣巴巴拉分校
UCSD	University of California, San Diego 加利福尼亚大学圣迭戈分校
UCSF	University of California, San Francisco 加利福尼亚大学旧金山分校
UDA	Ulster Defence Association 阿尔斯特防务协会
UDC	Universal Decimal Classification 国际十进制分类法
UDD	National United Front of Democracy Against Dictatorship 泰国反独裁民主联盟
UDDI	universal description, discovery, integration 通过描述、发现和集成
UDF	Union pour la Démocratie Française 法兰西民主联盟[法文]
UDF	United Democratic Front 南非民主统一战线
UDF	universal disk format 通用磁盘格式
UDP	Union pour la Démocratie et le Progrès 民主进步联盟[法文]
UDP/IP	User Datagram Protocol/Internet Protocol 用户数据报协议/因特网协议
UDS	unit dispatch system 机组调度系统
UDS	universal data system 通用数据系统
UEFA	Union Européenne de Football Association 欧洲足球联合会[法文]
UEFA	Union of European Football Associations 欧洲足球联合会
UESTC	University of Electronic Science and Technology of China 电子科技大学
UF	urea-formaldehyde resin 脲醛树脂
UFC	Ultimate Fighting Championship 终极格斗锦标赛/终极格斗冠军赛
UFC	Union Fédérale des Consommateurs 消费者联合会[法文]
UFC	urinary free cortisol 尿游离皮质醇
UFF	Ulster Freedom Fighters 阿尔斯特自由斗士
UFI	Union des Foires Internationales [英文: Union of International Fairs] 国际展览会联盟[法文]
UFO	Unidentified Flying Object 飞碟汽车[中国浙江]
UFO	Unidentified Flying Object 不明飞行体

UFP	Union des Forces du Progrès 进步力量联盟[法文]
UFTAA	United Federation of Travel Agents Associations 世界旅行社协会联合会
UG	Unigraphics NX EDS 公司的一个产品工程解决方案
UG	Ghent University 比利时根特大学
UGA	Uganda 乌干达[非洲国家]
UGC	Unit Gain Crossover 单位增益渡越
UGC	user generated content 用户原创内容
UGG	ugly sheepskin boots 雪地靴
UGL	Uniglory 立荣海运株式会社
UH	University of Helsinki 芬兰赫尔辛基大学
UHD	ultra high definition 超高清
UHF	ultra high frequency 超高频
UHFEW	ultra high frequency electromagnetic wave 超高频无线电磁波
UHMWPE	ultra-high molecular weight polyethylene 超高分子量聚乙烯[塑料]
UHT	ultra high temperature 超高温（瞬时灭菌）
UI	unemployment insurance 失业保险
UI	user interface 用户界面
UIA	Union Internationale des Architects [英文：International Alliance of Architects] 国际建筑同盟[法文]
UIC	University of Illinois at Chicago 伊利诺伊大学芝加哥分校
UICC	Union International Contre le Cancer [英文：International Union Against Cancer] 国际抗癌联盟[法文]
UICC	universal integrated circuit card 通用集成电路卡
UID	user identity 用户身份
UIDAI	Unique Identification Authority of India 印度独特身份识别管理
UIM	user identification module 用户识别模块
UIP	Union Internationale de Patinage [英文：International Skating Union] 国际滑冰联合会[法文]
UIRT	University Innovation Research and Training Program 大学生创新实验计划
UISA	United Inventors and Scientists of America 美国发明家和科学家联合会

U

UIT	Union Internationale de Tir 国际射击联合会[法文]
UITP	Union International des Transports Public 国际公共交通联会[法文]
UKAS	United Kingdom Accreditation Service 英国皇家认可委员会
UKISC	United Kingdom Industrial Space Committee 英国工业空间委员会
UKiset	United Kingdom Independent Schools Entry Test 英国私立寄宿学校入学考试
UKQCHE	UK Quality Code for Higher Education 英国高等教育质量标准
UKR	Ukraine 乌克兰[欧洲国家]
UKVI	United Kingdom Visas and Immigration 英国签证与移民（局）
UL	Underwriters Laboratories Incorporation 美国保险商实验室公司
UL	Underwriters Laboratories Incorporation 美国保险商实验室公司认证标志
ULC	Underwriters Laboratories Incorporation of Canada 加拿大安全标志
ULC	Underwriters Laboratories Incorporation of Canada 加拿大保险商试验室
ULCC	ultra large crude carrier 超大型油轮
ULE	ultra limited of electronic 超级电子控股有限公司
ULOC	ultra large ore carrier 超大型矿砂船
ULP	University of London Press 伦敦大学出版社[英国]
UM	Universidade de Macau 澳门大学[葡萄牙文]
UM	University of Macau 澳门大学
UM	University of Melbourne 澳大利亚墨尔本大学
UM	University of Michigan 密歇根大学
UM	University of Munich 德国慕尼黑大学
UMB	ultra mobile broadband 超移动宽带
UMF	Unique Manuka Factor 独特麦卢卡因子
UMF20＋	Unique Manuka Factor 20＋ 独麦素 20⁺（抗菌能力与苯酚 20％的水溶液抗菌效力相同）
UMOOCs	University MOOCs 中国高校外语慕课平台
UMP	Union pour un Mouvement Populaire 人民运动联盟[法文]
UMTS	universal mobile telecommunications system 通用移动通信系统
UN	United Nations 联合国
UNAIDS	The Joint United Nations Programme on HIV/AIDS 联合国艾滋病联合规划署

UNB	United Nations Bookshop 联合国书店
UNCAT	United Nations Convention Against Torture《联合国反酷刑公约》
UNCCD	United Nations Convention to Combat Desertification 联合国防治荒漠化公约
UNCD	United Nations Conference on Disarmament 联合国裁军谈判会议
UNCDF	United Nations Capital Development Fund 联合国资本开发基金会
UNCF	United Nations Children's Fund 联合国儿童基金
UNCITRAL	United Nations Commission on International Trade Law 联合国国际贸易法委员会
UNCSD	United Nations Commission on Sustainable Development 联合国可持续发展委员会
UNCTAD	United Nations Conference on Trade and Development 联合国贸易和发展会议
UNDP	United Nations Development Programme 联合国开发计划署
UNDRO	United Nations Disaster Relief Organization 联合国救灾组织
UNE	Una Norma Espanola 西班牙标准[西班牙文]
UNE	Una Norma Espanola 西班牙认证标志[西班牙文]
UNECE	United Nations Economic Commission for Europe 联合国欧洲经济委员会
UNEP	United Nations Environment Program 联合国环境计划署
UNESCO	United Nations Educational, Scientific and Cultural Organization 联合国教科文组织
UNEVOC	International Centre for Technical and Vocational Education and Training 国际职业技术教育培训中心
UNF	United Nations Forces 联合国部队
UNFCCC	UN (United Nations) Framework Convention on Climate Change《联合国气候框架公约》
UNFDAC	United Nations Fund for Drug Abuse Control 联合国管制药物滥用基金
UNFPA	United Nations Fund for Population Activities 联合国人口活动基金委员会
UNGA	United Nations General Assembly 联合国大会

U

UNGEGN	UN Group of Experts on Geographical Names 联合国地名专家组
UNHCR	United Nations Human Rights Council 联合国人权理事会
UNHCR	United Nations High Commissioner for Refugees 联合国难民事务高级专员办事处
uni	university 大学
UNIAN	Ukrainian Independent Information Agency of News 乌克兰独立通讯社
UNICEF	United Nations International Children's Emergency Fund 联合国儿童基金会
UNICJ	United Nations International Court of Justice (联合国)国际法院
UNIDO	United Nations Industrial Development Organization 联合国工业发展组织
UNIFIL	United Nations Interim Force in Lebanon 联合国驻黎巴嫩临时部队
UNISIST	World Science Information System 世界科学情报系统
UNITAR	United Nations Institute for Training and Research 联合国训练研究所
UNIX	UNiplexed Information and Computer Service 一种多任务多用户操作系统
UNL	universal network language 通用网络语言
UNLPP	United Nations Language Professionals Training Programme 联合国语言人才培训体系
UNO	United Nations Organization 联合国组织
UNODC	United Nations Office on Drugs and Crime 联合国毒品和犯罪问题办公室
UNON	United Nations Office at Nairobi 联合国内罗毕办事处
UNOPS	United Nations Office for Project Services 联合国项目事务署
unoreq	unless otherwise requested 除非另有要求
UNOV	United Nations Office at Vienna 联合国维也纳办事处
UNPO	The Unrepresented Nations and Peoples Organization 非联合国会员国家及民族组织
UNRWA	United Nations Relief and Works Agency 联合国难民救济和工程处
UNS	United Nations Secretariat 联合国秘书处
UNSAC	United Nations Scientific Advisory Committee 联合国科学咨询委员会
UNSC	United Nations Security Council 联合国安理会
UNSSC	United Nations System Staff College 联合国系统职员学院

UNSW	University of New South Wales 新南威尔士大学	
UNTAC	United Nations Transitional Authority in Cambodia 联合国柬埔寨临时权力机构	
UNTERM	United Nations Terminology Database 联合国术语库	
UNU	United Nations University 联合国大学	
UNV	United Unions Volunteers 联合国志愿人员组织	
UNWTO	Untied Nations World Tourism Organization 世界旅游组织	
UOB	United Overseas Banks 联合海外银行	
UOP	Universal Oil Products Company 美国环球石油产品公司	
UP	University of Pennsylvania 宾夕法尼亚大学	
UPC	Universal Products Code Committee 美国统一代码委员会	
UPC	UNESCO Publishing Centre 联合国教科文组织出版中心	
UPC	Universal Product Code 通用产品条码	
UPE	universal primary education 普及初等教育	
UPI	The United Press International 合众国际社［美国通讯社］	
UPI	Universal Pay Interface 统一支付界面	
UPI	Unwired Planet International UPI公司［靠收取专利费为生的公司］	
UPP	ubiquitin proteasome pathway 泛素蛋白酶体通路	
UPP	user partnership program 用户伙伴程序	
UPR	Union Pour la Republique 争取共和联盟［法文］	
UPS	uninterruptible power supply system 不间断电源	
UPS	United Package Service 联合包裹递送公司	
UPT	universal personal telecommunication 个人通信业务	
UPU	Universal Postal Union 万国邮政联盟	
UR	ultra rare 极度稀有	
UTR	ultra rare 极度稀有	
UR	Urban Revivo 知名快时尚品牌：港真	
UR	Uomini Rana 蛙人［意大利文］	
URA	Urban Renewal Authority (美国)市区重建局	
URL	Uniform Resource Locator 统一资源定位地址	
URO	urobilinogen 尿胆素原	
URRVS	urban rapid-rail-vehicle system 城市快轨车系统	

URU	Uruguay 乌拉圭[南美洲国家]
US	ultrasonic 超声波
US(A)	United States of America 美国[北美洲国家]
USA	United Stated Army 美国陆军
USAF	United States Air Force 美国空军
USAID	USA International Development 美国国际开发署
USAIPP	USA Intergration Pilot Programs 美国无人机融合试点计划
USAMRIID	the United States Army Medical Research Institute of Infectious Diseases 美国陆军传染病医学研究所
USB	universal serial bus 通用串行总线
USBP	United States Border Patrol 美国边防巡警[后来并入 CBP 海关及边境保护局]
USC	ultrasonic cleaning 超声波清洗
USC	United Ship Company 俄国联合造船公司
USC	United States Code《美国法典》
USCBC	United States-China Business Committee 美中贸易全国委员会
USCBP	U. S. Customs and Border Protection 美国海关与边境保护局
USCG	United States Coast Guard 美国海岸巡逻队
USCIS	United States Citizenship and Immigration Services 美国公民及移民服务局
USCP	United States Capitol Police 美国国会警察
USCPFA	US-China People's Friendship Association 美中人民友好协会[美国]
USD	United States Dollar 美元[货币]
USDA	United States Department of Agriculture 美国农产品认证标志
USDA	United States Department of Agriculture 美国农业部
USDILIN	United States Drug Induced Liver Injury Network 美国药物性肝损伤协作网络
USF	universal service fund 通用服务基金
USGBC	United States Green Building Council 美国绿色建筑委员会
USGPO	Untied States Government Printing Office 美国政府出版局
USGS	United States Geological Survey 美国地质勘探局
USIA	United States Information Agency 美国新闻署

USIU-Africa	United States International University-Africa 美国国际大学非洲分校	
USMC	United States Marine Corps 美国海军陆战队	
USMCA	United States-Mexico-Canada Agreement《美国—墨西哥—加拿大协定》[代替北美自由贸易协定 NAFTA]	
USML	US Munitions List 美国军火清单	
USMS	United States Marshals Service 美国执法处	
USN	United States Navy 美国海军	
USNCB	United States National Central Bureau 国际刑警组织美国国家中心局	
USNI	United States Naval Institute 美国海军研究协会	
USNWR	Untied States News and World Report《美国新闻与世界报道》	
USP	unique selling point 独特卖点	
USP	United States Pharmacopoeia《美国药典》	
USPACOM	United States Pacific Command 美国太平洋司令部	
USPP	United States Park Police 美国公园警察	
USPP	United States Probation and Parole 美国缓刑和假释	
USPS	United States Postal Service 美国邮政管理局	
USPTO	US Patent and Trademark Office 美国专利与商标局	
USR	unheated serum reagin test 不加热血清反应素试验	
USS	United States Ship 美国军舰	
USS	United States Standard 美国(工业)标准	
USSD	unstructured supplementary service data 非结构化补充数据业务	
USSOC	U. S. Special Operations Command 美国特种作战司令部	
USSR	Union of Soviet Socialist Republics 苏联	
USSS	United States Secret Service 美国密勤局	
USTR	United States Trade Representative 美国贸易代表办公室	
UT	Universal Time 世界时	
UT	The University of Texas MD Anderson Cancer Center 美国得克萨斯州大学 MD 安德森癌症中心	
UT	ultra thin 超薄	
UT	University of Tokyo 日本东京大学	
UT	University of Toronto 多伦多大学[加拿大]	

UTC	Universal Time Coordinated 协调世界时
Utd	united 联合的
UTI	urinary tract infection 尿路感染
UTM	Unmanned Aircraft System Traffic Management 无人机系统交通管理
UTS	University of Technology，Sydney 悉尼科技大学
UTTAS	utility tactical transport aircraft system 通用战术运输飞行器系统
UTV	utility vehicle 农夫车/多用途载运车
UUP	Ulster Unionist Party 北爱尔兰统一党
UV	ultraviolet 紫外光
UVA	ultraviolet A 长波紫外线
UVB	ultraviolet B 中波紫外线
UVC	ultraviolet C 短波紫外线
UVZ	Uhtomskii Vertoletneii Zavod 乌赫托姆直升机制造厂［俄文］
UVZ	Uraliskii Varonoctroitelineii Zavod 乌拉尔车辆制造厂［俄文］
UW	underwriters 保险公司
UWS	University of the West of Scotland 西苏格兰大学
UX	user experience 用户体验
UZB	Uzbekistan 乌兹别克斯坦［亚洲国家］

V	vanadium 钒［第 23 号化学元素］
V	victory 胜利
V	volt 伏(特)［法定电位、电压、电动势计量单位］
V	vornorm 暂行标准
V	versus 对(抗)
V	very 非常
V	Vladimir Putin 普京［俄罗斯总统］
V	Vauxhall 英国沃克斯豪尔汽车

V	vein 静脉
V	venous blood 静脉血
V	Venturi 法国文图瑞汽车
V	violet 紫色
V	vitamin 维生素
V&A	Victoria and Albert Museum 英国维多利亚与阿尔伯特博物馆
vac	vacation 假期
VAI	video-assisted instruction 电视辅助教学
VAN	Vanuatu 瓦努阿图[太平洋岛国]
VAP	ventilator-associated pneumonia 呼吸机相关性肺炎
VAT	Value-Added Tax 增值税
VAT	viscera adipose tissue 内脏脂肪组织
VBA	Visual Basic for Applications Visual Basic 宏语言
VBR	variable bit rate 动态比特率/可变比特率
VBS	Visual Basic Script Edition 基于 Visual Basic 的脚本语言
VC	Value Chain 价值链
VC	Venture Capital 风险投资(商)
VC	Video Conference 电视会议
VC	Virtual Community 虚拟社区
VC	Victoria Cross 维多利亚十字勋章
VC	vital capacity 肺活量
VC	vitamin C 维生素 C
vc/pe	venture capital/private equity 风险投资/私募股权
VCD	video compact disc 视频高密光盘；VCD 光盘；激光视盘
vcf	variant call format 变体调用格式
VCM	Venture Cycle Model 风险投资循环模型
VCM	variable code modulation 可变编码调制
VCO	voltage-controlled oscillator 压控振荡器
VCR	video cassette recorder 盒式磁带录像机
VCR	variable compression ratio 可变压缩比
VCU	vehicle control unit 整车控制器
VD	venereal disease 性病

VD	volume of dead space 死腔容积
VDA	variable digital amplifier 可变数字式滤波器
VDals	alveolar dead space 肺泡无效腔
VDalv	alveolar dead space 肺泡无效腔
VDanat	anatomic dead space 解剖无效腔
VDas	anatomic dead space 解剖无效腔
VDC	vehicle dynamic control 车辆动态控制
VDE	Verband Deutscher Elektrotechniker 德国电气产品质量认证标志[德文]
VDE	Verband Deutscher Elektrotechniker 德国电气工程师协会[德文]
VDH	Verband für das Deutsche Hundewesen 德国犬科学协会[德文]
VDIM	vehicle dynamics integrated management 车辆动态综合管理系统
VDR	voyage data recorder 船载航行数据记录仪[俗称船舶黑匣子]
VDSL	video digital subscriber line 视频数字用户线路
VDT	video display terminal 视频显示终端
VE	minute ventilation at rest 静息每分钟通气量
Veep	vice-president 副总统[口语用法,昵称]
VEGF	vascular endothelial growth factor 血管内皮细胞生长因子
VEN	Venezuela 委内瑞拉[南美洲国家]
Vet	veterinarian 兽医
VF	very fine 优美级(钱币)
VFA	Victoria Falls 维多利亚瀑布
VFA	Visiting Forces Agreement 访问部队地位协定
VG	Vici Gaming VG 电竞俱乐部
VG	very good 非常好的(钱币)
VGA	video graphics array 视频图形阵列
VHD	very high density 超高密度
VHF	very high frequency 甚高频
VHFRT	very high frequency radio telephone 甚高频无线电话
VHS	video home system 家用录像系统
VI	visual identity 视觉识别
VI	volume index 红细胞体积指数
VIAS	variable impedance aspiration system 可变阻抗吸气系统

VIC	very important customer 专人服务/贵宾
VIE	Vietnam 越南[亚洲国家]
VIG	video image generator 视频影像发生器
VIHC	Vancouver Immigration Holding Centre 温哥华移民拘留中心
VIK	value in kind 赞助商赞助的服务和现金等价物
VIN	vehicle identification number 车辆识别代码
VINTARS	The Vienna Internet Terminology and Reference System 维也纳网术语和参考系统
VIP	very important person 贵宾
VIPPU	Very Important Person Protection Unit 香港保护要人组
VIS	visual identity system 视觉识别系统
VIS	variable inlet(manifold)system 可变进气(歧管)系统
VISA	Visa International Service Association 维萨卡
VISI	visual identity system internate 网络形象识别系统
Viso-V	volume of isoflow 等流量容积
VIX	volatility index 波动率指数
VJ	video jockey 电视综艺节目主持人
VK	Vicno Keinl 英国卫裤
VK	vitamin K 维生素 K
VLCC	very large crude carrier 超大型油轮
VLDL	very low density lipoprotein 极低密度脂蛋白
VLE	virtual learning environment 虚拟学习环境
VLF	very low frequency 甚低频
VLOC	very-large ore carrier 超大型矿砂船
vlog	video weblog 视频博客
VLS	vertical launch system 垂直发射系统
VLSI	very large scale integration 超大规模集成电路
VLSIC	very large scale integrated circuit 超大规模集成电路
VLSIR	very large scale integrated research 超大规模集成研究(公司)
VLT	very large telescope 甚大望远镜
VM	Virtual Machine 虚拟机
VM	value-based management 价值管理

VM	vending manager 销售经理
VMA	vanillylmandelic acid 香草扁桃酸
V-mail	voice-mail 语音信箱
V-Mail	Victory Mail 胜利邮政
VMGW	virtual media gateway 虚拟媒体网关
VMP	value of marginal product 边际产品价值
VNA	vector network analyzer 矢量网络分析仪
VNA	virtual network architecture 虚拟网络结构
VND	Vietnam dong 越南盾[越南货币单位][越南文]
VO	virtual organization 虚拟组织
VOA	Voice of America 美国之音
VOA	Volunteers of America 美国志愿服务队
VOC	volatile organic compound 挥发性有机化合物
VOC	Verification of Conformity 伊拉克 VOC 符合性认证标志
VOD	video on demand 视频点播
VoIP	Voice over IP 网络语音通信技术
vol	volume 卷；册
VoLTE	voice over LTE 4G 数据传输技术[使用数据流量来打电话]
VP	vice president 副总经理,副总裁
VPN	virtual private network 虚拟专用网
VPO	Vienna Philharmonic Orchestra 维也纳爱乐交响乐团[奥地利]
VPS	virtual private service 虚拟专用服务
VQ	venture quotient 创业商数
VR	virtual reality 虚拟现实
VR	visual range 视程
VR	voice recognition 话音识别
VR/AR	virtual reality/augmented reality 虚拟现实/增强现实技术
VRE	vancomycin-resistant enterococcus 万古霉素耐药肠球菌
VS	versus 对（某人、某物、某集体）
VS	Vidal Sassoon 沙宣护发美发品（源于创始人维达·沙宣）
VS	very special 很特殊级别
VSA	Van Santen Associate 万山丹建筑表皮设计顾问公司

VSA	variable stability aircraft 变稳飞机验收	
VSA	vehicle stability assist 车辆稳定性辅助系统	
VSA	virtual server architecture 虚拟服务器架构	
VSA	visual scene analysis 可视影像分析	
VSA	voice stress analyser 人声压力分析计	
VSC	vehicle stability control 车身稳定控制系统	
VSO	voluntary service overseas 海外志愿者服务社	
VSO	Vienna Symphony Orchestra 维也纳交响乐团[奥地利]	
VSOP	very superior old pale 优质佳酿白兰地	
VSS	virtual studio system 虚拟演播系统	
VT	tidal volume 潮气量	
VTC	valve timing control 气门正时控制	
VTCS	variable turbulence control system 可变涡流控制系统	
VTM	virtual teller machine 远程视频柜员机	
VU	virtual university 虚拟大学	
VV	varicose vein 静脉曲张	
VVIP	very very important person 特殊贵宾/极重要的要人	
VVT	variable valve timing 可变气门正时技术	
VW	Volkswagen 德国大众汽车[德文]	
VX	persistent toxic nerve 持续性神经毒气[代字]	
VX	WeChat 微信[代字]	
VZF	Vision Zero Fund 零伤亡愿景基金

W

W	watt 瓦(特)[法定功率计量单位]	
W	west(ern) 西方(的)	
W	Wolfram [英文:tungsten] 钨[第74号元素][拉丁文]	
W	Wuling 五菱汽车[中国广西:汉语缩略语]	

W	warrant 许可证/执照
W	white 白色
W/C	week commencing 从（提到之）日开始的一周
W/M	weight and/or measurement at ship's option 重量和/或体积由船公司选择
w/o	without 没有
W/TAX	withholding tax 预扣税
w/v	weight in volume 单位体积的重量
W3C	World Wide Web Consortium 国际万维网联盟
WA	Wassenaar Arrangement《瓦森纳协定》
WAAS	wide area augmentation system 广域增强系统
WAAS	World Academy of Art and Science 世界艺术与科学协会
WAC	Women's Army Corps 陆军妇女队
WADA	World Anti-Doping Agency 世界反兴奋剂机构［组织］
WAF	with all faults 货物售出概不退换
WAIC	World Artificial Intelligence Conference 世界人工智能大会
WAM	weighted average mark 学分加权平均分［又称 GPA］
WAN	Wide Area Network 广域网
WAN	World Association of Newspapers 世界报业协会
wanna	want to 想要
WAP	Wireless Application Protocol 无线应用协议
Wash Pst	*Washington Post*《华盛顿邮报》［美国］
WASP	White Anglo-Saxon Protestant 白人盎格鲁-撒克逊新教徒［被认为是美国社会中实力最强的白人］
WAT	weight/altitude/temperature 重量/高度/温度
WATS	wide area telecommunication 长途电信业务
WAY	World Assembly of Youth 世界青年大会
Wb	weber 韦伯［磁通量单位］
WB	Winner Bitch 同品种同年龄段最佳母犬
WB	waste-book 流水账
WB	waybill 运单
WB	Weld Board 焊接产品认证标志
WB	Weld Board 焊接局

WB	World Bank 世界银行
WBA	World Boxing Association 世界拳击协会
WBA	white blood(cell) count 白细胞计数
WBA	World Biodiversity Association 世界生物多样性协会
WBA	World Boomerang Association 世界飞镖协会
WBC	White Blood Cell 白细胞
WBC	white blood(cell) count 白细胞计数
WBC	World Boxing Council 世界拳击理事会
WBC	World Barista Championship 世界咖啡师大赛
WBC-DC	white blood cell differential count 白细胞分类计数
WBDC	World Blockchain Digital Technology Conference 世界区块链数字科技大会
WBF	World Bridge Federation 世界桥牌联合会
WBG	World Bank Group 世界银行集团
WBL	World Brand Lab 世界品牌实验室
WBO	World Beauty Organization 世界美女组织
WBO	World Boxing Organization 世界拳击组织
WBSA	World Business Association 世界商务策划师联合会
WBUR	We're Boston University Radio 波士顿公共广播电台
WC	water closet 厕所(英美等英语国家现在一般不用作为"厕所"之意的WC,多用 toilet、washroom、restroom、bathroom 等,而男厕则多用 gents、men,女厕多用 ladies、women 等。)
WC	WeChat 微信
WC	will call 预订零售部
WC	without charge 免费
WC	working capital 流动资本
WC	World Champion 世界冠军
WC	World Class 世界级
WC	World Cup 世界杯
WCA	Waste Conducting Association 休斯敦废物处理协会
WCA	workplace conditions assessment 工厂条件评估
WCA	World Cyber Arena 世界电子竞技大赛

W

WCBA	Women Chinese Basketball Association 中国女子篮球协会
WCF	working capital fund 周转资金
WCG	World Cyber Games 世界电子竞技大赛
WCL	World Confederation of Labor 世界劳工联盟
WCO	World Customs Organization 世界海关组织
WCPA	World Commission on Protected Area 全球保育区域组织
WCPS	World Confederation of Productivity Science 世界生产力科学联盟
WCRF	World Cancer Research Foundation 世界癌症研究基金会
WCS	Wildlife Conservation Society 国际野生生物保护学会
WD	Winner Dog 同品种同年龄段最佳公犬
WD	working draft 工作草案
WDMS	World Directory of Medical Schools 世界医学院校名录
WDR	world development report 世界发展报告
WE	Team World Elite 世界精英
WED	Wednesday 星期三
WEF	World Economic Forum 世界经济论坛
WEG	World Electronic-sports Games 世界电子竞技比赛
WF	withdrawn failing 不及格停修
WFC	World Food Council 世界粮食理事会
WFC	weighted fractional count 加权的分数计数
WFC	World Financial Center 环球金融中心
WFC	World Future Committee 世界未来委员会
WFCMS	World Federation of Chinese Medicine Societies 世界中医药学会联合会
WFCMSM	Promotion Committee of Moxibustion of World Federation of Chinese Medicine Societies 世界中医药学会联合会艾灸保健推广委员会
WFDB	World Federation of Diamond Bourses 世界钻石交易所联盟
WFHVRAA	World Forum for Harmonization of Vehicle Regulation and its Administered Agreements 世界车辆法规协调论坛及其管理协定
WFME	World Federation for Medical Education 世界医学院校联合会
WFOE	wholly foreign owned enterprises 外资独资企业

WFP	World Food Program 联合国世界粮食计划署
WFR	Weil-Felix reaction 外-斐反应
WG	weight guaranteed 保证重量
WG	working group 工作组
WGA	Windows Genuine Advantage validation tool 微软视窗的正版验证工具
WGA	Writers Guild of America 美国编剧工会
WGC	World Gold Council 世界黄金协会
WH	white 白色
WHA	World Health Assembly 世界卫生大会
WHC	World Halal Council 世界清真委员会
WHC	World Heritage Committee 世界（文化）遗产委员会
WHFC	World Halal Food Conference 世界清真食品理事会
WHI	Women Health Initiative 妇女健康计划
WHIPS	Whole Head Impact Protect System 头颈部碰撞防护系统
WHO	World Health Organization 世界卫生组织
WI	West Indies 西印度群岛
WI	Women's Institute 妇女协会
WI	working instruction 作业指导书
WIBA	Women's International Boxing Association 世界女子拳击协会
WIBC	Women's International Bowling Congress 世界妇女保龄球联合会
WIBC	Women's International Boxing Council 女子国际拳击理事会
WIBF	Women's International Boxing Federation 国际女子拳击联合会
WIC	World Internet Conference 世界互联网大会
WIC	Women Infants and Children 美国农业部的妇幼婴儿计划
WIC	women, infants and children 妇婴幼儿
WIC	World Intelligence Conference 世界智能大会
WID	World Inequality Database 世界不平等数据库
Wi-Fi	wireless fidelity 无线保真技术
WIIC	World Internet Industry Conference 世界互联网工业大会
Wiki	wee kee wee kee 维基［源自夏威夷语"快点快点"］
WIM	wireless identification mould 无线识别模块
WiMax	Worldwide Interoperability for Microwave Access 万维微波

W

WIMAX	Worldwide Interoperability for Microwave Access 全球微波接入互操作性	
WIN	Women's Initiative Program 妇女进取计划	
WIN	Wireless Intelligent Network 无线智能网	
WINS	Windows Internet Name Service 视窗互联网服务的命名(微软)	
WIP	work in progress 在制品	
WIPO	World Intellectual Property Organization 世界知识产权组织	
WIR	World Inequality Report 世界不平等报告	
WIS	Weizmann Institute of Science 以色列魏茨曼科学研究所	
WITTA	World Interpreter and Translator Training Association 世界翻译教育联盟	
WIV	Wuhan Institute of Virus 武汉病毒研究所	
WIWT	What I Wore Today 今天我穿什么[网络用语]	
WLAN	Wireless Local Area Network 无线局域网	
WLF	wulinfeng 武林风[汉语拼音缩略语]	
WLS	Wild Life Sanctuary 野生动物保护区	
WLTM	would like to meet 愿意见面	
WM	work measurement 作业测定	
WM	warehouse management 库房管理	
WM	Web Money (Russian Internet Banking) 网络货币(俄罗斯网络银行)	
WMA	Windows Media Audio 一种音频媒体	
WMA	Worldwide MMA Alliance 世界综合格斗联盟冠军赛	
WMB	Word Magazine Bank 主要英语国家的出版物全文汇总	
WMC	World Memory Championship 世界脑力锦标赛	
WMC	Mobile World Congress 世界移动通信大会	
WMD	Weapon of Mass Destruction 大规模杀伤性武器	
WMDA	World Marrow Donor Association 国际骨髓供体协会	
WML	wireless markup language 无线标记语言	
WMO	World Meteorological Organization 世界气象组织	
WNBA	Women's National Basketball Association 美国国家女子篮球协会	
WNM	Washington National Monument 华盛顿国家纪念碑	
WOS	ISI Web of Science 国际论文数据库	
WOW	World of Warcraft 魔兽世界	
WP	weather permitting 雨天顺延	

WP	white power 白人至上
WPA	with particular average 水渍险
WPA	Wi-Fi Protected Access 无线网络安全保护系统
wpc	woman police constable 女警察
WPC	World Petroleum Congress 世界石油大会
WPF	World Peace Foundation 世界和平基金会
WPFG	World Police and Fire Games 世界警察和消防员运动会
WPI	Water Pollution Index 水质污染指数
WPI	Wholesale Price Index 批发价格指数
WPI	*World Patent Index*《世界专利索引》
WPkI	wireless public key infrastructure 无线公开密钥基础设施
wpm	words per minute 每分钟字数
WPMA	World Packaging Machinery Association 世界包装机械联盟
WPN	*World Press News*《世界报刊新闻》
WPOS	Western Pacific Ocean System 热带西太平洋海洋系统物质能量交换及其影响
WPS	women, peace and security 妇女、和平与安全
WPS	word processing system 字词处理系统
WPSI	Women, Peace and Security Index 女性、和平和安全指数
WPU	Witness Protection Unit 香港保护证人组
WPW	preexcitation syndrome 预激综合征
WQ	will quotient 志商
WR	world record 世界纪录
WR	war risk 战争险
WR	Wassermann reaction 乏色曼氏反应
WRAC	Women's Royal Army Corps 英国皇家陆军妇女队
WRAF	Women's Royal Air Force 英国皇军空军妇女队
WRC	World Rally Championship 世界汽车拉力锦标赛
WRF	Weather Research Forecast 气候研究预报
WRGB	white, red, green, blue 在三基色(红、绿、蓝)基础上加了白色
WRI	World Resource Institute 世界资源研究所
WS	woshan 涡扇[中国航空发动机型号,汉语拼音缩略语]

WS	Washington Star《华盛顿星报》[美国]
WSADS	Wind Support Airdrop System 风支持空投系统
WSC	Water and Sewerage Commission 给水与排污委员会
WSDE	World Stage of Digital Economy 世界区块链技术大会
WSDL	web service description language 网络业务描述语言
WSI	wafer scale integration 晶片规模集成电路
WSI	Wave & Soros International Ltd. 圣文森特和格林纳丁斯注册公司
WSJ	The Wall Street Journal《华尔街日报》
WSK	waiyu shuiping kaoshi 外语水平考试[汉语拼音缩略语]
WSU	Washington State University 美国华盛顿州立大学
WT	warrant 认股证
WT	weight 重量
WTA	Women's Tennis Association 国际职业女子网球协会
WTA	World Technological Association 世界科技城市联盟组织
WTCC	World Touring Car Championship 世界房车锦标赛
WTCC	World Touring Car Cup 世界房车杯赛
WTF	welcome to facebook 欢迎来到脸谱网
WTF	who to follow 关注谁
wtf	water front 滨水地区
WTI	World Trade Institute 世界贸易研究所
WTI	West Texas Intermediate 美国西得克萨斯中间基原油
WTO	World Trade Organization 世界贸易组织
WTO/SPS	World Trade Organization/Sanitary and PhytoSanitary（Measures）世界贸易组织实施卫生与植物卫生措施协定
WTSE	World Toilet Summit Expo 世界厕所峰会暨博览会
WTT	World Table Tennis 世界乒乓球职业大联盟
WTTC	World Tourism and Tourist Conference 世界旅游和旅行者协会
WU	wuzhuang 武装[汉语拼音缩略语]
WU	Wuhan University 武汉大学
WUN	World Universities Union 世界大学联盟
WUR	World University Rankings 世界大学排名
WUSTL	Washington University in St. Louis 圣路易斯华盛顿大学

WW	warehouse warrant 仓库收据
WWA	World Waterpark Association 国际水上乐园社团
WWC	World Water Committee 世界水资源委员会
WWDC	Worldwide Developers Conference 苹果全球开发者大会
WWDC	World War Debt Commission 世界大战债务委员会
WWE	World Wrestling Entertainment 世界摔跤娱乐公司
WWF	World Wildlife Fund 世界野生动物基金会
WWF	World Wrestling Federation 世界摔跤联合会
WWF	World Wildlife Fund 世界自然基金会
WWMHA	World-Wide Miniature Horse Association 全球迷你马协会
WWPSA	Western World Pet Supply Association 西方世界宠物提供协会
WWW	World Wide Web 万维网
WWW	World Weather Watch 世界天气监测网
WWW	Who Was Who《已故名人录》
WWW	Wood Wide Web 树联网
WYSIWYG	what you see is what you get 所见即所得

X	X-ray X 射线[一种波长很短的电磁辐射,由德国物理学家伦琴于1895年发现]
X	exit 退出
X. in	ex-interest 无利息
x. a.	ex all 一切除外
X. O.	extra old 非常久远(的酒);陈年特级的酒
xc	ex coupon 无息票
XD	XD picture card 一种专为储存数码照片开发的存储卡
XD	ex-dividend 无股息/无红利
Xe	xenon 氙[第54号化学元素]

XF	extremely fine 极美等级（钱币）
XISU	Xi'an International Studies University 西安外国语大学
XJU	Xi'an Jiaotong University 西安交通大学
XL	extra large 特大号（服装）
XLD	export levy duty 出口税
XML	extensible markup language 可扩展标记语言
XO	xanthine oxidase 黄嘌呤氧化酶
XP	Exercise Priority 运用优先权
XPR	ex privileges 不予优惠/无特权
XR	extended response 推迟答复
XSEZ	Xiamen Special Economic Zone 厦门经济特区
XTS	crosstell simulator 对话模拟器
XTS	extended test bench 扩展式测试台
XTX	export tax 出口税
XU	Xiamen University 厦门大学
XVP	executive vice president 执行副总裁
XXH	extra extra heavy 特超重
XXL	extra extra large 特特大号（服装）
XYZ	check your zipper 检查你的拉链[网络用语]

Y	YMCA (Young Men's Christian Association) 基督教青年会
Y	year 年
Y	yellow 黄色
Y	yttrium 钇[第 39 号化学元素]
y'all	you all 你们（都）
Y20	youth 20 countries 二十国集团青年会议
Yangkees	New York Yankees 纽约洋基队

yawns	young and wealthy but normal 富有但过着普通日子的年轻人
Yb	ytterbium 镱[第70号化学元素]
YCCI	the Yiwu China Commodity Index 义乌指数
YCPS	Yale Center for Parallel Supercomputing 耶鲁大学为中心的并行超级计算
YCT	Youth Chinese Test 中小学生汉语考试
YD	yard 码[长度单位]
yd(s)	yard(s) 码[英美长度单位=3英尺=0.914米]
YDY	yesterday 昨天
YE	yellow 黄色
YEM	Yemen 也门[亚洲国家]
YES	youth education service 青少年教育服务
YG	yellowish green 黄绿色
YG	YG Entertainment 韩国YG娱乐公司
YHA	Youth Hostels Association 青年旅舍协会
YHAMA	Yokohama 横滨市[日本城市]
YIL	yellow indicator lamp 黄色指示灯
YKK	Yoshida Kogyo Kabushikigaisha 日本YKK拉链[日文]
YLD	yield 收益
YLJ	*Yale Law Journal* 《耶鲁法学杂志》[美国]
YLL	Years of Life Lost 损失生命年数
YM	Yema 野马汽车[中国成都:汉语缩略语]
YMCA	Young Men's Christian Association 基督教青年会
YMMV	your mileage may vary 不同人有不同看法[网络用语]
YMP	Young Master Programme 环境小硕士[中国瑞典合作项目]
YNP	Yellowstone National Park 美国黄石国家公园
YO	yearly output 年产量
YOB	year of birth 出生年
YOCSEF	Young Computer Scientists & Engineers Forum 青年计算机科技论坛
YOLO	you only live once 你只会活一次[鼓励人们即使冒着生命危险也要奋斗一生和享受人生]
YOY	year over year 年环比
YP	yellow page 黄页

YPS	Young Professionals Scheme 年轻的专业人士计划
YR	yellow red 黄红色
yr(s)	year(s) 年
YRB	year book 年鉴
YRLY	yearly 每年的
YSL	Yarrow Shipbuilders Ltd 英国亚罗造船有限公司
YSL	Young Socialist League 青年社会主义者联盟
YSL	Yves Saint Laurent 伊夫·圣·罗兰名牌女装
YTB	yield to broker 经纪商收益
YTC	yield to call 至通知赎回时收益
YTM	yield to maturity 到期收益
YTN	Yonhap Television News 韩国电视台
YTN	youth transition network 青年网络
YU	Yale University 耶鲁大学
Yugo	Yugoslavia 前南斯拉夫[欧洲]
YUN	Yearbook of the United Nations《联合国年鉴》
YWCA	Young Women's Christian Association 基督教女青年会
YZ	yingzuo 硬座[汉语拼音缩略语]

Z	Zotye 众泰汽车[中国浙江永康]
Z	zero 不属上述的文献类型[参考文献标示字母]
Z	zone 区域
ZAM	Zambia 赞比亚[非洲国家]
ZAN	Zanzibar 桑给巴尔市[非洲坦桑尼亚城市]
ZAR	South African Rand 南非货币:兰特
ZBB	zero-based budgeting 免征点
ZD	zero defect 无差错
ZDD	zero defect program 无缺陷计划

ZEV	zero-emission vehicle 零排放车辆
ZEW	Zentrum für Europäische Wirtschafts forschung 经济景气指数[德文,由欧洲经济研究中心引申而来]
ZEW	Zentrum für, Europäische Wirtschaftsforschung 欧洲经济研究中心[德文]
ZF	zone of fire 交战区
ZFW	zero fuel weight 零燃油重量
ZGE	zero gravity effect 失重作用
ZHC	Zhongguo Hanyu Capacity 国家职业汉语能力测试[英汉混合缩略语]
ZI	zone interdit 禁区
ZIC	Zhuhai International Circuit 珠海国际赛车场
ZIM	Zimbabwe 津巴布韦[非洲国家]
ZIP	Zone Information Protocol 区域信息协议
ZL	zero line 基准线
Zn	zinc 锌[第30号化学元素]
ZO	zero output 零输出
ZOR	zone of responsibility 职责区域
ZOS	zone of separation 隔离带
ZPG	zero population growth 人口零增长
ZPMC	Shanghai Zhenhua Port Machinery Company Ltd. 上海振华重工(集团)股份有限公司
ZPR	zipper 拉链
ZR	zero coupon issue 零息发行
Zr	zirconium 锆[第40号化学元素]
ZSA	zero-set amplifier 调零放大器
ZSA	zone safety analysis 区域安全分析
ZST	zone standard time 地方标准时间
ZT	zero time 零时
ZTE	Zhongxing Telecommunication Equipment Corporation 中兴通讯
Z-time	zebra time 格林尼治平均时
ZU	Zhejiang University 浙江大学
ZUC	Zhengfa University of China (CUPL 为旧称) 中国政法大学
ZWEK	this week 本周
ZZB	zhongzubu 中共中央组织部[汉语拼音首字母]

希腊字母开头

α1-AT	α1-antitrypsin α1-抗胰蛋白酶
α2-AP	α2-antiplasmin α2-抗纤溶酶
α2-MG	α2-macroglobulin α2-巨球蛋白
α-HBDH	α-hydroxybutyrate dehydrogenase α-羟丁酸脱氢酶
α-NAE	α-naphthyl-acetate esterase α-乙酸萘酯酯酶
β2-MG	β2-microglobulin β2-微球蛋白
β-Gl	β-globulin β-球蛋白
β-MSH	β-melanocyte-stimulating hormone β-黑素细胞刺激素
γ-GT	γ-glutamyl transpeptidase γ-谷氨酰转肽酶

汉英部分

标点、数字、字母开头排序

- (US)美国教育传播与技术协会 **AECT**
  Association for Educational Communications and Technology
- (埃及)中东通讯社[埃及国家通讯社,设在开罗] **MENA**
  Middle East News Agency
- (保险)全险 **AAR**   against all risks
- (北京)宽带网公司 **BBN**   Broad Band Networks
- (北约)执行工作组 **EWG**   Executive Working Group
- (法国)国家科学研究中心[法文] **CNRS**
  Centre National de la Recherche Scientifique [英文：National Center for Scientific Research]
- (飞机)电子巡逻 **EP**   electronic patrol (aircraft)
- (飞机)短距离起落 **STOL**   short take-off and landing
- (港口的)自由区 **FZ**   Free Zone
- (高层管理人员)药业管理硕士课程班 **EMMA**
  Executive Master of Medicine Administration
- (公民网络)电子身份标识 **eID**   electronic identity
- (国际)信息系统审计与控制协会 **ISACA**
  Information System Auditing and Control Association
- (韩国)文化广播公司 **MBC**   Munhwa Broadcasting Corporation
- (航空)计算机订座系统 **CRS**   computer reservation system
- (计算机)硬盘 **HD**   hard disk

- (将受害者捆绑折磨后杀死的)变态连环杀手 **BTK killer**
  a serial killer who binds, tortures, and kills the victim
- (酒吧)领舞 **DS**   dancer
- (劳动和社会保障部)职业技能鉴定中心 **OSTA**
  Occupational Skill Test Association
- (联合国)国际法院 **UNICJ**
  United Nations International Court of Justice
- (联合国)亚洲及太平洋经济社会委员会 **ESCAP**
  Economic and Social Commission for Asia and the Pacific
- (联合国)战俘问题特设委员会 **AHCPW**
  Ad Hoc Commission on Prisoners of War
- (联合国教科文组织)国际科学协会理事会 **ICSU**
  International Council of Scientific Unions
- (两岸)经济合作框架协议 **ECFA**   Economic Co-operation Frame Agreement
- (美国)国际通信信息协会 **ICIA**
  International Communication Information Association
- (美国)大型燃料空气炸弹(或称炸弹之母) **MOAB**
  massive ordnance air burst
- (美国)个人退休账户 **IRA**   Individual Retirement Account
- (美国)工业和应用数学协会 **SIAM**
  Society for Industrial and Applied Mathematics
- (美国)公共广播公司 **PBS**   Public Broadcasting Service
- (美国)公共卫生署 **PHS**   Public Health Service
- (美国)国际安全顾问委员会 **ISAB**   International Safety Advice Bureau
- (美国)国际教育交流理事会 **CIEE**
  Council on International Educational Exchanges
- (美国)国际贸易委员会 **ITC**   International Trade Commission
- (美国)国家科学院 **NAS**   National Academy of Sciences
- (美国)国家宇航局 **NASA**
  National Aeronautics and Space Administration
- (美国)惠普公司 **HP**   Hewlett-Packard

(美国)教师助理[高等教育机构为研究生设置的支薪职位] **TA**
teaching assistant

(美国)军事技术情报局文献 **ASTIA**
(=Armed Service Technical Information Agency) Document

(美国)麻省理工学院 **MIT**
Massachusetts Institute of Technology

(美国)米高梅电影制片公司 **MGM**   Metro-Goldwyn-Mayer

(美国)免疫实施咨询委员会 **ACIP**
Advisory Committee on Immunization Practices

(美国)能源部 **DOE**   Department of Energy

(美国)全国职业橄榄球大联盟 **NFL**   National Football League

(美国)商务部 **DOC**   Department of Commerce

(美国)食品与药品管理局 **FDA**   Food and Drug Administration

(美国)市区重建局 **URA**   Urban Renewal Authority

(美国)天然产品协会 **NPA**   Natural Product Association

(美国)跳级考试 **APT**   Advance Placement Test

(美国)投资管理和研究协会 **AIMR**
Association of Investment and Management Research

(美国)微波通信公司 **MCI**   Microwave Communication Inc.

(美国)西北航空公司 **NWA**   Northwest Airlines

(美国)消费电子协会 **CEA**   Consuming Electronics Association

(美国)消费者联盟 **CU**   Consumers Union

(美国)学业能力倾向初步测验;大学预考 **PSAT**
Preliminary Scholastic Assessment Test

(美国)医学研究所 **IOM**   Institute of Medicine

(美国)英特尔芯片制造公司 **Intel**   Integrated Electronics

(美国)战略及国际问题研究中心 **CSIS**
Center for Strategic and International Studies

(美国国防部)高级研究计划署 **ARPA**   Advanced Research Project Agency

(美元的类似音)美元[网络用语] **BUX**   bucks

(南非)非洲人国民大会 **ANC**   African National Congress

(纽约)国际摄影中心 **ICP**   International Center of Photography

标点、数字、字母开头排序

- (拳击)击倒 **KO** — knock out
- (日本)东洋轴承制造公司 **NTN** — Toyo Bearing Manufacturing Co. Ltd
- (摄影)模量传递函数 **MTF** — modulation transfer function
- (摄影)显相纸 **DOP** — developing-out paper
- (台湾)海峡两岸交流基金会 **FEATS**
  Foundation for Exchange across the Taiwan Straits
- (台湾)无线卫星电视台 **TVBS** — Television Broadcast Satellite
- (泰国)人民民主联盟 **DAAD** — Democratic Alliance Against Dictatorship
- (统计)景气综合指数 **CI** — Composite Index
- (网络)点对点 **P2P** — point to point
- (印度)新德里电视台 **NDTV** — New Delhi Television
- (英国)独立电视新闻公司 **ITN** — Independent Television News
- (英国)高等教育咨询中心 **HEAC** — Higher Education Advisory Center
- (英国)国家高等教育文凭 **HND** — Higher National Diploma
- (英国)皇家律师 **KC** — King's Counsel
- (英国)皇家摄影学会 **RPS** — Royal Photographic Society
- (英国)军事情报(处) **MI** — Military Intelligence
- (英国)联合电视公司 **ATV** — Associated Television
- (英国剑桥大学)国际考试委员会 **CIE** — Committee of International Ex(am)
- (英国职业技术教育)国家高级合格证书 **HNC**
  Higher National Certificate
- (有本金交割)远期外汇合约 **DF** — Delivery Forward
- (宇航)出舱活动 **EVA** — extravehicular activity
- (中国)出国进修人员英语水平考试 **EPT** — English Proficiency Test
- (中国)国家教育考试委员会 **NEEA**
  National Education Examinations Authority
- (中国)全国人民代表大会 **NPC** — National People's Congress
- (中国)人民解放军 **PLA** — People's Liberation Army
- (中国)香港 **HK** — Hong Kong
- (中国)中央气象台 **CMO** — Central Meteorological Observatory
- (中国)中央人民政府 **CPG** — Central People's Government

- "奥运"流行语[反映了部分观众对 CCTV 和"奥运"的不满] CCAV
  CCTV＋Aoyun
- "海豹"队队员 SEALs　　　　　sea-air-lands
- "使世界清洁起来"组织 CUW　　Clean Up World
- "锁眼"-11 侦察卫星 KH-11　　　Key Hole-11
- "直观、有效地表达观点的工具"的简化版 Sway
  office sway
- 《澳港自由贸易协定》A-HKFTA
  Australia-Hong Kong Free Trade Agreement
- 《澳新更紧密经济关系贸易协定》ANICERTA
  Australia New Zealand Closer Economic Relations Trade Agreement
- 《不列颠百科全书》Ency Brit　　*Encyclopedia Britannica*
- 《出口管理条例》EAR　　　　　*Export Administration Regulation*
- 《穿越火线》[韩国游戏名] CF　　*Cross Fire*
- 《大不列颠百科全书》EB　　　　*Encyclopaedia Britannica*
- 《当代作家》CA　　　　　　　　*Contemporary Author*
- 《德国药典》[德文] DAB
  Deutsches Apothekerbuch[英文：*German Pharmacopoeia*]
- 《德黑兰日报》[伊朗] TJ　　　　*Teheran Journal*
- 《地球物理研究杂志》[美国] JGR　*Journal of Geophysical Research*
- 《读者文摘》[美国] RD　　　　　*Reader's Digest*
- 《法兰克福评论报》(德文) FR　　*Frankfurter Rundschau*
- 《商业法杂志》[英国] JBL　　　　*Journal of Business Law*
- 《反仿冒贸易协定》ACTA　　　　*Anti-Counterfeiting Trade Agreement*
- 《反恐精英》[电子游戏名] CS　　*Counter-Strike*
- 《纺织品与服装协定》ATC　　　　*Agreement on Textile and Clothing*
- 《哥伦比亚新闻评论》CJR　　　　*Columbia Journalism Review*
- 《工程索引》EI　　　　　　　　　*Engineer Index*
- 《公民身份修正法案》CAA　　　　*The Citizenship Amendment Act*
- 《公民身份修正议案》CAB　　　　*The Citizenship Amendment Bill*
- 《公平债务催收作业法》FDCPA　　*Fair Debt Collection Practices Act*

标点、数字、字母开头排序

- 《关于儿童安置的州际契约》**ICPC**
  Interstate Compact on the Placement of Children
- 《国防授权法案》**NDAA**　　　　　　National Defense Authorization Act
- 《国际环境研究与公共卫生》(杂志)**IJERPH**
  International Journal of Environmental Research and Public Health
- 《国际铁路货物运输公约》**CIM**
  Convention Concerning International Carriage of Goods by Rail
- 《国际铁路货物运输公约》[法文] **COTIF**
  Convention de relative aux Transports Internationaux Ferroviaires
- 《国际学位论文文摘》**DAI**　　　　*Dissertation Abstracts International*
- 《国际药学文摘》**IPA**　　　　　　International Pharmaceutical Abstracts
- 《韩日军事情报保护协定》**GSOMIA**
  Japanese and South Korean Military Intelligence Protection Agreement
- 《核不扩散条约》**NPT**
  Treaty on the Non-Proliferation of Nuclear weapons
- 《后勤交换协议备忘录》**LEMOA**
  Logistics Exchange Memorandum of Agreement
- 《华尔街日报》**WSJ**　　　　　　　*The Wall Street Journal*
- 《华盛顿星报》[美国] **WS**　　　　*The Washington Star*
- 《华盛顿邮报》[美国] **Wash Pst**　*The Washington Post*
- 《化学文摘》**CA**　　　　　　　　*Chemical Abstracts*
- 《基督教科学箴言报》(美国) **CSM**　*The Christian Science Monitor*
- 《简明牛津词典》**COD**　　　　　　*The Concise Oxford Dictionary*
- 《金融科技》**Fin Tech**　　　　　　*Finance Technology*
- 《金融时报》**FT**　　　　　　　　　*Financial Times*
- 《禁止生物武器公约》**BWC**　　　　Biological Weapons Convention
- 《经济评论》半月刊[英国] **Econ R**　*Economic Review*
- 《旧金山记事报》[美国] **SFC**　　　*San Francisco Chronicle*
- 《科技会议录索引》**ISTP**
  Index to Scientific & Technical Proceedings
- 《科学通讯》[英国季刊] **SN**　　　　*Science News*
- 《科学文摘》**SA**　　　　　　　　　*Science Abstracts*

- 《科学引文索引》网络版 **SCIE**   *Science Citation Index Expanded*
- 《跨太平洋伙伴关系协定》**TPP**   *Trans-Pacific Partnership Agreement*
- 《朗文当代英语辞典》**LDOCE**
  Longman Dictionary of Contemporary English
- 《联邦杀虫剂、杀真菌剂和灭鼠剂法案》**FIFRA**
  Federal Insecticide, Fungicide and Rodenticide Act
- 《联邦食品、药品及化妆品法案》**FFDCA**   *Federal Food, Drug and Cosmetic Act*
- 《联合国反酷刑公约》**UNCAT**
  United Nations Convention Against Torture
- 《联合国年鉴》**YUN**   *Yearbook of the United Nations*
- 《联合国宪章》**CUN**   *Charter of the United States*
- 《曼彻斯特卫报》[英国] **MG**   *Manchester Guardian*
- 《美国出版商目录年报》**PTLA**   *Publishers Trade List Annual*
- 《美国大学词典》**ACD**   *American College Dictionary*
- 《美国法典》**USC**   *United States Code*
- 《美国工具书年报》**ARBA**   *American Reference Books Annual*
- 《美国就业年龄歧视法案》**ADEA**   *Age Discrimination in Employment Act*
- 《美国科利尔百科全书》**CE**   *Collier's Encyclopedia*
- 《美国科学院院报》**PNAS**
  Proceedings of the National Academy of Sciences of the United States of America
- 《美国俚语词典》**DAS**   *Dictionary of American Slang*
- 《美国人名词典》**DAB**   *Dictionary of American Biography*
- 《美国新闻与世界报道》**USNWR**   *Untied States News and World Report*
- 《美国药典》**PUS**   *Pharmacopoeia of the United States*
- 《美国英语词典》**DAE**   *Dictionary of American English*
- 《美日共同防御援助协定》**MDAA**   *Mutual Defense Assistance Agreement*
- 《美语词典》**DA**   *Dictionary of Americanisms*
- 《魔兽世界》**WOW**   *World of Warcraft*
- 《南海各方行为宣言》**DOC**
  Declaration on the Conduct of Parties in the South China Sea
- 《能源研究文摘》**ERA**   *Energy Research Abstracts*
- 《年轻的荣耀》电竞俱乐部 **YG**   *Young Glory*

标点、数字、字母开头排序

- 《牛津大词典》[英国] NED
  New English Dictionary [=Oxford English Dictionary]
- 《牛津小词典》[英国] LOD　　　　　Little Oxford Dictionary
- 《牛津英语大词典》[英国] OED　　　Oxford English Dictionary
- 《牛津英语谚语词典》[英国] ODEP
  Oxford Dictionary of English Proverbs
- 《牛津英语语源学词典》[英国] ODEE
  Oxford Dictionary of English Etymology
- 《纽约时报》[美国] NYT　　　　　　The New York Times
- 《气候变化框架公约》FCCC
  Framework Convention on Climatic Change
- 《全面禁止核试验条约》CNTBT　　　Comprehensive Nuclear Test Ban Treaty
- 《日本药典》JP　　　　　　　　　　Japanese Pharmacopoeia
- 《日内瓦公约》(1864.8.22)[意大利文] CG
  Convenzione di Ginerra (22 Agosto, 1864)
- 《商业日报》[英国;美国] JOC　　　　Journal of Commerce
- 《社会科学百科全书》ESS　　　　　Encyclopedia of the Social Sciences
- 《世界报刊新闻》WPN　　　　　　　World Press News
- 《世界专利索引》WPI　　　　　　　World Patent Index
- 《泰晤士报文学副刊》[英国] TLS　　Times Literary Supplement
- 《通信兼容与安全协议》COMCASA
  Communication Compatible and Security Agreement
- 《瓦森纳协定》WA　　　　　　　　　Wassenaar Arrangement
- 《武器贸易条约》ATT　　　　　　　Arms Trade Treaty
- 《物理学文摘》[美国] PA　　　　　　Physics Abstracts
- 《心理学文摘》[美国] PA　　　　　　Psychological Abstracts
- 《新韦氏国际英语大词典》[美国] NID
  New International Dictionary (Webster's)
- 《星期六评论》[美国] SR　　　　　　Saturday Review
- 《削减战略武器条约》(美国与苏联签订的) START
  Strategic Arms Reduction Treaty
- 《耶鲁法学杂志》[美国] YLJ　　　　Yale Law Journal

355

- 《医师手册》[美国] **PDR**　　Physicians' Desk Reference
- 《已故名人录》**WWW**　　Who Was Who
- 《英国牛津人名大词典》**DNB**
  Oxford Dictionary of National Biography
- 《英国医学杂志》**BMJ**　　British Medical Journal
- 《英雄联盟》**LOL**　　League of Legends
- 《英语方言词典》**EDD**　　English Dialect Dictionary
- 《英语教学》[英国] **ELT**　　English League Teaching
- 《与贸易有关的知识产权协议》**TRIPs**
  Agreement on Trade-related Aspects of Intellectual Property Rights
- 《远东经济评论》**FEER**　　Far East Economic Review
- 《中导条约》**INF**
  Intermediate-Range Nuclear Forces Treaty
- 《中国国家地理》**CNG**　　China National Geography
- 《中国集邮报》**CPN**　　China Philately News
- 《中美洲投资法典范本》**CAMIC**　　Central American Model Investment Code
- 《中文社会科学引文索引》**CSSCI**
  Chinese Social Science Citation Information
- 《专利合作条约》**PCT**　　Patent Cooperation Treaty
- 《专利引文索引》**PQI**　　Patent Quotation Index
- 《罪恶王冠》**GC**　　Guilty Crown
- 10月 **Oct**　　October
- 11月 **Nov**　　November
- 12月 **Dec**　　December
- 17-羟皮质类固醇 **17-OHCS**　　17-hydroxycorticosteroids
- 17-酮类固醇 **17-KS**　　17-ketosteroid
- 17-酮类固醇实验 **17-KS**　　17-ketosteroid test
- 1月 **Jan**　　January
- 2月 **Feb**　　February
- 20尺标准集装箱 **TEU**　　twenty-foot-equipment unit
- 3C革命[指实现通信网络化、电脑化、自动控制化的过程] **3C**
  communication, computer, control

标点、数字、字母开头排序

- 3-磷酸甘油醛脱脂酶 **GAPDH**
  glyceraldehyde-3-phosphate dehydrogenase
- 3月 **Mar**   March
- 40标箱 **FEU**   forty foot equivalent unit
- 4D电影 **C4D**   cine 4D
- 4G数据传输技术［使用数据流量来打电话］**VoLTE**
  voice over LTE
- 4月 **Apr**   April
- 5'-核苷酸酶 **5'-NT**   5'-nucleotidase
- 500米口径球面射电望远镜 **FAST**
  Five-hundred-meter Aperture Spherical radio Telescope
- 5-氟尿嘧啶 **5-FU**   5-fluorouracil
- 5-羟色胺 **HT**   hydroxy tryptamine(serotonin)
- 5日生化需氧量 **BOD5**   five-day biochemical oxygen demand
- 5型磷酸二酯酶 **PDE-5**   phosphodiesterase-5
- 6S质量措施［实证、选题、安全、来源、标准化、结构］**6S**
  substantiation, selection, safety, sourcing, standardization, structure
- 6月 **Jun**   June
- 7月 **Jul**   July
- 80式新加坡突击步枪 **SAR80**   Singapore Assault Rifle 80
- 8月 **Aug**   August
- 9月 **Sep**   September
- AA制（香港人的）**AA**   all apart
- AA制 **AA**   acting appointment
- ABC分类控制法 **ABC**   ABC Analysis
- ACK赛制比赛中完成15个胜利积分的犬只，又称登陆冠军 V **CH**
  Champion
- B型超声诊断(仪) **B**   B type ultrasonic diagnose［examination］
- C++语言 **C++**   C plus plus
- CBI英语教堂 **CBI**   content Based instruction
- CG动画 **CG**   Computer Graphics
- CT扫描 **CT**   Computerized Tomography

- CT 血管造影 **CTA**   CT Angiography
- C 反应蛋白 **CRP**   C-reactive Protein
- C-反应蛋白抗血清 **CRPA**   C-reactive Protein Antiserum
- DNA 甲基转移酶 **DNMT**   DNA Methyltransferase
- DNA 指数 **DI**   DNA Index
- DR 戒指 **DR**   Darry Ring
- D-二聚体 **D-D**   D-dimer
- EBV 病毒 **EBV**   Epstein Barr Virus
- EDS 公司的一个产品工程解决方案 **UG**   Unigraphics NX
- EMC 公司 **EMC**   Richard Egan and Roger Marino's Company
- EPR 悖论(爱因斯坦、波多尔斯基和罗森为论证量子力学的不完备性而提出的一个悖论) **EPR**   Einstein Podolsky-Rosen paradox
- ERP 企业管理解决方案的软件名称 **SAP**   Systems, Applications and Product in Data Processing
- E 玫瑰花结形成试验 **ERET**   erythrocyte rosette formation test
- FCI 欧洲冠军[德文] **FCI-ES**   FCI—Europasieger
- G 点[指女性阴道中一个容易动情的敏感区域,在阴道前壁靠阴道口 2—3 厘米处] **G**   Grafenberg spot
- iG 电子竞技俱乐部 **IG**   Invictus Gaming
- K 粉[一种常见毒品] **K**   ketamine
- N 股[我国在纽约发行的股票] **N**   New York
- PA 指数 **PA**   Protection Grade of UVA
- RC 图书馆体系 **RCLS**   Ramapo Catskill Library System
- RNG 电子竞技俱乐部 **RNG**   Royal Never Give up
- TdT 介导的缺口末端标记法 **TUNEL**   TdT mediated dUTP nick end labeling
- TOP 计划 **TOP**   The Olympic Programme
- TOP 原则[要求穿戴与不同的时间、场合、地点相适应] **TOP**   time, occasion, place
- T-U 构型[美国用的氢弹构型,比我国于敏构型落后] **T-U**   Teller-Ulam

标点、数字、字母开头排序

- UPI 公司［靠收取专利费为生的公司］**UPI**   Unwired Planet International
- VG 电竞俱乐部 **VG**   Vici Gaming
- WD 和 WB 中的获胜者 **BOW**   Best of Winner
- X 代伙伴计划 **GPP**   Generation Partnership Plan
- X 光［一种波长很短的电磁辐射，由德国物理学家伦琴于 1895 年发现］**X**   X-ray
- $α_1$-抗胰蛋白酶 **$α_1$ AT** $α_1$-antitrypsin
- $α_2$-巨球蛋白 **$α_2$-MG** $α_2$-macroglobulin
- $α_2$-抗纤溶酶 **$α_2$-AP** $α_2$-antiplasmin
- α-羟丁酸脱氢酶 **α-HBDH**   α-hyroxybutyrate dehydrogenase
- $β_2$-微球蛋白 **$β_2$-MG** $β_2$-microglobulin
- β-半乳糖苷酶基因 **LacZ**   β-galactosidase gene
- β-黑素细胞刺激素 **β-MSH**   beta-melanocyte-stimulating hormone
- β-球蛋白 **β-Gl**   beta-globulin
- β-丁酮酸 **KET**   β-ketobutyric acid
- γ-谷氨酰转肽酶 **GGT**   gamma-glutamyl transferase
- γ-谷氨酰转移酶 **γ-GT**   γ-glutamyl transpeptidase
  - γ-羟基丁酸盐 **GHB**   gamma hydroxybutyrate

A

- 阿(托) **A** — atto
- 阿(托亨利)[电感单位] **aH** — atto Henry
- 阿巴合唱团[由四位音乐家姓名首字母组成] **ABBA**
  Agneth, Benny, Björn, Anni-Frid
- 阿布尼达尔恐怖组织 **ANO** — Abu Nidal Organization
- 阿布·萨耶夫恐怖组织 **ASG** — Abu Sayyaf Group
- 阿彻丹尼尔斯米德兰食品 **ADM** — Archer Daniels Midland Food
- 阿迪达斯服饰 **Adidas** — Adolf Adi Dassler
- 阿尔巴尼亚[欧洲国家] **ALB** — Albania
- 阿尔巴尼亚民主联盟党[阿尔巴尼亚文] **PADS/PDSH**
  Partia Aleanca Demokratike Shqiptare/Partia Demokratike Shqiptare
- 阿尔茨海默病 **AD** — Alzheimer's Disease
- 阿尔法·罗密欧汽车[意大利文] **ALFA Romeo**
  Anonoma Lombarda Fabbrica Automobili Romeo
- 阿尔及利亚[非洲国家] **ALG** — Algeria
- 阿尔斯特防务协会/阿尔斯特自由斗士组织 **UDA/UFF**
  Ulster Defence Association/Ulster Freedom Fighterso
- 阿富汗[亚洲国家] **AFG** — Afghanistan
- 阿根廷[拉丁美洲国家] **ARG** — Argentina
- 阿拉伯的 **AR** — Arabic
- 阿拉伯国家广播组织联盟 **ASBU** — Arab States Broadcasting Union
- 阿拉伯国家联盟 **LAS** — League of Arab States
- 阿拉伯航空 **UAA** — United Arab Airlines
- 阿拉伯联合酋长国[亚洲国家] **UAE** — The United Arab Emirates
- 阿拉伯联盟 **AL** — Arab League

A

- 阿拉伯石油输出国组织 **OAPEC**
  Organization of Arab Petroleum Exporting Countries
- 阿拉伯叙利亚通讯社 **SANA**　　　Syrian Arab News Agency
- 阿拉善 SEE 生态协会 **SEE**　　　Society of Entrepreneurs & Ecology
- 阿里云关系数据库 **RDS**　　　Relational Database Service
- 阿联酋阿布扎比公司 **ADCOM**　　　Abu Dhabi Company
- 阿曼[亚洲国家] **OMA**　　　Oman
- 阿塞拜疆[欧洲国家] **AZE**　　　Azerbaijan
- 阿司匹林耐量试验 **ATT**　　　aspirin tolerance test
- 阿斯麦 **ASML**
  Advanced semiconductor material lithography
- 阿斯麦尔 **ASML**
  Advanced Semiconductor Material Lithography[目前该全称已不作为公司标识，公司注册标识为 AML Holding N. V.]
- 阿西布朗勃法瑞公司[瑞典文] **ABB**　　　Asaa Brown Boveri Ltd
- 阿一宗二氏试验[妊娠检查] **A—Z Test**　　　Ascheim-Zondek Test
- 锕[第 89 号化学元素] **Ac**　　　actinium
- 埃[光波波长单位] **A**　　　Angström 或 angstrom
- 埃博拉出血热 **EBHF**　　　Ebola hemorrhagic fever
- 埃博拉幸存者综合计划 **CPSE**
  Comprehensive Plan for Survivors Ebola
- 埃尔顿·B. 斯蒂芬斯公司 **EBSCO**　　　Elton B. Stephens Company
- 埃及[非洲国家] **EGY**　　　Egypt
- 埃及标准化组织 **EOS**　　　Egyptian Organization for Standardization
- 埃及质量认证标志 **EOS**　　　Egyptian Organization for Standardization
- 埃尼阿克[电子数字积分计算机：第一台通用计算机] **ENIAC**
  Electronic Numerical Integrator And Computer
- 埃塞俄比亚[非洲国家] **ETH**　　　Ethiopia
- 埃索石油（根据首字母"S""O"的发音形成的缩略语）**ESSO**
  Standard Oil of New Jersey
- 埃索石油公司 **EPC**　　　Esso Petroleum Company
- 埃塔组织[西班牙文] **ETA**　　　Euskadi Ta Askatasuna

361

A

- 锿[第 99 号化学元素] **Es** — einsteinium
- 癌基因 **C-myc** — Cancer-myc
- 癌胚抗原 **CEA** — carcinoembryonic antigen
- 癌症的检测、流行病学及其最后结果 **SEER**
  surveillance, epidemiology, and end results
- 癌症分类法（根据肿瘤、淋巴结和转移情况）**TNM**
  primary tumor, regional nodes, metastasis (tumor staging)
- 癌症治疗等级的功能评估 **FACT**
  Functional Assessment of Cancer Therapy Scales
- 艾(可萨)[一个十进倍数的词头名称，其表示因数为 10^{18}] **E**
  exa
- 艾克斯—马赛大学[法文] **AMU** — Aix-Marseille Université
- 艾萨克·牛顿[英国物理学家] **Is N** — Isaac Newton
- 艾氏腹水癌 **EAC** — Ehrlich ascitic carcinoma
- 艾滋病[获得性免疫缺陷综合征] **AIDS** — Acquired Immune Deficiency Syndrome
- 艾滋病患者 **PWA** — person with AIDS
- 艾滋阻断药 **PEP** — post exposure prophylaxis
- 艾字节[1 **EB**＝10 亿 **GB**(千兆字节)] **EB** — Exabyte
- 砹[第 85 号化学元素] **At** — astatine
- 爱步鞋[丹麦产] **ECCO** — ECCO'let
- 爱尔兰[欧洲国家] **IRL** — Ireland
- 爱尔兰镑[爱尔兰货币] **IEP** — Ireland pound
- 爱尔兰产品质量认证标志 **IIRS**
  Institute for Industrial Research and Standards
- 爱尔兰工业研究和标准学会 **IIRS**
  Institute for Industrial Research and Standards
- 爱尔兰共和国的众议院议员[爱尔兰文] **TD**
  Teachta Dála
- 爱尔兰共和军 **IRA** — Irish Republican Army
- 爱尔兰有机认证标志 **IOA** — Irish Organic Association
- 爱尔兰有机商品委员会 **IOA** — Irish Organic Association
- 爱国者三型先进导弹系统 **PAC-3** — Patriot Advanced Capability-3

A

- 爱沙尼亚[欧洲国家] **EST**   Estonia
- 安(培)[电流的基本单位] **A**   ampere
- 安邦财产保险股份有限公司 **AB**
  Anbang Property & Casualty Insurance Co., Ltd
- 安保部 **SB**   Security Branch
- 安道尔[欧洲国家] **AND**   Andorra
- 安第斯共同市场 **ANCOM**   Andean Common Market
- 安哥拉[非洲国家] **ANG**   Angola
- 安哥拉乳业有限公司[葡萄牙文] **Lda**
  Sociedade Industrial de Lacticinios de Angola, Lda
- 安徽出版集团 **APG**   Anhui Publishing Group
- 安徽商业保理 **ABS**   Anhui Business Security
- 安静超音速技术 **QueSST**   quiet supersonic technology
- 安理会军事参谋团 **MSC**   Military Staff Commission
- 安全、高效、高质量 **SEQ**   safety, efficacy, quality
- 安全[汉语拼音"安全"的首字母] **AQ**   anquan
- 安全标识符 **SID**   security identifiers
- 安全标志[合乎标准之意] **AP**   Approved Product
- 安全电子交易协议 **SET**   Secure electronic transaction
- 安全防护系统 **SGS**   safe-guard system
- 安全分析报告 **SAR**   safety analysis report
- 安全服务 **SS**   security services
- 安全港 **SH**   security harbor
- 安全接入控制器 **SAC**   security access controller
- 安全评估计划 **SAP**   safety assessment plan
- 安全数据表 **SDS**   safety data sheet
- 安全数字卡 **SDC**   Secure Digital Card
- 安全数字卡协会[又称 **SD** 存储卡协会] **SDA**
  Security Digital Card Association
- 安全套接层 **SSL**   secure sockets layer
- 安全外壳协议 **SSH**   secure shell

A

- 安全玩具 **ST** — safe toy
- 安全系数 **FOS** — Factor of safety
- 安全协商会议 **SCM** — security consultative meeting
- 安全芯片 **TPM** — trusted platform module
- 安全性已认证[德国安全认证标识][德文] **GS** — Geprufte Sicherheit
- 安全账户管理 **SAM** — security account management
- 安全指标(行业) **SI** — safety index
- 安全总监,首席安全官 **CSO** — Chief Security Officer
- 安特卫普世界钻石中心 **AWDC** — Antwerp World Diamond Center
- 安提瓜和巴布达[北美洲国家] **ANT** — Antigua and Barbuda
- 安卓调试桥 **ADB** — Android Debug Bridge
- 氨基全氢喹啉 **TTX** — tetrodotoxin
- 氨基酸 **AA** — amino acid
- 氨基酸氮 **AAN** — amino acid nitrogen
- 按疾病诊断相关分担付费 **DFG** — Diagnosis Related Group
- 按计划、执行、检查、行动顺序进行质量管理 **PDCA** — plan, do, check, act
- 按价值 **PV** — per value
- 按摩医师 **DC** — doctor of chiropractic
- 按需分配宽带 **BOD** — bandwidth on demand
- 盎司[非法定质量计量单位,1盎司＝28.35克] **OZ** — ounce
- 奥地利[欧洲国家] **AUT** — Austria
- 奥地利标准化协会[德文] **ÖN** — Österreichischer Normunsinstitut
- 奥地利电气技术协会[德文] **ÖVE** — Österreichischer Verband für Elektrotechnik
- 奥地利电气认证标志[德文] **ÖVE** — Österreichischer Verband für Elektrotechnik
- 奥地利广播电视公司[德文] **ÖRF** — Österreichischer Rundfunk
- 奥地利联盟冠军[德文] **Ö-BS** — Österreichischer Bundessinger
- 奥地利联盟青年冠军[德文] **Ö-BJS** — Österreichischer Bundesjugendsiger

A

- 奥地利认证标志[德文] **ÖN**   Österreichischer Normunsinstitut
- 奥地利萨尔茨堡实验舞蹈学院 **SEAD**
  Salzburg Experiment Academy of Dance
- 奥地利先令[奥地利货币] **S/ATS**   Austrian Schiling
- 奥克托今[炸药] **HMX**   homocyclonite
- 奥利奥（夹心饼干）**OREO**   cream+chocolate
- 奥斯堡—纽伦堡机械工厂[德文] **MAN**   Maschinenfabrik Augsburg Nürnberg
- 奥尤陶勒盖铜金矿项目[蒙古文] **OT**   Oyu Tolgoi
- 奥运计划 **TOP**   The Olympic Programme
- 澳大利亚、新西兰、美国安全条约 **ANZUS**
  Australian, New Zealand and the United States Pacific Security Treaty
- 澳大利亚[大洋洲国家] **AUS**   Australia
- 澳大利亚安全情报组织 **ASIO**
  Australian Safety Information Organization
- 澳大利亚标准协会 **SAA**   Standards Association of Australia
- 澳大利亚产品质量认证标志 **SAA**   Standards Association of Australia
- 澳大利亚出生的华人 **ABC**   Australian Born Chinese
- 澳大利亚大学录取考试 **TEE**   Tertiary Entrance Examination
- 澳大利亚电信公司 **Telstra**   Telecom Australia
- 澳大利亚动物健康实验室 **AAHL**   Australian Animal Health Laboratory
- 澳大利亚翻译学院 **AITI**
  Australian Institute of Translation & Interpretation
- 澳大利亚翻译资格认可局 **NAATI**
  National Accreditation Authority for Translators and Interpreters
- 澳大利亚工业能力 **AIC**   Australian Industry Capacity
- 澳大利亚广播公司 **ABC**   Australian Broadcasting Corporation
- 澳大利亚国家标准 **AS**   Australian Standard
- 澳大利亚国民银行 **NAB**   National Australian Bank
- 澳大利亚和新西兰标准职业分类 **ANZSCO**
  Australian New, Zealand Standard Classification of Occupations
- 澳大利亚交通安全局 **ATSB**   Australian Traffic and Security Bureau

A

- 澳大利亚经济发展委员会 **CEDA**
  Committee for Economic Development of Australia
- 澳大利亚科技大学联盟 **ATN**　　Australian Technology Network
- 澳大利亚科学院 **AAS**　　Australian Academy of Science
- 澳大利亚联邦科学与工业研究组织 **CSIRO**
  Commonwealth Scientific and Industrial Research Organization
- 澳大利亚联合证券交易所 **AASE**　　Australian Associated Stock Exchanges
- 澳大利亚敏捷的狗协会 **ADAA**　　Agility Dog Association of Australia
- 澳大利亚墨尔本大学 **UM**　　University of Melbourne
- 澳大利亚频谱管理局 **SMA**　　Spectrum Manager of Australia
- 澳大利亚全国通用的职业与继续教育 **TAFE**
  technical and further education
- 澳大利亚人文学科研究委员会 **AHRC**　　Australian Humanities Research Council
- 澳大利亚商务联合会 **ACCA**
  Associated Chambers of Commerce of Australia
- 澳大利亚太平洋基础设施融资机构 **AIFFP**
  Australian Infrastructure Financing Facility for the Pacific
- 澳大利亚卫生与福利研究院 **AIHW**
  Australian Institute of Health and Welfare
- 澳大利亚医疗及福利学会 **AIHW**
  Australian Institute of Health and Welfare
- 澳大利亚医药科学家协会 **AIMS**　　Australia Institute of Medical Scientists
- 澳大利亚移民协会 **MIA**　　Migration Institute of Australia
- 澳大利亚应用语言学协会 **ALAA**
  Applied Linguistics Association of Australia
- 澳大利亚元(货币名称) **AUD**　　Australian dollar
- 澳大利亚战略政策研究所 **ASPI**　　Australian Strategic Policy Institute
- 澳大利亚足球联盟 **AFL**　　Australian Football League
- 澳加新英美情报联盟 **UKUSA**
  United States Communication Intelligence Agreement
- 澳抗,即乙型肝炎表面抗原 **Au**　　Australia antigen

B

- 澳门大学 UM — University of Macau
- 澳门大学[葡萄牙文] UM — Universidade de Macau
- 澳门理工学院[葡萄牙文] IPM — Instituto Politécnico de Macau
- 澳门理工学院 MPI — Macao Polytechnic Institute
- 澳门特别行政区 MSAR — Macao Special Administrative Region
- 澳门元[货币,葡萄牙语] MOP — Macao Patace de Macau
- 澳洲国立大学 ANU — The Australian National University
- 氥[第 118 号化学元素] Og — Oganesson

- 八国集团[即在 G7 的基础上加上俄罗斯] G8 Group of Eight
- 巴巴多斯[北美洲国家] BAR — Barbados
- 巴德监狱倡议 BPI — Bard Prison Initiative
- 巴哈马[北美洲国家] BAH — Bahamas
- 巴基斯坦[亚洲国家] PAK — Pakistan
- 巴基斯坦宝石贸易实验室 PGTL — Pakistan Gem Trade Laboratory
- 巴基斯坦标准学会 PSI — Pakistan Standards Institution
- 巴基斯坦产品认证标志 PSI — Pakistan Standards Institution
- 巴基斯坦国家联盟 PNA — The Pakistan National Alliance
- 巴基斯坦航空联合体 PAC — Pakistan Aeronautical Complex
- 巴基斯坦塔克西拉重工业 HIT — Heavy Industry, Taxilia
- 巴基斯坦先知之友[乌尔都文] SSP — Sipah-e-Sahaba Pakistan
- 巴拉圭[南美洲国家] PAR — Paraguay
- 巴拉索巴德拉中央合作银行 BBCCB Balasore Bhadra Central Cooperative Bank

- 巴勒斯坦[亚洲国家] **PLE**　　　　　Palestine
- 巴黎高等商业学院[法文] **HEC**　　　École des Hautes Etudes Commerciales
- 巴黎高翻学院[法文] **ESIT**
  École Supérieure d'Interprètes & de Traducteurs
- 巴黎高师[法文] **ENS**　　　　　　École Normale Superieure de Paris
- 巴黎国民银行[法文] **BNP**　　　　Banque Nationale de Paris
- 巴黎跨文化管理与公关学院[法文] **ISIT**
  Institut Supérieur d'interprétation et de traduction
- 巴黎全球物理研究所 **IPGP**　　　International Physics Group of Paris
- 巴黎世家服饰 **B**　　　　　　　　Balenciaga
- 巴黎统筹委员会 **COCOM**　　　　Coordinating Committee
- 巴林[亚洲国家] **BRN**　　　　　　Bahrain
- 巴拿马[北美洲国家] **PAN**　　　　Panama
- 巴塞尔行动网络 **BAN**　　　　　　Basel Action Network
- 巴氏财团 **BFG**　　　　　　　　　Buffett Financial Group
- 巴斯夫公司[德文] **BASF**　　　　　Badische Anilin-und-Soda-Fabrik
- 巴西[南美洲国家] **BRA**　　　　　Brazil
- 巴西产品质量认证标志[葡萄牙文] **ABNT**
  Associação Brasileire de Normas Técnicas
- 巴西技术标准协会[葡萄牙文] **ABNT**　　Associação Brasileire de Normas Técnicas
- 巴西地理统计局[葡萄牙文] **IBGE**
  Instituto Brasileiro de Geografia e Estatistica
- 巴西国家计量标准化和工业质量协会[葡萄牙文] **INMETRO**
  Instituto Nacional de Metrologia, Normalização e Qualidade Industrial
- 巴西石油公司[葡萄牙文] **PETROBRAS**　Petróleo Brasileiro
- 钯[第 46 号化学元素] **Pd**　　　　palladium
- 靶恩[非法定面积单位,1 靶恩$=10^{-28}$ m^2] **b**
  barn
- 白(俄)罗斯[欧洲国家] **BLR**　　　Belarus
- 白(俄)罗斯卢布[白(俄)罗斯货币] **BYR**　Belarusian Rouble

B

- 白蛋白/球蛋白比值 A/G　　albumin/globulin ratio
- 白蛋白［正常值35~50 g/L］Alb　　albumin
- 白藜芦醇 Res　　Resveratrol
- 白领女性 OL　　office lady
- 白人至上 WP　　white power
- 白色 W　　white
- 白色 WH　　white
- 白沙瓦到卡拉奇高速公路 PKM　　Peshawar to Karachi Motorway
- 白细胞 WBC　　White Blood Cell
- 白细胞 LEU　　leukocyte
- 白细胞分类计数 DC　　differential count
- 白细胞分类计数 WBC-DC　　white blood cell differential count
- 白细胞计数 WBC　　white blood(cell) count
- 白细胞计数 WBA　　white blood(cell) count
- 白细胞碱性磷酸酶 LAP　　leukocyte alkaline phosphatase
- 白细胞介素-2 IL-2　　interleukin-2
- 白细胞抑制因子 LIF　　leukocyte inhibitory factor
- 白种盎格鲁-撒克逊新教徒［被认为是美国社会中实力最强的白人］WASP White Anglo-Saxon Protestant
- 百［十进倍数的词头名称，其表示的因数为 10^2］h hecto
- 百安居（用公司两创始人的姓的首字母）B&Q Richard Block and David Quayle
- 百度、阿里巴巴、腾讯、京东为代表的巨头企业 BATJ Baidu, Alibaba, Tencent, Jingdong
- 百度［汉语拼音缩略语］BD　　Baidu
- 百度飞桨 PP　　PaddlePaddle
- 百分之五十补体溶血活性 CH50　　50% complement hemolytic activity
- 百视通 IPTV　　Internet Protocol TV
- 百万分之一 ppm　　part per million
- 百万伏（特）MV　　million volts

百万帕(斯卡) Mpa	megapascal
百万位/秒 MBPS	mega bits per second
百万像素 MP	megapixel
百万圆桌会议[全球寿险精英的最高盛会] MDRT	
The Million Dollar Round Table	
百威啤酒 Bud	Budweiser
班上最好的[网络用语] BIC	best in class
板上芯片 COB	chip on board
版本 Ed	edition
版权[符号] ©	copyright
办公室不宜[网络用语] NSFW	not safe for work
办公自动化 OA	office automation
半导体存储操作系统 SMOS	semiconductor memory operating system
半导体行业协会 SIA	Semiconductor Industry Association
半导体设施技术学院 SFTA	
Semiconductor Facilities Technology Academy	
半导体质数 SOX	semiconductor index
半乳糖 Gal	galactose
半数致死浓度 LC50	median lethal concentration
半主动激光器 SAL	semiactive laser
伴侣 OH	other half
帮厨兵 KP	kitchen police
磅/平方英寸 psi	pound per square inch
磅[拉丁文] lbs	librae
包括 inc/incl	including, included
饱和烃矿物油 MOSH	mineral oil saturated hydrocarbons
饱和指数 SI	saturation index
宝洁 P&G	Procter & Gamble
宝马汽车[原意为德国巴伐利亚汽车公司][德文] BMW	
Bayerishe Motoren Werke	
宝石 gem	gemstone

B

宝石贸易实验室 GTL	Gemological Trade Laboratory
宝石学协会会员 FGA	Fellowship of Gemological Association
宝缇嘉[意大利奢侈品牌] BV	Bottega Veneta
保安部(处) SW	Security Wing
保持健康[网络用语] kybo	keep your bowels open
保护证人计划公司[英国广告传播集团] WPP	Witness Protection Program Company
保加利亚[欧洲国家] BUL	Bulgaria
保加利亚标准局[保加利亚文] BDS	Bălgarski dár Žaven Standart
保加利亚船舶登记局 BRS	Bulgaria Register of Shipping
保健福利 HBP	health benefit program
保健与人事服务(部) HHS	Health and Human Services
保赔 P&I	protection and indemnity
保守政治行动会议 CPAC	Conservative Political Action Conference
保卫共和联盟[法文] PR	Rassemblement pour la République
保卫犹太人联盟[希伯来文] Kachi	Kahane chaio
保险(费) ince	insurance
保险单 IP	insurance policy
保险凭证 CI	certificate of insurance
保险统计师学会联合会 AIA	Associate of the Institute of Actuaries
保证重量 WG	weight guaranteed
报表程序的生成程序 RPG	report program generator
报酬率 ROR	rate of return
报告[参考文献标示字母] R	report
报纸文章[参考文献标示字母] N	newspaper article
报纸资源数据库 NS	Newspaper Resource
悲剧结尾 BE	bad ending
北爱尔兰防卫军 UDR	Ulster Defence Regiment
北爱尔兰防务协会 UDA	Ulster Defence Association
北爱尔兰统一党 UUP	Ulster Unionist Party
北大西洋公约组织 NATO	North Atlantic Treaty Organization

B

- 北斗导航系统 **BDS**   Beidou Navigation Satellite System
- 北京大学 **PKU/PU**   Peking University
- 北京大学国际 MBA 项目 **BIMBA**
  Beijing International Master of Business Administration at Peking University
- 北京电视台 **BTV**   Beijing Television
- 北京经济技术开发区 **BDA**
  Beijing economic-technological Development Area
- 北京理工大学 **BIT**   Beijing Institute of Technology
- 北京汽车制造有限公司 **BAW**   Beijing Automobile Works
- 北京师范大学 **BNU**   Beijing Normal University
- 北京外国语大学 **BFSU**   Beijing Foreign Studies University
- 北京文化 **BC**   Beijing Culture
- 北京银行 **BOB**   Bank of Beijing
- 北京正负电子对撞机 **BEPC**   Beijing Electron-Positron Collider
- 北马其顿[欧洲国家,前称:马其顿] **NMKD**
  North Macedonia
- 北美电子、电器产品质量认证标志 **CSA**   Canadian Standards Association
- 北美精算师 **FSA**   Fellow of the Society of Actuary
- 北美自由贸易协定[现在被 USMCA 代替] **NAFTA**
  North America Free Trade Agreement
- 贝可(勒尔)[法定放射性活度计量单位] **Bq**
  Becquerel
- 贝宁[非洲国家] **BEN**   Benin
- 贝塔斯曼亚洲投资基金 **BAI**   Bertelsmann Asia Investments
- 备用电源 **EPS**   emergency power supply
- 备用键 **Alt**   alternate key
- 背景误差 **BBE**   background block error
- 背景音乐 **BGM**   background music
- 背书不符 **EI**   endorsement irregular
- 背投电视 **PTV**   projection television
- 钡[第 56 号化学元素] **Ba**   barium

B

- 被动磁悬浮技术 HTT　　　　　　　Hyperloop Transportation Technologies
- 本白色 RW　　　　　　　　　　　　raw white
- 本土制造防御战机 IDF　　　　　　　indigenous defense fighter
- 本益比 P/E/PER　　　　　　　　　　price earnings ratio
- 本周 ZWEK　　　　　　　　　　　　this week
- 本周蛋白 BJP　　　　　　　　　　　Bence-Jones Protein
- 苯丙醇胺[曾用来做某些感冒药的一种成分] PPA
  phenylpropanolamine
- 苯丙酮尿症 PKU　　　　　　　　　　phenylketonuria
- 苯乙烯-α-甲基苯乙烯共聚物[塑料] SMS　styrene-α-methylstyrene copolymer
- 苯乙烯-α-甲基苯乙烯塑料 S/MS　　　　styrene-α-methylstyrene plastics
- 苯乙烯-丙烯腈共聚物[塑料] SAN　　　 styrene-acrylonitrile copolymer
- 苯乙烯-丙烯腈塑料 S/AN　　　　　　 styrene-acrylonitrile plastics
- 苯乙烯-丁二烯-苯乙烯嵌段共聚物[塑料] SBS
  styrene-butadiene-styrene block copolymer
- 苯乙烯-丁二烯共聚物[塑料] SB　　　　styrene-butadiene copolymer
- 泵喷嘴 EUI　　　　　　　　　　　　unit injector
- 鼻咽癌 NPC　　　　　　　　　　　　nasopharyngeal carcinoma
- 比较基因组杂交 CGH　　　　　　　　comparative genomic hybridization
- 比较主流的无线网络传输方式 E　　　　edge
- 比利时[欧洲国家] BEL　　　　　　　 Belgium
- 比利时标准化学会[法文] BN　　　　　Institut Belge de Normalisation
- 比利时电工技术委员会[法文] CEB　　　Comité Electrotechnique Belge
- 比利时法郎[比利时 2002 年前的货币] BF
  Belgian Franc
- 比利时根特大学 UG　　　　　　　　　University of Ghent
- 比利时银行家学会 BBA　　　　　　　 Belgium Banker Association
- 比利时钻石高阶议会 DHC　　　　　　 Diamond High Council
- 比例代表制 PR　　　　　　　　　　　proportional representation
- 比特/秒[数据传输速率单位] bps　　　　bits per second
- 比特币 BTC　　　　　　　　　　　　bitcion
- 比特币 BTC　　　　　　　　　　　　BitCoin

比特币黄金 BTG	Bitcoin Gold
比特流[pnp下载，又称变态下载] BT	Bit Torrent
比亚迪（车）[汉语拼音缩略语] BYD	Biyadi
比亚迪（英文意为：构筑你的梦想） BYD	Build Your Dreams
币值调整附加费 CAF	currency adjustment factor
毕尔巴鄂比斯开银行[西班牙文] BBVA	Banco Bilbao Vizcaya Argentaria
毕业前后用的实习许可 OPT	Optional Practical Training
毕兹 QNB	quinuclidinyl benzilate
闭合容积 CV	closed volume
闭合性颅脑损伤 CHI	closed-head injure
闭路电视 CCTV	Closed Circuit Television
闭塞性动脉硬化（症） ASO	arteriosclerosis obliterans
必须[口语] hafta	have to
铋[第83号化学元素] Bi	bismuth
秘鲁共产党[西班牙文] PCP	Partido Comunista del Perú
壁细胞抗体 PCA	parietal cell antibody
避雷针 LA	lightning arrester
避孕环 IUD	intrauterine device
边防保安队[印度] BSF	border security force
边际产品价值 VMP	value of marginal product
边际收益产品 MRP	marginal revenue of product
边际替代率 MRS	marginal rate of substitution
边际要素成本 MFC	marginal factor cost
边界税收调整 BTA	border tax adjustment
边境防务合作协议 BDCA	border defence cooperation agreement
边境交货 DAF	delivered at frontier
边境巡逻队 BP	Border Patrol
编号乐曲 Op	opus
变革请求 CR	change request
变速器控制系统 TCS	transmission control system
变速器控制装置 TCU	transmission control unit

B

变体调用格式 vcf	variant call format
变通的发展战略 ADS	alternative development strategies
变稳飞机验收 VSA	variable stability aircraft
便利店 CVS	convenience store
便士 P	penny
便携式媒体播放器 PMP	portable media player
便携式媒体中心 PMC	portable media center
便携式生命维持系统 PLSS	portable life-support system
便携式数据采集终端 PDT	portable data terminal
标签式图像文件格式 TIFF	tagged image file format
标准[参考文献标示字母] S	specification
标准必要专利 SEP	Standard Essential Patents
标准操作流程 SOP	standard operating procedure
标准大城市统计区 SMSA	standard metropolitan statistical area

标准大气压[非法定压力、压强、应力计量单位] atm
standard atmospheric pressure

标准电子自动计算机 SEAC	standard electronic automatic computer
标准发音 RP	received pronunciation
标准管理程序 SMP	standard management processor
标准汉字系统 SCS	Standard Chinese System

标准化测试与报告计划 STAR
Standardized Testing & Reporting Program

标准化管理局 SMB　　　The Standardization Management Board

标准化数据管理情报 SDMI
standardization data management information

标准检验程序 SIP	standard inspection procedure
标准碱过剩 SBE	standard base excess
标准开支评估 SSA	standard spending assessment
标准课业测评考试(现称 NCT) SAT	Standard Assessment Test
标准模板库 STL	standard template library
标准普尔(股票价格)指数 S&P	Standard & Poor's

- 标准普尔[美国的信用评级机构] **S&P**   Standard & Poor's
- 标准普尔500种股票指数 **S&P 500**   Standard & Poor's 500
- 标准企业分类法 **SIC**   standard industrial classification
- 标准清晰度 **SD**   standard definition
- 标准清晰度电视 **SDTV**   standard definition television
- 标准实验室规范 **GLP**   Good Laboratory Practice
- 标准碳酸氢根 **SBC**   standard bicarbonate radical
- 标准通用置标语言 **SGML**   Standard Generalized Markup Language
- 标准温度和压力 **STP**   standard temperature and pressure
- 标准制定组织 **SDO**   Standard Development Organization
- 标准制定组织 **SSO**   standard-setting organization
- 标准终端执行 **STEP**   standard terminal executive program
- 标准作业程序 **SOP**   standard operation procedure
- 表处理语言 **LISP**   list processing
- 表达序列标签 **EST**   express sequence tag
- 表没食子儿茶素没食子酸酯 **EGCG**   epigallocatechin gallate
- 表面传导电子发射显示 **SED**   surface conduction electron emitter display
- 表面声波 **SAW**   surface acoustic wave
- 表面贴装技术 **SMT**   surface mounting technology
- 表皮生长因子 **EGF**   epidermal growth factor
- 表皮生长因子受体 **EGFR**   epidermal growth factor receptor
- 表中数据单元 **TD**   table data cell
- 别相信任何人[网络用语] **DTA**   don't trust anybody
- 宾夕法尼亚大学 **UP**   University of Pennsylvania
- 滨水地区 **wtf**   water front
- 濒海战斗舰 **LCS**   littoral combat ship
- 濒死体验 **NDE**   Near Death Experience
- 濒危野生动植物种国际贸易公约 **CITES**   Convention on International Trade in Endangered Species
- 冰岛[欧洲国家] **ISL**   Iceland
- 冰箭 **LM5SLV**   Long March 5 Series Launch Vehicle

B

- 冰雾 **IF**   ice fog
- 丙肝抗体 **HCVAb**   hepatitis C virus antibody
- 丙酸倍氯米松 **BDP**   beclomethasone dipropionate
- 丙酸铜激酶 **PK**   pyruvate kinase (assay)
- 丙烯腈 **ABS**   acrylonitrile-butadiene-styrene
- 丙烯腈-苯乙烯-丙烯酸酯共聚物[塑料] **ASA**
  acrylonitrile-styrene-acrylates
- 丙烯腈-苯乙烯树脂 **AS**   acrylonitrile-styrene resin
- 丙烯腈-丁二烯-苯乙烯三元共聚物[塑料] **ABS**
  acrylonitrile butadiene-styrene terpolymers
- 丙烯腈-乙烯-苯乙烯共聚物(塑料) **AES**   acrylonitrile-ethylene-styrene
- 丙烯酰胺 **AM**   acrylamide monomer
- 丙种球蛋白 **GG**   gamma globulin
- 并购 **M&A**   mergers and acquisitions
- 并行处理操作系统 **SIPROS**   simultaneous processing operating system
- 并行自适应结构网格应用支撑软件框架 **PASMIN**
  Paralled Adaptive Structured Mesh Applications Infrastructure
- 并联混合动力电动汽车 **PHEV**   parallel-hybrid electric vehicle
- 病毒再生繁殖数 **RO**   reproduction number
- 病后护理和治疗中心协会 **CACA**   Central After-Care Association
- 病理学完全缓解 **PCR**   pathologic complete response
- 病例 **C/S**   case
- 病例报告表 **CRF**   case report form
- 病情稳定 **SD**   stable disease
- 病人自控镇痛 **PCA**   patient-controlled analgesia
- 病态自恋个性 **NPD**   narcissistic personality disorder
- 波波族[布尔乔亚和波希米亚缩写组合] **BOBO**
  Bourgeois Bohemian
- 波场虚拟机 **TVM**   TRON Virtual Machine
- 波动率指数 **VIX**   volatility index
- 波段显示 **BNDDIS**   band display
- 波多黎各[北美洲国家] **PUR**   Puerto Rico

波兰[欧洲国家] POL	Poland
波兰船舶登记局 PRS	Poland Register of Shipping
波士顿公共广播电台 WBUR	We're Boston University Radio
波士顿咨询公司(集团) BCG	Boston Consulting Group
波士顿咨询集团 BCG	Boston Consulting Group
波斯尼亚和黑塞哥维那[欧洲国家,又称波黑] B&H Bosnia and Herzegovina	
波伊茨-耶格 PJS	Peutz-Jeghers Syndrome
波音直升机 BH	Boeing helicopter
玻璃钢 FRP	fiberglass-reinforced plastic
玻璃增强塑料 GRP	glass reinforced plastic
玻利维亚[南美洲国家] BOL	Bolivia
𬭩[第107号化学元素] Bh	bohrium
播散肿瘤细胞 DTCs	disseminated tumor cells
伯克利软件设计[国际上一种广泛使用的免费操作系统] BSD Berkeley Software Design	
柏林航空展 BAS	Berlin Air Show
柏林机场会展中心 BECA	Berlin Expo Center Airport
铂[第76号化学元素] Pt	platinum
博鳌亚洲论坛 BAF	Bo'ao Asian Forum
博鳌亚洲论坛 BFA	Bo'ao Forum for Asia
博茨瓦纳[非洲国家] BOT	Botswana
博茨瓦纳标准局 BOBS	Botswana Bureau of Standards
博达克咨询有限公司 BDA	Dr Bohai Zhang, Duncan Alark Associates
博客 BLOG	web Log
博客服务提供商 BSP	Blog service provider
博览会 expo	exposition
博士 Dr	doctor
博思英语考试 BULATS	Business Language Testing Service
博斯—乔赫里—霍克文黑姆码 BCH Bose, Chaudhuri & Hocquenghem type of code	
薄利多销 SPQR	small profits and quick returns

B

薄膜场效应晶体管 TFT	thin film transistor
薄膜晶体管液晶显示屏 TFT-LCD	thin film transistor liquid crystal display
薄膜太阳能电池[由铜、铟、镓、硒组成] CIGS（Cu，In，Ga，Se）	
补偿性进口税 CID	Compensative Import Duty
补充说明 PS	post
补呼吸量 ERV	expiratory reserve volume
补体 C	complement
补吸气量 IRV	inspiratory reserve volume
不丹[亚洲国家] BHU	Bhutan
不得进一步参观[访问] NFV	no further visits
不懂察言观色[日文] Ky	kuuki ga yomenal
不动产 RP	real property
不动产投资信托公司 REITs	real estate investment trusts
不对称电子用户线路 ADSL	asymmetric digital subscriber line
不负责任的 DB	deadbeat
不负责任的爸爸 DBD	deadbeat dad
不规则的 irr	irregular
不过你已知道那件事了[网络用语] BYKTA	but you knew that already
不好 NBG	no bloody good
不及格停修 WF	withdrawn failing
不加热血清反应素试验 USR	unheated serum reagin test
不间断电源 UPS	uninterruptible power supply system
不间断自动驾驶系统 UA	uninterruptible autopilot
不结盟运动 NAM	Non-Aligned Movement
不结盟运动新闻网 NNN	Nonaligned News Network
不可用 N/A	not available
不可再分割性、一致性、隔离性与耐用性 ACID atomicity, consistency, isolation and durability	
不另行说明 NOS	not otherwise specified
不另行说明 NOE	not otherwise enumerated
不论真伪 FWIW	for what it's worth
不明飞行体 UFO	Unidentified Flying Object

- 不能重复刻录光盘 **DVD-RDL**　　DVD-Recordable data left
- 不时的创新思维,防御性技术,颠覆性商业模式 **3D**
  discontinuous innovation, defensible technology, disruptive business model
- 不适用 **N/A**　　not applicable
- 不受欢迎的人 **PNG**　　persona non grata
- 不属上述的文献类型[参考文献标示字母] **Z**
  zero
- 不同人有不同看法[网络用语] **YMMV**　　your mileage may vary
- 不须移民出境检查 **ECNR**　　emigration check not required
- 不要回信[网络用语] **DWB**　　don't write back
- 不依赖空气动力装置 **AIP**　　air-independent propeller
- 不予优惠 **XPR**　　ex privileges
- 不在办公室 **OOTO**　　out of the office
- 不在机旁 **AFK**　　away from keyboard
- 不正常终止[电脑] **ABEND**　　abnormal end
- 不正当竞争法[西班牙文] **LCD**　　Ley de Competencia Desleal
- 不知道[网络用语] **DK**　　don't [doesn't] know
- 不知道[口语] **dunno**　　don't [doesn't] know
- 布基纳法索[非洲国家] **BUR**　　Burkina Faso
- 布加迪汽车标志[源于艾托里·布加迪] **EB**
  Ettore Bugatti
- 布林线指标[其波动的上下限随股价浮动] **BOLL**
  Bolinger Band
- 布隆迪[非洲国家] **BDI**　　Burundi
- 布氏硬度 **HB**　　Brinell Hardness
- 布宜诺斯艾利斯行动计划[西班牙文] **PIBA**
  Programa de desarrollo Integrado de Buenos Aires
- 步兵战车[俄文] **BMP**　　Boyevaya Mashina Pekhoty
- 钚[第94号化学元素] **Pu**　　plutonium
- 部队登陆舰 **TLV**　　troop landing vessel
- 部分轨道轰炸系统 **FOBS**　　fractional orbital bombardment system
- 部分缓解 **PR**　　partial response
- 部门提前自愿自由化 **EVSL**　　early voluntary sectoral liberalization

材料安全数据一览表 MSDS	material safety data sheet
材料分析资料 MAD	material analysis data
材料评审委员会 MRB	material review board
材料强度试验研究价[智利,西班牙文] IDIEM	
Instituto de Investigaciones'y Ensayos de Materiales	
材料资源计划 MPR	materials resource planning
财产收入证书 PINC	property income certificate
财产税 ED	estate duty
财富论坛 FF	fortune forum
财商 FIQ	Financial Intelligence Quotient
财商 FQ	Financial Quotient
财务风险控制中心 FRCC	financial risk control center
财务管理 FICO	financial control
财务管理认证 CFM	Certified of Financial Management
财务经理 AE	account executive
财政部 DT	Department of the Treasury
财政规划系统 EPS	financial planning system
财政同盟 FU	fiscal union
财政效率 FE	Fiscal Efficiency
财政协调 FC	fiscal coordination
财政一体化 FI	fiscal integration
财政中性 FN	fiscal neutrality
裁军谈判会议 CD	conference on disarmament
裁军委员会会议(通称日内瓦裁军委员会) CCD	
Conference of Committee on Disarmament	

■ 裁判自行决定奖励给出色犬只［但又没被评上 BOB 或 BOS 的］**AOM**
Award of Merit
■ 采购经理人指数 **PMI**   Purchasing Manager Index
■ 彩电帕尔制 **PAL**   phase alternating (by) line
■ 彩色补偿滤光镜 **CC**   colour compensation filter
■ 彩色图形适配器 **CGA**   color graphics adapter
■ 彩妆艺术化妆品 **MAC**   make-up art cosmetics
■ 参见该条［拉丁文］**qv**   quod vide
■ 参考价格 **RP**   reference price
■ 参考与成人服务分会 **RASD**   Reference and Adult Services Division
■ 参考与用户服务协会 **RUSA**   Reference and User Services Association
■ 参数技术公司 **PTC**   Parameter Technology Corporation
■ 参议员 **Sen**   senator
■ 参照 **Ref**   reference
■ 餐馆 **HoReCa**   hotel, restaurant, cafe/catering
■ 餐桌慈善信任基金 **KTCT**   Kitchen Table Charities Trust
■ 残气容积 **RV**   residual volume
■ 仓库收据 **WW**   warehouse warrant
■ 藏在盒子里的宝藏 **KOZA**   Kooza
■ 操其他语言者的英语课程 **ESOL**   English for Speakers of Other Languages
■ 操纵特性增强系统 **MCAS**
maneucering characteristics augmentation system
■ 操作培训测试 **OTT**   operational training test
■ 操作试验与鉴定 **OPTEX**   operational test and evaluation
■ 操作说明书 **OS**   operational sheets
■ 操作系统 **OS**   operating system
■ 操作支持系统 **OSS**   Operating Support System
■ 草绿色 **OD**   olive drab
■ 厕所（作为"厕所"之意的 WC 在英美等英语国家现在一般不用，多用 toilet、washroom、restroom、bathroom 等，而男厕则多用 gent's、men；女厕多用 ladies、women 等。非英语国家有人用，英语国家的人一般也懂）**WC**
water closet

C

- 厕所文化研究中心 RCTC — Research Center for Toilet Culture
- 测距仪 DME — distance measuring equipment
- 测量单位 u/m — unit of measure
- 测试工程师 TD — Test Director
- 测试驱动开发 TDD — test-driven development
- 策略角色扮演游戏 SRPG — strategy role-playing game
- 策略品质保证 SQA — Strategic Quality Assurance
- 策略游戏 SLG — strategy game
- 层叠样式表 CSS — cascading style sheet
- 叉车 FLT — fork lift truck
- 插电式混合动力车 PHV — plug in hybrid vehicle
- 插入编辑 CUTIN — cutting
- 刹车辅助系统 BAS — brake assistant system
- 差[不好] D — dreadful
- 差错恢复程序 ERP — error recovery program
- 差等级（钱币）PR — poor
- 差示扫描量热法 DSC — differential scanning calorimetry
- 差速器 DIFF — differential
- 拆弹部队 EOD — explosive ordnance demolition
- 柴油机 D — diesel
- 柴油机和燃气轮机组合动力系统 CODAG — combined diesel and gas turbine (propulsion)
- 产房；分娩室 DR — delivery room
- 产品工程师 PE — production engineer
- 产品价值管理模式 PVM — products value management
- 产品来源国 COO — country of origin
- 产品设计的颜色、材质与工艺基础认知 CMF — color, material & finishing
- 产品生产周期管理 PLM — product lifecycle management
- 产品数据管理 PDM — product data management
- 产品责任 PL — product liability
- 产品质量工程师 PQE — product quality engineer

C

- 产前遗传学诊断 **PGD**   prenatal genetic diagnosis
- 产业颠覆联盟 **ISA**   Industry Subversive Alliance
- 产业政策研究院 **IPS**   Industry Policy Studies
- 昌河汽车[中国景德镇:汉语缩略语] **CH**   Changhe
- 肠内营养 **EN**   enteral nutrition
- 肠溶片剂 **ECT**   enteric coated tablet
- 肠易激综合征 **IBS**   irritable bowel syndrome
- 长安汽车[中国:汉语缩略语] **CA**   Chang'an
- 长波 **LW**   long wave
- 长波紫外线 **UVA**   ultraviolet A
- 长城国际心血管病会议 **GWICC**   Great Wall International Cardiovascular disease Conference
- 长丰汽车制造股份有限公司[中国] **CFA**   Changfeng Automobile
- 长航时多情报飞行器 **LEMV**   long-endurance multiplex vessel
- 长久性脱毛 **PHR**   permanent hair remove
- 长款或轴距加长 **Li**   lengthening or wheelbase lengthening
- 长期储备 **LTR**   long term reserve
- 长期储存 **LTS**   long term store
- 长期演进技术(2010年12月之后被正式称为4G) **LTE**   Long Term Evolution
- 长沙银行 **BCS**   Bank of Changsha
- 长途电话 **LDTEL**   long distance telephone
- 长途电信业务 **WATS**   wide area telecommunication
- 长途直拨电话 **STD**   subscriber trunk dialling
- 长途直接拨号 **DDD**   direct distance dialling
- 长征五号系列运输火箭 **LM5SLV**   Long March 5 Series Launch Vehicle
- 常备借贷便利 **SLF**   Standing Lending Facility
- 常规动力航母[代字] **CV-LX**   aircraft carrier, conventionally powered
- 常见问题及回答 **FAQs**   frequent asked questions
- 常染色体显性强迫型日光眼 **ACHOO**   Autosomal-dominant Compelling Helio-Ophthalmic Outburst
- 常识[日本人多用] **MANA**   manner

C

- 厂商建议提出的零售价 **MSRP**   manufacturer suggested retail price
- 场发射显示 **FED**   field emission display
- 场均进球数[足球] **GPG**   goals per game
- 场外交易 **OTCT**   over-the-counter trading
- 场外交易的证券 **OTCS**   over-the-counter securities
- 场外交易市场 **OTC**   over-the-counter
- 敞篷车和硬顶轿车的混合体 **CC**   cabrio-coupe
- 抄送 **CC**   carbon copy
- 超薄 **UT**   ultra thin
- 超大规模集成电路 **ELSI**   Extremely Large Scale Integrated circuit
- 超大规模集成电路 **VLSIC**   very large scale integrated circuit
- 超大规模集成研究(公司) **VLSIR**   very large scale integrated research
- 超大型矿砂船 **ULOC**   ultra-large ore carrier
- 超大型油轮 **ULCC**   ultra-large crude carrier
- 超大型油轮 **VLCC**   very large crude carrier
- 超大质量黑洞 **SMBH**   super massive black holes
- 超低频 **SLE**   super low frequency
- 超额负担 **EB**   excess burden
- 超高分子量聚乙烯[塑料] **UHMWPE**   ultra-high molecular weight polyethylene
- 超高密度 **VHD**   very high density
- 超高频 **SHF**   super high frequency
- 超高频 **UHF**   ultra high frequency
- 超高频无线电磁波 **UHFEW**
  ultra high frequency electromagnetic wave
- 超高清 **UHD**   ultra high definition
- 超高温(瞬时灭菌) **UHT**   ultra high temperature
- 超过限额 **OTT**   over the top
- 超行动宽带 **UMB**   ultra-mobile broadband
- 超乎期待 **E**   exceeds expectation
- 超乎寻常厉害的事物[以非典、艾滋病、人类免疫缺陷病毒引申] **SARS AIDS(HIV)**
  Severe Acute Respiratory Syndromes, Acquired Immune Deficiency Syndrome, Human Immunodeficiency Virus

C

- 超环面仪器 ATLAS — A Toroidal LHC Apparatus
- 超环线运输技术 HTT — Hyperloop Transportation Technologies
- 超激活和转录 TAT — transactivation and transcription
- 超级电子控股有限公司 ULE — ultra limited of electronic
- 超级高铁 H — hyperloop
- 超级高铁 PT — pneumatic tubes
- 超级计算大会 SC — Supercomputing Conference
- 超级男孩 SB — super boy
- 超级视频光盘 CVD — compact video disc
- 超级视频图形阵列 SVGA — super video graphic array
- 超级文件系统 EROFS — Extendable Read-Only File System
- 超级稀有 SR — super rare
- 特级超稀有[因为 super 无比较级] SSR — superior super rare
- 超级音频光盘 SACD — super audio compact disc
- 超媒体 Hypermedia — hypertext multimedia
- 超轻型 SL — super lightweight
- 超神联盟 LOL — League of Legends
- 超声波 US — ultra-sonic
- 超声波清洗 USC — ultra sonic cleaning
- 超声聚焦刀 HFU — high-intensity focused ultrasound
- 超声速燃烧冲压式发动机 SE — scramjet engine
- 超声心动图 UCG — ultrasonic cardiogram
- 超视距空对空导弹 BVRAAM — beyond-visual-range-air-air missile
- 超速离心机 UCF — ultracentrifuge
- 超脱沉思 TM — transcendental meditation
- 超微半导体公司 AMD — Advanced Micro Devices
- 超文本标记语言 HTML — hyper text markup language
- 超文本参考 HREF — hyper text reference
- 超文本传输协议 HTTP — hyper text transfer protocol
- 超文本传输协议服务器 HTTPS — hyper text transfer protocol server
- 超线程(技术) HT — hyper-threading
- 超氧化物歧化酶 SOD — superoxide dismutase

C

- 超一流规模的互联网公司[百度、阿里巴巴、腾讯] **BAT**
  Baidu, Alibaba, Tencent
- 超音速反舰导弹[法文] **ANS**   Anti-Navires-Supersonioue
- 超音速研究飞机 **HRA**   hypersonic research airplane
- 超音速运输机 **SST**   super-sonic transport
- 朝鲜 **KN**   Korea(North)
- 朝鲜[亚洲国家] **DPRK**   Democratic People's Republic of Korea
- 朝鲜经济研究所 **IBK**   Institute of Business of Korea
- 朝鲜退伍军人协会 **KVA**   Korean Veterans Association
- 朝鲜战争 **KW**   Korean War
- 朝鲜中央通讯社 **KCNA**   Korean Central News Agency[N. K.]
- 潮气量 **Vt**   tidal volume
- 车道偏离修正系统 **LDP**   lane departure prevention automotive
- 车辆动态控制 **VDC**   vehicle dynamic control
- 车辆动态综合管理系统 **VDIM**   vehicle dynamics integrated management
- 车辆及人员登陆艇 **LCVP**   landing craft, vehicle, personnel
- 车辆识别代码 **VIN**   vehicle identification number
- 车辆稳定控制技术 **VSA**   vehicle stability assist
- 车辆稳定性辅助系统 **VSA**   vehicle stability assistant
- 车辆自动识别系统 **ACI**   Automatic Car Identification System
- 车上交货价格 **FOR**   free on rail
- 车身稳定控制系统 **VSC**   vehicle stability control
- 车载自动诊断系统 **OBD**   on-board diagnostics
- 彻底改变美国的政治生态[引申义] **DIS**   drain the swamp
- 撤侨 **NEO**   non-combatant evacuation operation
- 沉默击破者 **SB**   Silence Breaker
- 陈年特级的酒 **XO**   extra old
- 衬套 **BUSH**   bushing
- 成本和管理会计师学会 **ICMA**
  Institute of Cost and Management Accountants
- 成本加保险费、运费价格 **CIF**   cost, insurance and freight
- 成本—效益分析 **CEA**   cost effectiveness analysis
- 成绩平均值 **GPA**   grade point average

成品线路板 PCBA	printed circuit board assembly
成人 A	adult
成人电影 AV	adult video
成人幽默 AH	adult humor
成人最低日需求量 MADR	minimum adult daily requirement
成熟的工业国 MIC	mature industrial countries
成纤维细胞生长因子 FGF	fibroblast growth factor
成长竞争力指数 GCI	Growth Competitiveness Index
承包商技术数据需求 CDRL	contractor data requirements list
承兑后若干天后付款 DA	day after acceptance
承兑交单 DA	document against acceptance
承认监管机构 RSB	Recognized Supervisory Body
承销人 U/W	underwriters
承运人箱 COC	carrier's owned container
城巴[香港] CTB	Citybus
城市空中交通 UAM	urban air transport
城市快轨车系统 URRVS	urban rapid-rail-vehicle system
城市气候领袖群 C40	40 Cities Climate Leadership's Group
城市休闲车 CR-V	city recreation vehicle
乘客姓名记录 PNR	passenger name record
乘用汽车厂[波兰文] FSO	Fabryka Samochodów Osobowych
程控交换 CBX	computerized branch exchange
程序处理表 PPT	program processing table
程序汇编语言 PAL	program assembly language
程序库 LIB	library
程序手册 PM	procedures manuel
橙黄色 OY	orange yellow
橙绿色 OG	orange green
橙色 O	orange
橙汁 OJ	orange juice
迟发型过敏反应 DTH	delayed type hypersensitivity
持久爱尔兰共和军 CIRA	Continuity Irish Republican Army

C

- 持久性有机污染物 **POPs** — persistent organic pollutants
- 持续减震控制（系统）**CDC** — Continuous Damping Control
- 持续性神经毒气［代字］**VX** — persistent toxic nerve
- 持续性植物人状态 **PVS** — persistent vegetative state
- 持证职业护士 **LVN** — licensed vocational nurse
- 齿轮传动涡扇发动机 **GTF** — geared turbofan
- 赤橙黄绿青蓝紫（色）**ROYGBIV** — red, orange, yellow, green, blue, indigo, violet
- 赤道几内亚［非洲国家］**GEQ** — Equatorial Guinea
- 冲突政策分析研究所 **IPAC** — Institute for Policy Analysis of Conflict
- 重新设计的杀伤器 **RKV** — re-design kill vehicle
- 宠物 **HHP** — household pet
- 宠物博览会 **FP** — Flocky Pet
- 宠物与动物运送机构 **IPATA** — Independent Pet and Animal Transportation Association
- 丑陋的鞋子的昵称 **UGG** — ugly boots
- 出版设计协会 **SPD** — Society of Publication Designers
- 出口管理公司 **EMC** — Export Management Company
- 出口加工区 **EPZ** — export processing zone
- 出口前产品与标准的符合性验证 **PVOC** — Pre-Export Verification of Conformity to Standards
- 出口申报单 **ED** — export declaration
- 出口税 **XLD** — export levy duty
- 出口税 **XTX** — export tax
- 出口退税 **ER** — export rebate
- 出口信贷机构 **ECA** — export credit agency
- 出票人 **Dr** — drawer
- 出生富有 **BR** — born rich
- 出生年 **YOB** — year of birth
- 出血时间 **BT** — bleeding time
- 初等教育三要素：读、写、算 **the three Rs** — reading, writing and arithmetic
- 初级工商管理 **EBA** — elementary business administration
- 初级护理机构 **PCP** — primary care provider

- 初级护理医师 **PCP**   primary care physician
- 初始化疗 **NAC**   neoadjuvant chemotherapy
- 初始货币供应 **ICO**   initial coin offerings
- 初学者通用指令码 **BASIC**   beginners all-purpose system instruction code
- 除非另有要求 **unoreq**   unless otherwise requested
- 储蓄和贷款 **S&L**   savings and loans
- 储蓄银行 **SB**   savings bank
- 储蓄账户 **SA**   savings account
- 处理器存储器 **PS**   processor storage
- 触地 **TD**   touchdown
- 穿甲试验 **APP**   Armor Piercing Proof
- 传导性角膜成形术 **CK**   conductive keratoplasty
- 传动比 **GR**   gear ratio
- 传动装置 **ACTR**   actuator
- 传感器 **SEN**   sensor
- 传媒学院[法文] **ICM**   Institut de la Communication et des Médias
- 传奇联盟 **LOL**   League of Legends
- 传染性非典型肺炎 **AP**   Atypical Pneumonia
- 传染性肝炎 **IH**   infectious hepatitis
- 传输单元 **TU**   transmission unit
- 传输单元传输完毕 **CTT**   completion of TU transmission
- 传输控制协议 **TCP**   transmission control protocol
- 传输衔接适配器 **TA**   transmission adapter
- 传统的无副翼旋翼头式 **FBL**   fly bar less(head)
- 传销 **MLM**   multi-level marketing
- 传真（系统） **FAX**   facsimile
- 传真通信系统 **FCS**   facsimile communications system
- 船上交货价格 **FOB**   free on board
- 船上卸货 **DA**   discharge afloat
- 船体与机械设备 **H&M/HM**   hull and machinery

C

- 船载航行数据记录仪［俗称船舶黑匣子］**VDR** voyage data recorder
- 串行 **SLIP** serial line IP
- 窗框媒介 **framedia** frame media
- 创 IV 国际论坛 **GIF** Gen IV International Forum
- 创办你的企业 **SYB** Start your business
- 创伤后应激障碍 **PTSD** post-traumatic stress disorder
- 创伤救治中心［印地文］**SMHS** Shri Maharaja Hari Singh
- 创业板 **GEM** Growth Enterprise Market
- 创业商数 **VQ** venture quotient
- 创造力商数 **CQ** creation quotient
- 创造性编辑［网络用语］**CE** creative editing
- 垂直发射系统 **VLS** vertical launch system
- 纯粹风险 **PR** pure risk
- 磁带［电子文献标示字母］**MT** magnetic tape
- 磁带操作系统 **TOS** tape operating system
- 磁带传输率 **DTR** disk transfer rate
- 磁带软件［电子文献标示略语］**CP/DK** computer program on disk
- 磁带数据库［电子文献标示略语］**DB/MT** data bank/magnetic tape
- 磁浮列车 **MLV** magnetic levitation vehicle
- 磁感应蛋白 **MagR** magnetoreceptor
- 磁共振成像/造影 **MRI** magnetic resonance imaging
- 磁盘操作系统 **DOS** disk operating system
- 磁随机读写存储器 **MRAM** Magnetic Random Access Memory
- 磁振造影 **MPI** Magnetic Particle Inspection
- 雌二醇 **E2** estradiol
- 雌激素受体 **ER** estrogen receptor
- 雌三醇 **E3** estriol
- 雌酮 **E1** estrone
- 次毫米波阵列望远镜 **SMA** Submillimeter Array (Radio Telescope)
- 聪明、漂亮、可爱、招人喜欢、酷［英语谐音缩略语］**Q** cute

从提到之日开始的一周 W/C	week commencing
从价税 AVT	ad valorem tax
从事工业工程的人 IE	industrial engineer
促黑激素 MSH	melanocyte-stimulating hormone
促红细胞生成素 EPO	erythropoietin
促黄体生成激素 LH	leuteinizing hormone
促黄体生成激素释放激素 LRH	
luteinizing hormone-releasing hormone	
促甲状腺激素 TTH	thyrotropic hormone
促甲状腺激素 TSH	thyroid-stimulating hormone
促甲状腺激素释放因子 TSH-RE	
thyroid-stimulating hormone-releasing factor	
促卵泡（成熟）激素 FSH	follicle-stimulating hormone
促肾上腺皮质激素 ACTH	adrenocorticotrophin hormone
促肾上腺皮质激素释放激素 CRH	corticotropin releasing hormone
促肾上腺皮质激素调节因子 CRF	corticotropin regulating factor
促销 SP	sales promotion
促销焦点（广告）POP	point of promotion
猝死综合征 SDS	sudden death syndrome
醋酸脱氧皮质酮 DOCA	deoxycorticosterone acetate
催泪瓦斯[乙烷基三碘乙酸] KSK	ethyl iodoacetate
催乳素 PRL	prolactin
催乳素释放抑制因子 PIF	prolactin release inhibiting factor
催乳素释放因子 PRF	prolactin releasing factor
存储标志 SM	storage mark
存储服务标识符 SSID	storage service identifier
存储器单元 SE	storage element
存储商数 MQ	memory quotient
存储数据协会 SDA	Storage Data Association
存款收条 DR	deposit receipt
存款账户 DA	deposit account

D

存款转账支票 DTC　　depositary transfer check
存托凭证 DR　　depositary receipts

钅达[第110号化学元素] Ds　　darmstadtium
打电话 PH　　phone
打扣码[法文] code promo　　un code promotionnel
打印机控制语言 PCL　　printer control language
打坐[佛教] TM　　transcendental meditation
大 Snr/Sr　　senior
大 Sr　　senior
大 Gt　　great
大不列颠 GB　　Great Britain
大不列颠哥伦比亚大学 UBC　　University of British Columbia
大道 Blvd　　boulevard
大电视 IPTV　　Internet Protocol TV
大都会运输署 MTA　　Metropolitan Transit Authority
大额可转让定期存单 CD　　Certificate Deposit
大发汽车[日本] D　　Daihatsu
大分子科学与工程奖 MSEA
　　Macromolecule Science and Engine Award
大副 F/O 或 FO　　first officer
大公司客户 LCA　　large corporation account
大规模集成电路 LSI　　large scale integration
大规模杀伤性武器 WMD　　Weapon of Mass Destruction
大湖研讨会的超大规模集成电路 GLSV　　Great Lakes Symposium on VLSIC

D

- 大火箭 **LM5SLV** — Long March 5 Series Launch Vehicle
- 大疆创新 **DJI** — Dajiang Innovations
- 大街 **Ave** — avenue
- 大连北大科技(集团)股份有限公司 **DBTC** — Dalian Beida Technology (Group)Co,LTD
- 大连外国语学院 **DUFL** — Dalian University for Foreign Languages
- 大楼综合征 **SBS** — sick building syndrome
- 大麻 **MJ** — marijuana
- 大马圣战组织[马来文] **KMM** — Kumpulan Mujahidin Malaysiao
- 大湄公河次区域经济合作 **GMS** — Great Mekong Subregion Economic Cooperation
- 大脑性麻痹 **CP** — cerebral palsy
- 大疱性表皮松解症 **EB** — epidermolysis bullosa
- 大气"激光笔" **APSOS** — Atmospheric Profiling Synthetic Observation System
- 大气模拟预测法规模式 **AERMOD** — AMS/EPA Regulatory Model
- 大容量内存卡 **SDHC card** — secure digital high capacity card
- 大赦国际[1961年成立于伦敦的国际人权组织] **AI** — Amnesty International
- 大数据房价指数 **BHPI** — big data house price index
- 大数据技术大会 **BDTC** — Big Data Technology Conference
- 大唐币 **DTC** — Datang Coin
- 大天区面积多目标光纤光谱天文望远镜 **LAMOST** — Large Sky Area Multi-Object Fiber Spectroscopy Telescope
- 大团圆结局 **HE** — happy ending
- 大西部公路[澳大利亚新南威尔士] **GWH** — Great Western Highway
- 大西洋标准时间 **AST** — Atlantic Standard Time
- 大西洋夏令时间 **ADT** — Atlantic Daylight Time
- 大西洋自由贸易区 **AFTA** — Atlantic Free Trade Area
- 大虾;大侠[网络,汉语拼音流行缩略语] **DX** — daxia

D

- 大笑 **LOL**   lots of laugh
- 大写 **UC**   upper case
- 大写字母和小写字母 **C&LC**   capitals and lower case
- 大型多人在线角色扮演游戏 **MMORPG**
  massive multiplayer online role playing game
- 大型轨道望远镜 **LOT**   large orbiting telescope
- 大型减速处理器 **LGBT**   large gear box treatment
- 大型旅游车 **GT**   grand tourer
- 大型强子对撞机 **LHC**   Large Hadron Collider
- 大型特写镜头 **LCU**   large close-up
- 大型天文望远镜 **GTC**   great telescope of celestial
- 大型拖船 **LT**   large tug
- 大型正负电子对撞机 **LEP**   large electron positron collider
- 大修结束 **EOH**   end of overhaul
- 大学 **uni**   university
- 大学二年级学生 **Soph**   sophomore
- 大学工艺研究所［法文］ **IUT**   l'Institut universitaire de technologie
- 大学和学院招生服务中心 **UCAS**   Universities and Colleges Admissions Service
- 大学入学事务局 **AO**   Admissions Office
- 大学生创新实验计划 **UIRT**
  University Innovation Research and Training Program
- 大学生职业发展协会 **SCDA**   Student Career Development Association
- 大学英语教学中强调人文教学：思想品德、文化修养和精神品格 **EDS**
  Education, demand, self-study
- 大学英语考试 **CET**   College English Test
- 大学英语协会 **CEA**   College English Association
- 大学预科的一年级学生 **Prep**   preparation
- 大学资源委员会 **CUR**   Committee of University Resource
- 大学资源委员会 **COUR**   Committee of University Resource
- 大血小板比值 **P-LCR**   platelet large cell ratio
- 大洋洲足球联合会 **OFC**   Oceanian Football Confederation
- 大洋钻探工程 **ODP**   Offshore Drilling Project

D

- 大英帝国大十字勋位夫人或骑士 **GBE**
  Dame or Knight of the Grand Gross of the British Empire
- 大英帝国统治的女士指挥官 **DBE**
  Dame Commander of the Order of the British Empire
- 大英帝国司令勋章 **CBE**
  Commander of the Order of the British Empire
- 大英帝国员佐勋章 **MBE** — Member of the Order of the British Empire
- 大众高速交通 **MRT** — mass rapid transit
- 大主教 **Abp** — archbishop
- 大宗商品信心指数 **CCI** — Continuous Commodity Index
- 代表 **rep** — representative
- 代数翻译程序与编译程序 **ALTAC** — algebraic translator and compiler
- 代数平均（AA 制：以前常等于 go Dutch）**AA**
  Algebraic Average
- 代谢当量 **MET** — metabolic equivalent
- 带给你我所有的祝福［网络用语］**AMBW**
  all my best wishes
- 带进位循环右移 **RRC** — rotate right through the carry flay
- 带薪实习课程 **Co-op** — Co-operative Education
- 带薪休假 **LWP** — leave with pay
- 贷记通知单 **CM** — credit memo
- 贷款（复数）**CRS** — credits
- 贷款基础利率 **LPR** — loan prime rate
- 贷款市场报价利率 **LPR** — loan price interest
- 贷款市场报价利率 **LPR** — loan prime rate
- 贷款违约保险 **CDS** — credit default swap
- 贷款支持计划 **LSP** — loans support plan
- 待定 **TBD** — to be decided［determined］
- 待确认 **TBC** — to be confirmed
- 待宣布 **TBA** — to be announced
- 待装运提单 **RECEIVED B/L** — received for shipment bill of landing
- 戴姆勒-奔驰股份公司［德文］**DB** — Daimler Benz AG

D

- 丹麦［欧洲国家］**DEN**   Denmark
- 丹麦 Gomspace 公司与欧洲航天局合作的 3 号微型卫星 **Gomx-3**
  Gomspace-3
- 丹麦标准协会［丹麦文］**DS**   Dansk Standardiseringsrad
- 丹麦电气认证标志［丹麦文］**D**   Danmarks Elektriske Materielkontrol
- 丹麦电气设备检验委员会［丹麦文］**D**   Danmarks Elektriske Materielkontrol
- 丹麦非电气产品质量认证标志［丹麦文］**DS**
  Dansk Standardiseringsrad
- 丹麦哥本哈根大学 **UC**   The University of Copenhagen
- 丹麦克朗［丹麦货币单位］［丹麦文］**DKr** Danish Krone
- 丹尼尔·琼斯［英国语音学家］**DJ**   Daniel Jones
- 担保抵押证券 **CMO**   collateralized mortgage obligation
- 担保债务凭证 **CDO**   collateralized debt obligation
- 单胺氧化酶 **MAO**   monoamine oxidase
- 单兵自卫武器 **PDW**   Personal Defense Weapon
- 单纯 **KISS**   keep it simple, stupid
- 单纯红细胞再生障碍性贫血 **PRCA**
  pure red blood cell regeneration barrier anemia
- 单点包机旅游（包括一切费用）**OTC**   one-stop inclusive tour charter
- 单对线高速数字用户线 **SHDSL**
  single-pair high bit rate DSL (digital subscriber line)
- 单个用户平均收入 **ARPU**   average revenue per user
- 单光子发射计算机断层摄影 **SPECT**
  single photon emission computerized tomography
- 单核白细胞 **M/Mon**   monocyte
- 单核苷酸多态性 **SNP**   single nucleotide polymorphism
- 单核细胞 **MONO**   monocyte
- 单极开关   single pole switch
- 单面单层光碟 **D5**   DVD5
- 单面双层光碟 **D9**   DVD9
- 单片机 **SCM**   single chip micyoco
- 单片微波集成电路 **MMIC**   monolithic microwave integrated circuit

- 单收入无子女夫妇 OINK　　one income no kids
- 单位 U　　unit
- 单位体积的重量 w/v　　weight in volume
- 单位增益渡越 UGC　　Unit Gain Crossover
- 单一混乱事件 SEU　　single event upsets
- 单一螺母 SLN　　single lock nut
- 单一犬种冠军[同 BOB] BOV　　Best of Variety
- 单一犬种冠军[同 BOV] BOB　　Best of Breed
- 单一犬种最佳相对性别[同 BOB 不同性别的最佳犬只] BOS　　Best Opposite Sex
- 胆(略)商(数) CQ　　courage quotient
- 胆固醇 Ch　　cholesterol
- 胆红素 BIL　　bilirubin
- 胆红素实验 BIL　　bilirubin test
- 胆碱酯酶 CHE　　cholinesterase
- 胆商 DQ　　daring quotient
- 但另一方面[网络用语] BTA　　but then again
- 淡褐色 HA　　hazel
- 淡水码头 FRWF　　fresh wharf
- 淡香精(香精含量15%)[法文] EDP　　eau de parfum
- 淡香精(香精含量15%)[法文] PDT　　parfum de toilette
- 淡香水(香精含量8%~15%)[法文] EDT　　eau de toilette
- 弹道导弹防御系统 BMD　　ballistic missile defence
- 弹射起飞/拦阻索助降系统 CATOBAR　　catapult-assisted takeoff/barrier operations
- 蛋白激酶 A AURKA　　Aurora (Kinase) A
- 蛋白激酶 B AURKB　　Aurora Kinase B
- 蛋白激酶 C AURKC　　Aurora Kinase C
- 蛋白结合碘 PBI　　protein bound iodine
- 蛋白质 PRO　　protein
- 蛋白质数据库 PDB　　protein data bank
- 氮[第7号化学元素] N　　nitrogen

D

- 氮化镓 **GaN** — gallium nitride
- 氮化上苯基四唑 **TTC** — triphenyl tetrazolium chloride
- 氮氧化合物 **NO** — nitrogen oxide
- 当代造船模式 **CSM** — contemporary shipbuilding model
- 当代作家最新修订版丛书 **CANR** — Contemporary Author New Revision Series
- 当量惯量 **IP** — inertia processional
- 当你不小心弄错时帮你改正[网络英语] **FTFY** — Fixed that for you
- 当前实力 **CS** — current strength
- 当然[网络用语] **BOC** — but of course
- 刀豆凝集素 A **ConA** — concanavalin A
- 导弹防御(系统) **MD** — missile defence
- 导弹护卫舰 **FFG** — frigate, frigate, guided-missile
- 导弹驱逐舰 **DDG** — guided missile destroyer
- 导弹应对能力委员会 **CMCC** — Committee of Missile Contingent Capacity
- 导轨接口系统 **RIS** — rail interface system
- 导轨适配系统 **RAS** — rail adapter system
- 导航战鉴定小组 **NET** — navigation warfare evaluation team
- 岛 **Is** — Island(s); Isle
- 倒挡 **R** — reverse
- 到岸价格[成本加保险费、运费] **CAF** — cost assurance and freight
- 到达 **arr** — arrival
- 到货通知 **NOA** — notice on availability
- 到期收益 **YTM** — yield to maturity
- 道德黑客认证 **CEH** — Certificated Ethical Hacker
- 道德商数 **MQ** — morals quotient
- 道路交通事故 **RTA** — road traffic accident
- 道·琼斯工业平均(股票价格指数) **DJIA** — Dow Jones Industrial Average (Stock Index)
- 道·琼斯公用事业平均指数 **DJUA** — Dow Jones Utility Average

D

- 道·琼斯指数 **DJI** — Dow Jones Index
- 得[口语] **hafta** — have to
- 得舒饮食[防高血压健康饮食] **DASH**
  Dietary Approaches to Stop Hypertension
- 锝[第43号化学元素] **Tc** — technetium
- 德尔福汽车系统 **DAS** — Delphi automotive systems
- 德法公共电视台[法文] **ARTE**
  Association Relativeà la Télévion Européenne
- 德国[欧洲国家] **GER** — Germany
- 德国 AMG 汽车制造公司[德文] **AMG** — Autrecht Melcher Grossaspach
- 德国 IBZ 德语培训学校[德文] **IBZ**
  Interkulturelles Bildungszentrum e. V. an der Universitaet Duisburg-Essen
- 德国 RWE 股份公司 **RWE**
  Rheinisch-Westfaetisches Elektriritaets-werk AG
- 德国安全(认证标志) **GS** — Germany Safety
- 德国安全认证标志之一[德文] **TüV** — Technischer Überwachungsverein
- 德国安特优(MTU)公司[德文] **MTU**
  Motoren und Turbinen Union GmbH
- 德国标准化学会[德文] **DIN** — Deutsche Institute für Normung
- 德国产品质量认证标志[德文] **DIN** — Deutsche Institute für Normung
- 德国船厂[德文] **DW** — Deutschen Werft AG
- 德国大众汽车[德文] **VW** — Volkswagen
- 德国电气产品质量认证标志[德文] **VDE** — Verband Deutscher Elektrotechniker
- 德国电气工程师协会[德文] **VDE** — Verband Deutscher Elektrotechniker
- 德国多卡模板公司[德文] **DOKA** — Doppelkabine
- 德国房车(大师)赛[德文] **DTM** — Deutsche Tourenwagen Meisterschaft
- 德国房车锦标赛 **GTCC** — German Touring Car Cup
- 德国非政府组织[德文] **Kiron** — Chiron
- 德国工程、信息科学、自然科学和数学专业认证机构 **ASIIN**
  German Accreditation Agency for Study Programs in Engineering, Informatics, Natural Sciences and Mathematics
- 德国工业标准[英文:German Industry Standards][德文] **DIN**
  Deutsche Industrie Normen

D

- 德国雇主协会联邦联合会［德文］**BDA**
  Bundesvereinigung der Deutschen Abeitgeberverbände
- 德国航空公司［德文］**DLH**　　　　　Deutsche Luft Hansa
- 德国豪车三巨头［奔驰、宝马、奥迪］**BBA**　Benz, BMW, Audi
- 德国霍瓦特造船厂［德文］**HDW**　　　Howaldtswerke-Deutsche Werft GmbH
- 德国建筑联合会［德文］**BDA**　　　　Bund Deutscher Architekten
- 德国精灵汽车 **Smart**　　　　　　　Swatch, Mercedes-Benz, art
- 德国劳氏船级社［德文］**GL**　　　　　Germanischer Lloyd
- 德国联邦风险评估研究所［德文］**BfR**　Bundesinstitut für Risikobewertung
- 德国联邦情报局［德文］**BND**　　　　Bundesnachrichtendienst
- 德国联邦宪法保卫局［德文］**BfV**　　　Bundesamt für Verfassungsschutz
- 德国量产房车赛［德文］**DPM**　　　　Deutsche Produktion Meisterschaft
- 德国马克［德国货币单位］［德文］**DM**　Deutsche Mark
- 德国马术奥委会［德文］**DOKR**　　　Deutsches Olympiadekomitee für Reiterei
- 德国马术协会［德文］**DRV**　　　　　Deutsche Reiterliche Vereinigung
- 德国马术协会［法文］**FEN**　　　　　Fédération Equestre Nationale
- 德国迈巴赫汽车 **MM**　　　　　　　Maybach
- 德国煤气与供水技术协会［德文］**DVGW**
  Deutsche Verein von Gas und Wasserfachmännern
- 德国煤气与自来水产品质量认证标志［德文］**DIN-DVGW**
  Deutsche Institue für Normung-Deutsche Verein von Gas und Wasserfachmännern
- 德国慕尼黑大学 **UM**　　　　　　　University of Munich
- 德国慕尼黑工业大学 **TUM**　　　　　Technical University of Munich
- 德国纳粹冲锋队［德文］**SA**　　　　　Sturmabteilung
- 德国纳粹党卫队［德文］**SS**　　　　　Schutzstaffel
- 德国纳粹党卫军［德文］**SS**　　　　　Schutzstaffel
- 德国汽车俱乐部［德文］**AD AC**　　　Allegemeiner Dentscher Automobil Club
- 德国犬科学协会［德文］**VDH**　　　　Verband für das Deutsche Hundewesen
- 德国犬运动协会［德文］**DHV**　　　　Deutscher Hundesportverband
- 德国人工智能研究中心［德文］**DFKI**
  Deutsche Forschungszentrum für Künstliche Intelligenz GmbH

- 德国认证机构［世界六家权威的国家认证机构之一，德文］**DAR**
  Deutsche Akkreditierungs Rat
- 德国社会民主党［德文］**SPD**　　　　　　Sozialdemokratische Partei Deutschlands
- 德国政府派驻北京的官方办事机构 **APS**　Akademiche Prüfstelle
- 德国重要的股票指数［德文］**DAX**　　　　Deutscher Aktienindex
- 德克斯长裤 **Daks**　　　　　　　　　　　Dad and Slacks
- 德拉维达进步联盟党［印地文］**DMK**　　　Dravida Munnetra Kazhagam
- 德雷克船长［包箱商标］**Dr**　　　　　　　Drake Captain
- 德意志新闻社［德文］**DPA**　　　　　　　Deutsche Presse Ageniur
- 德语托福考试［德文］**DaF**　　　　　　　Deutsch als Fremdsprache
- 德知航创：无人机研发团队 **TechX**　　　　technology X
- 登陆 **LDG**　　　　　　　　　　　　　　landing
- 等等［拉丁文］**etc**　　　　　　　　　　　et cetera
- 等离子体显示板 **PDP**　　　　　　　　　　plasma display panel
- 等流量容积 **Viso-V**　　　　　　　　　　　volume of isoflow
- 低促性腺素性功能减退症 **HH**　　　　　　　hypogonadotropic hypogonadism
- 低挡 **Lo**　　　　　　　　　　　　　　　low
- 低动态范围（图像）**LDR**　　　　　　　　low-dynamic range
- 低度多元化，相关多元化，不相关多元化，高度多元化 **LRUH**
  low diversity, related diversity, unrelated diversity, high diversity
- 低度酒精啤酒 **lab**　　　　　　　　　　　low-alcohol beer
- 低工资、无前途的工作 **McJobs**　　　　　　McDonald's Jobs
- 低密度聚乙烯［塑料］**LDPE**　　　　　　　low density polyethylene
- 低密度奇偶校验码 **LDPC**　　　　　　　　low density parity check code
- 低密度脂蛋白 **LDL**　　　　　　　　　　　low density lipoprotein
- 低密度脂蛋白胆固醇 **LDL-C(h)**　　　　　　low-density lipoprotein cholesterol
- 低密高密比 **LDL/HDL**
  low density lipoprotein/high density lipoprotein
- 低排放（污染）汽车 **LEV**　　　　　　　　low emission vehicle
- 低水位标志 **LWM**　　　　　　　　　　　low water mark
- 低温 **LT**　　　　　　　　　　　　　　　low temperature
- 低温相偏硼酸钡 **BBO**　　　　　　　　　　β-Bab204［Bete-Barium Borate］

D

- 低音大号、低音大喇叭[音响] **BT**   bass tuba
- 低油耗汽车 **EEV**   energy efficiency vehicle
- 低于平均[不佳] **P**   poor
- 低脂肪 **LF**   low fat
- 低脂肪饮食 **LFD**   low fat diet
- 滴滴涕[一种杀虫剂] **DDT**   dichloro-diphenyl-trichloroethane
- 迪奥女装 **CD**   Christain Dior
- 迪拜商品期货交易所 **DME**   Dubai Merchandise Exchange
- 迪比科移动电源[汉语拼音缩略语] **DBK**   dibike
- 镝[第66号化学元素] **Dy**   dysprosium
- 抵消性关税 **CVD**   countervailing duties
- 抵押补充贷款 **PSL**   pledged supplementary lending
- 底特律自动轨道交通系统 **DPM**   Detroit People Mover
- 地方标准时间 **ZST**   zone standard time
- 地方政府报告 **LGR**   Local government report
- 地理标示语言 **GML**   geography markup language
- 地理信息软件 **GIS**   geo-information software
- 地理信息系统[又称资源与环境信息系统] **GIS**   Geographical Information System
- 地面X战车技术 **GXV-T**   ground X vehicle technology
- 地面发射单元,燃料空气炸药 **SLUFAE**   surface-launched unit, fuel air explosive
- 地面交通中心 **GTC**   ground traffic centre
- 地面控制设备 **GCU**   ground control unit
- 地面数据终端 **GDT**   ground data terminal
- 地面通信(运输)线 **LL**   land line
- 地面无线 **DVB-H**   Digital Video Broadcasting-Terrestrial
- 地面显示系统 **GDS**   ground display system
- 地面运输系统 **AGTS**   Above Ground Transport System
- 地面战车 **GCV**   ground combat vehicle
- 地球观测组织 **GEO**   Group on Earth Observations
- 地球同步卫星运载火箭 **GSLV**   geosynchronous satellite launch vehicle
- 地球系统模式 **CESM**   Community Earth System Model

- 地鼠肝内胆管癌 ICC　　　　　　　　intrahepatic cholangiocarcinoma
- 地铁 MTR　　　　　　　　　　　　　metropolitan railway
- 地图信息服务中心 CIS　　　　　　　Cartographic Information Services
- 地下探宝游戏 D&D　　　　　　　　Dungeons and Dragons
- 地下铁道 Metro　　　　　　　　　　Metropolitan Railway
- 地形匹配（制导）TERCOM　　　　　terrain contour matching
- 地址 Add　　　　　　　　　　　　　address
- 地中海饮食 MIND　　　　　　　　　Mediterranean Diet
- 帝国化学公司［英国］ICI　　　　　　Imperial Chemical Industries
- 帝国理工大学［英国］ICL　　　　　　Imperial College London
- 帝国能源公司 IE　　　　　　　　　　Imperial Energy
- 第……代合作伙伴计划 GPP　　　　　generation partner program
- 第 3 梯队 E3　　　　　　　　　　　　Echelon 3
- 第二代（移动通信系统：含短信）2G　generation 2
- 第二语言习得 SLA　　　　　　　　　second language acquisition
- 第三代（移动通信系统：含短信、互联网接入）3G
  generation 3
- 第十届国际空间轨道设计大赛 GTOC X
  The 10th edition of the Global Trajectory Optimisation Competition
- 第四代（移动通信系统：含短信互联网接入，加视频）4G
  generation 4
- 第五代（移动通信系统：含短信、互联网接入、超高清视频、智能家居）5G
  generation 5
- 第一副总裁 FVP　　　　　　　　　　first vice president
- 第一人射击类游戏 FPS　　　　　　　first-person shooter game
- 碲［第 52 号化学元素］Te　　　　　　tellurium
- 典型肺炎 TP　　　　　　　　　　　　typical pneumonia
- 点播游戏 GOD　　　　　　　　　　　game on demand
- 点到点协议 PPP　　　　　　　　　　point to point protocol
- 点火 IGN　　　　　　　　　　　　　ignition
- 点击（通过）率 CTR　　　　　　　　click through ratio
- 碘［第 53 化学号元素］I　　　　　　　iodine

D

- 碘化钾 KI potassium iodide
- 碘耐量试验 ITT iodine tolerance test
- 碘缺乏症 IDD iodine deficiency disorders
- 碘值与皂化值因数 INS
  iodine number and saponification number factor
- 电磁辐射 EMR electromagnetic radiation
- 电磁兼容认证[现已被CCC认证代替] EMC
  Electromagnetic Certificate
- 电磁兼容性 EMC Electronic Magnetic Compatible
- 电磁脉冲 EMP electromagnetic pulse
- 电磁推进系统 Em-Drive electromagnetism drive
- 电磁阻拦索 EMAC electromagnetic arresting cable
- 电动汽车 EV electric vehicle
- 电动汽车安全 EVS electric vehicles security
- 电动汽车安全全球技术法规 EVS-GTR
  Electric Vehicles Security-Global Technology Regulation
- 电动助力转向系统 EPS electric power steering
- 电感式传感器 ITT inductance type transducer
- 电荷耦合器件 CCD charge coupled device
- 电化学疗法 ECT electrochemotherapy
- 电话（号码）Tel telephone
- 电话 PH phone
- 电话 T telephone
- 电话号码 tel telephone number
- 电话会议 con-call conference call
- 电汇 TT telegraphic transfer
- 电汇单 TMO telegraphic money order
- 电汇买进 TT telegraphic transfer bought
- 电机控制中心 MCC motor control center
- 电惊厥疗法 ECT electroconvulsive therapy
- 电离层加热器 IH Ionosphere Heater
- 电力碎片消除器 EDDE electric defragment dispelling equipment

405

D

中文	缩略语	英文
电力调节器	PLC	power line conditioner
电力线通信	PLC	power line communication
电力线载波	PLC	power-line carrier
电路测试	ICT	in circuit test
电路分析中常使用的晶体三极管等效电路的模型	E-M	ebers-moll (model)
电路交换数据网络	CSDN	Circuit Switching Data Network
电脑	C	computer
电脑成像技术	CGI	computer generated imagery
电脑电话	CT	Computer Telephone
电脑电话集成	CTI	computer telephone integration
电脑动漫	CG	computer game
电脑绘画	CG	computergraphics
电脑控制区[局]域网	CAN	computer area net
电脑排版系统	CTS	computerized typesetting system
电脑千年虫问题	Y2K	Year 2000 problem
电脑视频终端综合征	CVS	Computer Vision Syndrome
电脑语音合成技术	CTI	computer telephone integration
电脑直接印刷	CTP	Computer to Paper
电气测试实验室	ETL	Electrical Testing Laboratory
电气动力转向	EPS	electrical power steering
电气和电子工程师协会	IEEE	Institute of Electrical and Electronics Engineers
电气检验	EI	electrical inspectorate
电气描记图	EGG	electrogastrogram
电器产品安全规范	EPSR	Electrical Products Safety Regulation
电器制造商理事会[美]	EMC	Electrical Manufacturers Council
电商无线传输协议	eWTP	e-Commerce Wireless Transfer Protocol
电视(机)	TV	television
电视辅助教学	VAI	video-assisted instruction
电视广告影片	TVCF	television commercial film
电视会议	VC	Video Conference

D

电视机的机顶盒 STB	set top box
电视新闻 TVN	television News
电视综艺节目主持人 VJ	video jockey
电信、传媒、技术 TMT	
telecommunications, media and technology	
电信公司 telco	telecommunications company
电影广告 MVCF	movie commercial film
电影栏目主持人 MJ	movie jockey
电源线车 PLC	power-line carrier
电子 e/E	electronic
电子病历 EMR	Electronic Medical Record
电子差速锁 EDS	electronic differential lock system
电子差速锁定 EDL	electronic differential locking
电子出版系统 EPS	electronic publishing system
电子传递设备 ted	transferred electron device
电子道路收费 ERP	electronic road pricing
电子点火提前控制 ESAC	electronic spark advance control
电子电视节目指南 EPG	electronic program guide
电子对抗措施 ECM	electronic counter measures
电子对抗系统 ECS	electronic countermeasure system
电子防盗系统 EAS	electronic article system
电子伏(特)[能量单位名称] eV	electronic volt
电子港湾 Ebay	electronic bay
电子工程(学) EE	electronic engineering
电子工程设计发展联合会 JEDEC	Joint Electron Device Engineering Council
电子工程师 EE	electrical engineer
电子工业协会 EIA	Electronic Industries Association
电子公告[电子文献标示字母] EB	electronic bulletin board
电子公告栏系统 BBS	bulletin board system
电子-光学-红外 EO-IR	electro-optical-infrared
电子海图系统 ECS	electronic chart system
电子轰击式推进装置 EBV	electron bombarded vehicle

407

电子化商务中心区 **E-CBD**	electronic central business district
电子货运 **e-shipping**	electric shipping
电子绩效支持系统 **EPSS**	electronic performance support system
电子教室 **E-Class**	electronic class
电子教学产品 **ELP**	electronic learning product
电子竞技 **ES**	electronic sports
电子竞技人 **E-sportmen**	electronic sportmen
电子竞技世界杯 **ESWC**	Electronic Sports World Cup
电子竞技娱乐协会 **ESEA**	E-Sports Entertainment Association
电子刊物 **E-journal**	electronic journal
电子科技大学 **UESTC**	University of Electronic Science and Technology of China
电子控制单元 **ECU**	engine control unit
电子控制动力转向系统 **EPS**	electronic power steering
电子控制无级变速器 **ECVT**	electro-continuously variable transmission
电子控制装置 **ECU**	electronically controlled unit
电子控制装置 **ECU**	eletronic control unit
电子录像机 **EVR**	electronic video recorder
电子论坛 **e-talking**	electric talking
电子器件工程联合委员会 **JEDEC**	Joint Electron Device Engineering Council
电子前沿基金 **EFF**	electronic front fund
电子情报 **EL INT**	electronic intelligence
电子燃油控制系统 **EFM**	electronic fuel-management system
电子认证标志 **IECQ**	International Electrotechnical Commission of Quality
电子扫描雷达 **AESA**	active electronically scanned array radar
电子商店 **E-shop**	electronic shop
电子商务 **EB**	electronic business
电子商务 **EC**	electronic commerce
电子商务工程师认证考试 **CEBE**	Certified Exam of Business Engineers
电子商务顾问国际委员会 **EC-Council**	Electron Commercial Council
电子商务交易安全协议 **SET**	Secure Electronic Transfer

D

电子商务系统 ECS	electronic commerce system
电子设备 EL	electronics
电子设计自动化 EDA	electronic design automation
电子收费系统 ETC	electronic toll collection
电子书籍 E-book	electronic book
电子束 EB	electron beam
电子数据处理 EDP	electronic data processing
电子数据交换 EDI	electronic data interchange
电子数据系统 EDS	electronic data systems

电子数字积分计算机[1946年美国制造的第一台通用计算机的名称] ENIAC
electronic numerical integrator and calculator

电子文档 E-Paper	electronic paper
电子文体协会 ESEA	E-Sports Entertainment Association
电子稳定程序(系统) ESP	electronic stability program
电子稳定控制系统 ESC	electronic stability control
电子显微镜 EM	electron microscope
电子现场节目制作 EFP	electronic field program production
电子现金 E-cash	electronic cash
电子新闻采集 ENG	electronic news gathering
电子信息系统 EIS	Electronic Information System
电子学 EL	electronics
电子学位论文项目 ETD	Electronic Thesis and Dissertations
电子医疗记录 EMR	Electronic Medical Record
电子艺术 EA	electronic arts
电子音乐 EM	electronic music
电子银行 e-bank	electronic bank
电子邮件 E-mail	electronic mail
电子邮件营销 EDM	email direct marketing
电子娱乐博览会 E3	Electronic Entertainment Expo
电子杂志 E-zine	electronic magazine
电子战 EC	electronic combat
电子战 EW	electronic warfare

电子账单处理与支付系统 EBPP	electronic bill process and payment
电子职业联赛 CPL	Cyberathelete Professional League
电子制动(力)分配系统 EBD	electronic braking distribute
电子制动分配装置[德文] EBV	Elektronische Bremskraft vertung Gerät
电子制动可变多路传输器 EBV	electronic brake varioplex
电子制动力分配系统 EBD	electronic brakeforce distribution
电子制造服务业 EMS	electronical manufacturing services
电子资金转账 EFT	electronic funds transfer
电子自动开关 EAS	electronic automatic switch
垫圈 GSKT	gasket
淀粉酶 Am	amylase
靛氰绿滞留实验 ICG	indocyanine green
叠氮胸苷(一种抗艾滋病药物) AZT	azidothymidine
丁醇提取碘 BEI	butanol-extractable iodine
丁基羟基甲苯 BHT	Butylated Hydroxytoluene
丁克族[有双薪收入而没有孩子的夫妇] DINK Double Income and No Kids	
丁型肝炎抗体 HDVAb	hepatitis delta virus antibody
顶级美味大奖 STA	Superior Taste Award
顶置单凸轮轴发动机 SOHC	single overhead camshaft(engine)
顶置双凸轮轴(发动机) DOHC	double overhead camshaft(engine)
订单 PO	purchase order
订单评价 CF	customer feedback
订单缺陷率 ODR	Order Defect Rate
定量下限 LOQ	limit of quantity
定期存款 TD	time deposit
定期维修 PM	periodic maintenance
定位、导航与授时 PNT	position, navigation and timing
定位通信系统 LCS	located communications system
定位系统 LBS	location based services
定向刨花板 OSB	oriented strand board
定型产品 AP	approved product

D

- 定制研发生产 CDMO
  Contract Development Manufacture Organization
- 铥[第69号化学元素] Tm　　　　thulium
- 东北方(的) NE　　　　north-east(ern)
- 东部高科株式会社 DB HiTek　　　　Dongbu High Technology Co., Ltd
- 东部经济走廊 EEC　　　　East Economic Corridor
- 东方汇理银行 CACIB
  Credit Agricole Corporate and Investment Bank
- 东方经济论坛 EEF　　　　East Economic Forum
- 东方神起(代表永远在一起)[韩文] DBSK　　　　Dong Bang Shin Ki
- 东非共同市场 EACM　　　　East African Common Market
- 东风[汉语拼音缩略语] DF　　　　dongfeng
- 东海岸铁路 ECRL　　　　East Coast Rail Link
- 东京广播公司 TBS　　　　Tokyo Broadcasting System
- 东盟打击跨国犯罪部长级会议 AMMTC
  ASEAN Ministerial Conference on Transnational Crime
- 东盟打击跨国犯罪高官会议 SOMTC
  ASEAN Senior Officials Meeting on Transnational Crime
- 东盟地区论坛 ARF　　　　ASEAN Regional Forum
- 东盟学院 CAS　　　　College of ASEAN Studies
- 东盟自由贸易区 AFTA　　　　ASEAN Free Trade Area
- 东南方(的) SE　　　　south-east(ern)
- 东南非共同市场 COMSEA　　　　Common Market of Southeast Africa
- 东南亚国家联盟 ASEAN　　　　Association of Southeast Asian Nations
- 东西伯利亚—太平洋运输管道 ESPO
  The Eastern Siberia-Pacific Ocean Oil Pipeline
- 东西方协会 EWA　　　　East and West Association
- 东亚峰会 EAS　　　　East Asia Summit
- 氡[第86号化学元素] Rn　　　　radon
- 动感地带 M-zone　　　　Motive Zone
- 动画漫画游戏[通常指电玩游戏或美少女游戏的总称] ACG
  animation, comic, game

动力负载控制 PLC	power loading control
动力系统控制模块 PCM	power train control module
动脉 A	artery
动脉血二氧化碳分压 PaCO₂	partial pressure of carbon dioxide in artery
动脉血氧分压 PaO₂	arterial oxygen tension
动脉血氧含量 CaO₂	arterial oxygen content
动漫角色扮演 Cos	cosplay
动漫角色扮演 Cosplay	costume play
动态比特率 VBR	variable bit rate
动态服务器网页 ASP	active server pages
动态链接库 DLL	dynamic link library
动态流通语料库 DCC	dynamic circulation corpus
动态数据交换 DDE	dynamic data exchange
动态随机存取存储器 DRAM	dynamic random access memory
动态稳定性控制 DSC	dynamic stability control
动物解放阵线 ALF	Animal Liberation Front
动植物卫生检疫措施 SPS	sanitary and phytosanitary standard
动作角色扮演游戏 ARPG	action role playing game
动作类游戏 ACT	action game
动作冒险游戏 AAVG	action adventure game
冻干(技术) FD	freeze-drying
洞察号[利用地震、大地测量和热流的火星内部结构探测器] InSight	Interior Exploration using Seismic Investigations, Geodesy and Heat Transport
抖音 TT	TikTok
都柏林大学 UCD	University College Dublin
毒品管制局 DEA	Drug Enforcement Administration
毒品强制执行管理局 DEA	Drug Enforcement Administration
毒品调查科 NB	narcotics bureau
独立的 ind	independent
独立电视台[俄文] NTV	Niezavisimei Tielievidienie
独立腐败行为委员会 ICPC	Independent Corrupt Practice Commission

D

- 独立国家联合体 CIS　　　　　Commonwealth of Independent States
- 独立猫类联盟 ICF　　　　　　Independent Cat federation
- 独立软件开发商 ISV　　　　　independent software vendor
- 独立微机器人平台计划 SHRIMP
  Short-Range Independent Microrobotic Platforms
- 独立选修 ISP　　　　　　　　independent study program
- 独立组网 SA　　　　　　　　standalone
- 独生子 OS　　　　　　　　　only son
- 独特麦（卢卡因子）UMF　　　Unique Manuka Factor
- 独特卖点 USP　　　　　　　　unique selling point
- 赌场表的游戏 CTG　　　　　　Casino Table Game
- 杜比数码环绕声［美国杜比公司开发的家庭影院多声道数字音频系统］AC-3
  Dolby surround Coding-3
- 杜嘉［意大利奢侈品牌］D&G　Dolce & Gabbana
- 杜绝犯罪行为署 SOCA　　　　Stamp Out Crime Authority
- 杜克大学 DU　　　　　　　　Duke University
- 杜蕾斯（安全套）DUREX　　　durability, reliability, excellence
- 𬬻［第105号化学元素］Db　　 dubnium
- 短波 SW　　　　　　　　　　short wave
- 短波紫外线 UVC　　　　　　　ultraviolet C
- 短距离高频天线通信 NFC　　　near field communication
- 短距离起飞与垂直降落飞机 STOVL　short take-off and vertical landing aircraft
- 短期流动性调节工具 SLO　　　short-term liquidity operations
- 短信息服务 SMS　　　　　　　short message service
- 短暂性脑缺血发作 TIA　　　　transient ischemic attack
- 断念与脱离课程［项目］DDP　Desistance and Disengagement Programme
- 对（某人、某物、某集体）V/VS　versus
- 对氨基苯甲酸 PABA　　　　　para-aminobenzoic acid
- 对氨基马尿酸清除率 CPAH　　para-aminohippurate clearance
- 对苯二甲酸 PTA　　　　　　　purified terephthalic acid
- 对独联体技术援助 TACIS
  Technical Assistance to the Commonwealth of Independent States

对二甲苯 **PX**	p-xylene
对话模拟器 **XTS**	crosstell simulator
对话式代数语言 **CAL**	conversational algebraic language
对开信用证 **CC**	counter credit
对流免疫电泳 **CIEP**	counter immune electrophoresis
对欧洲出口委员会[英国] **ECE**	Export Council for Europe
对外汉语教学 **TCFL**	Teaching Chinese as a Foreign Language
对外汉语教学 **TCSOL**	Teaching Chinese to Speakers of Other Languages
对外经济开发局[美国] **FEDS**	Foreign Economic Development Service
对外英语教学 **TESOL**	Teaching English to Speakers of Other Languages
对象管理体系 **OMA**	object management architecture
多(内分泌)腺性自身免疫综合征 **PGAS** polyglandular autoimmune sydrome	
多巴胺 **DA**	dopamine
多边投资协议 **MAI**	Multilateral Agreement of Investment
多波段多大气成分主被动综合探测系统 **APSOS** Atmospheric Profiling Synthetic Observation System	
多不饱和脂肪酸 **PUFA**	polyunsaturated fatty acid
多层次信息网络营销 **MLM**	multilevel information network marketing
多层共轭自适应光学 **MCAO**	multi-congugate adaptive optics
多存取计算机 **MAC**	multiaccess computer
多地址代码 **MAC**	multiple address code
多点燃油喷射 **MFI**	multipoint fuel injection
多发性硬化(症) **MS**	multiple sclerosis
多哥[非洲国家] **TOG**	Togo
多功能轿车 **MPS**	multi-purpose sedan
多功能信息分发系统 **MIDL**	multiple information divided link
多功能元件 **MFC**	multifunction component
多功能主动传感器 **MFAS**	multifunction active sensor
多光谱瞄准系统 **MTS**	multispectral aiming system
多国性银行集团 **MBG**	Multinational Banking Group
多环芳烃 **PAH(s)**	polycyclic aromatic hydrocarbon(s)

D

- 多伦多大学[加拿大] UT　　　　University of Toronto
- 多氯联苯 PCB　　　　polychlorinated biphenyls
- 多媒体短信 MMS　　　　Multimedia Messaging Service
- 多媒体个人计算机 MPC　　　　multimedia personal computer
- 多媒体广播多播技术 MBMS　　　　multi broadcast multimedia service
- 多媒体计算机辅导教学系统 MCAI　　　　multimedia computer-assisted instruction
- 多媒体接口 MMI　　　　multimedia interface
- 多媒体卡 MMC　　　　multimedia card
- 多媒体控制器 MMC　　　　multimedia controller
- 多媒体口袋式个人电脑 MPPC　　　　multimedia pocket personal computer
- 多媒体内存卡 MMC　　　　multimedia memory card
- 多媒体网络运营商 MNO　　　　multimedia network operator
- 多媒体制作工具 CCT　　　　content creation tool
- 多米加共和国[北美洲国家] DOM　　　　The Dominican Republic
- 多目标杀伤器 MOKV　　　　multi-object kill vehicle
- 多囊卵巢综合征 PCOS　　　　polycystic ovary syndrome
- 多普勒(效应) Dop　　　　Doppler
- 多普勒导航系统 DNS　　　　Doppler Navigation System
- 多器官功能障碍评分 MODS　　　　multiple organ dysfunction score
- 多人对话 MUD　　　　multiple user dialogue
- 多输入多输出 MIMO　　　　many-input and many-output
- 多系统操作员 MSO　　　　multiple system operator
- 多协议标记交换 MPLS　　　　Multiple Protocol Label Switch
- 多药耐药 MDR　　　　multidrug resistance
- 多用户层面 MUD　　　　multiple user dimension
- 多用途汽车 MPV　　　　multi-purpose vehicle
- 多用途炸弹装置 GBU　　　　general-purpose bomb unit
- 多元智能 MI　　　　multiple intelligence
- 多脏器功能衰竭综合征 MOF　　　　multiple organ failure
- 多脏器功能障碍综合征 MODS　　　　multiple organ dysfunction syndrome
- 多种项目结算凭证 MCO　　　　miscellaneous charge order
- 多住户单元 MDU　　　　Multiple Dwellers Unit

俄国嘎斯汽车[俄文] **GAZ**	Gorkovsky Avtomobilny Zavod
俄国拉达汽车 **LD**	Lada
俄国联合造船公司 **USC**	United Ship Company
俄亥俄大学图书馆中心 **OCLC**	Ohio College Library Center
俄技集团[俄文] **Rostec**	Rossiiskaia Tehnika
俄罗斯[欧洲国家] **RUS**	Russia
俄罗斯船舶登记局 **RS**	Russian Maritime Register of Shipping
俄罗斯电视台 **RT**	Russian Television
俄罗斯杜布纳联合核研究所 **JINR**	Joint Institute for Nuclear Reseach
俄罗斯国家技术集团[俄文] **Rostec**	Rostekhnologii
俄罗斯国立莫斯科大学 **MSU**	Moscow State University
俄罗斯航空公司 **RAL**	Russian Airlines
俄罗斯联邦安全局 **FSB**	Federal Safety Bureau
俄罗斯卢布 **RUB**	Russian Ruble
俄罗斯商务委员会 **RBC**	Russia Business Council
俄罗斯新闻社 **RIA**	Russian Information Agency
俄罗斯移动通信系统公司 **MTS**	Mobile Tele Systems
俄罗斯直接投资基金 **RDIF**	Russia Direct Investment Fund
俄罗斯天然气工业股份公司[俄文] **Gazprom** Gazovaia promeishliennosti	
俄印第五代战斗机 **FGFA**	fifth generation fighter aircraft
锇[第76号化学元素] **Os**	osmium
额定电压 **RV**	rated voltage
厄尔尼诺现象[西班牙文] **EN**	El Niño
厄瓜多尔[南美洲国家] **ECU**	Ecuador
恶性黑色素瘤 **MM**	malignant melanoma

E

- 恩普雷萨国家汽车公司[西班牙文] **ENASA**
  Empresa Nacional de Autocamiones SA
- 儿茶酚胺 **CA**   catecholamine
- 儿童多动症 **ADD**   attention deficit disorder
- 儿童多动综合征[德文] **ADS**   Aufmer ksamkeitsdefizit-Syndrom
- 儿童家长教育中心 **CPEC**   Children Parenting Education Centre
- 儿童权利组织国际计划 **CROPI**
  Children's Rights Organization Plan International
- 儿童信托基金 **CTF**   Children Trust Fund
- 儿童重症监护室 **PICU**   pediatric intensive care unit
- 儿童专用安全装置 **CRS**   child restraint system
- 儿媳妇 **DIL**   daughter-in-law
- 耳鼻喉(科) **ENT**   ear, nose and throat
- 铒[第 68 号化学元素] **Er**   erbium
- 二〇一九新型冠状病毒 **2019-nCoV**   2019-novel coronavirus
- 二苯羟乙酸-3-奎宁环酯 **QNB**   3-quinuclidinyl benzilate
- 二丙酸倍氯米松 **BDP**   beclomethasone dipropionate
- 二代高通量测序技术 **mNGS**   metagenomics next generation sequencing
- 二等兵 **Pte**   private
- 二极管—晶体管逻辑电路 **DTL**   diode transistor logic
- 二价口服脊髓灰质炎疫苗 **BOPY**   bivalent oral poliovirus vaccine
- 二尖瓣关闭不全 **MI**   mitral insufficiency
- 二尖瓣狭窄 **MS**   mitral stenosis
- 二进制触发器 **BFF**   Binary Flip-Flop
- 二进制代码 **BC**   Binary Code
- 二进制相移键控 **BPSK**   binary phase shift keying
- 二磷酸腺苷 **ADP**   adenosine diphosphate
- 二氢睾酮 **DHT**   dihydrotestosterone
- 二巯基扁桃酸 **DMMA**   dimercaptomandelic acid
- 二十国集团青年会议 **Y20**   Youth 20 countries
- 二十三岁以下(国家队) **U23**   Under 23
- 二十岁以下(国家队) **U20**   Under 20

二十碳五烯酸 EPA	eicosa-pentaenoic acid
二维 2D	two dimensions
二维码 QR Code	Quick Response Code
二维码 QR	quick response
二硝基甲苯（炸药）2,4-DNT	2,4-Dinitrotoluene
二氧化硫 SO_2	sulphur dioxide
二氧化碳结合力 CO_2 CP	carbon dioxide combining power
二氧化碳总量 TCO_2	carbon dioxide
二乙基焦碳酸 DEPC	diethyl pyrocarbonate
二乙基磷化氢 DEHP	diethyl hydrogen phosphide

发动机传动装置(公司)[俄文] MTU	motorno-transmissionnaia ustanovka
发动机工业协会 EIA	Engineering Industries Association
发动机控制系统 EMS	engine management system
发动机控制装置 ECU	engine control unit
发光二极管 LED	light emitting diode
发货人装箱计数 SL&C	shipper's load and count
发明 inv	invention
发怒族[因工作过分紧张而精神抑郁和脾气暴躁的人] BO Burn Out	
发泡性聚苯乙烯[塑料] EPS	expandable polystyrene
发起组织委员会 COSO	Committee of Sponsoring Organizations
发射极耦合逻辑电路 ECL	emitter coupled logic
发射型计算机断层装置 ECT	emission computer tomography
发送请求 RTS	ready-to-serve
发展生产车间 PPS	Pre-Production Shop (development)
发展研究中心 DRC	development and research center

F

- 发展援助 DA development aid
- 发展中国家委员会 CDC committee for developing countries
- 乏色曼氏反应 WR Wassermann reaction
- 法(拉)[法定电容计量单位 F farad
- 法国[欧洲国家] FRA France
- 法国《世界报》[法文] LeM Le Monde[英文: The World]
- 法国 BPCE 银行集团[法文] BPCE Banque fédérale des banques populaires + Caisse nationale des caisses d'épargne
- 法国 NRJ 电台(法国最大电台)[法文] NRJ
  National Radio de Jeunes
- 法国 RTL 电台[法文] RTL Radio-Tolbiac (Zulpich)en Lutte
- 法国巴黎第六大学 PU6 University of Paris 6
- 法国标致雪铁龙[法文] PSA Peugot Société Anoryme
- 法国标准化协会[法文] AFNOR Association Française de Normalisation
- 法国标准化协会[法文] NF
  AFNOR (Association Française de Normalisation)
- 法国产品质量认证标志[法文] NF
  AFNOR (Association Française de Normalisation)
- 法国船级社[法文] BV Bureau Veritas
- 法国达飞海运集团[法文] CMA-CGM
  Companie Maritime d'Affertment-Companie General Maritime
- 法国大学科技学院院长联盟[法文] ADIUT
  Assemblée de directeurs des Instituts Universitaires de Technologie
- 法国法郎[法国 2002 年前的货币] FF/FRF
  French Franc
- 法国工会总同盟[法文] CGT Confederation Generale du Travail
- 法国国际广播电台[法文] RFI Radio France Internationale
- 法国国际生态认证中心 ECOCERT SA Ecological Certificate SA
- 法国国家电影中心[法文] CNC Centre National de la Cinematographie
- 法国国立行政学校[法文] ENA Ecole Nationale d'Administration
- 法国国立体育运动学院[法文] INSEP
  Institut National du Sport et de l'Education Physique

- 法国国营铁路公司[法文] **SNCF**
  Société Nationale des Chemins de Fer Français
- 法国航空公司 **AF**   Air France
- 法国民航安全调查局[法文] **BEA**   Le Bureau d'Enquêtes et d'Analyses
- 法国民意调查所[法文] **IFOP**   Institut Français de I'Opinion Publique
- 法国皮诺家族[法文] **PPR**   Pinault Printemps Redoute
- 法国葡萄酒质量检验特产名酒[法文] **AOC**
  appellation d'origine contrôlée
- 法国认证标志[法文] **SGS**   Société Générale de Surveillance S. A.
- 法国色康制[彩色电视系统][法文] **SECAM**
  Sequence de Couleurs avec Memoire
- 法国石油研究院[法文] **IFP**   Institut Français du Petrole
- 法国天然气公司[法文] **GDF**   Gaz de France
- 法国文图瑞汽车 **V**   Venturi
- 法国兴业银行[法文] **SG**   Société Générale
- 法国有机种植认证标志[法文] **AB**   Agriculture Biologique
- 法国最大的电信运营商之一[法文] **SFR**
  Société Française de Radiotéléphonie
- 法拉本多·马蒂民族解放阵线[西班牙文] **FMLN**
  Frente Farabundo Marti para la Liberación Nacional
- 法拉第未来[一家全球化互联网智能出行生态企业] **FF**
  Faraday's Future
- 法拉利车队[意大利文] **SF**   Scuderia Ferrari
- 法兰西民主联盟[法文] **UDF**   Union pour la Démocratie Française
- 法利雅调配威士忌 **FPT**   Faliya peach taste
- 法律代理人 **LA**   law agent
- 法律硕士[拉丁文] **LLM**   Legum Magister
- 法律效率 **LE**   law efficiency
- 法美资本公司 **FACC**   French American Capital Corporation
- 法术伤害 **AP**   ability power
- 法新社[法国通讯社][法文] **AFP**   Agence France-Presse
- 法学博士[拉丁文] **LLD**   Legum Doctor

F

法学博士［拉丁文］DJ	Doctor Juris
法语国家国际组织［法文］OIF	Organisation Internationale de la Francophonie
法语水平测试［法文］TEF	Test d'Evaluation de Francais
法语水平考试［法文］ELI	Examen Linguistique Individuel
法语知识测试［法文］TCF	Test de Connaissance du Français
翻译 TL	translation
翻译博士学位 DTI	Doctor of Translation and Interpreting
翻译家协会 TA	Translators' Association
翻译硕士 MTI	Master of Translation and Interpreting
翻译英语语料库 TEC	Translational English Corpus
钒［第 23 号化学元素］V	vanadium
反霸凌机车帮 BACA	Bikers Against Child Abuse
反帝国主义本土核心组织 NTA	Anti-imperialist Territorial Nuclei
反辐射导弹 ARM	Anti-Radiation Missile
反击 CS	counter strike
反舰导弹 ASM	anti-ship missile
反舰巡航导弹 ASCM	anti-ship cruise missile
反恐战争 ATW	Anti-terror(ism) war
反馈 FB	feedback
反雷（的）AM	Anti-mine
反潜战 ASW	antisubmarine warfare
反潜直升机 AH	anti-submarine helicopter
反潜直升机驱逐舰［代字］DDH	destroyer, anti-submarine helicopter
反倾销 AD	anti-dumping
反倾销和联合税收理事会 DGAD	anti-dumping and allied duties
反倾销税 CVD	countervailing duties
反情报活动局 CIFA	counter-intelligence field activity
反情报战地行动 CIFA	counter-intelligence field activity
反三碘甲腺原氨酸 rT3	reverse triiodothyronine
反社会行为令 ASBO	antisocial behaviour order
反卫星武器 SK	satellite killer

421

反卫星武器 ASAT　　　　　　　　　Anti-Satellite Weapon
反洗钱金融特别行动组[西方七国首脑会议设置的机构] FATF
Financial Action Task Force on Money Laundering
反向被动凝血反应 RPHA　　　　　reversed passive hemagglutination
犯罪现场调查 CSI　　　　　　　　crime scene investigation
饭前[拉丁文] ac　　　　　　　　　ante cibos
泛非通讯社 PANA　　　　　　　　Pan-African News Agency
泛美妇女协会 PAWA　　　　　　　Pan-American Women's Association
泛美技术标准委员会[西班牙文] COPANT
Comisión Pan-americana de Normas Técnicas
泛美商业仲裁委员会 IACAC
Inter-American Commercial Arbitration Commission
泛美卫生组织 PAHO　　　　　　　Pan-American Health Organization
泛欧实时全额自动清算系统 TARGET
The Trans-European Automated Real-time Gross settlement Express Transfer
泛欧证券交收综合技术平台 T2S　　TARGET 2-Securities
泛素蛋白酶体通路 UPP　　　　　　ubiquitin proteasome pathway
泛亚通讯社[设在香港] PANA　　　Pan-Asia News Agency
方法改善 ME　　　　　　　　　　method engineering
方正公司的中文网络出版整体解决方案[作者、出版社、网络书店渠道、读者、因特网] Apabi　　　　　　　　　　　author, publisher, area, buyer, Internet
方舟操作系统[鸿蒙操作系统] ARK OS
Noah's Ark Operating System
芳香烃矿物油 MOAH　　　　　　mineral oil aromatic hydrocarbons
钫[第87号化学元素] Fr　　　　　francium
防地雷反伏击车 MRAP　　　　　　mine resistant ambush protected vehicle
防滑驱动控制系统[德文] ASR　　anti-schlitten regelung
防滑制动系统 ABS　　　　　　　　anti-skid braking system
防刻死技术 BURN-Proof　　　　　buffer underrun proof
防空部队 ADF　　　　　　　　　　Air Defence Force
防空的 AA　　　　　　　　　　　antiaircraft
防空识别区 ADIZ　　　　　　　　Air Defense Identification Zone

F

防晒因子 SPF	Sun-protection factor
防守艾滋病套房 DAS	defensive Aids suites
防眩目系统 ADS	anti-dizzy system
防止滑转调节[控制]系统 ASR	anti-slip regulation (control)
防紫外线标准 PA	Protection Grade of UVA
房地产 RE/RLEST	real estate
房地产信托基金 REITs	real estate investment trusts
房间隔缺损 ASD	atrial septal defect
房间智能化系统 IRS	intelligent room system
房室全能型(心脏起搏器) DDD	double chambers-double chambers-double
房屋互助协会 S&L	savings and loan association
房租津贴 MAQ	money allowance for quarters
仿佛是说[拉丁文] q. d.	quasi dictum
仿人机器人[韩国产] Hubo	Humanoid Robot
访问部队地位协定 VFA	Visiting Forces Agreement
访问服务器 AS	access server
访问控制表 ACL	access control list
访问量 S	session
访问量百分比 SP	session percentage
纺织工程学士 BTE	bachelor of textile engineering
放射免疫导向手术 RIGS	radioimmunoguided surgery
放射免疫分析(法) RIA	radioimmunoassay
放射性碘摄取率 RAIU	radioactive iodine uptake

飞(母托)[十进分数单位的词头名称,其表示因数为 10^{-15}] F
femto

飞碟汽车[中国浙江] UFO	Unidentified Flying Object
飞行控制 FC	flight control
飞行试验中心 FTC	Flight Test Center
飞行数据记录器 FDR	flight data recorder
飞虎队 SDU	Special Duties Unit

飞机材料购买者委员会 CPAM
Committee of Purchasers of Aircraft Material

飞机库 **gar**	garage
飞机起落架 **LG**	landing gear

飞米[法定长度计量单位],1 飞米＝10^{-15} 米] **fm**
femtometer

非暴力行为和战略中心 **CANVAS**	
Center of Action of Non-Violence and Strategy	
非常 **V**	very
非常好的(钱币) **VG**	very good
非常滑稽的 **LOL**	laugh-out-loud
非常久远(的酒) **XO**	extra old
非常美的女人[网络用语] **BBW**	big beautiful woman
非处方药 **OTC**	Over the Counter
非典型肺炎 **SARS**	Severe Acute Respiratory Syndrome
非独立组网 **NSA**	non-stand alone
非法、不报告、不管制捕捞 **IUUF**	illegal, unreported, uncontrolled fishing
非法移民 **il**	illegal immigrant
非结构化补充数据业务 **USSD**	unstructured supplementary service data
非酒精性脂肪性肝病 **NAFLD**	non-alcoholic fatty liver disease
非类固醇类抗炎药 **NSAID(s)**	non-steroid antiinflammatory drug(s)
非联合国会员国家及民族组织 **UNPO**	
The Unrepresented Nations and Peoples Organization	
非临界相位匹配 **NCPM**	non-critical phase matched
非耐油 **N**	not resistant to oil
非浓缩还原汁 **NFC**	not from concentrate
非商业性质的新汽车安全试验组织 **IFL**	
Informed For Life	
非石油输出国组织成员国 **OPEC plus**	
Organization of Petroleum Exporting Countries plus	
非诉讼纠纷解决机制 **ADR**	alternative dispute resolution
非线性而指数级增比 **NXP**	nonlinear exponential increase ratio
非线性光学晶体 **KBBF**	

$KBe_2BO_3F_2$ [potassium fluoroboratoberyllate]

F

非相位匹配 NPM	non phase matched
非小细胞肺癌 NSCLC	non-small cell lung cancer
非医学教育和训练 NMET	non-medical education and training
非裔、亚裔及其他少数族裔 BAME	Black, Asian, and minority ethnic
非营利组织 NPO	non-profitable organization
非战斗人员撤离行动 NEO	non-combatant evacuation operation
非政府开发项目 NDI	Non-Government Development Item
非政府组织 NGO	Non-Governmental Organization
非洲、加勒比海和太平洋国家 ACP	African, Caribbean & Pacific Countries
非洲 Afr	Africa
非洲发展新伙伴计划 NEPAD	

The New Partnership for Africa's Development

非洲经济委员会 ECA	Economic Commission for Africa
非洲淋巴细胞瘤病毒 EB	Epstein Barr virus
非洲美国传记数据库 AABD	African American Biographical Database
非洲人 Afr	African
非洲统一组织 AUO	African Unity Organization
非洲统一组织 OAU	Organization of African Unity
非洲虚拟大学 AVU	The African Virtual University
非洲猪瘟病毒 ASFV	African swine fever virus
非洲猪瘟病毒毒株 Pig/HLJ/18	African swine fever virus strain
非洲足球联合会 AFC	African Football Confederation
非洲足球联合会 CAF	Confederation of African Football
菲朗氏调配威士忌 FW	Flylions whisky
菲律宾标准 PS	Philippine Standards
菲律宾产品标准局 PSA	Product Standards Agency
菲律宾产品认证标志 PS	Philippine Standards
菲律宾慈善博彩办公室 PCSO	Philippine Charity Sweepstakes Office
菲律宾共产党/新人民军 CPP/NPA	

Communist Party Philippines/New People's Army

| 菲律宾国家石油公司 PNOC | Philippine National Oil Co. |

F

- 菲律宾蕉农暨出口商协会 **PBGEA**
  Philippines Banana Growers and Exporters Association
- 菲律宾通讯社 **PNA**　　　　　Philippine News Agency
- 菲律宾伊斯兰教士理事会 **IDCP**　Islamic Dawah Council of the Philipines
- 菲律宾长途电话公司 **PLDTC**
  Philippine Long Distance Telephone Company
- 菲亚特汽车[原义:意大利都灵汽车厂][意大利文] **Fiat**
  Fabbrica Italiana Automobile Torino
- 肥厚型非梗阻性心肌病 **HNCM**
  hypertrophic nonobstructive cardiomyopathy
- 肥厚型心肌病 **HCM**　　　　　hypertrophic cardiomyopathy
- 斐济[大洋洲国家] **FIJ**　　　　Fiji
- 肺活量 **VC**　　　　　　　　vital capacity
- 肺结核病 **TB**　　　　　　　tuberculosis
- 肺科重症监护室 **PICU**　　　　pulmonary intensive care unit
- 肺泡气和动脉血氧分压差 **P(A-a) O_2**　alveolar-arterial oxygen tension difference
- 肺泡死腔 **VDals**　　　　　　alveolar dead space
- 肺泡氧分压 **PAO$_2$**　　　　alveolar oxygen partial pressure
- 肺心病 **CP**　　　　　　　　corpulmonale
- 肺氧弥散量 **DLO$_2$**　　　　diffusing capacity of the lungs for oxygen
- 肺一氧化碳弥散量 **DLCO**
  diffusing capacity of the lungs for carbon monoxide
- 废气处理系统 **TEG**　　　　　effluent gas treatment system
- 废气再循环 **EGR**　　　　　　exhaust gas recirculation
- 废气循环 **EGR**　　　　　　　exhaust gas recirculation
- 镄[第100号化学元素] **Fm**　　fermium
- 分贝[表示功率比和声音强度的单位] **dB**
  decibel
- 分布式对象计算架构 **DOCA**　　dynamic object computing architecture
- 分布式分类账技术 **DLT**　　　distributed ledger technology
- 分布式网络系统服务器 **DNS**　　distributed network server
- 分开同居者 **LAT**　　　　　　living apart together

F

分类 CAT	category
分类的 C	classified
分流管 MANIF	manifold
分流管空气压力 MAP	manifold air pressure
分散控制系统 DCS	dispose control system
分委员会 SC	subcommittee
分钟 min	minute（s）
芬兰标准协会[芬兰文] SFS	Suomen Standardisoimisliittory
芬兰电工标准委员会[芬兰文] SESKO	

Suomen Sahkötecknillinen Standardisoimiskomitea

| 芬兰电气认证标志 FI | Finland |
| 芬兰非电气产品质量认证标志[芬兰文] SFS | |

Suomen Standardisoimisliittory

芬兰赫尔辛基大学 UH	University of Helsinki
酚醛树脂 PF	phenol-formaldehyde resin
粉红色 P	pink
丰巢概念 TNGA	Toyota New Global Architecture
丰富的幽默感 GSOH	good sense of humour
风湿性关节炎 RA	rheumatic arthritis
风险调整后的绩效指标 RAPM	risk-adjusted performance measure
风险投资（商） VC	Venture Capital
风险投资/私募股权 vc/pe	venture capital/private equity
风险投资循环模型 VCM	Venture Cycle Model
风险优先数 RPN	risk priority number
风支持空投系统 WSADS	Wind Support Airdrop System
峰值 PV	peak value
蜂窝数字分组数据 CDPD	cellular digital packet data
佛得角[非洲国家] CPV	Cape Verde
否定的 neg	negative
夫精人工授精 AIH	artificial insemination by husband
夫妻配对[一般是漫画同人拿来自配的] CP	

couple

- 夫人[法文] **Mdme** — Madame
- 夫人 **Mdm** — Madam
- 夫人 **Mrs** — mistress
- 伏(特)[法定电位差、电压、电动势计量单位] **V** — volt
- 服务 **SV** — serve
- 发动机 **ENG** — engine
- 服务器平台服务 **PaaS** — platform-as-a-service
- 服务水平协议 **SLA** — Service-Level Agreement
- 服务提供商 **SP** — service provider
- 服役日期 **DOR** — date of rank
- 氟[第 9 号化学元素] **F** — fluorine
- 氟代硼铍酸钾 **KBBF** — $KBe_2BO_3F_2$
- 氟利昂 **CFCs** — chlorofluorocarbons
- 浮式生产储存卸货装置[西班牙文] **EPSO** — Ecuatorial, Escuela Profesional Socrates
- 浮式生产储油卸油装置 **FPSO** — floating production storage and offloading unit
- 符号最优汇编程序 **SOAP** — symbolic optimum assembly programming
- 符号汇编程序 **SAP** — symbolic assembly program
- 符合性评定机构 **CAB** — Conformity Assessment Body
- 辐射防护标准 **RPS** — Radiation Protection Standards
- 福迪汽车[中国佛山:汉语缩略语] **F** — Fudi
- 福建海峡高速客轮航运有限公司 **CSF** — Fujian Cross Strait Ferry Corporation
- 福克斯新闻频道 **FNC** — Fox News Channel
- 福特基金会 **FF** — Ford Foundation
- 辅酶 Q10/**CoQ10** — Coenzyme Q-10
- 辅助出版物 **SP** — support publications
- 辅助存储器 **AM** — auxiliary memory
- 辅助聚焦 **FA** — focus aid
- 辅助全球卫星定位系统 **AGPS** — assistant global positioning system

F

辅助生殖技术 ART	Assisted Reproductive Technologies
腐败控制指数 CC	corruption control (index)
讣闻 obit	obituary
付费电视 PTV	pay television
付款后装船 CBS	cash before shipment
付息抽税前收益 EBIT	earnings before interest and taxes
负债 L	liability
妇女、和平与安全 WPS	women, peace and security
妇女健康计划 WHI	Women Health Initiative
妇女进取计划 WIN	Women's Initiative Program
妇女协会 WI	Women's Institute
妇婴幼儿 WIC	women, infants and children
附加线路 EL	extra line
附加总值 GVA	gross value added
附言[拉丁文] PS	postscriptum
附言 ps	postscript
复旦大学 FU	Fudan University

复旦发展研究院金融研究中心 FDFRC
Fudan University Development Financial Research Center

| 复发性多发性硬化症 RMS | re-multiple sclerosis |

复方阿司匹林[由阿司匹林、非那西汀和咖啡因制成的一种解热镇痛药] APC
Aspirin-phenacetin-caffein

复合控制涡流燃烧式发动机 CVCC	compound vortex controlled combustion
复合年均增长率 CAGR	compound annual growth rate
复合通行卡 CPC	composite pass card
复数 pl	plural
复兴信贷银行[德文] KfW	Kreditanstalt für Wiederaufbau
复杂区域疼痛综合征 CRPS	complicated region pain syndrome
副本 CC	carbon copy
副官[法文] ADC	aide-de-camp
副总经理、副总裁 VP	vice president
副总统[口语用法,昵称] Veep	vice-president

傅丹[丹麦籍,越南出生] **Danh Vo**	Danish, Vietnam
富时指数公司 **FTSE**	Financial Times Stock Exchange
富时 100 指数[英国最权威最有代表性的股价指数] **FTSE100**	
Financial Times Stock Exchange 100 Index	
腹部主动脉瘤 **AAA**	abdominal aortic aneurysm
腹泻型肠易激综合征 **IBS—D**	irritable bowel syndrome with diarrhea

G

嘎斯汽车[俄国] **GAZ**	Gorkovsky Avtomobilny Zavod
钆[第 64 号化学元素] **Gd**	gadolinium
改进型联络支援装置 **ICSS**	improved contact support set
改良的热磨机械浆方法 **ATMP**	
Advanced Thermal Grinding Machanical Pulping Process	
钙[第 20 号化学元素] **Ca**	calcium
钙红色 **Cal-Red**	calcium-red
钙激活因子 **CAF**	calcium activated factor
概念层次网络 **HNC**	hierarchical network of concepts
概念设计报告 **CDR**	conceptual design report
概念验证 **POC**	proof of concept
甘胆酸 **CG**	cholyglycine
甘露糖 **Man**	mannose
甘油三(酸)酯 **TC**	triglyceride
肝癌 **HCC**	hepatocellular carcinoma
肝癌细胞 **HCC**	hepatoma carcinoma cell
肝功能残气量 **FRC**	functional residual capacity (of livers)
肝细胞癌 **HCC**	hepatic cellular cancer
肝细胞生长因子 **HGF**	hepatocyte growth factor
肝炎相关抗体 **HAA**	hepatitis associated antibody

G

肝炎相关抗原 HAA	hepatitis associated antigen
干热岩 DHR	dry hot rock
干热岩体 DGF	dry geothermal formation
干细胞因子 SCF	stem cell factor
干燥综合征 A 抗原 SS-A	sjögren syndrome-A antigen
干燥综合征 B 抗原 SS-B	sjögren syndrome-B antigen
干燥综合征 SS	sjögren syndrome
感染性心内膜炎 IE	infectious endocarditis
感谢 thx/tx	thanks
橄榄油 ol ol	olive oil
冈比亚[非洲国家] GAM	Gambia
刚果(布)[非洲国家] CGO	Congo
刚果(金)[非洲国家] COD	Congo(D. R.)
钢筋混凝土协会 CRSA	Concrete Reinforcement Steel Association
缸径/行程 B/S	bore/stroke
缸径行程比 B/S	bore-to-stroke
港元[货币] HKD	Hong Kong Dollar
高保真(度) HI-FI	high-fidelity
高层大气现象 UAP	upper atmosphere phenomena
高超音速常规打击武器 HCSW	hypersonic convention strike weapon
高超音速研究飞机 HRA	hypersonic research airplane
高出用户期望 ACE	above customer expectation
高等教育 HE	Higher Education
高等教育改善基金 FIPSE	
Fund for the Improvement of Postsecondary Education	
高等教育协会 AHE	Association for Higher Education
高等教育质量保证署 QAA	
Quality Assurance Agency for Higher Education	
高地球轨道 HEO	High Earth Orbit
高碘酸希夫染色 PAS	periodic acid-schiff stain
高动态范围(图像) HDR	high-dynamic rang
高度敏感的人[网络用语] HSP	highly sensitive person

高尔夫球俱乐部 GC	Golf Club
高分泌性慢性胃炎 HCG	hypersecretory chronic gastritis
高工锂电产业研究所 GBII	Gaogong lithium Battery Industry Institute
高功率微波 HPM	high power microware
高机动多用途轮式车辆 HMMWV	high mobility multipurpose wheeled vehicle
高级白兰地 VSOP	very superior old pale
高级编程语言 HPL	high-level programming language
高级编码标准的加密算法 AES	Advanced Encryption Standard
高级补充程度考试 AS	Advanced Subsidiary
高级操作系统 sup OS	superior operation system
高级持续性威胁 APT	Advanced Persistent Threat
高级访问内容系统 AACS	Advanced Access Content System

高级管理人员工商管理硕士学位 EMBA
Executive Master of Business Administration

高级人力资源专业认证 SPHR	Senior Profession of Human Resource
高级网络工程师 Master CNE	master computer net engineer
高级线性程序设计系统 ALPS	advanced linear programming system
高级移动电话服务 AMPS	advanced mobile phone service
高级音频编码技术 AAC	advanced audio coding
高级战斗头盔 ACH	advanced combat helmet
高级中学[美国] Sr HS	senior high school
高阶调制 PSK	phase shift keying
高精度驱动器 HDD	high-precision drive
高净值人士 HNWI	high-net-worth individual
高抗冲聚苯乙烯[塑料] HIPS	high impact polystyrene
高考英语 NMET	National Matriculation English Test
高科技 HT/Hi-Tech	high technology

高科技研究和发展项目 HTRDP
High Technology Research & Development Program

高空长航时的"碎片" Hale-D	high altitude, long-endurance-debris
高离层研究仪器 IRI	Ionosphere Research Instrument
高岭土部分凝血活酶时间 KPTT	kaolin partial thromboplastin time

G

高密度 HD	high density
高密度航空合金 HDF	high density ferroalloy
高密度聚乙烯［塑料］HDPE	high density polyethylene
高密度数据 HDD	high density data
高密度只读光盘 DVD-ROM	DVD-Read Only Memory
高密度脂蛋白 HDL	high density lipoprotein
高密度脂蛋白胆固醇 HDL-C(h)	high density lipoprotein cholesterol
高频 HF	high frequency
高频超视距雷达 HFOTHR	high frequency over-the-horizon radar

高频地波超视距雷达 HFGWOTHR
high frequency ground wave over-the-horizon radar

高频电磁仿真系统 HFESS
High Frequency Electromagnetic Simulation System

高频天波超视距雷达 HFSWOTHR
high frequency sky wave over-the-horizon radar

高频主动极光研究项目 HFAARP
High Frequency Active Auroral Research Program

高强度放电 HID	high intensity discharge
高强度间隙训练法 HIIT	high intensity interval training
高强度聚焦超声肿瘤治疗系统 HFU	high intensity focused ultrasound
高清广播 HDR	high definition radio
高清摄像机 HDR	high definition recorder
高清数字电影播放机 HVD	high definition video decoder
高清晰度 HD	high definition
高清晰度电视 HDTV	high definition TV
高清晰度多媒体接口 HDMI	high definition multimedia interface
高清晰度光碟 HDCD	high definition compact disk
高清晰度视频系统 HDVS	high definition video system
高射炮 AA	ack-ack
高速船 HSV	high speed vessel
高速打印机 HSP	High Speed Printer
高速数字用户线路 HDSL	high-speed digital subscriber line

G

- 高速铁路 HSR — high-speed railway
- 高速下行的分组接入 HSDPA — high-speed downlink packet access
- 高速装配 PTQ — put together quickly
- 高铁[法文] TGV — train à grande vitesse
- 高吞吐量计算 HTC — high-throughout computing
- 高香草酸 HVA — homovanillic
- 高效空气过滤器 HEFA — high efficient filter of air
- 高效能 HP — high potency
- 高新技术产品或服务 PS — product or service
- 高性能 HP — high performance
- 高性能计算 HPC — high performance computing
- 高性能计算机 HPC — high performance computer
- 高性能旅游乘用车 GTC — grand touring car
- 高压氧 HBO — hyperbaric oxygen
- 高中毕业文凭 GED — General Equivalency Diploma
- 睾(丸)酮 T — testosterone
- 糕点 TUC — tuck
- 锆[第 40 号化学元素] Zr — zirconium
- 哥伦比亚[南美洲国家] COL — Colombia
- 哥伦比亚产品质量认证标志[西班牙文] ICONIEC
  Instituto Colombiano de Normas Técnicas
- 哥伦比亚大学医学中心 CUMC — Columbia University Medical Center
- 哥伦比亚革命武装力量[西班牙文] FARC
  Fuerzas Armadas Revolucionarias de Colombia
- 哥伦比亚技术标准协会[西班牙文] ICONIEC
  Instituto Colombiano de Normas Técnicas
- 哥伦比亚民族解放军[西班牙文] ELN
  Ejército de Liberación Nacional
- 哥伦比亚中央抵押银行[西班牙文] BCH
  Banco Central Hipotecario
- 哥斯达黎加[北美洲国家] CRC — Costa Rica
- 鎶[第 112 号化学元素] Cn — copernicium

G

革命组织党[西班牙文] **PRI**	Partido Revolucionario Institucional
阁下 **HE**	Her/His Excellency
阁下 **Rt Hon**	Right Honourable
阁下[法文] **Mgr**	Monsignor
格斗锦标赛 **FC**	fighting championship
格斗类游戏 **FTG**	fight technology game
格林纳达[北美洲国家] **GRN**	Grenada
格林尼治(天文)平均时 **GMT**	Greenwich Mean (astronomical) Time
格林尼治平均时 **Z-time**	zebra time
格陵兰—冰岛—英国 **GIUK**	Greenland-Iceland-UK
格鲁吉亚[欧洲国家] **GEO**	Georgia

格鲁曼电子情报收集飞机[又名:入侵者收集飞机] **EA-6B**
Grumman electronic-intelligence-gathering aircraft named Intruder

格式标识符 **FI**	format identifier
格式接口管理系统 **FIMS**	form interface management system
隔离带 **ZOS**	zone of separation
隔热垫 **INSUL**	insulator
镉[第48号化学元素] **Cd**	cadmium

个人、社会、健康和经济教育 **PSHEE**
personal, social, health and economic education

个人储蓄账户 **ISA**	individual savings account
个人电脑 **PC**	personal computer
个人防护设备 **PPE**	personal protective equipment

个人计算机磁盘操作系统 **PC-DOS**
Personal Computer Disk Operating System

个人计算机存储卡国际协会 **PCMCIA**
Personal Computer Memory Card International Association

个人捷运 **PRT**	Personal Rapid Transit
个人解锁码 **PUK**	personal unlocking key
个人可支配收入 **DPI**	discretionary [disposable] personal income
个人可支配收入 **PDI**	personal disposable income
个人履历 **PR**	Personal Record

个人全能比赛 IAAC	individual all-around competition
个人全能决赛 IAAF	individual all-around finals
个人身份识别号码 PIN	Personal Identification Number
个人视频录像机 PVR	personal video recorder
个人数字助理 PDA	Personal Digital Assistant
个人通信网络 PCN	Personal Communication Network
个人通信业务 UPT	universal personal telecommunication
个人项目页 PPP	personal projects page
个人消费支出 PCE	personal consumption expenditure
个人信息管理 PIM	Personal Information Management
个人信息助理 PIA	Personal Information Assistant
个人移动通信 PMC	Personal Mobile Communication
个人知识管理 PKM	personal knowledge management
个人最好成绩 PB	personal best
个性化教学法 PSI	Personalized System of Instruction
各种各样的东西 AKT	all kinds of things
铬[第24号化学元素] Cr	chromium
给水与排污委员会 WSC	Water and Sewerage Commission
给我[口语] gimme	give me
跟单付款委托书 DPO	documentary payment order
跟踪控制系统 TCS	track control system
庚肝抗体 HGVAb	hepatitis G virus antibody
更改设计请求 CDR	change design request
工厂管理 PM	plant management
工厂条件评估 WCA	workplace conditions assessment
工厂自动化 FA	factory automation
工程-采购-合同施工总承包模式 EPC	engineering-procurement-contruction
工程变更通知 ECN	engineer change notice
工程变更需求 ECR	engineer change request
工程动力反应堆 EPR	engineering power reactor
工程管理指数 PMI	Project Management Index

G

- 工程教育模式设计制造及其自动化专业课程简介 **CDIO**
  Conceive Design Implement Operate
- 工程开发模型 **EDM**   engine development model
- 工程硕士 **ME**   Master of Engineering
- 工程物料清单 **E-BOM**   engineering bill of material
- 工党 **Lab**   Labour
- 工商管理博士 **DBA**   Doctor of Business Administration
- 工商管理硕士 **MBA**   Master of Business Administration
- 工商管理硕士协会 **AMBA**
  Association of Master of Business Administration
- 工商局 **AIC**   Administration of Industry and Commerce
- 工商协会 **CIA**   Commerce and Industries Association
- 工效学 **HFE**   Human Factors Engineering
- 工学士 **BE**   Bachelor of Engineering
- 工业(用)电视 **ITV**   industrial television
- 工业标准(体系)结构 **ISA**   industry standard architecture
- 工业发展委员会 **CID**   Committee for Industrial Development
- 工业管理 **IE**   industrial engineering
- 工业和安全局 **BIS**   Bureau of Industry and Security
- 工业机器人 **R**   industrial robot
- 工业教育委员会 **TEC**   Technical Education Council
- 工业界的一种颜色标准[三基色:红、绿、蓝] **RGB**
  red, green, blue
- 工业品质管理学 **IQM**   Industrial Quality Management
- 工业与安全局 **BIS**   Board of Industry and Security
- 工业咨询委员会[英国] **IAB**   Industry Advisory Board
- 工艺工程师 **PE**   process engineer
- 工作草案 **WD**   working draft
- 工作组 **WG**   working group
- 公安部公民网络电子身份标识 **SIMeID**
  Subscriber Identification Module electronic identity
- 公吨 **M/T**   metric ton

公公 **FIL**	father-in-law
公共（交通）车辆 **PSV**	public service vehicle
公共产品 **PG**	public goods
公共服务职业 **PSE**	Public Service Employment
公共关系 **PR**	public relation
公共管理博士 **DPA**	doctor of public administration
公共管理硕士 **MPA**	master of public administration
公共广播公司 **CPB**	Corporation for Public Broadcasting
公共科学图书馆 **PLOS**	Public Library of Science
公共利益科学中心 **CSPI**	Center for Science in the Public Interest
公共密钥密码系统 **PKC**	Public Key Cryptosystem
公共汽车快速个人客运 **PRT**	personal rapid transit
公共投资基金 **PIF**	public investment fund
公共卫生保健 **PHC**	public health care
公共卫生硕士 **MPH**	Master of Public Health
公共英语考试 **PET**	Public English Test
公共英语考试系统 **PETS**	Public English Test System
公关人士 **PRP**	public relation personnel
公海 **HS**	high seas
公斤 **kg**	kilogram
公开股份公司 **PLC**	public limited company
公开密钥基础设施 **PKI**	public key infrastructure
公开上市公司 **PLC**	public listed company
公里/小时 **km/h**	kilometer/hour
公亩［1公亩等于100平方米］**a** acre	
公平、合理和不带歧视性的条款 **FRAND** fair, reasonable, and non-discriminatory terms	
公平贸易委员会［英国］**FTC**	Fair Trade Commission
公顷［非法定面积计量单位，1公顷＝10 000平方米］**ha** hectare	
公认的会计准则 **GAAP**	generally accepted accounting principles

公认会计师 CA	chartered accountant
公式处理编译程序 FORMAC	formula manipulation compiler
公式转换语言 FORTRAN	formula translation
公司[多用于澳大利亚和南非] Pty	proprietary
公司[荷兰文] Mij/MPY	Maatschappij
公司管理认证 CICA	Certificate in Company Administration
公司形象 CI	Corporate Identity
公私合作模式 PPP	public-private-partnership
公用交换电话网 PSTN	Public Switched Telephone Network
公有潜在能力模型 CUP	common underlying proficiency model
公元[拉丁文] AD	Anno Domini
公元前 BCE	before the Common Era
公元前[拉丁文] AC	ante Christum
公元前 BC	before Christ
公园 P	park
公证员 NP	notary public
功夫 K	kung fu
功能核心 FCore	function core
功能检验装置 FCS	functional checkout set
功能强大、调用方便的底层图形库 open GL open graphics library	
功能性核磁共振 FMRI	Functional Magnetic Resonance Imaging
功能性消化不良 FD	functional dyspepsia
宫内避孕器 ICD	intrauterine contraceptive device
供精人工授精 AID	Artificial Insemination by Donor
汞[第 80 号化学元素][拉丁文] Hg	hydrargyrum
共产党 CP	Communist Party
共产主义青年团 CYL	Communist Youth League
共轭亚油酸 CLA	conjugated linoleic acid
共和党(党员) R	Republican
共和废品处理公司 RS	Republic Services
共同海关税则 CCT	Common Customs Tariff

共同农业政策 **CAP**	common agriculture policy
共同申报准则 **CRS**	Common Reporting Standard
共同税务汇报系统 **CRS**	common reporting standard
共同天线电视 **CATV**	community antenna television
共享无线接入协议 **SWAP**	Shared Wireless Access Protocol
共用天线电视 **MATV**	master antenna television
供参考 **FYR**	for your reference
供参考 **FYI**	for your information
供应管理协会 **ISM**	Institute for Supply Management
供应链管理 **SCM**	supply chain management
供应链管理经理 **SCM**	supply chain manager
供应商品质工程师 **SQE**	supplier quality engineer
供应商质量持续改善 **SCQI**	supporter continuous quality improvement
狗舍俱乐部［英国］**KC**	Kennel Club
购买力平价［相对购买力指标］**PPP**	Purchasing-Power Parity
购买力指数 **BPI**	Buying Power Index
够好就行 **JGE**	just good enough
孤儿药物认定 **ODD**	orphan drug Designation
古阿姆［由格鲁吉亚、乌克兰、阿塞拜疆、摩尔多瓦四国成立的非正式的地区联盟］**GUAM**	Georgia、Ukraine、Azerbaijan、Moldova
古巴［北美洲国家］**CUB**	Cuba
古巴国家标准化委员会［西班牙文］**NC** Comite Estatal de Normalization	
古龙水（香精含量4%～8%）［法文］**EDC** eau de cologne	
古琦时装 **GG**	Guccio Gucci
谷（氨酸）丙（酮酸）转氨酶 **GPT**	glutamic pyruvic transaminase
谷氨酸脱氢酶 **GDH/GLDH**	glutamic dehydrogenase
谷氨酰转肽酶 **GGT**	gamma-glutamyl transpeptidase
谷丙转氨酶 **ALT**	alanine aminotransferase
谷草转氨酶/天冬氨酸转氨酶 **GOT/AST** glutamic oxaloacetic transaminase/aspartate aminotransferase	

G

- 谷歌神经机器翻译系统 GNMT　　　　Google Neural Machine Translation
- 谷歌移动服务(认证) GMS　　　　　　Google Mobile Service(Certified)
- 谷歌邮件 Gmail　　　　　　　　　　　Google mail
- 谷胱甘肽-S-转移酶 GST　　　　　　　glutathione-S-transferase
- 谷丙转氨酶 GPT　　　　　　　　　　glutamic-pyruvic transaminase
- 谷草转氨酶 GOT　　　　　　　　　　glutamic-oxaloacetic transaminase
- 股本 CS　　　　　　　　　　　　　　capital stock
- 股本收益(股东权益报酬率) ROE　　　return on equity
- 股份公司(意大利文) SPA　　　　　　Società per Azioni
- 股份公司[德文] AG　　　　　　　　　Aktien Gesellschaft
- 股份公司[俄文] AO　　　　　　　　　Aktsionernoi Obshestvo
- 股份公司[葡萄牙文] SA　　　　　　　Sociedade Anónima
- 股份公司[西班牙文] SA　　　　　　　Sociedad Anónima
- 股份有限公司[德文] GmbH　　　　　　Gesellschaft mit beschränkter Haftung
- 股份有限公司[马来文] Bhd　　　　　　Berhad
- 股份有限公司[日文] KK　　　　　　　Kabushiki Kaisha
- 股份有限公司[西班牙文] SRL　　　　　Sociedad de Responsabilidad Limitada
- 股份有限公司[用于德国、瑞士、奥地利等国][德文] AG Aktien gesellschaft
- 股份有限公司 Inc　　　　　　　　　　incorporated
- 股票编号 SN　　　　　　　　　　　　stock number
- 股票除息除权 DR　　　　　　　　　　dividend right
- 股票价格指数期货 SPIF　　　　　　　Share Price Index Futures
- 股票交易所 SE　　　　　　　　　　　stock exchange
- 股票期权 ESO　　　　　　　　　　　executive stock options
- 股票市场 SM　　　　　　　　　　　　stock market
- 股票特别处理 ST　　　　　　　　　　special treatment
- 骨矿物质密度 BMD　　　　　　　　　bone mineral density
- 骨锚式助听器 BAHA　　　　　　　　bone anchored hearing aid
- 骨膜三角 CT　　　　　　　　　　　　codman triangle
- 骨髓增生异常综合征 MDS　　　　　　myelodysplastic syndrome
- 骨性关节炎 OA　　　　　　　　　　　osteoarthritis

骨源性碱性磷酸酶 BAP	blood bone alkaline phosphatase
骨质疏松症 O	osteoporosis
钴[第 27 号化学元素] Co	cobalt
固态技术协会 SSTA	Solid State Technology Association
固态驱动器 SSD	solid state driver
固态悬浮物 SS	solid suspension
固态硬盘 SSD	solid state disk
故障报告中心 FRC	Fault Reporting Center
故障分析报告 FAR	failure analysis report
故障模式与影响分析 FMEA	failure mode and effect analysis
故障影响分析 FEA	failure effect analysis
故障原因数据报告 FCDR	failure cause data reporting
故障指示器灯 MIL	malfunction indicator lamp
故障致命性分析 FCA	Failure Criticality Analysis
顾客满意指数 CSI	Customer Satisfaction Index
关岛[太平洋美国所属岛屿] GUM	Guam
关键绩效指标 KPI	Key Performance Indicator
关键系统操作中心 CSOC	Critical Systems Operations Center

关键意见领袖（微博上有话语权的人或微博红人大号）KOL
key opinion leader

| 关税合作理事会 CC | Customs Co-operation Council |

关税及贸易总协定（现已被 WTO 所取代）GATT
General Agreement on Tariffs and Trade

观察、熟悉[判断]、决策、行动（循环）OODA
observation, orientation, decision and action

观察研究基金会 ORF	observation research fund
官方代表基金 ORF	official representation fund
官方售价 OS	official selling price
管理层收购 MBO	management buyout

管理程序可靠性信息系统 PRISM
program reliability information system for management

G

- 管理发展研究所 IMD　　institute of management and development
- 管理工程学 ME　　Management Engineering
- 管理和金融办公室 OMF　　office of management and finance
- 管理会计师协会 SMA　　Society of Management Accountants
- 管理培训生 MT　　management trainee
- 管理信息系统 MIS　　management information system
- 管理员 Admin　　administrator
- 管理员控制台 SCC　　supervisor control console
- 管理者胜任素质测评（系统）MTS　　Manager Testing Solution
- 管理专业研究生入学考试 GMAT　　Graduate Management Admission Test
- 管理专业研究生入学考试委员会 GMAC　　Graduate Management Admission Council
- 冠心病 CAD　　coronary artery disease
- 冠心病监护病房 CCU　　Coronary Care Unit
- 冠状病毒研究小组 CSG　　coronavirus study group
- 惯性导航系统 INS　　inertial navigation system
- 光电系统 EOS　　electro-optical system
- 光碟 CD　　compact disc
- 光动力疗法 PDT　　photodynamic therapy
- 光分支存储器 LITASTOR　　light tapping storage
- 光符识别 OCR　　optical character recognition
- 光盘[电子文献标示字母] CD　　compact disc
- 光盘图书[电子文献标示略语] M/CD　　monograph/compact disc
- 光纤到办公室 FTTO　　fiber to the office
- 光纤到大楼 FTTB　　fiber to the building
- 光纤到家庭 FTTH　　fiber to the home
- 光纤到小区 FTTZ　　fiber to the zone
- 光纤滤波器技术 FBG　　fiber bragg gratings
- 光纤网络 FON　　fiber optic network
- 光学参量放大器 OPA　　optical parametric amplifier
- 光学参量振荡器 OPO　　optical parametric oscillator

- 光学纤维 **OF**   optical fibre
- 广播电台 **RD**   radio
- 广播卫星业务 **BSS**   Broadcast Satellite Service
- 广播系统 **PA**   public address system
- 广场 **Sq**   square
- 广东财经大学 **GDUFE**
  Guangdong University of Finance and Economics
- 广东发展银行 **GDB**   Guangdong Development Bank
- 广东金融学院 **GDUF**   Guangdong University of Finance
- 广东犬类俱乐部 **GKC**   Guangdong Kennel Club
- 广东外语外贸大学 **GUFS**   Guangdong University of Foreign Studies
- 广泛的概括[网络用语] **BSG**   broad sweeping generalization
- 广泛机构公告 **BAA**   broad-agency announcement
- 广告 **Ad**   advertisement
- 广告传媒业领域的行业贡献者 **ADMEN**
  Advertisement Men
- 广告黄金收视时间 **BTA**   Best Time Available
- 广告影片 **CF**   commercial film
- 广义货币(供应量) **M2**   Broad Money
- 广域海上无人监视 **BAMS**   Broad Area Maritime Surveillance
- 广域网 **WAN**   Wide Area Network
- 广域增强系统 **WAAS**   wide area augmentation system
- 广州大学城 **HEMC**   Higher Education Mega Center
- 广州青年组织 **CATO**   Cantonese Teenager Organization
- 广州纤维产品检测研究院 **GFPTRI**
  Guangzhou Fiber Products Testing and Research Institute
- 广州质量监督检测研究院 **GQT**
  Guangzhou Quality Supervision and Testing Institute
- 归国华侨联合会 **ROCA**   Returned Overseas Chinese Association
- 圭亚那[南美洲国家] **GUY**   Guyana
- 规格 **Spec**   specification
- 硅[第14号化学元素] **Si**   silicon

G

硅-蓝宝石集成电路 SOS	silicon-on-sapphire
硅质 SIL	silica
轨道轰炸器 FOBS	fractional orbital bombardment system
轨道线 ENV	envelopes
贵宾 VIP	very important person
贵金属 PM	precious metal
国防 D	defense
国防部 DOD	Department of Defense
国防部采购中心 DSC	Defense Supply Center

国防部情报信息系统 DODIIS
　　DOD (Department of Defense) Intelligence Information System

国防部战俘与失踪人员办公室 DPMO
　　Defense POW [Prisoner of War]/MP [Missing Personnel] Office

国防创新单元 DIU	defense innovating unit
国防地面核反应堆 DTR	defense terrestrial reactor
数字无线中继 DTR	digital trunked radio
国防航天局 DSA	Defense space Agency
国防贸易管制局 DOTC	Defense Office of Trade Control
国防情报局 DIS	Defense Intelligence Service
国防卫星计划 DSP	Defense Satellite Program
国防卫星通信系统 DSCS	defense-satellite communication system(s)
国防义勇军 TA	Territorial Army
国防战略评估 QDR	Quadrennial Defense Review

国会及行政当局中国委员会 CECC
　　Congressional and Executive China Committee

国会现代中国问题联合委员会[美国] JCCC
　　Joint Committee on Contemporary China

| 国会预算办公室 CBO | Congressional Budget Office |

国际癌症研究机构 IARC
　　International Agency for Research on Cancer

| 国际爱护动物基金会 IFAW | International Fund for Animal Welfare |
| 国际安全援助部队 ISAF | International Security Assistant Force |

国际奥林匹克运动委员会 **IOC**	International Olympic Committee
国际棒球联合会 **IBA**	International Baseball Association
国际宝石学协会 **IGI**	International Gemological Institute
国际宝石学院 **IGI**	International Gem Institute

国际比较文学协会[法文] **AILC**
Association Internationale de Littérature Comparée

国际比较文学协会 **ICLA**	International Comparative Literature Association
国际比较项目法 **ICP**	International Comparison Program
国际标准草案 **DIS**	Draft International Standard
国际标准化比率 **INR**	international normalized ratio
国际标准化组织 **IOS**	International Organization for Standardization
国际标准化组织 **ISO**	International Standardization Organization
国际标准化组织 **ISO**	International Organization of Standardization
国际标准化组织开发环境 **ISODE**	ISO development environment
国际标准连续出版物编号 **ISSN**	International Standard Serial Number
国际标准书号 **ISBN**	International Standard Book Number

国际标准箱单位(集装箱多式联运)**TEU**
Twenty-Foot Equivalent Units (inter modal shipping container)

国际标准协会 **ISA**	International Standards Association
国际标准音像制品编码 **ISRC**	International Standard Recording Code
国际标准最终草案 **FDIS**	Final Draft International Standard
国际冰球联合会 **IIHF**	International Ice Hockey Federation
国际铂金协会 **PGI**	Platinum Guild International

国际博硕士论文数字图书馆 **NDLTD**
Networked Digital Library of Theses and Dissertations

国际捕鲸委员会 **WC**	International Whaling Commission
国际财务报告准则 **IFRS**	International Financial Reporting Standards
国际财务管理协会 **IFMA**	International Financial Management Association
国际彩色宝石协会 **ICA**	International Colored Gemstone Association
国际残疾人奥林匹克委员会 **IPC**	International Paralympic Committee
国际残疾人体育联合会 **IDPSF**	International Disabled Persons's Sports Federation

G

- 国际残疾人体育协调委员会 **ICC**
International Committee for the Coordination of Sports for the Disabled
- 国际唱片业协会 **IFPI**
International Federation of the Phonographic Industry
- 国际超级计算大会 **ISC** International Supercomputing Conference
- 国际城市管理协会 **ICMA** International City Management Association
- 国际出版商协会 **IPA** International Publishers Association
- 国际传记中心 **IBC** International Biographical Centre
- 国际船级社协会 **IACS**
International Association of Classification Societies
- 国际床上用品协会 **ISPA** International Sleep Products Association
- 国际丛书资料系统 **ISDS** International Series Data System
- 国际打捞协会 **ISU** The International Salvage Union
- 国际大会与会议协会 **ICCA**
International Conference and Convention Association
- 国际大力士联盟 **IFSA** International Federation of Strength Athletes
- 国际大陆科学钻探计划 **ICDP**
International Continental Scientific Driving Plan
- 国际大学翻译学院联合会[法文] **CIUTI**
Conférence Internationale permanente d Instituts Universitaires de Traducteurs et Interprètes
- 国际大学生程序设计竞赛 **ICPC** International Collegiate Programming Contest
- 国际大学生体育联合会 **FISU** Federation of International Students of University
- 国际大洋发现计划 **IODP** International Ocean Development Program
- 国际大众传媒研究协会 **IAMCR**
International Association for Mass Communication Research
- 国际代理 **IA** international agent
- 国际单位 **IU** international unit
- 国际单位制[法文] **SI** Système International
- 国际的 **INT** international
- 国际地理奥林匹克竞赛 **IGEO** International Geography Olympiad
- 国际地理联合会 **IGU** International Geography Union

- 国际电报电话公司 **ITT**
  International Telephone and Telegraph Corporation
- 国际电报电话咨询委员会［法文］**CCITT**
  Comité Consultatif International pour Télégraphie et Téléphonie
- 国际电报电话咨询委员会 **CCITT**
  Consultative Committee on International Telegraph and Telephone
- 国际电工技术委员会(标志) **IEC**　International Electrotechnical Commission
- 国际电气技术质量委员会 **IECQ**
  International Electrotechnical Commission of Quality
- 国际电信局 **ITO**　　　　　International Telecommunication Office
- 国际电信联盟(标志) **ITU**　International Telecommunications Union
- 国际电信联盟通信部 **ITU-R**　International Telecom Union-Telecom
- 国际电信联盟无线部 **ITU-R**　International Telecom Union-Radio
- 国际电影传播文艺作品委员会[法文] **CIADLC**
  Comité International pour la Diffusion des Arts et des Letters par le Cinéma［英文］:International Committee for the Diffusion of Arts and Literature through Cinema］
- 国际电影和电视委员会[法文] **CICT**
  Conseil International du Cinéma et de la Télévision［英文］:International Film and Television Council］
- 国际电子商务师 **IEBS**　　　International Electronic Business Specialist
- 国际电子商务师职业资格认证 **CIECS**
  Certification of International E-Commerce Specialist
- 国际电子消费展 **CES**　　　International Consumer Electronics Show
- 国际冬季两项全能联盟 **IBU**　International Biathlon Union
- 国际动漫电影协会[法文] **ASIFA**
  Association Internationale du Film d'Animation
- 国际独立认证组织 **IIOC**
  Independent International Organization for Certification
- 国际儿童读物联盟 **IBBY**
  International Board on Books for Young People
- 国际儿童援助组织 **IHC**　　　International Help for Children

G

- 国际发展部 **DID**   Department of International Development
- 国际发展合作(组织) **ICD**   International Cooperation for Development
- 国际法委员会 **ILC**   International Law Commission
- 国际翻译工作者联合会[法文]**FIT**

   Fédéracion Internationale des Traducteurs [英文: International Federation of Translators]
- 国际翻译家联合会 **IFT**   International Federation of Translators
- 国际反兴奋剂组织 **WADA**   World Anti-Doping Agency
- 国际防务工业展 **IDEF**   International Defence Engineer Fair
- 国际防止油污证书 **IOPP**   International Oil Pollution Protection
- 国际肥胖症特别工作组 **IOTF**   International Obesity Task Force
- 国际废除核武器运动 **ICAN**

   International Campaign to Abolish Nuclear Weapons
- 国际风味暨品质评鉴所 **ITQI**   International Taste & Quality Institute
- 国际风险管理师协会 **PRMIA**

   Professional Risk Manager International Association
- 国际妇产科联盟[法文] **FIGO**

   Fédération Internationale de Gynecologie et d'Obstetrique
- 国际复兴开发银行 **IBRD**

   International Bank for Reconstruction and Development
- 国际高层建筑与城市住宅协会 **CTBUH**

   The Council on Tall Building and Urban Habitat
- 国际高尔夫球联盟 **IGF**   International Golf Federation
- 国际高性能计算机 **ISC**   International Supercomputing
- 国际工商管理硕士 **GMBA**   Global Master of Business Administration
- 国际工商管理硕士 **IMBA**   International Master of Business Administration
- 国际工商硕士 **MIB**   Master of International Business
- 国际公共广播电台 **PRI**   Public Radio International
- 国际公共交通联会[法文] **UITP**   Union International des Transports Public
- 国际公共交通联会 **IUPT**   International Union of Public Transport
- 国际公害品 **IPB**   International Public Bads

- 国际公益扶持组织 **ICSO**
  International Commonwealth Support Organization
- 国际共和研究所 **IRI**　　　International Republic Institute
- 国际骨髓供体协会 **WMDA**　World Marrow Donor Association
- 国际骨髓库 **BMDW**　　　Bone Marrow Devices of World
- 国际固态电路峰会 **ISSCC**　International Solid-State Circuits Conference
- 国际关注的突发公共卫生事件 **PHEIC**
  Public Health Emergency of International Concern
- 国际管道机械产品质量认证标志 **IAPMO**
  International Association of Plumbing and Mechanical Officials
- 国际管道机械理事会 **IAPMO**
  International Association of Plumbing and Mechanical Officials
- 国际管理集团 **IMG**　　　International Management Group
- 国际管理学院 **IMI**　　　International Management Institute
- 国际广播电视组织[法文] **OIRT**
  Organisation Internationale de Radiodiffusion et de Télévison
- 国际广播联合会(联盟) **IBU**　International Broadcasting Union
- 国际广播协会 **AIB**　　　Association of International Broadcasting
- 国际广播与电视协会 **IRTS**　International Radio and Television Society
- 国际广播中心 **IBC**　　　International Broadcast Center
- 国际规划局 **IPO**　　　　International Projects Office
- 国际海底地名管理机构 **SCUFN** Sub-Committee on Undersea Feature Names
- 国际海底管理(机构) **ISA**　International Seabed Authority
- 国际海事组织 **IMO**　　　International Maritime Organization
- 国际海豚保育计划 **IDCP**　International Dolphin Conservation Program
- 国际海洋计划 **IPSO**　　International Plan of Seas and Oceans
- 国际航空集团 **IAG**　　　International Aviation Group
- 国际航空联合会[法文] **FAI**　Fédération Aéronautique Interationale
- 国际航空协定 **IAC**　　　International Air Convention
- 国际航空运输协会 **IATA**　International Air Transport Association
- 国际合作联盟[法文] **ACI**　Alliance Coopérative Internationale
- 国际红十字会[法文] **CICR**　Comité International de la Croix-Rouge

G

- 国际红十字会[葡萄牙文] **CICV**   Comitê Internacional da Cruz Vermelha
- 国际红十字会[西班牙文] **CICR**   Comité Internacional de la Cruz Roja
- 国际红十字会 **IRC**   International Red Cross
- 国际红十字(委员)会 **ICRC**   International Committee of the Red Cross
- 国际滑冰联合会[法文] **UIP**
  Union Internationale de Patinage [英文：International Skating Union]
- 国际滑冰联盟 **ISU**   International Skating Union
- 国际滑雪联合会[法文] **FIS**
  Fédération Internationale de Ski [英文：International Ski Federation]
- 国际化学纤维标准局[法文] **BISFA**
  Bureau International pour la Standardisation des Fibres Artificielles
- 国际化妆品化学家学会联盟 **IFSCC**
  International Federation of Societies of Cosmetic Chemists
- 国际回收局 **BIR**   Bureau of International Recycling
- 国际会计师公会 **AIA**   Association of International Accountants
- 国际会计准则 **IAS**   International Accounting Standards
- 国际会议口译人员/译员协会[法文] **AIIC**
  Association Internationale des Interprétes de Conférence [英文：International Association of Conference Interpreters]
- 国际货币基金组织 **IMF**   International Monetary Fund
- 国际货币金融机构官方论坛 **OMFIF**
  Official Monetary Finance Institute Forum
- 国际击剑联合会[法文] **FIE**   Fédération Internationale d'Escrime
- 国际急救证书 **AHA**   American Heart Association
- 国际疾病分类(法) **ICD**   International Classification of Diseases
- 国际疾病分类学——肿瘤学 **ICD-O**
  International Classification of Diseases for Oncology
- 国际集成电路研讨会 **IIC**   International Integrated Circuit
- 国际计算机安全协会 **ICSA**   International Computer Security Association
- 国际计算机通信会议 **ICCC**
  International Conference on Computer and Communication
- 国际计算中心 **ICC**   International Computation Center

■ 国际技术移民职业列表 ISCO　　International Standard Classfication Occupations
■ 国际建筑同盟[法文] UIA
　　Union Internationale des Architects [英文：International Alliance of Architects]
■ 国际健美联合会 IFBB　　International Federation of Bodybuilders
■ 国际交易与衍生品协会 ISDA　　International Swaps and Derivatives Association
■ 国际教师证 ITIC　　International Teacher Identity Card
■ 国际教学调查 TALIS　　Teaching and Learning International Survey
■ 国际教育工作者协会 NAFSA
　　Association of International Educators [原全称为：National Association of Foreign Student Adviser]
■ 国际教育计划研究中心 IIEP　　International Institute of Educational Planning
■ 国际金融公司 IFC　　International Finance Corporation
■ 国际金融协会 IIF　　Institute of International Finance
■ 国际金融证书 CIF　　Certificate in International Finance
■ 国际金融中心 IFS　　International Finance Square
■ 国际紧急经济权利法案 IEEPA　　International Emergency Economic Powers Act
■ 国际经济合作会议 CIEC
　　Conference on International Economic Cooperation
■ 国际经济学与商学学生协会[法文] AIESEC
　　Association Internationale des Étudiants en Sciences Économiques et Commerciales [英文：International Association of Students of Economic and Commercial Sciences]
■ 国际经济增长委员会 CIEG　　Committee for International Economic Growth
■ 国际精算师协会 IAA　　International Association of Actuaries
■ 国际景观设计师协会 IFLA　　International Federation of Landscape Architects
■ 国际警察协会 IUPA　　International Union of Police Associations
■ 国际救援委员会 IRC　　International Rescue Committee
■ 国际举重联合会 IWF　　International Weightlifting Federation
■ 国际军火交易条例 ITAR　　International Traffic in Arms Regulation
■ 国际军事法庭 IMT　　International Military Tribunal
■ 国际军事体育理事会[法文] CISM　　Conseil International du Sport Militaire
■ 国际军事体育运动委员会[法文] CISM
　　Conseil International du Sport Militaire

G

- 国际咖啡品鉴大赛 **ICT** International coffee Tasting
- 国际咖啡品鉴者协会 **IICT** International Institute of Coffee Tasters
- 国际咖啡组织 **ICO** International Coffee Organization
- 国际开发金融公司 **IDFC** International Development Finance Co.
- 国际开发署 **IDP** International Development Program
- 国际开发委员会 **CID** Commission for International Development
- 国际开发协会［法文］**AID**
  Association Internationale de Développment［英文：IDA, International Development Association］
- 国际抗癌联盟［法文］**UICC**
  Union International Contre le Cancer［英文：IUAC, International Union Against Cancer］
- 国际科学电影协会 **ISFA** International Scientific Film Association
- 国际科学基金 **IFS** International Fund of Science
- 国际科学基金会 **IFS** International Foundation for Science
- 国际科学技术数据委员会 **CODATA**
  Committee on Data for Science and Technology
- 国际科学联合理事会 **ICSU** International Council of Scientific Union
- 国际空间站 **ISS** International Space Station
- 国际控制和自动化会议 **ICCA**
  International Conference on Control and Automation
- 国际口腔种植医师学会 **ICOI**
  The International Congress of Oral Implantologists
- 国际篮联［法文］**FIBA**
  Fédération Internationale de Basketball Amateur
- 国际篮球协会 **IBA** International Basketball Association
- 国际劳工大会［联合国］**ILC** International Labour Conference
- 国际劳工局 **ILO** International Labor Office
- 国际劳工组织 **ILO** International Labour Organization
- 国际垒球联合会 **ISF** International Softball Federation
- 国际理论和应用化学联合会 **IUPAC**
  International Union of Pure and Applied Chemistry

453

- 国际理论和应用物理联合会 **IUPAP**
  International Union of Pure and Applied Physics
- 国际联机计算机图书馆中心在线图书馆中心 **OCLC**
  On-Line Computer Library Center
- 国际联盟 **LN**   the League of Nation
- 国际粮食政策研究所 **IFPRI**   International Food Policy Research Institute
- 国际领袖基金会 **ILF**   International Leadership Foundation
- 国际聋哑人体育运动委员会[法文] **CISS**
  Comité International des Sports Silencieux
- 国际轮椅和截肢运动联合会 **IWAS**
  International Wheelchair and Amputation Sports Federation
- 国际论文数据库 **WOS**   ISI Web of Science
- 国际旅游联盟 **ITA**   International Touring Alliance
- 国际律师协会 **IBC**   International Bar Council
- 国际律师协会 **IBA**   International Bar Association
- 国际马术联合会[法文] **FEI**   Fédération Equestre Internationale
- 国际盲人体育联盟 **IBSA**   International Blind Sports Association
- 国际贸易博览会 **ITF**   International Trade Fair
- 国际贸易委员会[英国] **ITC**   International Trade Commission
- 国际贸易委员会 **ITM**   International Trade Commission
- 国际贸易中心 **ITC**   International Trade Centre
- 国际贸易组织[法文] **OIC**
  Organisation Internationale du Commerce [英文：International Trade Organization]
- 国际煤炭组织 **ICO**   International Coal Organization
- 国际美容整形外科学会 **ISAPS**
  International Society of Aesthetic Plastic Surgery
- 国际棉花咨询委员会 **ICAC**   International Cotton Advisory Committee
- 国际民航组织 **ICAO**   International Civil Aviation Organization
- 国际模式识别会议 **IAPR**
  The International Association for Pattern Recognition
- 国际魔术师协会 **IMS**   International Magicians Society
- 国际魔术协会 **IMS**   International Magic Society

G

- 国际穆斯林联盟 IMU　　　　　International Muslim Union
- 国际南北运输走廊 INSTC
  International North-South Transportation Corridor
- 国际南极旅游组织协会 IAATO
  International Association of Antarctic Tour Operators
- 国际难民组织 IRO　　　　　International Refugee Organization
- 国际脑瘫人体育和休闲运动协会 CP-ISRA
  Cerebral Palsy International Sport and Recreation Association
- 国际脑研究组织——凯默理 IBRO-Kemali
  International Brain Research Organization—Kemali
- 国际能源署 IEA　　　　　International Energy Agency
- 国际农业发展基金会 IFAD
  International Fund for Agricultural Development
- 国际女子拳击联合会 IWBF　　　International Women's Boxing Federation
- 国际女子拳击联合会 WIBF　　　Women's International Boxing Federation
- 国际排球联合会[法文] FIVB
  Fédération Internationale de Volley-Ball [英文:International Volleyball Federation]
- 国际排球联合会 IVF　　　　　International Volleyball Federation
- 国际皮划艇联合会[法文] FIC　　Fédération Internationale de Canoe
- 国际乒乓球联合会 ITTF　　　　International Table Tennis Federation
- 国际平面设计联盟 AGI　　　　Alliance Graphique International
- 国际葡萄与葡萄酒局[法文] OIV(V)
  Office Internationale de la Vigne et du Vin [英文:International Vine and Wine Office]
- 国际汽车大奖(最高奖) GP　　　grand-prix
- 国际汽车工业特别工作组 IATF　International Automotive Task Force
- 国际汽车俱乐部协会 IACF　　　International Automobile Club Federation
- 国际汽车联合会[法文] FIA　　　Fédération Internationale de l'Automobile
- 国际汽车联合会 IAF　　　　　International Automobile Federation
- 国际汽车音响超级职业巡回赛 AEA
  Auto Equipment Association

455

- 国际汽车制造商协会[法文] **OICA**
  Organisation Internationale des Constructeurs d'Automobile
- 国际青年成就组织 **JA**　　　　Junior Achievement
- 国际青年奖学金 **IYF**　　　　International Youth Fellowship
- 国际青年交流组织 **AFS**　　　The American Field Service
- 国际青年联盟 **IYF**　　　　　International Youth Federation
- 国际青少年读物委员会 **IBBY**　International Board on Books for Young People
- 国际清除持久性有机污染物网络 **IPEN**
  International POPs Elimination Network
- 国际清算银行 **BIS**　　　　　Bank for International Settlements
- 国际清真诚信联盟 **IHIA**　　　International Halal Integrity Alliance
- 国际清真食品理事会 **HFCI**　　Halal Food Council International
- 国际曲棍球联合会[法文] **FIH**
  Fédération Internationale de Hockey [英文：International Hockey Federation]
- 国际权威发行量认证机构 **BPA**　Business Publications Audit
- 国际拳击联合会 **IBF**　　　　International Boxing Federation
- 国际拳击联盟 **IBU**　　　　　International Boxing Union
- 国际拳击组织 **IBO**　　　　　International Boxing Organization
- 国际犬业协会[西班牙文] **FCI**　Federación Cynological Internacional
- 国际热带木材组织 **ITTO**　　　International Tropical Timber Organization
- 国际热核聚变实验堆(计划) **ITER**
  International Thermonuclear Experimental Reactor
- 国际人工智能中心 **IAIC**　　　International Artificial Intelligence Center
- 国际人民法庭 **IPT**　　　　　International People's Tribunal
- 国际人权联盟[法文] **FIDH**　　Fédération Internationale des Droits de l'Homme
- 国际人权委员会 **ICHR**　　　　International Council for Human Rights
- 国际人权组织 **IHO**　　　　　International Humanitarian Organization
- 国际认证财务顾问师协会 **IARFC**
  International Association of Registered Financial Consultants
- 国际认证协会 **IPCA**　　　　International Profession Certification Association
- 国际日期变更线 **IDL**　　　　International Date Line
- 国际柔道联合会 **IJF**　　　　International Judo Federation

G

- 国际乳制品业联合会 **IDF**   International Dairy Federation
- 国际伤残人体育组织 **ISOD**   International Sports Organization for the Disabled
- 国际商标协会 **INTA**   International Trademark Association
- 国际商会 **ICC**   International Chamber of Commerce
- 国际商业美术设计师协会 **ICADA**
  International Commercial Art Designer Association
- 国际商业美术设计师职业资格认证 **ICAD**
  International Commercial Art Designer
- 国际商业无线电委员会 **CRIC**   Commercial Radio International Committee
- 国际商业信贷银行 **BCCI**   Bank of Credit and Commerce International
- 国际商用机器公司 **IBM**   International Business Machines Corporation
- 国际上识别中风的 FAST 法［观察微笑时面部有无歪斜，双手平举，观察是否无力垂落，有无说话口齿不清，有上述情况第一时间求助］**FAST**
  face, arm, speech, time
- 国际少儿模特大赛 **IKMC**   International Kids Model Contest
- 国际设计大赛 **IDC**   International Design Contest
- 国际射击联合会［法文］**UIT**   Union Internationale de Tir
- 国际射箭联合会［法文］**FITA**
  Fédération Internationale de Tirà l'Arc［英文：International Federation for Archery］
- 国际摄影艺术联合会［法文］**FIAP**
  Fédération Internationale de l'Art photographique
- 国际神话学协会 **IMS**   International Mythological Society
- 国际生命科学研究所 **ILSI**   International Life Sciences Institute
- 国际生态纺织品研究与发展协会制定的安全测试标准［俄文］**ÖKO TEST**
  ÖKOtex Test
- 国际生物化学协会 **IUB**   International Union of Biochemistry
- 国际生物化学协会酶学委员会 **EC**   Enzyme Commission of IUB
- 国际生物学奥林匹克竞赛 **IBO**   International Biology Olympiad
- 国际十进制分类法 **UDC**   Universal Decimal Classification
- 国际实践管理硕士 **IMPM**   international master in practicing management
- 国际食品标准（认证）**IFS**   International Food Standard
- 国际食品法典委员会 **CAC**   Codex Alimentarius Commission

- 国际世界青年友谊会 **IWYF**　　International World Youth Friendship
- 国际事故文献(法文) **DIA**　　Documentation Internationale des Accidents
- 国际手球联合会 **IHF**　　International Handball Federation
- 国际兽疫学办公室 **OIE**　　Office of International Epizootics
- 国际数据 **ID**　　international data
- 国际数据公司 **IDC**　　International Data Corporation
- 国际数据集团 **IDG**　　International Data Group
- 国际数学奥林匹克竞赛;奥数 **IMO**
  International Mathematical Olympiad
- 国际数学家大会 **ICM**　　the International Congress of Mathematicians
- 国际数学联盟 **IMU**　　International Mathematics Union
- 国际水上乐园社团 **WWA**　　World Waterpark Association
- 国际水文学组织 **IHO**　　International Hydrographic Organization
- 国际私企中心 **CIPE**　　Center for International Private Enterprise
- 国际斯托克·曼德维尔轮椅运动联合会 **ISMWSF**
  International Stoke Mandeville Wheelchair Sports Federation
- 国际跆拳道联盟 **ITF**　　International Taekwondo Federation
- 国际泰拳理事会 **WMC**　　World Muay Thai Council
- 国际碳行动伙伴组织 **ICAP**　　International Carbon Action Partnership
- 国际糖尿病联盟 **IDF**　　International Diabetes Federation
- 国际陶器协会 **ICA**　　International Ceramic Association
- 国际体操联合会[法文] **FIG**
  Fédération Interationale de Gymnastique [英文: International Gymnastic Federation]
- 国际体验设计协会 **IEDC**　　International Experience Design Committee
- 国际天文学联合会 **IAU**　　International Astronomical Union
- 国际田径教练联合会 **ITFCA**
  International Track and Field Coaches Association
- 国际调查记者协会 **ICIJ**
  International Consortium of Investigative Journalist
- 国际铁路协会 **IRCA**　　International Railway Congress Association
- 国际通信卫星组织 **INTELSAT**
  International Telecommunications Satellite Organization

G

- 国际通信学会 **IIC** — International Institute of Communications
- 国际通用的民间故事类型分类法[由芬兰学者阿尔奈和美国学者汤普森提出并修订] **AT** — Aarne Thompson
- 国际通用的无线电求救信号的通俗写法 **SOS** — Save Our Souls
- 国际透明组织 **TI** — Transparency International
- 国际图书馆协会联合会 **IFLA** — International Federation of Library Associations
- 国际图书年 **IBY** — International Book Year
- 国际外科学会联合会 **IFSC** — International Federation of Surgical College
- 国际万维网联盟 **W3C** — World Wide Web Consortium
- 国际网球联合会 **ITF** — International Tennis Federation
- 国际危机组织 **ICG** — International Crisis Group
- 国际海运危险品编码 **IMDG Code** — International Maritime Dangerous Goods Code
- 国际危险品组织 **IDO** — International Dangerous Organization
- 国际卫生、体育与文娱理事会 **ICHPER** — International Council for Health, Physical Education and Recreation
- 国际文化产业博览交易会 **ICIF** — International Cultural Industries Fair
- 国际文化产业博览交易会 **ICITF** — International Cultural Industry Trade Fair
- 国际文凭 **IB** — International Baccalaureate
- 国际文凭组织 **IBO** — International Baccalaureate Organization
- 国际文献资料中心 **IDC** — International Documentation Center
- 国际无线电咨询委员会 **CCIR** — Consultative Committee on International Radio
- 国际物品编码协会(借用"欧洲物品编码协会"的 EAN) **EAN** — European Article Number
- 国际戏剧研究中心 **ICTR** — International Centre for Theatre Research
- 国际先进人工智能大会 **AAAI** — Association for the Advance of Artificial Intelligence
- 国际现代家具展 **ICFF** — International Contemporary Furniture Fair
- 国际项目管理专业资质认证 **IPMP** — International Project Management Profession
- 国际锌协会 **IZA** — International Zinc Association
- 国际新闻工作者联合会 **IFJ** — International Federation of Journalists
- 国际信息学奥林匹克竞赛 **IOI** — International Olympiad in Informatics

国际刑(事)警(察)组织 **ICPO/Interpol**
International Criminal Police Organization

国际刑警组织美国国家中心局 **USNCB**
United States National Central Bureau

国际刑事法院 **ICC**   International Criminal Court

国际虚拟媒体联盟 **IUVM**   International Union of Virtual Media

国际选美冠军[西班牙文] **CACIB**
Certificado de Aptitud al Campeonato Intenacional de Belleza

国际选美冠军资质证明[法文] **CACIB**
Certificate d' Aptitude au Championnat International de Beauté

国际学生服务处 **ISS**   International Student Service

国际学生证 **ISIC**   International Student Identity Card

国际雪橇滑雪联合会[法文] **FIBT**
Fédération Internationale de Bobsleigh et de Tobogganing [英文：International Bobsleighing and Tobogganing Federation]

国际研究型大学联盟 **IARU**   International Alliance of Research Universities

国际眼科理事会 **ICO**   International Council of Ophthalmology

国际羊毛秘书处 **IWS**   International Wool Secretariat

国际野生生物保护学会 **WCS**   Wildlife Conservation Society

国际业余拳击联合会[法语] **AIBA**
Association Internationale de Boxe Amateur [英文：International Amateur Boxing Association]

国际业余摔跤联合会[法文] **FILA**
Fédération Internationale de Lutte Amateur [英文：International Amateur Wrestling Federation]

国际业余田径联合会 **IAAF**   International Amateur of Athletics Federations

国际移动设备标识符 **IMEI**   International Mobile Equipment Identifier

国际移动通信 **IMT**   International Mobile Telecommunication

国际移动用户标识 **IMSI**   International Mobile Subscriber Identity

国际移动用户识别码 **IMSI**
International Mobile Subscriber Identification Number

国际移民组织 **IOM**   International Organization for Migration

G

- 国际艺术评论家协会［法文］**AICA**
  Association Internationale des Critique d'Art
- 国际译员协会 **III**　　　　　International Institute of Interpreters
- 国际易学风水研究中心 **IIFRC**
  International I-Ching Fengshui Research Center
- 国际音标 **IPA**　　　　　　International Phonetic Alphabet
- 国际音乐创作者委员会［法文］**CIAM**
  Confédération Internationale des Association de Musiciens
- 国际银行账户号码 **IBAN**　　International Bank Account Number
- 国际英语学习者语料库 **ICLE**　International Corpus of Learner English
- 国际英语语料库 **ICE**　　　　International Corpus of English
- 国际营养标准委员会 **CAC**　　Codex Alimentarius Commission
- 国际永久冠军 **Intl CH**　　　International Champion
- 国际泳联［法文］**FINA**　　　Fédération Internationale de Natation Association
- 国际有机农业运动联合会 **IFOAM**
  International Federation of Organic Agriculture Movement
- 国际宇航联合会 **IAF**　　　　International Astronautical Federation
- 国际羽毛球联合会 **IBF**　　　International Badminton Federation
- 国际羽绒羽毛检测实验室 **IDFL**　International Down & Feather Laboratory
- 国际语言学奥林匹克竞赛；奥语 **IOL**
  International Olympiad in Linguistics
- 国际原子能机构 **IAEA**　　　International Atomic Energy Agency
- 国际圆桌会议 **RTI**　　　　　Round Table International
- 国际运动安全中心 **ICSS**　　The International Centre for Sport Security
- 国际运输联盟 **ITF**　　　　　International Transport Federation
- 国际展览服务协会 **IFES**　　International Federation for Exhibition Services
- 国际展览会联盟［法文］**UFI**
  Union des Foires Internationales［英文：Union of International Fairs］
- 国际展览局 **BIE**　　　　　　Bureau of International Exhibition
- 国际展览年会 **IFA**　　　　　International Fair Annual
- 国际战略研究所 **IISS**　　　International Institute for Strategic Studies
- 国际招标 **IT**　　　　　　　international tender

- 国际照明委员会[法文] **CIE**　　Commission internationale de l'eclairage
- 国际证券识别编码 **ISIN**　　International Securities Identification Number
- 国际证券市场协会 **ISMA**　　International Securities Market Association
- 国际支付服务公司 **IPSC**　　International Payment Service Company
- 国际直拨(电话) **IDD**　　international direct dial
- 国际职业技术教育培训中心 **UNEVOC**
  International Centre for Technical and Vocational Education and Training
- 国际职业女子网球协会 **WTA**　　Women's Tennis Association
- 国际职业网球联合会 **ATP**　　Association of Tennis Professional
- 国际职业资格证书 **IVQ**　　International Vocational Qualification
- 国际植物保护公约 **IPPC**　　International Plant Protection Convention
- 国际志愿者协会[法文] **AVSI**
  Association de Volontaires pour le Service International
- 国际质量安全管理体系 **IQSCS**　　International Quality Safety Control System
- 国际智力残疾人体育联盟 **IFSIDP**
  International Federation of Sports for Intellectual Disabled Person
- 国际注册内部审计师 **CIA**　　Certified Internal Auditor
- 国际注册特许财务策划师 **FChFP**　　Fellow Chartered Financial Practitioner
- 国际注册资产管理师 **CPM**　　Certified Property Manager
- 国际专利分类法 **IPC**　　International Patent Classification
- 国际专利研究处 **IPRO**　　International Patent Research Office
- 国际专业婚礼摄影师协会 **ISPWP**
  The International Society of Professional Wedding Photographers
- 国际自行车联合会[法文] **UCI**
  Union Cycliste Internationale [英文: International Cycling Union]
- 国际自然保护联盟(国际自然保护协会) **IUCN**
  International Union for Conservation of Nature
- 国际自然及自然资源保护协会 **IUCNNR**
  International Union for Conservation of Nature and Natural Resources
- 国际自由人 **IF**　　international freeman
- 国际足球历史和统计联合会 **IFFHS**
  International Federation of Football History and Statistics

G

- 国际足球联合会［法文］**FIFA**
  Fédération Internationale de Football Associations ［英文：International Association Football Federation］
- 国际钻石制造商协会 **IDMA**
  International Diamond Manufactures Association
- 国际最佳工业设计奖 **IDEA**　　International Design Excellence Awards
- 国际作家和作曲家协会联合会［法文］**CISAC**
  Confédération Internationale des Sociétés d'Auteurs et Compositeurs
- 国家安全保障协会 **NSC**　　National Security Committee
- 国家安全部 **MSS**　　Ministry of State Security
- 国家安全分部 **NSB**　　National Security Board
- 国家安全委员会［美国］**NSC**　　National Security Council
- 国家北极野生生物保护区 **ANWR**　　Arctic Natural Wildlife Refuge
- 国家标准和技术协会 **NIST**　　National Institute of Standards and Technology
- 国家标准局 **NBS**　　National Board of Standards
- 国家标准扩展码［汉语拼音缩略语］**GBK**
  Guojia Biaozhun Kuozhanma
- 国家创新系统 **NIS**　　National Innovation System
- 国家催眠师协会 **NGH**　　National Guild of Hypnotists Inc.
- 国家打击犯罪局 **NCA**　　National Crime Agency
- 国家大气研究中心 **NCAR**　　National Center for Atmospheric Research
- 国家档案文件局 **NARS**　　National Archives and Records Service
- 国家导弹防御体系 **NMD**　　National Missile Defence System
- 国家地理情报局 **NGA**　　National Geography Agency
- 国家毒理学计划 **NTP**　　National Toxicology Program
- 国家毒品及酒精研究中心 **NDARC**
  National Drug and Alcohol Research Centre
- 国家毒品控制政策办公室 **ONDCP**
  Office of National Drag Control Policy
- 国家对外贸易委员会［美国］**NFTC**
  National Foreign Trade Council
- 国家工商行政管理局 **SAIC**　　State Administration for Industry and Commerce

- 国家公民登记册 **NRC**   National Register of Citizens
- 国家公务员考试 **NPSE**   National Public Servant Examination
- 国家公园管理处 **NPS**   National Park Service
- 国家海洋和大气管理局 **NOAA**
  National Oceanic and Atmospheric Administration
- 国家航天局 **CNSA**   China National Space Administration
- 国家环境预测中心 **NCEP**   National Center for Environment Predicting
- 国家计算机安全协会 **NCSA**   National Computer Security Association
- 国家计算机网格应急技术处理协调中心 **CNCERT/CC**
  China National Internet Emergency Center
- 国家开发银行 **CDB**   China Development Bank
- 国家科学基金会 **NSF**   National Science Foundation
- 国家科学研究委员会 **NRC**   National Research Council
- 国家科学研究中心［法文］**CNRS**   Centre National de la Recherche Scientifique
- 国家可再生能源实验室 **NREL**   National Renewable Energy Laboratory
- 国家课程考试 **NCT**   National Curriculum Test
- 国家空间研究委员会［西班牙文］**CONIE**
  Comisión Nacional de Investigación del Espacio
- 国家空域系统 **NAS**   national airspace system
- 国家篮球发展联盟 **NBDL**   NBA Development League
- 国家篮球联盟 **NBL**   National Basketball League
- 国家零售基金会 **NRF**   The National Retail Foundation
- 国家留学基金管理委员会 **CSC**   China Scholarship Council
- 国家秘密行动处 **NCS**   National Clandestine Activities Service
- 国家民主(捐赠)基金会 **NED**   National Endowment for Democracy
- 国家敏感症和传染病学会 **NIAID**
  National Institute of Allergies and Infectious Diseases
- 国家能源局 **NEA**   National Energy Agency
- 国家农业科研系统 **NARS**   National Agricultural Research System
- 国家气候中心 **NCC**   National Climate Center
- 国家汽车检测 **NCT**   National Car Test
- 国家情报局 **NIS**   National Intelligence Service

G

- 国家情报主任 **DNI** — Director of National Intelligence
- 国家情报主任办公室 **ODNI** — Office of the Director of National Intelligence
- 国家认可实验室 **NRTL** — National Recognized Testing Lab
- 国家森林种植发展规划 **NFPDP** — National Forest Plant and Development Plan
- 国家食品药品监督管理局 **SFDA** — State Food and Drug Administration
- 国家食品与药品管理局 **CFDA** — Country Food and Drug Administration
- 国家网络技术水平考试 **NCNE** — National Certification of Network Engineer
- 国家信息化计算机教育认证 **CEAC** — Computer Education and Certification
- 国家信息化指数 **NIQ** — National Informatization Quotient
- 国家选美冠军大赛[法文] **CAC** — Certificate d' Aptitute Au Championnat
- 国家选美冠军纸质证书[法文] **CAC** — Certificate d'Aptitude au Championnat
- 国家亚洲研究局(美国非营利组织) **NBAR** — National Bureau of Asian Research
- 国家药监局 **SDA** — State Drug Agency
- 国家移民管理局 **NIA** — National Immigration Administration
- 国家英语演讲比赛 **NESC** — National English Speaking Competition
- 国家战略研究所 **INSS** — Institute for National Strategic Studies
- 国家侦查局 **NRO** — National Reconnaissance Office
- 国家职业储蓄信托 **NEST** — National Employment Savings Trust
- 国家职业汉语能力测试[英汉混合缩略语] **ZHC** — Zhongguo Hanyu Capacity
- 国家职业资格(证书制度) **NVQ** — National Vocational Qualification
- 国家珠宝培训中心 **NGTC** — National Gem Training Center
- 国家珠宝玉石质量监督检测中心 **NGTC** — National Gemstone Testing Center
- 国家珠宝玉石质量监督检验中心 **NGTC** — National Gem Test Center
- 国家自然科学基金委员会 **NSFC** — National Science Fund Committee
- 国开行 **CDB** — China Development Bank
- 国库券 **TN** — treasury note

国库券 TB	treasury bond
国立癌症研究所 NCI	National Cancer Institute
国立老年研究所 NIA	National Institute Aging
国立情报学研究所 NII	National Institute of Informatics
国民财富总额 GNW	gross national wealth
国民待遇 NT	national treatment
国民党 KMT	Kuomintang
国民人口登记册 NPR	National Population Register
国民生产净值 NNP	Net National Product
国民生产总值 GNP	Gross National Product
国民收入 NI	national income
国民幸福总值 GNH	Gross National Happiness
国民账户制度 SNA	system of national accounts
国民志愿服务团[印地文] RSS	Rashtriya Swayamasevak Sangh
国民志愿服务团 NCC	National Cadet Corps
国民总福利 GNW	Gross National Welfare
国民总收入 GNI	Gross National Income
国民总支出 GNE	Gross National Expenditure
国内电话直拨 DDD	domestic direct dial
国内生产总值 GDP	Gross Domestic Product
国内市盈率,股价利润率 P/E	price-earnings
国内通信卫星 DOM-SAT	domestic satellite
国内信用膨胀 DCE	domestic credit expansion
国税局 IRS	Internal Revenue Service
国税局刑员调查处 IRSCI	Internal Revenue Service Criminal Investigation
国土安全部 DHS	Department of Homeland Security
国土安全部 HSD	Homeland Security Department
国土安全调查部门 HIS	Homeland Safety Investigation Bureau
国外航空邮件 FAM	foreign air mail
国外旅行通知书 NOFT	notification of foreign travel

H

- 国王[拉丁文] **R**   Rex
- 国务院 **DOS**   Department of State
- 国务院新闻办公室图片库 **CFP**   China Foto Press
- 国营军火工厂[比利时][法文] **FN**   Fabrique Nationale des Armes de Guerre
- 果糖 **Fru**   fructose
- 果糖胺 **FTS**   fructosamine
- 过得开心;玩得高兴[网络用语] **HAND**   have a nice day
- 过后跟你聊[网络用语] **CWYL**   chat with you later
- 过户转账代理人 **TA**   transfer agent
- 过境贸易 **TT**   transit trade
- 过量 **OD**   overdose
- 过敏性肠综合征 **IBS**   irritable bowel syndrome
- 过敏与传染病研究所 **NIAID**   National Institute of Allergy and Infectious Disease
- 过氧化物酶 **POX**   peroxidase
- 过氧化脂 **LPO**   lipid peroxides
- 过氧碳酸钠 **SPC**   sodium percarbonate

- 哈德洛克螺母 **HLN**   Hard Lock nut
- 哈德洛克螺丝 **HLS**   Hard Lock screw
- 哈尔滨工业大学 **HIT**   Harbin Institute of Technology
- 哈尔滨工业大学机器人集团 **HRG**   Harbin Industry University Robot Group
- 哈飞汽车[汉语缩略语] **H**   Hafei
- 哈佛大学、耶鲁大学和普林斯顿大学[美国] **HYP**   Harvard, Yale and Princeton Universities
- 哈哈大笑;纵情大笑[网络用语] **BL**   belly laugh

- 哈萨克斯坦[亚洲国家] **KAZ**   Kazakhstan
- 铪[第72号化学元素] **Hf**   hafnium
- 还原性谷胱甘肽 **GSH**   glutathione
- 孩之宝(玩具) **HASBRO**   Hassenfeld Brothers
- 孩子他爸 **BF**   baby's father
- 海岸监视部队 **CSF**   coastal surveillance force
- 海拔高度 **ALT**   altitude
- 海豹六队;海军特战开发小组 **NSWDG**   Naval Special Warfare Development Group
- 海恩斯与莫里斯服装、化妆品[瑞典] **H&M**   Hennes & Mauritz AB
- 海扶刀[高强度聚焦超声肿瘤治疗系统] **HIFU**   high-intensity focused ultrasound
- 海关编码[即《商品名称及编码协调制度的国际公约》] **HS**   International Convention for the Harmonized Commodity Description and Coding System
- 海关编码[简称,详称见另一个HS] **HS**   harmonized system
- 海关及边境保护局 **CBP**   Customs and Border Protection
- 海关警察 **CP**   customs police
- 海关联盟 **CU**   The Customs Union
- 海基会 **SEF**   Strait Exchange Foundation (of Taiwan, China)
- 海军部[英国] **Adm**   Admiralty
- 海军大西洋潜艇专用自动化数据网络系统 **SUBLAN/ADNS**   Submarine, Atlantic/Automated Data Network System
- 海军犯罪调查组 **NCIS**   Naval Criminal Investigation Service
- 海军海洋监视卫星 **NOSS**   Navy Ocean Surveillance Satellite
- 海军陆战队总部 **HQMC**   Headquarters, Marine Corps
- 海军上将 **Adm**   admiral
- 海军特种作战发展大队 **NSWDG**   Naval Special Warfare Development Group
- 海军特种作战人员 **SEALs**   sea-air-lands

H

- 海军元帅 **AF**   admiral of the fleet
- 海军运输船［代字］**AP**   navy transport ship
- 海军装载军官 **NEO**   naval embarkation officer
- 海空防卫及安全系统科技 **MAST**   marine and aerial safe technology
- 海拉癌细胞株 **HeLa**   Henrietta Lacks strain of cancer cells
- 海绿色 **SG**   sea green
- 海南航空 **HNA**   Hainan Airlines
- 海平面国际标准大气压 **ISASL**   International Standard Atmosphere Sea Level
- 海上浮式生产储卸油装置 **FPSO**   floating production, storage and offloading unit
- 海上钻井平台 **ODP**   Offshore Drilling Platform
- 海事局 **MSA**   Maritime Safety Administration
- 海外开发署 **ODA**   Overseas Development Administration
- 海外开发援助 **ODA**   Overseas Development Assistance
- 海外直接投资 **ODI**   overseas direct investment
- 海外志愿者服务社 **VSO**   voluntary service overseas
- 海外资产管理办公室 **OFAC**   Office of Foreign Assets Control
- 海湾(阿拉伯国家)合作委员会 **GCC**   Gulf Cooperation Council
- 海湾石化工业公司 **GPIC**   Gulf Petrochemical Industries Co.
- 海峡渡轮 **CSF**   Cross Strait Ferry
- 海峡交流基金会 **SEF**   Strait Exchange Foundation (of Taiwan, China)
- 海峡两岸关系协会(简称"海协会") **ARATS**   Association for Relations across the Taiwan Straits
- 海峡两岸综合性经济合作协议 **CECA**   Comprehensive Economic Co-operation Agreement
- 海牙常设仲裁法院 **PCA**   Permanent Court of Arbitration
- 海洋废物处理 **DAS**   disposal at sea
- 海洋工程局 **MEO**   marine engineering office
- 海洋迷彩服 **OCC**   ocean camouflage clothing
- 海洋热能转换 **OTEC**   ocean thermal energy conversion
- 海洋太阳能 **SSP**   sea solar power
- 氦［第2号化学元素］**He**   helium

含硫原油 SC	sour crude
含水量 MC	moisture content
含早餐旅馆 B&B	Bed & Breakfast
韩国［亚洲国家］KOR	Korea
韩国 DSP 娱乐公司 DSP	DSP Media
韩国 JYP（朴振英）娱乐公司 JYP	Jin Young Park Entertainment
韩国 LG 集团（直译：喜乐金星）LG	Lucky Goldstars
韩国 Line 公司的股票代码 LN	Line
韩国 YG 娱乐公司 YG	YG Entertainment
韩国标准局 KBS	Korean Bureau of Standards
韩国标准协会 KSA	Korean Standards Association
韩国步兵战车 KIFV	Korean infantry vehicle
韩国产品质量认证标志 KBS/K	Korean Bureau of Standards
韩国船级社 KR	Korean Register of Shipping
韩国第一女子乐团 Fin. K. L.	Fine Killing Liberty
韩国电器试验研究所 KETI	Korea Electrical Testing Institute
韩国电视台 KBS	Korean Broadcasting System
韩国电视台 YTN	Yonhap Television News
韩国对信息及通信产品质量的认证标志 MIC Ministry of Information and Communication	
韩国防空识别区 KADIZ	Korean Air Defense Identification Zone
韩国互联网集团［由 Naver 和 Hangame 两家公司组成］NHN Naver and Hangame Network Corp	
韩国开发研究院 KDI	Korea Development Institute
韩国科学技术情报研究院 KISTI Korea Institute of Science and Technology Information	
韩国科学技术研究院 KIST	Korean Institute of Science and Technology
韩国口笔译协会 KATI Korean Association of Translation and Interpretation	
韩国两栖装甲车 KAAV	Korea armoured amphibious vehicle
韩国流行音乐 K-POP	Korea-Pop
韩国旅游发展局 KTO	Korean Tourism Organization

H

- 韩国浦项制铁公司 **POSCO**　　Pohang Iron and Steel Co. Ltd
- 韩国食品 **K-Food**　　Korea-Food
- 韩国食品药品监督管理局 **KFDA**　　Korean Food and Drug Association
- 韩国首尔国立大学 **SNU**　　Seoul National University
- 韩国通信 **KT**　　Korea Telecom
- 韩国外国语大学 **HUFS**　　Hankuk University of Foreign Studies
- 韩国文化放送株式会社[韩国大型传媒企业] **MBC**　　Munhwa Broadcasting Corporation
- 韩国五大娱乐公司之一 **SM**　　Star Museum
- 韩国现代汽车 **H**　　Hyundai
- 韩国亚洲创意学院 **ACA**　　Asian Creation Academy
- 韩国有线收费电视台 **JTBC**　　Joongang Tongyang Broadcasting Company
- 韩国语能力测试 **KPT**　　Korean Profession Test
- 韩国证券交易所 **KSE**　　Korea Stock Exchange
- 韩国知识产权局 **KIPO**　　Korea Intellectual Property Office
- 韩国中小企业银行 **IBK**　　Industrial Bank of Korea
- 韩国综合指数 **KCI**　　Korea Composite Index
- 韩美驻军地位协定 **SOFA**　　ROK-US States of Forces Agreement
- 汉考国际 **CTI**　　Chinese Testing International
- 汉诺威工业设计论坛奖 **IF**　　Industries Forum Design
- 汉诺威国际信息及通信技术博览会[德文] **CeBIT**　　Centrum der Büro-und Informationstechnik
- 汉语框架网 **CFN**　　Chinese Frame Net
- 汉语拼音字母 **CPA**　　Chinese phonetic alphabet
- 汉语水平考试[汉语拼音缩略语] **HSK**　　Hanyu Shuiping Kaoshi
- 汉语研究中心 **CCS**　　Center for Chinese Studies
- 捍卫自由联盟 **ADF**　　Alliance Defending Freedom
- 焊接产品认证标志 **WB**　　Weld Board
- 焊接局 **WB**　　Weld Board
- 行[复数] **ll**　　line
- 行贿指数 **BPI**　　Bribe Payers Index

行事调调很酷 SWAG	swagger
行为驱动开发 BDD	behavior-driven development
行为商(数) BQ	behavior quotient
行为识别 BI	behaviour identity
行业质量保证体系 OS	occupation safeguard
杭州金融投资公司 HFI	Hangzhou Finance Investment Company
航班变更 FM	flight modification
航班取消 FX	flight cancellation
航空安全报告系统 ASRS	aviation safety reporting system
航空发展机构 ADE	aerial development establishment
航空公司运行控制中心 AOC	Airlines Operation Center
航空和航天的革新和领军者 ILA	Innovation and Leadership in Aerospace
航空监控雷达系统 ASRS	air-surveillance radar system
航空控制中心 ACC	Air Control Center
航空器拥有者及飞行员协会 AOPA	Aircraft Owners and Pilots Association
航空信汇 AMT	air-mail transfer
航空邮件[法文] PAV	Poste Avion [英文：air mail]
航空运送系统 ADS	aerial delivery system
航母打击部队 CSF	carrier strike force
航母打击群 CSG	carrier strike group
毫安时 mA·h	milli-Ampere/hour
毫克 mg	milligram(me)
毫克/千克 mg/kg	milligram(me)/kilogram
毫克/升 mg/l	milligram per liter
毫克 mg	milligram
毫米水银柱 mmHg	millimeter mercury column
毫摩尔/升 mmol/l	millimol/litre
毫升 ml	millilitre
毫微秒[一毫微秒等于十亿分之一秒] ns	nanosecond
毫西弗[辐射量单位，1毫西弗等于1000微西弗 μSV] mSV	millisievert
豪华汽车 LUX	luxury cars

H

- 好的 OK — okay
- 好运气[网络用语] BOL — Best of luck
- 好再交费[一种网络游戏模式] CSP — come-stay-pay
- 耗油率 SFC — specific fuel consumption
- 合成孔径雷达 SAR — synthetic aperture radar
- 合成血凝素, 血细胞凝集 HA — hemagglutination
- 合法 legit — legitimate
- 合格(德国人 Otto Kraste 是优秀质量检测员,他所检测的汽车无质量问题,每部合格车均写上他的姓名缩写 OK) OK — Otto Kraste
- 合格佳酿酒[法国葡萄酒质量管理标记][法文] AC — appellation contrôlée
- 合格境内机构投资者 QDII — Qualified Domestic Institutional Investors
- 合格境外机构投资者 QFII — Qualified Foreign Institutional Investors
- 合伙有限公司[荷兰文] CV — Commanditaine Vennootschap
- 合理化、标准化及相互适应性 RSI — rationalization, standardization, interoperability
- 合拍商数 CQ — collaboration quotient
- 合同管理官 ACO — administrative contracting officer
- 合同签订日期 CAD — contract award date
- 合同生产组织 CMO — Contract Manufacturing Organization
- 合同物流 CL — contract logistics
- 合同销售组织 CSO — Contract Sales Organization
- 合同研究组织 CRO — Contract Research Organization
- 合众国际社[美国通讯社] UPI — The United Press International
- 合资经营 JV — joint venture
- 和的平方根 rss — root-sum square
- 和平利用外层空间委员会 COPUOS — Committee on the Peaceful Uses of Outer Space
- 河流 R — river
- 河豚毒素 TTX — tetrodotoxin
- 荷兰[欧洲国家] NL/NED — Netherlands

473

- 荷兰阿姆斯特丹大学 **AU**   Amsterdam University
- 荷兰阿姆斯特丹证券交易所 **AEX**   Amsterdam Exchange
- 荷兰电工材料协会[荷兰文] **KEMA**
  N. V. tot Keuring van Electrotechnische Materiale
- 荷兰电工产品质量认证标志[荷兰文] **KEMA**
  N. V. tot Keuring van Electrotechnische Materiale
- 荷兰盾[荷兰货币] **F**   Florin
- 荷兰恩智浦半导体公司 **NXP**   NXP semiconductors
- 荷兰工业协会 **NII**   Netherlands Industrial Institute
- 荷兰国际集团 **ING**   International Netherlands Group
- 荷兰煤气认证标志[荷兰文] **HR**   Hoog Rendement
- 荷兰中央统计局[荷兰文] **CBS**   Centraal Bureau van Statistiek
- 核磁共振 **NMR**   Nuclear Magnetic Resonance
- 核磁共振血管造影 **MRA**   Magnetic Resonance Angiography
- 核管理委员会 **NRC**   Nuclear Regulatory Commission
- 核紧急支援组 **NEST**   nuclear emergency support team
- 核糖核蛋白 **RNP**   ribonuleoprotein
- 核糖核酸 **RNA**   ribonucleic acid
- 核糖核酸干扰 **RNAi**   ribonucleic acid interference
- 核威胁倡议 **NTI**   Nuclear Threat Initiative
- 核心视频共享 **KVS**   kernel video sharing
- 核因子-κB **NF-κB**   nuclear factor-κB
- 盒式磁带录像机 **VCR**   video cassette recorder
- 赫兹[法定频率计量单位] **Hz**   hertz
- 黑暗神殿 **BT**   Black Temple
- 黑格(脱咖啡因咖啡)[德文:原意为咖啡贸易公司] **HAG**
  Kaffee Handels Aktien Gesellschaft
- 黑海经济合作组织 **BSEC**   Black Sea Economic Cooperation
- 黑客马拉松 **Hackathon**   hacker marathon
- 黑色 **B**   black
- 黑索金[炸药] **RDX**   Hexogen
- 黑翼之巢 **BWL**   Blackwing Lair

H

𨭆[第108号化学元素] Hs	hassium
很快回来[网络用语] BBS	be back soon
很快就打起瞌睡[网络用语] DOS	dozing off soon
很特殊级别 VS	very special
亨(利)[法定电感计量单位] H	Henry
恒定角速度 CAV	constant angular velocity
恒定线速度 CLV	constant linear velocity
恒生指数 HSI	Hang Seng Index
恒温器 THERMO	thermostat
横滨市[日本城市] YHAMA	Yokohama

横向扩散金属氧化物半导体 LDMOS
Laterally-diffused metal oxide semiconductor

横越导航系统 TNS	Transit Navigation System
轰炸 BBT	bombardment
红斑狼疮 LE	lupus erythematosus
红斑狼疮细胞 LEC	lupus erythematosus cell
红黄色 RY	red yellow
红军旅 RAF	Red Army Faction
红绿蓝三原色 RGB	red, green, blue
红牛[饮料] RB	Red Bull
红色 R	red
红十字国际委员会 RCIC	Red Cross International Committee
红十字会 RC	Red Cross

红十字会与红新月会国际联合会 IFRCRCS
International Federation of Red Cross and Red Crescent Societies

红细胞 E	erythrocyte
红细胞 RBC	red blood cell
红细胞比积 Hct/Ht	haematocrit
红细胞沉降率 ESR	erythrocyte sedimentation rate
红细胞甲状腺浓度测定 RBCT4	red blood cell total thyronine concentration
红细胞平均常数 MCC	mean corpuscular constants

- 红细胞平均厚度 MCT　　　　　mean corpuscular thickness
- 红细胞平均体积 MCV　　　　　mean cell volume
- 红细胞平均血红蛋白浓度 MCHC
  mean corpuscular hemoglobin concentration
- 红细胞平均血红蛋白量 MCH　　mean corpuscular hemoglobin
- 红细胞平均直径 MCD　　　　　mean corpuscular diameter
- 红细胞葡萄糖-6-磷酸脱氢酶 G6PD　glucose 6-phosphate dehydrogenase
- 红细胞渗透脆性试验 EOFT　　　erythrocyte osmotic fragility test
- 红细胞体积指数 VI　　　　　　volume index
- 红细胞压积 HCT　　　　　　　haematocrit
- 红血球 RBC　　　　　　　　　red blood cell
- 宏达国际电子股份有限公司[台湾] HTC
  High Technology Computer Corporation
- 宏观审慎评估/管理框架 MPA　　macroprudential assessment
- 宏伟目标 BHAG　　　　　　　big, hairy, audacious goal
- 洪都拉斯[北美洲国家] HON　　Honduras
- 后部 RR　　　　　　　　　　rear
- 后卫 FB　　　　　　　　　　fullback
- 后效/后果 AE　　　　　　　　after effect
- 后效 AE　　　　　　　　　　after effect
- 厚片模塑料 TMC　　　　　　　thick molding compound
- 呼叫记录监视器 CRM　　　　　call recording monitor
- 呼叫者声纹识别 CAVE　　　　　Caller Verification
- 呼吸 R　　　　　　　　　　　respiration
- 呼吸机相关性肺炎 VAP　　　　ventilator associated pneumonia
- 呼吸指数 RQ　　　　　　　　respiratory quotient
- 胡萝卜素 Car　　　　　　　　carotene
- 蝴蝶网络公司 BNI　　　　　　Butterfly Network Inc.
- 互补 DNA CDNA　　　　　　　complementary DNA
- 互补金属氧化物半导体 CMOS　　complementary metal-oxide semi-conductor
- 互动数字软件协会 IDSA　　　　Interactive Digital Software Association
- 互联网 i　　　　　　　　　　Internet

H

- 互联网安全大会 ISC　　　　　　Internet Security Committee
- 互联网成瘾综合征 IAS　　　　　Internet addiction syndrome
- 互联网电话 IP　　　　　　　　Internet Phone
- 互联网电影数据库 IMDB　　　　The Internet Movie Database
- 互联网服务提供商 ISP　　　　　Internet Services Provider
- 互联网技术及方案供应商 ITP　　Internet technology provider
- 互联网接入提供商 IAP　　　　　Internet Access Provider
- 互联网名称与数字地址分配机构 ICANN
  The Internet Corporation for Assigned Names and Numbers
- 互联网目录提供商 IDP　　　　　Internet directory provider
- 互联网数据中心 IDC　　　　　　Internet Data Center
- 互联网通信引擎 ICE　　　　　　Internet Communication Engine
- 互联网网络信息中心 Internic　　 Internet Network Information Center
- 互联网协议 IP　　　　　　　　Internet Protocal
- 互联网协议版本 IPV　　　　　　Internet Protocol Version
- 互联网邮件访问协议 IMAP　　　Internet Mail Access Protocol
- 互联网域名系统 IDNS　　　　　Internet domain name system
- 互联网在线聊天 IRC　　　　　　Internet Relay Chat
- 互联网组管理协议 IGMP　　　　Internet Group Management Protocol
- 花卉商全球速递 FDT　　　　　　Florists' Transworld Delivery
- 华大基因(北京基因组研究中心) BGI　Beijing Genomics Institute
- 华侨 OC　　　　　　　　　　　Overseas Chinese
- 华侨城 OCT　　　　　　　　　Overseas Chinese Town
- 华润万家(超市) CRvanguard　　China Resource Vanguard Co., Ltd.
- 华盛顿国家纪念碑 WNM　　　　Washington National Monument
- 华氏(温度)[德文] F　　　　　　Fahrenheit
- 华为企业[中国著名民企] HW　　Huawei
- 华为手机操作系统[英文义:情感使用者界面] EMUI
  Emotion User Interface
- 华为移动服务 HMS　　　　　　Huawei Mobile Services
- 华娱电视台 CETV　　　　　　　China Entertainment Television

- 华中科技大学 **HUST**
  Huazhong University of Science and Technology
- 化学纯 **CP** — chemically pure
- 化学反应式数据库 **CCR-Expanded** — Current Chemical Reaction Expanded
- 化学机械抛光 **CMP** — chemical mechanical polishing
- 化学抛光 **CHP** — chemical polishing
- 化学品注册、评估、许可和限制 **REACH**
  Registration, Evaluation, Authorization and Restriction of Chemicals
- 化学热磨机械浆 **CTMP** — Chemi-thermal mechanical pulp
- 化学生物武器 **CBM** — chemical-biological munitions
- 化学文摘社 **CAS** — Chemical Abstract Service
- 化学需氧量 **COD** — chemical oxygen demand
- 化学与矿物学分析仪 **Che Min** — Chemistry and Mineralogy Analysis
- 化妆品安全报告 **CPSR** — Cosmetic Product Safety Report
- 画 3D 图形的软件 **3DMAX** — 3D studio max
- 话音识别 **VR** — voice recognition
- 话语加工研究所 **ILSP**
  The Institute for Language and Speech Processing
- 欢迎提出建议 **AAA** — any advice appreciated
- 环保 3R 原则[再回收、再利用、再填充] **3R**
  recycle, reuse, refill
- 环保木制汽车 **NCV** — nano cellulose vehicle
- 环保污染付费原则 **PPP** — Pollute Pays Principle
- 环境保护署 **EAP** — Environmental Agency of Protection
- 环境分析与规划 **EAP** — environmental analysis and planning
- 环境辅助生活 **AAL** — air auxiliary life
- 环境工作组织 **EWG** — environmental work group
- 环境管理体系[环境、健康、安全] **EHS** — Environment, Health, Safety
- 环境管理体系 **EMS** — environmental management system
- 环境可持续指数 **ESI** — Environmental Sustainable Index
- 环境控制系统 **ECS** — environmental control system
- 环境评估 **DEA** — draft environmental assessment

H

- 环境调查局 **EIA**　　Environmental Investigation Association
- 环境问题行动委员会［美国］**ENACT**　　Environmental Action for Survival
- 环境小硕士［中国—瑞典合作项目］**YMP**　　Young Master Programme
- 环境影响评估 **EIA**　　environmental impact assessment
- 环境友好汽车 **EEV**　　energy efficiency vehicle
- 环磷酸腺苷 **CAMP**　　cyclic adenosine monophosphate
- 环磷酰胺和泼尼松［化疗方案］**CP**　　cyclophosphamide and prednisone
- 环球金融集团 **GFG**　　Global Financial Group
- 环球金融中心 **WFC**　　World Financial Center
- 环球商务中心 **IBC**　　International Business Center
- 环球银行间金融通信协会/环球同业银行金融电讯协会 **SWIFT**　　Society for Worldwide Interbank Financial Telecommunication
- 环氧合酶 **Cox**　　cyclooxygenase
- 环氧树脂 **EP**　　epoxy resin
- 换言之［拉丁文］**i. e.**　　id est
- 皇后 **Q**　　queen
- 皇家荷兰航空公司［荷兰文］**KLM**　　Koninkijke Luchtvaart Maatschappij
- 黄疸指数 **II**　　icterus index
- 黄红色 **YR**　　yellow red
- 黄金购物车［购买按钮］**BB**　　Buy Box
- 黄金矿业服务公司 **GFMS**　　Gold Fields Mineral Services
- 黄金与其他金属熔合而成的合金［纯金为24K（即100%含金量）］**K**　　Karat Gold
- 黄绿色 **YG**　　yellow green
- 黄嘌呤氧化酶 **XO**　　xanthine oxidase
- 黄色 **Y/YE**　　yellow
- 黄色指示灯 **YIL**　　yellow indicator lamp
- 黄体生成激素 **LH**　　luteinizing hormone
- 黄体酮 **P**　　progesterone
- 黄页 **YP**　　yellow page
- 挥发性有机化合物 **VOC**　　volatile organic compound

回电[网络用语] CB	call back
回复 Re	reply
回顾商业研究 RBR	Review of Business Research
回来谈这个话题[网络用语] BOT	back on topic
回邮信封 SAE	stamped addressed envelope
回邮信封 SASE	self-addressed stamped envelope
回执 AR	Acknowledgement of Receipt
汇编 ASSEM	assemble
汇率 ROE	Rate of Exchange
汇率范围 ERM	exchange rate margin
汇率机制 ERM	exchange rate mechanism
汇率调整附加费 CAF	currency adjustment factor
汇票 BE	Bill of Exchange
会话式监督系统 CMS	conversational monitor system
会计学硕士 MACC	master of accounting
昏倒[网络用语] FT	faint
混合动力[内燃机、电动机]汽车 HEV	hybrid electric vehicle
混合光纤同轴电缆 HFC	hybrid fiber coax
混合现实 MR	mixture reality
混合氧化物[铀和钚] MOX	mixed-oxide (uranium and plutonium)
混合自动重传请求 HARQ	hybrid automatic repeat request
活化凝血时间 ACT	activated clotting time
活期存款账户 A/C	account current
火币全球通用积分 HT	Huobi Token
火箭助推榴弹发射器 RPG	Rocket-Propelled Grenade
火控系统 FCS	fire control system
火速 pdq	pretty damn(ed) quick
火星科学实验室 MSL	Mars Scientific Laboratory
火星立方星一号 Mar CO	Mars Cube One
火星手持透镜成像仪 MAHLI	Mars Hand Lens Imager
火星样本分析仪 SAM	Sample Analysis at Mars
火灾报警系统 FAS	fire alarm system

J

- 伙伴对伙伴的关系 **PTOP**   partner to partner
- 伙伴关系管理 **PRM**   Partner Relationship Management
- 伙伴合作协定 **PCA**   Partners Cooperation Agreement
- 钬[第67号化学元素] **Ho**   Holmium
- 货币(贬值)附加费 **CAF**   currency adjustment factor
- 货币和燃油附加费 **CAF**   currency and bunker adjustment factor
- 货币监理署 **OCC**   Office of the Control of the Currency
- 货币市场存单 **MMC**   money market certificate
- 货币政策委员会 **MPC**   monetary policy committee
- 货到付款 **COD**   collect on delivery
- 货物出口前符合性认证[东非国家常用] **PVOC**   Pre-Export Verification of Conformity
- 货物售出概不退换 **WAF**   with all faults
- 货已收到凭证 **ROG**   receipt of goods
- 货运吨公里 **FTKs**   Freight Ton Kilometers
- 货运协会 **FTA**   Freight Transport Association
- 获取特定情报办公室[或称"陶小组"] **TAO**   Office of Tailored Access Operations
- 霍尔木兹和平动议 **HOPE**   Hormuz Peace Effort
- 霍尔瑞斯型计算机 **HTC**   Hollerith Type Computer

J

- 机场保安组/机场特警队 **ASU**   Airport Security Unit
- 机场交货价 **FOA**   free on airport
- 机动保护火力 **MPF**   mobile protection fire
- 机动船 **M/V**   motor vessel
- 机动平台分析 **AMP**   analysis of mobility platform

- 机读目录，由美国国会图书馆销售 MARC machine-readable catalog
- 机器辅助服务部 MARS — the Machine-Assisted Reference Section
- 机器人大赛 Robocon — robot contest
- 机上宽带服务计划 AirCell — cell phones on aircraft
- 机械变速器 MT — mechanical transmission
- 机械生长因素 MGF — Mechanical Growth Factor
- 机械式自动变速器 AMT — automated mechanical transmission
- 机械研究中心 CRM — Centre of Research of Machine
- 机载电磁发射系统 EMALS — electro-magnetic aircraft launch system
- 机载数据终端 ADT — airborne data terminal
- 机载卫星接收站 ASRS — airborne satellite receiving station
- 机组调度系统 UDS — unit dispatch system
- 肌肤之钥 SKII — key is to the skin and cpb
- 肌肤之钥化妆品[日本品牌][法文] CPB Clé de Peau Beauté
- 肌酐(血)[生化检查项目之一] Cr — creatinine
- 肌红蛋白试验 MbT — myoglobin test
- 肌肉萎缩症 MD — muscular dystrophy
- 肌酸 CRE — creatinine
- 肌酸激酶 CK — creatine kinase
- 肌酸磷酸激酶 CPK — creatine phosphokinase
- 肌痛性脑脊髓炎 ME — Myalgic Encephalomyelitis
- 肌萎缩侧索硬化症 ALS — amyotrophic lateral sclerosis
- 肌型肌酸激酶同工酶 CK-MM — MM isoenzyme of creatine kinase
- 基本操作系统 BOS — basic operation system
- 基本科学指标 ESI — Essential Science Indicators
- 基本科学指标数据库 ESI — essential science indicators
- 基本输入输出系统 BIOS — Basic Input Output System
- 基层疾病保险金管理处[法文] CPAM — Caisse Primaire d' Assurance Maladie
- 基础代谢率 BMR — basal metabolic rate
- 基础设施即服务 IaaS — infrastructure as a service

J

- 基础套件 FS foundation suite
- 基础体温 BBT basal body temperature
- 基督教民主联盟[德文] CDU Christlich-Demokratische Union
- 基督教女青年会 YWCA Young Women's Christian Association
- 基督教青年会 Y/YMCA
  Young Men's Christian Association
- 基督教社会联盟[德文] CSU Christlich-Soziale Union
- 基金中的基金 FOF fund of fund
- 基因编辑技术/基因剪刀 CRISPR
  clustered regularly interspaced short palindromic repeats
- 基因组靶向定位诱导损伤技术 TILLING
  Targeting Induced Local Lesions IN Genomes
- 基于发行的跨平台计算机视觉库 open-CV
  open source computer vision library
- 基于风险控制的院校评审 RAA risk-based approach to assessment
- 基于风险资本 RBC risk-based capital
- 基于光子的全数字雷达 PHODIR photonic-based fully digital radar
- 基于计算机的音乐分析 CBMA computer-based music analysis
- 基于人工智能来实现智能助手的项目 CALO
  Cognitive Assistant that Learns and Organizes
- 基于 Visual Basic 的一种宏语言 VBA Visual Basic for Applications
- 基于 Visual basic 的脚本版 VBS Visual Basic Script Edition
- 基于需求搜集 RBC requirements-based collection
- 基于学科的信息门户 SBIGs subject-based information gateways
- 基质金属蛋白酶 MMP matrix metalloproteinase
- 基准线 ZL zero line
- 激光 LASER
  light amplification by the stimulated emission of radiation
- 激光捕获显微切割 LCM laser-captured microdissection
- 激光唱盘 CD compact disc
- 激光唱片交互式光盘 CD-I compact disc interactive
- 激光传输 LOT laser optical transmission

- 激光干涉引力波天文台 **LIGD**
  Laser Interferometer Gravitation-Wave Observatory
- 激光光学角膜切削术 **PRK**　　photorefractive keratectomy
- 激光皮光电会议 **CLEO**　　Conference on Lasers and Electro-Optics
- 激光扫描共聚焦显微镜 **LSCM**　　laser scanning confocal microscope
- 激光视盘 **LD**　　laser disc
- 激光视盘 **LV**　　laser vision
- 激光视听盘 **LCD**　　laser compact disc
- 激素替代疗法 **HRT**　　hormone replacement therapy
- 及格［合格］**A**　　acceptable
- 吉（伯）［磁通势单位］**Gi**　　gilbert
- 吉［咖］［十进倍数单位的词头名称，其表示的因数为 10^9］**G**
  Giga
- 吉布提［非洲国家］**DJI**　　Djibouti
- 吉尔吉斯斯坦［亚洲国家］**KGZ**　　Kyrgyzstan［或 Kirghizstan］
- 吉林大学 **JU**　　Jilin University
- 吉隆坡盛季酒店 **GSHKL**　　Grand Seasons Hotel Kuala Lumpur
- 吉隆坡证券交易所 **KLSE**　　Kuala Lumpur Stock Exchange
- 吉士美卡 **JCB**　　Japan Credit bureau Card
- 吉字节 **G**　　GB (1 GB=1 024 MB,1 MB=1 024 KB)
- 吉字节［千兆字节，计算机存储器容量单位］**GB**
  GigaByte
- 级联类型表［它是专门为 Web 网页设计者和用户开发的一种样式表机制］**CSS**
  Cascading Style Sheet
- 极低密度脂蛋白 **VLDL**　　very low density lipoprotein
- 极低频 **ELF**　　extra low frequency
- 极度稀有 **UR(R)**　　ultra rate
- 极高频 **EHF**　　extra high frequency
- 极美等级（钱币）**XF**　　extremely fine
- 极危 **CR**　　critical
- 极重要的要人 **VVIP**　　very very important person
- 极紫外线 **EUV**　　extreme ultraviolet

J

- 极紫线光刻机［第六代光刻机］EUVL extreme ultraviolet lithography
- 即插即用传感器 P&P — plug and play
- 即期汇票 DD — demand draft
- 即时聊天工具 QQ — Oh, I seek you→OICQ→QQ
- 即时通信 IM — instant messaging
- 即时战略类游戏 RSG — realtime strategy game
- 即时战术游戏 RTT — realtime tactics
- 急性骨髓性白血病 AML — acute myelogenous leukemia
- 急性冠心病 ACD — Acute Coronary Disease
- 急性呼吸道感染 ARTI — acute respiratory tract infection
- 急性呼吸窘迫综合征 ARDS — Acute Respiratory Distress Syndrome
- 急性黄斑变性 AMD — acute macular degeneration
- 急性淋巴细胞白血病 ALL — acute lymphocytic leukemia
- 急性心肌缺血 AMI — acute myocardial ischemia
- 急性早幼粒细胞白血病 APL — acute promyelocytic leukemia
- 疾病（预防）控制中心 CDC — Centers for Disease Control and Prevention
- 集成财经服务 IFS — integrated financial services
- 集成产品开发 IPD — integrated product development
- 集成产品开发团队 IPT — integrated project team
- 集成电路 IC — integrated circuit
- 集成电路卡 IC — integrated circuit card
- 集成多核架构处理器 MIC — many integrated cores
- 集成和协同办公 ICO — integration and coordination office
- 集成开发环境 IDE — integrated development environment
- 集成逻辑存储公司 IML — Integrated Memory Logic Limited
- 集成驱动器电子设备 IDE — integrated drive electronics
- 集成组合管理团队 IPMT — integrated portfolio management team
- 集合供应链 ISC — integrated supply chain
- 集换式卡牌游戏 TCG — trading card game
- 集落刺激因子 CSF — colony-stimulating factor
- 集中采购管理 CPM — Concentrated Purchasing Management

集中供热 CH	central heating
集中营[德文] KZ	Konzentrationslager
集装箱 TEU	twenty-foot-equipment unit
集装箱 CTR	container
集装箱堆场 CY	container yard
集装箱服务费 CSC	container service charge
集装箱货运站 CFS	container freight station
集装箱拼箱 CONSOL	consolidation
几内亚[非洲国家] GUI	Guinea
几内亚比绍[非洲国家] GBS	Guinea-Bissau
脊髓性萎缩 SMA	spinal muscular atrophy
计划评估审查技术 PERT	program evaluation and review technique
计量单位 CU	calculated unit
计算机(辅助)段层摄影术 CT	computerized tomography
计算机[空客的飞行警告] FWC	flight warning computer (airbus)
计算机程序[电子文献标示字母] CP	computer program
计算机断层血管造影术 CTA	CT angio(arterio)graphy
计算机分销商展览会 COMDEX	Computer Dealer Exhibition
计算机辅助测量 CAM	computer-aided measurement
计算机辅助测试 CAT	computer-assisted testing
计算机辅助电话调查(系统) CATI	computer-aided telephone investigation
计算机辅助翻译;电脑翻译 CAT	computer-aided translation
计算机辅助翻译与传播大赛 CATTC computer-aided translation and transmission competition	
计算机辅助工程 CAE	computer-aided engineering
计算机辅助管理 CAM	computer-aided management
计算机辅助和支持的协作学习 CSCL	computer-supported collaborative learning
计算机辅助交通管制 CATC	computer-aided traffic control
计算机辅助教学 CAI	computer-aided instruction
计算机辅助教育 CAE	computer-aided education
计算机辅助贸易 CAT	computer-assisted trading
计算机辅助软件工程 CASE	computer-aided software engineering

J

- 计算机辅助扫描技术 CAST　　computer-assisted scanning techniques
- 计算机辅助设计 CAD　　computer-aided design
- 计算机辅助实验 CAE　　computer-aided experiment
- 计算机辅助探测 CAD　　computer-aided detection
- 计算机辅助细胞学检查 CCT　　computer-assisted cytology test
- 计算机辅助系统工程 CASE　　computer-aided systems engineering
- 计算机辅助心电图描记 CAE　　computer-assisted electro-cardiography
- 计算机辅助学习 CAL　　computer-aided learning
- 计算机辅助制造 CAM　　computer-aided manufacture
- 计算机行业协会 CIA　　Computer Industry Association
- 计算机绘图 CPD　　computer-produced drawing
- 计算机集成制造 CIM　　computer-integrated manufacture
- 计算机集成制造系统 CIMS　　computer-integrated manufacturing system
- 计算机技术工业协会 CompTIA　　Computer Technology Industry Association
- 计算机技术研究所 ICT　　Institute of Computer Technology
- 计算机联机实时应用语言 CORAL
　　computer on-line real-time applications language
- 计算机模拟程序 CSP　　computer simulation program
- 计算机模拟技术 CST　　computer simulation technique
- 计算机模拟教学 CSI　　Computer-Simulated Instruction
- 计算机设备和软件系统的自动目录 ACCESS
　　automated catalog of computer equipment and software system
- 计算机输出缩微胶片 COM　　computer output microfilm
- 计算机数字控制(机床) CNC　　computer numerical control
- 计算机图形辅助三维交互应用 CATIA
　　Computer-graphics Aided Three-dimensional Interactive Application
- 计算机预订系统 CRS　　computer reservation system
- 计算机支持的协同工作 CSCW　　computer-supported cooperative work
- 计算机资源管理 CRM　　computer resources management
- 计算机自动图形接口机 MAGIC
　　machine for automatic graphics interface to a computer
- 计算机自适应测试 CAT　　computer adaptive test

- 计算流体动力学 CFD　　computational fluid dynamics
- 记录 recd　　recorded
- 记录管理 RM　　Record Management
- 记忆棒 MS　　memory stick
- 纪源资本 GGV　　Granite Global Ventures
- 技术 tech　　technology
- 技术、人才、宽容 3T　　technology, talent, tolerance
- 技术、娱乐、设计[美国一家私有非营利机构的名称] TED
  Technology, Entertainment, Design
- 技术报告 TR　　technical report
- 技术发展 TD　　technique development
- 技术管理 MOT　　management of technology
- 技术管理局 TMB　　Technical Management Board
- 技术规范 TS　　technical specification
- 技术监察协会[俄文] TüV　　Technischer Überwachungsverein
- 技术数据报告 TDR　　technical data report
- 技术网络 TN　　technology network
- 技术委员会 TC　　technical committee
- 技术咨询组 TAG　　technical advisory group
- 技术资料 TD　　technology data
- 技术资料中心 TDC　　technology data centre
- 季节性情感障碍 SAD　　seasonal affective disorder
- 季中邀请赛 MSI　　mid-season invitational
- 加班 OT　　overtime
- 加大推力的火箭 TAR　　thrust-augmented rocket
- 加勒比地区公约组织 CATO　　Caribbean Area Treaty Organization
- 加勒比共同市场/加勒比自由贸易同盟 CCM/CARIFTA
  Caribbean Common Market, Caribbean Free-Trade Association
- 加勒比共同体和共同市场 CARI
  Caribbean Community and Common Market
- 加利福尼亚大学旧金山校区 UCSF　　University of California at San Francisco
- 加利福尼亚大学 UC　　University of California

J

- 加利福尼亚大学洛杉矶校区 **UCLA**　University of California at Los Angeles
- 加利福尼亚大学圣巴巴拉分校 **UCSB**　University of California at Santa Barbara
- 加利福尼亚后学后教育委员会 **CPEC**
  California Post-secondary Education Commission
- 加利福尼亚空中资源委员会 **CARB**　California Air Resources Board
- 加仑[非法定液量单位]，1 加仑＝4.546 升 **gal**
  gallon
- 加密密钥 **SK**　secure key
- 加拿大[北美洲国家] **CAN**　Canada
- 加拿大爱德华王子岛 **PEI**　Prince Edward Island
- 加拿大爱德华王子岛国家公园 **PEINP**
  Prince Edward Island National Park
- 加拿大安全标志 **ULC**
  Underwriters Laboratories Incorporation of Canada
- 加拿大保险商试验室 **ULC**
  Underwriters Laboratories Incorporation of Canada
- 加拿大北美北极研究所 **AINA**　Arctic Institute of North America
- 加拿大边境服务局 **CBSA**
  Canada Border Services Agency/Administration
- 加拿大标准协会 **CSA**　Canadian Standards Association
- 加拿大标准协会 **SCC**　Standards Council of Canada
- 加拿大大不列颠哥伦比亚省移民服务协会 **ISS of BC**
  The Immigration Services Society of British Columbia
- 加拿大大专院校联盟；加拿大高等院校协会 **AUCC**
  Association of Universities and Colleges of Canada
- 加拿大电视新闻台 **CTV**　Canadian Television
- 加拿大多伦多艺术馆 **AGT**　Art Gallery of Toronto
- 加拿大多伦多证券交易所 **TSE**　Toronto Stock Exchange
- 加拿大防爆、电气等认证标志 **EMR**　Energy and Miner Region
- 加拿大高级研究院 **CIFAR**　Canadian Institute For Advanced Research
- 加拿大工程院院士 **FCAE**　Fellow of Canadian Academy of Engine
- 加拿大广播公司 **CBC**　Canadian Broadcasting Corporation

- 加拿大国际开发署 **CIDA**   Canadian International Development Agency
- 加拿大国家加速器实验室 **CNAL**   Canadian National Accelerator Laboratory
- 加拿大国家科学研究委员会 **NRCC**   National Research Council of Canada
- 加拿大国家研究委员会[法文] **CNRC**   Conseil national de recherches Canada
- 加拿大化学协会会员 **FCIC**   Fellow of the Chemical Institute of Canada
- 加拿大皇家警察 **CRM**   Canadian Royal Mounties
- 加拿大皇家骑警 **RCMP**   Royal Canadian Mounted Police
- 加拿大皇家协会会员 **FRSC**   Fellow of the Royal Society of Canada
- 加拿大皇家银行 **RBC**   Royal Bank of Canada
- 加拿大建材产品质量认证标志 **CGSB**   Canadian General Standards Board
- 加拿大教育协会 **CEA**   Canadian Education Association
- 加拿大教育研究委员会 **CCRE**   Canadian Council for Research in Education
- 加拿大昆特兰理工大学 **KPU**   Kwantlen Polytechnic University
- 加拿大联邦移民、难民及公民部 **IRCC**   Immigration, Refugees and Citizenship, Canada
- 加拿大麻醉师学会 **CAS**   Canadian Anesthetists' Society
- 加拿大青年协会 **CYA**   Canadian Youth Association
- 加拿大青少年团体 **JTC**   Junior Team Canada
- 加拿大社会科学研究委员会 **CSSRC**   Canadian Social Sciences Research Council
- 加拿大氢强度映射团队 **CHIME**   Canadian Hydrogen Intensity Mapping Experiment
- 加拿大石油地质工程技术有限公司 **PGI**   Petro-Geotech Incorporated
- 加拿大食品检验局 **CFIA**   Canada Food Inspection Agency
- 加拿大橡胶协会 **RAC**   Rubber Association of Canada
- 加拿大新闻社 **CNS**   Canadian News Service
- 加拿大新移民的语言教学 **LINC**   Language Instruction for Newcomers in Canada
- 加拿大信息处理学会 **CIPS**   Canadian Information Processing Society
- 加拿大移民顾问协会 **CSIC**   Canadian Society of Immigration Consultants

J

- 加拿大与欧盟全面经济与贸易协定 **CETA**
  Comprehensive Economical Trade Agreement
- 加拿大元[货币符号] **CAD/Can**   Canadian dollar
- 加拿大政府特别研究奖学金 **SCAS**
  Special Canadian Academic Scholarship
- 加拿大中国教育委员会 **CCEC**   Canada China Education Council
- 加拿大—中国科学技术协会 **CCSST**
  Canada-China Society for Science and Technology
- 加拿大中央标准理事会 **CGSB**   Canadian General Standards Board
- 加纳[非洲国家] **GHA**   Ghana
- 加纳标准局 **GSB**   Ghana Standards Board
- 加纳认证标志 **GSB**   Ghana Standards Board
- 加蓬[非洲国家] **GAB**   Gabon
- 加权的分数计数 **WFC**   weighted fractional count
- 加速并行处理技术 **APP**   accelerated parellel processing
- 加速器驱动次临界洁净核能系统 **ADS**
  accelerator driven sub-critical system
- 加值 **GVA**   gross value added
- 加州大学伯克利分校[美国] **UCB**   University of California, Berkeley
- 加州大学洛杉矶分校[美国] **UCLA**   University of California, Los Angeles
- 加州大学圣地亚哥分校 **UCSD**   University of California, San Diego
- 加州环境保护署 **CalEPA**   California Environmental Protection Agency
- 加州理工学院[美国] **CIT**   California Institute of Technology
- 家庭光纤网络 **HONET**   home optical network
- 家庭数据中心 **HDC**   Home Digital Center
- 家庭影院电脑 **HTPC**   home theater personal computer
- 家庭娱乐中心 **HET**   home entertainment center
- 家庭在线 **HOL**   Home On Line
- 家庭自动化 **HA**   home automation
- 家用录像机/家庭录像系统 **VHS**   video home system
- 家长、成人、小孩 **PAC**   parent, adult, children
- 家长教师联盟会 **PTA**   parent-teacher association

- 镓[第31号化学元素] **Ga**   gallium
- 甲苯胺蓝纠正试验 **TBT**   toluidine blue rectification test
- 甲醇 **MAL/Me alc**   methyl alcohol
- 甲酚-甲醛树脂 **CF**   cresol-formaldehyde(resin)
- 甲肝抗体 **HAV-IgM**   hepatitis A virus immunoglobulin M
- 甲基丙烯酸甲酯-丁二烯-苯乙烯共聚物[塑料] **MBS**   methyl methacrylate-butadiene styrene copolymer
- 甲基噻唑基四唑 **MTT**   methyl thiazolyl tetrazolium
- 甲基肾上腺素 **MN**   metanephrine 3-
- 甲基纤维素[塑料] **MC**   methyl cellulose
- 甲胎蛋白 **AFP**   alpha fetoprotein
- 甲烷 **meth**   methane
- 甲型肝炎病毒 **HAV**   hepatitis A virus
- 甲型肝炎抗体 **HAAb**   hepatitis A antibody
- 甲型肝炎抗原 **HAAg**   hepatitis A antigen
- 甲氧西林耐药金黄色葡萄球菌 **MRSA**   methicillin resistant staphylococcus aureus
- 甲状旁腺激素 **PTH**   parathyroid hormone
- 甲状旁腺激素相关蛋白 **PTHrP**   parathyroid hormone-related protein
- 甲状腺素结合球蛋白 **TBG**   thyroxine-binding globulin
- 钾[第19号化学元素][拉丁文] **K**   kalium
- 钾[第19号化学元素] **K**   potassium
- 假期 **vac**   vacation
- 假情报 **FI**   fake intelligence
- 价格表现指数 **CPI**   cost performance index
- 价格收益率 **Pe**   price-to-earnings(ratio)
- 价值创造型经营 **MBC**   management by creation
- 价值管理 **VM**   value-based management
- 价值链 **VC**   Value Chain
- 驾驶标准局 **DSA**   Driving Standards Agency
- 驾驶舱语音记录器 **CVR**   cockpit voice recorder
- 驾驶防瞌睡监视器 **DM**   drowsiness monitor

J

驾驶时燃料切断 FCDR	fuel-cutoff-in-drive
驾驶稳定性控制 DSC	drive stability control
架桥装甲车 AVLB	armored vehicle launched bridge
尖锐湿疣 CA	Condyloma Acuminatum
坚忍不拔的博弈 IG	invictus game
间变性淋巴瘤激酶 ALK	anaplastic lymphomatous kinase
间碘苄胍 MIBG	Meta-Iodo Benzy Guanidine
间接胆红素 I-Bil	indirect bilirubin
间接血细胞凝集抗体 IHA	indirect hemagglutination antibody
间接荧光抗体实验 IFA(T)	indirect fluorescent antibody test
监察长（公署）IG	Inspector General
兼并收购 M&A	mergers and acquisitions
兼职 PT	part-time
兼职助理 PTA	part-time assistant
柬埔寨[亚洲国家] CAM	Cambodia
柬埔寨救国党[已解散] CNRP	Cambodia National Rescue Party
减蛋综合征 EDS	egg drop syndrome

减少、再利用、再循环[环保者的格言] 3R
reduce, reuse, recycle

减少 dmsh	diminish
减震垫 INSUL	insulator
简单对象访问协议 SOAP	simple object access protocol
简单移动平均线 SMA	simple moving average
简单邮件传输协议 SMTP	simple message transfer protocol
简化指令集计算（机）RISC	reduced instruction set computing
简历[拉丁文] CV	curriculum vitae
简易爆炸装置 IED	improvised explosive device
简易凝血活酶生成试验 STGT	simplified thromboplastin generation test
简易信息聚合 RSS	really simple syndication
碱过量 BE	base excess
碱性成纤维细胞生长因子 BFGF	basic fibroblast growth factor
碱性磷酸酶 ALP	alkaline phosphatase

中文	缩略语	英文
见下页	PTO	please turn over
建行融资租赁	CCB Financial Leasing	China Construction Bank Financial Leasing
建设、运营、转让[是一种新兴的投资融资方式]	BOT	build, operate, transfer
建设-移交模式	BT	building-transfer
建筑工程师	Bldg E	building engineer
建筑工业协会	CIA	Construction Industries Association
建筑物的楼层	F	floor
建筑信息模型	BIM	building information modeling
剑桥秘书证书考试	BSC	British Secretary of Cambridge
剑桥大学	CU	Cambridge University
剑桥大学考试委员会	UCLES	University of Cambridge Local Examinations Syndicate
剑桥翻译委员会	CCT	Cambridge Committee of Translation
剑桥英语技能考试	CELS	Certificates in English Language Skills
健康、安全与环境一体化管理	EHS	environment, health, safety
健康、安全、环境一体化管理体系	HSE	Health, Safety, Environment
健康保险审查委员会	HIRC	health insurance review committee
健康财富规划师	HWP	health & wealth planner
健康风险评估	HRA	Health Risk Appraisal
健康风险评价	HRA	health risk assessment
健康商数[指一个人的健康智慧及对健康的态度]	HQ	Health Quotient
健康长寿,财源滚滚	LLAP	live long and prosper
舰船间无线电通话	TBS	talk between ships
舰队反恐安全组	FAST	Fleet Antiterrorist Security Team
舰载型 Shchuka 导弹[俄文]	KSS	Korabelny Snaryad "Strela"
渐冻人症	ALS	amyotrophic lateral sclerosis
渐进式动力转向机构	PPG	progressive power steering gear
键控穿孔操作员	KPO	key punch operator

J

- 江淮汽车[中国合肥] JAC　　Jianghuai Automobile Company
- 江苏自动化研究所 JARI　　Jiangsu Automation Research Institute
- 将军 Gen　　general
- 将要去 gonna　　going to
- 降低成本的管理 CRM　　cost reduction management
- 降低造价 RCO　　reduce the cost
- 降钙素 CT　　calcitonin
- 交错视频点播 SVOD　　Staggered VOD
- 交付前检查[售前服务] PDI　　pre-delivery inspection
- 交互式多媒体电视 IMTV　　interactive multimedia television
- 交互式视频点播 IVOD　　interactive video on demand
- 交互式语音应答 IVR　　interactive voice response
- 交货单存款证明 CD　　Certificate of Delivery
- 交货前付款 CBD　　cash before delivery
- 交流/直流/接地电流 AC/DC/EC
  alternating current/direct current/earth current
- 交流发电机 ALT　　alternator
- 交流发电机 ALTNTR　　alternator
- 交通安全性服务 TSS　　traffic safety service
- 交通部 DOT　　Department of Transportation
- 交通银行 BCM　　Bank of Communications
- 交响乐团 SO　　symphony orchestra
- 交易所交易基金 ETF　　Exchange Trading Fund
- 交易型开放式指数基金 ETF　　Exchange Trading Fund
- 交易总额 GMV　　gross merchandise value
- 交战区 ZF　　zone of fire
- 焦碳酸二乙酯 DEPC　　diethyl pyrocarbonate
- 角膜塑形镜,通过改变角膜形状来达到矫正近视目的的一种硬性隐形眼镜 OK orthokeratory
- 轿车 S　　sedan
- 较发达国家 MDC　　more developed country

495

较好 E	exceeds expectation
较好级（钱币）AG	about good
教练机 T	trainer
教学电视 ITV	instructional television
教育 Ed	education
教育部考试中心 NEEA	National Educational Examinations Authority
教育发展机会 EGO	educational growth opportunities
教育服务有限公司 ESI	Educational Services, Inc.
教育核心期刊全文数据库 PDC	Professional Development Collection
教育理学硕士 M. S. Ed	Master of Science in Education
教育模拟模型 ESM	educational simulation model
教育指数 EI	education index
教育咨询委员会 EAC	Education Advisory Committee
接地继电器盘 GRP	ground relay panel
接收信号强度 RSS	received signal strength
街 st/St	street
街道 Pl	place
街头篮球联盟 SBA	Street Basketball Association
节俭储蓄计划 TSP	thrifty savings plan
节目主持人 MC	Master of Ceremony
节奏蓝调[黑人流行音乐] R&B	Rhythm & Blues
杰西博挖掘装载机 JCB	Joseph Cyril Bamford
洁净空气量 CADR	clean air delivery rate
洁食认证 Kosher	Kosher certificate
结构工程师 ME	mechanical engineer
结构化编程 SP	structured programming
结构化查询语言 SQL	Structured Query Language
结构性植物蛋白 TVP	textured vegetable protein
结合胆酸 CCA	combining cholalic acid
结核菌素试验 OT	old tuberculin test

J

- 结转 B/O   brought over
- 捷孚凯[德文] GfK
  Gesellschaft für Konsum-, Markt-und Absatzforschung
- 捷克[欧洲国家] CZ   Czech
- 捷克电气产品质量认证标志[捷克文] ČSN
  Československých Státnich Norem
- 捷克共和国[欧洲国家] CZE   Czech Republic
- 截止日期 DD   deadline data
- 姐夫;妹夫;妻舅[网络用语] BIL   brother-in-law
- 解放 LIB   liberation
- 解放运动 LM   liberation movement
- 解谜类游戏 PZL   puzzle game
- 解剖死腔 Vdanat/VDas   anatomic dead space
- 借贷对照表 soc   statement of condition
- 借方 Dr   debtor
- 借方币 DBTC   debitcoin
- 借款通知单 DA   debit advice
- 借条 IOU   I owe you
- 借项清单 D/N   debit note
- 今日俄罗斯 RT   Russia Today
- 今日俄罗斯电视台 RTTV   Russia Today Television
- 今天我穿什么[网络用语] WIWT   What I wear today?
- 金[第79号化学元素][拉丁文] Au   aurum[英文为 gold]
- 金币[代字] AU   gold
- 金福饭店 KFKR   Kim Fook Korean Restaurant
- 金桥奖 GBA   Golden Bridge Award
- 金融创新与金融稳定 FIFS   financial innovation and financial stability
- 金融犯罪委员会 EFCC   Economic & Financial Crimes Commission
- 金融风险管理师 FR-M   Financial Risk Manager
- 金融风险管理师证书 FR-M   Financial Risk Manager
- 金融服务管理局 FSA   financial service authority

金融行动特别工作组 FATF	Financial Action Task Force
金融理财师 AFP	associate financial planner
金融贸易收支差额 BOT	balance of trade
金融信息传输系统[丹麦文] SPFA	Sparekassen Faaborg
金融英语证书考试 FECT	Financial English Certificate Test
金色 GLD	gold
金属孔眼 GROM	grommet
金属商品经理 MCM	metal commodity manager
金属陶瓷发热体 MCH	metal ceramics heater
金属硬度[代号] H	Hardness
金砖五国(指巴西、俄罗斯、印度、中国和南非) BRICS	the countries of Brazil, Russia, India, China and South Africa
津巴布韦[非洲国家] ZIM	Zimbabwe
仅差学校论文即可毕业 ABD	all but dissertation
仅供参考 FIO	for information only
紧凑式闪存 CF	compact flash
紧凑型轿车 C	coupe
紧急避孕 EC	emergency contraception
紧急发射指令 EAM	emergency action message
紧急行动的清单 EACL	emergency action checklist
紧急净化设备 EDF	emergency decontamination facility
紧急救生系统 ESS	emergency survival system
紧急情况缓解委员会 ERA	Emergency Relief Administration
紧急燃油附加费 EBAF	emergency bunker adjustment factor
紧急通知 APB	all points bulletin
紧急图像判读中心 IIIC	immediate imagery interpretation center
紧急制动辅助系统 EBA	emergency brake assistant
紧身舞衣 Danskin	dance+skin
紧身衣裤 BS	body suit
尽可能多[网络用语] AMAP	as much [many] as possible
进步力量联盟[法文] UFP	Union des Forces du Progrès

J

进场照明系统 ALS	approach-light system
进出口银行 EIB	Export-Import Bank
进阶精简报令集机器 ARM	Advanced RISC Machine
进口安全申报 ISF	Importer Security Filing
进口配额 IQ	import quota
进口许可证 IL	import license
进气 INT	intake
进气道燃油喷射系统 PFI	port fuel injected (system)
进气温度 ACT	air charge temperature
进气系统 AIS	air intake system
进展期疾病 PD	progressive disease
进展生存期 PFS	progression life survival
近场通信 NFC	near field communication
近地天体 NEO	Near Earth Object
近距离空中支援 CAS	Close Air Support
近距离无线电通信（技术）NFC	near field communication
近距离支援火力 CSF	close supporting fire
近未流通级（钱币）AU	about uncirculated
近战武器（游戏）CCW	close combat weapon
禁毒署 DEA	Drug Enforcement Agency
禁区 ZI	zone interdict
禁止化学武器组织 OPCW	Organization for the Prohibition of Chemical Weapons
禁止停车 NP	No Parking
京东［汉语拼音缩略语］JD	Jingdong
经常项目 C/A	current account
经常预算 RB	regular budget
经度 LONG	longitude
经管学院 SEM	School of Economics and Management
经纪商收益 YTB	yield to broker
经济规划机构 EPA	Economic Planning Agency
经济国际主义 EI	Economic Internationalism

经济国家主义 EN　　　　　　　　Economic Nationalism
经济合作与发展组织 OECD
　　Organization for Economic Cooperation and Development
经济互助委员会 CEMA　　　　　Council for Economic Mutual Assistance
经济伙伴关系协定 EPA　　　　　Economic Partnership Agreement
经济景气指数［德文，由欧洲经济研究中心引申而来］ ZEW
　　Zentrum für Europäische Wirtschafts forschung
经济开发区 BID　　　　　　　　Business Improvement District
经济特区 SEZ　　　　　　　　　Special Economic Zone
经济型的 E　　　　　　　　　　economic
经济研究局 ERS　　　　　　　　economic research service
经济研究学会［德文］ IFO　　　　Institut für Wirtschaftsforschung
经济与商业研究中心 CEBR
　　Centre for Economics and Business Research
经济增加值 EVA　　　　　　　　economic value added
经济政策委员会 EPC　　　　　　Economic Policy Committee
经静脉肾动脉造影术 IRA　　　　intravenous renal arteriography
经颅多普勒超声 TCD　　　　　　transcranial Doppler
经皮冠状动脉介入治疗 PCI　　　percutaneous coronary intervention
经皮经肝胆道镜检查 PTCS　　　percutaneous transhepatic cholangioscopy
经皮内镜下胃造瘘术 PEG　　　　percutaneous endoscopic gastrostomy
经皮心肺辅助法 PCPS　　　　　 percutaneous cardiopulmonary support
经前紧张征 PMT　　　　　　　　premenstrual tension
经前综合征 PMS　　　　　　　　premenstrual sydrome
经认可的葡萄产区［美国葡萄酒质量管理］ AVA
　　Approved Viticultural Area
经认证的经营者 AEO　　　　　　authorized economic operator
晶片规模集成电路 WSI　　　　　wafer scale integration
精氨酸琥珀酸裂解酶 ASL　　　　argininosuccinate lyase
精氨酸酶 ARG　　　　　　　　　arginase
精对苯二甲酸 PTA　　　　　　　pure terephthalic acid
精简指令集计算（机） RISC　　　reduced instruction set computing

J

- 精简指令系统计算机 RISC   Reduced instruction system computer
- 精美级（钱币）F   fine
- 精密模拟计算设备 PACE   precision analog computing equipment
- 精确定位器 PINPOINT   personal identification number+point
- 精神病学促进小组 GAP   Group for the Advancement of Psychiatry
- 精选极美级（钱币）CHXF   choice extremely fine
- 精选近未流通级（钱币）CHAU   choiced about uncirculated
- 精选未流通级（钱币）CHMS   choiced mint state
- 精选优美级（钱币）CHVF   choiced very fine
- 精英中的精英[网络用语] BOB   best of the best
- 精子低渗肿胀试验 HOS   sperm hypoosmotic swelling experiment
- 颈动脉 CP   carotid pulse
- 颈动脉-股动脉搏动波速度 C-FPWV   carotid-femoral pulse wave velocities
- 颈内动脉 CICA   cervical internal carotid artery
- 警察[网络用语] CT   counter terrorist
- 警察到达犯罪现场所需的时间 TAP   time of arrived police
- 警察局 PD   Police Department
- 警监会 IPCC   Independent Police Complaints Council
- 警犬队 PDU   Police Dog Unit
- 警司 Supt   superintendent
- 警员 PC   police constable
- 警员[对警察的一种幽默称呼] PC Plod   Police Constable Plod
- 净评级 NG   net grade
- 净推荐值 NPS   net promoter score
- 净重 N.W.   net weight
- 净资产收益率 ROE   return on equity
- 竞速类游戏 RAC   race game
- 竞争、消费和打击舞弊总局[法文] DGCCRF   Direction Générale de la Concurrence de la Consommation et de la Répression des Fraudes
- 静脉 V   vein

- 静脉葡萄糖耐量实验 **IGTT**　　intravenous glucose tolerance test
- 静脉曲张 **VV**　　varicose veins
- 静脉血 **V**　　venous blood
- 境外基金 **OSF**　　off-shore fund
- 境外企业人民币结算账户 **NRA**　　Non-Resident Account
- 纠错编码 **ECC**　　error correcting code
- 酒吧 **PH**　　public house
- 酒吧秀 **PS**　　pub show
- 酒精-麻醉剂综合预防教育 **CADPE**
  comprehensive alcohol-drug prevention education
- 酒泉宇航中心 **JSC**　　Jiuquan Space Center
- 救生 **R&R**　　rescue and resuscitation
- 救生船 **LB**　　life boat
- 就我来说［网络用语］**AFAIC**　　as far as I'm concerned
- 就我所能回忆的［网络用语］**AFAIR**　　as far as I recall
- 就业服务系统管理员 **ESSA**　　employment service systems administrator
- 居里(非法定放射性活度计量单位) **Ci**　　curie
- 居民消费调查 **RCI**　　resident cost inspection
- 居伊·拉罗希服装 **GL**　　Guy Laroche
- 锔［第 96 号化学元素］**Cm**　　curium
- 局域网络 **LAN**　　local area network
- 矩阵实验室 **MATLAB**　　matrix laboratory
- 巨幕(影像系统) **IMAX**　　Image Maximum
- 巨细胞病毒 **CMV**　　cytomegalovirus
- 巨型钻地弹 **MOP**　　Massive Ordnance Penetrator
- 据我所知［网络用语］**AFAIA**　　as far as I am aware
- 据我所知［网络用语］**AFAIK**　　as far as I know
- 聚 α-甲基苯乙烯［塑料］**PMS**　　poly(alpha-methyl styrene)
- 聚 α-烯烃 **PAO**　　polyalphaolefin
- 聚氨酯［塑料］**PU**　　polyurethane
- 聚苯 **PP**　　polyphenyl

J

J

聚苯砜[塑料] PPSU	polyphenylene sulfone
聚苯醚[塑料] PPO	polyphenylene oxide
聚苯烯腈[塑料] PAN	polyacrylonitrile
聚苯乙烯[塑料] PS	polystyrene
聚变相关设计研究 FDS	Fusion Design Study
聚丙烯[塑料] PP	polypropylene
聚丙烯无规共聚物[塑料] PP-R	polypropylene random copolymer
聚餐后的 AA 制 AA	each each
聚丁烯-[1][塑料] PB	polybutene-1
聚对苯二甲酸丁二醇酯[塑料] PBT	polybutylene terephthalate
聚对苯二甲酸乙二醇酯[塑料] PET	polyethylene terephthalate
聚芳砜[塑料] PASU	polyarylsulfone
聚芳醚[塑料] PAE	polyarylether
聚芳醚酮[塑料] PAEK	polyaryletherketone
聚芳酯[塑料] PAT	polyarylate
聚光光伏 CPV	concentrating photovoltaics
聚光太阳能发电 CSP	Concentrating Solar Power
聚合酶链反应 PCR	polymerase chain reaction
聚甲基丙烯酸甲酯[塑料] PMMA	polymethyl methacrylate
聚甲醛[塑料] POM	polyoxymethylene
聚邻苯二(甲)酰胺[塑料] PPA	polyphthalylamide
聚氯乙烯[塑料] PVC	polyvinyl chloride
聚醚砜[塑料] PES	polyether sulfone
聚醚醚酮[塑料] PEEK	polyetheretherketone
聚醚酮[塑料] PEK	polyether ketone
聚醚酰亚胺[塑料] PEI	polyetherimide
聚醚型聚氨酯[塑料] PEUR	polyether urethane
聚偏(二)氟乙烯[塑料] PVDF	polyvinylidene fluoride
聚偏(二)乙烯[塑料] PVDC	polyvinyl dichloride
聚四氟乙烯[塑料] PTFE	polytetrafluoroethylene
聚碳酸酯(塑料) PC	polycarbonate
聚烯烃低聚饱和烃 POSH	polyolefin oligomeric saturated hydrocarbons
聚酰胺尼龙 PA	polyamide nylon

- 聚酰胺-酰亚胺[塑料] **PAI**　　polyamide imide
- 聚酰亚胺[塑料] **PI**　　polyimide
- 聚腺苷二磷酸-核糖聚合酶 **PARP**　　poly（ADP-ribose）polymerase
- 聚亚苯基砜[塑料] **PSU**　　polyphenylene sulfone
- 聚亚苯基硫醚[塑料] **PPS**　　polyphenylene sulfide
- 聚乙烯[打包食品的塑料袋的标注] **PE**　　polyethylene
- 聚乙烯醇[塑料] **PVAL**　　polyvinyl alcohol
- 聚酯 **PET**　　polyester
- 聚酯醇酸树脂 **PAK**　　Polyester alkyd resins
- 聚酯型聚氨酯[塑料] **PAUR**　　polyester polyurethane
- 卷；册 **vol**　　volume
- 卷积神经网络 **CNN**　　Convolution Neural Network
- 决策支持系统 **DSS**　　decision support system
- 决定性打击 **CB**　　crushing blow
- 角色扮演游戏 **RPG**　　role-playing game
- 绝版 **OP**　　out of print
- 绝对平均 **AA**　　absolute average
- 绝缘体 **IL**　　insulator
- 绝缘栅双极型晶体管 **IGBT**　　insulated gate bipolar transistor
- 爵级司令勋位 **KBE**　　Knight Commander of the Order of the British Empire
- 爵士级别的司令勋章（女）**DBE**　　Dame Commander of the Order of the British Empire
- 军队自动化指挥系统（指挥、控制、通信、计算机、情报、监视、侦察）**C4ISR**　　command, control, communication, computer, intelligence, surveillance, reconnaissance
- 军情六处 **MI 6**　　Military Intelligence 6
- 军情五处 **MI 5**　　Military Intelligence 5
- 军士 **NCO**　　non-commissioned officer
- 军事革命 **RMA**　　Revolution in Military Affairs
- 军事牧师协会 **MCA**　　Military Chaplain's Association
- 军事外科医院 **MASH**　　medical army surgical hospital

军事系统报告 AD	Accession Document
军团菌抗体试验 anti-LP	legionella antibody test
军用防休克裤 MUST	military unshock trousers
军用国家标准(汉语拼音缩写) GJB	Guo Jun Biao
军用炸药[代字] C4	military explosive
均等就业机会委员会 EEOC	Equal Employment Opportunity Commission
均方位移 MSD	mean square displacement
均衡(音响) EQ	equalization
菌落形成单位 CFU	colony-forming unit

K

咖啡因 caff	caffeine
喀喇昆仑公路 KKH	Karakorum Highway
喀喇昆仑山 K	Klawquelen
喀麦隆[非洲国家] CMR	Cameroon
卡尔文·卡莱时装 CK	Calvin Klein
卡介苗 BCG	bacillus Calmette-Guerin
卡拉 OK 包房 KTV	Karaok TV
卡拉奇给水与排污委员会 KWSC	Karachi Water and Sewerage Commission
卡拉奇造船及机械制造厂 KSEW	Karachi Shipyard & Engineering Works
卡内基教育电视委员会 CCET	Carnegie Commission on Educational Television
卡内基音乐和戏剧委员会 CCMD	Carnegie Committee for Music and Drama
卡片类游戏 CAG	card game
卡片随机存取存储器 CRAM	card random access memory
卡塔尔[亚洲国家] QAT	Qatar
开(尔文)[法定温度计量单位] K	Kelvin

- 开发《星球争霸》竞赛时广泛使用的应用编程界面 **BWAPI**
  Brood War Application Programming Interface
- 开放大学 **TOU**　　　　　　　　The Open University
- 开放公共源码许可协议 **GPL**　　GNU Public License
- 开放获取期刊目录 **DOAJ**　　　 Directory of Open Access Journals
- 开放教育资源 **OER**　　　　　　open educational resource
- 开放金融交易 **OFE**　　　　　　open financial exchange
- 开放式的自然交互 **open NI**　　open natural interaction
- 开放网络基金会 **ONF**　　　　　open network foundation
- 开放系统互联 **OSI**　　　　　　open system interconnection
- 开放线性磁带 **LTO**　　　　　　linear tape-open
- 开放性实时以太网标准 **EPS**　　Ethernet for Plant Automation
- 开放运算语言 **open CL**　　　　open computer Language
- 锎[第 98 号化学元素] **Cf**　　 californium
- 坎(德拉)或新烛光[法定发光强度计量单位] **cd**
  candela
- 抗 O **ASO**　　　　　　　　　　antistreptolysin-O
- 抗病毒蛋白(质) **AVP**　　　　　antiviral protein
- 抗冲击聚苯乙烯[塑料] **IPS**　　impact-resistant polystyrene
- 抗骨骼肌抗体 **ASA**　　　　　　anti-skeletal muscle antibody
- 抗核抗体 **ANA**　　　　　　　　antinuclear antibody
- 抗甲状腺抗体 **ATA**　　　　　　anti-thyroid antibody
- 抗甲状腺球蛋白抗体 **ATGA**　　 antithyroglobulin antibody
- 抗碱血红蛋白测定 **HbF**　　　　Alkali-resistant hemoglobin determination
- 抗精子抗体 **AsAb**　　　　　　 antisperm antibody
- 抗菌能力与苯酚 20％的水溶液抗菌效力相同 **UMF20＋**
  Unique Manuka Factor 20＋
- 抗利尿激素 **ADH**　　　　　　　antidiuretic hormone
- 抗链球菌溶血素"O" **ASO**　　　antistreptolysin O
- 抗凝血酶 **AT**　　　　　　　　　antithrombin
- 抗平滑肌(自身)抗体 **ASMA**　　 anti-smooth muscle antibody
- 抗平滑肌抗体 **SMA**　　　　　　smooth muscle antibody

K

- 抗肾上腺皮质抗体 AAA　　anti-adrenal cortex antibody
- 抗肾小球基底膜抗体 AGBM
  antiglomerular basement membrane antibody
- 抗体依赖性细胞毒性 ADCC
  antibody-dependent cell mediated cytotoxicity
- 抗微生物药耐药性 AMR　　antimicrobial resistance
- 抗线粒体抗体 AMA　　anti-mitochondrial antibody
- 抗心肌抗体 AMA　　anti-myocardial antibody
- 抗心磷脂抗体 ACA　　anti-cardiac phospholipids antibody
- 抗心脂抗体 ACLA　　anti-cardiolipin antibody
- 抗胰岛细胞抗体 AICA　　anti-insulin cell antibody
- 抗着丝点抗体 ACA　　anticentromere antibody
- 抗中性粒细胞胞浆抗体 ANCA　　antineutrophil cytoplasmic antibody
- 抗组织蛋白抗体 AHA　　anti-histone antibody
- 钪[第 21 号化学元素] Sc　　scandium
- 考爱岛试验设施 KTF　　Kauai Test Facility
- 拷贝至中国 C2C　　copy to China
- 烤肉野餐 BBQ　　barbecue
- 靠近 nr　　near
- 科尔伯格-克拉维斯 KKR　　Kohlberg Kravis Roberts
- 科幻小说[或电影等] SF/sci-fi　　science fiction
- 科技、媒体、通信[以互联网联结起来的新兴行业] TMT
  technology, media, telecom
- 科技、娱乐、设计 TED　　technology, entertainment, design
- 科技大学 tech　　technical college
- 科技英语 EST　　English for Science and Technology
- 科伦坡国际集装箱码头 CICT　　Colombo International Container Terminal
- 科摩罗[非洲国家] COM　　Comoros
- 科斯达克[韩国创业板] KASDAQ
  Korean Association of Security Dealers Automated Quotations
- 科索沃阿尔巴尼亚保护部队[阿尔巴尼亚文] TMK
  Trupat Mbrojtese to Kosoves

- 科特迪瓦[非洲国家] **CIV** — Côte d'lvoire
- 科威特[亚洲国家] **KUW** — Kuwait
- 科威特认证标志 **GCC** — Gulf Cooperation Council
- 科学、技术、工程、数学 **STEM** — science, technology, engineering and maths
- 科学会议录引文索引 **CPCI-S** — Conference Proceedings Citation Index-Science
- 科学计划信息计算机检索 **CRISP** — computer retrieval of information on scientific projects
- 科学技术部门 **DST** — department of science and technology
- 科学情报研究所 **ISI** — Institute for Scientific Information
- 科学系统公司 **SSI** — Scientific Systems Co. Inc.
- 科学引文索引 **SCI** — Science Citation Index
- 科学与技术政策办公室 **OSTP** — Office of Scientific and Technical Policy
- 科学院 **AS** — Academy of Science
- 科学总委员会 **GESB** — The General Scientific Board
- 科研卓越框架 **REF** — Research Excellence Framework
- 颗粒细胞 **G** — granular cell
- 壳牌化学品公司英国分公司 **SCUK** — Shell Chemicals UK Limited
- 可背书债券 **EB** — endorsable bond
- 可编程逻辑控制器 **PLC** — Programmable Logical Controller
- 可编程只读存储器 **PROM** — programmable read-only memory
- 可变比特率 **VBR** — variable bit rate
- 可变编码调制 **VCM** — variable code modulation
- 可变进气(歧管)系统 **VIS** — variable inlet (manifold) system
- 可变气门正时技术 **VVT** — variable valve timing
- 可变数字式滤波器 **VDA** — variable digital amplifier
- 可变涡流控制系统 **VTCS** — variable turbulence control system
- 可变压缩比 **VCR** — variable compression ratio
- 可变阻抗吸气系统 **VIAS** — variable impedance aspiration system
- 可擦可编程逻辑器件 **EPLD** — erasable programmable logic device
- 可擦写光盘 **CD-RW** — compact disc-rewritable
- 可持续城市 **CS** — city of sustainability

K

- 可充电电池 **RBC**   rechargeable battery cell
- 可穿戴式人工肾脏 **AWAK**   automated wearable artificial kidney
- 可分解塑料 **dp**   degradable plastics
- 可公共提供的规范 **PAS**   publicly available specification
- 可还价 **o. n. o.**   or near/nearest offer
- 可行性研究报告 **FSR**   feasibility study report
- 可记录式光盘 **DVD-RW**   DVD-Rewritable
- 可见光通信 **Lifi**   Light Fidelity
- 可接受底线 **RWCS**   reasonable worst case scenario
- 可扩展标记语言 **XML**   extensible markup language
- 可录光盘 **CD-R**   compact discrecordable
- 可视影像分析 **VSA**   visual scene analysis
- 可吸入颗粒物 **IP**   inhalable particle
- 可写光盘 **CD-R**   compact discrecordable
- 可选择的实践训练 **OPT**   Optional Practical Training
- 可延期债券 **EB**   extendible bond
- 可移植数据文件 **PDF**   portable data file
- 可移植文档格式 **PDF**   portable document format
- 可以毁灭现有人类社会机构和规范的灾难性事件 **TEOTWAWKI**   The end of the world as we know it
- 克/平方厘米 g/cm^2 gram/square centimeter
- 克[法定质量计量单位] **g**   gram
- 克格勃[苏联国家安全委员会][俄文] **KGB**   Komitet Gosudarstvennoi Bezopasnosti
- 克拉[钻石计量单位] **Ct**   carat
- 克伦民族联盟[缅甸反政府武装] **KNU**   Karen National Union
- 克罗地亚[欧洲国家] **CRO**   Croatia
- 克罗地亚船舶登记局 **CRS**   Croatian Register of Shipping
- 克罗恩病 **CD**   Crohn's disease
- 刻录光盘 **DVD-R**   DVD Recordable
- 客车 **P. T.**   passenger train
- 客观缓解率 **ORR**   Objective relief rate

- 客观应答率 ORR　　　　　　　　　　objective response rate
- 客户对客户[电子商务的一种形式] C2C　　Customer to Customer
- 客户对商家[电子商务的一种形式] C2B　　Consumer to Business
- 客户共同投资计划 CCIP　　　　　　　customer common investment plan
- 客户关系管理 CRM　　　　　　　　　Customer Relationship Management
- 客户互动中心(系统平台) CIC　　　　　customer interaction center
- 客户机/服务器模式 C/S　　　　　　　client/server
- 客户质量指数 CQI　　　　　　　　　Customer Quality Index
- 客户中心能力成熟度模型 CC-CMM　　customer center-capability maturity model
- 客户忠诚指数 CLI　　　　　　　　　Customer Loyalty Index
- 氪[第36号化学元素] Kr　　　　　　　krypton
- 肯德基[炸鸡快餐] KFC　　　　　　　Kentucky Fries Chicken
- 肯尼亚[非洲国家] KEN　　　　　　　Kenya
- 肯尼亚标准局 KEBS　　　　　　　　Kenya Bureau of Standards
- 肯尼亚产品质量认证标志[旧称:KBS] KEBS
Kenya Bureau of Standards
- 空挡 N　　　　　　　　　　　　　　neutral
- 空对地导弹 ASM　　　　　　　　　air-to-surface missile
- 空对空导弹 AAM　　　　　　　　　air-to-air missile
- 空腹血糖[参见 FBG] FBS　　　　　　fasting blood sugar
- 空腹血糖 FBG　　　　　　　　　　　fasting blood glucose
- 空间和信息系统 SIS　　　　　　　　space and information system
- 空间环境纳米实验卫星 SENSE
Space Environment Nanometer Satellite of Experiment
- 空间机动飞行器 SMV　　　　　　　space motor vehicle
- 空间太阳望远镜 SST　　　　　　　　space sun telescope
- 空间研究委员会[法文] CRS　　　　　Comité des Recherches Spatiales
- 空间研究委员会 COSPAR　　　　　　Committee on Space Research
- 空军 AF　　　　　　　　　　　　　air force
- 空军基地 AFB　　　　　　　　　　　air force base
- 空军十字勋章 AFC　　　　　　　　　Air Force Cross

K

- 空客、波音（由中国轮流购买以求外交平衡）**AB**　Airbus，Boeing
- 空客、波音和中国商飞 **ABC**　Airbus，Boeing and COMAC
- 空滤器 **A/CL**　air cleaner
- 空气[德文] **L**　Luft
- 空气流量计 **AFM**　air flow meter
- 空气滤清器 **ACL**　air cleaner
- 空气喷射泵 **AIP**　air injection pump
- 空气探测器 **AE**　Air Explorer
- 空气调节系统 **a/c 或 AC**　air conditioning
- 空气调节系统[是包含温度、湿度、空气清净度及空气循环的控制系统]**HVAC**　heating，ventilation and air conditioning
- 空气污染指数 **API**　Air Pollution Index
- 空气质量控制系统 **AQS**　Air Quality System
- 空气质量指数 **AQI**　Air Quality Index
- 空燃比 **A/F 或 AFR**　air-fuel ratio
- 空调（器）**A/C**　air conditioning
- 空闲时间 **IT**　idle time
- 空中管制 **ATC**　air traffic control
- 空中技术情报中心 **ATIC**　Air Technology Information Center
- 空中加油 **AAR**　air to air refuelling
- 空中加油机 **AT**　aerial tanker
- 空中交通流量管理 **ATFM**　air traffic flow management
- 空中客车[欧洲制造的一种客机名称]**A**　airbus
- 空中拦截导弹 **AIM**　aerial intercept missile
- 空中下载 **OTA**　over the air
- 空中预警及控制系统 **AWACS**　airborne warning and control system
- 空中战术优势公司 **ATAC**　air tactics advantage company
- 孔子学院总部[国家汉办]**CIH**　Confucius Institute Headquarters (Hanban)
- 恐怖分子 **ter**　terrorist
- 恐怖主义情报预防系统 **TIPS**　Terrorism Information Prevention System

- 控股公司［匈牙利文］**RT**   részesedési társaság
- 控制 **CONT**   control
- 控制翻译程序 **CONTRAN**   control translator
- 控制麦克风的人［即说唱者］**MC**   microphone controller
- 控制数据汇编程序 **CODAP**   control data assembly program
- 控制自动化系统 **CAS**   Control Automation System
- 口服避孕药 **OC**   oral contracetive
- 口服葡萄糖耐量试验 **OGT(T)**   oral glucose tolerance test
- 口服营养增补剂 **ONS**   oral nutritional supplement
- 库(仑)［电荷量单位名称］**C**   coulomb
- 库存管理程序与控制技术 **IMPACT**   inventory management program and control technique
- 库存量单位 **SKU**   stock keeping unit
- 库尔德工人党 **KADEK**   Kurdistan Workers' Party
- 库尔德联盟党［库尔德文］**KeKîtî**   Partiya YeKîtî ya Kurdî l i Sûriyê
- 库尔德自由党［库尔德文］**Azadî**   Partiya Azadî ya Kurdî l i Sûriyê
- 库尔德最高委员会［库尔德文］**DBK**   Desteya Bilind a kurd
- 库房管理 **WM**   warehouse management
- 库克群岛［大洋洲新西兰属岛屿］**COK**   the Cook Islands
- 夸夸雷利·西蒙兹公司［英国高等教育研究机构，以世界大学排名最受关注］**QS**   Quacquarelli Symonds
- 夸脱［液量单位］**qt**   quart
- 跨大西洋贸易与投资伙伴协议 **TTIP**   Trans-Atlantic Trade and Investment Partnership
- 跨国公司 **TNC**   transnational company
- 跨国公司 **MNC**   multinational corporation
- 跨国界恐怖主义 **TNT**   transnational terrorism
- 跨国企业 **TNE**   transnational enterprise
- 跨膜压差 **TMP**   transmembrane pressure
- 跨太平洋战略经济伙伴关系协定［TPP 的前身］［由新西兰、新加坡、智利和文莱四国发起］**TPSEPA**   Trans-Pacific Strategic Economic Partnership Agreement

K

- 跨团队子系统间的集成测试 BBIT　　building block integrated test
- 跨职能团队 CFT　　cross-functional team
- 快餐 MRE　　Meal Ready to Eat
- 快递 SD　　special delivery
- 快冻食品 QFF　　quick frozen foods
- 快速粗制操作系统 QDOS　　quick and dirty operating system
- 快速电波爆发 FRB　　fast radio burst
- 快速反应 QR　　quick reaction
- 快速反应部队 QRF　　quick reaction force
- 快速傅立叶变换 FFT　　fast Fourier transform
- 快速公交系统 BRT　　Bus Rapid Transit
- 快速配额餐包 FSR　　fast supply (restaurant) ready
- 快速响应(码) QR　　quick response
- 快速消费品 FMCG　　fast-moving consumer goods
- 快速血浆反应素(实验) RPR　　rapid plasma reagent
- 快速眼动 REM　　rapid eye movement
- 快速展开式野战厨房 RDK　　rapid displaying kitchen
- 快速组装和混合设施 RFAB　　rapid facilities of assembly and blend
- 宽带数字网 BDN　　Broadband Digital Network
- 宽带远程接入服务 BRAS　　broadband remote access service
- 宽带综合业务数字网络 BISDN　　Broadband Integrated Services Digital Network
- 宽限期 GP　　grace period
- 框架网[计算机词典编纂项目] FN　　Frame Net
- 溃疡性结肠炎 UC　　ulcerative colitis
- 扩充转移网络 ATN　　augmented transition network
- 扩大贸易法[美国] TEA　　Trade Expansion Act
- 扩音器 LS　　loudspeaker
- 扩展工业标准结构 EISA　　extended industry standard architecture
- 扩展实景 AR　　augmented reality
- 扩展式测试台 XTS　　extended test bench
- 扩张宫颈和刮宫术 D&C　　dilatation and curettage

- 扩张型心肌病 **DCM**   dilated cardiomyopathy
- 廓尔喀人民族独立运动组织[印地语] **GJM**
  Gorkha Janmukti Morcha

- 拉达汽车[俄国] **LD**   Lada
- 拉丁美洲和加勒比地区经济委员会 **ECLAC**
  Economic Commission for Latin America and Caribbean
- 拉丁美洲和加勒比经济委员会[西班牙文] **CELAC**
  Comisión Económica de Latinoamérica yel Caribe
- 拉丁美洲经济委员会 **ECLA**   Economic Commission for Latin America
- 拉丁美洲自由贸易联盟 **LAFTA**   Latin American Free Trade Association
- 拉链 **ZPR**   zipper
- 拉什卡——简戈维组织[阿拉伯文] **LJ**   Lashkar l Jhangvi
- 拉什卡——塔伊巴组织[阿拉伯文] **LeT/LT**
  Lashkar-e-Tayyiba
- 拉脱维亚[欧洲国家] **LAT**   Latvia
- 辣根过氧化物酶 **HRP**   horseradish peroxidase
- 来电转接 **CF**   call forwarding
- 来源识别码 **SID**   source identification
- 莱索托[非洲国家] **LES**   Lesotho
- 莱泰克灯泡 **LITEX**   Light Technology Corp
- 铼[第75号化学元素] **Re**   rhenium
- 兰博基尼汽车[意大利文] **Lamb**   Lamborghini
- 蓝驰创投 **BRV**   Blue Run Ventures
- 蓝筹股 **BC**   blue chips
- 蓝光光盘 **BD**   Blue-ray Disc
- 蓝光光盘协会 **BDA**   Blue-ray Disc Association

L

- 蓝绿色 **GB** — green blue
- 蓝皮书 **BB** — Blue Book
- 蓝色 **B/BLU** — blue
- 蓝色高效能 **BE** — Blue Efficiency
- 镧[第 57 号化学元素] **La** — lanthanum
- 滥用 **A** — abuse
- 劳动力市场和职业研究所[德文] **IAB**
  Institut für Arbeitsmarkt-und Berufsforschung
- 劳伦斯·利弗莫尔国家实验室 **LLNL** — Laurence Livemore National Laboratory
- 劳斯莱斯汽车[英国] **R&R** — Rolls Royce
- 铹[第 103 号化学元素] **Lr** — lawrencium
- 老 **Sr/Snr** — senior
- 老大党[指美国共和党] **GOP** — Grand Old Party
- 老干妈辣酱 **ALS** — Angry Lady Sauce
- 老公[汉语拼音首字母缩略语] **LG** — lao gong
- 老年、遗嘱及残障保险[社会安全] **OASDI**
  old-age, survivors, and disable insurance [social security]
- 老年黄斑变性 **AMD** — aged-related macular degeneration
- 老年男子的荷尔蒙缺乏 **ADAM** — androgen deficiency in aging males
- 老挝[亚洲国家] **LAO** — Laos
- 老小孩 **kidult** — kid adult
- 铑[第 45 号化学元素] **Rh** — rhodium
- 酪氨酸激酶抑制剂 **TKI** — tyrosine kinase inhibitors
- 乐高玩具[丹麦文:意为"好好玩"] **LEGO**
  leg godt
- 乐器数字接口系统 **MIDI SYSTEM**
  Musical Instruction Digital Interface System
- 乐喜金星[由 Lucky Goldstars 衍生成] **LG**
  life's good
- 勒(克斯)[法定光照度计量单位] **Lx** — lux
- 雷达吸波材料 **RAM** — radar absorbing material
- 雷达信号特征分析 **RSA** — radar signature analysis

雷曼兄弟公司 LEH	Lehman Brothers Holdings Inc.
镭[第88号化学元素] Ra	radium
累进税 ED	extra duty
类风湿性关节炎 RA	rheumatoid arthritis
类风湿因子 RF	rheumatoid factor
冷藏 refr	refrigerate
冷凝集试验 CAT	cold agglutination test
冷却机组 UC	unit cooler
离岸加运费价格 CF	Cost and Freight
离岸价格 FOB	free on board
离岸人民币 CNH	Chinese Yuan in Hongkong
离车诊断 OBD	off-board diagnostics
离散变量自动电子计算机 EDVAC	electronic discrete variable automatic computer
黎巴嫩[亚洲国家] LB	Lebanon
礼貌回复邮件 CRM	courtesy reply mail
里昂化学工业公司[法文] ICL	Institut de Chimie de Lyon
里德-所罗门码 RS	Reed-Solomon
理工 STEM	science, technology, engineering and maths
理科硕士 MS	Master of Science
理念识别 MI	Mind Identity
理念识别 MI	mind identity
理赔率 CSR	claim settlement rate
理学博士 DSC	Doctor of Science
锂[第3号化学元素] Li	lithium
立邦漆 n	Nippon
立方米 CBM	cubic metre
立荣海运株式会社 UGL	Uniglory
立陶宛、波兰、乌克兰联合作战旅 LITPOLUKRBRIG	Lithuania, Poland, Ukraine Brigade
立陶宛[欧洲国家] LTU	Lithuania
立体电视 STV	stereoscopic television

L

- 利(息)率 **ROI** — rate of interest
- 利比里亚[非洲国家] **LBR** — Liberia
- 利比亚[非洲国家] **LBA** — Libya
- 利比亚国民军 **LNA** — Libyan National Army
- 利比亚民族团结政府 **GNA** — Government of National Accord
- 利弗莫尔自动研究计算机 **LARC** — Livermore Automatic Research Computer
- 利率风险 **IRR** — Interest Rate Risk
- 例如[拉丁文] **e. g. /ex gr** — exempli gratia [英文:for example]
- 粒细胞 **GRAN** — granulocyte
- 铊[第116号化学元素] **Lv** — livermorium
- 连接请求[网络用语] **CR** — connect request
- 连接肽[体检用语] **CP** — C-peptide
- 连续可变气门正时控制 **CVTC** — continuous variable timing control
- 连续膜过滤技术 **CMF** — continuous membrane filtration
- 连续凝血酶时间 **STT** — serial thrombin time
- 连续微滤 **CMF** — continuous micro filtre
- 连续性肾脏替代治疗 **CRRT** — continuous renal replacement therapy
- 联邦储蓄保险公司 **FDIC** — Federal Deposit Insurance Corporation
- 联邦公开/开放市场委员会 **FOMC** — Federal Open Market Committee
- 联邦航空管理局 **FAA** — Federal Aviation Administration
- 联邦监狱管理局 **FBP** — Federal Bureau of Prison
- 联邦快递公司 **FedEx** — Federal Express Corp.
- 联邦条例法规 **CFR** — Code of Federal Regulations
- 联邦通信委员会 **FCC** — Federal Communications Commission
- 联邦退休(节俭)储蓄投资委员会 **FTRIB** — the Federal Thrift Retirement Investment Board
- 联邦无线电委员会 **FRC** — Federal Radio Commission
- 联邦选举委员会 **FEC** — Federal Election Commission
- 联邦移民与难民(事务)局[德文] **BAMF** — Bundesamt für Migration und Flüchtlinge
- 联邦政府助学金免费申请 **FAFSA** — Free Application for Federal Student Aid

- 联邦住房贷款抵押公司[又称 FRE] **FHLMC**
  Federal Home Loan Mortgage Corporation
- 联邦注册会计师协会成员 **FACA**
  Fellow of the Association of Certified Accountants
- 联合包裹递送公司 **UPS**　　　　United Package Service
- 联合保护稳定部队[欧洲波黑军队] **SFOR**
  Stabilization Force
- 联合的 **Utd**　　　　　　　　　united
- 联合电子系统型号标志系统 **JETDS**
  joint electronics type designation system
- 联合工作组 **JWG**　　　　　Joint Working Group
- 联合股份公司[丹麦文] **A/S**　　Aktieselkab
- 联合国 **UN**　　　　　　　　United Nations
- 联合国艾滋病规划署 **UNAIDS**
  Joint United Nations Program on HIV/AIDS
- 联合国安理会 **UNSC**　　　United Nations Security Council
- 联合国安全理事会反恐怖主义委员会 **CTC**
  United Nations Security Council Counter-Terrorism Committee
- 联合国部队 **UNF**　　　　　United Nations Forces
- 联合国裁军谈判会议 **UNCD**　United Nations Conference on Disarmament
- 联合国裁军委员会(已被 UNCD 取代) **UNDC**
  United Nations Disarmament Commission
- 联合国常规军备委员会 **CCA**　Committee for Conventional Armaments
- 联合国大会(简称"联大") **UNGA**　United Nations General Assembly
- 联合国大学 **UNU**　　　　　United Nations University
- 联合国毒品和犯罪问题办公室 **UNODC**
  United Nations Office of Drug and Crime
- 联合国儿童基金 **UNCF**　　United Nations Children's Fund
- 联合国儿童紧急情况基金 **UNICEF**
  United Nations International Children's Emergency Fund
- 联合国法律事务厅 **OLA**　　Office of Legal Affairs

L

- 联合国防治荒漠化公约 **UNCCD**
  United Nations Convention to Combat Desertification
- 联合国非政府组织委员会 **CNGO**
  Committee on Non-Governmental Organization
- 联合国非洲经济委员会 **ECA**　　Economic Commission for Africa
- 联合国工业发展组织 **UNIDO**
  United Nations Industrial Development Organization
- 联合国管理事务部 **DM**　　Department of Management
- 联合国管制药物滥用基金 **UNFDAC**
  United Nations Fund for Drug Abuse Control
- 联合国国际法委员会 **ILCUN**
  International Law Commission of United Nations
- 联合国国际法院 **ICJ**　　International Court of Justice
- 联合国国际贸易法委员会 **UNCITRAL**
  United Nations Commission on International Trade Law
- 联合国国际医学教育研究促进基金会 **FAIMER**
  Foundation for Advancement of International Medical Education and Research
- 联合国海洋气象委员会 **CMM**　　Commission for Maritime Meteorology
- 联合国和平利用外层空间委员会 **CPUOS**
  Committee of the Peaceful Uses of Outer Space
- 联合国环境计划署 **UNEP**　　United Nations Environment Program
- 联合国技术信息促进系统 **TIPS**
  Technology and Information Promotion System
- 联合国际贸易中心 **JITC**　　Joint International Trade Center
- 联合国柬埔寨临时权力机构 **UNTAC**
  United Nations Transitional Authority in Cambodia
- 联合国教科文组织 **UNESCO**
  United Nations Educational, Scientific and Cultural Organization
- 联合国教科文组织出版中心 **UPC**　　UNESCO Publishing Centre
- 联合国经济及社会理事会 **ECOSOC**
  United Nations Economic and Social Council
- 联合国救灾总署 **UNDRO**　　United Nations Disaster Relief Office

- 联合国开发计划署 **UNDP**　　　United Nations Development Programme
- 联合国科学咨询委员会 **UNSAC**
  United Nations Scientific Advisory Committee
- 联合国可持续发展委员会 **UNCSD**
  United Nations Commission on Sustainable Development
- 联合国粮农组织 **FAO**
  Food and Agricultural Organization of the United Nations
- 联合国贸易和发展会议（**UN**）**CTAD**
  United Nations Conference on Trade and Development
- 联合国秘书处 **UNS**　　　United Nations Secretariat
- 联合国秘书长办公室 **EOSG**　　　Executive Office of the Secretary General
- 联合国难民救济和工程处 **UNRWA**　　　United Nations Relief and Works Agency
- 联合国难民事务高级专员办事处/联合国难民署高级专员 **UNHCR**
  United Nations High Commissioner for Refugees
- 联合国内部监督事务厅 **OIOS**　　　Office of Internal Oversight Services
- 联合国内罗毕办事处 **UNON**　　　United Nations Office at Nairobi
- 联合国欧洲经济委员会 **UNECE**
  United Nations Economic Commission for Europe
- 联合国气候框架协定 **UNFCCC**
  UN (United Nations) Framework Convention on Climate Change
- 联合国人道主义事务协调厅 **OCHA**
  United Nations Office for the Coordination of Humanitarian Affairs
- 联合国人口活动基金委员会 **UNFPA**
  United Nations Fund for Population Activities
- 联合国人权委员会（**UN**）**CHR**
  United Nations Committee on Human Rights
- 联合国世界粮食计划署 **WFP**　　　World Food Program
- 联合国书店 **UNB**　　　United Nations Bookshop
- 联合国术语库 **UNTERM**　　　United Nations Terminology Database
- 联合国特别大会 **SGA**　　　Special General Assembly
- 联合国托管理事会 **TC**　　　Trusteeship Council
- 联合国外勤资助部 **DFS**　　　Department of Field Support

L

- 联合国维持和平行动部 **DPKO**   Department of Peacekeeping Operations
- 联合国维和行动 **PKD**   Peace-keeping Deed (UN)
- 联合国维也纳办事处 **UNOV**   United Nations Office at Vienna
- 联合国西亚经济委员会 **ECWA**   Economic Commission for Western Asia
- 联合国系统职员学院 **UNSSC**   United Nations System Staff College
- 联合国项目事务厅 **UNOPS**   United Nations Office for Project Services
- 联合国训练研究所 **UNITAR**
  United Nations Institute for Training and Research
- 联合国语言人才培训体系 **UNLPP**
  United Nations Language Professionals Training Programme
- 联合国政府间气候变化专门委员会 **IPCC**
  Intergovernmental Panel on Climate Change
- 联合国政府网科技情报系统 **UNISIST**
  United Nations Intergovernmental System of Information in Science and Technology
- 联合国政治事务部 **DPA**   Department of Political Affairs
- 联合国志愿人员组织 **UNV**   United Nations Volunteers
- 联合国驻黎巴嫩临时部队 **UNIFIL**   United Nations Interim Force in Lebanon
- 联合国资本开发基金会 **UNCDF**   United Nations Capital Development Fund
- 联合国组织 **UNO**   United Nations Organization
- 联合海外银行 **UOB**   United Overseas Banks
- 联合技术委员会 **JTC**   Joint Technical Committee
- 联合警备区 **JSA**   Joint Security Area
- 联合轻型战术车辆 **JLTV**   joint light tactical vehicle
- 联合人工智能中心 **JAIC**   joint artificial intelligence center
- 联合商业情报 **ABI**   Associated Business Information
- 联合特遣队 **JTF**   Joint Task Force
- 联合调查小组 **JIT**   joint investigation team
- 联合图像专家组[一种图像压缩标准]**JP(E)G**
  joint photographic experts group
- 联合信息系统委员会 **JISC**   Joint Information Systems Committee
- 联合运输提单 **CTB/L**   combined transport bill of Lading

- 联合战俘和战斗失踪人员下落调查司令部 **JPAC**
  Joint POW [Prisoner of War]/MIA [Missing in action] Accounting Command
- 联合支持基金 **CSF**   combined support fund
- 联合直接攻击弹药 **JDAM**   joint direct attack munition
- 联机网络[电子文献标示字母] **OL**   on-line
- 联机网上的数据库[电子文献标示略语] **DB/OL**
  data bank on line
- 联运经营人 **CTO**   combined transport operator
- 廉价航空 **LCC**   low-cost carrier
- 廉价航空公司 **LCA**   low-cost airline
- 脸基尼 **Facekini**   face bikini
- 脸书 **F/FB**   Facebook
- 脸书人工智能研究 **FAIR**   Facebook Artificial Intelligence Research
- 恋爱养成游戏 **LVG**   love game
- 链路访问协议平衡 **LAPB**   line access protocol balanced
- 链路控制协议 **LCP**   link control protocol
- 良好级(钱币) **G**   good
- 良好农业规范 **GAP**   Good Agricultural Practice
- 良性前列腺增生 **BPH**   benign prostatic hyperplasia
- 粮食安全委员会 **CFS**   Committee of Foods Safety
- 两合公司[西班牙文] **SNC**   Sociedad en Comandita
- 两阶段进气系统 **DRS**   dual ram system
- 两轮驱动 **2WD**   two wheel drive
- 两栖突击车 **AAV**   Amphibious Assault Vehicle
- 两栖作战船坞登陆舰[代字] **LPD**   amphibious transport dock
- 两性关系和性教育 **RSE**   relationships and sex education
- 谅解备忘录 **MOU**   memorandum of understanding
- 量不足[拉丁文] **qns**   quantum ono sufficiat
- 量化宽松(货币政策) **QE**   quantitative easing
- 量子电子学 **QE**   quantum electronics
- 钌[第44号化学元素] **Ru**   ruthenium

L

列车自动保护系统 ATP	automatic train protection
列车自动停车(装置) ATS	automatic train stopping
列氏温标[法文] R	Échelle Réaumur Lieaomier
列支敦士登[欧洲国家] LIE	Liechtenstein
烈风警报 GW	Gale Warning
烈性酒 LIQ	liquor
邻苯二甲酸丁苄酸酯 BBP	butyl benzyl phthalate
邻苯二甲酸二(2-乙基己基)酯 DEHP	di (2-ethylhexyl) phthalate
邻苯二甲酸二丁酯[增塑剂] DBP	dibutyl phthalate
邻苯二甲酸二异癸酯[增塑剂] DIDP	di-iso-decyl phthalate
邻苯二甲酸酯 PAE	phthalic acid ester
邻苯二甲酸酯类化合物 PAEs	phthalic acid esters
临床管理信息化 CIS	Clinic Information System
临床医学学士 MBBS/BMBS	Bachelor of Medicine & Bachelor of Surgery
临床医学学士[拉丁文] MBBS/BMBS	Medicinae Baccalaureus/Baccalaureus Chirurgiae
临时保护身份 TPS	temporary protected status
临时雇员 temp	temporary employee
临时一般许可证 TGL	temporary general license
淋巴瘤相关抗原 LAA	lymphadenoma associated antigen
淋巴细胞 LYM	lymphocyte
淋巴细胞转化试验 LTT	lymphocyte transformation test
淋巴因子激活的杀伤细胞 LAK	lymphokine activated killer cells
磷[第15号化学元素] P	phosphorus
磷酸肌酸 CP	creatine phosphate
磷酸三(2-氯丙基)酯 TCPP	tris (2-chloropropyl) phosphate
磷脂酰肌醇-3-激酶 PI3K	phosphatidylinositol-3-kinase
鳞状细胞癌 SCC	squamous cell carcinoma
灵活反应战略 FRS	flexible response strategy
灵猫六国,其国名分别为:哥伦比亚、印尼、越南、埃及、土耳其和南非 CIVETS	Colombia, Indonesia, Vietnam, Egypt, Turkey, South Africa
灵商 SQ	soul quotient

- 零担货物装载 LCL   less than car load
- 零件目录 LOP   list of parts
- 零排放车辆 ZEV   zero-emission vehicle
- 零燃油重量 ZFW   zero fuel weight
- 零伤亡愿景基金 VZF   Vision Zero Fund
- 零时 ZT   zero time
- 零售价 RP   retail price
- 零售物价指数 RPI   retail price index
- 零输出 ZO   zero output
- 零息发行 ZR   zero coupon issue
- 岭南大学 LU   Lingnan University
- 领导能力评价 LAE   leadership ability evaluation
- 另外的 nother   another
- 浏览器/服务器模式 B/S   browser/server
- 流(明)[法定光通量计量单位] lm   lumen
- 流程虚拟机 PVM   Process Virtual Machine
- 流动检查站 MCS   mobile checkout station
- 流动资本 WC   working capital
- 流动资产 CA   current assets
- 流行病 EPI   epidemic
- 流行病应对创新联盟[挪威] CEPI   Coalition for Epidemic Preparedness Innovations
- 流行的 POP   popular
- 流行文化博物馆 MoPoP   Museum of Pop Culture
- 流行音乐节目主持人 DJ   Disc Jockey
- 流式微球技术 CBA   cytometric bead assay
- 流式细胞术 FCM   flow cytometry
- 流水账 WB   waste-book
- 琉球广播公司 RBC   Ryukyu Broadcasting Corporation
- 硫[第16号化学元素] S   sulfur
- 六A原则[积极正面的教育子女的原则:接纳、赞赏、关爱、有效性、责任、权威] 6A   acceptance, appreciation, affection, availability, accountability, authority

L

卢森堡[欧洲国家] LUX	Luxembourg
卢森堡广播电视台[法文] RTL	Radio Télévision Luxembourgecise
卢森堡广播电视台[德文] RTL	Radio-Télévision Luxembourg
卢森堡广播电视台 RTL	Radio and Television of Luxembourg
卢旺达[非洲国家] RWA	Rwanda
卢旺达解放军 ALIR	Army for the Liberation of Rwanda
𬬻[第104号化学元素] Rf	rutherfordium
鲁棒自适应波束 RABF	Robust Adaptive Beam Forming
镥[第71号化学元素] Lu	lutetium
陆风汽车[中国南昌] L	Landwind
陆基拦截器 GBI	Ground-Based Interceptor
陆军[法文] FT	forces terrestres
陆军参谋部二部[代字] G-2	military intelligence section of Army Corps
陆军妇女队 WAC	Women's Army Corps
陆军特种部队 SF	Special Forces
陆军中尉,海空军上尉 Lieut	lieutenant
路[用于书面地址] Rd	road
路透社[英国通讯社] Reuters	Reuter's News Agency
路易·威登集团[法文] LVMH	Louis Vuitton Moët Hennessy
路易·威登皮具 LV	Louis Vuitton
露齿大笑[网络用语] BSG	big smiling grin
卵磷脂-胆固醇酰基转移酶 LCAT	lecithin-cholesterol acyltransferase
伦敦(政治)经济学院 LSE London School of Economics and Political Science	
伦敦爱乐乐团 LPO	London Philharmonic Orchestra
伦敦贝斯丁的犹太教饮食分支机构 KLBD Kashrut Division of the London Beth Din	
伦敦大学出版社[英国] ULP	University of London Press
伦敦地下铁道[英国] LUR	London Underground Railway
伦敦帝国理工学院 ICL	Imperial College of London
伦敦工商会所 LCCI	London Chamber of Commerce and Industry

- 伦敦工商会所考试局 **LCCIEB**
  London Chamber of Commerce and Industry Exam Board
- 伦敦股票交易所 **LSE**　　London Stock Exchange
- 伦敦国际互联网交换中心 **LINX**　　London Internet Exchange
- 伦敦交易所 **RE**　　Royal Exchange
- 伦敦金属交易所 **LME**　　London Metal Exchange
- 伦敦美国记者协会 **AACL**
  Association of American Correspondents in London
- 伦敦塔[英国] **TOL**　　Tower of London
- 伦敦银行间拆放利率 **LIBOR**　　London Inter Bank Offered Rate
- 伦敦英语口语联盟 **ESU**　　English Speaking Union
- 伦琴(照射计量单位) **R**　　roentgen
- 轮[第111号化学元素] **Rg**　　roentgenium
- 轮船 **ss**　　steamship
- 论文集[参考文献标示字母] **C**　　collected papers
- 罗斯威尔派克纪念研究所开发的培养基 **RPMI-1640**
  Rosewell Pack Memorial Institute-1640
- 逻辑询问和更新系统 **LINUS**　　logical inquiry and update system
- 落基山学院 **CR**　　College of the Rocky
- 骆驼评级法(包括资本充足率、资产质量、经营管理水平、盈利状况、流动性) **CAMEL**
  capital adequacy, asset quality, management, earnings, liquidity
- 骆驼评级法的发展版(增加了"市场风险敏感度") **CAMEL＋**
  CAMEL＋sensitivity to market risk
- 旅行时间授权 **TTA**　　travel time authorized
- 旅客自动捷运系统 **APM**　　automated people mover systems
- 旅游目的地国家 **ADS**　　amusement destination state
- 旅游商业街 **RBD**　　Recreational Business District
- 铝[第13号化学元素] **Al**　　aluminium
- 绿黄色 **GY**　　green yellow
- 绿乐园[日本乐队] **TBG**　　The Brilliant Green
- 绿色 **G**　　green

绿色贝雷帽 SF	Special Forces
绿色荧光蛋白 GFP	green fluorescent protein
氯[第17号化学元素] Cl	chlorine
氯胺酮[一种具有镇痛作用的静脉全麻药物,是一种毒品] K	
ketamine	
氯氟烃 CFC	chloro fluorohydrocarbon
氯化聚氯乙烯 CPVC	chlorinated polyvinylchloride
氯化聚乙烯 CPE	chlorinated polyethylene
氯气无用 ECF	elemental chlorine free
滤过分数 FF	filtration fraction
滤清器 FLTR	filter

麻省理工学院的编译程序 COMIT
Compiler of Massachusetts Institute of Technology

马达加斯加[非洲国家] MAD	Madagascar
马丁·马吉拉服饰 MMM	Maison Martin Margiela
马尔代夫[亚洲国家] MDV	Maldives
马耳他[欧洲国家] MLT	Malta
马赫数[指某速度相对音速的倍数] M	Mach number
马科斯小汽车 MARCOS	Jem Marsh, Frank Costin
马拉维[非洲国家] MAW	Malawi
马拉维标准局 MBS	Malawi Bureau of Standards
马拉维认证标志 MBS	Malawi Bureau of Standards
马来西亚[亚洲国家] MAS	Malaysia

马来西亚标准与工业研究学会 SIRIM
Standards & Industrial Research Institute of Malaysia

马来西亚产品质量认证标志 **SIRIM**
Standards & Industrial Research Institute of Malaysia

马来西亚海事执法机构 **MMEA**
Malaysia Maritime Enforcement Agency

马来西亚石油公司[马来文] **Petronas**　Petroliam Nasional Bhd

马来西亚伊斯兰教发展署[马来文] **JAKIM**
Jabatan Kemajuan Islam Malaysia

马里[非洲国家] **MLI**　　　　　　　Mali

马尼拉城市发展局 **MMDA**　　　　Metro Manila Development Agency

马其顿[欧洲国家][现称 NMKD 北马其顿] **MKD**
Macedonia

马上回来[网络用语] **BRB**　　　　be right back

马中(北京)国际清真商品贸易中心 **MCBIHP**
Malaysia-China (Beijing) International Halal Products

玛莎公司 **M&S**　　　　　　　　Marks and Spencer

玛氏朱古力豆 **M&M's**　　　　　Forrest Mars and Bruce Murries

码[英美长度单位＝3 英尺＝0.914 米] **yd(s)**
yard(s)

码[长度单位] **YD**　　　　　　　yard

码分多路访问 **CDMA**　　　　　code division multiple access

码分多址 **CDMA**　　　　　　　code division multiple access

码间干扰 **ISI**　　　　　　　　　Inter-Symbol Interference

蚂蚁机器人 **ANTBOT**　　　　　ant robot

蚂蚁金服与马来西亚支付服务提供商 **TNG**
Touch'n Go

买方不负担卸货费用 **fo**　　　　free out

买方不负担装货费用 **fi**　　　　 free in

买方不负担装卸和理仓费 **fios**　free in, out and stow

买方不负担装卸货费用 **fio**　　　free in and out

买方信贷 **BC**　　　　　　　　　buyer's credit

买一送一 **BOGOF**　　　　　　　buy one, get one free

M

- 迈克尔·杰克逊[美国流行音乐巨星] **MJ** Michael Jackson
- 麦角酰二乙胺[一种迷幻药] **LSD**   lysergic acid diethylamide
- 麦金托希操作系统 **MACOS**   Macintosh Operating System
- 麦考瑞大学商业创新协会 **MIBS**   Macquarie Innovative Business Society
- 鿏[第109号化学元素] **Mt**   meitnerium
- 卖方集中度 **CR4**   Four-firm Concentration Rate
- 脉冲编码调制 **PCM**   pulse coding modulate
- 脉冲多普勒(雷达) **PD**   Pulse Doppler (radar)
- 脉中感应 **PI**   pulse interaction
- 曼彻斯特联合足球俱乐部/曼联 **Man Utd** Manchester United Football Club
- 曼古银珠宝佩饰 **MGS**   Marcasite
- 曼谷轨道交通系统 **BTS**   Bangkok rail transit system
- 曼卡车[原意:奥格斯堡·纽伦堡机械制造公司][德文] **MAN** Maschinen fabrica Augsburg Nürnberg
- 曼联电视台 **MUTV**   Manchester United Television
- 慢波睡眠 **SWS**   Slow Wave Sleep
- 慢性疲劳综合征 **CFS**   Chronic Fatigue Syndrome
- 慢性肾盂肾炎 **CP**   chloropurine
- 慢性中毒性脑病 **CTE**   chronic toxic encephathy
- 慢性阻塞性肺部疾病 **COPD**   chronic obstructive pulmonary disease
- 猫犬俱乐部 **RBC**   ragdoll breed club
- 毛里求斯[非洲国家] **MRI/MRU**   Mauritius
- 毛里塔尼亚[非洲国家] **MTN**   Mauritania
- 毛重 **GW**   gross weight
- 茂物农学院[印尼文] **IPB**   Institut Pertanian Bogor
- 冒险类游戏 **AVG**   adventure game
- 贸易发展理事会[香港] **TDC**   Trade Development Council
- 贸易合作组织 **OTC**   Organization for Trade Cooperation
- 贸易技术壁垒 **TBT**   trade barriers of technics
- 贸易投资区 **TIA**   trading investment area

贸易往来支持工具 INSTEX	Instrument for Supporting Trade Exchanges
贸易意向书 TP	trade protocol
贸易转向 TD	trade diversion
没头脑的人 P. A.	paper ass
没有 w/o	without
玫瑰花结形成细胞 EACRFC	EAC rosette forming cell
梅毒螺旋体血凝测定 TPHA	treponema pallidum haemagglutination assay
梅毒螺旋体制动测定 TPI	treponema pallidum immobilization assay
媒体新闻联络店 MRO	Media Relation Officer
媒体语言格式 MLF	media language format
煤气表 GFI	gas-flow indicator
煤气工业［俄文］Gazprom	Gazovaia promeishliennosti
酶联免疫吸附试验 ELISA	enzyme-linked immuno sorbent assay
酶免疫测定 EIA	enzyme immunoassay
镅［第95号化学元素］Am	americium
每分钟呼气量 VE	minute ventilation
每分钟转数 Rpm	revolutions per minute
每分钟字数 wpm	words per minute
每个［希腊文］aa	ana
每公斤的食用甲基乙二醛产品含量至少为400毫克,作用为帮助人体提高消化功能 MGO™ 400＋	methylglyoxal ™ 400＋
每股收益 EPS	earnings per share
每立方米空气［灰尘、烟气或雾霜］毫克数 mg/m^3	milligram per cubic meter of air
每秒百万次浮点运算 MFLOPS	million floating point operations per second
每秒百万条指令 MIPS	million instructions per second
每秒千万亿次浮点运算 PFLOPS	peta floating point operations per second
每秒英寸 IPS	inches per second
每秒帧数（电视图像的）FPS	frames per second
每秒钟画面数 PPS	pictures per second

M

每年[拉丁文] **p. a.**	per annum
每年的 **YRLY**	yearly
每平方英寸 **PSI**	per square inch
每日两次[拉丁文] **bid**	bis in die
每日四次[拉丁文] **qid**	quarter in die
每日推荐摄入量标准 **RDA**	recommended daily allowance
每日一考 **TD**	Test Daily
每收视一次付费 **PPV**	pay-per-view
每天[拉丁文] **qd**	quaque die
每天学点知识(在分享时加个TIL)[网络用语] **TIL** today I learned	
每小时[拉丁文] **qh**	quaque hora
每小时英里 **MPH**	mile per hour
每英寸的点数 **DPI**	dots per inch
每英寸像素 **ppi**	pixels per inch
每支香烟的(焦油)毫克数 **mg/cig**	milligrams per cigarette
每周 **pw**	per week
美国 **A**	America
美国(工业)标准 **USS**	United States Standard
美国[北美洲国家] **US(A)**	United States of America
美国Cisco公司网络设备操作系统注册商标 **iso** iPhone Operation System	
美国DC漫画公司 **DC**	Detective Comics
美国M24狙击步枪 **M24**	American Military Sniper Rifle
美国PVH服装集团(世界第二大服装集团) **PVH** Phillips-Van-Heusen	
美国癌症联合会 **AJCC**	American Joint Committee on Cancer
美国癌症协会 **ACS**	American Cancer Society
美国癌症研究院 **AICR**	American Institute for Cancer Research
美国艾奥瓦牛肉罐头 **IBP**	Iowa Beef Packers
美国安全委员会 **ASC**	American Security Council
美国巴博斯汽车 **B**	Brabus

- 美国芭蕾舞剧院 **ABT**　　American Ballet Theater
- 美国百路驰轮胎公司 **BFG**　　BF Goodrich
- 美国版权问题调查委员会 **CICP**
  Committee to Investigate Copyright Problems
- 美国版权协会 **CSUSA**
  Copyright Society of the United States of America
- 美国包装机械制造协会 **PMMI**
  The Packaging Machinery Manufactures Institute
- 美国宝洁公司[用两个创始人的姓的首字母] **P&G**
  Procter & Gamble
- 美国宝石学会 **AGS**　　American Gem Society
- 美国宝石学会签发的钻石证书 **AGS**　　American Gem Society
- 美国宝石学院 **GIA**　　Gem Institute of America
- 美国宝石研究所 **GIA**　　Gemological Institute of America
- 美国保守主义联盟 **ACU**　　American Conservative Union
- 美国保险商实验室公司 **UL**　　Underwriters Laboratories Incorporation
- 美国保险商实验室公司认证标志 **UL**
  Underwriters Laboratories Incorporation
- 美国报业协会 **NAA**　　Newspaper Association of America
- 美国边防巡警[后来并入 CBP 海关及边境保护局] **USBP**
  United States Border Patrol
- 美国编剧协会 **WGA**　　The Writers Guild of America
- 美国标准协会[现为 ANSI] **ASA**　　American Standards Association
- 美国波士顿大学 **BU**　　Boston University
- 美国波士顿交响乐团 **BSO**　　Boston Symphony Orchestra
- 美国波音飞机公司 **TBC**　　The Boeing Company
- 美国波音公司的"沉默鹰"战斗机 **F-15SE**
  Fighter-15 Silent Eagle
- 美国博硕士论文数据库 **PQDD**　　Pro Quest Digital Dissertation
- 美国步枪协会 **NRA**　　National Rifle Association
- 美国步枪协会—立法行动研究所 **NRA-ILA**
  National Rifle Association-Institute for Legislative Action

M

- 美国材料实验学会 **ASTM**   American Society of Testing Materials
- 美国财务会计准则委员会 **FASB**   Financial Accounting Standards Boards
- 美国参数技术公司旗下的 CAD/CAM/CAE 一体化的三维软件 **Pro-E**
  Pro-engineer
- 美国仓单系统 **AMS**   American Manifest System
- 美国出版商传播机构 **PCG**   publishers communication group
- 美国出版商协会 **AAP**   Association of American Publishers
- 美国出生的中国人 **ABC**   American-born Chinese
- 美国储蓄管理局 **OTS**   Office of Thrift Supervision
- 美国传统基金会 **HF**   The Heritage Foundation
- 美国船 **USS**   United States Ship
- 美国船舶局 **ABS**   American Bureau of Shipping
- 美国慈善施舍联合会 **Care**
  Cooperative for American Remittances to Europe/Everywhere
- 美国大西洋委员会 **ACUS**   Atlantic Council of the United States
- 美国大学公共关系协会 **ACPRA**
  American College Public Relations Association
- 美国大学教授协会 **AAUP**
  American Association of University Professors
- 美国大学理事会 **CB**   College Board
- 美国大学联合会 **AAC**   Association of American Colleges
- 美国大学联合会 **AAU**   Association of American Universities
- 美国大学能力测验 **CAT**   College Ability Test
- 美国大学入学考试 **ACT**   American College Testing
- 美国大学预修课程 **AP**   Advanced Placement
- 美国得克萨斯州大学 MD 安德森癌症中心 **UT**
  The University of Texas MD Anderson Cancer Center
- 美国地理学会 **AGI**   American Geographical Institute
- 美国地理学家协会 **AAG**   Association of American Geographers
- 美国地质勘探局 **USGS**   United States Geological Survey
- 美国典型培养物保存中心 **ATCC**   American Type Culture Collection
- 美国电话电报公司 **AT&T**   American Telephone & Telegraph Company

- 美国电脑协会 ACM　　　　　　　　　Association for Computing Machinery
- 美国电视学会 ATS　　　　　　　　　American Television Service
- 美国电影公司 AMC　　　　　　　　　American Movie Corporation
- 美国电影协会制定的电影分级制中的大众级，无裸体、性爱场面，吸毒与暴力场面也很少 G　　　　　　　　　General audiences all ages admitted
- 美国电影学会 AFI　　　　　　　　　American Film Institute
- 美国电子工业协会 EIA　　　　　　　Electronic Industry Association
- 美国电子元器件协会 ECA　　　　　　Electronic Components Association
- 美国对外关系委员会 CFR　　　　　　Council on Foreign Relations
- 美国对外文化交流协会 AIAS　　　　American Intercultural Affair Society
- 美国敦豪速递公司 DHL
  Adrian Dalsey, Larry Hillblom, Robert Lynn
- 美国躲避球协会[该虚拟组织源于电影躲避球] ADAA
  American Dodgeball Association of America
- 美国发明家和科学家联合会 UISA　　United Inventors and Scientists of America
- 美国翻译协会 ATA　　　　　　　　　American Translations Association
- 美国房地美公司[又称 FHLMC] FRE
  Freddie Mac
- 美国防虐待动物协会 ASPCA
  American Society for the Prevention of Cruelty to Animals
- 美国废品回收工业协会 ISRI　　　　Institute of Scrap Recycling Industries
- 美国佛罗里达国际大学 FIU　　　　　Florida International University
- 美国盖洛普民意测验 GP　　　　　　　Gallup Poll
- 美国肝脏病研究协会 AASLD
  American Association for the Study of Liver Disease
- 美国钢结构学会 AISC　　　　　　　　American Institute of Steel Construction
- 美国高等教育协会 AAHE
  American Association for Higher Education
- 美国哥伦比亚大学 CU　　　　　　　　Columbia University
- 美国哥伦比亚广播公司 CBS　　　　　Columbia Broadcast System
- 美国工程标准委员会 AESC　　　　　　American Engineering Standards Committee
- 美国工程师和建筑师协会 EAA　　　　Engineers Architects Association

M

- 美国工商管理学院联合会 **AACSB**
  American Assembly of Collegiate Schools of Business
- 美国公路和运输官员协会 **AASHTO**
  American Association of State Highway and Transportation Officials
- 美国公民及移民事务局 **USCIS**
  United States Citizenship and Immigration Service
- 美国公民自由联盟 **ACLU**　　American Civil Liberties Union
- 美国公园警察 **USPP**　　United States Park Police
- 美国公众兴趣科学中心 **CSPI**　　Center for Science in the Public Interest
- 美国共和党竞选委员会 **NRCC**　　National Republican Campaign Committee
- 美国共和党全国国会委员会 **NRCC**
  National Republican Congressional Committee
- 美国关键基础设施技术研究所 **ICIT**
  Institute for Critical Infrastructure Technology
- 美国关心亚洲学者委员会 **CCAS**　　Committee of Concerned Asian Scholars
- 美国官方分析化学家协会 **AOAC**　　Association of Official Analytical Chemists
- 美国管理学会 **AIM**　　American Institute of Management
- 美国广播公司 **ABC**　　American Broadcasting Corporation
- 美国广告代理协会 **AAAA**
  American Association of Advertising Agencies
- 美国国防部参谋长联席会议 **CCS**　　Combined Chiefs of Staff
- 美国国防部的标准编程语言［代字］**ADA**
  US DOD programming language
- 美国国防部高级研究计划署 **DARPA**
  Defense Advanced Research Projects Agency
- 美国国防部刑事调查局 **DCIS**　　Defense Criminal Investigation Service
- 美国国防情报局 **DIA**　　Defense Intelligence Agency
- 美国国防支援计划 **DSP**　　Defense Support Program
- 美国国会大厦警察 **USCP**　　United States Capitol Police
- 美国国会及行政当局中国委员会 **CECC**
  Congressional-Executive Commission on China
- 美国国会调查部 **CRS**　　Congressional Research Service

- 美国国会图书馆 L(O)C　　　　　　Library of Congress
- 美国国会图书馆手稿文献联合目录 NUCMC
  National Union Catalog of Manuscript Collections
- 美国国际大学—非洲分校 USIU-Africa
  United States International University-Africa
- 美国国际集团 AIG
  American International Group (Incorporated)
- 美国国际救援队 ARTI　　　　　American Rescue Team International
- 美国国际开发署 USAID　　　　　USA International Development
- 美国国际团体联合会 AFII
  American Federation of International Institutes
- 美国国际训练协会 AITA
  American International Training Association
- 美国国家安全局 NSA　　　　　　National Security Agency
- 美国国家安全太空战略 NSSS　　　National Safety Space Strategy
- 美国国家标准学会 ANSI　　　　　American National Standards Institute
- 美国国家标准研究所制定的 C 语言标准定义 ANSIC
  American National Standard Institute COBOL
- 美国国家超级计算机应用中心 NCSA
  National Center for Supercomputing Application
- 美国国家大学体育总会 NCAA　　National Collegiate Athletic Association
- 美国国家骨髓库 NMDP　　　　　National Marrow Donor Program
- 美国国家广播公司协会 ANAB
  American National Association of Broadcasters
- 美国国家海洋和大气局 NOAA
  National Oceanic and Atmospheric Administration
- 美国国家海洋渔业局 NMFS　　　National Marine Fisheries Service
- 美国国家篮球协会 NBA　　　　　National Basketball Association
- 美国国家女子篮球协会 WNBA　　Women's National Basketball Association
- 美国国家卫生基金会 NSF　　　　National Sanitation Foundation
- 美国国家作品协会 NCA　　　　　National Composition Association
- 美国国立生物信息中心 NCBI　　　National Centre of Biological Information

M

- 美国国立卫生研究院 **NIH** — USA National Institutes of Health
- 美国哈佛大学 **Harv** — Harvard University
- 美国海岸巡逻队 **USCG** — United States Coast Guard
- 美国海关与边境保护局 **USCBP** — U. S. Customs and Border Protection
- 美国海军 **USN** — United States Navy
- 美国海军陆战队 **USMC** — United States Marine Corps
- 美国海军学院 **USNI** — United States Naval Institute
- 美国海军研究协会 **USNRI** — United States Naval Research Institute
- 美国海姆立克急救法 **HM** — Heimlich Maneuvers
- 美国海洋生物实验室 **NBL** — Naval Biological Laboratory
- 美国航空驻华特遣队 **CATF** — China-Air Task Force
- 美国合金铸造学会 **ACI** — Alloy Casting Institute
- 美国钢铁学会 **AISI** — American Iron and Steel Institute
- 美国铝业公司 **ALCOA** — Aluminum Company of America
- 美国黑人文化及历史学会 **AACHS** — Afro-American Cultural and Historical Society
- 美国红十字会 **ARC** — American Red Cross
- 美国华人创业者协会 **CAEA** — Chinese-American Entrepreneurs Association
- 美国华盛顿州立大学 **WSU** — Washington State University
- 美国化学学会 **ACS** — American Chemical Society
- 美国环境保护署 **EPA** — Environmental Protection Agency
- 美国环球航空公司 **TWA** — Trans-World Airlines Inc.
- 美国环球石油产品公司 **UOP** — Universal Oil Products Company
- 美国缓刑和假释 **USPP** — United States Probation and Parole
- 美国黄石国家公园 **YNP** — Yellowstone National Park
- 美国会计协会 **AAA** — American Accounting Association
- 美国会议论文索引 **CPI** — Conference Papers Index
- 美国婚姻与家庭治疗师协会 **AAMFT** — American Association of Marriage and Family Therapists
- 美国婚姻与家庭治疗协会 **AAMFT** — American Association of Marriage and Family Therapy

美国机械学、力学联盟 **UAM**　　United American Mechanics

美国肌筋膜研究有限公司 **AIMS**
American Institute for Myofascial Studies LLC

美国计算机内存模块与主机板测试认证标志 **CMTL**
Computer Memory Test Labs

美国计算机协会国际大学生程序设计竞赛 **ACM-ICP**
ACM International Collegiate Programming Contest

美国技术学会 **ATS**　　American Technical Service

美国加速战略计算计划 **ASCI**　　Accelerated Strategic Computing Initiative

美国加州环境健康危害评估办公室 **OEHHA**
The Office of Environmental Health Hazard Assessment

美国加州浸会大学 **CBU**　　California Baptist University

美国建筑师学会 **AIA**　　American Institute of Architects

美国剑桥科学文摘社 **CSA**　　Cambridge Scientific Abstracts

美国焦虑症协会 **ADAA**　　Anxiety Disorders Association of America

美国教师教育学院联合会 **AACTE**
American Association of Colleges for Teacher Education

美国教师联合会 **AFT**　　American Federation of Teachers

美国教育考试服务中心 **ETS**　　Educational Testing Service

美国教育委员会 **ACE**　　American Council on Education

美国教育研究协会 **AERA**　　American Educational Research Association

美国教育资源信息中心 **ERIC**　　Education Resource Information Center

美国节能经济委员会 **ACEEE**
American Council for an Energy Efficient Economy

美国经济发展委员会 **CED**　　Committee for Economic Development

美国经济研究会 **ERA**　　Economic Research Association

美国军火清单 **USML**　　US Munitions List

美国军事援助计划 **MAP**　　Military Assistance Program

美国凯迪拉克汽车 **Cad**　　Cadillac

美国康奈尔大学 **CU**　　Cornell University

美国科技四巨头：谷歌、苹果、脸书、亚马逊 **GAFA**
Google, Apple, Facebook, Amazon

M

- 美国科学促进会 **AAAS**
  American Association for the Advancement of Science
- 美国科学促进协会 **AAPS**
  American Association for the Promotion of Science
- 美国科学工作者协会 **AASW**　　American Association of Scientific Workers
- 美国科学家联合会 **FAS**　　Federation of American Scientists
- 美国科学情报研究所 **ISI**　　Institute for Scientific Information
- 美国科学信息协会 **ASII**　　American Science Information Institute
- 美国科学院 **AAS**　　American Academy of Sciences
- 美国壳牌石油公司 **SOC**　　Shell Oil Company
- 美国肯尼迪文化中心 **KCC**　　Kennedy Cultural Center
- 美国空军 **USAF**　　United States Air Force
- 美国空军特别调查局 **OSI**　　Office of Special Investigation
- 美国篮球协会 **BAA**　　Basketball Association of America
- 美国劳工联合会 **AFL**　　American Federation of Labor
- 美国劳联-产联 **AFL-CIO**
  American Federation of Labor-Congress of Industrial Organizations
- 美国历史协会 **AHA**　　American Historical Association
- 美国利弗莫尔(峡谷)中学 **LVCP**　　Livemore Valley Charter Preparatory
- 美国联邦储备委员会 **Fed**　　Federal Reserve System
- 美国联邦储备银行 **FRB**　　Federal Reserve Bank
- 美国联邦海事委员会 **FMS**　　Federal Maritime Commission
- 美国联邦航空管理局航空数据交换协议 **FADE**
  FAA airline data exchange
- 美国联邦航空管理局云服务 **FCS**　　FAA Cloud Service
- 美国联邦贸易委员会 **FTC**　　Federal Trade Committee
- 美国联邦调查局 **FBI**　　Federal Bureau of Investigation
- 美国联邦通信委员会 **FCC**　　Federal Communications Commission
- 美国联合国协会 **AAUN**
  American Association for the United Nations
- 美国林肯纪念馆 **LM**　　Lincoln Memorial
- 美国临床肿瘤学会 **ASCO**　　American Society of Clinical Oncology

- 美国陆军 **USA**   United Stated Army
- 美国陆军传染病医学研究所 **USAMRIID**
  the United States Army Medical Research Institute of Infectious Diseases
- 美国旅行社 **ATS**   American Travel Service
- 美国铝业协会 **AA**   Aluminum Association
- 美国律师协会 **ABA**   American Bar Association
- 美国绿色建筑委员会 **USGBC**   United States Green Building Council
- 美国麻省总医院 **MGH**   Massachusetts General Hospital
- 美国马萨诸塞州海湾交通局 **MBTA**   Massachusetts Bay Transit Authority
- 美国贸易代表署 **USTR**   United States Trade Representative
- 美国美孚石油公司 **SOC**   Standard Oil Company
- 美国秘勤局 **USSS**   United States Secret Service
- 美国密歇根州立大学 **MSU**   Michigan State University
- 美国民建工程师协会 **ASCE**   American Society of Civil Engineers
- 美国民主党员 **D(em)**   Democrat
- 美国明尼苏达(大学)期刊联合目录 **MULS**
  Minnesota (University) Union List of Serials
- 美国明尼苏达私人学院协会 **MAPC**   Minnesota Association of Private Colleges
- 美国明晟指数公司 **MSCI**   Morgan Stanley Capital International
- 美国莫斯勒汽车 **M**   Mosler
- 美国-墨西哥-加拿大协定[代替北美自由贸易协定 NAFTA] **USMCA**
  United States-Mexico-Canada Agreement
- 美国南亚人联盟 **SAALT**   South Asian Americans Leading Together
- 美国能源信息署 **EIA**   Energy Information Administration
- 美国纽约证券交易所 **NYSE**   New York Stock Exchange
- 美国纽约中央火车站 **GCT**   Grand Central Terminal
- 美国农产品认证标志 **USDA**   United States Department of Agriculture
- 美国农业部 **USDA**   United States Department of Agriculture
- 美国农业部的妇幼婴儿计划 **WIC**   Women Infants and Children
- 美国培训与发展协会 **ASTD**
  American Society for Training and Development
- 美国皮肤病学会 **AAD**   American Academy of Dermatology

M

- 美国气象协会 AMS　　　　American Meteorological Society
- 美国汽车工程师学会 SAE　　Society of Automobile Engineers
- 美国汽车工人工会 UAW　　United Automobile Workers
- 美国汽车贸易政策委员会 APTC　American Policy Trade Council
- 美国汽车协会 AAA　　　　American Automobile Association
- 美国汽油、柴油发动机认证标志 EPA　Environmental Protection Agency
- 美国钱币鉴定、分级、评分的公司 NGC　Numismatic Guaranty Corporation
- 美国钱币协会 ANA　　　　American Numismatic Association
- 美国曲棍球联盟 AHL　　　American Hockey League
- 美国权力操弄的马基雅维利政治 M　Machiavellian Politics
- 美国全国癌症研究所 NCI　　National Cancer Institute
- 美国全国妇女组织 NOW　　National Organization of Women
- 美国全国公共广播电台 NPR　National Public Radio
- 美国全国广播公司 NBC　　National Broadcast Corporation
- 美国全国广播公司财经频道 CNBC　Consumer News and Business Channel
- 美国全国联合书目 NUC　　National Union Catalog
- 美国全国赛车协会 NASCAR
  The National Association for Stock Car Auto Racing
- 美国全国银行业协会 NBA　　National Banking Association
- 美国犬舍俱乐部 AKC　　　American Kennel Club
- 美国人工智能协会 AAAI
  International Association for Artificial Intelligence
- 美国人权委员会 ACHR　　American Council of Human Rights
- 美国认证协会 ACI　　　　American Certificate Institute
- 美国赛马协会 JA　　　　　Jockey Association
- 美国商品交易所 ACE　　　American Commodity Exchange
- 美国商学院协会 AACSB
  American Association of Collegiate Schools of Business
- 美国诗人协会 AAP　　　　Academy of American Poets
- 美国石油产品标志 IP　　　Institute of Petroleum
- 美国石油协会 API　　　　American Petroleum Institute
- 美国时尚设计委员会 CFDA　Council of Fashion Designers of America

- 美国实验生物学协会联盟 **FASEB**
  Federation of American Societies of Experimental Biology
- 美国数学竞赛 **AMC**   American Mathematics Competitions
- 美国数学竞赛委员会 **CAMC**
  Committee on the American Mathematics Competitions
- 美国数学协会 **MAA**   Mathematical Association of America
- 美国数学学会 **AMS**   American Mathematical Society
- 美国数学邀请赛 **AIME**
  American Invitational Mathematics Examination
- 美国数字千年版权法案 **DMCA**   Digital Millenium Copyright Act
- 美国司法部 **DOJ**   Department of Justice
- 美国斯坦福大学发起的机器阅读理解顶级赛事 **SQuAD**
  Stanford Question Answering Dataset
- 美国太空服务公司 **SSI**   Sky Service Incorporation
- 美国太平洋航空公司 **TPA**   Trans-Pacific Airlines
- 美国太平洋司令部 **USPACOM**   United States Pacific Command
- 美国糖尿病学会 **ADA**   American Diabetes Association
- 美国糖尿病研究与教育促进会 **CADRE**
  Committee of American Diabetes Research and Education
- 美国特斯拉汽车 **T**   Tesla
- 美国特许营业部经理 **CIAM**   Chartered Insurance Agency Manager
- 美国特种作战司令部 **USSOC**   U. S. Special Operations Command
- 美国通用汽车公司 **GM(C)**   General Motors Corporation
- 美国通用资本航空服务 **GECAS**   General Electric Capital Aviation Services
- 美国童子军 **BSA**   Boy Scouts of America
- 美国统一代码委员会 **UPC**   Universal Products Code Committee
- 美国统一代码委员会 **UCC**   Uniform Code Council
- 美国投资顾问协会 **ICAA**   Investment Counsel Association of America
- 美国图书馆协会 **ALA**   American Library Association
- 美国退休人员协会 **AARP**   American Association of Retired Persons
- 美国外国投资委员会 **CFIUS**
  The Committee on Foreign Investment in the United States

M

- 美国外交学院 FSI　　　　　　　　Foreign Service Institute
- 美国外语教学委员会 ACTFL
  American Council on the Teaching of Foreign Languages
- 美国网络联盟 NAI　　　　　　　　National Association of Internet
- 美国微软全国广播公司 MSNBC　　Microsoft National Broadcast Corporation
- 美国卫生、体育及娱乐协会 AAHPER
  American Association for Health, Physical Education and Recreation
- 美国卫星试验中心 STC　　　　　　Satellite Test Center
- 美国胃肠病学学会 ACG　　　　　　American College of Gastroenterology
- 美国胃肠病学杂志 AJG　　　　　　American Journal of Gastroenterology
- 美国文化教育委员会 CACE
  Committee of American Culture and Education
- 美国无人机融合试点计划 USAIPP　　USA Integration Pilot Programs
- 美国无损检测学会 ASNT
  American Society for Nondestructive Testing
- 美国无线电公司 RCA　　　　　　　Radio Corporation of America
- 美国无线电频率装置认证标志 FCC　Federal Communications Commission
- 美国无线电通信公司 RCAC　　　　RCA Communications Inc.
- 美国物理学会 AIP　　　　　　　　American Institute of Physics
- 美国西得克萨斯中间基原油 WTI　　West Texas Intermediate
- 美国现代语言协会 MLA　　　　　　Modern Language Association
- 美国现象级 IT 企业（谷歌、亚马逊、脸谱、苹果）GAFA
  Google, Amazon, Facebook, Apple
- 美国项目管理协会 PMI　　　　　　Project Management Institute
- 美国消费品安全委员会 CPSC　　　Consumer Product Safety Commission
- 美国消费者满意度指数 ACSI　　　American Consumer Satisfaction Index
- 美国小企业协会 AASB　　　　　　American Association of Small Business
- 美国心理学会 APA　　　　　　　　American Psychological Association
- 美国心血管学会学刊 JACC
  Journal of the American College of Cardiology
- 美国心脏病推广学会 ACCE　　　　American College Cardiology Extending

- 美国心脏病推广研究服务学会 ACCESS
American College of Cardiology Extending Study Services
- 美国心脏病学会 ACC　　　　　American College of Cardiology
- 美国心脏协会 AHA　　　　　　American Heart Association
- 美国欣斯代尔中心高中 HCHS　　Hinsdale Center High School
- 美国新安全中心 CNAS　　　　　Center of New America Safety
- 美国新闻署 USIA　　　　　　　United States Information Agency
- 美国信息交换标准代码 ASCII
American Standard Code for Information Interchange
- 美国胸科医师学会 ACCS　　　　American College of Chest Surgeons
- 美国学术团体委员会 ACLS　　　American Council of Learned Societies
- 美国巡回上诉法院 CCA　　　　　Circuit Court of Appeals
- 美国牙科协会 ADA　　　　　　　American Dental Association
- 美国牙科医师学会 AAD　　　　　American Academy of Dentists
- 美国研究生入学考试 GRE　　　　Graduate Record Examination
- 美国研究助理[高等教育机构为研究生设置的支薪职位] RA
research assistant
- 美国演员工会和广播电视艺人联合会 SAG-AFTRA
the Screen Actors Guild and the American Federation of Television and Radio Artists
- 美国养猫爱好者协会 ACFA　　　American Cat Fanciers Association
- 美国药品生产商联合会 ADM　　　American Drug Manufactures
- 美国药物性肝损伤协作网络 USDILIN
United States Drug Induced Liver Injury Network
- 美国伊斯兰食品营养委员会 IFANCA
Islamic Food and Nutrition Council of America
- 美国医疗保险协会 HIAA　　　　Health Insurance Association of America
- 美国医疗器械促进协会 AAMI　　America Association for Medical Instrument
- 美国医疗器械促进协会 AAMI
Association for the Advancement of Medical Instrumentation
- 美国医药协会杂志 JAMA
Journal of the American Medical Association
- 美国移民归化局 INS
Immigration and Naturalization Service, USA

M

M

- 美国移民律师协会 **AILA**   American Immigrate Lawyer Association
- 美国-以色列公共事务委员会 **AIPAC**   American-Israeli Public Affairs Committee
- 美国艺电公司[美国游戏巨头] **EA**   Electronic Arts
- 美国艺术和科学研究院 **AAAS**   American Academy of Arts and Sciences
- 美国艺术和文学学会 **AAAL**   American Academy of Arts and Letters
- 美国音乐公司 **MCA**   Music Company of America
- 美国音乐社团 **MCA**   Music Corporation of America
- 美国音乐学学会 **AIM**   American Institute of Musicology
- 美国印第安纳大学 **IU**   Indiana University
- 美国盈鹰控股有限公司 **PEH**   Premium Eagles Holding LLC
- 美国营养协会 **ADA**   American Dietetic Association
- 美国邮政(管理局) **USPS**   United States Postal Service
- 美国友邦保险有限公司 **AIA**   American International Assurance
- 美国有线(电视)新闻网 **CNN**   Cable News Networks
- 美国娱乐与体育节目电视网 **ESPN**   Entertainment and Sports Programming Network
- 美国语言学家协会 **AALS**   American Association of Language Specialists
- 美国语言自动处理咨询委员会 **ALPAC**   Automatic Language Processing Advisory Committee
- 美国原子能委员会 **AEC**   Atomic Energy Commission
- 美国运动医学会 **ACSM**   American College of Sports Medicine
- 美国运通卡 **AMEX**   American Express
- 美国运通信用卡 **AE**   American Express
- 美国在台协会 **AIT**   American Institute in Taiwan
- 美国在线服务公司 **AOL**   America On-Line
- 美国詹姆斯·布洛蓝星公司[以工程师名字命名] **JBL**   James Bullough Lansing
- 美国战略服务局 **OSS**   Office of Strategic Services
- 美国证券存托凭证 **ADR**   American Depositary Receipts
- 美国证券和交易委员会 **SEC**   Securities and Exchange Commission
- 美国证券交易所 **AMEX**   American Stock Exchange

美国政府出版局 USGPO	United States Government Printing Office
美国政府信息技术服务小组 GITS	Government Information Technology Service
美国政府允许学习期间使用的实习许可 CPT	
Curricular Practical Training	
美国之音 VOA	Voice of America
美国芝加哥交响乐团 CSO	Chicago Symphony Orchestra
美国芝加哥交易所 CBT	Chicago Board Trade
美国执法处 USMS	United States Marshals Service
美国职业安全与健康认证标志 ETL	Electrical Testing Laboratory
美国职业棒球大联盟 MLB	Major League Baseball
美国职业橄榄球大联盟 NFL	National Football League
美国职业高尔夫球协会 PGA	Professional Golfers Association of U.S.
美国职业篮球联赛 NBA	National Basketball Association
美国志愿服务队 VOA	Volunteers of America
美国志愿援华航空队 AVG	America Volunteer Group
美国质量控制学会 ASQC	American Society of Quality Control
美国质量协会 ASQ	American Society for Quality
美国中国语言、文化教师协会 AATCLC	
American Association of Teachers of Chinese Language and Culture	
美国中学入学考试 SSAT	Secondary School Admission Test
美国中央情报局 CIA	Central Intelligence Agency
美国中央情报局作战处 DO	Directorate of Operations
美国肿瘤病研究协会 AASND	
American Association for Study of Neoplast Diseases	
美国众议院 HR	House of Representatives
美国主战坦克[代字] M1A1	US main battle tank
美国注册管理会计师(认证) CMA	Certified Management Accountant
美国注册会计师协会 AICPA	
American Institute of Certified Public Accountants	
美国专利与商标局 USPTO	US Patent and Trademark Office
美国专业计算机内存测试实验室 CMTL	
Computer Memory Test Labs	

M

- 美国自动零售公司 ARA　　　　　Automatic Retailers of America
- 美国自然保护联盟 ACU　　　　　American Conservation Union
- 美国自然博物馆 AMNH　　　　　American Museum of Nature History
- 美国总审计局 GAO　　　　　　　General Accounting Office
- 美国足病医学协会 APMA　　　　American Pedopathy Medicine Association
- 美国足球联合会 AFC　　　　　　American Football Conference
- 美国足球联盟 AFL　　　　　　　American Football League
- 美国作曲家、作家与出版商协会 ASCAP

  American Society of Composers, Authors and Publishers
- 美联储 FRS　　　　　　　　　　Federal Reserve System
- 美联社 AP　　　　　　　　　　　Associated Press
- 美女、动物、幼儿[是广告大师奥格威从创意入手提出的广告表现三原则] 3B

  beauty, beast, baby
- 美属萨摩亚[太平洋群岛] AS　　　American Samoa
- 美术学士 BFA　　　　　　　　　Bachelor of Fine Arts
- 美印度(比较"人工智能") AI　　　America India
- 美英情报(局) ABI　　　　　　　American-British Intelligence
- 美元[货币] USD　　　　　　　　United States Dollar
- 美中贸易全国委员会 USCBC　　　United States-China Business Committee
- 美中人民友好协会[美国] USCPFA　US-China People's Friendship Association
- 美洲 A　　　　　　　　　　　　America
- 美洲国家组织 OAS　　　　　　　Organization of American States
- 美洲自由贸易区 FTAA　　　　　　Free Trade Area of Americas
- 镁[第 12 号化学元素] Mg　　　　magnesium
- 魅可[彩妆艺术化妆品] MAC　　　Make-up Art Cosmetics
- 钔[第 101 号化学元素] Md　　　 mendelevium
- 蒙古[亚洲国家] MGL　　　　　　Mongolia
- 蒙古国家公共电视台 MNB　　　　Mongolian National Broadcast
- 蒙古开发银行 DBM　　　　　　　Development Bank of Mongolia
- 猛击我[网络用语] BTHOOM　　　beats the hell out of me
- 锰[第 25 号化学元素] Mn　　　　manganese

- 孟加拉国[亚洲国家] **BAN**   Bangladesh
- 孟中印缅经济走廊 **BCIM**   Bangladesh, China, India, Myanmar
- 梦到你[网络用语] **DAY**   dreamed about you
- 迷你光盘 **MD**   mini disc
- 猕猴血型 **RH**   rhesus blood group
- 米[长度单位] **M**   metre
- 米格[苏联飞机设计师米高扬和格列维奇两人姓的首字母缩略语][俄文] **MiG**   Mikoyan i Gurevich
- 秘密的事情[希伯来文] **cabal**   cabbala
- 秘密副本,秘密抄送 **BCC**   blind carbon copy
- 秘密情报信源 **CHIS**   covent human intelligence sources
- 秘书 **Sec(y)**   secretary
- 密克罗尼西亚联邦政府[太平洋一地区] **FSM**   Federation States of Micronesia
- 密码系统 **CS**   cryptographic system
- 密纹唱片 **LP**   long-playing record
- 密歇根大学 **UM**   University of Michigan
- 密钥认证机构 **KCA**   Key Certification Authority
- 蜜胺/苯酚甲醛树脂[塑料] **MPF**   melamine/phenol formaldehyde resin
- 蜜胺甲醛树脂[塑料] **MF**   melamine-formaldehyde resin
- 免费 **WC**   without charge
- 免税 **TF**   tax free
- 免税商品商店 **DFS**   duty frees shop
- 免疫扩展计划 **EPI**   Expanded Programme on Immunization
- 免疫球蛋白(A,D,E,G,M) **Ig(A,D,E,G,M)**   immunoglobulin(A,D,E,G,M)
- 免疫细胞 **K**   killer cell
- 免疫粘连血凝反应测定 **IAHA**   immune adherence hemagglutination assay
- 免疫综合征 **ICD**   Immune Complex Disease
- 免疫组织化学 **IHC**   immunohistochemistry
- 免征点 **ZBB**   zero-based budgeting

M

- 缅甸[亚洲国家] **MYA** — Myanmar
- 缅甸克钦独立武装 **KIA** — Kachin Independent Army
- 缅甸克钦独立组织 **KIO** — Kachin Independent Organization
- 面向对象编程语言 **C#** — C SHARP
- 面向信息的语言 **INFOL** — information-oriented language
- 面向字符串的符号 **SNOBOL** — string-oriented symbolic language
- 秒[时间单位] **S/sec** — second
- 灭活的脊髓灰质炎疫苗 **IPV** — inactivated polio vaccine
- 民航 **CA** — Civil Aviation
- 民航与运输协会 **CATA** — Civil Aviation and Transport Association
- 民航总局[法文] **DGAC** — Direction Générale de l'Aviation Civile
- 民用导航辅助系统 **CNAS** — Civil Navigation Aids System
- 民主大会 **CFD** — Congress for Democracy
- 民主进步联盟[法文] **UDP** — Union pour la Démocratie et le Progrès
- 民主力量联盟[法文] **RFD** — Rassemblement des Forces Démocratiques
- 民主联盟党[土耳其文] **PYD** — Partiya Yekîtiya Demokrat
- 民主同盟军 **ADF** — Allies Democracy Forces
- 民主团结联盟[法文] **RDU** — Rassemblement pour la Démocratie et L'UNI
- 民主与发展全国同盟[法文] **PNDD** — Pacte National Pour la Démocratie et le Développement
- 民族解放军[西班牙文] **ELN** — Ejército de Liberación Nacional
- 敏捷制造 **AM** — agile manufacturing
- 名人迷[网络用语] **BNF** — big name fan
- 名人堂 **HF** — Hall of Fame
- 名义筹资 **ICO** — initial coin offering
- 名义上的共和党 **RINO** — Republicans in Name Only
- 明尼苏达矿业及制造公司 **3M** — Minnesota Mining & Manufacturing Co.
- 明天 **tmr** — tomorrow
- 明星;高层 **Glitterati** — glitter literati
- 明星博物馆[韩国一家娱乐公司名称] **SM** — Star Museum
- 模板元编程 **TMP** — template metaprogramming

模仿-借用-创新[翻译主张] ABC	Adapt-Borrow-Create
模块方式 BBA	building block approach
模拟经商[养成]游戏 SIM/SLG	simulation game

模拟联合国和平利用外层空间委员会 **MUNCOPUOS**
Model United Nations Committee on the Peaceful Uses of Outer Space

模拟数字语言 ADSL	analog to digital simulation
模拟—数字转换 A/D, D/A	analog-to-digital
模拟数字转换器 A/DC	analog-to-digital converter
模拟医学教育 SBME	simulation based medical education
模拟语言 SIMULA	simulation language
模式识别 PR	pattern recognition
模数转换器 ADC	analog-digital converter
摩(尔)[法定物质的量计量单位] Mol	molecule
摩拜单车 mobike	motorbicycle
摩尔/升 mol/l	mol/litre
摩尔多瓦[欧洲国家] MDA	Moldova
摩根大通银行 JPM	JP Morgan Chase Bank, New York
摩根士丹利 MS	Morgan Stanley
摩根士丹利资本国际 MSCI	Morgan Stanley Capital International
摩洛哥[非洲国家] MOR	Morocco
摩纳哥[欧洲国家] MON	Monaco
摩托罗拉(电子产品) MOTO	Motorola
莫里斯汽车[英国竞赛用车] M-G	Morris-Garage
莫桑比克[非洲国家] MOZ	Mozambique
墨西哥[北美洲国家] MEX	Mexico

墨西哥产品质量认证标志/墨西哥官方标准[西班牙文] **NOM**
Norma Oficial Mexicana

墨西哥联盟的国际刑事法院[西班牙文] **CMCPI**
Coalición Méxicana por la Corte Penal Internacional

墨西哥人权捍卫和促进委员会[西班牙文] **CMDPDH**
Comisión Méxicana de Defensay Promoción de los Derechos Humanos

N

- 墨西哥人权捍卫和促进委员会 **MCDPHR**　Mexican Commission for the Defence and Promotion of Human Right
- 墨西哥石油公司[西班牙文] **PEMEX**　Petróleos Mexicanos
- 默克齐[德国总理默克尔和前法国总统萨科奇的姓的合称,因他们以前常同时在欧盟会议上露面] **Merkozy**　Angela Merkel,Nicolas Sarkozy
- 某某[拉丁文] **NN**　Nomen nescio
- 某人健在 **L&W**　Living and well
- 某一犬种单独展的冠军 **BISS**　Best In Specialty Show
- 母基金 **FOF**　Fund of Fund
- 目标单兵作战武器 **OICW**　objective individual combat weapon
- 目标管理 **MBO**　management by object
- 目标管理的 SMART 原则[明确性、衡量性、可达到、相关性、期限性] **SMART**　specific,measurable,attainable,relevant,time-based
- 目标即时支付结算 **TIPS**　target instant payments settlement
- 目标链接嵌入 **OLE**　object lining and embedding
- 目标与关键结果法 **OKR**　Objective and Key Results
- 目标语言 **TL**　target language
- 目的地交货费 **DDC**　destination delivery charge
- 目录 **cat**　catalogue
- 目前[网络用语] **ATM**　at the moment
- 目前最有影响力的公钥加密算法(用三个发明人的姓氏的首字母) **RSA**　Ron Rivest,Adi Shamir,Leonard Adleman
- 钼[第 42 号化学元素] **Mo**　molybdenum
- 慕课[大规模网络公共课] **MOOCs**　massive open online courses

- 镎[第 93 号化学元素] **Np**　neptunium
- 哪里有这种东西吃? **WTF**　Where's the food?

- 纳米[又称毫微米＝10亿分之一米] **nm**　nanometer
- 纳米比亚[非洲国家] **NAM**　Namibia
- 钠-葡萄糖协同转运蛋白2 **SGLT-2**　sodium-dependent glucose transporters 2
- 纳斯达克(指数) **Nasdaq**　National Association of Securities Dealers Automated Quotations
- 纳斯达克股票代码 **CDN**　Cadence Design System, Inc.
- 纳斯达克证券交易所 **NTRI**　Nutrisystem Inc.
- 纳维叶-斯托克斯(方程) **NS**　Navier-Stokes
- 钠(第11号化学元素)[拉丁文] **Na**　natrium [英文：sodium]
- 钠尿肽受体 **NPR**　natriuretic peptide receptor
- 奶牛生长激素 **rBGH**　recombinant bovine growth hormone
- 奶牛生长激素 **rBST**　recombinant bovine somatotropin
- 奶业20强 **D20**　Dairy 20
- 奶制品王后(连锁快餐店) **DQ**　Dairy Queen
- 氖[第10号化学元素] **Ne**　neon
- 耐甲氧西林性表皮葡萄球菌 **MRSE**　meticillin resistant staphylococcus epidermidis
- 男女恋 **BG**　boy and girl
- 男人 **M**　man
- 男同性恋者 **MSM**　men who have sex with men
- 男性更年期 **ADAM**　androgen deficiency in aging males
- 男性化妆品 **MMUK**　Men's Make-Up UK
- 男性间的恋爱[或称蔷薇；耽美；少年爱。不完全等同于男同性恋] **BL**　Boy's Love
- 男性易怒综合征 **IMS**　irritable male syndrome
- 男优 **AVA**　adult video actor
- 男友 **BF**　boy friend
- 男子勃起功能障碍 **ED**　erection dysfunction
- 南大西洋异常区 **SAA**　South Atlantic Anomaly
- 南德国技术监督联合会[德文] **TÜV SÜD**　Technischer Überwachungsverein, süddeutsch

N

- 南方的 So/S south(ern)
- 南方科技大学 SUSTech South University of Science and Technology
- 南非 SA South Africa
- 南非[非洲国家] RSA Republic of South Africa
- 南非标准规范 SASS South African Standard Specifications
- 南非产品认证标志 SASS South African Standard Specifications
- 南非标准局 SABS South African Bureau of Standards
- 南非产品质量认证标志 SABS South African Bureau of Standards
- 南非地面站 ESSA Earth Station, South Africa
- 南非国家动物园 NZG National Zoological Gardens of South Africa
- 南非航空公司 SAA South African Airways
- 南非货币:兰特 ZAR South African Rand
- 南非民主统一战线 UDF United Democratic Front
- 南海岸空气质量管理区 SCAQMD South Coast Air Quality Management District
- 南海行为准则 COC Codes of Conduct
- 南极 μ 介子和高能中微子探测器阵列望远镜 AMANDA Antarctic Muon and Neutrino Detector Array
- 南京大学 NU Nanjing University
- 南开大学 NU Nankai University
- 南美洲足球协会/南美足联[西班牙文] CONMEBOL Confederación Sudamericana de Fútbol
- 南斯拉夫[欧洲] Yugo Yugoslavia
- 南斯拉夫标准 JUS Jugoslovenski Standard
- 南斯拉夫船舶登记局 JR Jugoslav Register (of Shipping)
- 南斯拉夫联邦标准化协会[塞尔维亚-克罗地亚文] SZS Savezni Zavodza Standardizaciju
- 南斯拉夫认证标志 JUS Jugoslovenski Standard
- 南亚地区性合作联盟:[由孟加拉国,不丹,马尔代夫,尼泊尔,印度,巴基斯坦,斯里兰卡等国组成] SAARC South Asian Association for Regional Co-operation—Bangladesh, Bhutan, Maldives, Nepal, India, Pakistan, Sri Lanka
- 南亚洲联合目录 SAUC South Asia Union Catalogue

脑电图 EEG	electroencephalogram
脑机接口 BCI	brain computer interface
脑脊液 CSF	cerebrospinal fluid
脑脊液蛋白电泳 PE	protein electrophoresis
脑脊液寡克隆区带 OCBs	oligoclonal bands
脑力激荡 BS	brain storming
脑钠肽 BNP	brain natriuretic peptide
脑型肌酸激酶同工酶 CK-BB	creation kinase BB isoenzyme
脑源性神经营养因子 BDNF	brain-derived neurotrophic factor
瑙鲁[太平洋岛国] NRU	Nauru
内部 int	interior
内部保密文件 ISE	internal secret file
内部计算选项 ICO	in-house computing option
内部节点 IN	internal node
内部联运 ipi	interior point intermodal
内部收益率 IRR	Internal Rate of Return
内地香港青年联合会 AMHKY	Association of Mainland and Hong Kong Youth
内地与港澳地区关于建立更紧密经贸关系安排 CEPA	Closer Economic Partnership Arrangement
内阁安全委员会 CCS	Cabinet Committee on Security
内华达州自主系统研究所 NIAS	Nevada Institute of Autonomic System
内镜逆行胰胆管造影 ERCP	endoscopic retrograde cholangiopancreatography
内镜下括约肌乳头切开术 EST	endoscopic sphincteropapillectomy
内陆运输委员会 ITC	Inland Transport Committee
内容分发网络 CDN	content delivery network
内容数字版权加密保护技术 DRM	digital rights management
内生肌酐清除率 Ccr	endogenous creatinine clearance rate
内务部 DOI	Department of the Interior
内线股票补偿 ISC	insider stock compensation
内脏脂肪组织 VAT	viscera adipose tissue

N

- 内置的变量(管道) **BIV**　　built-in variable (plumbing)
- 能力发展计划 **CDP**　　capability development plan
- 能量效率比 **EER**　　energy efficiency ratio
- 能效与生产维护管理 **EPM**　　Energy Efficiency & Productive Maintenance
- 能源矿产局 **EMR**　　energy and miner region
- 能源研究和发展署报告[美国四大科技报告之一] **ERDA**
  Energy Research and Development Administration
- 能源与环境设计认证 **LEED**
  Leadership in Energy and Environmental Design
- 尼泊尔[亚洲国家] **NEP**　　Nepal
- 尼加拉瓜[北美洲国家] **NCA**　　Nicaragua
- 尼康相机[日文,意为:日本光学工业株式会社] **NIKON**
  Nippon Kogaku KK
- 尼莫地平[药] **NMD**　　Nimodipine
- 尼日尔[非洲国家] **NIG**　　Niger
- 尼日利亚[非洲国家] **NGR**　　Nigeria
- 尼日利亚标准局 **SON**　　Standard Organization of Nigeria
- 尼日利亚标准局认证 **SONCAP**
  Standard Organization of Nigeria Conformity Assessment Programme
- 尼日利亚标准组织 **NSO**　　The Nigerian Standards Organization
- 尼日利亚工业标准 **NIS**　　Nigerian Industrial Standards
- 尼日利亚强制性合格评定程序 **SONCAP**
  Standards Organization of Nigeria Conformity Assessment Program
- 尼特族[指一些不升学,不就业,不参加培训无所事事的青年族群] **NEET**
  Not in Employment, Education or Training
- 尼亚加拉学院 **NC**　　Niagara College
- 铌[第41号化学元素] **Nb**　　niobium
- 你/你们[网络用语] **U**　　you
- 你们(都) **y'all**　　you all
- 你只会活一次[鼓励人们即使冒着生命危险也要奋斗一生和享受人生] **YOLO**
  you only live once
- 你知道(的谐音) **UC**　　you see

钅尔[第113号化学元素] Nh	nihonium
逆境情商 AQ	Adversity Quotient
逆转录聚合酶链反应 RT-PCR	
reversetranscription-polymerase chain reaction	
年 yr(s)	year(s)
年[拉丁文] a	annum
年 Y	year
年产量 YO	yearly output
年初 BOY	beginning of year
年度百分比利率 APR	annual percentage rate
年度报告 AR	Annual Report
年度采购计划 AAP	annual acquisition plan
年度股东大会 AGM	Annual General Meeting
年环比 YOY	year over year
年会 AGM	annual general meeting
年鉴 YRB	year book
年金的现值系数 PVIFA	present value interest factors of annuity
年金的终值系数 FVIFA	final value interest factors of annuity
年龄/性别/位置[网络用语] A/S/L	age/sex/location
年龄/性别[网络用语] A/S	age/sex
年龄相关黄斑变性 ARMD	aged-related macular degeneration
年平均降雨量 AAR	average annual rainfall
年轻的荣耀 YG	young glory
年轻的专业人士计划 YPS	Young Professionals Scheme
年轻富有,但看起来很平常的人 yawns	
young and wealthy but normal	
年轻专业人士论坛 FYP	Forum for Young Professionals
年少者 Jnr/Jr	junior
鸟氨酸氨甲酰基转移酶 OCT	ornithine carbamoyl transferase
鸟类国际 BI	Birds International
鸟嘌呤酶 GD	guanase
尿 17-生酮类固醇 17-KGS	17-ketogenic steroids

N

尿白蛋白/肌酐比率 ACR	albumin-to-creatinine ratio
尿白细胞 LEU	leucocyte
尿比重 SG	specific gravity
尿胆红素 BIL	bilirubin
尿胆素原/尿胆原 UBG/URO	urobilinogen
尿蛋白 PRO	urine protein
尿淀粉酶 UAMY	urine amylase
尿儿茶酚胺 UCA	urine catecholamine
尿含铁血黄素试验 ROUS	urine hemosiderin
尿路感染 UTI	urinary tract infection
尿潜血 BLD	urine occult blood
尿素清除率 CUR	urea clearance rate
尿酸 UA	uric acid
尿酸碱度 pH	potential hydrogen
尿糖 GLU	glucose
尿酮体 KET	urine ketone body
尿酮体 KET	β-ketobutyric acid
尿透明度 TURB	turbidity
尿微量白蛋白 UALB	urinary albumin
尿亚硝酸盐 NIT	nitrite
尿亚硝酸盐定性 NIT	nitrite
尿液颜色 COL	colour
尿游离皮质醇 UFC	urinary-free cortisol
脲醛树脂 UF	urea-formaldehyde resin
镍[第28号化学元素] Ni	nickel
您[网络用语] U	you
凝血活酶生成实验 TGT	thromboplastin generation test
凝血酶原活性 PA	prothrombin activity
凝血酶原消耗时间 PCT	prothrombin consumption time
凝血时间 CT	clotting time
牛(顿)[法定力、重力计量单位] N	Newton

■ 牛海绵状脑病［即疯牛病］ BSE
Bovine Spongiform Encephalopathy（即 mad cow disease）
■ 牛津＋剑桥 Oxbridge　　　　　　Oxford＋Cambridge
■ 牛津大学［英国］ OU　　　　　　Oxford University
■ 牛津大学出版社［英国］ OUP　　Oxford University Press
■ 牛津饥荒救济物质委员会 Oxfam　Oxford Committee for Famine Relief
■ 牛津语料库 OCC　　　　　　　　Oxford Corpus Collection
■ 牛免疫缺损病毒 BIV　　　　　　Bovine Immunodeficiency Virus
■ 牛奶碱性蛋白 MBP　　　　　　　milk basic protein
■ 牛奶碱性蛋白成分 BMBPF　　　　bovine milk basic protein fraction
■ 牛皮癣性关节炎 PSA　　　　　　psoriatic arthropathy
■ 纽约 NY/N　　　　　　　　　　New York
■ 纽约大都会队 Mets　　　　　　　New York Mets
■ 纽约大都会运输署 MTA　　　　　Metropolitan Transportation Authority
■ 纽约期货交易所 NYBOT　　　　　New York Board of Trade
■ 纽约商品交易所 NYMEX　　　　　New York Mercantile Exchange
■ 纽约市 NYC　　　　　　　　　　New York City
■ 纽约市公共交通局 NYCT　　　　　New York City Transit
■ 纽约洋基队 Yangkees/Nyy　　　　New York Yankees
■ 农村教育行动项目 REAP　　　　　Rural Education Action Program
■ 农村宽带联盟 RBC　　　　　　　rural broadband coalition
■ 农村无线运营商协会 RWA　　　　rural wireless operator association
■ 农夫车 UTV　　　　　　　　　　utility vehicle
■ 农杆菌介导转基因 Bt　　　　　　Bt cry 1 Ah
■ 农牧业的 A&P　　　　　　　　　Agricultural and Pastoral
■ 农业科学学士 BSA　　　　　　　Bachelor of Science in Agriculture
■ 农业综合生产能力 ACPC
agricultural comprehensive production capability
■ 挪威［欧洲国家］ NOR　　　　　Norway
■ 挪威标准［挪威文］ NS　　　　　Norsk Standard
■ 挪威标准化协会［挪威文］ NSF　　Norges Standardiserings-Forbund

N

- 挪威产品质量认证标志[挪威文]**NS**   Norsk Standard
- 挪威船级社[挪威文]**DNV**   Det Norske Veritas
- 挪威电气材料检验所[挪威文]**N/NEMKO** Norges Elektriske Materiell Kontroll
- 挪威电气产品质量认证标志[挪威文]**N/NEMKO** Norges Elektriske Materiell Kontroll
- 挪威建筑标准化委员会[挪威文]**NBR**   Norges Byggstandardiseringsrad
- 挪威克朗[货币单位]**NKr**   Norwegian Krone
- 挪威游轮 **NCL**   Norwegian Cruise Line
- 挪亚方舟 **ARK**   Noah's Ark
- 诺顿命令管理器 **NC**   Norton Commander
- 诺基亚西门子公司 **NSN**   Nokia Siemens Network Company
- 诺唯真游轮 **NCL**   Norwegian Cruise Line
- 诺维真游轮控股公司 **NCLH**   Norwegian Cruise Line Holding Company
- 锘[第102号化学元素]**No**   nobelium
- 女警察 **wpc**   woman police constable
- 女朋友 **GF**   girl friend
- 女同性恋 **GL**   girl's love
- 女王 **Q**   queen
- 女王[拉丁文]**R**   Regina
- 女性,和平和安全指数 **WPSI**   Women, Peace and Security Index
- 女性机器人 **Fembot**   female type robot
- 女优 **AVA**   adult video actress
- 女子国际拳击理事会 **WIBC**   Women's International Boxing Council
- 钕[第60号化学元素]**Nd**   neodymium

讴歌汽车[日本] A	Acura
欧共体有机产品质量认证标志[法文] CE	Communauté Européenne
欧陆卡 EMVCo	Europay, Mastercard Visa Cooperation
欧盟[法文] CE	Communauté Européenne
欧盟独立交易登记系统 CITL	The Community Independent Transaction Log
欧盟内部的术语库 IATE	Interactive Terminology for Europe
欧盟食品安全局 EFSA	European Food Safety Authority
欧盟碳排放交易体系 ETS	Emission Trading Scheme
欧盟知识产权局 EUIPO	European Union Intellectual Property Office
欧盟质量认证标志 CE	Conformity of Europe
欧盟中国商会 CCCEU	China Chamber of Commerce in European Union
欧松板 OSB	oriented strand board
欧亚大陆 Eurasia	Europe and Asia
欧亚经济体联盟 EAEU	Eurasian Economical Union
欧元[货币符号] EUR/€	Euro
欧元区 EZ	Euro Zone
欧洲、中东和非洲 EMEA	Europe, Middle-East and Africa
欧洲安全与防务政策 ESDP	European Safety and Defence Policy
欧洲安全与合作组织 OSCE	Organization for Security and Cooperation in Europe
欧洲包装机械协会 EUROPAMA	The European Packaging Machinery Association
欧洲标准 EN	European Standards
欧洲标准化委员会[法文] CEN	Comité Européen de Normalisation

O

- 欧洲的 **EN**　　European
- 欧洲的中国语言学会 **EACL**　　European Association of Chinese Linguistics
- 欧洲电工标准化委员会[法文] **CENELEC**
  Comité Européen de Normalisation Electrotechnique
- 欧洲电工标准化委员会电子器件委员会 **CECC**
  CENELEC Electronic Components Committee
- 欧洲电气标准协调委员会[现已改为：CENELEC][法文] **CENEL**
  Comité Européen de Coordination des Normes Electriques
- 欧洲电子元器件质量认证标志 **CECC**
  CENELEC Electronic Components Committee
- 欧洲翻译中心[法文] **CET**
  Centre Européen de Traduction[英文：European Translation Center]
- 欧洲反恐中心 **ECTC**　　the European Counter-Terrorism Centre
- 欧洲犯罪记录信息系统 **ECRIS**　　European Crime Record Information System
- 欧洲防务共同体 **EDC**　　European Defense Community
- 欧洲防务局 **EDA**　　European Defence Administration
- 欧洲肺癌会议 **ELCC**　　European Lung Cancer Conference
- 欧洲妇女联合会[德文] **EFU**
  Europaische Frauenunion[英文：European Union of Women]
- 欧洲高尔夫球协会 **EGA**　　European Golf Association
- 欧洲歌唱大赛 **ESC**　　Eurovision Song Contest
- 欧洲工业联合会委员会 **CEIF**　　Council of European Industrial Federation
- 欧洲共同市场[德文] **EWG**　　Europäische Wirtschaftsgemeinschaft
- 欧洲共同市场 **ECM**　　European Common Market
- 欧洲共同体[法文] **CE**　　Communauté Européenne
- 欧洲共同体 **EC**　　European Community
- 欧洲共同体联合聚变中心 **JET**　　Joint European Torus
- 欧洲共同体新闻处 **ECIS**　　European Community Information Service
- 欧洲共同体自由工会联合会 **ECFTUC**
  European Confederation of Free Trade Unions in the Community
- 欧洲管理发展基金会 **EFMD**
  European Foundation for Management Development

- 欧洲广播联盟 EBU　　　　　European Broadcasting Union
- 欧洲国际银行 EBIC　　　　　European Banks of International Company
- 欧洲航空安全局 EASA　　　　European Aviation Safety Agency
- 欧洲航天局 ESA　　　　　　 European Space Agency
- 欧洲核子研究委员会[法文] CERN
  Conseil Européen pour la Recherche Nucleaire
- 欧洲核子研究中心 ECRN　　　European Center of Research Nuclear
- 欧洲烘烤机械协会 EBMA　　　The European Baking Machinery Association
- 欧洲化学品管理局 ECHA　　　European Chemicals Agency
- 欧洲货币单位 ECU　　　　　 European currency unit
- 欧洲货币体系 EMS　　　　　 European Monetary System
- 欧洲货币协定组织 EMA　　　　European Monetary Agreement
- 欧洲计算机制造商协会 ECMA　　European Computer Manufactures Association
- 欧洲计算语言学协会 EACL
  European Chapter of the Association for Computational Linguistics
- 欧洲技术认可[认证] ETA　　　European Technical Approvals
- 欧洲技术认可组织 EOTA　　　 European Organisation for Technical Approvals
- 欧洲加热和冷却应用技术的可持续项目 ASTECH
  European Sustainable Project for Heating and Cooling Applications
- 欧洲金融稳定机构 EFSM　　　 European Financial Stable Frame
- 欧洲金融稳定基金 EFSP　　　 European Financial Steady Fund
- 欧洲经济共同体[法文] CEE
  Communauté Économique Européenne [英文: European Economic Community]
- 欧洲经济共同体 EEC　　　　　European Economic Community
- 欧洲经济合作联盟 ELEC　　　　European League for Economic Cooperation
- 欧洲经济区 EEA　　　　　　　European Economic Area
- 欧洲经济委员会[法文] CEE
  Commission Économique pour l'Europe
- 欧洲经济委员会 ECE　　　　　Economic Commission for Europe
- 欧洲经济研究中心[德文] ZEW
  Zentrum für, Europäische Wirtschaftsforschung
- 欧洲开发基金会 EDF　　　　　European Development Fund

O

- 欧洲理事会 **CE**   Council of Europe
- 欧洲联盟 **EU**   European Union
- 欧洲林农业 **SAFE**   Silvoarable Agroforestry For Europe
- 欧洲贸易促进组织 **EOTP**   European Organization for Trade Promotion
- 欧洲盟军司令部 **ACE**   Allied Command Europe
- 欧洲民航联盟 **ECAC**   European Civil Aviation Community
- 欧洲南方天文台[法文] **OEA**   Observatoire Européen Austral
- 欧洲南方天文台 **ESO**   European South Observation
- 欧洲七国证券交易所的运营商和所有者 **OMX**   Office Max
- 欧洲青少年儿童局 **EBYC**   European Bureau for Youth and Childhood
- 欧洲氢协会 **EHA**   European Hydrogen Association
- 欧洲拳击联合会 **EBU**   European Boxing Union
- 欧洲人口问题研究中心[法文] **CEEP**   Centre Européen d'Études de Population [英文：European Center for Population Studies]
- 欧洲人口研究中心 **ECPS**   European Centre for Population Studies
- 欧洲人权法院 **ECHR**   European Court of Human Rights
- 欧洲食品安全机构 **EFSA**   European Food Safety Agency
- 欧洲太阳能联盟 **SAFE**   Solar Energy Association For Europe
- 欧洲太阳能制造业联合会 **EU Pro Su**   Europe Production Sun
- 欧洲体育媒体联盟 **ESM**   European Sports Media
- 欧洲田径协会 **EAA**   European Athletic Association
- 欧洲调查协调署 **EUREKA**   European Research Coordination Agency
- 欧洲通信标准协会 **ETSI**   European Telecommunications Standards Institute
- 欧洲投资银行 **EIB**   European Investment Bank
- 欧洲委员会 **CE**   Council of Europe
- 欧洲委员会议会大会 **PACE**   Parliamentary Assembly of the Council of Europe
- 欧洲未来交通系统 **EBSF**   European Bus System of the Future

- 欧洲文化中心［法文］**CEA**
Centre Européen de la Culture［英文：European Cultural Center］
- 欧洲稳定机制 **ESM**   European Steady Mechanism
- 欧洲问题研究联合会［法文］**AIEE**
Association des Instituts d'Études Européennes［英文：Association of Institutes for European Studies］
- 欧洲物品编码协会 **EAN**   European Article Number
- 欧洲协调委员会 **ECC**   European Coordinating Committee
- 欧洲心脏病学年会 **ESC**   European Society of Cardiology
- 欧洲新车评估体系 **E-NCAP**   Europe-New Car Assessment Program
- 欧洲新车评估体系 **Euro N CAP**   European New Car Assessment Program
- 欧洲新奢侈时装品牌［1976年创建于慕尼黑］**MCM**
Mode Creation Munich
- 欧洲信息服务中心 **EIS**   European Information Service
- 欧洲学术研究网 **EARN**   European Academic and Research Network
- 欧洲研究项目 **ESP**   European Studies Project
- 欧洲研究型大学联盟 **LERU**   League of European Research Universities
- 欧洲央行 **ECB**   European Central Bank
- 欧洲药品管理联合会 **EDMF**   European Drug Management Federation
- 欧洲药品质量管理局 **EDQM**   European Drug Quality Management
- 欧洲药物管理局 **EMA**   European Medicine Association
- 欧洲移民问题研究组织 **REMP**
Research Group for European Migration Problems
- 欧洲议会 **EP**   European Parliament
- 欧洲音乐奖 **EMA**   Europe Music Awards
- 欧洲宇航防务公司 **EADS**   European Aero Defence System
- 欧洲羽毛球联合会 **EBU**   European Badminton Union
- 欧洲原子能机构 **EAEA**   European Atomic Energy Agency
- 欧洲政治研究中心 **CEPS**   Centre for European Policy Studies
- 欧洲质量管理基金 **EFQM**   European Foundation for Quality Management
- 欧洲质量奖 **EQA**   European Quality Award
- 欧洲质量奖金 **EQP**   European Quality Premium

P

欧洲质量改进系统 EQULS	European Quality Improvement System
欧洲质量组织 EOQ	European Organization for Quality
欧洲肿瘤内科学会 ESMO	European Society for Medical Oncology
欧洲肿瘤年会 ECCO	European Cancer Conference
欧洲肿瘤研究协会 EACR	European Association for Cancer Research
欧洲专利局 EPO	European Patent Office
欧洲专利条约 EPC	European Patent Convention
欧洲自由贸易协会[法文] AELE	Association Européenne de Libre-Échange [英文: European Free Trade Association]
欧洲自由贸易协会[联盟] EFTA	European Free Trade Association
欧洲自由贸易协会 FTA	Free Trade Association
欧洲足球联合会[法文] UEFA	Union Européenne de Football Association
欧洲足球联合会 UEFA	Union of European Football Association
欧洲足球联盟 EFU	European Football Union

帕(斯卡)[标准压强单位 1 帕＝1 牛顿/米²] Pa	Pascal
帕金森病 PD	Parkinson's disease
帕拉瓜河的炼油中心 CRP	Center of Refinery in Paragua
帕劳[大洋洲国家][代字] PLW	Palau
怕错过 FOMO	fear of missing out
排放 EM	emission
排光沼泽里的水 DTS	drain the swamp
排气 EXH	exhaust
抛物线指标 SAR	stop and reverse
抛物转向[止损]指标 SAR	stop and reverse

炮击 BBT	bombardment
锫[第97号化学元素] Bk	berkelium
配对 CP	coupling
配音演员 CV	voice character
配置转换控制 CSC	configuration switching control
喷气机驾驶员 SB	superboy
喷气推进实验室 JPL	Jet Propulsion Laboratory
喷油器 INJ	injector
硼[第5号化学元素] B	boron
硼酸钡 BBO	barium borate
批发价格指数 WPI	Wholesale Price Index
皮肤病研究学会 SID	Society for Investigative Dermatology
皮下脂肪组织 SAT	subcutaneous adipose tissue
铍[第4号化学元素] Be	beryllium
匹兹堡冠状病毒疫苗 Pitts Co Vacc	Pittsburgh Coronavirus Vaccine
偏硼酸钡 BBO	barium metaborate
片刻 sec	second
片上系统 soc	system on chip
片状模塑料 SMC	sheet molding compound
票面金额,面值 FA	face amount
票面金额 FV	face value
拼箱 LCL	less than car load
频道 CH	channel
频繁的 FRQ	frequent
频分多路 FDMA	frequency division multiple access
频分多址 FDMA	frequency division multiple address
频分双工方式 FDD	frequency division duplex
频率依赖顺应性 Cfd	frequency dependent compliance
品牌管理系统 BMS	Brand Management System
品质保证 QA	quality assurance
品质成本交期服务 QCDS	Quality Cost Delivery Service
品质工程师 QE	quality engineer

P

品质管理 QC	quality control
品质管理圈 QCC	quality control circle
品质手册 QM	quality manual
平板电脑 Tablet PC	tablet personal computer
平板显示器 EPD	electronic plane display
平等权利修宪案 ERA	Equal Rights Amendment
平方 sq	square
平方公里射电阵 SKA	Square Kilometre Array
平方公里阵列望远镜探测器 ASKAP	Australian Square Kilometer Array Pathfinder
平衡记分卡 BSC	balanced scorecard
平均保费等值 APE	average premium equivalence
平均故障间隔时间 MTBF	mean time between failure
平均红细胞体积 MCV	mean corpuscular volume
平均红细胞血红蛋白（含量）MCH	mean corpuscular hemoglobin
平均绝对误差 MAE	mean absolute error
平均血小板体积 MPV	mean platelet volume
平均指数月收入 AIME	average indexed monthly earnings
平均最大呼气流量 MMEF	mean maximum expiratory flow
评估等级 AL	assessment level
评价中心 AC	assessment center
苹果根据 iPhone 等产品的认证 MFi	made for iPhone[或 iPod 或 iPad]
苹果全球开发者大会 WWDC	World Developers Conference
凭单据付款 CAD	cash against documents
屏幕菜单调节 OSD	on-screen display
钋[第 84 号化学元素] Po	polonium
钷[第 61 号化学元素] Pm	promethium
破伤风抗毒素 TAT	tetanus antitoxin
破伤风类毒素 TT	tetanus toxoid
破伤风免疫球蛋白 TIG	tetanus immunoglobulin
葡萄球菌凝集试验 SCT	staphylococcal clumping test
葡萄糖 GLU/Glu	glucose

- 葡萄糖耐量试验 **GTT**   glucose tolerance test
- 葡萄糖耐受因子 **GTF**   glucose tolerance factor
- 葡萄牙[欧洲国家] **POR**   Portugal
- 葡萄牙工业协会 **AIP**   Association of Industry of Portugal
- 葡萄牙投资银行[葡萄牙文] **BPI**   Banco Português de Investimento
- 镤[第 91 号化学元素] **Pa**   Protactinium
- 普遍的基本收入 **UBI**   universal basic income
- 普遍增资 **GCI**   general capital increase
- 普惠制 **GSP**   Generalized System of Preference
- 普及初等教育 **UPE**   universal primary education
- 普京[俄罗斯总统] **V**   Vladmir Putin
- 普林斯顿大学[美国] **PU**   Princeton University
- 普适文本格式 **RTF**   rich text format
- 普通 **gen**   general
- 普通包装协议 **GPP**   generic packetized protocol
- 普通的适合所有观众的影片 **U**   universal
- 普通话水平测试[汉语拼音缩略语] **PSC**   putonghua shuiping ceshi
- 普通教育证书 **GCE**   General Certificate of Education
- 普通术语学 **GTT**   The General Theory of Terminology
- 普通信托基金 **GTF**   general trust fund
- 普通液压助力动力转向系统 **HPS**   hydraulic power steering
- 普通优惠关税 **GPT**   general preferential tariff
- 镨[第 59 号化学元素] **Pr**   prasceodymium

- 七国集团[1975 年由美国、日本、法国、英国、德国、意大利和加拿大七国组成] **G7**   Group of Seven
- 七一型肠道病毒 **EV71**   enterovirus type 71

Q

期货交易管理委员会 CFTC	Commodity Futures Trade Committee
期刊文章[参考文献标示字母] J	journal
期刊引证报告 JCR	Journal Citation Report
期中支付系统 IPS	Interim Payment System
齐多夫定[一种抗艾滋病药物] AZT	zidovudine
其他交易授权 OTA	other trading authority
其他落后阶层 OBCs	other backward classes
其他事项 AOB	any other business
奇瑞汽车有限公司[中国] CAC	Chery Automobile Corporation Limited
脐血造血干细胞移植 CBSCT	cord blood stem cell transplantation
企业标准[汉语拼音缩略语] Q	qiyebiaozhun
企业并购 MA	merger and acquisition
企业防务联合基础设施 JEDI	Joint Enterprise DoDIIS Infrastructure
企业管理中心 EMC	Enterprise management center
企业家形象识别系统 EPIS	Entrepreneur Personal Identity System
企业家移民计划 FEP	Federal Entrepreneur Immigration Program
企业竞争力指数 BCI	Business Competitiveness Index
企业决策管理 EDM	enterprise decision management
企业联合组织 synd	syndicate
企业商品交易价格指数 CGPI	corporate goods price index
企业社会责任 CSR	corporate social responsibility
企业生产能力成熟度模型 CMM	Capability Maturity Models
企业识别 CI	Corporate Identity
企业识别系统 CIS	corporation identity system
企业信息门户 EIP	enterprise information portal
企业形象设计 CIS	corporate identify system
企业应用集成 EAI	enterprise application integration
企业应用系统 EAS	enterprise application system
企业资产管理 EAM	enterprise asset management
企业资金结算中心 ECSC	enterprise capital settlement center
企业资源计划 ERP	enterprise resource planning
起居室 LR	living room

- 气垫登陆艇 LCAC　　　　　　　　landing craft air cushion
- 气动空气分配系统 PADS　　　　　pneumatic air distribution system
- 气缸 CYL　　　　　　　　　　　 cylinder
- 气候研究预报 WRF　　　　　　　 Weather Research Forecast
- 气门室 CHMBR　　　　　　　　　chamber
- 气门正时控制 VTC　　　　　　　 valve timing control
- 气体绝缘全封闭组合电器 GIS　　　gas insulator switchgear
- 气体绝缘输电线路 GIL　　　　　　gas-insulated transmission line
- 气相沉积法 CVD　　　　　　　　 chemical vapor deposition
- 汽车电器协会 AEA　　　　　　　 Automotive Electric Association
- 汽车防抱死制动系统 ABS　　　　　anti-lock brake system
- 汽车库 gar　　　　　　　　　　　garage
- 汽车拉力赛中为观众及方便电视转播而设的路段 SSS
  Super Special Stage
- 汽车拖车稳定系统 TSS　　　　　　trailer stability system
- 汽车修理厂 gar　　　　　　　　　garage
- 汽轮机跳闸保护系统 ETS　　　　　emergency trip system
- 汽油 gas　　　　　　　　　　　　gasoline
- 汽油 PET　　　　　　　　　　　 petrol
- 千(＝1000) K　　　　　　　　　 kilo
- 千比特 kb/kbit　　　　　　　　　 kilobit
- 千比特/秒[数据传输速率] Kbps　　 kilobits per second
- 千吨(相当于千吨 TNT 的爆炸力) kt　kiloton(s)
- 千赫[法定频率计量单位] kHz　　　 kilohertz
- 千焦耳[功的单位] kj　　　　　　　 kilojoule
- 千克/平方厘米 kg/cm²　　　　　　kilogram/square centimeter
- 千米 [长度单位] km　　　　　　　kilometer
- 千米每小时 kph　　　　　　　　　kilometres per hour
- 千帕斯卡[压强单位] Kpa　　　　　kilopascal
- 千瓦[功率单位] kW　　　　　　　kilowatt
- 千瓦时 kWh　　　　　　　　　　kilowatt hour
- 千位每秒 kbps　　　　　　　　　 kilobits per second

Q

- 千字节 **Kbit** — Kilobyte
- 千字节/秒[数据传输速率] **Kbps** — kilobytes per second
- 千字节[计算机存储单位][另参 **GB**] **KB/Kb** kilo byte
- 牵引力控制系统 **TCS** — traction control system
- 铅[第 82 号化学元素][拉丁文] **Pb** — plumbum
- 签收短信通知 **MSG** — message
- 前部 **FR** — front
- 前端总线 **FSB** — front side bus
- 前海投资控股公司 **QIHC** — Qianhai Investment Holding Company
- 前捷克斯洛伐克标准化与计量局[捷克文] **ČSN** Československých Státnich Norem
- 前进挡 **D** — drive
- 前列腺酸性磷酸酶 **PAP** — prostate acid phosphatase
- 前列腺特异抗原 **PSA** — prostate-specific antigen
- 前轮驱动 **FWD** — front wheel drive
- 前哨淋巴结活检 **SLNB** — sentinel lymph node biopsy
- 潜能 **LE** — latent energy
- 潜水员 **dvr** — diver
- 潜艇[德文] **U-boot** — Unterseeboot
- 潜血 **OB** — occult blood
- 浅蓝色 **LB** — light blue
- 浅绿色 **LG** — light green
- 欠发达国家 **LDC** — less developed country
- 嵌合抗原受体 T 细胞免疫疗法 **CAR-T** chimeric antigen receptor t-cell immunotherapy
- 嵌入式 SIM 卡 **eSIM** — embedded subscriber identification module
- 嵌入式视窗操作系统 **CE** — compact embedding
- 强动力自动战术机器人 **EATR** — enhancing automatic tactics robot
- 强度调制适性放疗 **IMRT** intensity modulated conformal radiation therapy

571

- 强化的环境友好车辆和发动机 EEV
  enhanced environmentally friendly vehicles and engines
- 强迫进化病毒 FEV   forced evolutionary virus
- 强迫症 OCD   obsessive compulsive disorder
- 强生医药公司 JNJ   Johnson and Johnson
- 强直性脊椎炎 AS   ankylosing spondylitis
- 羟甲基戊二酰辅酶 A HMG—CoA   hydroxyl-methylglutaryl coenzyme A
- 亲切的照顾 TLC   tender loving care
- 勤劳、聪明、宁静 HIS   hard-working, intelligence, silence
- 青岛大学 QU   Qingdao University
- 青绿色 BG   bluish green
- 青绿色 T   turquoise
- 青年计算机科技论坛 YOCSEF
  Young Computer Scientists & Engineers Forum
- 青年剧院西北 YTN   youth theatre northwest
- 青年旅舍协会 YHA   Youth Hostels Association
- 青年男子基督教协会 YMCA   Youth Men's Christian Association
- 青年社会主义者联盟 YSL   Young Socialist League
- 青年网络 YTN   youth transition network
- 青年专业人员 JPO   junior professional officer
- 青少年教育服务 YES   youth education service
- 青少年领袖能力培养计划[包括:明确具体的、可衡量评估的、可实现的、结果导向的、有时间限制的几个方面] SMART
  special, measurable, achievable, result-oriented, timed
- 青少年训练中心 JTC   Junior Training Center
- 轻轨 LRT   light rail transit
- 轻轨列车 LRT   light rail train
- 轻量级水净化器 LWP   light water processor
- 轻柔地[意大利文] P   piano
- 轻微脑机能障碍 MBD   minimal brain dysfunction
- 轻型商务用车 LCV   light commercial vehicle

Q

- 氢[第1号化学元素] H — hydrogen
- 氢离子浓度指数 pH — potential hydrogen
- 倾斜地球同步卫星 IGSS — Inclined Geosynchronous Satellite
- 倾斜地球同步轨道 IGSO — Inclined Geosynchronous Orbit
- 清淡香水（香精含量1‰～3％）[法文] EF — eau fraiche
- 清华大学 TU — Tsinghua University
- 清华领导力[汉语拼音缩略语] THLDL — Tsinghua lingdaoli
- 清洁发展机制 CDM — Clean Development Mechanism
- 清洁发展机制执行理事会 CDM-EB — Executive Board of Clean Development Mechanism
- 清酒罐 BBT — bright beer tank
- 清廉指数 CPI — clear and pure index
- 清算所 CH — clearing house
- 清真产业发展局 HDC — Halal Industry Development Corporation
- 清真认证 HC — Halal certification
- 清真食品研究中心（总部在香港）HFC — Halal Foundation Center
- 情报部门 SS — secret service
- 情报监视和侦察 ISR — Intelligence Surveillance and Reconnaissance
- 情报研究局 BIR — Bureau of Intelligence and Research
- 情商 EQ — Emotion Quotient
- 情形 C/S — case
- 请购单 PR — purchase requirement
- 请回复[法文] RSVP — Répondez s'il vous plaît
- 请求报价单 RPQ — request for price quotation
- 球迷身份证 FANID — fan identification
- 区块链共识网络 BCN — Blockchain Consensus Network
- 区议会[英国] DC — District Council
- 区域 Z — zone
- 区域安全分析 ZSA — zone safety analysis
- 区域建设委员会 RBC — regional business center

区域宽带联盟 RBC	regional broadband consortia
区域淋巴结清扫 RLND	regional lymph node dissection
区域全面经济伙伴关系 RCEP	Regional Comprehensive Economic Partnership
区域商业文献全文数据库 RBN	Regional Business News
区域商业中心 RBC	regional building committee
区域信息协议 ZIP	Zone Information Protocol
驱动力控制系统 TCS/TRAC/TRC	traction control system
驱动马达 DM	driver motor
屈光度 D	diopter
趋向指数 DMI	directional movement index
曲轴强制通风器 PCV	positive crankshaft ventilation
曲轴位置 CKP	crank shaft position
取款通知 AR	Advice of Receipt
取消资格 DQ	disqualify
去[口语] gotta	got to
去甲肾上腺素 NE	noradrenaline
去污和服役[停用] D&D	Decontamination and Decommissioning
去中心化应用 DAPP	decentralized application
全场犬类后备总冠军[即亚军] RBIS	Reserve Best In Show
全场犬类总冠军 BIS	Best In Show
全场特幼犬冠军 BJPIS	Best Junior Puppy In Show
全肠外营养 TPN	total parenteral nutrition
全场幼犬冠军 BPIS	Best Puppy In Show
全程微距 CF Micro	continue focus micro
全地形车 ATV	All Terrain Vehicle
全地形自行车 ATB	all terrain bicycle
全动态影像 FMV	full-motion video
全断面硬岩掘进机 TBM	full face rock tunnel boring machine
全高清 FHD	full high definition
全公司质量控制 CWQC	company-wide quality control
全国冰球联盟 NHL	National Hockey League

Q

- 全国步枪协会 **NRA**　　　　　　　　National Rifle Association
- 全国出国培训备选人员外语考试 **BFT**　Business Foreign Language Test
- 全国大学生英语竞赛 **NECCS**
  National English Contest for College Students
- 全国大学体育协会 **NCAA**　　　　　National Collegiate Athletic Association
- 全国电视制式委员会 **NTSC**　　　　National Television Systems Committee
- 全国翻译专业资格(水平)考试 **CATTI**
  China Accreditation Test for Translators and Interpreters
- 全国房地产经纪人协会 **NAR**　　　　National Association of Realtors
- 全国改革与发展联盟[法文] **RNRD**
  Rassemblement National pour la Réforme et le Developpement
- 全国公路交通安全管理局 **NHTSA**
  National Highway Traffic Safety Administration
- 全国计算机等级考试 **NCRE**　　　　National Computer Rank Examination
- 全国计算中心 **NCC**　　　　　　　　National Computing Center
- 全国纪录 **NR**　　　　　　　　　　national record
- 全国金融综合信息服务网 **CFN**　　　countrywide finance net
- 全国进口商协会 **NCI**　　　　　　　National Council of Importers
- 全国经济研究所 **NBER**　　　　　　National Bureau of Economic Research
- 全国开放源代码高校推进联盟 **LUPA**
  Leadership of Open Source University Promotion Alliance
- 全国冷冻食品包装商协会 **NAFFP**
  National Association of Frozen Food Packers
- 全国领养协会 **NAS**　　　　　　　　National Adoption Society
- 全国民主协会 **NDI**　　　　　　　　National Democratic Institute
- 全国普通高等学校英语统一招生考试 **NMET**
  National Matriculation English Test
- 全国期货协会 **NFA**　　　　　　　　National Futures Association
- 全国青少年卡丁车运动委员会(K 为 carting car 的变异缩略语) **CNYK**
  China Youth K
- 全国青少年信息学奥林匹克竞赛 **NOI** National Olympiad in Informatics

- 全国青少年信息学奥林匹克联赛 **NOIP**
  National Olympiad in Informatics in Provinces
- 全国人民大会党［塞拉利昂］**APC**　　All People's Congress
- 全国人民代表大会和中国人民政治协商会议（简称"两会"）**NPC&CPCC**
  National People's Congress and Chinese People's Political Consultative Conference
- 全国认定的评级组织 **NRSRO**
  Nationally Recognized Statistical Rating Organization
- 全国生物科技管理专业委员会 **NCB**
  National tech Committee of the Biotechnology
- 全国实习号证书 **NTN**　　National Training Number Certificates
- 全国税号证书 **NTN**　　National Tax Number Certificates
- 全国糖业股份公司［智利，西班牙文］**IANSA**
  Instituto Azucarero Nacional, S. A.
- 全国统计与经济研究所［法文］**INSEE**
  Institut national de la statistique et des études économiques
- 全国外国留学生指导教师协会 **NAFSA**
  National Association of Foreign Student Advisers
- 全国外国学生事务协会 **NAFSA**
  National Association of Foreign Student Affairs
- 全国外语翻译证书考试 **NAETI**
  National Accreditation Examinations for Translators and Interpreters
- 全国信息安全标准化技术委员会 **TC260**
  National Information Security Standardization Technical Committee
- 全国印第安人基金［葡萄牙文］**FUNAI** Fundação Nacional dos Indios
- 全国英语等级考试 **PETS**　　Public English Test System
- 全国有色人种促进会 **NAACP**
  National Association for the Advancement of Colored People
- 全国运输安全委员会 **NTSB**　　National Transportation Safety Board
- 全国证券交易自动报价系统 **STAQ**
  Securities Trading Automated Quotation System
- 全国咨询中心 **NRC**　　National Referral Center
- 全国自动回复系统 **NARS**　　National Automated Response System

Q

- 全景式监控影像系统 AVM　　around view monitor
- 全局码 GTT　　Global Title Translation
- 全科医生 GP　　general practitioner
- 全无氯 TCF　　totally chlorine-free
- 全美移民律师协会 AILA　　American Immigration Lawyer Association
- 全美证券交易商协会 NASD　　National Association of Securities Dealers
- 全面与进步跨太平洋伙伴关系协定 CPTPP
　　Comprehensive and Progressive Agreement for Trans-Pacific Partnership
- 全面禁止核试验条约组织 CTBTO
　　Comprehensive Nuclear-Test-Ban Treaty Organization
- 全面禁止核试验条约组织筹备委员会 CTBTO
　　Preparatory Commission for the Comprehensive Nuclear-Test-Ban Treaty Organization
- 全面客户体验 TCE　　total customer experience
- 全面评级 FG　　full grade
- 全面质量服务 TQS　　Total Quality Service
- 全面质量管理 以前用 TQC(Total Quality Control) TQM
　　Total Quality Management
- 全球[万维]网 WWW　　World Wide Web
- 全球半导体联盟 GSA　　Global Semiconductor Association
- 全球保育区域组织 WCPA　　World Commission on Protected Area
- 全球采购经理指数 GPMI　　Global Purchasing Manager Index
- 全球产业展望 GIV　　Global Industry Vision
- 全球创业观察 GEM　　Global Entrepreneurship Monitor
- 全球导弹防御系统 GMD　　Global Missile Defence(system)
- 全球导航卫星系统 GNSS　　Global Navigation Satellite System
- 全球定位系统 GPS　　Global Positioning System
- 全球翻译社区 GTC　　global translator community
- 全球反垃圾焚烧联盟 GAIA　　The Global Anti-Incinerator Alliance
- 全球分类系统 GCS　　Globe Classification System
- 全球分销系统 GDS　　Global Distribution System
- 全球服务关系代码 GSRN　　Global Service Relation Number

- 全球公共政策研究所 **GPPI**   Global Public Policy Institute
- 全球硅谷 **GSV**   Global Silicon Valley
- 全球海上遇险与安全系统 **GMDSS**   global maritime distress and safety system
- 全球核能伙伴计划 **GNEP**   Global Neuclear Energy Partnership
- 全球化、国际化、本地化和翻译 **GILT**
  globalization, internationalization, localization, translation
- 全球化及世界城市研究网络 **GaWC**
  Globalization and World Cities Research Network
- 全球环境基金 **GEF**   Global Environment Facility
- 全球环境监测系统 **GEMS**   Global Environmental Monitoring System
- 全球基础设施中心 **GIH**   Global Infrastructure Hub
- 全球基准指数 **ACWI**   All Country World Index
- 全球金融诚信组织 **GFI**   Global Financial (Integrity) Institute
- 全球金融中心指数 **GFCI**   Global Finance Center Index
- 全球竞争力指数 **GCI**   Global Competitiveness Index
- 全球跨境电商人才培训联盟 **GET**   Global Ecommerce Training
- 全球垃圾焚烧替代联盟 **GAIA**
  The Global Alliance for Incinerator Alternatives
- 全球迷你马协会 **WWMHA**
  World-Wide Miniature Horse Association
- 全球目录识别 **GCID**   Global Catalog Identifier
- 全球配送服务 **GDS**   Global Distribution Service
- 全球拳击队 **GBU**   Global Boxing Unit
- 全球人工智能技术大全 **GAITC**
  Global Artificial Intelligence Technology Conference
- 全球人脸识别挑战赛 **FRPC**   Face Recognition Prize Challenge
- 全球商品交易中心 **GTC**   global trade centre
- 全球社会风险竞赛 **GSVC**   Global Social Venture Competition
- 全球食品安全倡议（认证）**GFSI**   Global Food Safety Initiative
- 全球铁路数字移动通信系统 **GSMR**
  Global System for Mobile Communication of Railway
- 全球通用证书项目 **PGA**   Project of Global Access

Q

- 全球网 **WWW**　　World Wide Web
- 全球微波接入互操作性 **WIMAX**
  Worldwide Interoperability for Microwave Access
- 全球卫星通信系统 **GSCS**　　Global Satellite Communication System
- 全球卫星移动个人通信 **GMPCS**
  Global Mobile Personal Communication by Satellite
- 全球哮喘防治创议 **GINA**　　Global Initiative for Asthma
- 全球信息基础设施 **GII**　　Global Information Infrastructure
- 全球学生阅读能力进展研究 **PIRLS**
  Progress in International Reading Literacy Study
- 全球一体化框架 **GIF**　　Global Integration Framework
- 全球医疗复兴基金 **IAEGHCRF**
  IA Ecoflex Global Health Care Renaissance Fund
- 全球移动宽带论坛 **MBBF**　　Globe Mobile Broadband Forum
- 全球移动通信系统 **G/GSM**　　Global System for Mobile Communications
- 全球邮政特快专递 **EMS**　　express mail service
- 全球战力 **GFP**　　global fighting power
- 全日本航空公司 **ANA**　　All Nippon Airways
- 全日本劳动总同盟 **JCL**　　Japanese Confederation of Labor
- 全三态覆盖 **KTTC**　　K Tatal Tri-state Coverage
- 全身性淋巴结肿大 **GGE**　　generalized glandular enlargement
- 全生命周期成本 **LCC**　　Life Cycle Cost
- 全世界银行(间)金融电信学会 **SWIFT**
  Society for Worldwide Interbank Financial Telecommunication
- 全损 **T/L/TL**　　total loss
- 全息磁盘驱动器 **HDD**　　holographic disk drive
- 全息平视显示器 **HUD**　　holographic up display
- 全印学生委员会[印地文] **ABVP**　　Akhil Bharatiya Vidyarthi Parishad
- 全英高校中国研究中心 **BICC**　　British Institute Centre of China
- 全自动编译技术 **FACT**　　fully automatic compiling technique
- 醛固酮 **ALD**　　aldosterone
- 醛脱氢酶 **ALDH**　　aldehyde dehydrogenase

- 犬组冠军 BIG/G1　　　　　　　Best In Group
- 缺铁性贫血 IDA　　　　　　　iron deficiency anemia
- 缺铁症 ID　　　　　　　　　　iron deficiency
- 缺氧诱导因子-1 HIF-1　　　　hypoxia inducible factor-1
- 确认,应答[是通信中的一个控制码,常在计算机间通联使用] ack
acknowledgment code

- 然而我可能又错了[网络用语] BTAICBW
but then again I could be wrong
- 燃料电池混合动力汽车 FCHV　　fuel cells hybrid vehicle
- 燃料电池汽车 FCV　　　　　　fuel cell vehicle
- 燃料电池提供动力来源的电动汽车 FC(E)V
fuel cell electric vehicle
- 燃气轮机压缩机 GTC　　　　　gas turbine compressor
- 燃烧室 CC　　　　　　　　　　combustion chamber
- 燃油附加费 BAF　　　　　　　bunker adjustment factor
- 燃油直接喷射 GDI　　　　　　gasoline direct injection
- 让·路易·雪莱服饰 JLS　　　Jean-Louis Scherrer
- 让我[口语] lemme　　　　　　let me
- 让我大吃一惊[网络用语] BTSOOM　bears the shit out of me
- 热带西太平洋海洋系统物质能量交换及其影响 WPOS
Western Pacific Ocean System
- 热电发电机 TEG　　　　　　　thermo-electric generator
- 热量限制类药物 cr　　　　　　calorie restricted
- 热流和物理性质探测仪 HP3　　heat flow and physical properties probe
- 热磨机械浆 TMP　　　　　　　thermal mechanical pulp
- 热平衡 TB　　　　　　　　　　thermal balance

R

- 热塑性弹性件 TPE　　thermoplastic elastomer
- 热塑性聚氨酯(弹性体) TPU　　thermoplastic urethane (elastomer)
- 热休克蛋白 HSPs　　heat shock proteins
- 热休克反应 HSR　　heat shock response
- 人T细胞白血病-淋巴瘤病毒 HTLV　　human T-cell leukemina-lymphoma virus
- 人表皮生长因子受体-2 HER2　　human epidermal growth factor receptor-2
- 人才定向推荐 TDR　　talent directional recommendation
- 人的因素工程学 HFE　　Human Factors Engineering
- 人工半自动收费通道 MTC　　manual semi-automatic toll collection
- 人工股票市场 ASM　　artificial stock market
- 人工输入,机器输出 MIMO　　man in, machine out
- 人工通用智能 AGI　　Artificial General Intelligence
- 人工智能 AI　　artificial intelligence
- 人工智能机器人 AIBO　　Artificial Intelligence Robot
- 人工智能实验室 CSAIL
  Computer Science and Artificial Intelligence Laboratory
- 人工智能研究的基础 FAIR
  Fundamentals of Artificial Intelligence Research
- 人工智能研究所[法文] IDSIA
  Instituto Dalle Molle di Studi sul l'Intelligenza Artificiale
- 人工智能研究院 AITC　　Artificial Intelligence Technology Center
- 人工智能与交互式数字娱乐大会 AIIDE
  Artificial Intelligence and Interactive Digital Entertainment
- 人机交互 HCI　　human-computer interaction
- 人口零增长 ZPG　　zero population growth
- 人口问题参考资料局 PRB　　Population Reference Bureau
- 人口增长率 PGR　　population growth rate
- 人类白细胞A抗原 HLA-A　　human leukocyte antigen-A
- 人类白细胞抗原 HLA　　Human Leucocyte Antigen
- 人类发展指数 HDI　　Human Development Index
- 人类基因组计划 HGP　　Human Genome Project

人类基因组组织 **HUGO**	Human Union of Gene Organization
人类免疫缺陷病毒；艾滋病病毒 **HIV**	human immunodeficiency virus
人类嗜T[淋巴]细胞病毒-1 **HTLV-1**	human T-cell lymphotropic virus type-1
人类受精与胚胎学管理局 **HFEA**	Human Fertilisation and Embryology Authority
人力及人事委员会 **MPC**	Manpower and Personnel Council
人力资源 **HR**	Human Resource
人力资源管理 **HRM**	human resource management
人力资源会计 **HRA**	human resource accounting
人力资源开发 **HRD**	human resource development
人力资源配置 **HRA**	human resource allocation
人力资源专业认证 **PHR**	Profession of Human Resource
人力资源总监 **CHO**	Chief Human Resource Officer
人力资源总监 **HRD**	human resource director
人脸数据库 **LFW**	Labeled Faces in the Wild
人民币(符号) **CNY**	Chinese Yuan
人民币[汉语拼音缩略语] **RMB**	renminbi
人民币合格境外投资者 **RQFII**	RMB Qualified Foreign Institutional Investors
人民币跨境支付(业务)系统 **CIPS**	Cross-border Interbank Payment System
人民行动党 **PAP**	People's Action Party
人民进步联盟[法文] **APP**	Alliance Populaire Progressiste
人民联盟[马来文] **PR**	Pakatan Rakyat
人民运动联盟[法文] **UMP**	Union pour un mouvement populaire
人脑蛋白 **HBP**	human brain protein
人脐静脉内皮细胞 **HUVEC**	human umbilical vein endothelial cell
人权 **HR**	human right
人权国际联合会 **IFHR**	International Federation for Human Rights
人权监察站 **HRW**	human rights watch
人权劳动局 **DRL**	Department of Right and Labour
人权协会 **HRA**	Human Rights Association

R

人绒毛膜促性腺素 HCG	human chorionic gonadotrophin
人乳头瘤病毒 HPV	human papilloma virus
人声压力分析计 VSA	voice stress analyser
人事自动数据系统 PADS	personnel automatic data system
人寿保险 LI	life insurance
人寿保险单 LIP	life insurance policy
人体克隆 HC	human clone
人体密码 HC	human code
人体设计工程学 DHE	design human engineering
人体生长激素 HGH	human growth hormone
人血清白蛋白 HSA	human serum albumin
人与生物圈保护区 MAB	Man And Biosphere Reserve
人造地球卫星 AES	Artificial Earth Satellite
人质救援组 HST	Hostage Supply Team
认股证 WT	warrant
认可的供应商名单 AVL	approved vendor list
认识你的客户 KYC	knowing your consumer
认证互联网络大师 CIW	Certified Internet Webmaster
认证机构 CB	certification body
认证机构体系 CB	Certification Bodies' Scheme
认知行为疗法 CBT	Cognitive Behavioral Therapy
认知教学法 CTM	Cognitive Teaching Method
认知学术语言能力 CALP	cognitive academic language proficiency
任何情况下[网络用语] AE	in any event
任家萱、田馥甄、陈嘉桦三人组合 SHE	Selina、Hebe、Ella
任务执行率 M-CR	mission capable rate
任务组 TF	task force
日本[亚洲国家] JPN	Japan
日本 IKO 轴承(I 表示革新、K 表示技术、O 表示创意) IKO Innovation, Knowhow and Originality	
日本 TDK 集团[日文] TDK	Tokyo Denki Kagaku
日本 YKK 拉链[日文] YKK	Yoshida Kogyo Kabushikigaisha

- 日本本田汽车 H　　　　　　　　Honda
- 日本产品质量认证标志 PSE　　　Public Service Employment
- 日本川崎重工 KRC　　　　　　　Kawasaki Rail Car
- 日本大发汽车 D　　　　　　　　Daihatsu
- 日本的5s管理法的英文表达法 CAN-DO
   Cleaning up, Arranging, Neatness, Discipline, Ongoing Improvement
- 日本的5S管理法[即：整理、整顿、清扫、清洁、素养]（日文）5S
   Seiri, Seiton, Seisou, Seiketsu, Shitsuke
- 日本地貌联盟 JGU　　　　　　　Japanese Geomorphological Union
- 日本电气公司 NEC　　　　　　　Nippon Electric Company
- 日本电视台 NTV　　　　　　　　Nippon Television
- 日本电信电话株式会社 NTT
   Nippon Telegraph and Telephone Corporation
- 日本电影公司[日文] NIKKATSU　Nippon Katsudo Shashin
- 日本东京大学 UT　　　　　　　　University of Tokyo
- 日本东京电力公司 TEPCO　　　　Tokyo Electric Power Co. Ltd.
- 日本东京谷物交易所 TGE　　　　Tokyo Grain Exchange
- 日本东京票据交易所 TCH　　　　Tokyo Clearing House
- 日本东京证券交易所 TSE　　　　Tokyo Stock Exchange
- 日本东洋电气公司 TEC　　　　　Toyo Electric Co
- 日本东洋工程公司 TEC　　　　　Toyo Engineering Corp
- 日本二人组合乐队 C&A　　　　　Chage & Aska
- 日本丰田公司生产系统管理模式 TPS　TOYOTA production system
- 日本丰田汽车 T　　　　　　　　Toyota
- 日本工业标准 JIS　　　　　　　Japanese Industrial Standards
- 日本工业标准委员会 JISC　　　　Japanese Industrial Standard Committee
- 日本狗舍俱乐部 JKC　　　　　　Japan Kennel Club
- 日本广播公司 JBC　　　　　　　Japan Broadcasting Corporation
- 日本广播公司[日文] NHK
   Nippon Hoso Kyokai [英文:Japan Broadcasting Corporation]
- 日本国际电气通信基础技术研究所 ATR
   Advanced Telecommunications Research Institute International

R

- 日本国际协力机构 JICA
  Japanese International Co-operation Agency
- 日本国际贸易促进协会 JITPA
  Japan International Trade Promotion Association
- 日本国际商品展览会 JITF　　　Japanese International Trade Fair
- 日本国际协力银行 JBIC　　　　Japanese Bank of International Co-operation
- 日本国际银行 JIB　　　　　　 Japan International Bank
- 日本国家癌症中心 JNCC　　　 Japan's National Cancer Centre
- 日本国家剧院 NTJ　　　　　　National Theatre of Japan
- 日本国内最有影响的搏击比赛 K-1　Karate-1
- 日本海军 JN　　　　　　　　　Japan Navy
- 日本海事协会[日文] NK　　　　Nippon Kaijikyokai
- 日本海外协力事业团 JOCV　　　Japan Overseas Cooperation Volunteer
- 日本航空公司 JAL　　　　　　 Japan Airlines Co., Ltd
- 日本航线 JL　　　　　　　　　Japan Airlines
- 日本航运中心 JSC　　　　　　 Japan Ship Centre
- 日本红十字会 JRC　　　　　　 Japan Red Cross
- 日本货物编码 JAN　　　　　　 Japanese Article Number
- 日本教育协会 JEA　　　　　　 Japan Education Association
- 日本经济研究所 JERI　　　　　 Japan Economic Research Institute
- 日本经济研究中心 JERC　　　　Japan Economic Research Center
- 日本科学家和工程师联合会 JUSE　Japanese Union of Scientists and Engineers
- 日本矿产品、工业品质量认证标志 JIS　Japanese Industrial Standards
- 日本雷克萨斯汽车 L　　　　　　LEXUS
- 日本理化学研究所[日文] RIKEN
  RIkagaku Kenkyusho [英文：Institute of Physical and Chemical Research]
- 日本铃木汽车 S　　　　　　　 Suzuki
- 日本马自达汽车 M　　　　　　 Mazda
- 日本贸易申诉局 OTO　　　　　 Office of Trade Ombudsman
- 日本贸易振兴机构 JETRO　　　 Japan Extention Trade Organization
- 日本农林标准 JAS　　　　　　 Japanese Agricultural Standard
- 日本讴歌汽车 A　　　　　　　 Acura

日本汽车研究所 JARI	Japan Automobile Research Institute
日本犬舍俱乐部 JKC	Japanese Kennel Club
日本三井住友银行 SMBC	The Sumitomo Mitsui Banking Corporation
日本三菱国际公司 MIC	Mitsubishi International Co. Ltd.
日本胜利公司 JVC	Japan Victor Company
日本特许情报中心 JAPATIC	Japan Patent Information Center
日本铁路(公司) JR	Japanese Railway
日本玩具质量认证标志 ST	safe toy
日本维克托公司 JVC	Japan Victor Company
日本显示公司 JDI	Japan Display Inc.
日本新闻网 NNN	Nihon News Network
日本亚洲经济研究所 IAEA	Institute of Asian Economic Affairs
日本有机产品、食品质量认证标志 JAS	Japanese Agricultural Standard
日本资生堂中高端护肤品牌:肌肤之钥 cpb clé de peau BEAUTÉ	
日财卡 JCB	Japan Credit bureau Card
日常不宜[网络用语] NSFL	not safe for life
日电 NEC	Nippon Electric Company
日东电工有限公司 Nitto	Nitto Denko co., Ltd.
日裔美国人 AJA	Americans of Japanese Ancestry
日语能力测试 JLPT	Japanese Language Proficiency Test
日元[货币] JPY	Japanese Yuan
日中经济协会 JCEA	Japan-China Economic Association
融化再制制皂法 MP	melt & pour
荣获大英帝国勋章的军官 OBE	Officer of the Order of the British Empire
熔火之心 MC	molten core
溶酶体 Lys	lysosome
荣威汽车[中国:汉语缩略语] Rw	Rongwei
溶血性尿毒综合征 HUS	hemolytic-uremic syndrome
融资收购 LBO	leveraged buy out
柔性电路板 FPC	flexible plate of circuit
肉毒杆菌毒素 BT	botulinus toxin

R

- 铷[第37号化学元素] **Rb**   rubidium
- 乳点 **BP**   bust point
- 乳胶颗粒凝集试验 **LPAT**   latex particle agglutination test
- 乳糜微粒 **CM**   chylomicron
- 乳酸脱氢酶 **LDH**   lactate dehydrogenase
- 乳糖 **LaC**   lactose
- 乳腺癌易感基因 **BRCA**   breast cancer susceptibility gene
- 入侵检测系统 **IDS**   intrusion detecting system
- 软磁盘 **FD**   floppy disc
- 软件定义网络 **SDN**   software definition network
- 软件和信息业协会 **SIIA**
  Software & Information Industry Association
- 软件开发工具包 **SDK**   software development kit
- 软件配置管理 **SCM**   software configuration management
- 软件运营服务模式 **SaaS**   software-as-a-service
- 软件质量保证 **SQA**   Software Quality Assurance
- 软盘驱动器 **FDD**   floppy disk driver
- 软银集团 **SBGC**   SoftBanK Group Corp
- 软银集团 **SG**   SoftBank Group
- 软银中国资本 **SBCVC**   SoftBank China Venture Capital
- 瑞典[欧洲国家] **SWE**   Sweden
- 瑞典电气产品质量认证标志[瑞典文] **SEMKO**
  Svenska Elektriska Materiel-kontroll-Anstalten
- 瑞典电气设备检验所[瑞典文] **SEMKO**
  Svenska Elektriska Materiel-kontroll-Anstalten
- 瑞典非电气产品质量认证标志[瑞典文] **SIS**
  Sveriges Industriens Standardiserings kommission
- 瑞典工业标准化委员会[瑞典文] **SIS**
  Sveriges Industriens Standardiserings kommission
- 瑞典皇家理工学院[瑞典文] **KTH**
  Kungliga Tekniska Hogskolan [英文：Royal Institute of Technology]

- 瑞典卡罗琳斯卡学院 **KI**   Karolinska Institute
- 瑞典克朗[货币] **SEK**   Swedish krona
- 瑞典民主党 **SD**   Swedish Democrat
- 瑞典人[丹麦—挪威文] **SV**   svensk
- 瑞典人类学和地理学会 **SSAG**
  Sweden Society of Anthropology and Geography
- 瑞典萨博汽车公司[瑞典文] **SAAB**   Svenska Aeroplan Aktiebolaget
- 瑞典显示器产品质量认证标志[瑞典文] **TCO**
  Tjänstemannens Central Orgnisation [Tjanstemannens Central Orgnisation]
- 瑞典专业雇员协会 **FPE**
  Swedish Federation of Professional Employees
- 瑞阁堡葡萄酒 **RH**   Regal House
- 瑞麒汽车[中国:汉语缩略语] **R**   Riich
- 瑞士[欧洲国家] **SUI**   Switzerland
- 瑞士产品质量认证标志 **S**   SEV[见 SEV 条]
- 瑞士产品质量认证标志[德文] **SEV**   Schweizerischen Elektrotechnischen Verein
- 瑞士持股银行 **HHAG**   Helvetia Holding AG
- 瑞士电工协会(＝ASE)[德文] **SEV**   Schweizerischen Elektrotechnischen Verein
- 瑞士电工协会[法文] **ASE**   Association Suisse des Electriciens
- 瑞士电气产品质量认证标志 **S**   SEMKO(见 SEMKO 条)
- 瑞士法郎[法文] **CHF**   Confederatio Helvetico fran(s)
- 瑞士法郎[瑞士 2002 年前的货币] **SF**   Swiss Franc
- 瑞士广播公司 **SBC**   Swiss Broadcast Corporation
- 瑞士国际管理发展学院 **IMD**
  International Institute for Management and Development
- 瑞士国家电视台[德文] **SF**   Schweizer Fernschen
- 瑞士国家广播电视集团[德文] **SRF**   Schweizer Radio and Fernschen
- 瑞士国家旅游局 **SNTO**   Swiss National Tourist office
- 瑞士国家银行 **SNB**   Swiss National Bank
- 瑞士联邦理工学院[德文] **ETH**   Eidgenössische Technische Hochschule
- 瑞士联合银行 **UBS**   Union Bank of Switzerland

S

- 瑞士苏黎世药妆开发公司 **BBCC** — Beauty and the Best Cosmeceutical Company Ltd.
- 瑞士通用公证行［法文］**SGS** — Société Générale de Surveillance Holding S. A.
- 瑞士英语 **Swinglish** — Swiss English
- 瑞星软件 **RX** — rising
- 润滑剂 **lub** — lubrication
- 润滑油 **LO** — lubricating oil
- 若开邦洛兴亚救世军 **ARSA** — Arakan Rohingya Salvation Army

- 萨尔瓦多［南美洲国家］**SV** — El Salvador
- 塞尔维亚［欧洲国家］**SRB** — Serbia
- 塞拉利昂［非洲国家］**SLE** — Sierra Leone
- 塞拉利昂人民党 **SLPP** — The Sierra Leone People's Party
- 塞内加尔［非洲国家］**SEN** — Senegal
- 塞浦路斯［欧洲国家］**CYP** — Cyprus
- 塞浦路斯标准与质量管理局 **CYS** — Cyprus Organization for Standards and Control of Quality
- 塞浦路斯产品质量认证标志 **CYS** — Cyprus Organization for Standards and Control of Quality
- 3,5,3′-三碘甲腺原氨酸 **T3** — 3,5,3′-triiodothyronine
- 三碘甲状腺原氨酸摄取试验 **T_3U** — triiodothyronine uptake test
- 三价口服脊髓灰质炎疫苗 **TOPV** — trivalent oral poliovirus vaccine
- 三角贸易 **TT** — triangular trade
- 三磷酸腺苷 **ATP** — adenosine triphosphate
- 三菱支线喷气式飞机 **MRJ** — Mitsubishi Regional Jet
- 三硼酸锂晶体 **LBO** — LiB305［Lithium Triborate crystal］

三十二位精简指令集 **ARM**   Acorn RISC Machine
三维:长、宽、高 **three D**   length, width, depth
三维 **3D**   three dimensions
三维建模软件 **3Dmax**   3-Dimensional Studio Max
三硝基甲苯炸药[又名:梯恩梯炸药] **TNT**   trinitrotoluene
三星综合技术院 **SAIT**
   Samsung Aggregative Institute of Technology
三英国(电信公司) **Three UK**   three United Kingdom
三元乙丙橡胶 **EPDM**   ethylene-propylene-diene monomer
三坐标测量仪器 **CMM**   coordinate measuring machine
伞兵援救员 **PJ**   pararescue jumper
桑给巴尔市[非洲坦桑尼亚城市] **ZAN**   Zanzibar
扫描隧道显微镜 **STM**   scanning tunnel microscope
铯[第55号化学元素] **Cs**   caesium
森林管理委员会 **FSC**   forest stewardship council
沙滩车 **ATV**   all terrain vehicle
沙特阿拉伯[亚洲国家] **KSA**   Saudi Arabia
沙特阿拉伯标准局 **SASO**   Saudi Arabian Standards Organization
沙特阿拉伯航空公司 **SV/SAA**   Saudi Arabian Airlines
沙特基础工业公司 **SABIC**   Saudi Arabian Basic Industry Company
沙特认证标志 **GCC**   Gulf Cooperation Council
沙宣护发美发品 **VS**   Vidal Sassoon
沙宣洗发水(源于发明人维达·沙金) **VS**   Vidal Sassoon
厦门大学 **XU**   Xiamen University
厦门经济特区 **XSEZ**   Xiamen Special Economic Zone
晒伤防护剂 **SPA**   sunburn preventive agent
山梨醇脱氢酶 **SDH**   sorbitol dehydrogenase
钐[第62号化学元素] **Sm**   samarium
汕头国际集装箱码头有限公司 **SICT**
   Shantou International Container Terminal Co., Ltd.
善待动物的人 **PETA**
   people for the ethical treatment of animals

S

- 善待动物组织 PETA
People for the Ethical Treatment of Animals Association
- 伤残调整生命年 DALY Disability Adjusting Life Years
- 商标 TM trade mark
- 商标注册 TMR trademark registration
- 商家到商家到客户[电子商务的一种形式] B to B to C
business to business to customer
- 商家对客户[电子商务的一种形式] B2C business to customer
- 商家对商家[电子商务的一种形式] B to B/B2B/BTB
business to business
- 商家对消费者[电子商务的一种形式] BTC business to customer
- 商家对政府[电子商务的一种形式] B to G business to government
- 商家对政府[电子商务的一种形式] B2G Business to Government
- 商品价格指数 CPI commodity price index
- 商品交易所 COMEX commodities exchange
- 商品调查局 CRB Commodity Research Bureau
- 商品调查指数 CRBI Commodity Research Bureau Index
- 商品与服务税 GST goods and services tax
- 商品期货交易委员会 CFTC
Commodity Futures Trading Commission
- 商品期货交易委员会 CFTC Commodity Futures Trade Committee
- 商务汉语考试 BCT Business Chinese Test
- 商务软件联盟 BSA Business Software Association
- 商务网络智能 BNI business network intelligence
- 商务印书馆 CP The Commercial Press
- 商务英语翻译考试 BETT Business English Translation Test
- 商务英语翻译证书考试 ETTBL
English Translation Test of Business Language
- 商务英语证书[澳大利亚政府和其他英联邦国家认可] CBE
Certificate of Business English
- 商务英语证书 BEC Business English Certificate
- 商务支持系统 BSS Business Support System

商务智能 BI	business intelligence
商学士 BC	Bachelor of Commerce
商学硕士 MC	Master of Commerce
商学院 B-school	business school
商业(信息)仓库 BW	business warehouse
商业标准[汉语拼音缩略语] SB	shangyebiaozhun
商业参考与服务小组 BRASS	Business Reference and Services Section
商业服务供应商 CSP	commercial service provider
商业服务平台 BSP	Business Service Platform
商业公司 CC	commercial company
商业管理人员范畴 CBM	category business management
商业管制清单 CCL	Commerce Control List
商业流程外包 BPO	business process outsourcing
商业票据 CP	commercial paper
商业频道 BFM	business frequency modulation
商业情报系统 BIS	Business Information System
商业软件技术 BST	Business Software Technology
商业社会标准认证 BSCI	Business Social Compliance Initiative
商业银行 CB	Commercial Bank
商业知识管理 BKM	business knowledge management
商业智能 BI	business intelligence
商业周刊公司 BWC	Business Weekly Corporation
商业资源电子文献全文数据库 BSP	Business Source Premier
商用彩色 CIO	color in the office
商用翻译程序 COMTRAN	commercial translator
熵炸药 TATP	triacetone triperoxide
上船 em	embark
上等销售品质 GMQ	Good Merchantable Quality
上海大学 SU	Shanghai University
上海大众 SVW	Shanghai Volkswagen
上海大众汽车公司 SVAC	Shanghai Volkswagen Automotive Company
上海国际能源中心 INE	Shanghai International Energy Exchange

S

上海合作组织 SCO	Shanghai Cooperation Organization
上海华普汽车 SMA	Shanghai Maple Automobile
上海化学工业园区 SCIP	Shanghai Chemistry Industry Park
上海交通大学 SJU	Shanghai Jiaotong University
上海浦东发展银行 SPDB	Shanghai Pudong Development Bank
上海浦发银行 SPD Bank	Shanghai Pudong Development Bank
上海汽车集团股份有限公司 SAIC	Shanghai Automotive Industry Corp. Group

上海市工商管理局 SAIC
Shanghai Administration of Industry and Commerce

上海市英语中级口译资格证书 CSIAT
Certificate of Shanghai Interpretation Accreditation Test (Intermediate Level)

上海外国语大学 SISU	Shanghai International Studies University
上海外语频道 ICS	International Channel Shanghai
上海微电子装备公司 SMEE	Shanghai Microelectronics Equipment Co
上海音乐学校 SCM	Shanghai Conservatory of Music

上海振华港口机械股份有限公司 ZPMC
Shanghai Zhenhua Port Machinery Company Ltd.

上海证券交易所 SSE	Shanghai Securities Exchange
上皮内癌 IEC	intraepithelial carcinoma
上皮细胞向间质转换 EMT	epithelial-mesenchymal transition

上汽集团 SAIC
Shanghai Automotive Industry Corporation (Group)

上市型开放式基金 LOF	Listed Open-ended Fund
上市许可申请 MAA	market allowance application
上午[拉丁语] AM	ante meridiem
上下文内关键词 KWIC	key word in context
上下文中的关键字母 KLIC	key letters in context
上议院[英国] HOL	House of Lords
少校 Maj	major
少于整箱装载 LCL	less than car load
奢侈 Lux	luxury; luxurious
设备工程师 ME	machine engineer

- 设备管理 **PM**   plant management
- 设计、采购、施工、运营一体化 **EPCO**
  excogitation, purchaser, construction, operation
- 设计、测量、评价[是把流行病学、医学统计学原理和方法应用于临床研究的设计、数据的测定,效果的评价] **D. M. E.**
  design, measure, evaluate
- 设计、勘察管理、采购、施工和运营一体化 **EPCO+PM**
  excogitation, purchaser, construction, operation and prospecting management
- 设计变更通知 **DCN**   design change notice
- 设计变更需求 **DCR**   design change request
- 设计手册 **DM**   Design Manual
- 设计资料手册 **DIM**   design information manual
- 社会安全卡 **SSC**   social security card
- 社会安全卡号码 **SSN**   social security number
- 社会保险号 **SIN**   social insurance number
- 社会保障总署 **SSA**   Social Security Administration
- 社会工作硕士 **MSW**   master of society work
- 社会行政管理硕士 **MSSM**   master of society servant management
- 社会科学统计软件包,统计产品与服务解决方案 **SPSS**
  Statistical Package for the Social Science, Statistical Product and Service Solution
- 社会科学引文索引 **SSCI**   Social Science Citation Index
- 社会民主工党[北爱尔兰] **SDLP**   Social Democratic and Labour Party
- 社会与人文科学会议录引文索引 **CPCI-SSH**
  Conference Proceedings Citation Index-Social Science & Humanities
- 社会责任 **SA**   social accountability
- 社会责任标准体系[一种质量认证] **SA8000**
  Social Accountability 8000
- 社会责任国际组织 **SAI**   Social Accountability International
- 社会责任投资 **SRI**   socially responsible investing
- 社交电商链 **SEC**   Social Ecommerce Chain
- 社交网络服务 **SNS**   Social Networking Services
- 社交网站 **SNS**   social networking site

S

- 社区服务警察 PCSO　　police community support officer
- 社区健康协会 CHA　　Community Health Association
- 社区支持农业 CSA　　Community Supported Agriculture
- 射击类游戏 STG　　shooting game
- 射频 R/射频技术 RF　　radio frequency
- 射频识别技术 RFID　　radio frequency identification
- 摄氏度[法定摄氏温度计量单位] ℃　　centigrade
- 摄像系统 PPS　　picture pickup system
- 麝香草酚浊度试验 TTT　　thymol turbidity test
- 伸缩套管 TCF　　telescopic tube
- 身份证 ID　　identity card
- 身体健康指数 PFI　　Physical Fitness Index
- 砷[第 33 号化学元素] As　　arsenic
- 深部静脉血栓形成 DVT　　deep veinous thrombosis
- 深层卷积世代对抗网络 DCGAN　　Deep Convolutional Generative Adversarial Networks
- 深度、距离和时间 DDT　　depth, distance and time
- 深度集成数字仿真 FDS　　Fusion Digital Simulation
- 深红色 DR　　dark red
- 深空天线网络 DSN　　deep space network
- 深蓝 UB　　ultra blue
- 深绿色 DG　　dark green
- 深潜系统 DDS　　Deep Diving System
- 深色 DK　　dark
- 深色磁盘[电子文献标示字母] DK　　disk
- 深吸气量 IC　　inspiratory capacity
- 深圳发展银行 SDB　　Shenzhen Development Bank
- 深圳广播电影电视集团 SZMG　　ShenZhen Media Group
- 深圳国际公益学院 CGPI　　China Global Philanthropy Institute
- 深圳犬类保护协会 SDPA　　Shenzhen Dogs Protection Association
- 深圳小姐 Miss SZ　　Miss Shenzhen

神经内分泌型的非小细胞肺癌 NSCLC-NE	non-small cell lung caner with neuroendocrine properties
神经生长因子 NGF	nerve growth factor
神经元特异性烯醇化酶 NSE	neurone specific enolase
神经网络处理单元 NPU	neural-network processing unit
神秘顾客访问 MMP	mysterious motorist program
神童 IGC	intellectually gifted children
审查人 OR	official referee
审计总署 GAO	General Auditing Office
肾小球过滤率 GFR	glomerular filtration rate
肾血浆流量 RPF	renal plasma flow
肾血流量 RBF	renal blood flow
甚大望远镜 VLT	very large telescope
甚低频 VLF	very low frequency
甚高频 VHF	very high frequency
甚高频无线电话 VHFRT	very high frequency radio telephone
渗透型内因脑干胶质瘤 DIPG	diffuse intrinsic pontine glioma
渗透性 Osm	osmosis
升[容量与体积单位] L/l	liter
生产管理 PC	production control
生产管理 PM	Production Management
生产规范要求 MSR	manufacturing specification request
生产和物料控制 PMC	production & material control
生产计划 PP	product plan
生产控制 PC	production control
生产失效模式与效应分析 PFMEA	production failure mode & effect analysis
生产物料控制 PMC	production material control
生产物料清单 P-BOM	production bill of material
生产许可证 PC	production certification
生产者物价指数 PPI	Producer's Price Index
生成式对抗网络 GANS	generative adversarial networks
生化需氧量 BOD	biochemical oxygen demand

S

生活垃圾 HR	household refuse
生理年龄 CA	chronological age
生命力 HP	hit point
生命质量/生存质量/生活质量 QOL	quality of life
生态产品和服务(功能) EG & S	ecological goods and service
生物安全四级实验室的不规范简称 P4	Protect 4
生物反馈疗法 BFT	Biofeedback Therapy
生物应答调节剂 BRM	Biological Response Modifier

生物分子资源实验室协会 ABRF
The Association of Biomolecular Resource Facilities

生物技术 biotech	biology technology
生物假阳性 BFP	biologic false positive
生物识别学会年会 BIC	Biometrics Institute Congress
生物选择剂和毒素 BSATs	biological select agents and toxins

生物学数学模型[易感者、感染而未发病者,染病者,恢复者] SEIRS
susceptibles, exposed, infectives, recovered

生物学与其他学科相结合形成的交叉学科 Bio-X
Biology-X

生物医学中心 BMC	Bio Med Centre
生意 biz	business
生长激素 GH	growth hormone
生长激素 STH	somatotropic hormone

生长激素释放抑制激素 GHRIH
growth hormone-releasing-inhibiting hormone

生长激素释放因子 GHRE	growth hormone-releasing factor
生长激素抑制素 SS	somatostatin
生长介素 SM	somatomedin
声道 CH	channel
声光可调谐滤光器 AOTF	acousto-optical tunable filter
声音/调制调解插卡 AMR	audio/modem riser

省紧急协调中心 PECC
Provincial Emergency Coordination Centre

省销售税 PST	provincial sales tax
省油车 EEV	energy efficiency vehicle
圣安东尼奥联合基地 JBSA	Joint Base San Antonio
圣彼得堡国际经济论坛 SPIEF	St. Petersburg International Economic Forum
圣迭戈超级计算中心 SDSC	San Diego Supercomputer Center
圣路易斯华盛顿大学 WUSTL	Washington University In St. Louis
圣马力诺[欧洲国家] SMR	San Marino
圣人 S	Saint
圣人 St	saint
圣徒 SS	saints
圣文森特和格林纳丁斯注册公司 WSI	Wave & Soros International Ltd.
胜利 V	victory
胜利邮政 V-Mail	Victory Mail
失去平衡 OOB	out of balance
失事飞机报告 MACR	missing aircraft report
失效模式与效应分析 FMEA	failure mode & effect analysis
失效期 EXp. Date	expiry date
失业保险 UI	unemployment insurance
失重作用 ZGE	zero gravity effect
狮王 KOL	Kings of Lion
十二烷基硫酸钠—聚丙烯酰胺凝胶电泳 SDS-PAGE	sodium dodecyl sulfate-polyacrylamide gel electrophoresis
十进倍数单位的词头名称"十"的符号,表示的因数为 10^1 da	deca
十进分数单位的词头名称"分",表示的因数为 10^{-1} d	deci
十九岁以下(国家队) U19	Under 19
十亿 bn	billion
石英 qtz	quartz
石油 PET	petrol
石油经纪公司 PBC	petroleum brokerage company

S

- 石油生产国 OPC　　　　　　　　oil producting countries
- 石油输出国 PEC　　　　　　　　petroleum exporting countries
- 石油输出国组织 OPEC
  Organization of Petroleum Exporting Countries
- 石油天然气公司 ONGC　　　　　Oil and Natural Gas Company
- 石油消费国 OCC　　　　　　　　oil consuming countries
- 石油协会 IP　　　　　　　　　　Institute of Petroleum
- 时常 oft　　　　　　　　　　　often
- 时分多路 TDMA　　　　　　　　time division multiple access
- 时分多址 TDMA　　　　　　　　time division multiple address
- 时分双工 TDD　　　　　　　　　time division duplex
- 时间延迟反射 TDR　　　　　　　time relay reflectometry
- 时髦 IN　　　　　　　　　　　in fashion
- 时尚健儿健身俱乐部 FAFC　　　Fashion Athletes Fitness Club
- 时尚商务总会 FBA　　　　　　　Fashion Business Association
- 时域反射 TDR　　　　　　　　　time domain reflectometry
- 识别 ID　　　　　　　　　　　identification
- 实际到达时间 ATA　　　　　　　actual time of arrival
- 实际碱过剩 ABE　　　　　　　　actual base excess
- 实际控制线 LAC　　　　　　　　line of actual control
- 实际控制线 LOC　　　　　　　　line of control
- 实际身体伤害(罪) ABH　　　　actual bodily harm
- 实际碳酸氢盐 AB　　　　　　　actual bicarbonate
- 实际重量,实际权数 AW　　　　actual weight
- 实时全额支付系统 RTGS　　　　Real Time Gross Settlement
- 实时物流 RTL　　　　　　　　　real time logistics
- 实体肿瘤疗效评估标准 RECIST
  Response Evaluation Criteria in Solid Tumor
- 实验电动机械模块[意大利文] Mose　Modulo Sperimentale Elettromeccanico
- 实验飞机项目 EAP　　　　　　　Experiment Aeroplane Program
- 实验管理系统 EMS　　　　　　　experiment management system
- 实验设计 DOE　　　　　　　　　design of experiments

- 实验室 **LAB**   laboratory
- 食品、药品和化妆品研究协会[印尼文] **LPPOM**
  Lembaga Pengkajian Pagan, Obat-obatan dan Kosmetika
- 食品安全和应用营养中心 **CFSAN**
  Center for Food Safety and Applied Nutrition
- 食品安全研究信息办公室 **FSRIO**   Food Safety Research Information Office
- 食品安全中心 **CFS**   The Center for Food Safety
- 食品接触材料 **FCM**   food contact material
- 食用甲基乙二醛 **MGO**   methylglyoxal
- 史密斯航空俱乐部 **SAC**   Smith Aviation Club
- 矢量网络分析仪 **VNA**   vector network analyzer
- 使用此技术编码的音频格式 **AAC**   advanced audio coding
- 世界(文化)遗产委员会 **WHC**   World Heritage Committee
- 世界癌症研究基金会 **WCRF**   World Cancer Research Foundation
- 世界版权公约 **UCC**   Universal Copyright Convention
- 世界包装机械联盟 **WPMA**   World Packaging Machinery Association
- 世界报业协会 **WAN**   World Association of Newspapers
- 世界杯 **WC**   World Cup
- 世界不平等报告 **WIR**   World Inequality Report
- 世界不平等数据库 **WID**   World Inequality Database
- 世界厕所峰会暨博览会 **WTSE**   World Toilet Summit Expo
- 世界超算大会 **ISC**   International Supercomputing Conference
- 世界车辆法规协调论坛及其管理协定 **WFHVRAA**
  World Forum for Harmonization of Vehicle Regulations and its Administered Agreements
- 世界城市评级机构 **GaWC**   Globalization and World Cities
- 世界大学联盟 **WUN**   World Universities Union
- 世界大学排名 **WUR**   World University Rankings
- 世界大学排名中心 **CWUR**   Center for World University Rankings
- 世界大学学术排名 **ARWU**   Academic Ranking of World Universities
- 世界大战债务委员会 **WWDC**   World War Debt Commission

S

- 世界地质地图委员会 **CGMW**
  Commission for the Geological Map of the World
- 世界电子竞技比赛 **WEG**　　　　World Electronic-sports Games
- 世界电子竞技大赛 **WCA**　　　　World Cyber Arena
- 世界电子竞技大赛 **WCG**　　　　World Cyber Games
- 世界发展报告 **WDR**　　　　　　world development report
- 世界翻译教育联盟 **WITTA**
  World Interpreter and Translator Training Association
- 世界反酷刑组织 **WOAT**　　　　Worst of All Time
- 世界反兴奋剂机构[组织] **WADA**　the World Anti-Doping Ageney
- 世界房车杯赛 **WTCC**　　　　　World Touring Car Cup
- 世界房车锦标赛 **WTCC**　　　　World Touring Car Championship
- 世界飞镖协会 **WBA**　　　　　　World Boomerang Association
- 世界妇女保龄球联合会 **WIBC**　Women's International Bowling Congress
- 世界冠军 **WC**　　　　　　　　World Champion
- 世界海关组织 **WCO**　　　　　World Customs Organization
- 世界和平基金会 **WPF**　　　　World Peace Foundation
- 世界互联网大会 **WIC**　　　　World Internet Conference
- 世界互联网工业大会 **WIIC**　　World Internet Industry Conference
- 世界黄金协会 **WGC**　　　　　The World Gold Association
- 世界级 **WC**　　　　　　　　　World Class
- 世界纪录 **WR**　　　　　　　　world record
- 世界经济论坛 **WEF**　　　　　World Economic Forum
- 世界精英 **WE**　　　　　　　　Team World Elite
- 世界警察消防队员运动会 **WPFG**　World Policemen and Firemen Game
- 世界咖啡师大赛 **WBC**　　　　World Barista Championship
- 世界科技城市联盟组织 **WTA**　World Technological Association
- 世界劳工联盟 **WCL**　　　　　World Confederation of Labor
- 世界粮食理事会 **WFC**　　　　World Food Council
- 世界粮食四巨头[全世界粮食产量的 80% 都掌握在世界粮食市场的四大巨头手中],[它们是:ADM(美国阿彻丹尼斯米德兰公司),Bunge(荷兰邦吉集团)Cargill(美国嘉吉公司),Dreyfus(Louis Dreyfus)(法国路易达孚公司)] **ABCD**
  ADM, Bunge, Cargill, Dreyfus

- 世界旅行社协会联合会 **UFTAA**
  United Federation of Travel Agents Associations
- 世界旅游和旅行者协会 **WTTC**　　World Tourism and Tourist Conference
- 世界旅游组织 **UNWTO**　　Untied Nation World Tourism Organization
- 世界贸易电子平台 **eWTP**　　electronic World Trade Platform
- 世界贸易研究所 **WTI**　　World Trade Institute
- 世界贸易组织 **WTO**　　World Trade Organization
- 世界贸易组织实施卫生与植物卫生措施协定 **WTO/SPS**
  World Trade Organization/Sanitary and Phytosanitary（Measures）
- 世界美女组织 **WBO**　　World Beauty Organization
- 世界明星对抗赛 **GSL**　　Global Star League
- 世界脑力锦标赛 **WMC**　　World Memory Championship
- 世界女子拳击协会 **WIBA**　　Women's International Boxing Association
- 世界品牌实验室 **WBL**　　World Brand Lab
- 世界乒乓球职业大联盟 **WTT**　　World Table Tennis
- 世界气象组织 **WMO**　　World Meteorological Organization
- 世界汽车拉力锦标赛 **WRC**　　World Rally Championship
- 世界桥牌联合会 **WBF**　　World Bridge Federation
- 世界青年大会[法文] **AMJ**
  Assemblée mondiale de la Jeunesse［英文：World Assembly of Youth］
- 世界青年大会 **WAY**　　World Assembly of Youth
- 世界清真食品理事会 **WHFC**　　World Halal Food Conference
- 世界清真委员会 **WHC**　　World Halal Committee
- 世界区块链数字科技大会 **WBDC**
  World Blockchain Digital Technology Conference
- 世界拳击理事会 **WBC**　　World Boxing Council
- 世界拳击协会 **WBA**　　World Boxing Association
- 世界拳击组织 **WBO**　　World Boxing Organization
- 世界犬业联盟[法文] **FCI**　　Fédération Cynologique Internationale
- 世界人工智能大会 **WAIC**　　World Artificial Intelligence Conference
- 世界商务策划师联合会 **WBSA**　　World Business Association
- 世界生产力科学联盟 **WCPS**　　World Confederation of Productivity Science

S

- 世界生物多样性协会 **WBA**   World Biodiversity Association
- 世界石油大会 **WPC**   World Petroleum Congress
- 世界时 **UT**   Universal Time
- 世界摔跤联合会 **WWF**   World Wrestling Federation
- 世界摔跤娱乐公司 **WWE**   World Wrestling Entertainment
- 世界水上极速运动大赛 **IAC**   International Aquatic-speed Competition
- 世界水资源委员会 **WWC**   World Water Committee
- 世界斯诺克球员巡回锦标赛 **PTC**   World Snooker Player Tour Championship
- 世界体育舞蹈协会 **IDSF**   International Dance Sport Association
- 世界天气监测网 **WWW**   World Weather Watch
- 世界卫生大会 **WHA**   World Health Assembly
- 世界卫生组织[法文] **OMS**   Organisation Mondiale de la Santé
- 世界卫生组织 **WHO**   World Health Organization
- 世界未来委员会 **WFC**   World Future Committee
- 世界野生动物基金会 **WWF**   World Wildlife Fund
- 世界一级方程汽车锦标赛 **Fl**   Formula One (Grand Prix) 1
- 世界医学院校联合会 **WFME**   World Federation for Medical Education
- 世界医学院校名录 **WDMS**   World Directory of Medical Schools
- 世界移动通信大会 **WMC**   Mobile World Congress
- 世界艺术与科学协会 **WAAS**   World Academy for Art and Sciences
- 世界银行 **WB**   World Bank
- 世界银行集团 **WBG**   World Bank Group
- 世界英语教师协会中国大会 **TCA**   TESOL International Association China Assembly
- 世界语 **Esp**   Esperanto
- 世界语协会 **EA**   Esperanto Association
- 世界知识产权组织 **WIPO**   World Intellectual Property Organization
- 世界智能大会 **WIC**   World Intelligence Conference
- 世界中医药学会联合会 **WFCMS**   World Federation of Chinese Medicine Societies

- 世界中医药学会联合会艾灸保健推广委员会 **WFCMSM**
  Promotion Committee of Moxibustion of World Federation of Chinese Medicine Societies
- 世界著名快递与物流公司,总部位于荷兰 **TNT**
  Thomas National Transport
- 世界资源研究所 **WRI**   World Resource Institute
- 世界自然保护联盟 **IUCN**
  International Union for Conservation of Nature
- 世界自然基金会 **WWFN**   World-Wide Fund for Nature
- 世界综合格斗大赛 **WMA**   World Mixed Martial Arts
- 世界钻石交易所联盟 **WFDB**   World Federation of Diamond Bourses
- 世界最权威的宝石（鉴定书）[荷兰文] **HRD**
  Hoge Raad voor Diamant
- 世界最权威的宝石鉴定书 **GIA**   Gemological Institute of America
- 世界最权威的宝石鉴定书 **IGI**   International Gemological Institute
- 市场干预基金 **MIF**   Market Intervention Fund
- 市场总监 **MD**   marketing director
- 市净[账]率 **P/B/PBR**   price-to-book ratio
- 市盈率 **PE/P/EPER**   price earnings ratio
- 事件视界望远镜 **EHT**   Event Horizon Telescope
- 事实上[网络用语] **AAMOF**   as a matter of fact
- 事务处理机制 **TPF**   transaction processing facility
- 试验数据 **D**   trial data
- 试验治疗 **TOC**   test of cure
- 视程 **VR**   visual range
- 视窗互联网服务的命名（微软）**WINS**   Windows Internet Name Service
- 视光学院 **CO**   College of Optometry
- 视黄素 X 受体 **RXR**   retinoid x receptor
- 视觉识别 **VI**   visual identity
- 视觉识别系统 **VIS**   visual identity system
- 视频博客 **vlog**   video weblog
- 视频博客 **VLOG**   Video weblog

视频点播 VOD	video on demand
视频高密光盘：VCD 光盘；激光视盘 VCD	video compact disc
视频光盘 OVD	Optical Video Disc
视频会议硬件 HVC	hardware video conference
视频数字用户线路 VDSL	video digital subscriber line
视频图形阵列 VGA	video graphics array
视频显示终端 VDT	video display terminal
视频影像发生器 VIG	video image generator
适航证 AC	airworthiness certification
室内数字系统 DIS	digital indoor system
铈[第58号化学元素] Ce	Cerium
视黄醛 R	retinene
嗜碱性粒细胞 BASO	basophil
嗜酒者互助协会 AA	Alcoholics Anonymous
嗜酸粒细胞直接计数 EOSC	eosinophil count
嗜酸性粒细胞 EO/EOS	eosinophil
嗜异性凝集试验 HAT	heterophil agglutination test
嗜中性粒细胞 N	neutrophil
收到 recd	received
收费电视 STV	subscription television
收费电视 Pay-TV	pay television
收据 Rec(p)t	receipt
收据 RV	receipt voucher
收入指数 II	income index
收缩压 SP	shrinkage pressure
收益 YLD	yield
手柄驱动轴 SDA	shaft drive axis
手持地面无线 DVB-H	Digital Video Broadcasting-Handheld
手术室 OR	operational room
手提个人电脑 HPC	hand personal computer
手性固定相法 CSP	chiral stationary phase

手性流动相法 CMP	chiral mobile phase
手性试剂衍生化法 CRP	chiral reagent derivatization
手足口病 HFMD	hand, foot, mouth disease
守护古物[树,遗址] DOTA	defense of the ancients
首次代币发售 ICO	initial coin offering
首次公开发行股票 IPO	Initial Public Offering
首次公开募股 IPO	Initial Public Offering
首尔电视台 SBS	Seoul Broadcasting System
首席财务官,财务总经理 CFO	Chief Financial Officer
首席采购官 CPO	chief procurement officer
首席程序官 CPO	chief programme officer
首席分析官 CRO	chief research officer
首席风险控制投资师 CRO	chief risk officer
首席工程师 LE	lead engineer
首席沟通官 CGO	Chief Government Officer
首席行政官 CAO	chief administrative officer
首席会计师团体 CAG	chief accountant group
首席技术官 CTO	chief technology officer
首席价值官[网络用语] CVO	Chief Value Officer
首席检察官 AG	attorney general
首席经营官 COO	chief operation officer
首席精算官 CAO	chief accuracy officer
首席路演官[网络用语] CRO	chief roadshow officer
首席律师 CLO	chief law officer
首席培训官 CLO	chief learning officer
首席品牌官 CBO	Chief Brand Officer
首席商务官 CBO	Chief Business Officer
首席市场官 CMO	chief market officer
首席谈判官 CNO	chief negotiating officer
首席外交官 CDO	Chief Diplomatism Officer
首席网络官 CWO	chief web officer
首席网页制作官 CHO	Chief Homepage Officer

S

首席文化官 CCO	Chief Culture Officer
首席系统官 CSO	Chief System Officer
首席信息官 CIO	Chief Information Officer
首席信息技术官 CITO	chief information technology officer
首席宣传官 CCO	Chief Communications Officer
首席艺术官 CAO	chief art officer
首席隐私官 CPO	chief privacy officer
首席游戏官 CGO	Chief Game Officer
首席知识官 CKO	chief knowledge officer
首席执行官 CEO	Chief Executive Officer
首席质量官 CQO	chief quality officer
受保护的地理标志 PGI	protected geographical indication
受保护的原产地名称 PDO	protected designation of origin
售后服务 AS	after sales support
兽医 Vet	veterinarian
书中冰冻切片检查 FSA	frozen section analysis
舒适、好奇和挑战 3C	comforting curiosity challenge
舒张压 DP	diastolic pressure
输电线载波 PLC	power-line carrier
输入/输出 I/O	input/output
输入输出开关 IOS	input-output switch
输入——转换——输出 ITO	input-transformation-output
熟练英语证书考试 CPE	Cambridge English: Proficiency
树联网 WWW	Wood Wide Web
树突细胞 DC	dendritic cell
树突状细胞 DC	dendritic cell
数据处理管理协会 DPMA	data processing management association
数据处理机 DPM	data processing machine
数据处理平台 DPP	data processing platform
数据处理设备 Dpi	data processing installation
数据管理程序 DMR	data management routines
数据管理系统 DBMS	Data Base Management System

数据记录控制 DRC	data record control
数据加密标准 DES	Data Encryption Standard
数据库[电子文献标示字母] DB	data bank
数据库管理系统 DMS	database management system
数据路径软件 DPS	data path software
数据入口装置 DAA	data access arrangement
数据收集平台 DCP	data collection platform
数据收集设备 DCD	data collecting device
数据网 DATANET	data network
数据网络业务 DNS	data network service
数据载波检测 DCD	data carrier detection
数据增强输出内存 EDO	enhanced data-out ram
数据终端 DT	data terminal
数据终端设备 DTE	data terminal equipment
数控机床 CNC	computerized numerical control machine
数量性状遗传位点 QTL	quantitative trait loci
数码光处理 DLP	digital light processor
数码航电系统 DAS	digital avionics system
数码盒式磁带 DCC	digital compact cassette
数码精密显像 DRC	Digital Reality Creation
数码媒体集团 DMG	digital media group
数码相机 DSC	digital system camera
数学分析器、数值积分器和计算机 MANIAC	mathematical analyzer, numerical integrator and computer
数字版权管理 DRM	digital rights management
数字逼真重建 DRC	Digital Reality Creation
数字病毒性疾病 DVD	digital virus disease
数字波束形成 DBF	digital beam former
数字操作系统 DOS	digital operating system
数字串行接口 SDI	Serial Digital Interface
数字电视 DTV	digital television
数字电影倡导联盟(规范) DCI	digital cinema initiators

S

数字动态高清芯片 DDHD	digital dynamic high device
数字多功能光盘 DVD	digital versatile disc
数字多媒体广播 DMB	digital multimedia broadcasting
数字放射线照相术 DR	digital radiography
数字化货币 DC/EP	digital currency electronic payment
数字化设备在网络接连中的应用 DNA	digital network application
数字化同步话音和数据 DSVD	Digital Simultaneous Voice and Data
数字化种植示范基地 DPDB	digital planting demonstration base
数字货币 DCEP	Digital Currency Electronic Payment
数字货币 DIGICCY	digital currency
数字家庭工作组 DHWG	Digital Home Working Group
数字减影血管造影术 DSA	digital subtraction angiography
数字录像机 DVR	digital video recorder
数字模拟语言 DSL	digital simulation language
数字模拟转换器 D/AC	digital-analog converter
数字模拟转换器 DAC	digital-to-analog converter
数字生活网协会 DLNA	Digital Life Network Association
数字视频;数字摄像机 DV	digital video
数字视频带宽 DVB	digital video bandwidth
数字视频光盘 DVD	digital video disc
数字视频广播 DVB	digital video broadcasting
数字视频广播——地面 DVB-H	Digital Video Broadcasting-Terrestrial
数字视频广播——手持 DVB-H	Digital Video Broadcasting-Handheld
数字视频广播系统 DVBS	Digital Video Broadcasting System
数字数据网 DDN	digital data network
数字图像存储模板 DIMM	digital image memory module
数字网络结构[一种用于网络体系结构的协议] DNA	digital network architecture
数字网络系统 DNS	digital network system
数字微波系统 DMS	digital microwave system
数字微镜芯片 DMD	digital micromirror device
数字卫星广播系统 DSBS	Digital Satellite Broadcasting System

数字相机 **DC**	digital camera
数字信号处理（技术）**DSP**	digital signal processing
数字信号处理器 **DSP**	digital signal processor
数字信号处理芯片 **DSP**	digital signal process
数字虚拟磁盘 **DVD**	digital virtual disc
数字音频磁带 **DAT**	digital audio tape
数字音频广播 **DAB**	Digital Audio Broadcasting
数字音频视频编解码技术标准 **AVS**	Audio Video Coding Standard
数字影院立体声系统 **DTS**	digital theater system
数字用户线路 **DSL**	digital subscriber line
数字指示索引 **NDI**	Numerical Designation Index
数字终端就绪 **DTR**	data terminal ready
数字资源内容提供者 **DCP**	digital content provider
衰变因子 **DAF**	decay accelerating factor
双倍速数据（传输速）率 **DDR**	Double Data Rate
双边航空安全协定 **BASA**	Bilateral Air Safety Agreement
双边投资协定 **BIT**	bilateral investment treatment
双酚 A **BPA**	bisphenol A
双环汽车[中国石家庄:汉语缩略语] **S**	Shuanghuan
双机仓[德文] **DOKA**	Doppelkabine
双极型晶体管 **BJT**	bipolar junction transistor
双极型三极管 **BJT**	bipolar junction triode
双极性偏移 **BPO**	bipolar offset
双卡双待 **DS&DS**	dual sim & dual standby
双离合器变速器 **DCT**	double clutch transmission
双链脱氧核糖核酸 **dsDNA**	double-stranded DNA
双氢睾酮 **DHT**	dihydrotestosterone
双音多频 **DTMF**	dual tone multi-frequency
水晶 **QZ**	quartz
水疗[拉丁文] **SPA**	Solus Par Aqua
水陆两用汽车[代字] **DUKW**	amphibious truck
水泥和混凝土协会[英] **CCA**	Cement and Concrete Association

水平起飞和着陆 HTOL	horizontal takeoff and landing
水文地质风险评估 HRA	hydrogeological risk assessment
水银 Mer	mercury
水质污染指数 WPI	Water Pollution Index
水渍险 WPA	with particular average
税后利润 PAT	profit after tax
税后现金流量 CFAT	cash flow after taxes
税务人员 T-men	tax men
睡眠障碍 SD	sleeping disturbance
顺便问一下[网络用语] BTW	by the way
顺丁烯二酸二（2-乙基己 酯）DEHM	di (2-ethylhexyl) maleate
顺时针方向 CW	clockwise
顺势指标 CCI	Commodity Channel Index
顺序彩色与存储电视制式[法文] SECAM	sequence couleur a memorie
顺序彩色与存储电视制式 SECAM	Sequential colour and memory
顺序传送彩色与存储[法文] SECAM	Sequential Couleur a memoire
说明书 INST	instruction
说实话 TBH	to be honest
硕士学位 MS	Master Degree
司法部 DJ	Department of Justice
司法通信网 JCN	justice communication network
司法危机网 JCN	justice crisis network
司令勋章 CBE	Commander of the Order of the British Empire
丝米[非法定长度计量单位 1 丝米=0.1 毫米=0.00001 米] Dmm	decimillimetre(s)
丝裂原激活的蛋白激酶 MAPK	mitogen-activated protein kinase
私募股本 PE	private equity
私募及创投 PEVC	private equity venture capital fund
私人抵押保险 PMI	private mortgage insurance
私人有限公司[荷兰文] BV	Besloten Vennootschap
私人助理 PA	personal assistant

- 私营事业最高委员会［西班牙文］**COSIP**
  Consejo Superior de la Iniciativa Privada
- 思科认证设计工程师 **CCDA**   Cisco Certified Design Associate
- 思科认证网络工程师 **CCNA**   Cisco Certified Network Associate
- 思科认证网络专家 **CCIE**   Cisco Certified Internetwork Expert
- 思科认证网络资深设计工程师 **CCDP**   Cisco Certified Design Professional
- 思科认证资深网络工程师 **CCNP**   Cisco Certified Network Professional
- 斯德哥尔摩国际和平研究所 **SIPRI**
  Stockholm International Peace Research Institute
- 斯里兰卡［亚洲国家］**SRI**   Sri Lanka
- 斯里兰卡标准局 **BCS**   Bureau of Ceylon Standard
- 斯里兰卡产品质量认证标志 **SIS**   Sri Lanka Industry Standards
- 斯里兰卡工业标准 **SIS**   Sri Lanka Industry Standards
- 斯里兰卡卫星公司 **Supreme SAT**   Supreme Satellite
- 斯洛伐克［欧洲国家］**Slo(v)**   Slovakia
- 斯洛文尼亚［欧洲国家］**SLO/Slo(v)**   Slovenia
- 斯坦福大学［美国］**SU**   Stanford University
- 斯威士兰［非洲国家］**SWZ**   Swaziland
- 锶［第38号化学元素］**Sr**   strontium
- 死腔容积 **VD**   volume of dead space
- 死亡的蓝屏［网络用语］**BSOD**   blue screen of death
- 四 D 打印 **4DP**   four dimensional printing
- 四川省泰国研究中心 **SPRITS**
  Sichuan Provincial Research Institute of Thai Studies
- 四川外国语大学 **SISU**   Sichuan International Studies University
- 四碘甲腺原氨酸 **T4**   tetraiodo thyronine
- 四轮驱动 **4WD**   four wheel drive
- 四氢大麻酚 **THC**   tetrahydrocannabinol
- 四十英尺当量单位 **FEU**   Forty-foot Equivalent Units
- 四维   由空间的长、宽、高和时间坐标组成 **4D**
  four dimensions
- 搜索救援队 **SAR**   search and Rescue

S

- 搜索救援服务 SAR　　　　　　　　Search and rescue
- 搜索引擎 LSE　　　　　　　　　　local search engine
- 搜索引擎营销 SEM　　　　　　　　search engine marketing
- 搜索引擎优化 SEO　　　　　　　　search engine optimization
- 苏丹[非洲国家] SUD　　　　　　　Sudan
- 苏格兰国民党 SNP　　　　　　　　Scottish Nationalist Party
- 苏格兰和伦敦（支持英国不脱欧的）ScotLond
  Scotland and London
- 苏格兰皇家银行 RBS　　　　　　　Royal Bank of Scotland
- 苏格兰交响乐团 SSO　　　　　　　Scottish Symphony Orchestra
- 苏格兰民族党 SNP　　　　　　　　Scottish National Party
- 苏格兰学分和学历体系 SCQF
  Scottish Credit and Qualifications Framework
- 苏格兰住房协会联盟 SFHA　　　　 Scottish Federation of Housing Association
- 苏格兰资格证书 SQC　　　　　　　Scottish Qualification Certificate
- 苏联 USSR　　　　　　　　　　　 Union of Soviet Socialist Republics
- 苏联的水陆两栖坦克 PT-76　　　　Soviet amphibious tank
- 苏联国家标准[俄文] GOST　　　　 Gosudarstvennyj Obscesojuznyi standart
- 苏联狙击步枪 SVD　　　　　　　　Soviet sniper rifle
- 苏联民用航空公司[＝Soviet Air Lines] AEROFLOT
  Aero Flotilla
- 苏联内务人民委员会[俄文] NKVD　 Narodnei Kamisariat Vnutrennih Diel
- 苏伊士运河使用者合作协会 CASU
  Cooperative Association of Suez Canal Users
- 素肉 TVP　　　　　　　　　　　　textured vegetable protein
- 塑料炸弹[代字] C4　　　　　　　 plastic bomb
- 塑身 BM　　　　　　　　　　　　 Body Maintenance
- 宿舍舍监 RA　　　　　　　　　　 residence advisor
- 酸性磷酸酶 ACP　　　　　　　　　acid phosphatase
- 算法加密系统[以发明者的姓氏首字母命名] RSA
  Ron Rivest, Adi Shamir, Leonard Adleman
- 算法语言 ALGOL　　　　　　　　　algorithmic language
- 虽然 tho'　　　　　　　　　　　　though

613

- 随机存取存储器 RAM　　Random Access Memory
- 髓鞘碱性蛋白 MBP　　myelin basic protein
- 碎片 frag　　fragment
- 损失生命年数 YLL　　years of life lost
- 羧甲基纤维素 CMC　　carboxymethyl cellulose
- 缩略语 abbr(ev)　　abbreviation
- 所罗门群岛[太平洋岛国] SOL　　Solomon Islands
- 索福瑞集团 TNS　　Taylor Nelson Sofres
- 索马里[非洲国家] SOM　　Somalia
- 索引 Ind　　index

- 它过去是 't was　　it was
- 它将是 't wil　　it will
- 铊[第81号化学元素] Tl　　thallium
- 塔吉克斯坦[亚洲国家] TJK　　Tajikistan
- 塔吉特[参见 TARGET 条] TGT　　TARGET
- 塔内防守 TD　　tower defence
- 塔斯社[苏联通讯社][俄文] TASS
  Telegrafnoie Agenstvo Sovietskavo Soyuza
- 塔温陶勒盖(巨型煤矿)[蒙古文] TT　　Tavan Tolgoi
- 胎儿酒精综合征 FAS　　fetus alcohol syndrome
- 台北[中国台湾地区] TPE　　Taipei
- 台湾地区 TWN　　Taiwan
- 台湾积体电路制造股份有限公司 tsmc
  Taiwan Semiconductor Manufacturing Company
- 太安[炸药] PETN　　pentaerythritol tetranitrate
- 太比特 Tb　　terabit

T

- 太比特[二进制计算机内存或数据单位] **Tibit/Tib**
  tebibit
- 太空磁谱仪计划 **AMS** — atmospheric magnetic spectrometer
- 太空望远镜 **ST** — space telescope
- 太平洋标准时间 **PST** — Pacific Standard Time
- 太平洋导弹靶场设施 **PMRF** — Pacific Missile Range Facility
- 太平洋经济合作理事会 **PECC** — Pacific Economic Cooperation Conference
- 太平洋天文学会 **PAS** — Pacific Astronomical Society
- 太平洋投资管理公司 **PIMCO** — Pacific Investment Management Co.
- 太平洋夏令时间 **PDT** — Pacific Daylight Time
- 太平洋证券交易所 **PCX** — Pacific Exchange (stocks)
- 太阳井高地 **SW** — Sunwell Plateau
- 太阳能光伏应用博览会 **SPE**
  Solar-Energy & Photovoltaic Application Expo
- 太阳能建筑系统 **SPBS** — solar power building system
- 太字节[二进制计算机内存或数据单位] **TiB**
  tebibyte
- 钛[第22号化学元素] **Ti** — titanium
- 泰国[亚洲国家] **THA** — Thailand
- 泰国产品质量认证标志 **TISI** — Thai Industrial Standards Institute
- 泰国反独裁民主联盟 **UDD**
  National United Front of Democracy Against Dictatorship
- 泰国工业标准协会 **TISI** — Thai Industrial Standards Institute
- 泰国航空公司 **TAC** — Thai Airways Company
- 泰国航空公司 **TAC** — Thai Airways Co., Ltd
- 泰国证交所指数 **SETI** — Stock Exchange of Thailand Index
- 泰国铢[货币] **B/THB** — Thailand Baht
- 泰拳业余爱好者国标联合会 **IFMA**
  International Federation of Muay Thai Amateur
- 谈判5W2H法则[目标、策略、原因、合适时间、地点、关键人、进展程度,然后达目标] **5W2H**
  what, how, why, when, where, who, how much

- 坦克火力支援战车[俄文] BMPT　　Boievaia mashina poddierzhki tankov
- 坦率、建设性、合作 3C　　candid, constructive, cooperative
- 坦桑尼亚[非洲国家] TAN　　Tanzania
- 坦桑尼亚标准局 TBS　　Tanzania Bureau of Standards
- 坦桑尼亚产品质量认证标志 tbs　　Tanzania Burean of Standards
- 钽[第73号化学元素] Ta　　tantalum
- 探矿机器人[海底无人深潜器] Minero　　mine robot
- 碳[第6号化学元素] C　　Carbon
- 碳罐净化阀 CPV　　canister purge valve
- 碳化硅 SIC　　silicon carbide
- 碳氢化合物 HC　　hydrocarbon
- 碳水化合物 carbo　　carbohydrate
- 碳酸氢盐 HCO_3^-　　bicarbonate
- 碳氧血红蛋白试验 Hb COT　　carboxyhemoglobin test
- 唐璜[转义:淫荡者] DJ　　Don Juan
- 唐可娜儿时装 DKNY　　Donna Karan New York
- 糖化血红蛋白 GHb　　glycosylated hemoglobin
- 糖化白蛋白 GA　　glycated albumin
- 糖化血红蛋白[另见 GHb] HbA1C　　glycosylated hemoglobin
- 糖化血红蛋白 HGB　　glycosylated hemoglobin
- 糖化血浆蛋白 GPP　　glycosylated plasma protein
- 糖化血清蛋白测定 GSP　　glycated serum protein assay
- 糖基化血红蛋白 GHbA1　　glycosylated hemoglobin A1
- 糖抗原 CA　　Carbohydrate Antigen
- 糖抗原 19-9 CA19-9　　carbohydrate antigen 19-9
- 糖尿病 DM　　diabetes mellitus
- 糖尿病并发骨质疏松症 DOP　　diabetes osteoporosis
- 糖尿病及其并发症控制试验 DCCT　　diabetes control and complications trial
- 糖原合成酶激酶 GSK　　glycogen sythase kinase
- 糖原染色 PAS　　periodic acid-schiff stain
- 糖原指数 GI　　glycogen index
- 淘汰检出限 LOD　　limit of detection

套利定价理论 APT	Arbitrage Pricing Theory
特(斯拉)[法定磁感应强度计量单位] T	Tesla
特别反应组 SRT	special reaction team
特别行动反应组 SORT	special operations reaction team
特别行动勤务组 GIS	Special Interventions Group
特别行政区 SAR	Special Administrative Region
特别活动科 SAD	special action department
特别进口许可证 SIL	special import license
特别任务连 SDU	Special Duties Unit
特别搜集服务 SCS	special collection service
特别提款权 SDR	Special Drawing Rights
特别指定国民 SDN	specially designated national
特别转让 PT	Particular Transfer
特超重 XXH	extra extra heavy
特陈(酒) XO	extra old
特大号(服装) XL	extra large
特恩斯市场研究公司 TNS	Taylor Nelson Sofres
特发性肺纤维化 IPF	idiopathic pulmonary fibrosis
特氟龙(不粘塑料)[聚四氟乙烯] TEFLON polytetrafluoroethylene	
特惠贸易区 PTA	preferential trade area
特惠贸易协定 PTA	preferential trade agreement
特技效果 SFX	special effects
特警队 SDU	Special Duties Unit
特雷弗汽车[英] TVR	Trevor
特立尼达和多巴哥[北美洲国家] TRI	Trinidad and Tobago
特立尼达和多巴哥标准局 TTBS	Trinidad and Tobago Bureau of Standards
特立尼达和多巴哥产品质量认证标志 TTBS Trinidad and Tobago Bureau of Standards	
特纳电视网 TNT	Turner Network Television
特纳经典电影 TCM	Turner Classic Movie
特色淡啤 SA	Special Ale

- 特设证券 SPS   special purpose securities
- 特殊贵宾 VVIP   very very important person
- 特殊线路 EL   extra line
- 特殊用途媒介物；特别目的载体 SPV   special-purpose vehicle
- 特特大号（服装）XXL   extra extra large
- 特许（证）lic   licence
- 特许财富管理师 CWM   certified wealth manager
- 特许公认会计师成员 FCCA
  Fellowship of Chartered Certified Accountants
- 特许公认会计师公会 ACCA
  The Association of Chartered Certified Accountants
- 特许会计师 CA   chartered accountant
- 特许金融分析师 CFA   chartered［certified］financial analyst
- 特许连锁 FC   franchise chain
- 特许市场技术师 CMT   chartered market technocrat
- 特许专利代理人 CPA   chartered patent agent
- 特异性酯酶染色 SPE   specific esterase stain
- 特应性皮炎，又称遗传过敏性皮炎；自身致敏性皮炎 AD
  atopic dermatitis
- 特种空中勤务团 SAS   special air service regiment
- 特种武器和战术 SWAT   special weapons and tactics
- 特种作战航空团 SOAR   special operations aviation regiment
- 特种作战气象队 SOWT   special operations weather team
- 铽［第65号化学元素］Tb   terbium
- 腾落指标［股市的一种大势分析指标］ADL
  advance decline line
- 腾讯操作系统 TOS   Tencent operating system
- 梯恩梯炸药 TNT   trinitrotoluene
- 锑［第51号化学元素］［拉丁文］Sb   stibium
- 踢拳击 K   kickboxing
- 提单 B/L   bill of lading
- 提货单 D/O   delivery order

■ 提前商业信息 ACI	Advanced Commercial Information
■ 提问环节 Q&A	question and ask
■ 体表面积 BSA	body surface area
■ 体臭 BO	body odour
■ 体格锻炼 PT	physical training
■ 体检 PE	physical examination
■ 体内不变的自然杀伤 T 细胞 iNKT	internal Natural Kill T-cell
■ 体商 BQ	body quotient
■ 体声波 BAW	bulk acoustic wave
■ 体外冲击波碎石术 ESWL	extracorporeal shockwave lithotripsy
■ 体外膜氧合器 ECMO	extracorporeal membrane oxygenator
■ 体外受精 IVF	in vitro fertilization
■ 体育课 PE	physical education
■ 体育类游戏 SPG	sport game
■ 体育硕士 MPE	Master of Physical Education
■ 体育仲裁法庭 CAS	Court of Arbitration for Sports
■ 体重变化 BWC	body weight change
■ 体重指数[以体重 kg/身高 m² 表示] BMI	Body Mass Index
■ 天冬氨酸转氨酶 AST	aspartate aminotransferase
■ 天冬氨酸转氨甲酰酶 ACT	aspartate carbamyl transferase
■ 天基航天监视（系统）SBSS	space-based space surveillance
■ 天津大学 TU	Tianjin University
■ 天蓝色 az	azure
■ 天蓝色 SB	sky blue
■ 天马汽车[中国保定:汉语缩略语] TM	Tianma
■ 天文单位[地球到太阳的距离＝149 600×10⁶ 米] Au astronomical unit	
■ 天知道 gkw	God knows what
■ 天知道 gok	God only knows
■ 天主教 RC	Roman Catholic
■ 鿬[第 117 号化学元素] Ts	tennesson

- 挑战赛 CC　　　　　　　　　　　Challenge Certificate
- 条件反射 CR　　　　　　　　　　conditioned reflex
- 条码(技术) BC　　　　　　　　　bar code
- 调幅 AM　　　　　　　　　　　　amplitude modulation
- 调换线路 EL　　　　　　　　　　exchange line
- 调节器 ADJ　　　　　　　　　　adjuster
- 调零放大器 ZSA　　　　　　　　zero-set amplifier
- 调频 FM　　　　　　　　　　　　frequency modulation
- 跳级(生) AP　　　　　　　　　　advanced placement
- 跳舞机 DDR　　　　　　　　　　Dance Dance Revolution
- 贴现率 Dr　　　　　　　　　　　discount rate
- 铁[第 26 号化学元素][拉丁文] Fe　　ferrum [英文:iron]
- 铁路交货价格 FOR　　　　　　　free on rail
- 铁路现代化管理系统 MMI　　　　modernization management system
- 停泊待命[船舶到港口后,听候指令] CFO
  Calling For Orders
- 停车场 P　　　　　　　　　　　park
- 停车挡 P　　　　　　　　　　　parking
- 停车换乘 P&R　　　　　　　　　park and ride
- 停车换乘 P+R　　　　　　　　　park and ride
- 停放处;车辆停放、船只停泊的标志 P　　parking
- 停止营业 COB　　　　　　　　　close of business
- 通过描述、发现和集成 UDDI
  universal description, discovery, integration
- 通过推动创新型神经技术的大脑研究 BRAIN
  brain research through advancing innovative neurotechnologies
- 通话结束 EOT　　　　　　　　　End of Transmission
- 通信和多媒体委员会 CMC
  Communication and Multimedia Commission
- 通信技术卫星 CTS　　　　　　　communication technology satellite
- 通信输入输出控制系统 CIOCS
  communications input/output control system

T

- 通信网络控制 CNC — communication network control
- 通信自动化系统 CAS — Communication Automation System
- 通讯控制协议和互联网协议 TCP/IP
  transmission control protocol/internet protocol
- 通讯欺诈管理 CFM — communications fraud management
- 通用编译程序 GECOM — general compiler
- 通用产品条码 UPC — Universal Product Code
- 通用处理器 GPU — general processing unit
- 通用串行总线 USB — universal serial bus
- 通用磁盘格式 UDF — universal disk format
- 通用登陆艇 LCU — landing craft, utility
- 通用电气公司 GE — General Electric Company
- 通用电器公司[德文] AEG — Allgemeine Elektrizitats Geselächaft
- 通用电子信息服务 GEIS — General Electric Information Services
- 通用服务基金 USF — universal service fund
- 通用航空航天飞行器 CAV — common aerospace vehicle
- 通用集成电路卡 UICC — universal integrated circuit card
- 通用鉴定公司[法文] SGS — Société Général de Surveillance
- 通用聚苯乙烯[塑料] GPPS — general purpose polystyrene
- 通用美国英语 GAE — General American English
- 通用商业语言 COBOL — common business-oriented language
- 通用时间计数器 GTC — general time counter
- 通用数据系统 UDS — universal data system
- 通用网关接口 CGI — common gateway interface
- 通用网络语言 UNL — universal network language
- 通用无线分组业务 GPRS — general packet radio service
- 通用系统模拟程序 GPSS — general purpose systems simulator
- 通用纤维素塑料 CE — cellulose plastics, general
- 通用移动通信系统 UMTS — universal mobile telecommunications system
- 通用英语 EGP — English for General Purposes
- 通用战术运输飞行器系统 UTTAS — utility tactical transport aircraft system
- 通用准则 CC — common code

通知付款 **AP**	advice and pay
同伴式父母 **Peerenting**	peer＋parent
同步动态存储器 **SDRAM**	
Synchronous Dynamic Random Access Memory	
同济大学 **TU**	Tongji University
同品种同年龄段最佳公犬 **WD**	Winner Dog
同品种同年龄段最佳母犬 **WB**	Winner Bitch
同人配对 **CP**	coterie partner
同一税率 **FAK**	freight all kinds
铜[第 29 号化学元素][拉丁文] **Cu**	cuprum
铜币[代字] **AE**	copper
童年抵美国者暂缓遣返 **DACA**	Deferred Action for Childhood Arrivals
统计分析系统(语言) **SAS**	Statistical Analysis System
统一报告标准 **CRS**	common reporting standard
统一成本的会计标准 **UCAS**	uniform cost accounting standards
统一对外税率 **C. E. T.**	Common External Tariff
统一计算机系统 **UCS**	Unified Computing System
统一通信[指把计算机技术与传统通信技术融为一体的新通信模式] **UC**	
Unified Communications	
统一支付界面 **UPI**	Universal Pay Interface
统一资源定位地址 **URL**	Uniform Resource Locator
头孢酊 **CFX**	cefoxitin
头颈部碰撞防护系统 **WHIPS**	Whole Head Impact Protect System
头脑奥林匹克 **OM**	Odyssey of the Mind
投机性风险 **SR**	speculative risk
投诉警方独立监察委员会 **IPCC**	Independent Police Complaints Council
投影 **PPT**	powerpoint
投影胶片 **OHT**	overhead transparency
投影仪 **OHP/OYH**	overhead projector
投资 **inv**	investment
投资回报 **ROI**	return on investment

T

- 投资回报率 ROI — return on investment
- 投资利润 ROI — return of investment
- 投资人与国家的纷争解决条款 ISDS — Investor-State Dispute Settlement
- 投资者关系 IR — investor relations
- 透明网络底层 TNS — transparent network substrate
- 透射电子显微镜 TEM — transmission electron microscope
- 凸轮轴位置 CMP — camshaft position
- 凸缘 FLG — flange
- 突尼斯[非洲国家] TUN — Tunisia
- 突尼斯战斗团 TCG — The Tunisian Combatant Group
- 突破性药物资格 BTD — breaking talent and ability of drug
- 图示均衡器（音响）GE — graphic equalizer
- 图书馆 LIB — library
- 图书馆学情报学文摘 LISA — Library and Information Science Abstracts
- 图书馆因特网索引 LII — Librarian's Internet Index
- 图像处理器 GPU — graphic processing unit
- 图像倒转诱发电位 prep — pattern reversal evoked potential
- 图像感知系统 PPS — picture perception system
- 图像理解和模式识别 IUPR — Imagery Understanding and Pattern Recognition
- 图形加速接口 AGP — accelerated graphics port
- 图形交换格式 GIF — graphics interchange format
- 图形文件系统 GFS — graphical file system
- 图形用户界面 GUI — graphical user interface
- 土地整治及乡村建设公司[法文] SAFER — Société d'Aménagement Foncier et d'Etablissement Rural
- 土耳其[亚洲国家] TUR — Turkey
- 土耳其标准学会[土耳其文] TSE — Turk Standardlari Enstitusu
- 土耳其产品质量认证标志[土耳其文] TSE — Turk Standardlari Enstitusu
- 土耳其伊斯坦布尔银行[土耳其文] IB — Istanbul Banka

- 土库曼斯坦[亚洲国家] **TKM**　　　Turkmenistan
- 钍[第 90 号化学元素] **Th**　　　thorium
- 钍基熔盐堆核能系统 **TMSR**
  Thorium Molten Salt Reactor Nuclear Power System
- 团队竞技 **TD**　　　team death match
- 团队战 **CW**　　　Clan War
- 团结工会[波兰文] **SC**　　　Solidarność
- 团结中心 **SC**　　　solidarity center
- 推迟答复 **XR**　　　extended response
- 推荐性国家标准[汉语拼音缩略语] **GB/T**
  Guo Biao/Tui
- 推力矢量控制 **TVC**　　　thrust vectoring control
- 推力矢量转换器 **TVC**　　　thrust vector converter
- 腿碰球[极球运动] **lbw**　　　leg before wicker
- 退出 **X**　　　exit
- 退还保险费 **RP**　　　return premium
- 托福考试[指美国举办的母语为非英语者的英语水平考试] **TOEFL**
  Test of English as a Foreign Language
- 托福学术口语考试 **TAST**　　　TOFEL Academic Spoken Test
- 托业考试[国际交流英语考试] **TOEIC**
  Test of English for International Communication
- 脱氢表雄酮 **DHEA**　　　dehydroepiandrosterone
- 脱氢抗坏血酸 **DHA**　　　dehydroascorbic acid
- 脱氢乙酸 **DHA**　　　dehydroacetic acid
- 脱氧核糖核酸[俗称脑黄金] **DNA**　　　deoxyribonucleic acid
- 脱脂奶粉 **NFDM**　　　non-fat dry milk
- 陀螺俯仰位 **GPP**　　　gyro pitch position
- 拓扑绝缘 **TI**　　　topological insulators
- 唾液流率 **SFR**　　　saliva flow rate
- 唾液免疫球蛋白 **ASIgA**　　　salivary immunoglobulin A
- 唾液免疫球蛋白 **GSIgG**　　　salivary immunoglobulin G

挖大脑网络认证服务 DNA	Digbrain Network Authentication
蛙人［意大利文］UR	Uomini Rana
蛙人推进器 DPV	diver propulsion vehicle
蛙人推进装置 DPD	diver propulsion device
蛙人支援艇 SSB	swimmer support boat
瓦（特）［法定功率计量单位］W	watt
瓦/平方米·度（传热系数）$W/m^2 K = w/m^2 ℃$ watt/square meter, degree Celsius	
瓦努阿图［太平洋岛国］VAN	Vanuatu
外表化语言 E	Externalized language
外宾楼（办公室）FBO	foreign building office
外发加工方式 OPA	Outward Processing Arrangement
外国记者协会 FCC	Foreign Correspondents Club
外国技术处 FTD	Foreign Technology Department
外国侨民 FN	foreign national
外国申请留学德国人员高校入学德语考试［德文］DSH Deutsche Sprachpruefung für den Hochschulzugang auslaendischer Studienbewerber	
外国医学毕业生考试 FMGE	Foreign Medical Graduate Exam
外国在美国投资委员会 CFIUS	Committee on Foreign Investment in U. S.
外国账户税收遵从法 FATCA	Foreign Account Tax Compliance Act
外国直接投资 FDI	foreign direct investment
外汇 Forex/FX	foreign exchange
外汇兑换券 FEC	Foreign Exchange Certificate
外籍职业女性协会 EPWS	Expatriate Professional Women's Society
外交保安局 DSS	Diplomatic Security Service
外交部 FAO	Foreign Affairs Office

外交关系委员会 **FRC**	Foreign Relations Committee
外交关系协会 **CFR**	Council on Foreign Relations
外交贸易部 **DFAT**	Department of Foreign Affairs and Trade
外交政策 **FP**	foreign policy
外来词 **exot**	exotic
外来移民 **immig**	immigration
外贸仲裁委员会［中国］**FTAC**	Foreign Trade Arbitration Commission
外围部件互连 **PCI**	peripheral component interconnect
外围控制器接口 **PCI**	peripheral controller interface
外围设备互连专业组 **PCISIG**	
peripheral component interconnect special interest group	
外星人 **E. T.**	extraterrestrial
外星智能通讯 **METI**	Messaging to Extra-Terrestrial Intelligence
外-斐反应 **WFR**	Weil-Felix reaction
外用［拉丁文］**ad. us. ext**	ad usum externum
外语水平考试［汉语拼音缩略语］**WSK**	waiyu shuiping kaoshi
外语学院 **SFL**	School of Foreign Languages
外语与文化学院 **CFLC**	College of Foreign Languages and Cultures
外周动脉疾病 **PAD**	peripheral arterial disease
外资独资企业 **WFOE**	wholly foreign owned enterprises
外资企业 **FIE**	foreign invested enterprise
外资投资风险审查现代化法案 **FIRRMA**	
The Foreign Investment Risk Review Modernization Act	
完美［杰出］**O**	outstanding
完全缓解 **CR**	complete response
完税后交货价 **DDP**	delivered duty paid
玩家对抗环境 **PVE**	player vs environment
玩家工会 **PLU**	player labour union
晚安 **GN**	Good night
万古霉素耐药肠球菌 **VRE**	vancomycin-resistant enterococcus
万国手表［瑞士］**IWC**	International Watch Company
万山丹建筑表皮设计顾问公司 **VSA**	Van Santen Associate

W

| 万事达卡 EMVCo | Europay, Mastercard Visa Cooperation |
| 万维网 WWW | World Wide Web |

万维微波 **WiMax**　　Worldwide Interoperability for Microwave Access

万向节 CVJ	constant velocity joint
万一[网络用语] BAC	by any chance
万亿字节 TB	terabyte
王室的 R	royal
王室法律顾问 QC	Queen's Counsel
王者荣耀韩国职业联赛 KRKPL	Korea King Professional League
王者荣耀职业发展联赛 KGL	KPL G-League
王者荣耀职业联赛 KPL	King Professional League
网关应用软件编程接口 GAPI	gateway application programming interface
网卡 NIC	Network Interface Card
网络操作系统 NOS	network operating system
网络成瘾症 IAD	Internet addictive disease
网络电视 IPTV	Internet Protocol TV
网络附属存储 NAS	network affiliated storage
网络工程师 CNE	computer net engineer
网络功能虚拟化 NFV	Network Function Virtualization
网络货币（俄罗斯网络银行）WM	Wed Money (Russian Internet Banking)
网络计算机 NC	network computer
网络技术官 ITO	Internet technology officer
网络接入点 NAP	network access point
网络节目主持人 NJ	Network Jocker
网络控制协议 NCP	network control protocol
网络路由选择控制中心 NRCC	network routing control center
网络论坛中的站内短消息 PM	Private Message
网络名人 KOL	key opinion leader
网络内容服务商 ICP	Internet Content Provider

网络内生安全试验场 **NEST**　　network endogenous security testing ground

网络平台提供商 IPP	internet platform provider
网络入侵检测系统 NIDS	Network Intrusion Detection System
网络设备提供商 IEP	internet equipment provider
网络通信插卡 CNR	communication network riser
网络图形格式 PNG	Portable Network Graphic Format
网络新闻传送协议 NNTP	Network News Transfer Protocol
网络信息联盟 CNI	Coalition for Networked Information
网络形象识别系统 VISI	visual identity system internate
网络虚拟化 FV	Network Virtualization
网络业务描述语言 WSDL	web service description language
网络游戏 OG	online game
网络语音通信技术 VOIP	Voice Over IP
网络执法分队 CPT	computer network police team
网络作战部队 CMF	computer network military force
网上 OL	online
网上报纸[电子文献标示略语] N/OL	newspaper on line
网上电子公告[电子文献标示略语] EB/OL	electronic bulletin board on line
网上会议录[电子文献标示略语] C/OL	conference proceeding on line
网上期刊[电子文献标示略语] J/OL	journal on line
网上银行 E-BANK	electronic bank
网页级别 PR	page rank
网友媒体与言论平台 cb	cnBeta. COM
网址 NA	network address
网状细胞(计数) RC/Ret	reticular cell
往来账户 A/C	account current
往来账户 CA	current account
危地马拉[南美洲国家] GUA	Guatemala
危害分析和关键控制点 HACCP	Hazard Analysis and Critical Control Point
危机管理中心 CMC	Crisis Management Center

W

- 危机性新闻故事中的三个主要报道对象：坏人、辩护人、受害者 **3Vs** villain, vindicator, victim
- 危急的 **CR** — critical
- 危险污染物质 **HPS** — hazardous polluting substance
- 威尔士国家交响乐团 **NOW** — National Orchestra of Wales
- 威力斯万能车 **GPW** — general purpose Willys
- 威麟汽车[中国] **R** — Rely
- 微波 **MCRWV** — microwave
- 微波通信系统 **MCS** — microwave communication system
- 微处理器 **MPU** — micro-processing unit
- 微处理器系统 **MPS** — microprocessor system
- 微电子机械系统 **MEMS** — micro electronic mechanic system
- 微克 **mcg** — microgram
- 微量免疫电泳 **IEP** — immunoelectrophoresis
- 微软的积极保护项目 **MAPP** — Microsoft Active Protections Program
- 微软公司 **MS** — Microsoft
- 微软开发者网 **MSDN** — Microsoft Developer Network
- 微软认证产品专家 **MCPS** — Microsoft Certified Product Specialist
- 微软认证方案开发员 **MCSD** — Microsoft Certified Solution Developer
- 微软认证教师 **MCT** — Microsoft Certified Teacher
- 微软认证数据库管理员 **MCDBA** Microsoft Certified Data-Base Administrator
- 微软认证系统工程师 **MCSE** — Microsoft Certified System Engineer
- 微软认证专家 **MCP** — Microsoft Certified Professional
- 微软视窗的正版验证工具 **WGA** Windows Genuine Advantage Validation Tool
- 微软授权视窗应用学习中心 **MLC** Microsoft (Authorized Window) Learning Center
- 微软网络服务 **MSN** — Microsoft Service Network
- 微通道结构 **MCA** — micro channel architecture
- 微信 **WC** — WeChat
- 微星公司 **MSI** — Micro Star International

微型 SD 卡（安全数字卡）TF	Trans Flash
微型碟，微型唱片 MD	mini disc
微型计算机程序设计语言 PLM	programming language for microcomputer
微信［代字］VX	WeChat
微血管密度 MVD	microvessel density
韦（伯）［法定磁通量计量单位］WB/Wb	weber
围产期重症监护室 PICU	perinatal intensive care unit
桅杆相机 Mastcam	mast camera
维多利亚女王［别称］GOW	Grand Old Woman
维多利亚瀑布 VFA	Victoria Falls
维多利亚十字勋章 VC	Victoria Cross
维护、维修和使用 MRO	Maintenance, Repair and Operations
维基［源自夏威夷语"快点快点"］Wiki	wee kee wee kee
维萨卡 VISA	Visa International Service Association
维萨卡联合组织 EMVCo	Europay, Mastercard Visa Cooperation
维生素 C VC	vitamin C
维生素 K VK	vitamin K
维生素 V	vitamin
维修与供应 MANDS	maintenance and supply
维也纳爱乐交响乐团［奥地利］VPO	Vienna Philharmonic Orchestra
维也纳交响乐团［奥地利］VSO	Vienna Symphony Orchestra
维也纳网术语和参考系统 VINTARS	
The Vienna Internet Terminology And Reference System	
纬度 L	latitude
委内瑞拉［南美洲国家］VEN	Venezuela
委内瑞拉石油公司［西班牙文］PDVSA	Petroleo de Venezuela SA
委托代工 OEM	original equipment manufacture
委托权益证明 DPOS	delegated proof of stake
委员会草案 CD	Committee Draft
委员会投票草案 CDV	Committee Draft for Vote
为开发人员和 IT 团队提供安全、耐久且扩展性高的对象存储 AWS S3	
Amazon Simple Storage Service	
卫生及公共服务部 HHS	Department of Health and Human Services

W

- 卫生维护组织 **HMO** — Health Maintenance Organization
- 卫星导航系统 **NSS** — navigation satellite system
- 卫星电视 **STV** — satellite television
- 卫星对卫星跟踪 **SST** — satellite-to-satellite tracking
- 卫星广播服务 **SBS** — Satellite Broadcasting Service
- 卫星控制中心 **SCC** — Satellite Control Center
- 卫星连线 **SNG** — satellite news gathering
- 卫星通信 **SATCOM** — satellite communications
- 卫星新闻采集 **SNG** — satellite news gathering
- 卫星运载火箭 **SLV** — satellite launching vehicle
- 卫星直播 **DBS** — direct broadcasting by satellite
- 未成年人犯罪指数 **JDI** — Juvenile Delinquency Index
- 未计利息、税收、折旧、摊销前时收入 **EBITDA** — earning before interest, taxes, depreciation and amortization
- 未来和新兴技术 **FET** — future and emerging technology
- 未来建筑实验室 **FALab** — Future Architecture Lab
- 未来十年的产业趋势：娱乐、财富管理、教育、安全、健康 **FRESH** — fun, rich, education, safety, health
- 未来作战航空系统 **FCAS** — future combat aviation system
- 未另行规定 **NOS** — not otherwise specified
- 未另行授权 **NOA** — not otherwise authorized
- 未流通级（货币）**MS** — mint state
- 位图 **BMP** — Bitmap
- 胃电图 **EGG** — electrogastrogram
- 胃动素 **MOT** — motilin
- 胃酸分泌峰值 **PAO** — peak acid output
- 温差发电机 **TEG** — thermo-electric generator
- 温度 **temp** — temperature
- 温哥华移民拘留中心 **VIHC** — Vancouver Immigration Holding Centre
- 温和急性呼吸综合征 **MARS** — Mild Acute Respiratory Syndrome
- 文本结束符 **ETX** — end of text character
- 文化创意产业集聚 **CCIC** — cultural and creative industrial clustering

- 文化创造族[指反对物欲享受、追求心理健康,希望以自身价值创造新文化方式的人] CC　　　　　　　　Cultural Creative
- 文件传输协议 FTP　　　　　　file transfer protocol
- 文件分配表 FAT　　　　　　　file allocation table
- 文件号 FN　　　　　　　　　　file number
- 文件库 LIB　　　　　　　　　　library
- 文控中心 DCC　　　　　　　　document control center
- 文莱[亚洲国家] BRU　　　　　Brunei
- 文学士[拉丁文] AB　　　　　　Artium Baccalaureus
- 文学学士 BA　　　　　　　　　Bachelor of Arts
- 文娱与健康 2H　　　　　　　　happy and healthy
- 文字识别 OCR　　　　　　　　optical character recognition
- 文字—语言转换 TTS　　　　　text to speech
- 稳态视觉诱发电位 SSVEP　　　steady-state visual evoked potentials
- 问卷评估法 MEQ　　　　　　　morningness eveningness questionnaire
- 问题 Q　　　　　　　　　　　　question
- 问责与公民信任基金 FACT foundation for accountability and civic trust
- 涡轮增压器 T　　　　　　　　turbo
- 涡扇[中国航空发动机型号,汉语拼音缩略语] WS woshan
- 我的天啊! OMG　　　　　　　Oh, my God
- 我国自主版权的嵌入式操作系统[希望+开放] HOPEN hope+open
- 我将[口语] I'mma　　　　　　I'm going to
- 我们(已经)过得很愉快吗?[网络用语] AWHFY Are we having fun yet?
- 我欠你的 IOU　　　　　　　　I owe you
- 我要[口语] I'mma　　　　　　I'm going to
- 我也是 me too　　　　　　　　that applies to me, too
- 我再说一次,以防万一[网络用语] ICYMI In case you missed it

W

- 我在哪儿可得一个？［网络用语］**AWCIGO**
  and where can I get one
- 乌干达［非洲国家］**UGA**　　　　　Uganda
- 乌赫托姆直升机制造厂［俄文］**UVZ**　Uhtomskii Vertoletneii Zavod
- 乌克兰［欧洲国家］**UKR**　　　　　Ukraine
- 乌克兰独立民意调查机构 **RGU**　　　Rating Group Ukraine
- 乌克兰独立通讯社 **UNIAN**
  Ukrainian Independent Information Agency of News
- 乌克兰格里夫纳［乌克兰货币单位］**UAH**
  Ukrainian Hryvnia
- 乌克兰国际商业电视台 **ICTV**　　　International Commercial Television
- 乌拉尔车辆制造厂［俄文］**UVZ**　　Uraliskii Varonoctroitelineii Zavod
- 乌拉圭［南美洲国家］**URU**　　　　Uruguay
- 乌拉圭中央银行［西班牙文］**BCU**　Banco Central del Uruguay
- 乌里扬诺夫汽车制造厂［俄文］**UAZ**　Ulianovskii Avtomobilinei Zavod
- 乌兹别克斯坦［亚洲国家］**UZB**　　Uzbekistan
- 污染标准指数 **PSI**　　　　　　　pollutant standard index
- 污染控制指数 **PCI**　　　　　　　Pollution Control Index
- 钨［第 74 号元素］［拉丁文］**W**　　Wolfram［英文：tungsten］
- 无病生存（时间）**DFS**　　　　　disease-free survival
- 无病生存率 **DFS**　　　　　　　disease-free survival
- 无差错 **ZD**　　　　　　　　　　zero defect
- 无处不在的电脑 **UC**　　　　　　ubiquitous computer
- 无船经营的公共承运人 **NVOCC**　　non-vessel operating common carrier
- 无此账 **N/A**　　　　　　　　　no account
- 无法解释的空中现象 **UAP**　　　　unidentified aerial phenomena
- 无副翼系统/无平衡标系统 **FBL**　　fly bar less system
- 无股息/无红利 **XD**　　　　　　ex-dividend
- 无国界医生组织［法文］**MSF**
  Medecins Sans Frontiers［英文：Doctors without Borders］
- 无核（武器）国家 **NNC**　　　　non-nuclear countries

633

无痕植发 FUE	follicle unit extration
无极变速传动/无极自动变速器 CVT	continuously variable transmission
无极自动变速器控制单元 CVTCU	CVT control unit
无酒精啤酒 nab	no-alcohol beer
无利息 X. in	ex-interest
无频率变换 NFC	no frequency conversion
无缺陷计划 ZDD	zero defect program
无人机系统交通管理 UTM	Unmanned Aircraft System Traffic Management
无人机系统交通管理平台 UASUTM	Unmanned Aircraft System UTM
无人驾驶飞行器 PAC	pilotless aircraft
无人驾驶飞机 UAV	unmanned air vehicle
无人空中监视 UAS	Unmanned aerial surveillance
无人认领行李中心 UBC	unclaimed baggage centre
无人天空监视 UAS	Unmanned aerospace surveillance
无收入多子女（家庭）NILK	no income lots of kids
无损音频压缩编码 FLAC	free lossless audio code
无碳复写纸(不用复写纸可复写) NCR	no carbon required (paper)
无特权 XPR	ex privileges
无息票 xc	ex coupon
无限、有限股份两合公司[德文] KG	Kommanditgesellschaft
无线保真技术 Wi-Fi	wireless fidelity
无线标记语言 WML	wireless markup language
无线电传输技术 RTT	radio transfers technology
无线电话 PHS	personal handyphone system
无线电技术研究所[俄文] RTI	radiotehnicheskii institut
无线电控制 RC	radio control
无线电资源控制器 RRC	radio resource controller
无线公开密钥基础设施 WPkI	wireless public key infrastructure
无线局域网 WLAN	Wireless Local Area Network
无线射频识别 RFID	radio frequency identification
无线识别模块 WIM	wireless identification mould

W

- 无线数据系统 **RDS**   Radio Data System
- 无线通信网络技术组 **TNT**   Traffic Network Technology
- 无线网络安全保护系统 **WPA**   Wi-Fi Protected Access
- 无线寻呼机 **BP**   beeper
- 无线应用协议 **WAP**   Wireless Application Protocol
- 无线智能网 **WIN**   Wireless Intelligent Network
- 无学习能力 **LDs**   learning disabilities
- 无用 **NG**   no good
- 无用 **OOU**   out of use
- 无源相控阵雷达 **PPAR**   passive phased array radar
- 无源相控阵雷达 **PESA**   passive electronically scanned array（radar）
- 五A智能化［通信、办公、保安、楼宇、消防］写字楼 **5A**   CA、OA、SA、BA、FA
- 五R笔记法［记录、简化、背诵、思虑、复习］**5R**   record，reduce，recite，reflect，review
- 五个国家（哈萨克斯坦、乌兹别克斯坦、土库曼斯坦、吉尔吉斯斯坦、塔吉克斯坦）与美国的对话机制 **C5+1**   5 countries (Kazakhstan, Uzbekistan, Turkmenistan, Kyrgyzstan, Tajikistan)+USA
- 五国联防协议［包括澳大利亚、新西兰、新加坡、马来西亚和英国］**FPDA**   Five-Power Defense Arrangements
- 五菱汽车［中国广西:汉语缩略语］**W**   Wuling
- 五人公司［1972年创］［德文］**SAP**   Systemalyse und Programmentwicklung
- 五人制世界杯足球 **F5WC**   Football 5 World Cup
- 五星安全认证 **C-ncap**   China-New Car Assessment Programme
- 五眼联盟（由美、英、加、澳、新组成）**FVEY**   Five Eyes
- 午前广播 **BAM**   broadcasting AM
- 武汉病毒研究所 **WIV**   Wuhan Institute of Virus
- 武汉大学 **WU**   Wuhan University
- 武器装备总署［法文］**DGA**   Délégation Générale à l'Armement
- 武装［汉语拼音缩略语］**WU**   wuzhuang
- 舞台上带动气氛的人 **MC**   microphone controller

- 勿倒置 TSU　　　　　　　　　this side up
- 戊肝抗体 HEVAb　　　　　　　hepatitis E virus antibody
- 物控 MC　　　　　　　　　　material control
- 物理疗法 phys ther　　　　　　physical therapy
- 物理伤害 AD　　　　　　　　attack damage
- 物理世界 PW　　　　　　　　Physics World
- 物理学会 IP　　　　　　　　　Institute of Physics
- 物联网 IoT　　　　　　　　　Internet of Things
- 物料管理 MC　　　　　　　　material control
- 物料管理 MM　　　　　　　　material management
- 物料控制 MC　　　　　　　　material control
- 物料清单 BOM　　　　　　　　bill of material
- 物料需求计划 MRP　　　　　　Material Requirement Plan

X

- 𨭎[第106号化学元素] Sg　　　seaborgium
- 西安交通大学 XJU　　　　　　Xi'an Jiaotong University
- 西安外国语大学 XISU　　　　　Xi'an International Studies University
- 西班牙[欧洲国家] ESP　　　　　Spain [西班牙文为：España]
- 西班牙巴塞罗那大学 UB　　　　University of Barcelona
- 西班牙比塞塔[西班牙货币符号][西班牙语] ESP
  Espanola Pesaeta
- 西班牙毕尔巴鄂比斯开银行[西班牙文] BBAV
  Banco Bilbao Vizcaya Argentaria
- 西班牙标准[西班牙文] UNE　　Una Norma Espanola
- 西班牙标准化协会[西班牙文] IRANOR
  Instituto Español de Normalizacion

X

- 西班牙国际饮用水开发股份有限公司［西班牙文］**EIA**
  Agua Sierra de Cazorla S. A. Explotaciones Internacionales Acuiferas
- 西班牙国王 **K of S**   King of Spain
- 西班牙认证标志［西班牙文］**UNE**   Una Norma Espanola
- 西北方(的) **NW**   north-west(ern)
- 西北工业大学 **NPU**   Northwestern Polytechnical University
- 西方(的) **W**   west(ern)
- 西方世界宠物提供协会 **WWPSA**   Western World Pet Supply Association
- 西门子［电导单位］**S**   siemens
- 西南方(的) **SW**   south-west(ern)
- 西苏格兰大学 **UWS**   University of the West of Scotland
- 西雅衣家(荷兰人布伦尼克迈耶兄弟品牌服装) **C&A**
  Clemens and August Brenninkmeyer
- 西印度群岛 **WI**   West Indies
- 希腊［欧洲国家］**GRE**   Greece
- 希腊标准化组织 **ELOT**
  The Hellenic Organization for Standardization
- 希腊船级社 **HR**   Hellenic Register
- 希腊技术协会 **TEE**   Technical Chamber of Greece
- 希腊术语协会 **ELETO**   The Hellenic Society for Terminology
- 希沃特［辐射剂量单位］**Sv**   sievert
- 硒［第 34 号化学元素］**Se**   selenium
- 悉尼科技大学 **UTS**   University of Technology Sydney
- 稀有 **R**   rare
- 锡［第 50 号化学元素,英文为 tin］［拉丁文］**Sn**
  stannum
- 洗手间 **LAV**   lavatory
- 喜剧结尾 **HE**   happy ending
- 系统担保程序 **SAP**   system assurance program
- 系统单晶片 **SoC**   system-on-chip
- 系统管理服务器 **SMS**   systems management server
- 系统汇编程序 **SAP**   system assembly program

- 系统网络架构 SNA　　　　　　　system network architecture
- 系统信息服务 SIS　　　　　　　system information service
- 系统性红斑狼疮 SLE　　　　　　systemic lupus erythematosus
- 系统应用技术和产品的数据处理 SAP
  systems applications and products in data processing
- 细胞毒性 T[淋巴]细胞 CTL　　　cytotoxic T lymphocyte
- 细胞分布宽度 RDW　　　　　　　red cell distribution(width)
- 细胞角质蛋白片段 19 抗原 21- CYERA21-1
  cyto-keratin 19 fragment antigen21-1
- 细胞外基质 ECM　　　　　　　　extracelluar matrix
- 细胞亚群 CD4/CD8　　　　　　　CD4/CD8 T helper cells/T killer cells
- 细碟[时长 15～20 分] EP　　　 extended playing record
- 细颗粒物(如 PM2.5 指大气中直径小于或等于 2.5 微米的颗粒物，PM10 指可吸入颗粒物) PM　　　　　　fine particulate matter
- 下班前 EOD　　　　　　　　　　end of the day
- 下一代测序 NGS　　　　　　　　next generation sequencing
- 下一代互联网 NG　　　　　　　 Next Generation Internet
- 夏威夷修订的律例 HRS　　　　　Hawaii Revised Statutes
- 仙人 CB　　　　　　　　　　　　Celestial Being
- 先交费[一种网络游戏模式] CPS　come-pay-stay
- 先进半导体物质光刻机 ASML
  advanced semiconductor material lithography
- 先进的交通信息服务系统 ATIS　 advanced traffic information service
- 先进电视制式委员会 ATSC　　　 Advanced Television System Committee
- 先进防空导弹 AAD　　　　　　　advanced air defense
- 先进公共交通系统 APTS　　　　 advanced public transport (traffic) system
- 先进极高频 AEHF　　　　　　　 advanced extremely high frequency
- 先进计量基础设施 AMT　　　　　advanced metering infrastructure
- 先进技术 AT　　　　　　　　　　advanced technology
- 先进驾驶信息系统 ADIS　　　　 advanced driver information system
- 先进交通管理系统 ATMS　　　　 advanced traffic management system
- 先进量测仪 AMI　　　　　　　　advanced measurement instrument

先进汽车控制系统 AVCS	Advanced Vehicle Control System
先进任务增程器 AMXD	advanced mission extender device
先进摄影系统 APS	advanced photo system
先进生命信息系统 ALIS	advanced life information system
先进坦克火炮技术展示车 ATAC	advanced tank and artillery chariot
先进先出（法）FIFO	first-in first-out
先进意念力学 AIM	advanced idea mechanics
先进战术艇[一种核潜艇] ATV	advanced tactics vessel
先进智能磁带 AIT	advanced intelligent tape
先期开发 AD	advanced development
先生 Mr	mister
先生[法文] M	monsieur
先天性心脏病 CHD	congenital heart disease
先修课程 AP	advanced program
纤溶酶原 PG	plasminogen
纤溶酶原 PLG	plasminogen
纤溶酶原活性 PLGA	plasminogen activity
纤维蛋白单体 FM	fibrin monomer
纤维蛋白原 Fb	fibrinogen
纤维蛋白原降解产物 FDP	fibrinogen degradation product
纤维素纳米纤维 CNF	cellulose nano fibre
氙[第54号化学元素] Xe	xenon
显卡挖矿 BTG	Bitcoin Gold
现场可编程门阵列 FPGA	field programmable gate array
现场装配 CKD	completely knocked down
现成为电子邮件地址中的分隔符 @	at
现代造船模式 BSM	modern shipbuilding model
现金订货 C/O	cash order
现金管理服务 CMS	cash management service
现金管理账户 CMA	cash management account
现金结汇 CS	cash settlement
现金流量贴现 DCF	discounted cash flow

现金自动存款机 CDM	cash deposit machine
现实生活中［网络用语］IRL	in real life
现役［军］AD	active duty
限制级的 R	restricted
限制热卡 cr	calorie restricted
线路终端设备 LTE	line terminator equipment
线上线下 O2O	online to offline
线型低密度聚乙烯［塑料］LLDPE	linear low density polyethylene
线型中密度聚乙烯［塑料］LMDPE	linear medium density polyethylene
线性的 LIN	linear
腺苷脱氨酶 ADA	adenosine deaminase
腺相关病毒 AAV	adeno-associated virus
相对平均偏差 RSD	relative standard deviation
相对强弱指标 RSI	relative strength index
相对湿度 RH	relative humidity
相互间连接系统 IS	Interlinking System
相互信息 MI	mutual information
相控阵雷达 PAR	phrased array radar
相位变化线 PAL	phase alternation (by) line
香草扁桃酸 VMA	vanillylmandelic acid
香港保护儿童政策组 CPPU	Child Protection Policy Unit
香港保护要人组 VIPPU	Very Important Person Protection Unit
香港保护证人组 WPU	Witness Protection Unit
香港爆炸品处理课 EOD	Explosive Ordnance Disposal
香港城市大学 City U	City University of Hong Kong
香港惩教署 CSD	Correctional Services Department
香港冲锋队 EU	Emergency Unit
香港大学 HKU	The University of Hong Kong
香港电视广播有限公司 TVB	Television Broadcasts Limited
香港反恐特勤队 CTRU	Counter Terrorism Response Unit
香港工会联合会 HKFTU	Hong Kong Federation of Trade Unions
香港工业总会 FHKI	Federation of Hong Kong Industry

- 香港海关 **CED**　　　　　　　　Customs and Excise Department
- 香港汇丰银行 **HSBC**　　　　　Hong Kong and Shanghai Banking Corporation
- 香港机场特警队 **ASU**　　　　 Airport Security Unit
- 香港纪律部队 **DSHK**　　　　　Disciplined Services of Hong Kong
- 香港技术支援组 **TSD**　　　　 Technical Service Department
- 香港鉴证科 **IB**　　　　　　　 Identification Bureau
- 香港交易所 **HKEX**　　　　　　Hong Kong Exchange
- 香港教育大学 **EduHK**　　　　 The Education University of Hong Kong
- 香港金融风险管理师协会 **HKFRMA**
  Hong Kong Financial Risk Manager Association
- 香港金融管理局 **HKMA**　　　　Hong Kong Monetary Authority
- 香港浸会大学 **HKBU**　　　　　Hong Kong Baptist University
- 香港浸会大学持续教育学院 **SCE HKBU**
  School of Continuing Education Hong Kong Baptist University
- 香港警察公共关系科 **PPRB**　　Police Public Relation Bureau
- 香港警察机动部队 **PTU**　　　 Police Tactical Unit
- 香港警察谈判小组 **PNC**　　　 Police Negotiation Circle
- 香港警队护送组 **FEG**　　　　 Force Escort Group
- 香港警区反三合会行动组 **DATS**　District Anti-Triad Squad
- 香港警务处 **HKPF**　　　　　　Hong Kong Police Force
- 香港警校 **DTS**　　　　　　　 Detective Training School
- 香港警校 **PTS**　　　　　　　 Police Training School
- 香港康乐及文化事务署 **LCSD**　Leisure and Cultural Services Department
- 香港科技大学 **HKUST**
  The Hong Kong University of Science and Technology
- 香港理工大学 **Poly U**　　　　 The Hong Kong Polytechnic University
- 香港廉政公署 **ICAC**　　　　　Independent Committee Against Corruption
- 香港贸易发展局 **TDC**　　　　 Trade Development Council
- 香港民众安全服务队 **CASHK**　 Civil Aid Service of Hong Kong
- 香港虐儿罪案调查组 **CAIU**　　Child Abuse Investigation Unit
- 香港认证服务中心 **HKAS**　　　Hong Kong Attestation Service
- 香港入境事务处 **ID**　　　　　 Immigration Department

香港商业罪案调查科 **CCB**	Commercial Crime Bureau
香港社区组织协会 **SOCO**	Society for Community Organization
香港失踪人口调查组 **RMPU**	Regional Missing Person Unit
香港双语法例资料系统 **BLIS**	Bilingual Laws Information System
香港特别行政区 **HKSAR**	Hong Kong Special Administration Region
香港特别职务队 **RSDS**	Regional Special Duty Squad
香港特遣队 **TF**	Task Force
香港投资基金 **HKIF**	Hong Kong Investment Fund
香港消防处 **HKFSD**	Hong Kong Fire Service Department
香港小艇队 **SBU**	Small Boat Unit
香港刑事记录科 **CRB**	Criminal Record Bureau
香港刑事情报科 **CIB**	Criminal Intelligence Bureau
香港医疗辅助队 **AMS**	Auxiliary Medical Service
香港艺术发展局 **HKADC**	Hong Kong Arts Development Council

香港有组织罪案及三合会调查科 **OCTB**
Organised Crime and Triad Bureau

香港政府飞行服务队 **HKGFS**	Hong Kong Government Flying Service
香港职工会联盟 **HKCTU**	Hong Kong Confederation of Trade Unions
香港中国旅行社 **HCTS**	Hong Kong China Travel Service
香港中文大学 **CUHK**	The Chinese University of Hong Kong

香港中学会考 **HKCEE**
Hong Kong Certificate of Education Examination

香港中学文凭考试 **DSE**　　　Diploma of Secondary Education

香港中药检定中心 **HKCMAC**
Hong Kong Chinese Medicine Authentication Centre

香港重案组 **RCU**	Regional Crime Unit
香港重点及搜查队 **FSC**	Force Search Cadre
香港专才教育中心 **GEC**	Genius Education Centre
香港专业辅导协会 **HKPCA**	Hong Kong Professional Coaching Association
香港总区反三合会行动组 **RATU**	Regional Anti Triad Unit
香港总区跟踪及支援队 **RSSS**	Regional Surveillance & Support Squad
香港总区情报组 **RIU**	Regional Intelligence Unit

X

厢式小汽车 S	saloon
想要[口语] wanna	want to
项目、计划和政策 PPP	projects, plans and policy
项目风险评估委员会 PRAB	Program Rick Assessment Board
项目风险评估委员会 PRAC	Program Risk Assessment Committee
项目工程师 PE	project engineer
项目管理 PM	project management
项目管理办公室 PMO	Project Management Office
项目管理承包 PMC	project management contract
项目管理专业人员认证 PMP	Project Management Professional
项目数量检验 PQS	project quantity surveyor
项目委员会 PC	project committee
像婴儿一样地哭[网络用语] CLAB	crying like a baby
橡胶 RUB	rubber
枭龙[中巴联合生产的战斗机] JF	Joint Fighter

消费、市场及销售研究协会[德文] GfK
Gesellschaft für Konsum-, Markt- und Absatzforschung

消费超低压处理器笔记本 CULV	consumer, ultra, low, voltage
消费电子产品展览会 CES	consumer electronics show
消费电子展 FA	Electronics Fair

消费行为学领域的理论模型之一[引起注意,产生兴趣,唤起欲望,留下记忆,购买行动] AIDMA　　attention, interest, desire, memory, action

消费类电子产品 CE	Consumer Electronics
消费品安全改进法案 CPSIA	Consumer Product Safety Improvement Act
消费者;最终用户 C	consumer
消费者保护局 CPB	Consumer Protection Bureau
消费者报告 CR	consumer reports

消费者对工厂[电子商务的一种形式] C2F
consumer to factory

消费者对消费者[电子商务的一种形式] C2C
consumer to consumer

消费者价格指数 CPI　　consumer price index

■ 消费者联合会[法文] **UFC**	Union Fédérale des Consommateurs
■ 消费者协会 **C. A.**	Consumers' Association
■ 消费者信息与商业频道 **CNBC**	Consumer News and Business Channel
■ 消声器 **MFLR**	muffler
■ 消息应用处理接口 **MAPI**	Message Application Process Interface
■ 硝化甘油[炸药] **NG**	nitro glycerine
■ 硝基蓝四氮试验 **NBT**	nitroblue tetrazolium
■ 硝酸铵(炸药) **AN**	ammonium nitrate
■ 硝酸纤维素 **CN**	cellulose nitrate
■ 硝酸异丙酯 **IPN**	isopropyl nitrate
■ 销售点终端机;电子收款机 **POS**	point of sale (terminal)
■ 销售经理 **VM**	vending manager
■ 销售配置系统 **SCS**	sales configuration system
■ 销售收益率 **ROS**	return on sales
■ 销售与分销 **SD**	sales and distribution
■ 小规模集成电路 **SSI**	small scale integration
■ 小号 **S**	small
■ 小号的 **s**	small
■ 小陆桥运输 **MLB**	miniland bridge
■ 小轮车 **BMX**	bicycle motocross
■ 小旅馆 **LDG**	lodge
■ 小卖部 **PX**	post exchange
■ 小时 **h**	hour
■ 小时 **hr**	hour
■ 小写字体 **LC**	lower case
■ 小型多功能汽车 **SMPV**	small multi-purpose vehicle
■ 小型机动牵引汽艇 **MT**	motor towboat
■ 小型探索者计划 **SMEX**	small explorer
■ 小型休闲车 **SRV**	small recreation vehicle
■ 小于或等于 **LE**	less or equal
■ 小于或等于 **LEQ**	less than or equal
■ 小直径制导炸弹 **GBU-39SDB**	guided bomb unit-39 small diameter bomb

X

校友 OB	old boy
校园里的大人物[网络用语] BMOC	big man on campus
校园信息技术和教育服务 CITES	campus information technologies and educational services
校正(航空)炸弹[俄文] KAB	korrektiruemaia aviachionnaia bomba
校准器 ADJ	adjuster
笑破肚皮[网络用语] BWL	bursting with laughter
协会 Assoc	association
协会 SOC	society
协调世界时 UTC	Universal Time Coordinated
协调制编码 H. S. Code	The Harmonized System Code
协同决策 CDM	collaborative decision making
协议交换邮件 MTP	mail transfer protocol
协议书 LOA	list of agreement
胁迫蛋白 SP	stress protein
写博客的人 BLOGGER	Web Logger
谢天谢地，又是星期五了。TGIF	Thank God. It's Friday.
谢谢 ta	thank you
心电图 ECG	electrocardiogram
心房抑制型起搏 AAI	atrial inhibited pacing
心肺复苏术 CPR	cardiopulmonary resuscitation
心肌型肌酸激酶同工酶 CK-MB	MB isoenzyme of creation kinase
心理压力测评器 PSE	psychological stress evaluator
心灵商 MQ	mental quotient
心灵支配者 MM	mind master
心律不齐 DAH	Disordered Action of the Heart
心钠素 ANP	atrial natriuretic polypeptide
心血管疾病 CVD	cardiovascular disease
心音图 PCG	phonocardiogram
心源性猝死 SCD	sudden cardiac death
心脏监护病房 CCU	Cardiac Care Unit
心脏每分钟搏出量 HMO	heart minute output

■ 心脏骤停后综合征 PCAS	post-cardiac arrest syndrome
■ 心阻抗图 ICG	impedance cardiogram
■ 芯片 MC	microcircuit
■ 辛迪加 synd	syndicate
■ 辛烷 OCT	octane
■ 锌[第30号化学元素] Zn	zinc
■ 新巴[香港] NWFB	New World First Bus
■ 新产品导入 NPI	new product introduction
■ 新产品工程师 NPE	new product engineer
■ 新产品开发 NPD	new product development
■ 新车鉴定程序 NCAP	New Car Assessment Program
■ 新蛋白脂质 NPL	neoproteolipid

■ 新的欧洲行驶（油耗）循环（综合油耗计算循环）NEDC
new European driving cycle

■ 新工作项目提案 NWIP	New Work Item Proposal
■ 新冠肺炎 NCP	novel coronavirus pneumonia
■ 新冠肺炎 COVID	coronavirus disease
■ 新华通讯社 NCNA	New China News Agency
■ 新基准轿车 NBC	new basic car
■ 新加坡[亚洲国家] SIN	Singapore

■ 新加坡标准与工业研究院 SISIR
Singapore Institute of Standards and Industrial Research

■ 新加坡产品质量认证标志 SISIR
Singapore Institute of Standards and Industrial Research

■ 新加坡国立大学 NUS	National University of Singapore
■ 新加坡航空公司 SINGAIR	Singapore Airlines Ltd

■ 新加坡剑桥A水准考试 A
Cambridge General Certificate of Education Advanced Level

■ 新加坡南洋理工大学 NTU	Nanyang Technological University

■ 新加坡惹勒南国际研究院 RSIS
Singapore Rajaratnam School of International Studies

■ 新加坡认证标志 PSB	Productivity and Standards Board

- 新加坡生产力及标准委员会 **SPRING**
  Standards, Productivity and Innovation Board
- 新加坡生产力及标准质量会议 **PSB**　Productivity and Standards Board
- 新加坡石油公司 **SPC**
  Singapore Petroleum Company Limited
- 新加坡星展银行 **DBS**　　　　Development Bank of Singapore
- 新加坡研发的仿人机器人 **RE**　Robot Erectus
- 新加坡伊斯兰宗教理事会[印尼文] **MUIS**
  Majils Ugama Islam Singapura
- 新加坡英语 **Singlish**　　　　Singapore English
- 新民主党 **NDP**　　　　　　　New Democratic Party
- 新模式/新式样 **NP**　　　　　new pattern
- 新南威尔士大学 **UNSW**　　　University of New South Wales
- 新能源与智能公交系统 **CBSF**　China Bus System of the Future
- 新生代哈里斯科州卡特尔[西班牙文] **CJNG**
  Cartel de Jalisco Nueva Genracion
- 新生儿加强监护病房 **NICU**　Neonatal [Newborn] Intensive Care Unit
- 新闻艺术博物馆[国际赌神 David Walsh 所设] **MONA**
  Museum of Old and New Art
- 新西兰[大洋洲国家] **NZL**　　New Zealand
- 新西兰标准协会 **S**　　　　　Standards Association of New Zealand
- 新西兰标准协会 **SANZ**　　　Standards Association of New Zealand
- 新西兰产品质量认证标志 **S**　Standards Association of New Zealand
- 新西兰产品质量认证标志 **SANZ**　Standards Association of New Zealand
- 新西兰电视台 **TVNZ**　　　　Television, New Zealand
- 新西兰高等教育联盟 **NZHEA**　New Zealand Higher Education Alliance
- 新西兰学历认证局 **NZQA**　　New Zealand Qualifications Authority
- 新西兰元[货币] **NZD**　　　　New Zealand Dollar
- 新型冠状病毒 **nCoV**　　　　novel coronavirus
- 新型冠状病毒感染的肺炎 **NCIP**　novel coronavirus-infected pneumonia
- 新型兴奋剂[四氢乙基羟基二降孕三烯炔酮] **THD**
  tetra hydro destrinone

新兴工业化国家 NIC	newly-industrializing country
新兴工业化经济 NIE	newly-industrializing economics
新兴市场 GEM	Growth and Emerging Market
新药申报 NDA	New Drug Application
新一代地铁车辆 NGSC	new generation of subway car
新一代高密度数字激光视盘 EVD	enhanced versatile disc
信不信由你[网络用语] BION	believe it or not
信封背面[网络用语] BOTE	back of the envelope
信号采集控制模块 SAM	signal acquisition/activation module
信汇 M/T	mail transfer
信托收据 TR	trust receipt
信息、协调及组织 ICO	information, coordination and organization
信息安全管理体系 ISMS	information security management system
信息处理(程序) IP	information processing
信息处理编译程序语言 CLIP	compiler language for information processing
信息处理集团 HIS	information handling services
信息处理平台 IPP	information processing platform
信息处理系统 IPS	information processing system
信息处理语言 IPL	information processing language
信息传输系统 ITS	information transmission system
信息传送业务 MTS	message transfer service
信息服务组 ISG	Information Service Group
信息高速公路 ISH	Information Super Highway
信息管理系统 IMS	information management system
信息过多 TMI	too much information
信息和通信技术标准委员会 ICTSB	Information and Communiction Technologies for Standardization Board
信息化家电 IA	information appliance
信息及通信部门 MIC	Ministry of Information and Communication
信息技术 IT	information technology
信息技术产业委员会 ITIC	Information Technology Industry Council
信息技术即服务 ItaaS	information technology as a service

信息技术协会 **ITA**	Information Technology Association
信息技术与创新基金会 **ITIF**	Information Technology & Innovation Foundation
信息检测系统 **IDS**	information detection system
信息检索 **IR**	information retrieval
信息检索系统 **IRS**	information retrieval system
信息交换用汉字编码集,一种汉字编码 **CCII**	Chinese Character Code for Information Interchange
信息搜索排名 **ISR**	Information Search Ranking
信息通信技术 **ICT**	information communication technology
信息系统服务管理 **ISSM**	Information System Service Management
信息系统审计师 **CISA**	commissioner of information system audit
信息选择传播 **SDI**	Selective Dissemination of Information
信息邀请书 **RFI**	request for information
信息与通信部 **MIC**	Ministry of Information and Communication
信息与通信技术 **ICT**	information and communication technology
信息摘录 **IE**	information extraction
信息自动储存与检索系统 **ASRS**	automatic storage/retrieval system
信用卡 **CC**	credit card
信用卡客服 **CCSVC**	credit card service
信用违约互换/信用违约交易 **CDS**	credit default swap
信用证 **LC**	Letter of Credit
信噪比 **SNR**	signal notice ratio
星基增强服务 **SBAS**	satellite-based augmentation system
星期六 **SAT**	Saturday
星期日 **SUN**	Sunday
星期三 **WED**	Wednesday
星期四 **THU**	Thursday
星期天、星期一、星期二、星期三、星期四、星期五、星期六 **SMTWTFS**	Sunday, Monday, Tuesday, Wednesday, Thursday, Friday, Saturday
星期五 **FRI**	Friday
星期一 **MON**	Monday

星球大战计划 SWP	Star Wars Program
星体惯性测量系统 SIMS	stellar inertial measurement system
兴业银行 CIB	Industrial Bank Co., Ltd.
刑事侦查局 CID	Criminal Investigation Division
型号合格证 TC	type certification
幸福家庭的秘诀[宽恕,欣赏,榜样,亲密,聆听,爱你自己] Family	forgiveness, appreciation, model, intimacy, listening, you
性病 VD	venereal disease
性传播感染 STI	sexually transmitted infection
性传染疾病 STD	sexually transmitted disease
性能分析显示系统 PADS	performance analysis display system
性商 SQ	sexual quotient
性少数群体 LGBTQ	lesbian, gay, bisexua, transgender, queer
凶案调查组 IHIT	integrated homicide investigation team
匈牙利[欧洲国家] HUN	Hungary
匈牙利标准化局[匈牙利文] MSZ	Magyar Szabvány
匈牙利标准局[匈牙利文] MSZH	Magyar Szabvány ügyi Hivatal
匈牙利电工协会[匈牙利文] MEE	Magyar Electrotechnikal Egyesulet
匈牙利认证标志[匈牙利文] MSZ	Magyar Szabvány
胸肌 pec	pectorals
胸围/腰围/臀围[简称三围] B/W/H	bust/waist/hips
胸腺 T	thymus
胸罩 BRA	brassiere
熊猫电子集团有限公司 PEG	Panda Electronic Group
休假 LOA	leave of absence
休斯敦废物处理协会 WCA	Waste Conducting Association
休闲车 RV	recreation vehicle
修图 P	photoshop
修正总吨 CGT	compensated gross ton
修正总吨 CGT	compensated gross tonnage
袖珍红外报警器 HIRA	handheld infrared alarm
袖珍家庭企业 TOHO	Tiny Office Home Office

溴［第 35 号化学元素］**Br**	bromine
虚拟大学 **VU**	virtual university
虚拟服务器架构 **VSA**	virtual server architecture
虚拟公共图书馆 **IPL**	Internet Public Library
虚拟货币 **IM**	ideal money
虚拟机 **VM**	Virtual Machine
虚拟媒体网关 **VMGM**	virtual media gateway
虚拟社区 **VC**	Virtual Community
虚拟数字资产 **IMO**	initial miner offerings
虚拟网络结构 **VNA**	virtual network architecture
虚拟现实/增强现实技术 **VR/AR**	virtual reality/augmented reality
虚拟现实 **VR**	virtual reality
虚拟学习环境 **VLE**	virtual learning environment
虚拟演播系统 **VSS**	virtual studio system
虚拟专用服务 **VPS**	virtual private service
虚拟专用网 **VPN**	virtual private network
虚拟组织 **VO**	virtual organization
需监管的孩子 **CINS**	child in need of supervision
需监护的未成年人 **MINS**	minor(s) in need of supervision
需求最大值 **DMAX**	demand maximum
许可证 **W**	warrant
旭硝子玻璃集团公司［日本］**AGC**	Asahi Glass Company
序号 **SN**	serial number
叙利亚［亚洲国家］**SYR**	Syria
叙利亚阿拉伯标准化与计量组织 **SASMO** Syrian Arab Organization for Standardization and Metrology	
叙利亚阿拉伯陆军 **SAA**	Syria Arabia Army
叙利亚阿拉伯人联盟 **SAC**	Syria Arabian Coalition
叙利亚阿拉伯通讯社 **SANA**	Syrian Arab News Agency
叙利亚产品质量认证标志 **SNS**	Syrian National Standard
叙利亚革命阵线 **SRF**	Syria Revolutionary Front
叙利亚国家标准 **SNS**	Syrian National Standard

- 叙利亚联盟党 **SUP** — Syriac Union Party
- 叙利亚民主军 **SDF** — Syria Democratic Forces
- 叙利亚全国民主变革力量民族协调机构 **NCC** — National Coordination Committee for the Forces of Democratic Change
- 叙利亚全国委员会 **SNC** — Syrian National Council
- 叙利亚武装力量 **SAF** — Syria Armed Forces
- 叙利亚自由军 **FSA** — Free Syria Army
- 蓄电池 **BAT** — Battery
- 旋转和内部结构实验 **RISE** — rotation and interior structure experiment
- 选区 **AD** — assembly district
- 选择性终止妊娠 **ETP** — elective termination pregnancy
- 学分加权平均分[又称 GPA] **WAM** — weighted average mark
- 学分加权平均分[又称 WAM] **GPA** — grade point average
- 学科测评系统 **KAS** — Knowledge Assessing System
- 学生贷款资金 **SLT** — student loan institution
- 学生能力国际评估计划 **PISA** — Programme for International Student Assessment
- 学生与人员互访信息系统 **SEVIS** — student and exchange visitor information system
- 学术 **A** — academic
- 学术导师 **al** — academic leader
- 学术能力评估测试 **SAT** — Scholastic Assessment Test
- 学术期刊集成全文数据库 **ASP** — Academic Search Premier
- 学术用英语 **EAP** — English for Academic Purpose
- 学位论文[参考文献标示字母] **D** — dissertation
- 学位论文 **diss** — dissertation
- 学习管理系统 **LMS** — learning management system
- 学习障碍 **LD** — learning disorder
- 学业指数 **AI** — Aptitude Index
- 学院 **A** — academy
- 雪地靴 **UGG** — ugly sheepskin boots
- 血(液)尿素氮 **BUN** — blood urea nitrogen

X

- 血沉降率 BSR — Blood Sedimentation Rate
- 血管紧张素转化酶 ACE — angiotensin converting enzyme
- 血管紧张素转化酶抑制剂 ACEI — angiotension converting enzyme inhibitor
- 血管内皮细胞生长因子 VEGF — vascular endothelial cell growth factor
- 血红蛋白A2 HbA2 — minor fraction of adult hemoglobin
- 血红蛋白 HB — hemoglobin
- 血红蛋白 Hb — hemoglobin
- 血红蛋白 HGB — hemoglobin
- 血红蛋白半饱和分压 P_{-50} — oxygen half-saturation pressure of hemoglobin
- 血浆复钙时间 PRT — plasma recalcification time
- 血浆复钙时间 PCAT — plasma recovery-calcium time
- 血浆肾素活性 PRA — plasma renin activity
- 血浆铜蓝蛋白 CP — ceruloplasmin
- 血浆纤维蛋白原 fg — fibrinogen
- 血浆鱼精蛋白沉淀 PPP — plasma protamine precipitating
- 血块收缩试验 CRT — clot retraction test
- 血清丙酮酸 PA — pyruvic acid
- 血清胆红素 Bil — bilirubin
- 血清蛋白电泳 SPE — serum protein electrophoresis
- 血清过氧化脂质 LPO — lipid peroxides
- 血清黄嘌呤氧化酶 SXO — serum xanthine oxidase
- 血清肌红蛋白 Mb — myoglobin
- 血清肌红蛋白 MYO — myoglobin
- 血清肌红蛋白 SMb — serum myoglobin
- 血清肌酸酐 SCr — serum creatinine
- 血清可提取的核抗原抗体 ENA — extractable nuclear antigens
- 血清亮氨酸氨基肽酶 SLAP — serum leucine aminopeptidase
- 血清尿素氮 SUN — serum urea nitrogen
- 血清尿酸 SUA — serum uric acid
- 血清凝血酶原时间 SPT — serum prothrombin time
- 血清前白蛋白 SPA — serum prealbumin

血清乳酸 LA	lactic acid
血清铁蛋白 FEN	ferroprotein
血清铜［拉丁文］Cu	cuprum
血清心肌肌钙蛋白 CTnI	serum troponin I
血清脂蛋白(a) LP(a)	lipoprotein
血清脂肪酶 LPS	lipase
血清总胆固醇 TC	total cholesterol
血清总胆红素 STB	serum total bilirubin
血清总铁结合力 TIBC	total iron-binding capacity
血清总唾液酸 TSA	total sialic acid
血清总脂 STL	serum total lipoid
血色指数 CI	color index
血栓素A2 TXA2	thromboxane A2
血糖 GLU	blood glucose
血小板(计数) PLT	platelet
血小板比积 PCT	platelet constrict volume
血小板第三因子试验 PF_3T	platelet factor Ⅲ test
血小板活化因子 PAF	platelet activating factor
血小板计数 BPC	blood platelets count
血小板聚集试验 PAgT	platelet agglutination test
血小板黏附试验 PAdT	platelet adherence test
血小板体积分布宽度 PDW	platelet distribution width
血小板相关补体 PAC	platelet associated complement
血小板相关免疫球蛋白A PAIGA	platelet associated IgA
血小板相关免疫球蛋白G PAIGG	platelet associated IgG
血小板相关免疫球蛋白M PAIGM	platelet associated IgM
血型 BG	blood group
血压 BP	blood pressure
血液缓冲碱 BBB	blood buffer base
血液酒精浓度 BAC	Blood Alcohol Concentration
熏猪肉、生菜加番茄三明治 BLT	bacon, lettuce and tomato
寻找外太空星球智慧生命计划 SETI	Search for Extraterrestrial Intelligence
巡航导弹潜艇 CMS	cruise missile submarine

循环免疫复合体 CIC　　　circulating immune complexes
循环冗余码校验 CRC　　　cyclic redundancy check

压控振荡器 VCO　　　voltage controlled oscillator
压缩版视频光盘 HDVD　　　high-density digital video disk
压缩比 CR　　　compression ratio
压缩内存[又叫 CF 卡,是一种在掌上电脑和数码相机上使用的大容量存储设备] CF　　　compact flash
压缩天然气 CNG　　　compressed natural gas
压缩天然气汽车 CNGV　　　compressed natural gas vehicle
鸭尾巴式发型 DA　　　duck's arse
牙齿种植复杂病例诊断设计中心 IDDC
　　　Implanting Complex Cases Diagnosis Design Center
牙买加[北美洲国家] JAM　　　Jamaica
雅典国立科技大学 NTUA　　　The National Technical University of Athens
雅加达证券指数 JSX　　　Jakarta Stock Index
雅思考试 IELTS　　　International English Language Testing System
亚非共同市场 AACM　　　African-Asian Common Market
亚非经济合作组织 AFRASEC
　　　Afro-Asian Organization for Economic Cooperation
亚广联地区机器人大赛 ABU Robocon
　　　Asian Broadcasting Union Robot Contest
亚甲基二氧甲基苯丙胺 MDMA　　　methylenedioxymethylamphetamine
亚历山大·丹尼斯公司[英国最大巴士公司之一] ADL
　　　Alexander Dannis
亚马逊标准标识号[亚马逊随机生成的字母数字组合] ASIN
　　　Amazon Standard Identification Number

亚马逊的产品广告 SP	sponsored products
亚马逊物流 FBA	Fulfillment by Amazon
亚美尼亚[欧洲国家] ARM	Armenia
亚欧会议 ASEM	Asia-Europe Meeting

亚瑟士[日本跑鞋名品牌,源于拉丁语格言,意为健全的精神寓于强健的体魄]
[拉丁文] Asics　　anima sana in corpore sano

亚太地区男科学联合会 AAFA	Asia Pacific Association of Andrology
亚太地区学生企业家精神峰会 ASES	Asia-Pacific Student Enterprise Spirit
亚太顾客服务协会 APCSC	Asia Pacific Customer Service Commission
亚太互联网交换中心 APIX	Asia Pacific Internet Exchange
亚太经合组织 APEC	Asia-Pacific Economic Cooperation
亚太经济协调委员会 APECC	

Asian-Pacific Economic Consultative Committee

亚太清真理事会 APHC	Asia Pacific Halal Council
亚太心脏大会 APHC	Asia Pacific Heart Commission
亚太心脏医学研讨会议 APCA	Asian and Pacific Cardiac Association
亚太音乐创作者联盟 APMA	Asia-Pacific Musician Association
亚太证券交易所 APX	Asia Pacific Exchange
亚信峰会 ACS	Asia Credit Summit
亚裔婚前摄影 APP	Asian Prewedding Photo
亚洲、北美向东费率协定 ANERA	

Asia, North America Eastbound Rate Agreement

亚洲、非洲、拉丁美洲(的) AAA	Asian-African-Latin American
亚洲奥林匹克理事会 OCA	Olympic Committee of Asia
亚洲大奖赛 AGP	Asia Grand Prix
亚洲当代艺术展 ACAS	The Asia Contemporary Art Show
亚洲电视 ATV	Asia Television Limited
亚洲反病毒研究协会 AAVR	Asian Anti Virus Researchers
亚洲公司治理协会 ACGA	Asian Corporate Government Association
亚洲管理教育论坛 AFBE	Asian Forum on Business Education
亚洲广播联盟 ABU	Asian Broadcasting Union
亚洲合作对话 ACD	Asian Co-operative Dialogue

Y

- 亚洲货币单位 **ACU**   Asian Currency Unit
- 亚洲基础设施投资银行 **AIIB**   Asian Infrastructure Investment Bank
- 亚洲基础设施投资银行［法文］**BAII**
  La Banque asiatique d'investissement pour les infrastructures
- 亚洲及远东经济委员会 **ECAFE**
  Economic Commission for Asia and the Far East
- 亚洲决算货币 **ACD**   Asian Clearing Dollar
- 亚洲开发银行 **ADB**   Asian Development Bank
- 亚洲青少年发明展 **AYIE**   Asian Youth Invent Expo
- 亚洲睡眠研究会 **ASRS**   Asian Society for Research in Sleeping
- 亚洲太平洋（地区）**APAC**   Asia & Pacific
- 亚洲-太平洋通讯社组织 **OANA**   Organization of Asia-Pacific News Agencies
- 亚洲太平洋网络 **APN**   Asian and Pacific Network
- 亚洲投资基金 **AIF**   Asian Investment Fund
- 亚洲文明对话 **CDAC**   Conference on Dialogue of Asian Civilizations
- 亚洲问题研究学会［美国］**AAS**   Association for Asian Studies
- 亚洲相互协作与信任措施会议 **CICA**
  Conference on Interaction and Confidence-Building Measures in Asia
- 亚洲新闻国际通讯社 **ANI**   Asian News International
- 亚洲议会和平协会 **AAPP**   The Association of Asian Parliaments for Peace
- 亚洲有线与卫星电视广播协会 **CASBAA**
  Cable and Satellite Broadcasting Association of Asia
- 亚洲足球联合会 **AFC**   Asian Football Confederation
- 氩［第 18 号化学元素］**A(r)**   argon
- 烟酒火器管理局 **ATE**   Bureau of Alcohol, Tobacco & Firearms
- 烟酰胺单核苷酸［延缓衰老的药］**NMN**
  Nicotinamide Mononucleotide
- 烟酰胺腺嘌呤二核苷酸 **NAD**   nicotinamide adenine dinucleotide
- 延程运行 **ETOPS**   extended operations
- 延迟存储自动电子计算机 **EDSAC**   electronic delay storage automatic computer
- 延迟性肌肉酸痛 **DOMS**   delayed onset muscle soreness
- 延时 **TD**   transmission delay

| 延长航程 ER | extended range |

严重急性呼吸道感染［新型冠状病毒］SARI
Severe Acute Respiratory Infection

| 严重急性呼吸综合征 SARS | severe acute respiratory syndrome |

严重急性呼吸综合征冠状病毒 2 型 SARS-CoV-2
SARS-coronavirus-2

严重综合性免疫缺陷 SCID	severe combined immunodeficiency
炎症性肠病 IBD	inflammatory bowel disease
研发部 R&D	Research and Development Department
研发和创新 RDI	research, development and innovation

研究和文献中心［世界语］CDE
Centro de Espoloro kaj Dokument［英文：Research and Documentation Center］

研究与发展咨询委员会 ACORD	Advisory Council on Research and Development
研究与开发 R&D	research and development
颜色 COL	colour
演示,示范 DEMO	demonstration
演示板 Demo	demonstration
央视调查咨询公司 CVSC	Central Viewer Survey & Consulting Company
阳光英语俱乐部 SEC	Sunshine English Club
氧［第 8 号化学元素］O	oxygen
氧饱和度 O_2 sat	oxygen saturation
氧饱和度 $SatO_2$	oxygen saturation
氧分压 PO_2	partial pressure of oxygen
氧含量 O_2-C	oxygen content
氧化石墨 GO	graphite oxide
氧化石墨烯 GO	graphene oxide
摇摆不定男生［英国男孩团体］JLS	Jack the Lad Swing
摇头表示失望［网络用语］SMH	shaking my head

摇头丸/亚甲基二氧甲基苯丙胺 MDMA
methylenedioxymethamphetamine

遥感技术 RS	remote sensing
遥感图像理解 RSIU	Remote Sensing Imagery Understanding
遥控门锁系统 RKE	remote keyless entry system

Y

Y

- 药品不良反应 ADR — adverse drug reaction
- 药品福利管理 PBM — pharmacy benefit management
- 药品经营质量管理规范 GSP — Good Supplying Practice
- 药品临床试验管理规范 GCP — Good Clinical Practice
- 药品上市许可持有人制度 MAH — Marketing Authorization Holder
- 药品生产商协会 PMA — Pharmaceutical Manufacturers Association
- 药物安全委员会 CSM — Committee on Safety of Medicines
- 药物评价与研发中心 CDER — Center of Drug Evaluation and Research
- 药用化妆品 cosmeceutical — cosmetic pharmaceutical product
- 要点 KP — key point
- 要回来[网络用语] BB — be back
- 耶鲁大学 YU — Yale University
- 耶鲁大学为中心的并行超级计算 YCPS — Yale Center for Parallel Supercomputing
- 也叫作 AKA — also known as
- 也门[亚洲国家] YEM — Yemen
- 也许[网络用语] BAC — by any chance
- 野马汽车[中国成都:汉语缩略语] YM — Yema
- 野生动物保护区 WLS — Wild Life Sanctuary
- 业务集团 BG — business group
- 业务流程重组 BPR — business process reengineering
- 业务数据分析 BDA — Business Data Analysis
- 业务运营支持系统 BOSS — Business & Operation Support System
- 业余篮球国际联盟[法文] FIBA — Fédération Internationale de Basketball Amateur
- 页 P — page
- 页码 PP — pages
- 液化气储罐 LGT — liquid gas tank
- 液化石油 LP — liquefied petroleum
- 液化石油气 LPG — liquefied petroleum gas
- 液化天然气 LNG — liquefied natural gas

- 液化沼气 **LMG** — liquefied methane gas
- 液晶二极管 **LCD** — liquid crystal diode
- 液晶聚合物［塑料］**LCP** — liquid crystal polymer
- 液晶可变延迟器 **LCVR** — liquid crystal variable retarder
- 液晶模块 **LCM** — liquid crystal module
- 液晶拼接屏 **BSV** — boshivideo
- 液晶显示（器）**LCD** — liquid crystal display
- 液晶显示器 **LD** — liquid display
- 液力变扭离合器 **TCC** — torque converter clutch
- 一般毒性标准 **CTC** — common toxicity criteria
- 一般工厂项目 **GPP** — general plant projects
- 一般合伙人 **GP** — general partner
- 一般级（钱币）**FA** — fair
- 一般认为安全［美国食品药品管理局常用］**GRAS** — Generally Recognized as Safe
- 一般信贷安全保护协会［德文］**Schufa** — Schutzgemeinschaft für allgemeine Kroditssicherung
- 一茶匙（的量）**tsp(s)** — teaspoon
- 一次二阶矩法 **FOSM** — first-order second-moment
- 一次性的电子邮箱地址 **DEA** — disposable e-mail address
- 一次性费用 **NRO** — Non Recurring Charges
- 一代"朝不保夕、压力巨大、负担沉重、债台高筑"的人 **iPod generation** — Insecure, Pressured, Overtaxed and Debt-ridden generation
- 一带一路 **B&R** — The Belt and Road
- 一带一路，尊重，创新，合作，求同存异 **BRICS** — The Belt and Road, respect, innovation, cooperation, seeking common ground while shelving differences
- 一个地球自然基金会 **OPF** — One Planet Foundation
- 一个人或事物 **'un** — one
- 一会儿回来［德文］**BG** — Bis Gleich
- 一会儿就回来［网络用语］**BBIAB** — be back in a bit
- 一会儿就回来［网络用语］**BBIAM** — be back in a minute[moment]

Y

Y

- 一会儿就回来[网络用语] **BBIAS**   be back in a second
- 一级方程式锦标赛 **F1**   formula I
- 一览表 **cat**   catalogue
- 一路一带倡议 **BRI**   The Belt and Road Initiative
- 一秒钟用力呼气量 **FEV1**

  forced expiratory volume in one second
- 一切除外 **x. a.**   ex all
- 一清二吹三压[口对口呼吸和心脏按压抢救心肌梗死的方法:气道通畅、改善通气、恢复循环] **ABC**   airway, breathing, circulation
- 一丘之貉[网络用语] **BOF**   birds of a feather
- 一氧化碳 **CO**   carbon monoxide
- 一种测试管理工具 **TD**   Test Director
- 一种创建交互式网页应用的网页开发技术 **AJAX**

  Asynchronous JavaScript and XML
- 一种多任务多用户操作系统 **UNIX**

  Uniplexed Information and Computing Service
- 一种蜂浆纸[源于汉语拼音"好好爱"] **HHA**   hao hao ai
- 一种国际流行的网络即时通信软件 **ICQ**   I seek you
- 一种机器人 **ASIMO**   Advanced Step Innovative Mobility
- 一种色彩模型[色调+饱和度+亮度] **HSB**   hue, saturation, brightness
- 一种心理恐怖战术[由"恐惧""不确定""怀疑"的英文首字母组成] **FUD**

  fear, uncertainty, doubt
- 一种演示文稿图形程序 **PPT**   PowerPoint
- 一种音频媒体 **WMA**   Windows Media Audio
- 一种音频压缩格式[或称第三代声音文件压缩格式] **MP3**

  MPEG 1 Layer 3
- 一种音视频压缩格式[或称第四代声音文件压缩格式] **MP4**

  MPEG 1 Layer 4
- 一种营销理论[顾客、消费、便利、交流 4 个英语单词皆以 C 开头] **4C**

  customer, cost, convenience, communication
- 一种专为储存数码照片开发的存储卡 **XD**   XD picture card
- 伊夫·圣·罗兰名牌女装 **YSL**   Yves Saint Laurent

伊拉克 [亚洲国家] IRQ	Iraq
伊拉克 COC 符合性认证标志 COC	Certificate of Conformity
伊拉克 VOC 符合性认证标志 VOC	Verification of Confirmity
伊朗 [亚洲国家] IR	Iran
伊朗电信公司 TCI	Telecommunications Corporation of Iran
伊朗交易法规 ITR	Iranian Transaction Regulations
伊朗伊斯兰革命卫队 IRGC	Islamic Revolutionary Guard Corps
伊丽莎白女王号 HMS	Her Majesty's Ship Queen Elizabeth
伊利诺伊大学芝加哥分校 UIC	University of Illinois at Chicago
伊利诺伊视光学院 ICO	Illinois College of Optometry
伊利诺伊自动计算机 ILLIAC	Illinois Automatic Computer
伊斯兰共和国通讯社 IRNA	Islamic Republic News Agency
伊斯兰会议组织 OCI	Organization of the Islamic Conference
伊斯兰教纪元 [拉丁文] AH	Anno Hegirae
医疗辅助计划 Medicaid	Medical Aid
医生 Dr	doctor
医学博士 MD	Medicine Doctor
医学计算机服务管理处 MCSA	Medical Computer Services Administration
医学实验室科学协会 IMLS	Institute of Medical Laboratory Sciences
医学文摘数据库 EMBASE	Excerpta Medica Database
医学影像传送与储存系统 PACS	Picture Archiving and Communication System
医院船 HS	hospital ship
医院获得性肺炎 HAP	hospital acquired pneumonia
医院信息系统 HIS	hospital information system
依我带偏见的看法 [网络用语] IMBO	in my biased opinion
依我看 [网络用语] AISI	as I see it
铱 [第 77 号化学元素] Ir	iridium
仪表着陆系统 ILS	instrument landing system
宜家家居 (公司创始人姓名和位置的首字母组合) [瑞典文] IKEA	Ingvar Kamprad Elmtaryd Agunnaryd

Y

- 胰岛素 **INS** — insulin
- 胰岛素放射免疫测定 **IRI** — insulin radioimmunoassay
- 胰岛素耐量实验 **InTT** — insulin tolerance test
- 胰岛素样生长因子 **IGF** — insulin-like growth factors
- 移动办公[任何时间地点,利用 **IT** 工具都可上班,甚至兼职数份工作] **MO** — mobile office
- 移动博客 **Mrabo** — Mobile Rabo
- 移动存储盘 **U** — USB Flash Disk
- 移动电视发送卫星 **DVB-SH** — Digital Video Broadcasting-Satellite Services to Handhelds
- 移动多媒体技术联盟 **MMTA** — Mobile Multimedia Technology Alliance
- 移动号码携带 **MNP** — mobile number portability
- 移动交换中心 **MSC** — mobile switch center
- 移动设备管理 **MDM** — Mobile Device Management
- 移动世界大会 **MWC** — Mobile World Congress
- 移动式清洁回收与循环系统 **MCRRS** — Mobile Clean Recovery and Revolving System
- 移动运营商 **MNO** — Mobile Network Operator
- 移动站 **MS** — Mobile Station
- 移交—经营—移交[一种国际流行的项目融资方式] **TOT** — Transfer-Operate-Transfer
- 移居 **immig** — immigration
- 移民并加入国籍 **I&N** — immigration and naturalization
- 移民出境检查 **ECR** — emigration check required
- 移民法律行动计划 **MLAP** — migrant legal action program
- 移民局 **INS** — Immigration and Naturalization Service
- 移民与海关执法(局) **ICE** — Immigration and Customs Enforcement
- 颐养康复中心[意为:颐康、颐乐、颐和] **3H** — Healthy, Happy, Harmonious
- 乙(型)肝(炎)病毒 **HBV** — hepatitis B virus
- 乙醇凝胶试验 **EGT** — ethanol gelatin test

- 乙酸纤维素 **CA** — cellulose acetate
- 乙烯丙烯共聚物［塑料］**EPM** — ethylene propylene copolymer
- 乙烯-乙酸乙烯酯共聚物［塑料］**EVA** — ethylene-vinyl acetate copolymer
- 乙酰胆碱 **ACh** — acetylcholine
- 乙型肝炎 e 抗体 **HBeAb** — hepatitis B e antibody
- 乙型肝炎 e 抗原 **HbeAg** — hepatitis B e antigen
- 乙型肝炎表面抗体 **HBsAb** — hepatitis B surface antibody
- 乙型肝炎表面抗原 **HBsAg** — hepatitis B surface antigen
- 乙型肝炎核心抗体 **HBcAb** — hepatitis B core antibody
- 乙型肝炎核心抗原 **HBcAg** — hepatitis B core antigen
- 已经过时 **OOTD** — outfit of the day
- 以后再聊 **TTYL** — talk to you later
- 以及别的［拉丁文］**et al** — et alib
- 以人为本的公司领导模式［由四部分组成：人、流程、合作伙伴、绩效］**4P** — people, process, partner, performance
- 以色列［亚洲国家］**ISR** — Israel
- 以色列标准学会 **SII** — Standards Institution of Israel
- 以色列产品质量认证标志 **SII** — Standards Institution of Israel
- 以色列航空航天工业公司 **IAI** — Israel Aircraft Industries, Ltd.
- 以色列魏茨曼科学研究所 **WIS** — Weizmann Institute of Science
- 以事实为依据［网络用语］**BIF** — basis in fact
- 以四位一体为核心的汽车特许经营模式［包括整车销售（Sale），零配件供应（Sparepart），售后服务（Service）和信息反馈（Survey）］**4S** — sale, sparepart, service, survey
- 以微电子技术为中心的社会自动化革命［工厂自动化、办公自动化、家庭自动化］**3A** — FA, OA, HA
- 以吻封信 **SWAK** — sealed with a kiss
- 钇［第 39 号化学元素］**Y** — yttrium
- 艺术、传媒与技术学院 **CAMT** — College of Arts, Media and Technology
- 艺术属公众 **PubArt** — Art for Public
- 艺术硕士专业学位 **MFA** — master of fine arts
- 艺术与人文科学引文索引 **A&HCI** — Arts & Humanities Citation Index

Y

议会私人秘书 **PPS**	Parliamentary Private Secretary
议会议员 **MHA**	Member of the House of Assembly
异步传输模式 **ATM**	asynchronous transfer mode
异硫氰酸荧光素 **FITC**	fluorescein isothiocyanate
异柠檬酸脱氢酶 **ICD**	isocitrate dehydrogenase
异性恋 **BG**	boy and girl
译码器 **DCD**	decoder
易安信公司 **EMC**	Richard Egan and Roger Marino Co.
易趣 **Ebay**	electronic bay
易燃的 **infl**	inflammable
益智类游戏 **PUZ**	puzzle game
意大利[欧洲国家] **ITA**	Italy

意大利产品质量认证标志[意大利文] **IMQ**
　　Instituto Italiano del Marchio di Qualita

意大利船级社[意大利文] **RINA**	Registo Italiano Navade

意大利国际旅游局[意大利文] **ENIT**
　　Ente Nazionale Industrie Turistiche [英文: Italian State Tourist Office]

意大利空军特别行动勤务组[意大利文] **GIS**
　　Gruppo d'Intervento Speciale

意大利里拉[货币] **Lit**	lire italiane
意大利信鸽饲养者协会[意大利文] **FCI**	Federazione Colombotila Italiana
意大利一家跑车制造商[意大利文] **ATS**	Automobili Turisme e Sport SpA

意大利质量标志学会[意大利文] **IMQ**
　　Instituto Italiano del Marchio di Qualita

意大利总工会[意大利文] **CGIL**
　　Confederazione Generale Italiana de Lavoro [英文: Italian General Confederation of Labor]

意法半导体集团 **ST**	SGS＋Thomson
意外事故伤害赔偿局 **ACC**	Accident Compensation Corporation
翼身融合体 **BWB**	blended wing body
镱[第70号化学元素] **Yb**	ytterbium

义乌指数 YCCI　　the Yiwu China Commodity Index
因特网操作系统 IOS　　Internet Operation System
因特网接入点 POP　　point of presence
因特网连接安全网服务系统 ICSS　　Internet Connection Secure Server
因特网商业论坛 IBA　　Internet Business Forum
因特网协议 IP　　Interface Protocol
因特网协议版本 IPV　　Internet Protocol Version
因特网研究资源评价的著名指标体系［包括：可信性、准确性、合理性、支持度］ CARS　　credibility, accuracy, reasonableness, support
因为［根据英文单词读音缩略］［网络用语］ BK　　because
阴极射线管 CRT　　cathode ray tube
音乐电视 MTV　　music television
音乐和蓝调咖啡馆［美国辛辛那提］ RBC　　Rhythm and Blues Cafe
音乐会管弦乐团 CO　　Concert Orchestra
音乐教学数字界面 MIDI　　musical instruction digital interface
音乐类游戏 MUG　　music game
音乐视频［一种用动态画面配合歌曲演唱的艺术形式］ MV　　Music Video
音乐舞蹈影片 MDV　　Music Dance Video
音乐学士 BMus　　Bachelor of Music
音频 AF　　audio frequency
音频-视频 AV　　audio-visual
铟［第49号化学元素］ In　　indium
银［第47号化学元素］［拉丁文］ Ag　　argentums
银币［代字］ AG　　silver
银行、改革、包容、信心和获得感 BRICS　　bank, reform, inclusiveness, confidence, sense of gain
银行标识号 BIN　　bank identification number
银行担保 BG　　bank guarantee
银行间票据交换支付系统 CHIPS　　Clearing House Interbank Payment System

Y

- 银行卡消费信心指数 BCCI　　Bankcard Consumption Confidence Index
- 银行卡协会 ICA　　Interbank Card Association
- 银行同业拆借利率 IBOR　　interbank offered rate
- 引擎评价系统 EES　　engine evaluation system
- 引文中[拉丁文] lc　　loco citato
- 隐血 OB　　occult blood
- 印藏边境警察部队 ITBP　　Indo-Tibetan Border Police
- 印度[亚洲国家] IND　　India
- 印度报业托拉斯 PTI　　Press Trust of India
- 印度标准局 BIS　　Bureau of Indian Standards
- 印度标准学会 ISI　　Indian Standards Institution
- 印度产品质量认证标志 ISI　　Indian Standards Institution
- 印度船级社 IRS　　Indian Register of Shipping
- 印度次大陆 ISC　　Indian subcontinent
- 印度独特身份识别管理 UIDAI　　Unique Identification Authority of India
- 印度公民国家登记簿 NRIC　　National Register of Indian Citizen
- 印度管理学院 IIM　　Indian Institutes of Management
- 印度国家信息技术研究院 NIIT　　National Institute of Information Technology
- 印度国家议会 INC　　Indian National Congress
- 印度国家银行 SBI　　State Bank of India
- 印度航空公司 IAC　　Indian Airlines Corporation
- 印度廓尔喀兰领地管理局 GTA　　Gurkland Territory Administration
- 印度理工学院 IIT　　Indian Institute of Technology
- 印度孟买巴拉特钻交所 BDB　　Bharat Diamond Bourse
- 印度民主青年联合会 DYFI　　Democratic Youth Federation of India
- 印度男性避孕药[英文意为:在引导下对精子进行可逆抑制] RISUG　　Reversible Inhibition of Sperm Under Guidance
- 印度尼西亚[亚洲国家] INA　　Indonesia
- 印度尼西亚船级社[印尼文] BKI　　Biro Klasifikasi Indonesia
- 印度尼西亚乌拉玛委员会 ICU　　Indonesian Council of Ulama
- 印度尼西亚乌拉玛委员会[印尼文] MUI　　Majelis Ulama Indonesia

- 印度普里特维防御飞行器 PAD　　Prithvi Air Defense
- 印度全国民主联盟 NDA　　National Democratic Alliance
- 印度人民党 BJP　　Bharatiya Janata Party（India）
- 印度石油公司 IOC　　Indian Oil Company
- 印度斯坦航空有限公司 HAL　　Hindustan Aeronautics Ltd.
- 印度塔塔汽车 T　　Tata
- 印度外交部 MEA　　Ministry of External Affairs（India）
- 印度新德里电视台 NDTV　　New Delhi Television
- 印度洋偶极子 IOD　　Indian Ocean Dipole
- 印度医学协会 IMA　　Indian Medical Association
- 印度医学咨询委员会 MCC　　Medical Consulting Committee
- 印度中央后备警察部队 CRPF　　Central Reserve Police Force（India）
- 印度钻石交易中心 IDTC　　Indian Diamond Trade Center
- 印尼《大学生周报》[印尼文] MM　　Mingguan Mahasiswa
- 印刷电路板 PCB　　printed circuit board
- 印刷电路板 PWB　　print wiring board
- 印刷电路板组件 PCBA　　printed circuit board assembly
- 印刷电路卡 PC card　　printed circuit card
- 印刷对比度 PCS　　print contrast signal
- 英镑[英国货币] GBP　　Great Britain Pound
- 英尺[非法定长度计量单位 1 英尺＝12 英寸＝0.3048 米] Ft　　foot
- 英寸 in　　inch
- 英帝国 BE　　British Empire
- 英帝国勋章 OBE　　Order of the British Empire
- 英帝国勋章获得者 MBE　　Member（of the Order）of the British Empire
- 英帝国勋章奖的司令勋位 CBE　　Commander of the Order of the British Empire
- 英格兰保龄球协会 EBA　　English Bowling Association
- 英格兰桥牌联合会 EBU　　English Bridge Union
- 英格兰银行 BOE　　Bank of England

英国[欧洲国家] **GBR**	Great Britain
英国 ARM 公司 **ARM**	Advanced RISC Machines
英国 ARM 技术 **ARM**	Advanced RISC Machines
英国 ARM 微处理器 **ARM**	Advanced RISC Machines
英国多林金德斯利出版社 **DK**	Dorling Kindersley
英国 EE 电信公司 **EE**	Everything Everywhere
英国 O2 电信公司 **O2**	On & On
英国奥委会 **BOA**	British Olympics Association
英国宝石测试实验室 **GTL**	Gem Testing Laboratory of Great Britain
英国宝石协会会员 **FGA**	Fellowship of Gemological Association
英国报纸联合社 **PA**	Press Association Ltd
英国标准规范 **BSS**	British Standard Specification
英国标准学会 **BSI**	British Standards Institution
英国宾利汽车 **B**	Bentley
英国伯恩茅斯交响乐团 **BSO**	Bournemouth Symphony Orchestra
英国伯明翰交响乐团 **BSO**	Birmingham Symphony Orchestra
英国慈善援助基金会 **CAF**	Charities Aid Foundation
英国大学及研究图书馆联盟 **CURL**	Consortium of University and Research Libraries
英国大学及研究图书馆联盟在线联合目录 **COPAC**	the CURL Online Public Access Catalogue
英国德温特世界专利索引 **DII**	Derwent Innovations Index
英国的 **Br**	British
英国电信公司 **BT**	British Telecommunications
英国电影和电视艺术学院 **BAFTA**	The British Academy of Film and Television Arts
英国独立电视台 **ITV**	Independent Television
英国儿童投资基金 **TCI**	The Children's Investment Fund
英国发展教育委员会 **CEA**	Council for Educational Advance
英国防止虐待动物协会 **RSPCA**	Royal Society for the Prevention of Cruelty to Animals
英国房车赛 **BTCC**	British Touring Car Cup

英国纺织品协定 **BTA**	British Textile Agreement
英国高等教育质量标准 **UKQCHE**	UK Quality Code for Higher Education
英国葛兰素史克公司 **GSK**	Glaxo Smith Kline
英国工党 **LP**	Labour Party
英国工业空间委员会 **UKISC** United Kingdom Industrial Space Committee	
英国公函免付邮费戳记 **OHMS**	On His [Her] Majesty's Serve
英国公职人员联合会 **CSU**	Civil Service Union
英国广播公司 **BBC**	British Broadcast Corporation
英国广告标准局 **ASA**	Advertising Standards Authority
英国国际发展部 **DFID**	Department for International Development
英国国际壳牌石油公司 **SIPC**	Shell International Petroleum Company
英国国家芭蕾舞团 **NBT**	National Ballet Theatre
英国国家出口委员会 **BNEC**	British National Export Council
英国国家党 **BNP**	British National Party
英国国家书目 **BNB**	British National Bibliography
英国国家卫生局 **NHS**	National Health Service
英国国民(海外)护照 **BN(O)**	British National (Overseas) Passport
英国海军舰艇 **HMS**	Her[His] Majesty's Ship
英国海外教育发展中心 **CEDO**	Centre for Educational Development Overseas
英国海外领土公民 **BOTC**	British Overseas Territories Citizen
英国航空事故调查局 **AAIB**	Air Accidents Investigation Branch
英国航空研究委员会 **ARC**	Aeronautical Research Council
英国化学工业公司 **ICI**	Imperial Chemical Industries
英国皇家空军 **RAF**	Royal Air Force
英国皇家陆军妇女队 **WRAC**	Women's Royal Army Corps
英国皇家汽车俱乐部 **RAC**	Royal Automobile Club
英国皇家认可委员会 **UKAS**	United Kingdom Accreditation Service
英国皇家特许保险学会 **CII**	Chartered Insurance Institute
英国皇家特许会计师 **ACA**	The Associate Chartered Accountant
英国皇家艺术学会 **RSA**	Royal Society of Arts
英国皇家空军妇女队 **WRAF**	Women's Royal Air Force

Y

- 英国吉列塔汽车 G　　　　　　　　Ginetta
- 英国加工与包装机械厂商贸易协会 PPMA
  The Process and Packaging Machinery Association
- 英国剑桥大学 CU　　　　　　　　Cambridge University
- 英国剑桥翻译协会 CAT　　　　　　Cambridge Academy of Translation UK
- 英国剑桥信息技术 CIT　　　　　　Cambridge Information Technology
- 英国金融服务管理局 FSA　　　　　Financial Service Authority
- 英国金融行为监管局 FCA　　　　　Financial Conduct Authority
- 英国精算师协会 IFoA　　　　　　　Institute and Faculty of Actuaries
- 英国科技集团 BTG　　　　　　　　British Tecnology Group
- 英国科学史学会 BSHS　　　　　　　British Society for the History of Science
- 英国科学作家协会 ABSW　　　　　Association of British Science Writers
- 英国空军上校 Gp Capt　　　　　　　Group Captain
- 英国空军特种部队 SAS　　　　　　Special Air Service Regiment
- 英国劳氏船级社 LR　　　　　　　　Lloyds Register of Shipping
- 英国劳斯莱斯汽车 RR　　　　　　　Rolls-Royce
- 英国老年协会 BGA　　　　　　　　British Geriatrics Association
- 英国立达公司 RSL　　　　　　　　Rieter-Scragg Ltd
- 英国零售商协会（认证）BRC　　　British Retail Consortium
- 英国伦敦机场 LAP　　　　　　　　London Airport
- 英国旅行社协会 ABTA　　　　　　Association of British Travel Agents
- 英国旅游局 BTA　　　　　　　　　British Tourist Authority
- 英国美学学会 BSA　　　　　　　　British Society of Aesthetics
- 英国秘密情报局［又称军情六处 MI6］SIS
  Secret Intelligence Service
- 英国名爵汽车 MG　　　　　　　　Morris Garage
- 英国年轻人的时装品牌 FCUK　　　French Connection United Kingdom
- 英国骑士官勋章［男］KBE
  Knight Commander of the Order of the British Empire
- 英国签证与移民（局）UKVI　　　　United Kingdom Visas and Immigration
- 英国情报部 BID　　　　　　　　　British Intelligence Department
- 英国情报处 BIS　　　　　　　　　British Information Service

- 英国认证标志 **BSI**　　British Standards Institution
- 英国商会联合会 **ABCC**　　Association of British Chambers of Commerce
- 英国审计师资格 **RQB**　　Recognized Qualifying Bodies
- 英国石油公司 **BP**　　British Petroleum
- 英国食品标准局 **FSA**　　Food Standards Agency
- 英国私立寄宿学校入学考试 **UKiset**
United Kingdom Independent Schools Entry Test
- 英国糖尿病协会 **BDA**　　British Diabetes Association
- 英国特雷弗汽车 **TVR**　　Trevor
- 英国特许公认会计师公会 **ACCA**
The Association of Chartered Certified Accountants
- 英国特许人事和发展协会 **CIPD**
Chartered Institute of Personnel and Development
- 英国天空广播公司 **BSkyB**　　British Sky Broadcasting
- 英国图书馆与信息专家注册协会 **CILIP**
the Chartered Institute of Library and Information Professionals
- 英国脱欧 **Brexit**　　Britain exiting from the EU
- 英国微处理器企业 **ARM**　　Advanced RISC Machines
- 英国维多利亚与阿尔伯特博物馆 **V&A**
Victoria and Albert Museum
- 英国卫裤 **VK**　　Vicno Keinl
- 英国卫生防护局 **HPA**　　Health Protection Agency
- 英国沃克斯豪尔汽车 **V**　　Vauxhall
- 英国五大名校：牛津大学（University of Oxford），剑桥大学（University of Cambridge），帝国理工（Imperial College London），伦敦政治经济学院（London School of Economics and Political Science）和伦敦大学学院（UCL：London's Global University）**G5**
Group of Five (Universities)
- 英国星际航行学会 **BIS**　　British Interplanetary Society
- 英国牙科协会 **BDA**　　British Dental Association
- 英国亚罗造船有限公司 **YSL**　　Yarrow Shipbuilders Ltd
- 英国医学委员会 **BMC**　　British Medical Council

Y

- 英国银行家学会准会员 **AIB**   Associate of the Institute of Bankers
- 英国营养协会 **BDA**   British Dietetics Association
- 英国邮政总局 **BPO**   British Post Office
- 英国运输部 **MoT**   Ministry of Transport
- 英国政府通信总部 **GCHQ**   Government Communications Headquarters
- 英国职工大会 **TUC**   Trades Union Congress
- 英国肿瘤研究协会 **BACR**   British Association for Cancer Research
- 英国咨询和心理治疗协会 **BACP**   British Association for Counselling and Psychotherapy
- 英国咨询调解与仲裁局 **ACAS**   Advisory, Conciliation and Arbitration Service
- 英国自由党 **LP**   Liberal Party
- 英里每加仑 **mpg**   miles per gallon
- 英里每小时 **mph**   miles per hour
- 英联邦大学协会 **ACU**   Association of Commonwealth Universities
- 英联邦电信委员会 **CTB**   Commonwealth Telecommunications Board
- 英联邦科学署 **CSO**   Commonwealth Scientific Office
- 英联邦文学和语言研究会 **ACLALS**   Association for Commonwealth Literature and Language Studies
- 英联邦议会联合会 **CPA**   Commonwealth Parliamentary Association
- 英美旅游协会 **AATA**   Anglo-American Tourist Association
- 英美烟草公司 **BAT**   British American Tobacco
- 英石［英国重量单位＝14磅或6.35千克］ **st**   stone
- 英属维尔京群岛 **BVI**   British Virgin Islands
- 英特尔（微型电子计算机） **Intel**   intelligence
- 英特尔极限大师杯赛 **IEM**   Inter Extreme Masters
- 英伟达半导体公司 **NVDA**   NVIDIA Corporation
- 英文式中文 **Engnese**   English Chinese
- 英文写作测试 **TWE**   test of written English
- 英雄联盟职业联赛 **LPL**   League of Legends Pro League
- 英雄所见略同［网络用语］ **BMTIPG**   brilliant minds think in parallel gutters
- 英语程度不足 **LEP**   limited English proficiency

英语翻译语料库 GloWbE	The Corpus of Global Web-Based English
英语国家语料库 BNC	British National Corpus (Collection)
英语角 EC	English Corner
英语口语测试 SET	Spoken English Test
英语口语测试 TSE	Test of Spoken English
英语入门考试 PET	Primary English Test
英语协会 EA	English Association
英语学习 ELL	English language learning
英语学校游泳协会 ESSA	English School Swimming Association
英语语言教学 ELT	English Language Teaching
英语作为第二语言的教学 TESL	Teaching English as a Second Language
婴儿 BB	baby
婴儿急性死亡综合征 SIDS	sudden infant death syndrome
婴儿死亡率 IMR	infant mortality rate

荧光密螺旋体抗体吸收试验 FTA-ABS
fluorescent treponemal antibody absorption (test)

荧光原位杂交 FISH	fluorescence in situ hybridization
营养素参考值 NRV	nutrient reference value
营养学国际研修 NIAS	Nutrition International Advanced Studies
营业停止[网络用语] EOB	End of Business

营运车辆调度管理系统 CVOM
commercial vehicle operation/fleet management

影像平滑 STF	smooth trans focus
影子公司 FC	front company
应急电源 EPS	emergency power supply
应急开关 Ems	emergency switch
应收票据 B/R	bill receivable
应收账款 A/R	Account Receivable
应用(程序) app	application
应用程序接口 API	application program interface
应用程序内购买 IAP	In-App Purchase
应用服务器 AS	application server

Y

- 应用服务提供商 **ASP** — application service provider
- 应用技术卫星 **ATS** — Applications Technology Satellite
- 应用生产性软件包 **APP** — application productivity package
- 应用研究系统 **ARS** — Applied Research System
- 硬 X 射线调制望远镜 **HXMT** — Hard X-ray Modulation Telescope
- 硬件描述语言 **HDL** — Hardware Description Language
- 硬盘驱动器 **HDD** — hard disk drive
- 硬座[汉语拼音缩略语] **YZ** — yingzuo
- 拥有高达战士的私设武装组织[天人] **CB** — Celestial Being
- 永久的结构性合作 **PESCO** — permanent structural cooperations
- 永久性正常贸易关系 **PNTR** — Permanent Normal Trade Relations
- 永远 **BF** — be forever
- 永远是你的[网络用语] **AY** — always yours
- 永远最好的朋友 **BFF** — best friend forever
- 勇气、资本、能力(＋沟通)[一种商业成功经验] **3Cs(＋1C)** — courage, capital, capacity (＋communication)
- 用传真机传送 **FAX** — facsimile
- 用户工程师 **CE** — Customer Engineer
- 用户回线 **EL** — exchange line
- 用户伙伴程序 **UPP** — user partnership program
- 用户界面 **UI** — user interface
- 用户码 **UC** — user code
- 用户身份 **UID** — user identity
- 用户识别模块 **SIM** — subscriber identification module
- 用户识别模块 **UIM** — user identification module
- 用户识别模块卡开发工具包 **STK** — SIM Card Tool Kit
- 用户数据报协议/因特网协议 **UDP/IP** — User Datagram Protocol/Internet Protocol
- 用户体验 **UX** — user experience
- 用户研究与体验设计中心 **CDC** — Customer Research & User Experience Design Center

- 用户原创内容 **UGC** — user generated content
- 用户直连工厂 **C2M** — Consumer to Manufacturer
- 用户终端设备 **CPE** — customer premise equipment
- 用于印刷的四分色：青、洋红、黄、黑 **CMYK** — cyan, magenta, yellow, black
- 优良制造标准 **GMP** — Good Manufacturing Practice
- 优美级（钱币）**VF** — very fine
- 优普丰敏捷教练认证 **CSM** — Certified Scrum Master
- 优球蛋白溶解试验 **ELT** — euglobulin lysis test
- 优势、劣势、机会、威胁［前两者是内部条件的优劣，后两者是外部条件的优劣，通过分析，制定策略］**SWOT** — strengths, weaknesses, opportunities, threats
- 优秀设计 **GD** — good design
- 优质佳酿白兰地 **VSOP** — very superior old pale
- 忧思科学家联盟 **UCS** — The Union of Concerned Scientists
- 幽门螺杆菌 **HP** — helicobacter pylori
- 由……改编 **arr** — arranged by
- 由 Adobe 公司开发的一种图像编辑软件 **PS** — Photoshop
- 由 Dulbecco 改良的 Eagle 培养基 **DMEM** — Dulbecco's Modified Eagle Medium
- 由美国 Be 公司研制的一种个人计算机操作系统 **BeOS** — BE Operating System
- 由于［根据英文单词读音缩略］［网络用语］**BK** — because
- 邮购 **m.o.** — mail order
- 邮政办公协议 **POP** — post office protocol
- 邮政编码 **PC** — postal code
- 邮政部门 **PO** — the Post Office
- 邮政汇票 **PMO** — Postal Money Order
- 邮资和包装费 **p and p** — postage and packing
- 邮资和手续费 **p and h** — postage and handling
- 犹太认证 **Kosher** — Kosher Certificate

Y

Y

- 油船 **TS** — tank ship
- 油价调整指数附加费 **BAF** — bunker adjustment factor
- 铀［第 92 号化学元素］**U** — uranium
- 游离甲状腺素 **FT4** — free thyroxine
- 游离甲状腺指数 **FT4I** — free thyroxine index
- 游离前列腺特异性抗原 **FPSA** — free prostate-specific antigen
- 游离三碘甲腺原氨酸 **FT3** — free triiodothyronine
- 游离脂肪酸 **FFA** — free fatty acid
- 游手好闲、浪费时间、无所事事的人 **B. T. O.** — big time operator
- 游戏成瘾 **GD** — gaming disorder
- 游戏工作站 **PS** — play station
- 游戏管理员 **GM** — game manager
- 游戏软件协会 **ESA** — The Entertainment Software Association
- 友好的露齿大笑［网络用语］**BFG** — big friendly grin
- 有点儿 **kinda** — kind of
- 有高级视听设备的餐厅 **RTV** — restaurant television
- 有关产品颜色、材质与工艺基础的认知 **CMF** — color, material & finishing
- 有害生物防治 **PCO** — pest control operation
- 有核（武器）国家 **NWS** — nuclear weapon states
- 有核红细胞 **NRBC** — Nucleated Red Blood Cells
- 有机玻璃 **OG** — organic glass
- 有机发光二极管 **OLED** — organic light-emitting diode
- 有机硅塑料 **Si** — silicone plastics
- 有人跟我想法一样吗？［网络英语］**DAE** — Dose anyone else?
- 有问必答［网络英语］**AMA** — ask me anything
- 有限傅立叶变换 **FFT** — finite Fourier transform
- 有限公司［法文］**SA** — Société Anonyme
- 有限公司［芬兰文］**O/Y** — Osakeyhtiö
- 有限公司［芬兰文］**OY** — Osakeyhtiö

有限公司［马来文］SDN BHD	Sendirian Berhad
有限公司［瑞典文］AB	Aktiebolag
有限公司［瑞典文］A/B	Aktiebolag
有限公司［意大利文］S. A.	Società Anonima
有限公司［印尼文］PT	Perséroan Torbetas
有限公司［印尼文］Pt	Perséroan Torbetas
有限股份公司［荷兰文］NV	Naamloze Vernootschap
有限合伙公司 LP	Limited Partnership
有限合作人 LP	limited partner
有限元分析 FEA	finite element analysis
有限责任公司 Ltd	limited
有限责任公司［丹麦—挪威文］APS	Anparts Selskab
有限责任公司［挪威文］AS	Aksjeselskap
有限责任公司［葡萄牙文］SARL	Sociedade Anónima de Responsabilidadem Limitada
有限责任公司［意大利文］SRL	Società a responsabilità limitata
有线电视 CATV	community antenna television
有线电视网络媒体公司 HBO	home box office
有效功率 EHP	effective horsepower
有效剂量 ED	effective dose
有效市场假说 EMH	Efficient Market Hypothesis
有效微生物群 EM	effective microbe
有效消费者反应 ECR	efficient consumer response
有源矩阵有机发光二极管 AMOLED	active matrix organic light emitting diode
有源相控阵雷达 AESA	active electronically scanned array（radar）
有资质的车辆改装商 QVM	Qualified Vehicle Modifier
铕［第63号化学元素］Eu	europium
又及［拉丁文］PS	postscriptum
又名 AKA	also known as
右边 RH	right
右后卫（足球）RF	right fullback

右手 r. h.	right hand
右心室肥大 RVH	right ventricular hypertrophy
右眼/左眼（测试眼睛时的标志）OD/OS	oculus dexter/oculus sinister
诱导多能干细胞 iPS cell	induced pluripotent stem cell
余割 csc	cosecant
余切 cot	cotangent
余弦 cos	cosine
鱼肉毒素 CFP	Ciguatera Fish Poisoning
宇宙航行科技报告 STAR	Scientific and Technical Aerospace Report
宇宙探测污染委员会 CETEX	Committee on Contamination of Extra-Terrestrial Exploration
宇宙微波背景辐射 CMB	cosmic microwave background
雨天顺延 WP	weather permitting
语料分析计算工具 TACT	textual analysis computing tools
语言大数据联盟 LBDA	Language Big Data Alliance
语言能力综合测评 LAT	Language Ability Test
语言与学术评估中心 CELA	Center of Evaluation of Language and Academics
语音、视频及集成数据架构 AVVID	architecture for voice, video and integrated data
语音识别系统 SRS	speech recognition system
语音信箱 V-mail	voice-mail
语音用户界面 LUI	language user interface
玉米膳食纤维 CDF	corn dietary fiber
预备役军官训练团 ROTC	Reserve Officers' Training Corps
预订零售部 WC	will call
预激综合征 WPW	preexcitation syndrome
预计到达时间 ETA	estimated time of arrival
预计离开时间 ETD	estimated time of departure
预扣税 W/TAX	withholding tax
预料课程 IB	initial program

中文	缩写	英文
预期寿命指数	LEI	life expectancy index
预申报制	AFR	Advance Filing Rules
预算控制法案	BCA	budget control act
预涂感光版，一种预先涂有感光性膜层的印刷版	PS	presensitized plate
预置气门	OHV	overhead valve
域名	DN	domain name
域名解析服务器	DNS	domain name server
域名系统	DNS	Domain Name System
员工帮助计划	EAP	Employee Assistance Program
员工持股计划	ESOP	Employee Stock Ownership Plan
员工辅助计划	EAP	employee assistance program
员工关系管理	ERM	employee relations management
员佐勋章	M. B. E	Member of the Order of the British Empire
原肌球蛋白受体激酶	TRK	tropomyosin receptor kinase
原上海港机股份有限公司	SPMC	Shanghai Port Machinery Co., Ltd.
原声碟	OST	Original Sound Track
原始品牌制造商	OBM	Original Brand Manufacturer
原始设备制造商	OEM	original equipment manufacturer
原始设计制造商	ODM	original design manufacturer
原位导管癌	DCIS	ductal carcinoma in situ
原位肿瘤	Tis	tumor in situ
原子力显微镜	AFM	atomic force microscope
原子量	AW	atomic weight
原子武器	AW	atomic weapon
源语言[被译语言]	SL	source language
远程反舰导弹	LRASM	long-range antiship missile
远程访问服务	RAS	Remote Access Service
远程高超音速武器	LRHW	long-range hypersonic
远程视频柜员机	VTM	virtual teller machine
远程通信程序	TCP	telecommunication program
远东货运工会	FEFC	Far East Freight Conference

Y

- 远红外辐射 **FIR**　　　　far infrared radiation
- 远红外线 **FIR**　　　　far infrared
- 远景 **LS**　　　　long shot
- 远期汇票 **TD**　　　　time draft
- 愿灵安息[拉丁文] **RIP**　　　　Requiescat In Pace
- 愿意见面 **WLTM**　　　　would like to meet
- 约旦[亚洲国家] **JOR**　　　　Jordan
- 约旦投资促进局 **JIPO**　　　　Jordan Investment Promotion Office
- 约翰·霍普金斯大学 **JHU**　　　　Johns Hopkins University
- 约翰逊航线 **JL**　　　　Johnson Line
- 月球勘测轨道器 **LRO**　　　　Lunar Reconnaissance Orbiter
- 岳父[网络用语] **FIL**　　　　father-in-law
- 越快越好[网络用语] **ASAP**　　　　as soon as possible
- 越南[亚洲国家] **VIE**　　　　Vietnam
- 越南电子商务网 **ECVN**　　　　Electronic Commerce, Vietnam
- 越南盾[越南货币单位][越南文] **VND**　　　　Vietnam dong
- 越野车辆 **ORV**　　　　off-road vehicle
- 越野自行车 **BMX**　　　　Bicycle Motocross
- 云服务器 **ECS**　　　　elastic compute service
- 云呼叫中心 **CCC**　　　　Cloud Call Center
- 孕酮 **P**　　　　progesterone
- 运单 **WB**　　　　waybill
- 运动类游戏 **SPT**　　　　sport
- 运动图像专家组[一种压缩比较大的活动图像和声音压缩标准] **MPEG**　　　　Moving Picture Experts Group
- 运动心率 **HER**　　　　exercise heart rate
- 运动型多功能车 **SUV**　　　　sports utility vehicle
- 运动型休闲车 **SRV**　　　　sport recreational vehicle
- 运动娱乐和豪华型汽车 **SL**　　　　sport & luxurious
- 运费吨 **R/T**　　　　revenue ton
- 运输安全管理局 **TSA**　　　　Transportation Security Administration

运输安全局 TSA	Transportation Security Agency
运输代理人 TA	traffic agent
运输服务管理局 TSA	Transportation Service Authority
运营 OP	operation
运营商标识码 CIC	Commerce Identification Code
运营总监 OD	operations director
运用优先权 XP	Exercise Priority
运油汽车[船] MT	motor tanker

杂合性丢失 LOH	loss of heterozygosity
杂志广告 MG	magazine advertising
载人飞行系统 MFS	manned flying system
载体 CARR	carrier
载噪比 CNR	carrier to noise ratio
载脂蛋白 A1 APO A-1	apolipoprotein A-1
载脂蛋白 B APO-B	apolipoprotein B
再次公开发行新股票 SPO	secondary public offering
再见 BFN	bye for now
再见,我的朋友[adios 源于西班牙文][网络用语] AMF adios, my friend	
再见[网络用语] B4N	bye for now
再见[网络用语] BB	bye-bye
再见[网络用语] BBFN	bye bye for now
再见[网络用语] BBN	bye bye now
再见[网络用语] CU	see you
在版编目 CIP	cataloging in publication

Z

- 在大城市,人们出门上班,不少人是先乘公交车到最近的地铁站,出了地铁,再走一段路才到单位,这些人被称为 BMW 一族 **BMW**
  bus, metro, walk
- 在家办公 **SOHO**　　　　　　　　small office home office
- 在三基色(红、绿、蓝)基础上加了白色 **WRGB**
  white, red, green, blue
- 在我看来[网络用语] **IMHO**　　　in my humble opinion
- 在我看来[网络用语] **IMO**　　　　in my opinion
- 在线 **OL**　　　　　　　　　　　online
- 在线测试仪 **ICT**　　　　　　　　in circuit tester
- 在线分析处理 **OLAP**　　　　　　online analysis and processing
- 在线离线 **O2O**　　　　　　　　online to offline
- 在线旅行社 **OTA**　　　　　　　online travel agent
- 在线旅游代理商 **OTA**　　　　　online travel agent
- 在职人员硕士研究生入学资格考试 **GCT**　　Graduate Candidate Test
- 在制品 **WIP**　　　　　　　　　work in progress
- 在……外 **outta**　　　　　　　　out of
- 暂行标准 **V**　　　　　　　　　vornorm
- 赞比亚[非洲国家] **ZAM**　　　　Zambia
- 赞同(别人的话)(引用别人话时"以此为证")[网络用语] **QFT**
  quoted for truth
- 赞助商赞助的服务和现金等价物 **VIK**　　value in kind
- 糟糕 **D**　　　　　　　　　　　dreadful
- 早老性痴呆 **AD**　　　　　　　　Alzheimer's Disease
- 早期反射[指只经过一次反射的回声][音响] **ER**
  Early Reflection
- 皂土絮状试验 **BF**　　　　　　　bentonite flocculation test
- 造骨牛奶蛋白 **OMP**　　　　　　osteoblast milk protein
- 造血干细胞 **HSC**　　　　　　　hematopoietic stem cell
- 造纸工业联合会 **PIF**　　　　　　Paper Industry Federation
- 噪声控制协会 **NAS**　　　　　　Noise Abatement Society
- 噪音指数 **NI**　　　　　　　　　noise index

增强热塑性塑料 RTP	reinforced thermoplastics
增强塑料 RP	reinforced plastics
增强现实技术 AR	augmented reality
增强型短信服务 EMS	enhanced message service
增强型速率 GSM 演进技术 EDGE	enhanced data rate for GSM Evolution
增强型图形适配器 EGA	enhanced graphics adapter
增强型小设备接口 ESDI	enhanced small device interface
增强性并行端口 EPP	enhanced parallel port
增强性地热系统 EGS	enhanced geothermal system
增压器(超增压的) SC	super charger (super charged)
增值税 VAT	Value-Added Tax
增殖细胞核抗原 PCNA	proliferating cell nuclear antigen
增殖细胞相关抗原 Ki67	proliferating cell-associated unclear antigen
乍得[非洲国家] CHA	Chad

炸弹之母[或称大型燃料空气炸弹] MOAB
mother of all bombs

战斗管理/指挥,控制,通信,计算机和情报[军队自动化指挥系统] BMC4I
battle management/command, control, communications, computers, and intelligence

战斗型多用无人艇[源于江苏自动化研究所] JARI
Jiangsu Automation Research Institute

战斗支援部队 CSF	combat support force
战略安全部 SSD	Strategy Security Department
战略防御计划 SDI	Strategic Defense Initiative
战略石油储备 SPR	strategic petrol reserve
战略与防务研究中心 SDSC	Strategic and Defense Studies Centre
战略与防务研究中心 CSDR	Center for Strategic and Defense Research

战略与预算评估中心 CSBA
Center for Strategic and Budgetary Assessments

战区导弹防御系统 TMD	theater missile defense (system)
战术分析系统 TAS	tactical analysis system
战术技术办公室 TTO	tactics technology office
战术中心 TC	tactical center

Z

- 战术助推滑翔 TBG　　　　　　　　　tactics boosting glide
- 战争险 WR　　　　　　　　　　　　war risk
- 张量处理器 TPU　　　　　　　　　　tensor processing unit
- 掌上电脑 PDA　　　　　　　　　　　Personal Digital Assistant
- 掌上游戏机 PSP　　　　　　　　　　play station portable
- 账户编号 a/c NO　　　　　　　　　　account number
- 账户管理中心 CAC　　　　　　　　　center of account control
- 招聘流程外包 RPO　　　　　　　　　recruitment process outsourcing
- 招商银行 CMB　　　　　　　　　　　China Merchants Bank Co., Ltd.
- 兆,十进倍数单位词头名称[其表示的因数为 10^6] M　　　mega
- 兆比特 Mib　　　　　　　　　　　　mebibit
- 兆赫(兹)[法定频率计量单位] MHz　　megahertz
- 兆帕[压强单位,1 帕＝1 牛顿/米²] mpa　　mega pascal
- 兆瓦(特) MW　　　　　　　　　　　megawatts
- 兆位(比特)每秒 Mbps　　　　　　　　megabits per second
- 兆字节 MiB　　　　　　　　　　　　mebibyte
- 兆字节每秒 Mbps　　　　　　　　　　megabytes per second
- 兆字节[计算机存储单位] MB　　　　　megabyte
- 照片处理 ps　　　　　　　　　　　　photoshop
- 照片服务 PS　　　　　　　　　　　　photo service
- 照片墙(一款社交应用) INS　　　　　 instagram
- 照我的意思做[网络用语] DWIM　　　do what I mean
- 照我看来[网络用语] AFAICS　　　　　as far as I can see
- 照我说[网络用语] AFAICT　　　　　　as far as I can tell
- 照相排字 PTC　　　　　　　　　　　photographic type composition
- 遮瑕膏 BB　　　　　　　　　　　　blemish balm
- 锗[第 32 号化学元素] Ge　　　　　　germanium
- 浙江大学 ZU　　　　　　　　　　　Zhejiang University
- 浙商银行 CZBANK　　　　　　　　　China Zheshang Bank Co., Ltd.
- 针对产品的评价 PR　　　　　　　　　product review

- 侦察门户工具包 **SPT**   Scout Portal Toolkit
- 珍宝级（钱币）**Gem MS**   Gem Mint State
- 真沸点 **tbp**   true boiling point
- 真皮标志产品 **GLP**   genuine leather product
- 真实发展指数 **GPI**   genuine progress indicator
- 真相与调解委员会[南非组织] **TRC**   Truth and Reconciliation Commission
- 诊断相关组 **DRG**   diagnosis related group
- 上海振华重工（集团）**ZPMC**
  Shanghai Zhenhua Port Machinery Company Ltd.
- 争端解决规则和程序 **DSU**   dispute settlement usage
- 争端解决机构 **DSB**   dispute settlement body
- 争取共和联盟[法文] **UPR**   Union Pour la Republique
- 争取民主社会运动[库尔德文] **Tev-Dem**   Tevgera Civaka Demokratîk
- 争取民主与革新共和党[法文] **PRDR**
  Parti Républicain pour la Démocratie et Ranouveau
- 蒸发 **EVAP**   evaporate
- 蒸汽船 **S/S**   steam ship
- 拯救 **SV**   save
- 整备质量 **C. W.**   curb weight
- 整车控制器 **VCU**   vehicle control unit
- 整个髋关节成形术 **THA**   total hip arthroplasty
- 整合行销传播 **IMC**   integrated marketing communications
- 整合灵性心理学 **ISP**   integral spiritual psychology
- 整箱 **FCL**   full container load
- 整形外科 **PS**   plastic surgery
- 正常 **N**   normal
- 正常费用 **NCH**   normal charge
- 正电子发射断层扫描装置 **PET**   positron emission tomography
- 正电子发射断层摄影术 **PET**   positron emission tomography
- 正电子发射计算机断层显像 **PET-CT**
  positron emission tomography-computed tomography
- 正割 **sec**   secant

Z

- 正交频分复用 **OFDM**
  orthogonal frequency division multiplexing
- 正交相移键控 **QPSK**   quadrature phase shift keying
- 正交振幅调制 **QAM**   quadratUre amplitude modulation
- 正能量 **PE**   positive energy
- 正切 **tan**   tangent
- 正如你所知道的[网络用语] **AKA**   also know as
- 正弦 **sin**   sine
- 证明完毕[拉丁文] **QED**   quod erat demonstrandum
- 证券交易所 **St Ex(ch)**   Stock Exchange
- 证券经纪人公司[法文] **CAC**   compagnie des agents de change
- 证券委员会 **SC**   securities commission
- 证书颁发机构授权 **CAA**   Certificate Authority Authorization
- 证书授权中心 **CA**   Certificate Authority
- 政策研究院 **IPS**   Institute of Policy Studies
- 政府出版物 **GI**   government issue
- 政府担保的投资 **GGI**   government-guaranteed investment
- 政府对企业[电子商务] **G2B**   Government to Business
- 政府和社会资本合作模式[法文] **PPP**   partenarist public-privé
- 政府间版权委员会[法文] **CIDA**
  Comité Intergouvernmental du Droit d'Auter [英文：Intergovernmental Copyright Committee]
- 政府间海事协商组织[现改为："国际海事组织"IMO] **IMCO**
  Inter-Government Maritime Consultative Organization
- 政府监督项目组织 **POGO**   Project on Government Oversight
- 政府经济发展办公室 **GOED**
  Government Office of Economic Development
- 政府开发援助 **ODA**   Official Development Assistance
- 政府培训中心 **GTCs**   Government Training Centres
- 政府批准委员会 **GAB**   Government Approval Board
- 政府清真产品认证机构[印尼文] **BPJPH**
  Badan Penyelenggara Jaminan Produk Halal

- 政府信息处理 **GIPC**   Government Information Processing
- 政府优惠贷款 **GCL**   Government Confessional Loan
- 政府与社会资本合作 **PPP**   public-private-partnership
- 政府支持的企业 **GSE**   Government-Sponsored Enterprise
- 政府组织的非政府组织 **GONGO**   Government Organized NGO
- 政治部 **SB**   special branch
- 政治行动委员会 **PAC**   political action committee
- 政治行动委员会[特殊利益集团的代言人] **PACs**   Political Action Committees
- 政治行情看涨 **PUMP**   Political Upwardly Mobile Personality
- 政治上正确:能符合大多数选民的立场,引申不得罪人的立场,有时有挖苦意 **PC**   politically correct
- 支撑移植物植入失败 **FTSE**   failed to sustain engraftment
- 支持开源和自由软件运动的计划 **MOSS**   Mozilla Open Source Support
- 支付宝无处不在 **AE**   Alipay Everywhere
- 支付差额 **PB**   payment balance
- 支付对支付 **PVP**   payment v payment
- 支付所得税 **PAYE**   pay as you earn
- 支架 **BRKT**   bracket
- 芝加哥大学 **UC**   University of Chicago
- 芝加哥贸易委员会 **CBOT**   Chicago Board of Trade
- 芝加哥商品交易所 **CMT**   Chicago Merchandise Trade
- 芝加哥商业交易所 **CME**   Chicago Mercantile Exchange
- 知道 **knw**   know
- 知名快时尚品牌:港真 **UR**   Urban Revivo
- 知识产权 **IP**   intellectual property
- 知识产权 **IPR**   intellectual property right
- 知识创新管理 **KIM**   knowledge and innovation management
- 知识工程与知识科学 **KEKS**   knowledge engineering and knowledge science
- 知识共享组织公共许可 **CCPL**   Creative Commons Public License
- 知识管理 **KM**   knowledge management

Z

- 知识获取系统 KAS — Knowledge Acquisition System
- 知识机器人 Know-bot — knowledge robot
- 知识引擎 Kengine — knowledge engine
- 知识资产管理系统 IPAM — intellectual property asset management
- 知行合一成就领导力[知识思考、连接、行动、领导力] THLDL
  think, link, do, leadership
- 脂蛋白 X LP-X — lipoprotein-X
- 脂肪酶 SL — lipase
- 脂肪酸 FA — fatty acid
- 执行法律顾问 ACTG — acting legal advisor
- 执行副总裁 XVP — executive vice president
- 执行文件的扩展名 EXE — executable file
- 执照 W — warrant
- 直到 'til — until
- 直到 thru — through
- 直到 til — until
- 直观有效的表达观点的工具 PPT — powerpoint
- 直接存取存储器 DMA — Direct Memory Access
- 直接胆红素 D-Bil — direct bilirubin
- 直接到户 DTH — direct to home
- 直接方式存储 DAS — disposal attached storage
- 直接飞行控制 DFC — direct flight control
- 直接观察治疗策略 DOTS — Directly-Observed Treatment Strategy
- 直接换挡变速器 DSG — direct shift gearbox
- 直接驱动 DDR — direct drive
- 直接热轧制 HDR — hot direct rolling
- 直接数字控制 DNC — direct numerical control
- 直接提问 dq — direct question
- 直接投资基金 DIF — direct investment fund
- 直接荧光抗体技术 DFAT — Direct Fluorescent Antibody Technique
- 直接邮件广告 DM — direct mail advertising
- 直流电 DC — direct current

- 直投广告 DM   direct marketing
- 职业安全健康管理体系 OSHMS
  Occupational Safety and Health Management System
- 职业保龄球手协会 PBA   Professional Bowlers Association
- 职业电子竞技职业选手联赛 PGL   ProGamer League
- 职业岗位培训合格证书 CETTIC
  China Employment Training Technical Instruction Center
- 职业技术教育与培训学院 TVET
  Technical and Vocational Education and Training College
- 职业健康安全管理体系 OHSMS
  Occupational Heath Safety Management Systems
- 职业介绍所 LE   labour exchange
- 职业经理人资格证书 CCMC   Chinese Career Manager Certification
- 职业清单 SOL   Skilled Occupation List
- 职业人员争取妇女平等权利组织[象征该组织有力量] POWER
  Professional Organized for Women's Equal Rights
- 职业网球协会 ATP   Association of Tennis Professional
- 职业卫生安全体系 OHSA   Occupational Health Safety System
- 职业英语考试[美国为母语为非英语国家的企业、政府部门和英语学习者开发的一项考试] TOPE   Test of Professional English
- 职责区域 ZOR   zone of responsibility
- 只读存储器 ROM   Read Only Memory
- 只读光盘 CD-ROM   compact disc read-only memory
- 只读数字激光视盘机 DVD-ROM   DVD-Read Only Memory
- 只是看看(并非真正购物) JL   just looking
- 纸质书 p-book   paper-book
- 指定经营实体 DOE   designated operational entities
- 指挥、控制、通信和情报系统[军队自动化指挥系统] C3I
  system of command, control, communication and information
- 指挥:现代海空行动 CMANO   Command Modern Air/Naval Operations
- 指令集架构 ISA   instruction set architecture

Z

- 指面孔多变的年轻女子，她们一会儿是美女，一会儿是野兽，一会儿是婴儿 **3B**
  beauty，beast，baby
- 指示剂/指示器 **Ind**　　　　　　　indicator
- 指数 **Ind**　　　　　　　　　　　index
- 指数平滑移动平均线 **MACD**　　　moving average convergence divergence
- 指数系数 **MQ**　　　　　　　　　merit quotient
- 指游戏中玩家相互格斗，引申指对决 **PK**　　player killing
- 至进展时间 **TTP**　　　　　　　　time to progression
- 至通知赎回时收益 **YTC**　　　　　yield to call
- 志商 **WQ**　　　　　　　　　　　will quotient
- 制空权团队合作系统 **ATS**　　　　air control team cooperation system
- 制造 **MFG**　　　　　　　　　　manufacturing
- 制造业活动指数 **MI**　　　　　　 manufacturing index
- 制造执行系统 **MES**　　　　　　 manufacturing execution system
- 制造资源计划（系统）**MRP**　　　manufacturing resource plan
- 质化和量化的货币宽松政策 **QQE**
  quantitative and qualitative monetary easing
- 质量 **Q**　　　　　　　　　　　　quality
- 质量安全 **QS**　　　　　　　　　 quality safety
- 质量保证 **QA**　　　　　　　　　quality assurance
- 质量保证局 **QAO**　　　　　　　 Quality Assurance Office
- 质量服务 **QS**　　　　　　　　　 quality service
- 质量管理 **QM**　　　　　　　　　quality management
- 质量管理圈 **QCC**　　　　　　　 Quality Control Circle
- 质量管理体系 **QMS**　　　　　　 Quality Management System
- 质量和数量证书 **QQC**　　　　　 quality and quantity certificate
- 质量检查 **QR**　　　　　　　　　quality review
- 质量检查处 **QCD**　　　　　　　 quality control division
- 质量控制 **QC**　　　　　　　　　quality control
- 质量控制特别指令 **QCDS**　　　　Quality Control Directive Special
- 质量评价 **QA**　　　　　　　　　quality assessment
- 质量水平 **QL**　　　　　　　　　quality level

- 致癌物质鉴定委员会 CIC　　carcinogen identifying commission
- 致病性大肠杆菌 EPEC　　enteropathogenic escherichia coli
- 智慧城市代表企业：平安、阿里巴巴、腾讯、华为 PATH
  Ping'an, Alibaba, Tencent, Huawei
- 智慧停车 ETCP　　electronic toll collection park
- 智利[南美洲国家] CHI　　Chile
- 智利工厂发展协会[西班牙文] SOFOFA　　Sociedad de Fomento Fabril
- 智利国家标准局[西班牙文] INN　　Instituto Nacional de Normalizacion
- 智能测评系统 IAS　　intelligent assessing system
- 智能车路系统 IVHS　　intelligent vehicle highway system
- 智能创作系统 IAS　　intelligent authoring system
- 智能电网 SG　　smart grids
- 智能多功能终端 IMT　　intelligence multi-functional terminal
- 智能个人电视 IPTV　　intelligent personal television
- 智能计量嵌入式通用集成电路卡 eUICC
  embedded universal integrated circuit card
- 智能交通系统 ITS　　intelligent transport system
- 智能卡 IC　　integrated circuit card
- 智能控制系统 ECS　　electronic control system
- 智能手持设备 SHD　　smart handheld devices
- 智能芯片 IC　　intelligence chip
- 智商 IQ　　intelligence quotient
- 中阿(拉伯)合作论坛 CASCF　　China-Arab States Cooperation Forum
- 中爱联合纯种犬文化发展中心 CKU　　China Kennel Union
- 中巴经济走廊 CPEC　　China-Pakistan Economic Corridor
- 中版药品福利管理 CPBM　　Chinese Pharmacy Benefit Management
- 中北美及加勒比足球联合会[西班牙文] CONCACAF
  Confederación Norte-Centroamericana y del Caribe de Fútbol
- 中北美及加勒比足球协会 CONCACAF
  Confederation of North, Central American and Caribbean Football
- 中波 MW　　medium wave
- 中波紫外线 UVB　　ultraviolet B

Z

- 中部标准时间 **CST** — Central Standard Time
- 中部圣经学院 **CBC** — Central Bible College
- 中层管理人才发展计划 **MDP** — management development plan
- 中程空对地导弹[法文] **ASMP** — air-sol moyenne portée
- 中船重工 **CSSC** — China State Shipbuilding Corporation Limited
- 中等教育证书[英国] **CSE** — Certificate of Secondary Education
- 中东呼吸综合征 **MERS** — Middle East Respiratory Syndrome
- 中东经济委员会 **ECME** — Economic Commission for the Middle East
- 中东贸易委员会[英国] **COMET** — Committee for Middle East Trade
- 中东贸易咨询委员会 **ACMET** — Advisory Council on Middle East Trade
- 中东欧国家 **CEEC** — Central East Europe Countries
- 中毒控制中心;毒品控制中心 **PCC** — poison control center
- 中俄 **CR** — China, Russia
- 中俄韩 **CRK** — China, Russia, Korea
- 中俄联合开发的 CR929 宽体客机 **CR929** — China Russia 929
- 中非共和国[非洲国家] **CF** — Central African Republic
- 中非关税和经济同盟 **CEUCA** — Customs and Economic Union of Central Africa
- 中非合作论坛 **FOCAC** — Forum on China-Africa Cooperation
- 中风判断三个词[要求:患者笑一下,说一个简单句子,举起双手。如果患者不能做好其中任何一个,请立即送患者入医院] **STR** — smile, talk, raise
- 中风判断五要素:力量,感觉,吞咽,说话,看东西 **5S** — strength, sense, swallow, speak, seeing
- 中共中央党校 **CCPS** — Party School of the Central Committee of CPC
- 中规模集成电路 **MSI** — medium scale integration
- 中国(国家)标准[汉语拼音缩略语] **GB** — Guobiao
- 中国(深圳)国际品牌内衣展 **SIUF** — China (Shenzhen) International Brand Underwear Fair

- 中国(消费者)生活形态模型 **CHINA-VALS**
  CHINA-value and life style
- 中国 **CHN** China
- 中国 TCL 电子有限公司 **TCL** Today China Lion
- 中国澳门汽车总会[葡萄牙文] **AAMC**
  Associaçia Geral Automobile de Macau-China
- 中国保险集团 **CIG** China Insurance Group
- 中国保险与社会保障研究中心 **CCISSR**
  Center of China Insurance and Society Security Research
- 中国北斗卫星导航系统 **BDS** Beidou Navigation Satellite System
- 中国北方机车厂 **CNR** China Northern Railway
- 中国标准化协会 **CAS** China Association for Standardization
- 中国标准技术开发公司 **CSTC** China Standard Technical Services Co., Ltd.
- 中国不间断骑行协会 **ROCN** Randonneurs of China
- 中国残疾人联合会 **CDPF** China Disabled Persons' Federation
- 中国仓鼠卵巢 **CHO** Chinese Hamster Ovary
- 中国产品质量认证委员会 **CNACPQ**
  China National Accreditation Council for Products Quality
- 中国成套工程有限公司 **CCEC**
  China National Complete Engineering Corporation
- 中国出口商品交易会 **CECF** Chinese Export Commodities Fair
- 中国出入境检验检疫局 **CIQ** China Entry-exit Inspection and Quarantine
- 中国传记数据库 **CBD** China Biographical Database
- 中国传媒大学 **CUC** Communication University of China
- 中国船舶工业贸易公司 **CSTC** China Shipbuilding Trade Co.
- 中国船级社 **CCS** China Classification Society
- 中国船级社质量认证公司 **CCSC** China Classification Society Certification
- 中国船贸 **CSOC**
  China Shipbuilding and Offshore International Corporation
- 中国存托凭证 **CDR** Chinese Depository Receipt
- 中国大陆科学钻探工程 **CCSD** Chinese Continental Scientific Drilling
- 中国大学生篮球协会 **CUBA** China University Basketball Association

- 中国大学生追踪调查 **PSCUS** Pursuing Tracing Survey of Chinese University Students
- 中国大宗商品发展研究中心 **CDRC**   Commodity Development Research Centre
- 中国的道德与贤能政治 **M**   morality and political meritocracy
- 中国低活化马氏体钢 **CLAM**   China Low Activation Martensitic
- 中国电信集团公司 **CHINA TELECOM**   China Telecommunications Corporation
- 中国电信认证中心 **CTCA**   China Telecom Certification Authority
- 中国电子技术标准化研究所 **CESI**   Chinese Electronics Standardization Institute
- 中国电子竞技运动会 **CEG**   China E-Sports Game
- 中国电子科技集团公司 **CETC**   China Electronic Technology Corporation
- 中国电子商业汇票系统 **ECDS**   Electronic Commercial Draft System
- 中国电子消费展 **CES**   China Electronics Show
- 中国电子信息产业发展研究院 **CCID** China Center for Information Industry Development
- 中国电子信息产业集团公司 **CEC**   China Electronic Company
- 中国电子学会 **CIE**   Chinese Institute of Electronics
- 中国翻译职业交流大会 **CTPF**   China Translation Profession Forum
- 中国犯罪信息中心 **CCIC**   China Crime Information Center
- 中国房车锦标赛 **CTCC**   China Touring Car Championship
- 中国非处方药物协会 **CNMA**   China Non-prescription Medicine Association
- 中国佛教协会 **CBA**   Chinese Buddhist Association
- 中国福利会 **CWI**   China Welfare Institute
- 中国高等教育博览会 **HEEC**   Higher Education Expo of China
- 中国高等教育学会 **CAHE**   China Association of Higher Education
- 中国高速铁路 **CRH**   China Railway High-speed
- 中国高校外语慕课平台 **UMOOCs**   University MOOCs
- 中国高新技术交易会 **CHTF**   China HI-TECH Fair
- 中国工商银行 **ICBC**   Industrial and Commercial Bank of China
- 中国工业标准 **CIS**   Chinese Industrial Standards
- 中国公民信息登记系统 **CNRS**   Chinese National Registration System
- 中国公用计算机互联网 **CHINANET**   China Network
- 中国共产党 **CPC**   Communist Party of China

- 中国共产党中央委员会 CCCPC
Central Committee of the Communist Party of China
- 中国关怀生命协会 CALC　　　China Association of Life Concerning
- 中国光大银行 CEB　　　China Everbright Bank
- 中国广播局 CNR　　　China National Radio
- 中国广播影视集团 CRFTG　　　China Radio Film and Television Group
- 中国广告的诺贝尔奖 ADMEN　　　Advertisement Men
- 中国国际房地产与建筑科技展览会(简称"中国住交会") CIHAF
China International Real Estate & Architectural Technology Fair
- 中国国际服装博览会 CHIC
China International Clothing & Accessories Fair
- 中国国际服务贸易交易会 CIFTIS
China International Fair for Trade in Services
- 中国国际工业博览会 CIIF　　　China International Industrial Fair
- 中国国际广播电台 CRI　　　China Radio International
- 中国国际进口博览会 CIIE　　　China International Import Expo
- 中国国际经济交流中心 CCIEE
China Center for International Economic Exchanges
- 中国国际救援队 CISAR　　　China International Search and Rescue
- 中国国际旅行社 CITS　　　China International Travel Service
- 中国国际贸易促进委员会 CCPIT
China Council for the Promotion of International Trade
- 中国国际能源控股有限公司 CIEC　　　China International Energy Center
- 中国国际品牌设计(年展) BDCI　　　Brand Design of China International
- 中国国际商会 CCOIC　　　China Chamber of International Commerce
- 中国国际投资贸易洽谈会 CIFIT
China International Fair for Investment and Trade
- 中国国际信托投资公司 CITIC
China International Trust and Investment Corporation
- 中国国家标准化管理委员会 SAC
Standardization Administration of the P. R. C.
- 中国国家代码 CN　　　China

Z

Z

- 中国国家顾客满意度指数 CNCSI　　China National Customer Satisfaction Index
- 中国国家禁毒委员会 NNCC
  China National Narcotics Control Commission
- 中国国家开发投资公司 SDIC
  State Development & Investment Corp Group
- 中国国家开发银行 CDB　　China Development Bank
- 中国国家认证认可监督管理委员会 CNCA
  Certification and Accreditation Administration of the P. R. C.
- 中国国家图书馆 NLC　　National Library of China
- 中国国家信息安全漏洞共享平台 CNVD
  China National Vulnerability Database
- 中国海关总署 GACC
  Customs General Administration of Customs, P. R. China
- 中国海警部队 CCG　　China Coast Guard
- 中国海事仲裁委员会 CMAC　　China Maritime Arbitration Commission
- 中国海洋石油总公司 CNOOC　　China National Offshore Oil Corp
- 中国航空工业集团公司 AVIC　　Aviation Industry Corporation of China
- 中国航天科技集团公司 CASC
  China Aerospace Science and Technology Corporation
- 中国合格评定国家认可委员会 CNAS
  China National Accreditation Service for Conformity Assessment
- 中国和印尼的合资公司 KCIC　　Kereta Cepat Indonesia China
- 中国核电力研究所 NPIC　　Nuclear Power Institute of China
- 中国互联网安全大会 ISC　　China Internet Security Conference
- 中国互联网集团 CIG　　China Internet Group
- 中国互联网金融联盟 CIFC　　China Internet Finance Conference
- 中国互联网数据中心 DCCI　　Data Center of China Internet
- 中国互联网协会 ISC　　Internet Society of China
- 中国互联网信息中心 CNNIC　　China Internet Network Information Center
- 中国华源集团有限公司 CWGC　　China Worldbest Group Co., Ltd.
- 中国环球电视网 CGTN　　China Global Television Network
- 中国货物编码 CAN　　Chinese Article Number

- 中国机读目录格式 **China MARC**
  China Machine Readable Cataloging Format
- 中国机械进出口(集团)有限公司 **CMC**
  China National Machinery Import and Export Corporation
- 中国疾病预防控制 **CDPC**   Chinese Disease Prevention and Control
- 中国计量认证 **CMA**   China Metrology Accreditation
- 中国计算机大会 **CNCC**   China National Computer Congress
- 中国计算机协会 **CCF**   China Computer Federation
- 中国加拿大研究会 **ACSC**   Association for Canada Studies in China
- 中国检验认证(集团)有限公司 **CCIC**
  China Certification & Inspection (Group) Co., Ltd.
- 中国建设银行 **CCB**   China Construction Bank
- 中国建筑传媒奖 **CAMA**   China Architecture Media Award
- 中国建筑装饰装修材料协会 **CADBM**
  China Association of Decorative Building Materials
- 中国健美协会 **CBBA**   Chinese Bodybuilding Association
- 中国交通运输协会 **CCTA**
  Chinese Communications and Transportation Association
- 中国教育电视台 **CETV**   China Education Television
- 中国教育和科研计算机网 **CERNET**   China Education and Research Network
- 中国教育科研网 **CERNET**
  China Educational and Scientific Research Network
- 中国节能产品认证中心 **CECP**   China Energy-saving Center of Products
- 中国金桥网 **China GBN**   China Golden Bridge Network
- 中国金融期货交易所 **CFFEX**   China Financial Futures Exchange
- 中国金融认证中心 **CFCA**   China Finance Certification Authority
- 中国进出口商品检验总公司 **CCIC**
  China National Import and Export Commodities Inspection Corporation
- 中国进出口质量认证中心 **CQC**
  China Quality Certification Centre
- 中国进出口总公司 **CNIEC**
  China National Import and Export Corporation

Z

- 中国经济高峰会 CES　　　　　　China Economic Summit
- 中国经济情报委员会 CEIC　　　　China Economic Intelligence Committee
- 中国经济调查 CEP　　　　　　　China Economy Probe
- 中国经济信息（网）CEI　　　　　China Economic Information
- 中国经济研究中心 CCER　　　　　China Center of Economic Research
- 中国精密机械进出口总公司 CPMIEC
  China Precision Machinery Import-Export Corporation
- 中国救捞 CRS　　　　　　　　　China Rescue & Salvage
- 中国抗菌材料及制品行业协会 CIAA
  Chinese Industry Association for Antimicrobial Materials & Products
- 中国抗中子辐照钢 CLAM　　　　　China Low Activation Martensitic
- 中国科技论文与引文数据库 CSTPCD
  Chinese Science and Technology Papers and Citation Databases
- 中国科技网 CSTNET　　　　　　 China Science and Technology Network
- 中国科学技术协会 CAST
  China Association for Science and Technology
- 中国科学技术信息研究院 ISTIC
  Institute of Scientific and Technical Information of China
- 中国科学院 CAS　　　　　　　　Chinese Academy of Sciences
- 中国科学院大学 UCAS　　　　　　University of Chinese Academy of Sciences
- 中国篮球公开赛 CBO　　　　　　 Chinese Basketball Open
- 中国篮球协会 CBA　　　　　　　Chinese Basketball Association
- 中国篮球组织 CBO　　　　　　　China Basketball Organization
- 中国历代人物传记资料库 CBDB　　China Biographical Database
- 中国粮油食品进出口（集团）有限公司 CNCOFIEC
  China National Cereals, Oils and Foodstuffs Import and Export Corporation
- 中国留学生 OSCs　　　　　　　　overseas Chinese students
- 中国路桥工程公司 CRBC　　　　　China Railway and Bridge Company
- 中国旅行社 CTS　　　　　　　　China Travel Service
- 中国煤炭设备成套有限公司 CCCEC
  China Coal Complete Sets of Equipment Co., Ltd.
- 中国棉花价格指数 CC Index　　　China Cotton Index

- 中国免税 **CDF**   China Duty Free
- 中国民用航空局［其前身为 General Administration of Civil Aviation of China（中国民用航空总局）］**CAAC**   Civil Aviation Administration of China
- 中国民生银行 **CMBC**   China Minsheng Bank Co., Ltd.
- 中国农业银行 **ABC**   Agricultural Bank of China
- 中国女子篮球协会 **WCBA**   Women Chinese Basketball Association
- 中国欧盟商会 **EUCCC**   European Union Chamber of Commerce in China
- 中国企业品牌竞争力指数 **CBI**   China Business Index
- 中国企业社会责任同盟 **CFCSR**   Chinese Federation to Corporate Social Responsibility
- 中国气候观测系统 **CCOS**   China Climate Observation System
- 中国汽车系统股份公司 **CAAS**   China Automotive Systems, Inc.
- 中国汽车技术研究中心 **CATARC**   China Automotive Technology and Research Center
- 中国强制性产品认证标志 **CCC**   China Compulsory Certification
- 中国强制性产品认证制度 **3C**   China Compulsory Certification
- 中国青年大使 **CYA**   China Youth Ambassador
- 中国青年旅行社 **CYTS**   China Youth Travel Service
- 中国轻工业设计师 **CDLI**   China Designer of Light Industry
- 中国区域定位系统 **CAPS**   China Area Position System
- 中国全国读者调查 **CNRS**   China National Reader Survey
- 中国拳击锦标赛 **CBC**   China Boxing Champion
- 中国人才热线 **CJOL**   China Job Online
- 中国人民保险公司 **PICC**   People's Insurance Company of China
- 中国人民大学 **RUC**   Renmin University of China
- 中国人民对外文化协会 **CPACRFC**   Chinese People's Association for Cultural Relations with Foreign Countries
- 中国人民解放军 **PLA**   People's Liberation Army of China
- 中国国际救援队 **CISRT**   China International Search and Rescue Team
- 中国人民外交学会 **CPIFA**   Chinese People's Institute of Foreign Affairs

Z

- 中国人民银行 **PBC**   The People's Bank of China
- 中国人民争取和平与裁军协会 **CPAPD**
  Chinese People's Association for Peace and Disarmament
- 中国人民政治协商会议 **CPPCC**
  Chinese People's Political Consultative Conference
- 中国人权捍卫者网络 **CHRD**   Chinese Human Rights Defenders
- 中国人文社会科学论文索引 **CHSSCI**
  China Humanities Social Sciences Citation Index
- 中国认证人员国家注册委员会 **CRBA**
  China National Registration Board for Auditors
- 中国软件开发中心 **CSDC**   China Software Development Centre
- 中国软件联盟 **CSA**   China Software Association
- 中国软件运营服务 **SaaS**   Software as a Service
- 中国商检标志 **CCIB**   China Commercial Inspection Bureau
- 中国商品检验公司 **CCIC**   China Commodity Inspection Corporation
- 中国商品交易中心 **CCEC**   China Commodity Exchange Center
- 中国商业美术设计师 **CCAD**   China Commerce Art Designer
- 中国商用飞机有限责任公司 **COMAC**
  The Commercial Aircraft Corporation of China, Ltd.
- 中国社会发展互联网 **CSDN**   China Social Development Network
- 中国社会科学院 **CASS**   Chinese Academic of Social Sciences
- 中国社会科学院大学 **UCASS**
  University of Chinese Academy of Social Sciences
- 中国生物医学文献数据库 **CBM**   Chinese Biological Medicine
- 中国石化(公司) **Sinopec**   China Petroleum & Chemical Corporation
- 中国石油勘探开发数据模型 **PCEDM**
  Petro China Exploration Development Model
- 中国石油天然气集团有限公司 **CNPC**   China National Petroleum Corporation
- 中国实验室国家认可委员会 **CNAL**
  China National Accreditation Board for Laboratories
- 中国市场调查 **CEP**   China Economic Panel
- 中国市场与媒体研究 **CMMS**   Chinese Market and Media Study

- 中国术语学建设暨术语规范化 **NCTFS**
  National Conference on Terminological Formation and Standardization
- 中国数控机床展览会 **CCMT**　　China CNC Machine Tool Fair
- 中国数字多媒体广播 **CDMB**　　China Digital Multimedia Broadcasting
- 中国税收征管信息系统 **CTAIS**
  China Taxation Administration Information System
- 中国台湾股票交易所 **TSE**　　Taiwan Stock Exchange
- 中国太平洋保险公司 **CPIC**　　China Pacific Insurance Corporation
- 中国太阳石油公司 **CSOC**　　China Sun Oil Company
- 中国探月 **CLEP**　　China Lunar Exploration Program
- 中国体育舞蹈联合会 **CDSF**　　Chinese Dance Sport Federation
- 中国天眼 **FAST**
  Five-hundred-meter Aperture Spherical Radio Telescope
- 中国铁道建筑总公司 **CRCC**　　China Railway Construction Corporation
- 中国铁路互联网 **CRNET**　　China Railway Network
- 中国铁路时刻 **CRS**　　China Railway Schedule
- 中国投资发展促进会 **CAPI**
  China Association for the Promotion of Investment
- 中国投资银行 **CIB**　　China Investment Bank
- 中国图片代理机构 **CFP**　　China Foto Press
- 中国网络电视 **CWTV**　　China Web TV
- 中国网络电视台 **CNTV**　　China Network Television
- 中国网络营销职业经理人认证（管理办公室）**CEMPMC**
  China E-Marketing Professional Managers Certification
- 中国卫星导航定位协会 **GLAC**　　GNSS and LBS Association of China
- 中国卫星网络 **CSNet**　　China Satellite Network
- 中国文化大数据产业项目 **CCDI**　　China Culture Data Industry
- 中国文学艺术界联合会 **CFLAC**
  China Federation of Literary and Art Circles
- 中国无线电运动协会 **CRSA**　　Chinese Radio Sports Association

Z

- 中国物流与采购联合会 **CFLP**
  China Federation of Logistics & Purchasing
- 中国物品编码中心 **ANCC**　　　　Article Numbering Center of China
- 中国物业管理协会 **CPMI**　　　　China Property Management Institute
- 中国下一代互联网工程 **CNGI**　　China Next Generation Internet
- 中国现代国际关系研究院 **CICIR**
  China Institute for Contemporary International Relations
- 中国现代化支付系统 **CNAPS**　　China National Automatic Payment System
- 中国枭龙战斗机 **FC**　　　　　　Fighter China
- 中国消费者协会 **CCA**　　　　　China Consumer's Association
- 中国小康建设研究会 **CWSA**　　China Well-off Society Association
- 中国新车评价规程 **C-NCAP**　　China-New Car Assessment Programme
- 中国信息安全认证中心 **ISCCC**
  China Information Security Certification Center
- 中国刑事警察学院 **CIPUC**
  Criminal Investigation Police University of China
- 中国行为艺术平台 **CAPP**　　　China Art Platform of Performance
- 中国兴业银行 **CIB**　　　　　　Industrial Bank Co., Ltd.
- 中国野生动物经营利用管理专用标识 **CNWM**
  China National Wildlife Management
- 中国业余篮球公开赛 **CBO**　　　Chinese Basketball Open
- 中国医疗保健国际交流促进会 **CPAM**
  China International Exchange and Promotion Association for Medical and Health-care
- 中国医疗自媒体联盟 **CMWA**　　China Medical We-media Association
- 中国医院信息系统 **CHIS**　　　Chinese Hospital Information System
- 中国移动多媒体广播 **CMMB**　　China Mobile Multimedia Broadcasting
- 中国移动互联网 **CMN**　　　　China Mobile Net
- 中国移动通信集团有限公司 **CMCC**
  China Mobile Communications Group Co., Ltd.
- 中国音乐剧 **CMO**　　　　　　Chinese music opera
- 中国音乐著作权协会 **MCSC**　　Music Copyright Society of China

- 中国银行 **BOC** — Bank of China
- 中国银行保险监督管理委员会 **CBIRC** — China Banking and Insurance Regulatory Commission
- 中国英语能力等级量表 **CSE** — China's Standards of English
- 中国营销经理人职业资格认证 **CMMQ** — Chinese Career Manager Certification
- 中国营养学会 **CNS** — Chinese Nutrition Society
- 中国用户满意度指数 **CCSI** — Chinese Customer Satisfaction Index
- 中国油脂学会 **COA** — China Oil Association
- 中国与全球化智库 **CCG** — Center for China and Globalization
- 中国语言模型 **CLM** — Chinese language module
- 中国语言智能大会 **CLIC** — China Language Intelligence Conference
- 中国远洋运输(集团)总公司 **COSCO** — China Ocean Shipping Group
- 中国运输生产指数 **CTSI** — China Transport Production Index
- 中国证券监督管理委员会 **CSRC** — China Securities Regulatory Commission
- 中国政法大学 **CUPL** — China University of Political Science and Law
- 中国政法大学[旧称,现称 ZUC] **CUPL** — China University of Political science and Law
- 中国知识管理中心 **KMC** — Knowledge Management Center
- 中国知识基础设施(工程) **CNKI** — China National Knowledge Infrastructure
- 中国知网 **CNKI** — China National Knowledge Infrastructure
- 中国职业技能鉴定中心 **OSAT** — Occupation Skill Association of Test
- 中国质量检验联盟 **CTA** — China Testing Alliance
- 中国中车股份有限公司 **CRRC** — China Railway Rolling Stock Corporation
- 中国中期投资股份有限公司 **CIFCO** — China International Futures Investment Co., Ltd.
- 中国中央电视台 **CCTV** — China Central Television
- 中国气象局 **CMA** — China Meteorological Administration
- 中国专利局 **CPB** — China Patent Bureau
- 中国综合格斗联盟 **CMFA** — China Mixed Fighting Alliance
- 中国总会计师协会[原名 CIGA] **CFO** — China Association of Chief Financial Officers
- 中国钻石管理局 **DAC** — Diamond Administration of China

Z

- 中海洋石油集团有限公司 **CNOOC**　China National Offshore Oil Corporation
- 中航技进出口有限责任公司 **CATIC**
  China National Aero-Technology Import & Export Corporation
- 中华口腔医学会 **CSA**　Chinese Stomatological Association
- 中华全国体育总会 **ACSF**　All-China Sports Federation
- 中华全国总工会 **ACFTU**　All-China Federation of Trade Unions
- 中华人民共和国 **PRC**　the People's Republic of China
- 中华人民共和国国家质量监督检验检疫总局 **AQSIQ**
  General Administration of Quality Supervision, Inspection and Quarantine of the People's Republic of China
- 中华文化海外传播论坛 **CCOCF**
  China Culture Overseas Communication Forum
- 中华医学会 **CMA**　China Medical Association
- 中华医学会骨科学分会 **COA**　Chinese Orthopaedic Association
- 中华预防医学会 **CPMA**　Chinese Preventive Medical Association
- 中华总商会[属香港特别行政区] **CGCC**
  Chinese General Chamber of Commerce
- 中科院国家科学数字图书馆 **CSDL**　Chinese Science Digital Library
- 中老年男性雄激素部分缺乏综合征 **PADAM**
  partial androgen deficiency of aging men
- 中美国 **Chimerica**　China America
- 中美联合培养物理类研究生计划 **CUSPEA**
  China-US Physics Examination and Application
- 中美洲共同市场 **CACM**　Central American Common Market
- 中美洲国家组织 **OCAS**　Organization of Central American States
- 中美洲自由贸易协定 **CARTA**　Central American Free Trade Agreement
- 中密度聚乙烯[塑料] **MDPE**　medium density polyethylene
- 中密度纤维板 **MDF**　medium density fibre board
- 中南大学 **CSU**　Central South University
- 中南民族大学 **SCUFN**　South-Central University for Nationalities
- 中年富翁[指头发苍白、有闲的、富有的已婚者] **GLAM**
  graying, leisured, affluent and married

- 中欧法学院 CESL　　　　　　　China-Europe School of Law
- 中欧国际工商管理学院 CEIBS
  China Europe International Business School
- 中频 MF　　　　　　　　　　medium frequency
- 中期借贷便利 MLF　　　　　　medium-term lending facility
- 中山大学 SYSU　　　　　　　Sun Yat-Sen University
- 中士 Sgt　　　　　　　　　　sergeant
- 中式朋克,一种摇滚乐 CnPunk　China Punk
- 中枢神经系统 CNS　　　　　　central nervous system
- 中文期刊全文数据库 CJFD　　 China Journals Full-text Database
- 中文式英文 Chinglish　　　　　Chinese English
- 中小企业 MSB　　　　　　　　medium-small business
- 中小企业 SMSE　　　　　　　small and medium scale enterprise
- 中小企业发展指数 SMEDI
  small and medium-sized enterprise development index
- 中小型企业 SME　　　　　　　small and medium-sized enterprise
- 中小学及学前教育的 K-12　　　kindergarten to 12th grade
- 中小学教师资格考试 NTCE
  National Teacher Certificate Examination
- 中小学生汉语考试 YCT　　　　Youth Chinese Test
- 中心 C　　　　　　　　　　　center
- 中心非特异性酯酶染色 NSE　　non-specific esterase
- 中心频率 CF　　　　　　　　　Center Frequency
- 中芯国际集成电路制造有限公司 SMIC
  Semiconductor Manufacturing International Corporation
- 中信银行 CITIC
  China International Trust and Investment Corporation
- 中型登陆艇 LCM　　　　　　　landing craft medium
- 中型战术车族 FMTV　　　　　family of medium tactical vehicles
- 中兴通讯 ZTE
  Zhongxing Telecommunication Equipment Corporation
- 中性粒细胞 NEUT　　　　　　neuter granulocyte

Z

- 中性粒细胞碱性磷酸酶 NAP　　neutrophil alkaline phosphatase
- 中学毕业证书[英国] Sc　　school certificate
- 中学(大学)二年级学生 Soph　　sophomore
- 中学教育普通证书 GCSE　　General Certificate of Secondary Education
- 中央处理器 CPU　　Central Processing Unit
- 中央动态存储器 CDS　　central dynamic store
- 中央公园区 CPD　　center park district
- 中央广播电视总台 CMG　　China Media Group
- 中央交换设施 CSF　　central switching facility
- 中央控制室 CCR　　central control room
- 中央人民广播电台 CNR　　China National Radio
- 中央商务区 CBD　　central business district
- 中央生活区 CLD　　Central Living District
- 中央数据处理系统 CDPS　　central data processing system
- 中央文化区 CCD　　Central Cultural District
- 中央信息区 CID　　central information district
- 中央预订系统 CRS　　central reservation system
- 中医 TCM　　Traditional Chinese Medicine
- 中医药研究促进会传统文化翻译与国际传播专业委员会 COTIP
Committee of Translation and International Promotion of Traditional Chinese Culture
- 中医药研究所 IACM
The Institute for the Advancement of Chinese Medicine Ltd.
- 中银国际 BOCI　　Bank of China International
- 中印[中国+印度] Chindia　　China+India
- 中印尼高铁合同承包商联合体 HSRCC
High Speed Railway Contractor Consortium
- 中长期战略技术清单 MLTSSL
Medium and Long-term Strategic Skills List
- 中置输出(音响) CO　　Center Output
- 中资企业赴美投资 CBIUS
Chinese Buyer Investment in the United States

■ 终端打印 TP	terminal printing
■ 终极格斗冠军赛/终极格斗锦标赛 UFC	
Ultimate Fighting Championship	
■ 肿瘤坏死因子 TNF	tumor necrosis factor
■ 肿瘤坏死因子-α TNF-α	tumor necrosis factor-α
■ 肿瘤进展时间 TTP	time to progress
■ 肿瘤浸润淋巴细胞 TIL	tumor infiltrating lymphocyte
■ 肿瘤雷达 PET-CT	
positron emission tomography-computed tomography	
■ 肿瘤抑制基因 TSG	tumor suppressor gene
■ 肿瘤诱导 Ti	tumor inducing
■ 仲裁委员会 PAC	press arbitration commission
■ 众泰汽车[中国浙江永康] Z	Zotye
■ 重复性外力伤害 RSI	repetitive strength injure
■ 重工业研究协会 HERA	Heavy Engineering Research Association
■ 重力 GF	gravity force
■ 重力恢复和内部实验室 GRAIL	gravity recovering and interior library
■ 重量、颜色、切割、透明度[国际上衡量钻石的4个标准] 4C	
carat, color, cut, clarity	
■ 重量/高度/温度 WAT	weight/altitude/temperature
■ 重量 WT	weight
■ 重量和/或体积由船公司选择 W/M	
weight and/or measurement at ship's option	
■ 重庆工商大学 CTBU	
Chongqing Technology and Business University	
■ 重型设备运输车 HET	heavy equipment transporter
■ 重债国 HIPC	heavily indebted poor countries
■ 重症病房 ITU	Intensive Therapy Unit
■ 重症肌无力 MG	myasthenia gravis
■ 重症监护病房 EICU	emergency intensive care unit
■ 重症监护室 ICU	intensive care unit

Z

州 St	state
州儿童医疗保险 SCHIP	State Children Health Insurance Program
周[非法定频率计量单位] C	cycle
周转资金 WCF	working capital fund
洲际交易所 ICE	Intercontinental Exchange
轴 SHF	shaft
轴承 BRG	bearing
珠宝鉴定资格证书 GIC	Gem Identification Certificate
珠宝资产评估师 CPVG	certified public valuer of gem
珠海国际赛车场 ZIC	Zhuhai International Circuit
逐行倒相制 PAL	phase alternating (by) line
主从追随式机甲系统 AS	armored mobile master-slave system
主动矩阵有机发光二极体 AMOLED	active-matrix organic light-emitting diode
主动式底盘稳定性装置 AFS	active frame stability
主缸 M/C	master cylinder
主权风险 SR	sovereign risk
主生产计划 MPS	master production schedule
主数据的管理 MDM	master data management
主题音乐 TM	theme music
主要经济指标 MEI	main economic indicators
主要设备清单 MEL	master equipment list
主要研究者 PI	principal investigator
主要英语国家的出版物全文汇总 WMB	World Magazine Bank
主战坦克 MBT	main battle tank
助理/助手[印尼文] ASST	assisten
助理 Asst	assistant
助理工程师 AE	assistant engineer
住院医生助手 RA	resident assistant
住宅体制 HS	House System
住宅质量保证保险[又称"潜在缺陷保险"] IDI Inherent Defects Insurance	
注册(公共)会计师 CPA	certified public accountant

注册财务顾问 RFC	Registered Financial Consultants
注册国际商务谈判专家认证 CIBNE	Certified International Business Negotiation Expert
注册国际心理咨询师 CIPC	Certified International Psychological Consultant
注册护士 LPN	licensed practical nurse
注册环境研究院 CEI	Certified Environmental Institute
注册会计师 CGA	certified general accountant
注册机构 RA	Registration Authority
注册金融策划师 CFP	Certified Financial Planner
注册金融风险管理师 CFRM	Certified Financial Risk Manager
注册普通护士 RGN	registered general nurse
注册商标 R	registered trade mark
注册商标 RTM	registered trade mark
注册商业投资师 CCIM	Certified Commercial Investment Member
注册退休储蓄计划 RRSP	registered retirement saving plan
注册信贷风险分析师 CCRA	certified credit risk analyst
注意[拉丁文] NB	nota bene
注意缺陷多动症 ADHD	attention deficit hyperactivity disorder
注意事态变化 KIV	keep it view
驻华外国记者协会 FCCC	the Foreign Correspondents' Club of China
驻科索沃国际安全部队 KFOR	Kosovo Peacekeeping Force
驻留时间、温度和速度 RTS	residence time, temperature and speed
驻外事务处机构 FSI	foreign serve institute
祝好 BR	best regards
祝一切顺利[网络用语] ATB	all the best
专案组合优化管理系统 PPP	project portfolio prioritization
专利[参考文献标示字母] P	patent
专利商标局 PTO	patent and trademark office
专利引文索引 PCI	Patent Citation Index
专门出版物 SP	Special Publications
专门用途英语 ESP	English for Special Purposes
专门用途英语教学 TESP	Teaching English for Specific Purposes

Z

州 St	state
州儿童医疗保险 SCHIP	State Children Health Insurance Program
周[非法定频率计量单位] C	cycle
周转资金 WCF	working capital fund
洲际交易所 ICE	Intercontinental Exchange
轴 SHF	shaft
轴承 BRG	bearing
珠宝鉴定资格证书 GIC	Gem Identification Certificate
珠宝资产评估师 CPVG	certified public valuer of gem
珠海国际赛车场 ZIC	Zhuhai International Circuit
逐行倒相制 PAL	phase alternating (by) line
主从追随式机甲系统 AS	armored mobile master-slave system
主动矩阵有机发光二极体 AMOLED	active-matrix organic light-emitting diode
主动式底盘稳定性装置 AFS	active frame stability
主缸 M/C	master cylinder
主权风险 SR	sovereign risk
主生产计划 MPS	master production schedule
主数据的管理 MDM	master data management
主题音乐 TM	theme music
主要经济指标 MEI	main economic indicators
主要设备清单 MEL	master equipment list
主要研究者 PI	principal investigator
主要英语国家的出版物全文汇总 WMB	World Magazine Bank
主战坦克 MBT	main battle tank
助理/助手[印尼文] ASST	assisten
助理 Asst	assistant
助理工程师 AE	assistant engineer
住院医生助手 RA	resident assistant
住宅体制 HS	House System
住宅质量保证保险[又称"潜在缺陷保险"] IDI	Inherent Defects Insurance
注册(公共)会计师 CPA	certified public accountant

- 注册财务顾问 **RFC**   Registered Financial Consultants
- 注册国际商务谈判专家认证 **CIBNE**
 Certified International Business Negotiation Expert
- 注册国际心理咨询师 **CIPC**
 Certified International Psychological Consultant
- 注册护士 **LPN**   licensed practical nurse
- 注册环境研究院 **CEI**   Certified Environmental Institute
- 注册会计师 **CGA**   certified general accountant
- 注册机构 **RA**   Registration Authority
- 注册金融策划师 **CFP**   Certified Financial Planner
- 注册金融风险管理师 **CFRM**   Certified Financial Risk Manager
- 注册普通护士 **RGN**   registered general nurse
- 注册商标 **R**   registered trade mark
- 注册商标 **RTM**   registered trade mark
- 注册商业投资师 **CCIM**   Certified Commercial Investment Member
- 注册退休储蓄计划 **RRSP**   registered retirement saving plan
- 注册信贷风险分析师 **CCRA**   certified credit risk analyst
- 注意[拉丁文] **NB**   nota bene
- 注意缺陷多动症 **ADHD**   attention deficit hyperactivity disorder
- 注意事态变化 **KIV**   keep it view
- 驻华外国记者协会 **FCCC**   the Foreign Correspondents' Club of China
- 驻科索沃国际安全部队 **KFOR**   Kosovo Peacekeeping Force
- 驻留时间、温度和速度 **RTS**   residence time, temperature and speed
- 驻外事务处机构 **FSI**   foreign serve institute
- 祝好 **BR**   best regards
- 祝一切顺利[网络用语] **ATB**   all the best
- 专案组合优化管理系统 **PPP**   project portfolio prioritization
- 专利[参考文献标示字母] **P**   patent
- 专利商标局 **PTO**   patent and trademark office
- 专利引文索引 **PCI**   Patent Citation Index
- 专门出版物 **SP**   Special Publications
- 专门用途英语 **ESP**   English for Special Purposes
- 专门用途英语教学 **TESP**   Teaching English for Specific Purposes

Z

- 专人服务 VIC — very important customer
- 专属经济区 EEZ — Exclusive Economic Zone
- 专业采购经理认证 CPPM — Certified Purchasing Professional Manager
- 专业采购人员认证 CPP — Certified Purchasing Professional
- 专业风险管理 PRM — professional risk management
- 专业工程师 pro-e — professional engineer
- 专业会计硕士 MPAcc — master of professional accounting
- 专业集成电路 ASIC — application specific integrated circuit
- 专业人员 Pro — professional
- 专业英语考试 PET — Professional English Test
- 专业用户原创内容 PUGC — professional user generated content
- 专业原创内容 PGC — professional generated content
- 专著[参考文献标示字母] M — monograph
- 专著或论文中析出的文献[参考文献标示字母] A — article from anthology
- 转发 FW — forward
- 转基因（遗传改造）GM — genetically modified
- 转基因食品 GMF — genetically modified food
- 转基因有机体 GMO — genetically modified organism
- 转矩 TORQ — torque
- 转入 C/O — carried over
- 转推[用于所转发的消息前] RT — retweet
- 装货单 S/O — shipping order
- 装甲多用途车辆 AMPV — armored multi-purpose vehicle
- 装甲修理车 ARV — armored recovery vehicle
- 装甲运兵车 APC — armored personnel carrier
- 装配 ASSEM — assemble
- 装运单 S/N — shipping note
- 装运单 SN — shipping note
- 准备发送 RTS — ready-to-send
- 准备基金 RF — reserve fund
- 准精算师 ASA — Associate of Society of Actuary

准男爵 Bart	baronet
准时化 JIT	just-in-time
准天顶卫星系统 QZSS	Quasi Zenith Satellite System
桌面操作系统 DOS	desktop operation system
桌面附件 DA	desk accessory
桌面管理接口 DMI	desktop management interface
桌面类游戏 TAB	table game
桌面类游戏 TBG	table game
桌面演习 TTX	table top exercise
桌上角色扮演游戏 TRPG	table role playing game
浊色 D	dark
着陆 LDG	landing
资本货物 CG	capital goods
资本利润率 RR	rate of return on capital
资本收益率 ROC	return on capital
资本所得税 CGT	capital gains tax
资本与债务比率 CDR	capital-to-debt ratio
资本账户 C/A	capital account
资本支出 CAPEX	capital expenditure
资本转移税 CTT	capital transfer tax
资本资产定价模型 CAPM	capital asset pricing model
资产(通常是房地产)抵押债券 ABS	asset-backed securities
资产财货 CG	capital goods
资产担保证券 ABS	asset-backed security
资产管理公司 AMC	Asset Management Companies
资产回报率/资产收益(率) ROA	return on assets
资产评估师 CPV	certified public valuer
资产评估硕士 MV	Master of Valuation
资金投资集团 CIG	capital investment group
资金转移定价 FTP	funds transfer pricing
资料汇编[参考文献标示字母] G	general
资源获取就是初始化 RAII	resource acquisition is initialization
子宫颈长度 LCU	length of the cervix uteri

Z

紫光红色 **PR**	purple red
紫红色 **RP**	reddish purple
紫蓝色 **PB**	purple blue
紫色 **P**	purple
紫色 **PU**	purple
紫色 **V**	violet
紫外光 **UV**	ultraviolet
自备购物袋[环保人士常用] **BYOB**	Bring Your Own Bag
自带酒 **BYOB**	Bring Your Own Booze
自动(循环)存取款机 **CRS**	cash recycling system

自动/紧急锁止收卷器[安全带] **A/ELR**
automatic/emergency locking retractor

自动编码系统 **ACS**	automatic coding system
自动变速器 **AT**	automatic transmission
自动变速箱用油 **ATF**	automatic transmission fluid
自动仓储物流系统 **ASRS**	automated support requirements system
自动仓单系统 **AMS**	automated manifest system
自动操作和调度程序 **AOSP**	automatic operating and scheduling program
自动测试装置 **ATE**	automatic test equipment
自动存款机 **AD**	automatic depositor
自动导轨运输系统 **AGTS**	Automated Guideway Transit System
自动发音分析系统 **ASAS**	Automatic Speech Analysis System
自动跟踪 **AF**	automatic following
自动工程设计 **AED**	automated engineering design
自动公路系统 **AHS**	automated highway system
自动柜员机 **ATM**	Automated Teller Machine
自动过程控制 **APC**	automatic process control
自动号码识别 **ANI**	automatic number identification

自动呼叫分配[是一种用于处理许多来话呼叫的特殊电话系统] **ACD**
automatic call distribution

自动化仓储系统 **AS/RS**	automatic storage and retrieval system
自动化订座系统 **ASRS**	automatic seat reservation system

- 自动化翻译研究中心[法文] **CETA**
Centre d'Études pour la Traduction Automatique [英文:Center for the Study of Automatic Translation]
- 自动货运飞船 **ATV**   Automatic Transport Vehicle
- 自动计算机辅助设计 **AUTO CAD**   automatic computer aided design
- 自动驾驶系统 **AMD**   automatic master device
- 自动交换中心 **ASC**   Automatic Switch Center
- 自动缴费机 **APM**   automated payment machine
- 自动清算所 **ACH**   automated clearing house
- 自动商业环境 **ACE**   Automated Commercial Environment
- 自动识别系统 **AIS**   Automatic Identification System
- 自动适应性发动机技术发展 **AETD**   adaptive engine technique development
- 自动收款机 **ACM**   automated checkout machine
- 自动售检票 **AFC**   Automatic Fare Collection
- 自动售票机 **ATV**   Automatic Ticket Vendor
- 自动售票机 **TIM**   ticket issue machine
- 自动输出控制 **AOC**   Automatic Output Control
- 自动数据处理 **ADP**   automatic data processing
- 自动数据系统 **ADS**   automated data system
- 自动数据再调度技术 **DART**   data automatic rescheduling technique
- 自动数学翻译 **AMTRAM**   automatic mathematic translation
- 自动数字编码系统 **ADES**   automatic digital encoding system
- 自动数字牌识别 **ANPR**   automatic number plate recognition
- 自动数字网络 **AUTODIN**   automatic digital network
- 自动速度调节 **ASR**   automatic speed regulation
- 自动提款机 **ATM**   Automated Teller Machine
- 自动体外除颤器 **AED**   automated external defibrillator
- 自动体外除颤仪起搏器 **AEDP**   automated external defibrillator pacemaker
- 自动调节系统 **SRS**   self-regulating system
- 自动同步鉴别器 **ASD**   automatic synchronized discriminator
- 自动图像传输 **APT**   automatic picture transmission
- 自发性知觉经络反应 **ASMR**   autonomous sensory meridian response
- 自动译码机 **ACT**   automatic code translation

Z

自动引导车 AGV	automatic guided vehicle
自动语音识别 ASR	automatic sound recognition
自动重传请求 ARQ	automatic repeat-request
自动转换开关电器 ATS	automatic transfer switching equipment
自动转账制度 ATS	automatic transfer system
自动装置,不用手动 HOA	hands off-automatic
自动装置与自动控制 AAC	automat and automatic control
自发循环恢复 ROSC	restoration of spontaneous circulation
自行车俱乐部 BC	bicycle club
自己动手做 DIY	Do It Yourself
自然语言处理 NLP	natural language processing
自然语言理解 NLU	natural language understanding
自然语言生成 NLG	natural language generation
自然资源保护协会 NRDC	Natural Resources Defense Council
自适应编码调制 ACM	adaptable code modulation
自适应脉冲编码调制 ADPCM	adaptive differential pulse code modulation
自适应声学转换编码技术 ATRAC	Adaptive Transform Acoustic Coding
自我确认交易 ACT	automated confirmation transactions
自由贸易区 FTA	Free Trade Area
自由贸易协定 FTA	Free Trade Agreement
自由民主党[法文] PLD	parti liberal démocrate
自主移动应用系统 AMAS	autonomous mobile application system

自主远射程巡航导弹[法文] SCALP
système de croisière conventionnel autonome à longue portée

字词处理系统 WPS	word processing system
字节/秒[传输速率单位] Bps	bytes per second
宗教教育 RE	religious education
综合财务报表 IFS	integrated financial statement
综合大洋钻探计划 IODP	Integrated Ocean Drilling Program
综合度假区 IR	integrated resort
综合服务广告集团 CCG	Cross Communication Group

综合格斗[是一种规则极为开放的竞技格斗运动] MMA
mixed martial arts

综合交通换乘中心 GTC	general traffic centre
综合年度财政报告 CAFR	comprehensive annual financial report
综合农业和生物多样性区域 IFBAS	integrated farming and biological areas
综合驱动器电子设备 IDE	integrated drive electronics
综合社会调查 GSS	General Social Survey
综合业务数据网 ISDN	integrated service digital network
综合业务数字广播-地面传输 ISDB-T	
Integrated Services Digital Broadcasting-Terrestrial Transmissions	
综合自校验 CSC	comprehensive self-check
棕红色 brPK	brownish pink
棕色 BRN	brown
总部/总公司 HO	head office
总部位于纽约的有线网络媒体公司 HBO	
Home Box Office	
总成 ASSY	assembly
总胆固醇 TC	total cholesterol
总胆汁酸 TBA	total bile acid
总蛋白 TP	total protein
总吨位 GT	gross tonnage
总固定成本 TFC	total fixed costs
总挥发性有机物 TVOC	total volatile organic compounds
总会计师 GAO	general accounting officer
总经理 GM	general manager
总决赛最有价值运动员 FMVP	Final Most Valuable Player
总可变成本 TVC	total variable costs
总空中悬浮物 TSP	total suspended particle
总理 PM	Prime Minister
总前列腺特异性抗原 TPSA	tissue polypeptide specific antigen
总生存率 OS	overall survival
总收视点 GRP	gross rating point
总输入量 GI	general input
总所有成本 TCO	total cost of ownership
总脂肪组织 TAT	total adipose tissue

Z

Z

总重量 GW	gross weight
走进朝鲜 INDPRK	In Democratic People's Republic of Korea
足量［拉丁文］qs	quantum sufficiat
足球俱乐部 AFC	Association Football Club
足球俱乐部 FC	football club
足球协会 FA	Football Association
阻塞性睡眠呼吸暂停 OSA	obstructive sleep apnea
组蛋白脱乙酰酶 HDAC	histone deacetylase
组合（编辑）ASSEM	assemble
组合信托 TOT	trust of trusts
组织多肽抗原 TPA	tissue peptide antigen
组织管理 MBO	management by organization
祖母绿［宝石］em	emerald
钻石 HRD 证书［荷兰文］HRD	Hoge Raad voor Diamant
钻石生产商协会 DPA	Diamond Production Association
最不发达国家 LDC	least developed country
最迟停止营业时间 LCT	latest closing time
最迟完成时间 LCT	latest completing time
最大传输单元 MTU	maximum transport unit
最大肺活量 FVC	Forced Vital Capacity
最大公因子 HCF	highest common factor
最大呼气流量容积曲线 MEFV	maximal expiratory flow volume curves
最大密度 DMAX	density maximum
最大努力 ME	maximum effort
最大通气量 MVV	maximal ventilatory volume
最大影像 IMAX	image maximum
最大有效率 MER	maximum efficient rate
最大允许总质量 PTW	permissible total weight
最大值 MAX	maximum
最低国际劳保标准 MILS	minimum international labour standards
最低进口价格 MIP	minimum import price
最低有效功率 LEP	lowest effective power

- 最高级贵宾 **PTVIP** — platinum very important person
- 最高优先级的抗菌药物 **HPCIA** — highest priority critically important antimicrobials
- 最好的朋友 **BF** — best friend
- 最惠国 **MFN** — Most Favored Nations
- 最简 **KISS** — keep it simple, stupid
- 最受益国家 **MAIC** — most advantageously involved country
- 最小的 **min** — minimum
- 最小电话服务标准 **MTSS** — minimum telephone service standard
- 最小公倍数 **LCM** — least common multiple
- 最小公分母 **LCD** — lowest common denominator
- 最小红斑量 **MED** — minimal erythema dose
- 最优生产技术 **OPT** — Optimized Production Technology
- 最有价值的运动员 **MVP** — Most Valuable Player
- 最终、完全、可验证的无核化 **FFVD** — final, fully-verified denuclearization
- 最终委员会草案 **FCD** — final committee draft
- 醉酒开车 **DWI** — driving while intoxicated
- 尊敬的 **Revd** — reverend
- 尊敬的[尊称主教] **Rt Rev(d)** — Right Reverend
- 昨天 **YDY** — yesterday
- 左手 **lh** — left hand
- 作为第二语言的英语 **ESL** — English as a Second Language
- 作为外语的英语 **EFL** — English as a Foreign Language
- 作为外语的英语教学 **TEFL** — Teaching English as a Foreign Language
- 作业测定 **WM** — work measurement
- 作业成本法 **ABC** — activity-based costing
- 作业指导书 **WI** — working instruction
- 作战引导队 **CCT** — combat control team
- 作战阵亡人士 **KIA** — killed in action
- 作战中失踪人员 **MIA** — missing in action
- 坐在这里歇斯底里地笑[网络用语] **SHLH** — sitting here laughing hysterically

参考文献

[1] 北京外国语学院法语系《法汉缩略语词典》编辑组. 法汉缩略语词典[M]. 北京:商务印书馆,1983.

[2] 池肇春,司君利,季光,等. 现代医学英汉缩略语词典[M]. 北京:军事医学科学出版社,2016.

[3] 霍恩比. 牛津高阶英汉双解词典[M]. 9版. 北京:商务印书馆,2018.

[4] 蒋兆明. 英汉信息技术缩略语词典[M]. 香港:红蓝(香港)出版公司,2007.

[5] 李虹. 世界各国与地区不同机构缩略语辞典[M]. 北京:外文出版社,2008.

[6] 南京大学《德汉缩略语词典》编写组. 德汉缩略语词典[M]. 南京:江苏人民出版社,1981.

[7] 戚建平,邹江兴. 英汉网络空间缩略语大词典[M]. 北京:国防工业出版社,2015.

[8] 斯塔尔,克奇里希. 英文缩略语词典[M]. 北京:知识产权出版社,2006.

[9] 殷汝祥. 英汉澳大利亚缩略语词典[M]. 北京:中国经济出版社,2003.

[10]《英汉军事缩略语大辞典》编纂委员会. 英汉军事缩略语大辞典[M]. 北京:解放军出版社,2008.

[11] 余富林. 中国媒体常用字母词词典[M]. 上海:上海大学出版社,2012.

[12] 朱和中,陶立三. 新英语外来语词典[M]. 北京:商务印书馆国际有限公司,2014.

[13] 朱玉富. 俄语外来语百科词典[M]. 哈尔滨:黑龙江大学出版社,2017.

后 记

《实用英汉-汉英缩略语手册》在华中科技大学外国语学院许明武院长、刘泽华副院长、唐旭日主任和外语学院全体同仁的关心、支持下,终于完成了。

在本手册出版的时候我们还要感谢恩师——翻译理论家刘重德教授和翻译界的翘楚李亚舒教授。我的恩师——泸江一支笔王重稼教授和恩师——北大才子程铭教授、罗祚韦教授、张怀骞老师、熊锦林老师及老友熊介桂先生在英语缩略语方面给了我极大的帮助、支持和指导。

我的学生文劲宇、刘卫东、徐诗玉、樊海蓉在收集缩略语方面提供了极大的帮助。

我的学生李其在提供资料、解决大量疑难方面做出了十分突出的贡献。

十分感谢东南大学周菊编辑,没有她和她的同事们的帮助,这本手册不可能出版。还要感谢打字员丁志良女士,她一边工作还一边打字,十分辛苦!

华中科技大学外国语学院 余富林
2020 年 8 月